P9-CRO-166

Mason A. Carpenter • Wm. Gerard Sanders
Kenneth F. Harling

Strategic Management
A Dynamic Perspective
Concepts

Custom Canadian Edition

Taken from:
Strategic Management:
A Dynamic Perspective - Concepts, Canadian Edition
by Mason A. Carpenter, Wm. Gerard Sanders, and Kenneth F. Harling

Pearson Learning Solutions, 501 Boylston Street, Suite 900, Boston, MA 02116
A Pearson Education Company
www.pearsoned.com

Printed in the United States of America

6 7 8 9 10 V0UD 19 18 17 16 15

000200010271914567

MS

ISBN 10: 1-269-92976-3
ISBN 13: 978-1-269-92976-9

Dedication

My work on this book is dedicated to my wife, Lisa, and to our boys, Wesley and Zachary.

—M.A.C.

This book is dedicated to my family—my wife, Kathy, and our children, Ashley, Adam, and Noelle—for providing the patience and support necessary to complete this project.

—W.G.S.

I dedicated my work herein to my wife, Charlene.

—K.F.H.

Brief Contents

Contents

PART FOUR   STRATEGY VEHICLES FOR NEW DIRECTIONS

11

12

CASE Title	Primary	Secondary	Primary Chapter	INDUSTRY	Retail	Mfg	Svc	Tech	COUNTRY
1 ABS Global-Canada	1	8,13	Introduction	Genetic Technologies			x	x	Canada/Global
2 The Puzzle Store	2	1	Strategic Leadership	Toy	x				Canada
3 SciCan Scientific Inc.: Sell Out or Persist?	3	4,11	Internal Environment	Scientific Glassware		x			Canada
4 MacTara Limited and the Wood Products Industry in Nova Scotia	4	9	External Environment	Wood Products		x			Canada
5 Handshake VR: Innovating with Touch	5	3,4	Creating Business Strategies	Telehaptic Technology				x	Canada
6 Chateau des Charmes Wines Ltd.	6	3,4	Crafting Business Strategy	Wine	x	x			Canada
7 H&R Sewing Machine Co.	6	3,4,13	Crafting Business Strategy	Distribution-industrial equipment	x		x		Canada
8 Research in Motion: Entering a New Era	6	3,4	Crafting Business Strategy	Mobile Communication		x		x	Canada/Global
9 Summervale Farms: A Financial Analysis, Forecasting, and Valuation Case	7	3,4	Performance of the Strategy	Agriculture		x			Canada
10 Plant Nutrients Inc.	8	3,4	Strategy Implementation	Agricultural Inputs		x			USA
11 Super AM Food Markets	8	5,9	Strategy Implementation	Food retailing	x		x		USA
12 Ganong Bros. Limited	9	4,13	Corporate Strategy	Confectionery	x	x			Canada
13 NuComm International: Making a Call on China	10	8	International Strategies	Call Centre			x		Canada/Global
14 Novelis, Alcan's Spin-off: Staying Competitive?	12	7,9	Mergers and Alliances	Aluminum Products		x			Canada
15 Walter Hundhausen GmbH	13	4,10,14	New Ventures and Corporate Renewal	Iron Foundary		x			Germany
16 Board Games at Lutherwood	14	12	Corporate Governance	Not-for-Profit			x		Canada
17 Zarlink Semiconductor Inc.	14	7,8	Corporate Governance	Semiconductor				x	Canada
18 Gammon Lake Resources Inc.	7	4	Performance of the Strategy	Gold Mining		x			Canada/Global
19 Wal-Mart in China	10	9	International Strategies	Retailing	x				US/Global

FIRM SIZE	Formulation	Evaluation	Implementation	Entrepreneurship	Environmental change	Industry	International	Resource-based view	Ethics
M		x	x		x	x			
S	x			x					x
S	x					x			
L		x			x	x	x		
S	x								
M		x	x		x	x		x	
M	x	x			x				
L	x	x				x		x	
S		x							
L		x	x						
L		x	x						x
M		x							
L	x	x					x		
L		x							
L		x	x		x	x	x	x	
M		x	x						
M		x				x			x
M		x					x		
L							x		

Preface

I agreed to take on the job of developing the Canadian edition of Mason A. Carpenter and W. Gerard Sanders's text *Strategic Management: A Dynamic Perspective* because the book captures recent developments in strategic thought. Of particular merit is its recognition that the formulation of a strategy is never finished as the business world seems ever more dynamic. This means that top management continually modifies strategy even as it implements it.

Two principles guided the writing of the Canadian edition of *Strategic Management: A Dynamic Perspective*. The first principle said that we were not simply "Canadianizing" the text by replacing "Seattle" with "Vancouver," "New York" with "Toronto," and the "U.S. dollar" with "loonies." Our editors at Pearson Canada granted us freedom to utilize the material in Carpenter and Sanders's original book, along with our own material, in the manner we saw fit. This included reducing the CEO as hero, introducing many Canadian examples, and reflecting the impact of the Canadian context on business management. This freedom allowed us to pick and choose from the 13 chapters, and well over 460 pages in the U.S. edition. Content of the chapters was altered to recognize the insights that Canadian reviewers provided into the U.S. edition, recent developments in strategic thought, and issues particularly relevant to Canadian business.

The second principle directed us to maintain the orientation of the book, with the first eight chapters focusing on business strategy and the last six chapters focusing on various topics that extend beyond business into additional topics that instructors may want to include in a course.

We took on this endeavour because we are passionate about our beliefs in the importance of business strategy. We hope that you will take the opportunity this course provides to experience strategy today, so that you are prepared to participate in the incredible adventures ahead of you. Strategy makes a profound impact on businesses, and you will experience its effect on organizations throughout your career.

Key Features

In creating this book, we focused each chapter on a topical issue for which supporting literature is readily available. Our intention was to highlight fresh ideas in the literature rather than to provide a comprehensive overview. We viewed this approach as the way to capture student interest and motivate them to "dig into" the subject. Various features within each chapter encourage students to take an active role in developing their understanding of strategic management so that they can better understand, and better make a contribution to, a business' pursuit of a strategy. Specific features include:

LEARNING OBJECTIVES

The chapter structure begins with learning objectives that are presented again at the conclusion of the chapter, along with a summary of what students learned in relation to that objective. These objectives provide students with the opportunity to take stock of what they have learned, as well as an opportunity to rehearse their new knowledge. In addition, the feedback students receive from these objectives will allow them to take a targeted approach toward their studies.

CHAPTER OPENING VIGNETTE

Each chapter begins with a vignette that deals with real people and companies. The vignettes provide a clear perspective from which to appreciate the concepts presented in the chapter. They lead students through an integrated view of competitive environments and help students to see the interdependence of firms and environments. Most examples are Canadian, but telling examples are drawn from companies around the world.

SUSTAINABILITY AND ETHICS BOXES

Chapters in the book contain one or two boxes, providing an ethical situation or a sustainability issue. In this way, areas of topical interest are highlighted while simultaneously incorporated into the discipline of strategic management. Like the chapter opening vignettes, the majority of the boxes cover Canadian issues, but issues are gleaned from the United States and beyond.

STRATEGY DIAMOND

The "strategy diamond" introduced in Chapter 1 teaches students to seek internal coherence and consistency in changing external environments. The strategy diamond considers the five elements of strategy—*arenas*, *vehicles*, *differentiators*, *staging*, and *economic logic*—to reinforce for students the idea that questions concerning all five elements are required to determine whether their strategy represents an integrated whole.

CHAPTER REVIEW QUESTIONS

Study questions at the end of each chapter will help students organize the material they learned in the chapter.

EXPERIENTIAL ACTIVITIES

Group activities and ethical debates presented at the end of each chapter provide opportunities for students to engage in activities with each other. These activities help students to focus on the implications, ethical and otherwise, of strategic decision making.

HOW WOULD YOU DO THAT?

In each chapter, How Would You Do That? boxes place students in the role of strategic decision maker, affording them the opportunity to engage in the practical application of tools picked up over the course of their reading. The practice offered by these boxes will make students better able to connect the relevance of topics under discussion to strategic thinking.

CASE STUDIES

A volume of selected case studies accompanies the *Concepts* volume. These case studies provide another opportunity for students to consider and evaluate how strategic management decisions are made in real organizations. In selecting cases for this volume, we sought to include cases focused on small, medium, and large companies in order that students would become familiar with differences across a spectrum of organizations. The case studies were also chosen with a view toward covering as much of the book as possible.

Opportunities to engage with the material and to promote the development of a personal perspective on strategic management will make any course more meaningful to students. The features provided in this book are designed to support this development, while at the same time providing a stimulating introduction to the world of strategic management. In this way, the book provides information and develops skills that will stand the test of time and help students be successful in their careers.

Resources for Instructors

At Pearson Canada, instructors can access a variety of print and presentation resources available for download with this text. The following supplements are available:

- Instructor's Resource CD Instructor's Resource CD-ROM (ISBN 978-0-13-515331-4): This resource CD includes the following instructor supplements:

  - Instructor's Manual: The instructor's manual includes chapter descriptions and outlines, along with detailed discussions of the chapter opening vignettes. Discussion of the chapter content is correlated to the learning objectives, and additional teaching and discussion points are highlighted throughout. Helpful guides to boxed features and end-of-chapter material are also included.

- Testbank (Test Item File): The testbank provides more than 1300 test questions, including multiple choice, true/false, short answer, and essay. The Test Item File enables instructors to view and edit the existing questions, add questions, and generate tests.
- Pearson MyTest: MyTest is a powerful assessment generation program that helps instructors create quizzes, study guides, and exams, and then save them as MS Word documents. Questions and tests can be authored online, affording instructors flexibility and the ability to manage assessments at any time from anywhere.
- PowerPoint Slides: PowerPoint lecture slides provide instructors with notes and figures to supplement their in-class lectures. More than 300 slides are available as an indispensible teaching tool for instructors.
- Image Library

Instructor supplements are also available for download from Pearson Canada's online catalogue. Navigate to your book's catalogue page to view a list of those supplements that are available. See your local sales representative for details and access.

CourseSmart eTextbooks

CourseSmart goes beyond traditional expectations to provide instant, online access to the textbooks and course materials you need at a lower cost for students. And even as students save money, you can save time and hassle with a digital eTextbook that allows you to search for the most relevant content at the very moment you need it. Whether it's evaluating textbooks or creating lecture notes to help students with difficult concepts, CourseSmart can make life a little easier. And with online tools like highlighting and note-taking, students will save time and study efficiently. See how when you visit www.coursesmart.com.

Acknowledgments

This edition is built upon the foundation provided by Carpenter and Sanders but is more than the efforts of the three authors identified with this text. It is the product of inputs provided by other academic colleagues, by the professionals at Pearson Canada, and by those closest to us—our families.

In addition, two graduate students at Wilfrid Laurier University helped find cogent Canadian examples. They were Mike Dotter and Brad Miller. A former student, Irem Ali, also provided constructive criticism of several chapters.

The editorial team at Pearson Canada consisted of Nicole Lukach, Editor-in-Chief; Darryl Kamo, Developmental Editor; Imee Salumbides, Project Manager; and Heather Sangster (Strong Finish), Production Editor and Copy Editor, who all contributed greatly to bringing this work to a successful conclusion. They did a masterful job of keeping the project on track and ensuring that the project had the polish on it that it required.

Most importantly, I acknowledge the support of my wife, who commented on each chapter and drove home the need for strategy professors to recognize the importance of finance when determining whether a company really has a competitive advantage.

Specific thanks go to academic reviewers across the country who provided thorough and constructive comment. They suggested areas that needed more emphasis, areas that needed less, and provided corrections. They include:

Ian Anderson, *Algonquin College*
Kamal Argheyd, *Concordia University*
Alan Chapelle, *Vancouver Island University*
Mark Fuller, *St. Francis Xavier University*
Eric Gedajlovic, *Simon Fraser University*
Judith Holton, *Mount Allison University*
Joe Ilsever, *Douglas College*
Knud Jensen, *Ryerson University*
Terry Power, *Royal Roads University*
Clem Ramchatesingh, *Humber College*

Norman T. Sheehan, *University of Saskatchewan*
Josephine Stomp, *University of Windsor*
Steve Tissenbaum, *Ryerson University*
Erna van Duren, *University of Guelph*
Jaana Woiceshyn, *Haskayne School of Business*
Julie Wong, *Dawson College*
Jisun Yu, *Concordia University*
Vasile Zamfirescu, *Kwantlen Polytechnic University*

About the Authors

Mason A. Carpenter

Professor Carpenter is the M. Keith Weikel Professor of Leadership at the Wisconsin School of Business. He has a BS in business administration from California State University (Humboldt) and University of Copenhagen, Denmark, and an MBA from California State University (Bakersfield). He also completed graduate studies in enology at the University of Bordeaux, France. Before obtaining his PhD in strategy at the University of Texas, Austin, he worked in banking, management consulting, and software development. His research concerns corporate governance, top management teams, and the strategic management of global firms, and is published in *Strategic Management Journal*, *Academy of Management Journal*, *Academy of Management Review*, *Academy of Management Executive*, *Journal of Management*, and *Human Resource Management*. He serves on the editorial boards of the *Academy of Management Journal*, *Academy of Management Review*, *Journal of Management Studies*, and the *Strategic Management Journal*, was voted Professor of the Year by MBA students, and identified as one of the most popular professors in the *BusinessWeek* MBA poll. He recently received the Larson Excellence in Teaching award from the School of Business, and the University of Wisconsin's Emil H. Steiger Distinguished Teaching Award.

Wm. Gerard Sanders

Professor Sanders is an associate professor and the department chair in Organization Leadership and Strategy at the Marriott School of Management at Brigham Young University. He earned a PhD in strategic management from the University of Texas at Austin. In 1996, Professor Sanders joined the faculty at BYU, where he teaches strategic management. He has also been a visiting professor at Penn State University. His research is in the area of corporate governance and its affects on firm strategy and performance. He has published extensively in the *Academy of Management Journal*, *Strategic Management Journal*, *Journal of Management*, *Human Resource Management*, among other outlets. His work on the effects of stock option pay has been featured in such outlets as the *New York Times*, the *Economist*, *BusinessWeek*, *CFO*, and on National Public Radio's *Marketplace*. Professor Sanders is an associate editor of the *Academy of Management Journal*. In 2001, he received the Marriott School's J. Earl Garrett Fellowship and in 2003 he was designated a University Young Scholar. Prior to entering graduate school, Dr. Sanders spent twelve years in industry managing the acquisitions and financing of large portfolios of commercial real estate.

Kenneth F. Harling

Kenneth Harling is a professor at the School of Economics and Business, Wilfrid Laurier University, Ontario. He received a BSc from the University of Guelph and an MSc and PhD from Purdue University. Dr. Harling has previously taught at the University of Guelph, Pennsylvania State University, Purdue University, University of Waterloo, and the German International School of Management and Administration in Hanover, Germany. He has also served on the staff of the National Academy of Sciences, Washington, D.C. and the Organization for Economic Cooperation and Development, Paris, France. In recent years, his teaching interests have focused on strategy execution.

The author of numerous articles, in recent years he has turned his attention to case teaching and writing. In addition, he initiated the Maple Leaf Conference and managed it for four years. This conference assists authors developing cases dealing with issues facing the food system. He has also served on the editorial boards of Agribusiness and of the International Food and Agribusiness Management Association. He has consulted with international organizations, governmental agencies, for profit companies and cooperatives in Canada and the United States. He has also performed executive training in Canada, China, Nigeria, and the United States.

CANADIAN EDITION

STRATEGIC MANAGEMENT

·····································

A DYNAMIC PERSPECTIVE

CONCEPTS

1 Introducing Strategic Management

In this chapter, we challenge you to:

1. Understand what a *strategy* is and identify the difference between business-level and corporate-level strategy.

2. Understand why we study *strategic management*.

3. Understand the relationship between *strategy formulation* and *implementation*.

4. Describe the determinants of *competitive advantage*.

5. Recognize the difference between the *fundamental* view and the *dynamic* view of *competitive advantage*.

Doughnut Wars

Canada has the highest per capita consumption of doughnuts in the world. In 2000, Tim Hortons, the largest seller of doughnuts in Canada, had 1860 stores (mostly franchise operations) and was expanding in the United States, where it had 120 stores. It was considered one of the best managed quick-service restaurants in Canada.

That year, Krispy Kreme Doughnut Inc. (KKD), a fast-rising star in the U.S. doughnut business and a darling of Wall Street, announced that it was coming to Canada. At the time, KKD had 200 units and system sales in the United States of $448 million. The Canadian market looked perfect: Canada was right next door and Canadians loved doughnuts. KKD's management thought that its great-tasting product would quickly take business away from the established competitors. Roly Morris was charged with spearheading KKD's Canadian expansion through KremeKo, an exclusive franchisee, area developer, and holder of licensing rights to all provinces except British Columbia. Morris said that KKD would be successful because it offered a unique doughnut and coffee operation that did not confuse its image by peddling croissants, bagels, muffins, and espresso. KKD's five-year plan for Canada was to open 40 stores that would employ more than 5000 people.

How would this contest play out?

Tim Hortons

The foundation for Tim Hortons (TH) was laid by Jim Charade, who, after touring Mister Donut's headquarters in Massachusetts in 1962, decided he could grow a similar business. He opened his first doughnut store in Scarborough in 1963. The next year, in partnership with National Hockey League defenceman Tim Horton, Charade opened the chain's first store in Hamilton, Ontario. In 1965, Ron Joyce became the third franchisee, operating three stores by 1967. Joyce became Horton's new partner that year. Joyce said, "Jim Charade was the guy who dreamed up the idea of TH—but he couldn't execute. There were lots of financial problems. So Tim bought him out and I became his partner."[1] After Tim Horton died in an automobile crash in 1974, Joyce acquired the shares held by Horton's widow and became the sole owner of TH.

Joyce saw the customer—not the competition—as the point of focus and kept management honed in on serving the customer. This meant providing products that the customer wanted and having systems that delivered those products efficiently. TH adjusted to cultural changes throughout the years by evolving from a doughnut shop into a quick-service restaurant. It expanded into other baked goods and into lunch items such as soup, sandwiches, and chili. Coffee, however, continued to represent almost half of total sales revenue. And coffee was important because often it drove multiple daily customer visits, which produced the sales volume that allowed TH to locate more stores much closer together than its fast-food competitors were able to do.

Under Joyce's leadership, TH developed an efficient, profitable, and systematic business that delivered a strong and consistent customer experience, despite the occasional bad location or mediocre franchisee. Franchisees were instructed to brew coffee every 20 minutes to reflect the company's core value of "Always Fresh." "'Always Fresh' meant concepts, ideas, thoughts. We are talking about TH being always fresh, whether it be uniforms, quality of the products, chains, and so on."[2] "Always Fresh" produced an appropriately priced menu that was served up efficiently. Another core value TH demonstrated was a commitment to communities though various charitable activities, most notably TH's Memorial Camp, which ran summer camps for underprivileged children.

Joyce was always interested in growing the business. He said, " . . . if we are going to lead this brand in this segment of the industry, we had to move the numbers up. In 1992 we made the decision that we would have 1000 stores by 1995. So that became our goal. Then we said our next goal was 2000 stores by 2000, and we accomplished that. After that we just ramped up everything. The real estate department had to have more people. We had four regional offices . . . It allowed us to focus on those key parts of the country and each was given a goal to achieve in more stores to open."[3]

TH developed its stronghold in southwestern Ontario and then quickly spread across Canada, virtually eliminating independent doughnut shops while producing a doughnut shops–to–population ratio that surpassed all other countries. In 2000, doughnuts accounted for around 25 percent of TH's sales and TH accounted for 13 percent of the Cdn$7 billion in Canadian sales of quick-serve restaurants.[4]

No leader stays forever. Partly as an estate planning move, Joyce sold his ownership of TH to Wendy's International, a fast-food chain based in the United States. He left behind an experienced management team that he had put together. Paul House, whom Joyce had recruited into marketing in 1985, became TH's CEO, and six of the seven executives reporting to him had worked at TH for more than five years. The shares that Joyce received in the sale made him Wendy's largest shareholder, and he was made a member of Wendy's board of directors. As one of many directors, he had less say in what happened at TH. We'll consider the consequences of this loss of power in the epilogue.[5]

Krispy Kreme

Krispy Kreme Doughnuts Inc. (KKD) was founded in 1937 and vertically integrated in the doughnut business, making, retailing, and wholesaling the finished product as well as producing its own doughnut mixes and manufacturing its own doughnut-making machinery. In 1982, a group of investors led by Joseph McAleer Sr. bought the company. By the early 1990s, KKD's approach to making doughnuts in volume at stores and then shipping 75 percent of them to local grocery stores was not working. At this time, Mac Joseph McAleer Jr., then president, and Scott Livengood, then chief operating officer, decided to pursue growth by "reconcepting" the business. They built up the KKD brand through an emotional bond with customers. Key elements included a one-of-a-kind taste, stores that were doughnut-making theatres, and "Hot Doughnuts Now" signs. Located in the middle of the store, each doughnut theatre had windows that allowed the customer to see the equipment and watch the entire manufacturing process. And production was scheduled so that doughnuts were being made when most customers visited the store—between 6 and 11 in the morning. Whenever a fresh batch was ready, a neon sign outside the store lit up, announcing, "Hot Doughnuts Now." The doughnut theatres produced sufficient doughnuts to be shipped to other retail stores. This built the brand in the market, gave consumers a chance to try the product, and gave KKD stores additional revenue.

KKD used a number of low-cost publicity gimmicks instead of direct advertising. For more than a year before a store's opening, it was hyped, pumping media interest to a fever pitch prior to each opening. Immediately prior to the opening, large quantities of doughnuts were distributed for free, particularly to the media, and consumers formed lines at the store days before the official opening.

Coffee had been a feature of KKD stores since the 1960s. In 1996, KKD introduced its proprietary blend, named "America's Cup of Coffee." This took advantage of the fact that "Americans are drinking more coffee and becoming more knowledgeable about coffee," according to Jack McAleer, then vice-president of concept development. In the early 2000s, KKD vertically integrated into the beverage business with its acquisition of Digital Java Inc., a Chicago-based buyer and micro-roaster of premium-quality coffee. The overall goal of KKD was to increase sales from beverages from 10 percent to about 20 percent by 2008.

Scott Livengood, who became CEO in 1998 and then chairman of the board in 1999, was the key spokesperson for this new approach. He spoke calmly, passionately, and thoughtfully about the company, presenting what many saw as a shrewd and successful strategic vision that would support aggressive expansion. He earned industry kudos as leader of the company, including the 2001 Executive of the Year award from *Restaurants & Institutions* magazine.

To support KKD's expansion strategy, new management talent was drafted in the 1990s and KKD became a publicly traded company in 2000 to acquire the capital needed for expansion. Going public when it did allowed KKD to capitalize on investors' appetite for growth stocks as the stock-market boom for high-tech stocks withered. KKD enticed investors by setting earnings-per-share targets and then beating them by a penny each quarter—this was a common practice of the 1990s. KKD's executives profited greatly from this practice because their bonuses were tied to exceeding earnings growth targets.

When KKD announced that it was entering the Canadian market, some felt that TH had better get ready for an all-out war on its home turf. Joyce was less concerned. His view was that, "The KKD phenomenon is on the order of the Tim Hortons phenomenon when we first started. We used to have those huge lineups. It was a novelty. When the novelty wears off, what's their staying power? I don't think they have staying power. Obviously they've done fairly well in the United States. But how many stores can they open in Canada and survive?"[6] KKD expanded into Canada through KremeKo, a franchisee that was 40 percent owned by KKD. It opened the first Canadian store in Mississauga, Ontario, in December 2001. Before the opening 250 000 free doughnuts were distributed. KKD's first Canadian customers lined up in eager anticipation and were happy to spend $70 000 on doughnuts on the opening day. Over the next several years, 12 more stores opened in eastern and central Canada and seven opened in British Columbia.

Epilogue

Tim Hortons' growth in Canada continued, though its expansion in the United States was slower than planned. Joyce resigned from Wendy's board in 2003 because he disagreed with decisions made by Wendy's management—one being the decision to start using par-baked products, including doughnuts. These were partially cooked at a plant in Brantford, Ontario, and then shipped frozen to the shops. TH's management viewed these products as fresh because the individual stores finished the cooking and then iced the products. In 2006, Wendy's spun off TH as a standalone public company. By January 2010, TH had 3015 locations across Canada (73 percent were stores) and 563 restaurants in the United States.

While TH continued to grow, KKD experienced difficulty in Canada. KremeKo incurred a significant loss of US$2.1 million in 2003 and filed for bankruptcy in April 2005. In December, Krispy K Canada Co., a subsidiary of KKD, bought all assets of KremeKo Inc. for Cdn$17 million. The remaining operations consist of five factory stores (Mississauga, Laval, Greenfield Park [Quebec], Quebec City, and Vancouver) and wholesaling operations in eastern and central Canada. In British Columbia, only one store in Delta remains open.

KKD's Canadian adventure was not helped by events in the United States. There, its financial fortunes started dimming in spring 2004 as sales growth stalled. In May, KKD gave its first-ever profit warnings. In 2005, sales were 19 percent below the previous year, and in 2006 sales were 22 percent below the previous year. Questions about KKD's accounting practices started as the company's sales growth stalled. Investigators discovered that Scott Livengood had fudged financial results starting in the late 1990s. Correcting this required a reduction in pre-tax income from 2001 through the third quarter of fiscal year 2005 of US$25.6 million. By January 2010, KKD had only 582 stores system-wide.

A special committee of independent auditors placed primary responsibility for the company's failure on Livengood and John W. Tate, the chief operating officer. "In our view, [they] bear primary responsibility for the failure to establish the management tone, environment, and controls essential for meeting the company's responsibilities as a public company."[7] Problems were made worse by KKD's failure to employ general counsel for two years and its hiring of three chief financial officers in four years—including one who told investigators that he was not comfortable in the job.

Why are some companies incredibly successful while others are not? And why is it that once they are successful, few can sustain a high level of success? In this text, we will introduce you to the concepts that you will need to answer questions about achieving and sustaining success in the world of business competition. ■

Introducing Strategic Management

A company's performance is directly related to the quality of its strategy and its competency in implementing it. Concerns about strategy, sometimes referred to as *business policy*, preoccupy the minds of most top executives. Their responsibility is to see that the company's whole is ultimately greater than the sum of its parts—whether these parts are distinct business units or simply the functional areas that contribute to the performance of one particular business. Good strategies are affected by, and affect all of, the functional areas of the company, including marketing, finance, accounting, and operations. We will also introduce you to the concepts and tools that you will need to analyze the conditions of a company and its industry, to formulate appropriate strategies, and to determine how to go about implementing a chosen strategy.

Three themes that run throughout this book are critical to developing competency in the field of strategic management.

1. **Companies and industries are *dynamic* in nature.** In recent years, emerging theories and research have recognized that markets are dynamic and that dynamic capabilities are needed if businesses are to create continuing value. Our first theme then is the dynamic nature of both companies and their competitive environments. The current situation of a company is a result of past decisions made by its managers, customers, and competitors. And the decisions made today will alter the future situation that company finds itself in. At KKD, management shifted the company from being largely a wholesale doughnut bakery with thin margins to a retail store providing customers with a theatrical experience and the company with higher margins. This new approach had considerable appeal and so attracted franchisees, customers, and investors. But as the novelty wore off, so did customer interest. At TH, management recognized and responded to the cultural shift in society before its competitors. As Canadian consumers shifted from consuming snacks to consuming meals outside the home, TH moved from being a coffee and doughnut business to being a quick-service food business. The company was rewarded with rapid and profitable growth.

2. **To succeed, the *formulation* of a good strategy and its *implementation* should be inextricably connected.** Unfortunately, many managers tend to focus on formulating a plan of attack and give too little thought to implementing it until it's too late. Likewise, they may give short shrift to the importance of strategic leadership in effectively bridging strategy formulation and implementation. Research suggests that, on average, managers are better at formulating strategies than they are at implementing them. This problem has been described as a "knowing–doing gap."[8] Effective managers realize that successfully implementing a good idea is at least as important as generating one. To implement strategies, the organization's leaders have numerous levers at their disposal. Levers such as organizational structure, systems and processes, and people and rewards are tools that help strategists achieve alignment—that is, having all of the company's activities to complement one another and support the strategy. At TH, management had the organization and resources in place to support the perceptive changes its leadership made to strategy. The success of TH in the quick-service business should have attracted competitors, but TH has been able to continue to dominate that business because it beat competitors to good locations and continued to execute its strategy well. KKD's situation is an example of a company that did not have a sound strategy. Using "doughnut theatres" and assigning geographical franchises was initially successful as sales surged. But as sales started to slide, the strategy appeared to be based on perpetuating a fad rather than following a fundamental trend in consumer tastes. And as the sales and profits slumped, management became engaged in questionable behaviour. Top management was replaced in 2005, but the company is still struggling and numerous of its U.S. franchisees have flirted with bankruptcy.

3. **Strategic leadership is essential if a company is to both formulate and implement strategies that create value.** Strategic leaders are those responsible for formulating companies' strategy and for making sure that it is implemented. This responsibility comes to them because they are high in the management hierarchy within the company. In formulation they define a strategy so that the company creates value in a way that rivals cannot. In implementation they (1) make substantive decisions about implementation levers and

resource allocation and (2) develop support for the strategy from key stakeholders. Without leadership on both counts, what is needed is unlikely to be done. Ron Joyce of TH, on the one hand, is an example of a strong strategic leader. He stepped in when Jim Charade proved unable to implement his dream of a doughnut chain. He then pushed for growth and modified TH's strategy to take advantage of changing consumer culture. He also developed a strong management structure focused on delivering quality. This team continued to deliver superior results even after Joyce left active management in TH. The company continues to draw support both from customers and from shareholders. Scott Livengood of KKD, on the other hand, is an example a weak strategic leader. The new business model that he developed with Mac McAleer did not provide a sustainable competitive advantage. Moreover, the poor design of systems and breeches of ethics by individuals showed poor implementation. The failures led various stakeholders, including shareholders and franchisees, to challenge what was happening at the company.

What Is Strategic Management?

Strategic management is the process by which the leader of a company manages the formulation and implementation of its strategy. We still need to consider the *goal* of strategic management, what it means to "have a *strategy*," and how to know whether a strategy is a good one or a bad one.

strategic management
Process by which a company manages the formulation and implementation of a strategy.

A HOLISTIC PERSPECTIVE

The word *strategy* is derived from the Greek *strategos* and can be translated roughly as "the general's view." The general is at the top of the military hierarchy and in that position contends with situations that are much more difficult and complex than those of the soldier. The important thing about the Greek derivation of the word *strategy* is that the big-picture perspective is fundamentally different from the detail of operational tactics.

Those who form the top management team of large corporations face much more complex problems than those encountered by employees at the bottom of the organizational hierarchy. They have to make infrequent decisions with long-term consequences. They must weigh many pieces of information when making their decisions and also consider the primary and secondary effects of those decisions before committing to a particular alternative. Such a comprehensive view is said to be holistic in that one has a whole or total appreciation for the situation when making a decision.

The holistic perspective is what sets strategic management apart from functional management such as accounting, finance, marketing, and operations. In these studies, decisions were made from what was the correct functional answer. But at the top of the organization, the best functional answers can be incompatible or even contradictory. What top management has to do is determine what is best for the company as a whole. Finding this usually requires tradeoffs among the functional areas. Some of the "best" functional answers are seen as inappropriate given the broader situation as understood when one has a holistic perspective.

WHY STUDY STRATEGY?

You may wonder why it is important to study strategy when your career is unlikely to begin at the level of strategic leadership. From a practical standpoint, employers expect you to be functionally fluent in accounting, marketing, or some other specialization. So why study strategy?

Early in your career you can benefit in four ways from understanding strategic management.

- First, you will be more effective in carrying out the general manager's plans because your functional contributions will fit better with those of other functions.
- Second, you will appreciate why strategic leaders do not do what you think is best because they have to make tradeoffs in pursuit of what is best for the company. This makes you more understanding of the roles of others in the company and more accommodating of their needs.

■ Third, framing your needs in strategic terms makes it more likely that you will get the resources and authority that you need to perform your assigned tasks.

■ Fourth, you will have a framework for collecting experiences and testing the thinking you need to move higher in the management hierarchy.

When you are a strategic leader, possibly because you have chosen to be an entrepreneur, understanding strategy provides three benefits.

■ First, you have a holistic way of thinking about the company and what it seeks to accomplish. This helps you integrate the various dimensions of the company so that you make better decisions and promote actions that improve the performance of the company.

■ Second, you have a vocabulary and set of tools for framing discussions with others about the future of the company. This makes the discussion more effective and efficient.

■ Third, you have a framework for putting experience in perspective. This helps you learn from what happens around you and so build the ability to develop insights into business situations as they occur.

Everyone in the management hierarchy has a role to play in formulating and implementing strategy. Lower-level managers collect and analyze data regarding competition and commercial opportunities, and then they make functional decisions that implement the strategy. Meanwhile, senior managers put together the big picture, making the various tradeoff decisions that allow the business to make the best of the future. This means that everyone in the business is better off understanding strategic management.

WHAT IS STRATEGY?

strategy The coordinated means by which an organization pursues its goals and objectives.

Strategy means different things to different people (and a lot of these ideas are not particularly accurate).[9] In fact, experts in the field have formulated various definitions of *strategy*. We've adopted the simple and direct definition: **strategy** is the coordinated means by which an organization pursues its goals and objectives.[10] A strategy thus encompasses the pattern of actions that have been taken and those that are planned to be taken by an organization in pursuit of its objectives.[11]

Exhibit 1.1 outlines the strategic management process that you will be exploring and applying throughout this textbook.[12] You can see how vision, goals and objectives, internal and external analysis, and implementation levers can be used to help formulate and implement strategy.

Exhibit 1.1 The Strategic Management Process

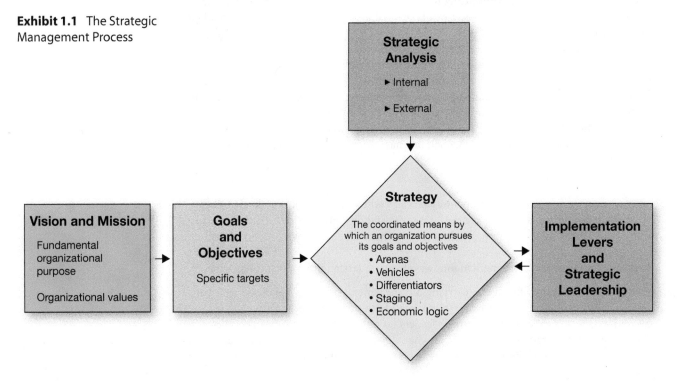

Strategy outlines the means by which a company intends to create unique value for customers and other important stakeholders.[13] This definition of strategy is important because, as you will see later, it forces managers to think holistically and dynamically about what the company does and why those activities consistently lead customers to prefer the company's products and services over those of its competitors.

BUSINESS STRATEGY VERSUS CORPORATE STRATEGY

In studying strategy, a distinction is made between strategic issues at the business level and those at the *corporate level*. Some companies are focused sharply on their *business* strategy: Companies such as TH and KKD compete in only one or very few industries. Other companies such as GE and Vivendi compete in many industries—companies having a portfolio of businesses in unrelated industries are called *conglomerates*.

Two companies can compete in the same industry, but when that business is part of a corporation, what it does to compete in its industry is influenced by the corporate strategy as well. Consider the two largest competitors in the aircraft-engine industry. In 2009, the largest was GE, with US$18.8 billion in aircraft-engine sales that accounted for 18 percent of its overall revenues. The second largest was Rolls-Royce PLC, with US$10.1 billion in engine sales that accounted for 64 percent of its overall revenues. Rolls-Royce had sold its luxury car operations to BMW and Volkswagen in 1998. In contrast, GE diversified into enterprises manufacturing light bulbs, medical devices, and commercial jet engines; providing home mortgages; broadcasting (it owns NBC); and operating self-storage facilities. Within the aircraft-engine industry, both GE and Rolls-Royce face the same competitive pressures, such as determining how to compete against such rivals as Pratt & Whitney (the third-largest company in the industry). In managing its portfolio of businesses, GE faces strategic issues that are less relevant to Rolls-Royce, which is more focused on its aircraft-engine business.

Business Strategy

Business strategy refers to the ways in which a company goes about achieving its objectives within *a particular industry or industry segment*. In other words, one of GE's business strategies would be how it pursues its objectives within the jet-engine business. This strategy may encompass such things as how it competes against Rolls-Royce for contracts from Boeing and Airbus, how it cooperates with other suppliers of technology it uses in designing its engines, and the decision to ramp up scale in an effort to reduce its costs. When TH's managers decide how to compete with KKD for consumer dollars, they, too, are engaged in business strategy.

business strategy Strategy for creating value while competing with rivals in a particular industry.

You might be more familiar with Rolls-Royce's automobiles than its jet engines. Ironically, Rolls-Royce PLC no longer makes luxury automobiles. Its core business is now jet engines, which generate 64 percent of its revenues.

Business strategy, therefore, focuses on *achieving a company's objectives within a particular business line.*

Increasingly, business strategy also takes into account the changing competitive landscape in which a company is located. Two critical questions that business strategy must address are (1) how the company will achieve its objectives *today*, when other companies may be competing to satisfy the same customers' needs, and (2) how the company plans to compete *in the future.* Later chapters will focus on specific issues associated with business strategy.

Corporate Strategy

Many companies grow by diversifying into other industries. TH and KKD both diversified into the coffee-roasting industry while large corporations such as 3M and GE have diversified into dozens of industries. A company that chooses to be in multiple industries needs to understand how it will increase performance of the business units it has beyond what they might achieve independently. Otherwise, there is no point in holding the businesses. Wal-Mart, for example, started with general retail stores and diversified into the grocery business. It has found that having combined grocery and general retail stores, increases retail foot traffic and boosts sales of non-grocery retail products by 30 percent.

corporate strategy Strategy for creating value by diversifying into various industries.

Corporate strategy requires that management decide which industries the corporation will be in, when and how to enter and leave these industries, and the strategies that are used by its businesses in each of these industries. Thinking at the corporate level adds another level of strategic decisions. Corporate strategy is such a significant subject that a whole chapter (Chapter 9) is devoted to it later in this text.

Strategy Formulation and Implementation

Earlier, we stated that *strategy* is the means by which an organization pursues its goals and objectives. **Strategy formulation** is the process of *deciding what the strategy will be*; while **strategy implementation** is the process of performing all the activities necessary *to make the strategy a reality.*[14] The chapter's opening vignette focused mostly on strategy implementation as it described management activities in the two companies as they worked to put their strategies in place. Presenting strategic management as having two separate processes hides the fact that the two are interdependent because the strategy formulated determines the work that has to be done to put it in place while what can be done to put strategy in place limits the strategic alternatives that can be considered.

strategy formulation Process of developing a strategy.

strategy implementation Process of executing a strategy.

STRATEGY FORMULATION

We know that strategy formulation means deciding what to do. Some strategies result from rational and methodical planning processes based on analyses of both internal resources and capabilities and the external environment. Others emerge over time and are adopted only after an unplanned pattern of decisions or actions suggests that an unfolding idea may unexpectedly lead to an effective strategy. Sometimes the recognition of a strategically good idea is accidental or "lucky," but corporate innovation and renewal are increasingly the products of controlled experiments and the opportunistic exploitation of surprise.[15] As you can see in Exhibit 1.2, these different aspects of strategy are referred to as intended, deliberate, realized, emergent, and unrealized.[16] You can think of intended strategy as the initial plan, whereas the realized strategy is what actually is put in place and succeeds. Thus, parts of the realized strategy can be credited to deliberate choices and actions (i.e., intended strategies that are realized), and parts are due to unplanned ones (i.e., realized strategies that were not deliberate but nevertheless emerged). Finally, some aspect of the initial strategic plan is not realized at all, and drops by the wayside.

The various aspects of intended and realized strategy are illustrated by the experience of the chipmaker Intel. During its early years, Intel was consciously focused on the design and manufacture of dynamic, random-access memory chips (DRAMs), and through the 1970s and early 1980s virtually all of the company's revenue came from DRAMs. Intel's participation in the DRAM market was intentional and planned virtually from the moment of its founding. By 1984, however, 95 percent of the company's revenue came from the microprocessor segment

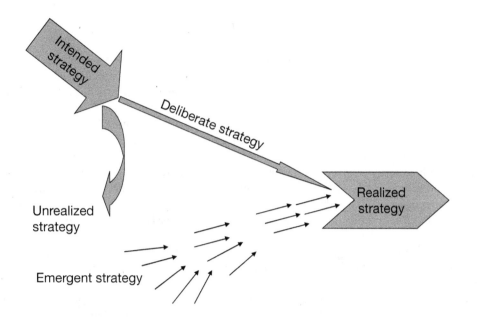

Exhibit 1.2 Intended and Realized Strategies

of the industry. Ironically, Intel's participation in this segment of the industry was not planned by senior management. Rather, it evolved from an experimental venture to make processors for Busicom, a Japanese maker of calculators.[17] Unbeknownst and unforeseen by top management was the fact that market demand was shifting dramatically from DRAMs to microprocessors. Only through the Busicom experiment—and Intel's willingness to follow the signals this experiment sent them in terms of market-demand shifts—was the company able to dramatically change its business strategy. To this day, Intel officials give credit for the company's dominance in the microprocessor market to a strategy that emerged originally from a lower-level management initiative—one that, at the time, was not greeted with unanimous enthusiasm by senior management.[18]

Since their lucky foray into the microprocessor market, Intel managers have obviously focused on effective strategies for maintaining the company's advantages in the segment while at the same time promoting experiments and exploiting surprises like Busicom to keep abreast of significant underlying market-demand shifts.

FOCUS ON ETHICS 1.1
Responding to Strategic Failures

A successful business is one that performs well. Key to such performance is formulating a sound strategy and then implementing that strategy. When the business does not perform well because the strategy is not sound or is poorly implemented, or both, management feels the pressure of the situation. Sometimes management responds by attempting to bolster performance through illegal actions. Investigators at Krispy Kreme found that, as its performance started to decline in the United States, its CEO, Scott Livengood, had fudged financial results even during the company's meteoric rise starting in the late 1990s. Improper accounting practices were used to satisfy the investors' hunger for growth. For example, management manipulated KKD's earnings through "channel stuffing"—booking increased revenue by delivering more doughnuts to retailers than they ordered at the end of a reporting period, then taking the unsold doughnuts back at the beginning of the next reporting period. And franchises that KKD bought back

were put on the books as intangible assets that it did not have to amortize, though most of the value was for property, plant, and equipment the franchisees had bought from KKD.

KKD also failed to reveal conflicts of interest as it acquired franchises. It did not disclose that one of the owners of a Northern California franchise it bought back was Livengood's ex-wife. Nor did it identify two of the owners of the Dallas and Shreveport franchises it bought back as being owned by the brother and cousin of a senior executive. For these franchises, it paid more than US$11 million a store while months earlier it was paying an average of US$6.5 million a store.

Suppose you were managing a business in which performance was poor for the quarter but you were certain that the business would recover. Would you make some "adjustments" that disguised this temporary setback so that shareholders would not be confused by events? After all, the poor performance was only temporary.

THE STRATEGY DIAMOND AND THE FIVE ELEMENTS OF STRATEGY

Good strategy formulation means refining the elements of the strategy.[19] Remember, first of all, not to confuse *part* of a strategy—for example, being a low-cost provider or first mover in an industry—for strategy itself. Being a low-cost provider or first mover may be part of a strategy, but it is not a complete strategy.

As we noted earlier, a strategy is the means by which a company will achieve its goals and objectives. This is, of course, the *intended strategy* (referring back to Exhibit 1.2), although through this process managers have a good chance of shaping the *realized strategy* as well. In a for-profit company, a business strategy will generally address how it will compete against its rivals and make a profit. For instance, if a company has an objective to be one of the top two companies in a particular industry, this is a complex objective. As result, a strategy designed to pursue this objective will consist of an *integrated set of choices*. These choices can be categorized as five related elements of strategy based on decisions that managers make regarding *arenas, vehicles, differentiators, staging,* and *economic logic*. We refer to this constellation of elements, which are central to the strategic management process outlined in Exhibit 1.3, as the *strategy diamond*. Unfortunately, many naïve managers only focus on one or two such elements, often leaving large gaps in the overall strategy. Or they may have all five pieces but not understand how they need to fit together. Only when you have answers to your questions about *each of these five elements* can you determine whether your strategy is an integrated whole. You will also have a better idea of the areas in which your strategy needs to be revised or overhauled. As Exhibit 1.3 shows, a good strategy diamond provides answers to all five questions:[20]

1. **Arenas.** Where will we be active?
2. **Vehicles.** How will we get there?
3. **Differentiators.** How will we win in the marketplace?
4. **Staging and pacing.** What will be our speed and sequence of moves?
5. **Economic logic.** How will we obtain our returns?

The five elements of strategy are related to both formulation and implementation. Good implementation means that an organization coordinates resources and capabilities and uses structure, systems, processes, and strategic leadership to translate a deliberate strategy into a realized strategy and to positive, bottom-line results. Let us take a closer look at each of these elements.

Exhibit 1.3 The Business Strategy Diamond

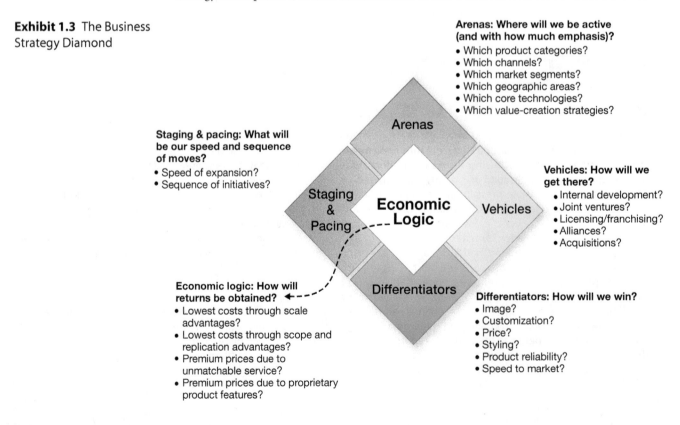

Arenas

By **arenas**, we mean areas in which a company will be active. Decisions about a company's arenas may encompass its products, services, distribution channels, market segments, geographic areas, technologies, and even stages of the value-creation process. The identification of arenas must be very specific, since it tells managers what the company should and should not do. In addition, because companies can contract with outside parties for everything from employees to manufacturing services, the choice of arenas can be fairly narrowly defined for some companies.

For example, as the largest U.S. bicycle distributor, Pacific Cycle owns the Schwinn, Mongoose, and GT brands and sells its bikes through big-box retail outlets and independent dealers, as well as through independent agents in foreign markets. In addition to these arena choices, Pacific Cycle has entirely outsourced the production of its products to Asian manufacturers. In outsourcing shoes and apparel lines, Nike follows a similar strategy in terms of arenas. One key difference, however, is that Nike, through its Nike Town retail outlets, has also chosen a direct retail presence in addition to its use of traditional retail distribution channels.

arena Area (product, service, distribution channel, geographic markets, technology, etc.) in which a company participates.

Vehicles

Vehicles are the means for participating in targeted arenas. For instance, a company that wants to go international can achieve that objective in different ways. In a drive to enter certain international markets such as China, Wal-Mart has opened new stores and grown organically—meaning that it developed all the stores internally as opposed to by acquisition. Elsewhere, Wal-Mart has purchased existing retailers and has transferred its unique way of doing business to the acquired companies. It has done so successfully in Canada, where it bought the discounter Woolco, and in England, where it bought the ASDA supermarket chain, but not so in Germany, where it bought the Wertkauf and Interspar supermarket chains. Likewise, a company that requires a new technology could develop it through investments in R&D, or it could opt to form an alliance with a competitor or supplier who already possesses the technology, thereby accelerating the integration of the missing piece into its set of resources and capabilities. Finally, one company could buy another company that owns the technology it wants. Waterloo, Ontario–based Research In Motion (RIM) did exactly this when it bought Dash Navigation to acquire valuable GPS capabilities to incorporate in RIM's devices. The possible vehicles for entering a new arena, then, include acquisitions, alliances, and organic growth.

vehicles Means for entering new arenas (e.g., through acquisitions, alliances, internal development, etc.).

Differentiators

The company that understands why its customers regularly choose its products or services over those of competitors has identified its **differentiators**. The output of differentiators can be seen in the features and attributes of a company's products or services that help it win sales. Companies can be successful in the marketplace along a number of common dimensions, including *image, customization, technical superiority, price,* and *quality and reliability.* TH has gained sales in the marketplace through the flavour of its coffee, convenience, its range of food items, and quick service. KKD gained sales through its "doughnut theatre" and "hot doughnuts now." Toyota and Honda have done well by providing effective combinations of differentiators. They sell both inexpensive cars and high-end cars. In each case, many consumers find the value that these Japanese companies provide hard to match. Effective strategies often combine differentiators, and specific choices have to be made about which differentiators are used. Providing everything that consumers want is impossible. Imagine, for instance, providing a single product that boasts both state-of-the-art technology and the lowest price on the market. Part of the problem is perceptual—consumers often associate low quality with low price. Part of it is practical—leading-edge technologies cost money to develop and command higher prices because of their uniqueness or quality.

differentiator Feature or attribute of a company's product or service (e.g., image, customization, technical superiority, price, quality, and reliability) that helps it beat its competitors in the marketplace.

There are two critical factors in selecting differentiators:

- **These decisions must be made early.** Key differentiators rarely materialize without significant up-front decisions, and without valuable differentiators, companies tend to lose marketplace battles.
- **Identifying and executing successful differentiators means making tough choices—tradeoffs.** Managers who can't make tough decisions about tradeoffs often end up trying to satisfy too broad a spectrum of customer needs; as a result, they make too many strategic compromises and execute poorly on most dimensions.

Audi is a company that has aligned these two factors successfully. In the early 1990s, Audi's management realized that its cars were perceived as low-quality, high-priced German automobiles—a poor position from which to compete. Given limited resources, the company could not produce cars in both the low-price and high-quality strata. Management had to move the Audi brand either upmarket or downmarket. Moving upmarket required improving quality sufficiently to justify premium pricing. Moving downmarket required lowering costs so that the pricing was consistent with customers' perceptions of the product quality. Management decided to move upmarket by improving quality and image; it invested in quality programs and in refining its marketing efforts. Ten years later, the quality of Audi cars has increased significantly, and customers perceive Audi closer to the level of BMW and Mercedes. Audi has reaped the benefits of premium pricing and improved profitability, but the decisions behind the strategic upmarket move entailed significant tradeoffs.[21]

Differentiators are what drive potential customers to choose one company's offerings over those of competitors. The earlier and more consistent the company is at defining and driving these differentiators, the greater the likelihood that customers will recognize them.

Staging

staging Timing and pace of strategic moves.

Staging refers to the timing and pace of strategic moves. Staging choices typically reflect available resources, including cash, human capital, and knowledge. At what point, for example, should a company enter specific international markets? Pursuing global opportunities too early can redirect resources that are needed to exploit its existing opportunities in Canada. And when the time comes to expand internationally, management has to decide which countries to enter first and which will come later. Furthermore, as product lines are expanded, management has to decide which products to offer first and which to offer later. For instance, RIM chose to focus first on producing products for the business market and later turned to developing products for the consumer market. Wal-Mart explicitly decided to delay its international moves so that it could focus first on dominating the U.S. market, which is, after all, the largest retail market in the world. Despite mixed results overseas, Wal-Mart is the undisputed leader in global retailing and has recently increased its emphasis on international markets as the basis for future growth.[22]

Staging decisions are driven by several factors: resources, urgency, credibility, and the need for early wins. Because few companies have the resources to do everything they would like to do immediately, they usually have to match opportunities with available resources. In addition, not all opportunities to enter new arenas are permanent; some windows of opportunity are open only for a short time. In such cases, early wins and the credibility with key stakeholders may be necessary to implement a strategy.

Economic Logic

economic logic Means by which a company will earn an excess profit by implementing a strategy.

Most of the companies you will study are likely to be for-profit companies and so will have earning an economic profit as a key objective. The previous four elements of strategy just reviewed (arenas, vehicles, differentiators, and staging) will only make sense for a for-profit company to the extent that they combine to produce a superior profit. Earning a normal profit, of course, requires a company to meet all of its operating and financing costs. Achieving a superior profit is a tall order for any organization. **Economic logic** is the fifth element of strategy and it refers to *how* the company will earn a profit—that is, how the company will generate positive returns over and above its cost of capital. Economic logic is the "fulcrum" for profit creation. In analyzing a company's economic logic, think of both costs and revenues. Sometimes economic logic resides primarily on the *cost* side of the equation. WestJet Airlines, for example, can fly passengers for significantly lower costs per passenger mile than Air Canada. At other times, economic logic may rest on the company's ability to increase the customer's willingness to pay premium prices for products (in other words, prices that significantly exceed the costs of providing enhanced products). Such is the case with RIM's BlackBerry and Apple's iPhone.

The strategy diamond is a powerful and flexible tool in a strategic management toolkit. You can apply the diamond at multiple levels—at a product level (product strategy), business level (business strategy), corporate level (corporate strategy), and global level (international strategy). When the five elements of strategy are aligned and mutually reinforcing, the company is generally in a position to perform well. The discussion in How Would You Do That? 1.1 demonstrates how to apply the strategy diamond to the highly successful airline WestJet. High performance levels indicate that a strategy was well conceived and is being well executed.

STRATEGY IMPLEMENTATION LEVERS

Whatever the origin of a strategic idea, successful strategies are dependent on effective implementation. As discussed earlier, *strategy implementation* is the process of executing the strategy—of taking the actions that put the strategy into effect and ensuring that organizational decisions are consistent with it.[24] The process of implementation also encompasses the refinement, or change, of a strategy as more information is made available through early implementation efforts. The goal of implementation is twofold:

- To make sure that strategy formulation is comprehensive and well informed.
- To translate good ideas into actions that can be executed (and sometimes to use execution to generate or identify good ideas).

The value of a company's strategy is determined by its ability to carry it out. "Any strategy," says Michael Porter, one of the pre-eminent writers on the subject, " . . . is only as good as its execution."[25] Adds Peter Drucker, one of the most prolific writers on management: "The important decisions, the decisions that really matter, are strategic. . . . [But] more important and more difficult is to make effective the course of action decided upon."[26]

To implement strategies, organization leaders have numerous levers at their disposal. The framework summarizing these levers is shown in Exhibit 1.4.[27] We categorize these levers into three broad categories: (1) *organization structure*, (2) *systems and processes*, and (3) *people and rewards*. The strategist uses these levers to bring the human side of the organization into alignment with the resources and capabilities of the company so that the tasks needed to realize the strategy are performed.

In addition, strategic leadership engages in activities related to implementing the strategy that are unique to their positional authority. As the exhibit suggests, implementation includes the activities carried out by the organization that are aimed at executing a particular strategy. Often, the strategy that is realized through these implementation efforts is somewhat different from the original plan. Ideally, these deviations from the original plan are the result of explicit alterations to the strategy that result from feedback during early implementation efforts, as well as from the exploitation of serendipitous opportunities that were not anticipated when the strategy was formulated.

Organization Structure

Structure is the manner in which responsibilities, tasks, and people are organized. It includes the organization's authority, hierarchy, units, divisions, and coordinating mechanisms. Use of the

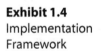

Exhibit 1.4
Implementation
Framework

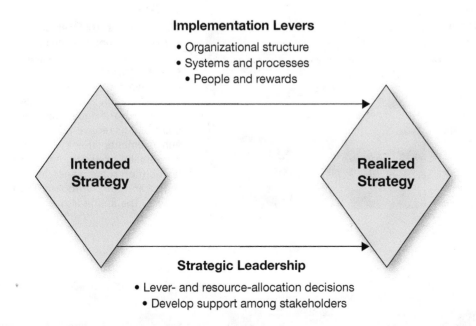

et's consider a recent entrepreneurial success story to see how the strategy diamond can be applied.

WestJet was founded in 1996 by a group of business executives in Western Canada who saw the potential for a low-fare carrier after experiencing the high travel costs for their executives who flew around the region. They modelled the airline after Southwest Airlines, an airline headquartered in Texas that was highly successful as a low-cost carrier. The competitive situation changed as the airline grew and Air Canada challenged WestJet's value offer. In response, WestJet copied some features of JetBlue, a successful American start-up based in New York, such as providing more amenities to its "guests" (passengers), including leather seating and individual in-seat live-satellite TV. This positioned it to provide more than simply low fares. In 2006, the airline served 23 Canadian cities, 11 U.S. cities, and one Caribbean destination. It generated a pre-tax operating profit of 11.2 percent, one of the best in the North American airline industry.

As you can see from the graph in Exhibit 1.5, WestJet has done something right. Its growth in revenues, earnings, and cash flow has trended upward. In 2004, it had a hiccup in terms of performance as ACE (Air Canada) came out of bankruptcy and WestJet modified its strategy to meet a more aggressive competitor. Then in 2008 and 2009 it was hurt by the financial crisis.

To begin applying the strategy diamond to WestJet, let's quickly review WestJet's mission, which is "to enrich the lives of everyone in WestJet's world by providing safe, friendly, and affordable air travel." Its vision includes that, "By 2016, WestJet will be one of the five most successful international airlines in the world, providing our guests with a friendly and caring experience that will change air travel forever." It intends to accomplish this mission by offering travellers a high-value product through prudent cost control, high-frequency service, and friendly customer service, while offering low fares that stimulate air traffic.[23]

Using the strategy diamond and public documents posted at www.westjet.com and www.sedar.com, we can describe the strategy that West-

Jet pursued in order to meet its stated objectives.

- **In what arenas does WestJet compete?** The company competes as a low-fare commercial air carrier in the North American market. It has two hubs serving the market: a western hub in Calgary and an eastern hub in Toronto.

- **What vehicles does WestJet use to enter the arenas in which it competes?** WestJet started from scratch and grew organically. Over time it pursued alliances to improve revenues and lower costs. One revenue-improving alliance was with Transat A.T. Transat offered all-inclusive vacation packages for which WestJet provided flights. One cost-reducing alliance was with the Loyalty Management Group. WestJet used Loyalty's "Air Miles" reward program rather than run its own.

- **What are its differentiators?** WestJet developed the image of a low-fare airline with high-quality service. Although it offers only one class of service, it betters Air Canada through friendly and caring interaction with the "guest" at every point. Guests receive value-added enhancements such as onboard live-satellite television, enhanced legroom on some planes, leather seats, and buy-on-board food service. The airline also provides attractive flights because they are frequent and point-to-point.

- *How does WestJet's staging—the speed of its expansion and the sequence of its growth initiatives—reflect its timetable for achieving its objectives?* WestJet grew from being a low-cost regional carrier to a national airline. In 1996, it started with short-haul, point-to-point flights in Western Canada. In 1999, it expanded to Eastern Canada to provide low-fare capacity on long-haul routes. In 2004, it began flights to the United States. In 2007, WestJet added flights to Nassau in the Bahamas, and it has aspirations to fly to other international destinations as well.

- *What's the economic logic of WestJet's strategy?* On the revenue side, WestJet works to maximize revenues by balancing maximum passenger revenues with optimal load factors. This is done by offering multiple fare levels, with fares increasing as the time of the flight approaches. Temporary seat sales are used to stimulate demand. Last-minute fares are highest but are generally lower than competitors

and offer good value for money. The airline added routes that were attractive to passengers and dropped those that proved unprofitable. It also pursued other sources of revenue, using planes for charter and cargo flights.

On the cost side, WestJet holds a low-cost structure. This is accomplished through numerous decisions, some of which follow. West-jet flies point-to-point so flights can be run as frequently as volume supports full planes. WestJet also keeps costs down by offering a single class of service, and by not offering meal service, city ticket offices, or airport lounges, nor interlining baggage and ticketing with other airlines. West-Jet uses a single type of aircraft, Boeing 737s, because this provided greater efficiency in crew training, crew scheduling, and maintenance than multi-aircraft airlines. And making reservations is low cost because they are made using ticketless automated systems.

WestJet has found a way to prosper by effectively aligning the five elements of its strategy so that they are internally consistent and externally generate market demand.

Walking through the WestJet's strategy diamond helps illustrate its

strategy. The plan looks sound, but what is required to implement such a plan? The next sections of this chapter provide an overview of this critical issue.

1. Go to Warren Buffett's Letters to Berkshire Shareholder's webpage at www.berkshirehathaway.com/letters/letters.html and read the most recent letter. How many of the strategy topics covered in this chapter can you find references to in the letter? Pick one of the businesses owned by Berkshire Hathaway and draft a strategy formulation diamond for it similar to the one outlined in the WestJet example in this How Would You Do That? box.

2. Use the strategy implementation model in Exhibit 1.5 to identify what would be necessary to successfully implement WestJet's strategy. How would the implementation levers be different for WestJet than for Air Canada?

Exhibit 1.5 Performance of Westjet, 1997–2009

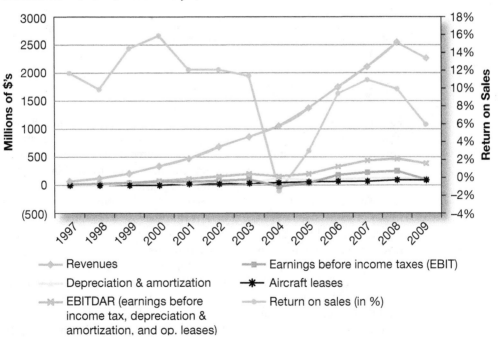

- ◆— Revenues
- —— Depreciation & amortization
- —✳— EBITDAR (earnings before income tax, depreciation & amortization, and op. leases)
- —■— Earnings before income taxes (EBIT)
- —✳— Aircraft leases
- —— Return on sales (in %)

structural lever involves restructuring the organization. At this point, we need to remind our-selves of key structural questions that managers must consider when implementing a strategy:

- Is the current structure appropriate for the intended strategy?
- Are reporting relationships and the delegation of authority set up to execute the strategic plan?
- Is the organization too centralized (or decentralized) for the strategy?

Systems and Processes

Systems and processes are all the organizational processes and procedures that plan, coordinate, and control the work of people in the organization. They include control and incentive systems, resource-allocation procedures, information systems, budgeting, distribution, and so forth.

People and Rewards

The *people and rewards* lever of the model underscores the importance of using all of the orga-nization's members to implement a strategy. Regardless of the strategy, at the end of the day, the people in the organization will have to implement it. Competitive advantage is generally tied to the company's human resources.[28] According to WestJet Airlines, competitors may be able to replicate its technologies, products, and low-cost infrastructure; however, assembling a team that can rival its highly motivated people is much more difficult. Hence, WestJet considers attracting, training, motivating, and retaining the right individuals as very important. Well-trained and highly motivated employees are critical to the development and execution of its strategy, especially in a highly competitive environment.[29]

STRATEGIC LEADERSHIP

Strategic leadership plays two critical roles in successful implementation of a strategy: (1) mak-ing substantive implementation-lever and resource-allocation decisions and (2) developing and maintaining support for the strategy from key stakeholders. These roles are highlighted here so that you can incorporate them into your own assessment of a strategy's feasibility, as well as ensure that you include these roles in your implementation plans. These roles will be discussed in greater detail in Chapter 12.

A successful strategy is not generally formulated just by a single person or a small group of leaders. Strategic leadership requires involving the right people in critical decisions because key information may be widely dispersed within the company. In addition, successful strategy implementation requires active leadership to ensure that what emerges and what is realized are desirable and that needed changes are detected before it is too late.

What Is Competitive Advantage?

Earlier, we defined *strategy* as the means by which a company will achieve its objectives. We noted that within a company's business operations, its objectives generally encompass some notion of being successful where success is measured by its return on the capital invested in it. The more successful company earns more on the capital invested in it that its competitors do. It accomplishes this by providing an offer that customers find more attractive to relative to the cost of creating the offer than the competitors do. The result is that more customers are willing to buy or are willing to pay the company considerably more than the company's cost of creat-ing the offer or both. The company that accomplishes this has a higher return on the capital invested in it and so has a **competitive advantage**.

competitive advantage A company's ability to create *value* in a way that its rivals cannot.

Why are some companies able to achieve greater advantage over rivals? All companies are not alike. Dell, for example, had capabilities that computer manufactures, such as Hewlett-Packard and IBM, were unable to duplicate. Thus Dell had a competitive advantage that only recently appears to have been neutralized by Hewlett-Packard and IBM. Toyota enjoyed a simi-lar advantage in the automotive industry until recent concerns over quality. In some industries, we see new entrants quickly gain a competitive advantage by outmanoeuvring incumbents. For instance, RIM was able to enter the mobile phone industry, which has formidable incumbents, and yet still earn substantial profits because it offered a unique service.

No competitive advantage lasts forever, however, as other competitors are always seeking to increase the return on capital invested in them. As they make their offer more attractive, their performance improves and this erodes the competitive advantage of those with it. Economists argue that eventually all companies achieve normal returns on the capital invested in them so that no company has a competitive advantage. The goal of every company with a competitive advantage, however, is to sustain its advantage for as long as possible so that it obtains abnormally high returns on the capital invested in it. [30, 31]

DETERMINANTS OF COMPETITIVE ADVANTAGE

The field of strategic management focuses on explanations of competitive advantage—on the reasons why companies experience above- and below-normal rates of returns and on the ways that companies can exploit the limits of perfect competition. The three primary perspectives on this issue are summarized in Exhibit 1.6. The perspectives, as we shall see, reflect contrasting but complementary points of view:

■ The *internal perspective* focuses on companies and potential internal sources of uniqueness.
■ The *external perspective* focuses on the structure of industries and the ways in which companies can position themselves within them for competitive advantage.
■ The *dynamic perspective*, which bridges the internal and external perspectives, is a third view of competitive advantage. This view helps explain why competitive advantage typically does not last for long periods.

Let's examine each of these perspectives, or theories, more closely.

The Internal Perspective

The first perspective on competitive advantage is an internal one. It is often called the *resource-based view of the company.* This perspective suggests that no two companies are identical because they possess resources and capabilities of different qualities. The advantage goes to the companies with superior resources and capabilities. Proponents of this theory argue that a company gains an advantage by obtaining valuable and rare resources and then developing the capability to utilize these resources to attract customers toward their products and services at the expense of competitors. As a result, the companies with superior resources and capabilities enjoy a competitive advantage over other companies.[32] This advantage makes it relatively easier for these companies to achieve consistently higher levels of performance than competitors. Competitive advantage, therefore, arises when a company's resources allow its products, services, or

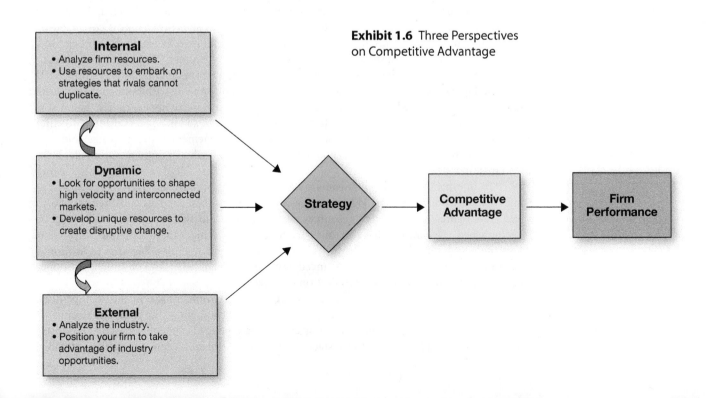

Exhibit 1.6 Three Perspectives on Competitive Advantage

businesses to compete successfully against rival companies in the same industries. According to this perspective, the objective for managers is to determine what resources and capabilities offer the most potential value, to acquire them if they are lacking, and then to leverage those specific resources and capabilities in executing the company's strategy. The resource-based view also holds that a company's bundle of resources may either hinder or help its entry into new businesses—an idea that we will explore further in later chapters.[33]

The External Perspective

The second perspective on competitive advantage contends that variations in companies' competitive advantage and performance are primarily a function of industry attractiveness and the *position* of companies within the industry relative to competitors. Thus, this external perspective suggests that competitive advantage comes from a company's positioning within the competitive business environment.

The seminal work supporting this approach is Michael Porter's work on competitive strategy.[34] Porter's theory—based on *industrial organization economics* (I/O economics)—suggests that companies should do one of two things: (1) position themselves to compete in attractive industries or (2) adopt strategies that will make their current industries more attractive. In some countries, for instance, carmakers lobby for import tariffs in order to make their domestic markets more attractive. When the strategy works, the access of foreign manufacturers to the market is limited, and the cost of participating in it is higher. (In later chapters, we will explore in more detail the theoretical models and tools that help managers analyze, understand, and shape a company's competitive environments.)

The Dynamic Perspective

The third perspective combines both the internal and external determinants of competitive advantage as it sees the interplay between the two. Consider the management of a company which identifies an attractive opportunity in an industry. It then builds the resources and capabilities needed to exploit this opportunity. Over time the situation of the industry changes so that the position held by the business is less attractive and its resources and capabilities create less value. The implication is that competitive advantage is not sustained as changes in the environment and in resources and capabilities occur. To accommodate change, strategy needs to be dynamic and to change so that the company's competitive advantage is sustained over time.

Note that the dynamic perspective provides a useful explanation of what happened in the chapter's opening vignette. TH started as a doughnut store that differentiated itself through good service and products that customers wanted. As customer wants changed, TH altered its products and locations. With its success, TH was able to alter the arenas it competed in, becoming a quick-service restaurant across Canada and the United States. KKD, a much older company, reinvented its business by altering what it offered customers. The concept of "doughnut theatres" was something that differentiated the company from other doughnut stores. KKD was also highly successful in altering the perception of the company with both consumers and investors. This provided a temporary surge in sales due to fad-like appeal rather than a sustained growth in sales. KKD was able to disguise this problem so long as it continued to enter new markets, and so expand its arena. But eventually management could no longer hide the lack of sustained profitable growth, and the company collapsed, becoming a much smaller business than it had been.

The internal drivers of dynamism are assets such as knowledge and technology as well as information from customers. When employees learn from these sources and then transform and reconfigure the company's resources and capabilities so that competitive advantage is strengthened, the company has dynamic capabilities. Risk taking, experimentation, improvisation, and continuous learning are key features of successful companies. Research In Motion is an example of a company that has enhanced its competitive advantage by continually introducing new technology into its communication products.

The external drivers of dynamism are found in the environment and include competitors, customers, and costs. These change slowly in a stable environment so the company's competitive advantage can be maintained by slow changes in strategy. The global chocolate industry provides an example of a relatively stable environment because a few companies—notably,

Hershey, Kraft, M&M/Mars, and Nestlé—dominate it in terms of both size and brands. In addition, demand for chocolate is relatively stable, growing with population growth. To stimulate growth, large companies formulate new candy bars. However, this type of growth is rather incremental and predictable. Smaller companies have carved out niches by offering differentiated products such as Ganong Brothers Ltd. with its Chicken Bones candies, but this rarely results in any significant upheaval of market position. But when environmental conditions change rapidly, as with "hyper-competition" and in "high velocity markets," the company's competitive advantage can only be sustained by rapid changes in strategy.[35]

From the dynamic perspective, a company's current competitive advantage is not an accurate predictor of future performance. The reason is that the current advantage is the outcome of past competitive activities. As the competitive environment changes, the company's advantage is not sustainable because of changes in the attractiveness of opportunities and the resources and assets needed to exploit them. With the dynamic perspective in mind, we look to the past for clues about how the company arrived at its current position and to the future to predict what the new competitive landscape will look like. The challenge is then to determine what management needs to do to sustain the competitive advantage of the company for the long-term.

Summary of Challenges

1. *Understand what strategy is and identify the difference between business-level and corporate-level strategy. Strategic management* is the process by which a company manages the formulation and implementation of its strategy. A *strategy* is the central, integrated, externally oriented concept of how a company will achieve its objectives. Strategies typically take one of two forms: business strategy or corporate strategy. The objective of a business strategy is to spell out how the company plans to compete. This plan integrates choices regarding arenas (where the company will be active), vehicles (how it will get there), differentiators (how it will win), staging (the speed and sequence of its moves), and economic logic (how it obtains its returns). The objective of corporate strategy is to spell out which businesses a company will compete in, how ownership by the corporate parent adds value to the business, and how this particular diversification approach helps each business compete in its respective markets.

2. *Understand why we study* strategic management. It should be clear to you by now that strategic management is concerned with company performance. Strategic management holds clues as to why companies survive when performance suffers. Strategy helps you to understand which activities are important and why and how a plan, absent good execution, is perhaps only as valuable as the paper it's printed on.

3. *Understand the relationship between* strategy formulation *and* implementation. Strategy formulation is the determination of what the company is going to do; strategy implementation is how the company goes about doing it. These two facets of strategy are linked and interdependent. This interdependence is made strikingly clear by the strategic management process (Exhibit 1.1) you are introduced to in this chapter, examples throughout the text, and the specific treatment of implementation levers in Chapter 11.

4. *Describe the determinants of* competitive advantage. Competitive advantage is realized when one company creates value in ways that its competitors cannot, such that the company clearly performs better than its competitors. Advantage is not simply higher relative performance; rather, superior performance signals the ability of a company to do things in ways its direct competitors cannot. The two primary views of competitive advantage—internal and external—are complementary and together are used to help formulate effective strategies. The internal view portrays competitive advantage to be a function of unique, company-specific resources and capabilities. The external view holds that a company's performance is largely a function of its position in a particular industry or industry segment given the overall structure of the industry. Profitable industries are considered attractive, and therefore, high company performance is attributed to a company's position in the industry relative to the characteristics of the industry or industry segment.

5. *Recognize the difference between the* fundamental *and* dynamic views of competitive advantage. The two fundamental views of competitive advantage are characterized by a largely internal or external orientation toward competitive advantage. Research shows that few companies persist in their dominance over competitors over prolonged periods of time so for most companies, competitive advantage is considered to be temporary. The dynamic perspective assumes that a company's current market position is not an accurate predictor of future performance because position alone does not provide a competitive advantage. Instead, the dynamic perspective looks at the past for clues about how the company arrived at its present position and to the future to divine what the new competitive landscape might look like. It also holds that it's possible for the company to influence the future state of the competitive landscape.

Review Questions

1. What is strategic management?
2. What are the key components of the strategic management process?
3. How does business strategy differ from corporate strategy?
4. What is the relationship between strategy formulation and strategy implementation?
5. What five elements comprise the strategy formulation diamond?
6. What are the internal and external perspectives of competitive advantage?
7. What are the fundamental and dynamic perspectives of competitive advantage?
8. Why should you study strategic management?

Experiential Activities

Group Exercises

1. Identify the characteristics of a company that the members of your group would like to work for and try to identify an example of this type of company. What's the difference between business and corporate strategy at this company? How might that affect your experiences and opportunities in that organization? Use your knowledge of the company's strategy to construct a high-impact job application cover letter to apply for a job with this company.
2. How is international expansion related to business and corporate strategy? Identify a company that may be thinking of expanding into new international markets. Apply the staging element of the strategy diamond to the company's international expansion opportunities or plans. Which markets should it target first and why?

Ethical Debates

1. Should ethics be a formal and explicit part of strategy formulation and implementation? What would you do to ensure that ethics are included in both activities?
2. For many of the companies you will study in this class, competitive advantage is measured by some form of financial profitability. How should you evaluate ethical choices in terms of accounting costs and benefits?

Endnotes

1. Monte Stewart, "Former Coffee Czar Brews Bittersweet Tale," *Business Edge* (B.C. edition) 3:25 (December 8, 2006): 8. From Business Edge News Magazine.

2. Alex Mlynek, "Ron Joyce," *Canadian Business* 76:12 (June 23, 2003): 22.

3. Stewart, "Former Coffee Czar Brews Bittersweet Tale," 9.

4. Kevin Libin, "Holey War," *Canadian Business* 73:15 (August 21, 2000): 34.

5. Stewart, "Former Coffee Czar Brews Bittersweet Tale," 9.

6. Mlynek. "Ron Joyce."

7. "Committee Points Finger at Krispy Kreme Chief," *Toronto Star*, August 11, 2005.

8. J. Pfeffer and R. I. Sutton, The Knowing-Doing Gap: How Smart Companies Turn Knowledge into Action (Boston: Harvard Business School Press, 2000).

9. M. Porter, "What Is Strategy?" *Harvard Business Review* 74:6 (1996): 61–78.

10. D. C. Hambrick and J. W. Fredrickson, "Are You Sure You Have a Strategy?" *Academy of Management Executive* 15:4 (2001): 48–59.

11. K. R. Andrews, *The Concept of Corporate Strategy* 3rd ed. (Homewood, IL: Irwin, 1987).

12. Adapted from Hambrick and Fredrickson, "Are You Sure You Have a Strategy?"

13. R. H. Waterman, T. J. Peters, and J. R. Phillips, "Structure Is Not Organization," *Business Horizons* 23:3 (1980): 14–26.

14. Andrews, *The Concept of Corporate Strategy.*

15. S. Brown and K. Eisenhardt, *Competing on the Edge* (Boston: Harvard Business School Press, 1998); R. A. Burgelman and L. Sayles, *Inside Corporate Innovation* (New York: Free Press, 1986).

16. Adapted from H. Mintzberg, "The Strategy Concept I: Five Ps for Strategy" *California Management Review* 30:1 (1987): 11–24.

17. R. A. Burgelman, "Fading Memories: A Process Theory of Strategic Business Exit in Dynamic Environments," *Administrative Science Quarterly* 39 (1993): 24–56.

18. Burgelman, "Fading Memories"; A. Grove, *Only the Paranoid Survive* (New York: Doubleday, 1996).

19. This section draws extensively from Hambrick and Fredrickson, "Are You Sure You Have a Strategy?"

20. Adapted from Hambrick and Fredrickson, "Are You Sure You Have a Strategy?"

21. Personal interviews with company executives.

22. T. Carl, "After Growing on Small Towns, Wal-Mart Looks to World for More Expansion," Associated Press Newswires, March 26, 2003.

23. WestJet Annual Information Form, 2006; Issued March 14, 2007. Accessed through www.sedar.com.

24. The Strategy Execution Imperative: Leading Practices for Implementing Strategic Initiative (Washington, D.C.: Corporate Executive Board, 2001); C. M. Christensen, "Making Strategy: Learning by Doing," *Harvard Business Review* (November-December 1997): 141–142, 144, 146, 148, 150–154, 156.

25. M. F. Porter, "Know Your Place: How to Assess the Attractiveness of Your Industry and Your Company's Position in It," *Inc.* (September 1991): 90.

26. P. F. Drucker, *The Practice of Management* (New York: HarperCollins, 1954): 352–353.

27. Adapted from D. Hambrick and A. Cannella, "Strategy Implementation as Substance and Selling," *Academy of Management Executive* 3:4 (1989): 278–285.

28. See J. B. Barney and P. M. Wright, "On Becoming a Strategic Partner: The Role of Human Resources in Gaining Competitive Advantage," *Human Resource Management* 37:1 (1998): 31–46; J. Pfeffer, *Competitive Advantage Through People* (Boston: HBS Press, 1994).

29. WestJet, Annual Information Form 2007, 9.

30. J. B. Barney, "Firm Resources and Sustained Competitive Advantage," *Journal of Management* 17:1 (1991): 99–121; M. A. Peteraf, "The Cornerstones of Competitive Advantage: A Resource-Based View," *Strategic Management Journal* 14:3 (1993): 179–191.

31. R. R. Wiggins and T. W. Ruefli, "Sustained Competitive Advantage: Temporal Dynamics and the Incidence and Persistence of Superior Economic Performance," *Organization Science* 13:1 (2002): 82–105.

32. Barney, "Firm Resources and Sustained Competitive Advantage"; Peteraf, "The Cornerstones of Competitive Advantage"; B. Wernerfelt, "A Resource Based View of the Firm," *Strategic Management Journal* 5:2 (1984): 171–180.

33. Peteraf, "The Cornerstones of Competitive Advantage"; C. A. Montgomery and S. Hariharan, "Diversified Expansion by Large Established Companies," *Journal of Economic Behavior* 15:1 (1991): 71–99.

34. M. Porter, *Competitive Strategy* (New York: Free Press, 1980).

35. Brown and Eisenhardt, *Competing on the Edge*.

2 The Process of Strategic Leadership

Fixing the Strategy at Xerox

Long before people Googled anything, they Xeroxed everything. The Xerox Corporation had a near monopoly that was first challenged in 1970 when IBM introduced its first copier and Japanese companies entered the market. During the 1980s Xerox struggled, but in the 1990s it recovered. The price of common shares rose from US$5 in October 1990 to US$66 in January 1999. But by November 2000 the price was back down to US$4, and questions were raised about its ability to survive. Dividends were cut for the first time in 53 years. Meanwhile, debt holders were also affected as the rating of Xerox's US$18 billion debt dropped from A- to BBB. Active speculation stirred that the company could go bankrupt.

In May 2000, Anne Mulcahy was appointed president and chief operating officer (COO) of Xerox at the age of 56. She replaced Rick Thoman, who, in one year as CEO, failed to address the declining performance of Xerox Corporation and made organizational changes that hurt its performance. Under Mulcahy's leadership, top management spent six months doing a deep, critical assessment of Xerox's competitiveness. It examined the company's expertise and competency and reached a consensus on what it did not do well. And it determined what Xerox needed to do to turn its performance around.

In October 2000, Mulcahy announced that Xerox's "business model is unsustainable." This was followed by management's turnaround plan, which outlined five actions. First, management focused on aggressively reducing costs, cutting them by US$600 million as 7000 jobs were eliminated and some manufacturing was outsourced. Second, non-core assets were sold, with the proceeds used to reduce debt. Third, actions were taken in core businesses to improve productivity in operations and research. Fourth, plans were made to reduce the amount of risk the company faced. Fifth and finally, innovation was encouraged in the core business by engaging in intense customer focus, creating and leveraging the world's best technologies, and using disciplined processes.

Employees asked Mulcahy to describe what Xerox would look like when it emerged from the turnaround. Initially she was incredulous.

> "I would think to myself, Why aren't you asking me whether or not we're going to make it?" Nonetheless, she committed her vision of the company's future to paper. She did not issue a traditional vision statement, but in 2001 presented a ficti-tious *Wall Street Journal* article describing Xerox in the year 2005—she had earned a Bachelor of Arts degree in English/Journalism. In the article, "We outlined the things we hoped to accomplish as though we had already achieved them. We included performance metrics—even quotes from Wall Street analysts. It was really our vision of what we wanted the company to become."[1]

To this day people reflect on the vision and ask when the rest of the dream will be realized even though it was made up.

To ensure that people felt part of the company, Mulcahy trav-elled continually. "Effective communication, especially in a time of crisis, was perhaps the single most important com-ponent of the company's successful turnaround strategy."[2] Mulcahy was honest with employees. "When your organiza-tion is struggling, you have to give people the sense that you know what's happening, and that you have a strategy to fix it. Beyond that, you have to tell people what they can do to help."[3] For the first year, she engaged employees in "turnaround talk," keeping them abreast of progress and enlisting their support. In the following years, Xerox became profitable again and positioned itself with new rules and an operating style that allowed top management to drop the turnaround mantra.[4]

Mulcahy empowered people to find cost savings. She told everyone to think big numbers, big reductions, and then to go make big savings happen. Employees came up with thou-sands of suggestions, allowing Xerox to reduce costs dramatically.

Over time performance improved. Xerox met or exceeded earning forecasts in nearly every quarter. Its global business produced substantial cash, debt was virtually eliminated, and costs were driven down. In 2005, sales were US$15.9 billion, on which it earned US$1 bil-lion. Innovative activities produced new printing technologies, as well as greener products that produced less waste and used fewer consumables. Ninety-five percent of its products were new and accounted for a significant portion of sales. Finally, customers were being better serviced through Xerox's Global Services, which continues to provide customers with end-to-end solutions.

Mulcahy, speaking at the World Investment Conference in La Baule, France, in 2004, said, "As proud as I am of our financial turnaround at Xerox, what gives me even greater satisfaction is the progress we have made on strengthening our core business to ensure future growth. Even as we dramatically reduced our cost base, we maintained research and development investments. In fact, we didn't take a single dollar out of R&D in our core business—not one."[5,6] In 2009, Mulcahy stepped down as CEO. That year, Xerox was the world's biggest supplier of office printers, copiers, and related services with sales of US$15 billion.

What do we see? We see that Anne Mulcahy mixed together three different approaches to strategic leadership: planned, visioned, and discovered. By using multiple methods, she was able to ensure that all employees were functioning around the strategy and that the strat-egy was making the best of the situation. ■

The Process of Strategic Leadership

This chapter presents the processes used by management to provide strategic leadership. This discussion is separated into three components: who the leaders are, what processes they use, and what human factors influence the process.

The top management team leads strategy because it represents the only level in the organization at which managers possess the breadth of view needed to determine what choices make the most sense for the business. Each member of management contributes to strategy making, but the chief executive officer bears the ultimate responsibility for formulating and implementing the strategy. Our detailed discussion starts with the role of top management in the process.

Top management can use the planned, visioned, and discovered approaches to strategic leadership. Because organizations are complex, management does not rely on a single process but uses a blend of the three approaches to ensure that the strategy is being followed and is appropriate to the situation. This requires that top management integrate the three processes in appropriate proportions so that they are mutually reinforcing and fit the context within which management must manage. To appreciate the three approaches, this chapter breaks each one down into a series of sequential steps. It then illustrates how the three are integrated.

The chapter concludes by describing how humans engaged in this process influence it. Human characteristics—including cognition, power and politics, and values and ethics—all produce results that differ according to the people involved.

Top Management

While leaders influence other people's pursuit of goals, strategic leaders influence others so that they produce organizational outcomes such as company-wide performance, competitive superiority, innovation, strategic change, and survival. **Strategic leadership** is often associated with individuals such as Xerox's Anne Mulcahy but is really exercised by teams of top executives. Given the complexity and speed of competitive change and uncertainty facing most firms today, this should not be surprising.

strategic leadership Managing an overall enterprise and influencing key organizational outcomes.

The top management team, typically led by the chief executive officer (CEO or president), is responsible for managing the strategy of the business. The ultimate authority to decide what the business will do is found at this level of the organization. Failure to use this authority can lead to lack of direction and internal conflict. Proper use of this authority provides direction and produces the coordination and control needed for a smooth working organization that meets the goals of the business.

Fit

fit Condition in which all decisions made by management may support each other but at a minimum do not contradict each other.

An implicit assumption of top management is that when various decisions "fit together," the organization will perform better. The idea of **fit** has also been called alignment and coherence. Without fit, decisions contradict each other, causing confusion, ineffectiveness, and inefficiency.

Sometimes, initial decisions relating to strategy may not seem to fit but do so as further decisions are made that line up with the initial decisions. This is said to be "stretching the organization." An example of stretch appears in Exhibit 2.1, which shows Matsushita Electric, the Japanese parent company of Panasonic, stretching the company to become a "Super Manufacturing Company." Such a company, explains Matsushita CEO Kunio Nakamura, "must in essence be 'light and speedy.' Now when the nature of business is changing, emphasis will be placed on the maintenance, broadening and strengthening of IT, on R&D, and marketing. Moreover, Matsushita at present is like a heavy lead ball loaded with assets. In the future we need to cast off superfluous assets and become a company that can move lightly like a soccer ball."[7]

Matsushita's Goal: To Become a 21st-Century "Super Manufacturing Company"		
	Today: A Conventional Manufacturing Company	**Tomorrow: A 21st-Century Super Manufacturing Company**
Role	Providing goods	Providing solutions
Investment	Principally capital investment	Expansion of R&D, marketing, and IT investment
Information	From the company	Interactive/direct contact with customers
Organization	Pyramid	Flat and web

Exhibit 2.1 Creating Strategic Purpose at Matsushita

Source: "In the Pursuit of a Super Manufacturing Company," Panasonic. Accessed July 18, 2005, at www.matsushita.co.jp/corp/vision/ president/interview2/en/index.html.

MISFITS

A business always has a strategy because strategy is defined in terms of the decisions that management has made about the arena, differentiators, economic logic, staging, and vehicles. Every operating business has made decisions about these either explicitly or implicitly. However, the strategy might not be a good one because it does not fit with the environment or because decisions about the resources and organization of the business do not fit with the strategy. Misfits that are strategically important will either cause poor performance of the business now or in future. For example, management may be making investments that move the business into new markets, although the business has nothing that differentiates it from the competitors in those markets. As a consequence, the return on investment made is likely small and will lower performance for the business.

We now turn to the three leadership approaches that top management can use to develop and administer strategy. We characterize each approach as a process that ensures that the decisions made fit together.

Processes for Leading

Top management uses three processes to determine what the business should do in the future: the planned, visioned, and discovered approaches. Each one is considered as a pure form because it helps us understand what is involved with that particular process. In reality, most management teams use a combination of all three processes, as we read in the opening vignette about Xerox.

THE PLANNED PROCESS

With the **planned process**, top management assumes that it can determine through keen analysis what will happen in the future and then design a strategy that will produce the best performance. It leads management in drawing up a plan of action that puts the strategy in place by moving the business from where it is in terms of resources and organization to where it needs to be. Anne Mulcahy, for example, used the planned process when she announced that Xerox's business model was unsustainable and so had Xerox's top management put together a turnaround plan that focused on five actions.

planned process A plan of actions that will put strategy in place is created by top management.

THE VALUE OF THE PLANNED PROCESS

The planned process implies relatively high certainty about what needs to be done so it works well in static and stable situations such as those found in mature industries. It can also be called the designed approach because management has crafted a strategic approach to the situation facing the business. Keen analysis is able to identify where problems lie and what actions need to be taken.

Exhibit 2.2 The Planned
Process

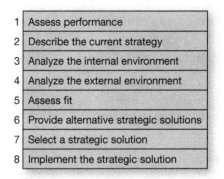

The appeal of the planned process is that it can be applied at the corporate, business, functional, and product level. The sophistication of the analysis can be tailored as desired so that it can be done relatively quickly using qualitative analysis or more slowly and thoroughly using considerable quantitative analysis. The process also forces managers to better understand and respond to factors that have the greatest actual and potential impact on the business's performance.

HOW THE PLANNED PROCESS WORKS

The process of planning as a way of preparing for the future involves eight steps (see Exhibit 2.2).

1. Assess Performance

The first step in any strategic analysis is always to determine how well the business has been performing. If performance is satisfactory, then the strategic challenges the business faces are likely in the future and the business has time to adjust to them. If performance is unsatisfactory, then the business has a serious strategic problem that must be addressed in the near future. When performance is so weak that the survival of the business is in question, the strategic problem has to be addressed immediately.

2. Describe the Current Strategy

The essential decisions about strategy described in terms of the business strategy diamond presented in Chapter 1: arenas, vehicles, differentiators, staging and pacing, and economic logic. Describing these five elements of strategy provides a rich understanding of the business at the present time and where it is going. A description of what the business is doing is frequently called the business's mission.

3. Analyze the Internal Environment

Its resources and capabilities are what the business has to work with. These are combined in the functional activities of the value chain. The resources and capabilities are assessed to see whether they create a value curve of differentiators that provides a sustainable competitive advantage.

4. Analyze the External Environment

The business operates in an evolving industry that is subject to competitive forces. The driving forces of evolution include politics, the economy, society, and technology. Knowing where the industry is in its evolution and the dynamism of that evolution has implications for the nature of competition and the available opportunities. As a player in the industry, the business's continuing success depends on having a strategy that pursues opportunities before competitors recognize them and, once competitors recognize them, makes it difficult for competitors to match the business competitively.

5. Assess Fit

Management has made many decisions about how certain resources and capabilities will be combined to satisfy a business strategy that positions the business in a selected environment. And decisions that management has made about the pursuit of that business strategy will require specific resources and capabilities in the future.

In this step, the interrelationships among all these decisions are tested to determine whether they are mutually supporting. This testing includes relationships within strategy, resources and capabilities, and the environment. When they are compatible, they are said to fit, and when they are not, they are said to misfit. Performance is usually inadequate when there are serious misfits. The fits and misfits are catalogued to provide input to the next step.

6. Provide Alternative Strategic Solutions

Sometimes the strategic alternatives that the business can pursue are clear to top management because it has spent a lot of time thinking about the situation and what might be done. Other times the management team has to design alternative solutions. When creating alternatives, each needs to be mutually exclusive so that the choice is either one alternative or another. If management chooses to accept all alternatives, the alternatives are not mutually exclusive. Rather they form the steps in a plan of action. The viability of each alternative is tested to ensure that it is feasible (that is, it can be accomplished or implemented) and that it is acceptable to those making the selection.

7. Select a Strategic Solution

Typically, selecting one strategic alternative over others is an exercise in judgment because the criteria used to assess each one differ. From an analytical perspective, the right answer is based on the strength of the argument given the underlying facts and analysis. From a real-world perspective, the alternative chosen must also have people within the company ready to support and execute it. Whatever the choice, risk is associated with the choice because the future is uncertain.

8. Implement the Strategic Solution

The final step is putting the solution in place, which starts with the preparation of a plan of action. In this plan, the necessary strategic, organizational, and resource changes are identified. Individuals with the appropriate level of authority are assigned responsibility for putting the changes in place, given a time frame for accomplishing their responsibilities, and given the resources needed to perform their responsibilities. Results are projected so that management can determine whether the plan is being achieved, and contingency plans are developed so that they are available if the plan is not being achieved. Contingency plans are often related to the riskiest aspects of the choice.

WEAKNESSES OF THE PLANNED PROCESS

The planned/designed process assumes that the information needed is available for analysis and can be used to produce a rational decision. But the necessary tools, concepts, and information are not always available to do complete analysis. And it gets worse when one recognizes that uncertainty, complexity, and ambiguity are common when dealing with strategic situations. Still, the design/planning process is attractive because it allows management to consider how it might make the business both effective and efficient.

FOCUS ON ETHICS 2.1
Considering Ethics When Planning

Robert Finocchio, the former president, CEO, and chairman of Informix Corp., says that ethics are not integrated into strategy by proclamation. He recommends using an ethics checklist when doing planning. Each year management can examine its actions over the past year to see whether they were consistent with the company's purpose and values. This includes looking at how the organization actually behaved, including whether behaviour was transparent and took advantage of opportunities for celebrating ethical behaviour. In planning for the next year, the company can ask itself a series of questions, including:

- Is our purpose sufficiently well articulated?
- Do we face new legal requirements?

- Do we have new constituents?
- If we acquire another organization, how will it be ethically assimilated?
- Are our rewards structures appropriate?
- Is there any need to change the mechanics (constituent communication, employee training, organizational structure, issue resolution processes)?
- How will we measure our performance?
- Do we have new goals/objectives in the ethical domain?

Do you think that using a list such as this will solve ethical issues found in businesses?

Source: Miriam Schulman, "Incorporating Ethics into the Organization's Strategic Plan," Markkula Center for Applied Ethics, Santa Clara University, March 22, 2006. Accessed September 3, 2009, at www.scu.edu/ethics/practicing/focusareas/business/strategic-plan.html.

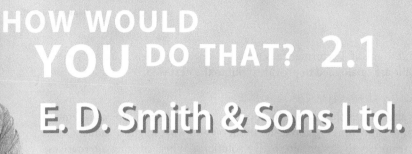

The planning process is commonly used in case study analysis, so an illustration of this process will help you understand how to tackle many of the cases you will face in strategic management. The situation to consider was faced by Lewellen Smith, the CEO of E. D. Smith & Sons Ltd. in 1992. At the time, the company was a family-owned Canadian company more than 100 years old. Its sales of $76 million that year were produced by products manufactured in its single plant in Winona, Ontario. The strategic issue that year was that Dave Nichols, president of Loblaw International Merchants and the creator of President's Choice and No-Name Generics, asked Smith to build a plant in the United States to support Nichol's expansion of Loblaw's merchandising program into that country. Smith had only weeks to decide whether his company would cooperate, since Nichols was quickly pushing ahead with his merchandising plans. Let's go through the steps of our planning process.

1. Assess Performance
Company sales dropped from $100 million in 1987 following the ratification of free trade between Canada and the United States to $60 million in 1990, but performance was recovering and sales by 1992 were $72 million. The net profit, however, was still weak at only 2 percent of sales.

2. Describe the Strategy
Arena: E. D. Smith produced pie fillings, jams, and sauces, which it sold to retailers under its own national brands and increasingly under retailer's controlled labels. The primary markets were Ontario and Quebec, while experimental sales were being made into the United States. Thirty-three percent of the company's sales were the President's Choice sauces E. D. Smith made for Loblaw.

Vehicles: E. D. Smith had national licences for half the sauces it sold. It used no other vehicles.

Differentiators: E. D. Smith had a national brand that was recognized for its superior quality. The company's advertising also featured the fact that the company was a family-owned Canadian business. In addition, the company did custom manufacturing of products for food retailers. These products were of superior quality, often using novel recipes, and were competitively priced.

Staging and Pacing: E. D. Smith had excess capacity in Winona so it was growing sales as quickly as possible.

Economic Logic: E. D. Smith had slowly declining volume in national brands and increasing sales in controlled labels. The national brand was losing market position against larger U.S.–based competitors' sales that were driving prices and profitability down. The controlled

labels had moderate profitability because prices were strong relative to high production costs incurred to produce quality products.

3. Analyze the Internal Environment
E. D. Smith had made numerous improvements in functional activities since free trade was approved in 1988. It promoted its uniqueness as a family-owned Canadian business. It improved manufacturing processes so products would meet buyer specifications at lower cost. It lowered costs by outsourcing administrative activities and procuring lower-cost, semi-processed ingredients. The capability to produce controlled labels was enhanced as that business grew. Everything it did internally was what a management consultant would recommend. E. D. Smith, however, had limited financial resources as it recovered from the dramatic increase in competition due to free trade.

4. Analyze the External Environment
E. D. Smith competed with national brand manufacturers such as Kraft Foods and manufacturers of controlled brands (also known as private labels) for retailers. The net profit margins of the former were nearly 7 percent on average while that of the latter was 5 percent.

E. D. Smith's primary customers were five major food chains: Loblaw and the Great Atlantic & Pacific Tea Company in Ontario, Metro-Richelieu and Provigo in Quebec, and Oshawa Group, which competed in both Ontario and Quebec.

Loblaw International Merchants intended to license its highly successful President's Choice merchandising program to food retailers in the United States. Nichols's ability to sell this program there would be greatly improved if companies supplying Loblaw in Canada were able to manufacture in the United States. The U.S. market was attractive to Loblaw and E. D. Smith because it was 10 times larger than Canada's, but U.S. food retailers were regional companies and U.S. customers were not familiar with the E. D. Smith brand.

5. Assess Fit

The shift to controlled label made sense given that these sales were more profitable and growing. Management had improved its ability to pursue this business by expanding product development capabilities in this area.

The financial resources were limited, but this was not a problem because no major changes appeared necessary. Financing a major investment such as a plant in the United States would have to be done through debt, however.

E. D. Smith had few alternative customers in Canada because food retailers would not purchase controlled label products from a manufacturer that also made them for a competitor. Losing Loblaw's controlled label business would be particularly harmful to E. D. Smith because it was so dependent on that business.

If Nichols was serious about entering the U.S. market, the danger that E. D. Smith ran by not expanding into the United States was that Nichols would line up a U.S. supplier that might then become Loblaw's supplier in Canada as well.

6. Create Alternative Strategic Solutions

One alternative was to decline the offer and continue growing the controlled label business in Canada. Two other alternatives, both involving serving Loblaw and other customers in the United States, were building a new plant or buying an existing U.S. plant.

7. Select a Strategic Solution

Lewellen Smith decided to buy a plant in the United States to manufacture President's Choice and other controlled label products. The justification was that E. D. Smith had to move quickly to hold on to Loblaw's business. Doing so created potential for E. D. Smith in a much larger market that it would find very difficult to enter on its own—in other words, Loblaw provided an alliance (a vehicle) that helped it enter the U.S. market.

8. Implement the Strategic Solution

Before buying the plant, E. D. Smith marketing had to establish sales forecasts for the U.S. market. Then operations had to calculate what assets and capabilities were needed to produce the volume. Following this, finance had to raise sufficient capital to buy the plant. Next, senior management had to find the plant and buy it. Then, operations had to set up appropriate equipment and processes, human resources had to find and train local employees, procurement had to find local suppliers, and marketing had to develop local customers. Only after all this was done would the U.S. plant be making sales.

Follow Up

E. D. Smith acquired a plant in Byhalia, Mississippi. Nichols was unsuccessful in selling the President's Choice merchandising program in the United States, however. After spending approximately Cdn$10 million and various corporate resources over a two-year period, E. D. Smith sold all of its interest in the U.S. plant. In 2001, E. D. Smith was sold to Imperial Capital, which in 2007 sold the company to TreeHouse Foods Inc., a producer based in suburban Chicago.

HOW WOULD YOU DO THAT? QUESTIONS

1. Pick a company that has recently been in the press. Perform a simple analysis of the issues that present lack of fit among decisions. Based on your analysis do you think that its performance will improve or decline in the future?

THE VISIONED PROCESS

Management's intent is provided through a vision statement, which is produced through the **visioned process.**[8] The vision statement is a description of the desired future state of the company. It is the answer to the question "What will this business be in 10 or 20 years?" Anne Mulcahy provided Xerox employees with a fictitious description of what the company had become some years in the future. Andy Grove, former CEO of Intel, had a similar view. He described the vision as a mental image of what the company should look like when you get to the other side.[9] The vision statement in practice ranges from a word, to a statement three pages long, or even a picture. Better statements are usually simple and brief, thus easily understood and remembered. Longer statements are more of a plan that, while rich in strategic content, is more directive and less likely to resonate with people and motivate their contributions. Grove said that the statement has to be clear enough for people to visualize but also crisp enough that it can be communicated simply to tired, demoralized, and confused staff.[10]

While the statement is the immediately visible result of the visioning process, the process is more important than the statement itself. By using a vision statement, management allows flexibility since it does not impose conditions on how the business gets there.

THE VALUE OF THE VISIONED PROCESS

The visioned process provides a strategic intent that calls for managers to set ambitious goals and then to develop the resources and capabilities needed to achieve those goals. The tension between where it wants to be and where the business is both energizes people and encourages their creativity. Having a vision also helps simplify conflict resolution because it provides a common superior goal. Without a vision of where the business is trying to go, managers are more concerned with today's problems while focused competitors are building new resources and capabilities to pursue future opportunities. The result is that the company loses its competitive advantage to these competitors.

HOW THE VISIONED PROCESS WORKS

The vision statement is produced through the visioning process. While a vision statement is important, it has little effect unless the stakeholders agree with it and are willing to participate in pursuing it. Getting their cooperation means actively engaging them in a multi-step process. The alternative view is that the business can rely on one or two gifted individuals to decide where the business is headed. This view can hold for a business that is started by an entrepreneur or run by an autocratic leader, but it is a dangerous one for larger businesses as they have resource commitments and stakeholders who want the business to serve their interests.

Exhibit 2.3 shows the key steps of the visioning process: establish the pre-conditions needed for visioning to be successful, create the vision, sell the vision, and enact the vision.

1. Establish Pre-Conditions

Six conditions need to be achieved before visioning can be conducted successfully. First, the organization has to have top managers who feel responsible for the direction of the company. Second, those members engaged in visioning need the relevant information to construct the vision. Third, members need to understand why the vision is being created. Fourth, open and clear communication is needed so that creative ideas and individual differences can be discussed. Fifth, the key stakeholders in the business need to be identified so that their interests are considered when setting the vision. Sixth and finally, all members need to understand that the vision is a prediction and that conditions may require changes to the vision. Once these conditions have been established, it is possible to conduct a visioning exercise.

Exhibit 2.3 The Visioned Process

1	Establish pre-conditions
2	Create the vision
3	Sell the vision
4	Enact the vision

2. Create the Vision

Creating the vision starts with a lot of analysis, thinking, and discussion and typically culminates with a seemingly sudden crystallization of a vision in one "eureka-like" flash. Most often, the vision is initiated by one person rather than a group and then negotiated through with others. The others should be convinced by their own reasoning and appreciate the opportunities the vision holds. The CEO, if not the creator, acts as the catalyst in crafting the vision. Once the vision has been created, the business's present situation needs to be re-examined to ensure that the vision can be achieved given the company's strategy, resources, capabilities, and competition. Exhibit 2.4 provides examples of vision statements for some Canadian companies.

3. Sell the Vision

Those involved in creating the vision can be excited about it, but it will not have much meaning to other stakeholders until the vision is sold to them. John Galt, on becoming CEO of Husky Injection Molding Systems in 2005, set sharing the vision with people as a top priority. "It is important that everyone understands where we are going and embrace their role in achieving our goals."[11] Those selling the vision are more likely to be successful in doing so when they have passion, emotion, and conviction. One knows that people have bought the vision when they can define what they need to do in their jobs to contribute to the pursuit of the vision.

4. Enact the Vision

Leaders demonstrate their commitment to the vision by behaving in ways consistent with the vision and the values associated with it. They also ensure that others are acting in accordance with the vision and its supporting values. If people are not acting in ways consistent with the vision, it is simply an empty expression.

WEAKNESSES OF THE VISIONED PROCESS

A weakness to this approach is that the vision is an abstraction that may not be concrete enough to be useful by itself. And translating it into behaviours for workers at all levels of the organization is hard work. Furthermore, even an abstract vision is not possible when the future is unknowable. But a concrete vision can be a problem when management gets caught in the "tunnel vision trap." Then the vision drives their actions even though it is no longer achievable. Finally, the vision encourages behaviours that are seen as glorious and energizing but can also be pathological (producing obsessive behaviour) and even demotivating.

Exhibit 2.4 Examples of Vision Statements by Canadian Companies

Agrium:
To be one of the world's leading providers of inputs for plant growth by creating value for each of our stakeholders.

Corus Entertainment:
To be globally recognized as Canada's most influential entertainment company.

Enbridge:
To be North America's leading energy delivery company.

Intrawest:
To being the best in the world at guiding our guests through an evolving range of great experiences which connect them to fun, a sense of discovery and rejuvenation.

Manulife Financial:
To be the most professional life insurance company in the world: providing the very best financial protection and investment management services tailored to customers in every market where we do business.

Sun Life Financial:
To be an international leader in protection and wealth management.

Tim Hortons:
To be the quality leader in everything we do.

Westjet:
To become one of the five most successful international airlines by 2016.

THE DISCOVERED PROCESS

discovered process
People throughout the company
have generated strategic ideas from
which top management has selected
some to further.

The **discovered process** assumes that the environment is too complex and/or rapidly changing for consensus about strategy to be reached. When this is the case, strategy needs to emerge through an iterative and evolutionary process that is continually redefining the strategy. Decisions that help craft strategy may be urgent, interim, and piecemeal, while those making the decisions may not appreciate the full implications of what they are deciding. The steady accumulation of these small steps or interventions produces a pattern that gives rise to the strategy. The pattern is evident in retrospect by examining the direction, consistency, and reinforcement of the decisions made.[12]

With this process, individuals throughout the organization are allowed to make the innovations they think are appropriate. Anne Mulcahy, for example, used the discovered process at Xerox when she encouraged and empowered people to find new things to do and new ways of doing old things. Innovation includes the following forms: continuous process improvement, as occurs with six sigma programs at companies such as General Electric and Ford Motor Co.; process revolution, as occurs at Wal-Mart with its investment in Radio Frequency Identification (RFID) tagging technology; product and service innovation, as commonly occurs in consumer product companies; and strategic innovation that involves new business models, as we see in the evolving music and "newspaper" industries.

Using the discovered process may be more appropriate than the planned process. In 1984, Honda entered the U.S. motorcycle market. Its executives found themselves involved in "miscalculation, serendipity, and organizational learning."[13] Honda's success was due to the adaptability and hard work of its staff rather than any long-term plan. For example, Honda's initial plan on entering the United States was to compete in large motorcycles with engines of around 300 cc's. Only when the team found that the scooters they were using to get around Los Angeles attracted positive interest from consumers did they come up with the idea of selling Super Cub, which had a much smaller 50 cc engine.

The discovered process does not distinguish between formulation and implementation, unlike the planned process, which emphasizes the importance of formulation and sees implementation decisions that follow as instrumental because they "put" strategy in place. The discovered process also focuses on the results of innovative decisions rather than on decision making itself.

THE VALUE OF THE DISCOVERED PROCESS

The discovered process produces a business strategy that evolves over time as the business adapts to changes in society, technology, and politics. The business that adapts quickly is able to "beat" other businesses to opportunities as they appear. Another advantage is that the discovered process allows those with the best information about the opportunities to make the decisions that are fundamental to the success of the business.

HOW THE DISCOVERED PROCESS WORKS

Knowledgeable employees who sense opportunities and shape them through their activities generate ideas. They attempt to set in place innovations that are often considerably different from those encouraged by existing rules and norms, as well as only partially rational. This is not surprising when innovators are operating in environments where uncertainty and ambiguity are high.[14] Even though innovation comes from employees, top management plays an important role as it sets the climate for innovation and orchestrates the process. Exhibit 2.5 illustrates the four steps of the innovation process: establish pre-conditions, find ideas, develop ideas, and prune/fertilize innovations.

Exhibit 2.5 The Discovered Process

1	Establish pre-conditions
2	Find ideas
3	Develop ideas
4	Prune/fertilize innovations

1. Establish Pre-Conditions

For the discovered process to work, top management needs to establish a culture that supports innovation. In such a culture, employees have to be open-minded to the irrational and offbeat, be nonconformist and flexible, be inquisitive and enterprising, be willing to think the unthinkable, be willing to take a chance on being wrong and failing, and shun perfectionism. Another responsibility of management is to support employees as they create and exercise options. This involves giving them the resources and freedom they need for continuous innovation and reality testing. Sometimes employees will make mistakes. Management has to accept these so that it does not stifle creativity and learning.

2. Find Ideas

Ideas that contribute to the development of strategy can come from anywhere in the organization as individuals see the need to do something different or differently. Other times individuals may act on serendipitous discoveries or react to unanticipated events. As employees act on their ideas, they contribute to the definition of the business's strategy, though no one knows at the time what the impact will be.

A higher level of ideas is encouraged by staffing the organization with diverse individuals. The ability of individuals to generate ideas can also be enhanced through various techniques such as brainstorming, cross-fertilization (putting employees with very different perspectives together), encouraging the pursuit of curiosity, customer interviewing, and mining proprietary technology.

Ideas and their consequent innovations are more often seen in industries where businesses are fragmented and new because conditions are more dynamic, creating a changing and unpredictable environment. This generates a diversity of ideas and innovation because different people in different companies will respond in different ways.

3. Develop Ideas

Initially, ideas may not be well formed or well informed. They have to be refined and improved. This is made possible through feedback about what it takes to make the idea work and how well it works. When the innovation occurs, further ideas can be stimulated and lead to further innovations that support and extend the value created by the initial idea.

Innovation requires a diversity of ideas because no one knows which will prove valuable. The lack of consensus over which ideas will be beneficial means that an idea will only survive if it has a champion. The champion supports the development of an idea and its installation as an innovation. The character of champions is that they identify with the idea as their own, and with its promotion as a cause, to a degree that goes far beyond the requirements of their job. They inspire others with their enthusiasm and persist in promoting their idea despite strong opposition.

The development of ideas requires commitment from both employees and management. An idea initially comes from employees, often an individual who champions the idea and gets others to commit to it and put it into practice.[15] Management also has to show commitment by allowing employees to have the time and resources to experiment, sometimes by allowing them to "bootleg" resources.

4. Prune/Fertilize Innovations

Management imposes some rationale on the innovations the business accepts and builds. This is necessary because the business does not have sufficient resources to support all innovations, and the variety of innovations must be reconciled or coordinated so that they are reasonably compatible. The challenge management faces is that making this decision early runs the danger of limiting innovation and making it late allows creeping commitment to less desirable ideas. Still, management needs to intervene, when appropriate, quashing poor emergent innovations but nurturing potentially beneficial ones.[16]

Management can select innovations using one of several different processes. It can treat newly formed solutions as tentative until they prove themselves. As they are developed, intentions are gradually made concrete and tied to particular details. Alternatively, it can sort solutions based on effort needed to install the solution, the impact of the solution, and the ease of undoing the solution. Innovations quickly installed are those that require little effort, have a big impact, and are easily reversed if they prove wrong. This approach has been called "fail early, fail often."[17] This process closes off fewer options, leaving open more opportunities to adjust what has been done should the circumstance change. This process is superior to the technical rationality in conditions of great uncertainty. Using the technically rational process leads one to search for the right decision, intentionally avoiding the search for error and delaying its recognition. This approach requires that management searches for errors and responds to them once discovered.[18]

Weaknesses of the Discovered Process

Innovation can be stymied in at least four different ways. First, a strong hierarchy working with an elaborate and bureaucratic (top-down) control system gives managers greater ability to block ideas and innovations that do not fit with their own views. Second, a strong organizational culture that prefers stability can limit innovation by challenging new ideas and demeaning them based on previous experience. Third, individuals in the organization may not have the necessary mindset for innovation. Considerable personal psychological adjustment may be required as individuals throw out the logic that they spent an entire career carefully constructing and living by. Innovation also requires admitting mistakes as soon as possible and avoiding attempts to justify them. Most of us are used to being judged by whether we made the right choice. If it turns out to be wrong, we devote much energy concealing this fact, or in justifying our original decision. Fourth, championing an idea requires individuals with certain talents. They have to overcome cultural inertia and political barriers by inspiring others to support their new ideas. Such individuals are not common in an organization, since many managers often prefer employees who do their assigned work while following the business's rules and regulations.

A TOTAL APPROACH

While there are alternative processes that can be used in strategic leadership, the complexity of businesses and the benefit of having all in an organization pursuing the strategy prompts leaders to use all three processes at the same time. The opening vignette, described how Anne Mulcahy blended the three processes at Xerox. She engaged the company in planning when the top management explored what was happening to the company and what needed to be done to turn it around. She provided the company with a vision that had a lasting impact. And she called on the people throughout the company to find innovative solutions to help improve performance of the business.

Another example of an integrated approach is provided by Don Pether, former president and CEO of Dofasco. During his tenure, the company became one of the most profitable steel operations in North America based on earnings per tonne. This performance was the result of top management's revision of company strategy after the recessions of the early 1980s and 1990s followed by the development of excess supply of steel, enhanced by emerging global competition, which drove prices down. Top management saw the need to reinvent the company, making it less vulnerable to the movement of the general steel market and providing margins in excess of commodity steel.[19]

In 1993, Dofasco's top management team spent seven months identifying a new vision that would allow Dofasco to create real value and grow its business in a sustainable way. It started by looking at the evolving needs of customers and of the end-users of Dofasco's products in target markets: automotive, construction, and packaging. It then focused on making Dofasco more profitable in these markets by selecting a unique market position. The outcome

Donald A. Pether, president and CEO,
Dofasco Inc., 2003–2006.

was the idea that Dofasco would become a niche producer, supplying large but very specific market segments. In the core business, steel coil products, Dofasco would produce superior products more efficiently, thereby offsetting the challenges aluminium would present in the automotive business. The key to growth in value of the company, however, came from an unwavering focus on the unmet needs of its customers. Opportunities were pursued where Dofasco could take cost out of the customer's value chain and add value to its value chain. This required innovation in steel products, technologies, and applications. Examples included hydroforming parts for automotive customers, laser-welding steel blanks to be stamped into auto parts, and producing a unique galvanized steel product for exposed use. This new approach to the business was expressed in the vision "Solutions in Steel." Associated with this, the corporate goal shifted from measuring growth by capacity of production to growth in value added or, in other words, profit.

Implementing Dofasco's new corporate vision "Solutions in Steel" required a commitment to modernizing facilities and fostering innovation. This involved taking leadership in developing innovative products and technologies within the industry. An ongoing and evolving process was used to help the company stay ahead of the next wave of change. As Don Pether said, "In today's market, if you are not technologically advanced and in a position to build solutions, you will not be capable of differentiating yourself from other commodity suppliers."

While technology may drive the company forward, the great catalyst within Dofasco was its culture and the adaptability of the people. Pether said, "Your business can have the best technology in the world, but if you fail to make your strategy inclusive, you will not be successful. You need people to drive those objectives forward and commit to ongoing growth. This requires that everyone understands what direction the company is heading toward, so they can become fully engaged and see the value in executing their work."[20] Pether added that management needs to be clear in demonstrating the value of innovation if it wants workers to accept it.

The implication of the Dofasco and Mulcahy examples is that strategic leadership should not be seen as using a singular process to lead. In practice, top management blends the three processes to improve the quality of strategic decisions and their implementation. Each of the processes runs continuously and in parallel with the others. By recognizing that multiple processes are being used, one is better able to disentangle the complex processes that are in use in most companies. Looking at strategic leadership in this way also helps explain why intended strategy is not the same as realized strategy. While an intended strategy can be planned, a dynamic environment in which conditions are forever changing means that pursuing the plan can produce disappointing performance. Better to deal with the dynamics by allowing people the flexibility to adjust actions according to the vision and even discover new actions so that the company takes the best advantage of the overall situation.

The Human Influence On Strategic Leadership Processes

We have described three processes for leading strategically. Because people are involved in each process, their behaviour influences how the processes operate. The challenge facing the strategic leader is recognizing when and how human factors are influencing the processes. That people influence the process is not good or bad in its own right. That is determined by the consequences of their behaviour. But top management needs to assess this so it knows whether it needs to deal with behavioural problems. The three major aspects of human behaviour affecting the processes are cognition, power and politics, and values and ethics.

COGNITIVE BIASES

Cognition is the process of thought, which includes perception, reason, and memory. It determines how humans process information and reach decisions.[21] These mental capabilities affect how we regard things, how we judge or choose, how we draw conclusions from premises, and how we recall or stick with details.

Robert Campeau, a highly successful builder in Canada, had his decision making affected by cognitive biases. In Ottawa, Campeau constructed both office complexes and residential subdivisions to accommodate Canada's rapidly expanding civil service starting in 1950. Campeau developed a reputation as a high-quality builder and became the most successful in the city. Campeau's success in real estate development soon spread to Toronto and included the Scotia Tower and the Harbour Castle hotel. Campeau then ventured into the United States, looking for acquisitions that would add shopping mall real estate to his portfolio of assets— he thought that retailing would complement real estate development. Through his Campeau Corporation, in 1986 he gained control of Allied Stores by paying more than US$4 billion for a company that was later worth about US$2 billion. In 1988 he gained control of Federated Department Stores, owner of Bloomingdale's, by paying a little more than US$8 billion for the company, which later had a market value of US$3 billion. The debt obligations following the mergers were huge, and an economic downturn after the acquisitions hurt retail sales. Campeau Corporation was unable to meet its debt obligations, and Federated and Allied filed for bankruptcy reorganization. Campeau Corporation was eventually acquired by the Reichmann brothers' Olympia & York Developments Ltd.

The failed mergers likely occurred in part because of Campeau's multiple biases. First, he assumed that his success in Canada would transfer to the United States and that his success in real estate would transfer to retailing. Second, he drew on his one experience with Wall Street, when doing the Allied deal, to dominate the negotiation of the Federated deal. Third, he found information that confirmed his expectations about the success of the mergers. He likely ignored any information that indicated he was overestimating Federated's potential. And because the other bidder—Macy's—was in the retailing business and kept increasing the price, he assumed that the price was justified.

From this example we see that personal factors of strategic leaders influence their perception, information processing, and decision making. Moreover, in complex situations several biases may interact.[22] These personal biases are called cognitive biases and have been verified in laboratory experiments. Here we are interested in those biases that lead to poor strategic decisions. They include:

1. *prior hypothesis bias:* A decision maker with a strong prior belief about the relationship between two variables makes decisions based on that belief even though evidence has been presented that it is wrong. Moreover, the decision maker tends to seek and use information that is consistent with prior beliefs while ignoring information that contradicts those beliefs. This can lead one to believe in a strategy even though others see it as inappropriate.

    Presently, executives in the music industry are working hard to keep this industry operating largely according to the rules of the past: They will develop artists and then distribute the product of these artists. This worked well when technology was expensive and new music was promoted over the radio and sold on records and compact discs through retail stores. Musicians now have many alternative venues because of digital technology and the internet. They can sell their music directly to the public and provide private concerts over the internet. Yet the traditional music companies are stridently seeking enforcement of their copyrights with the apparent assumption that this will bring the customers back to them and their traditional way of doing business.

2. *escalating commitment:* A decision maker, having already committed significant resources to a strategy, will commit more resources to the project even after receiving feedback that it is failing. The feeling of personal responsibility for the strategy apparently induces the decision maker to continue with the strategy even when stopping it would improve performance.

    Executives at Motorola fell into this trap. Motorola offered the first commercial cellular phone system based on analog technology. By 1994, Motorola had 60 percent of the U.S. cellular market. At that time telephone carriers told Motorola that they wanted to shift to digital technology because it was superior. The first wave of digital systems was commercialized in 1996. Ironically, Motorola had clear evidence of the increasing popularity of digital because it had licensed out its patents for digital technology to competitors, including Nokia and Ericsson. Yet, even with customer requests and clear data on market trends, Motorola's divisional managers of cellphones believed that customers really wanted better, sleeker analog phones and so presented a Star-TAC phone to the market—it was small but still an analog phone. Motorola finally launched its first digital phone in 1997 after competition was far ahead.

3. *reasoning by analogy:* When faced with a complex or novel situation, the decision maker thinks back to a similar situation and then transfers the lessons from that situation to the present one. Analogies are beneficial when the situations are similar and can spark creative thinking. A weakness of analogies is that the two situations may be similar in only superficial ways but different in causal traits. Hence, the analogy will misguide decision making. Mental maps are an attempt to deal with this by producing more complex thought structures behind an analogy.

   The supermarket, a retail format pioneered during the 1930s, has served as an analogy many times. Charles Lazarus was inspired by the supermarket when he founded Toys "R" Us in the 1950s. Thomas Stemberg, the founder of Staples and a former supermarket executive, reports in his autobiography that Staples began with an analogical question: "Could we be the Toys "R" Us of office supplies?" Since then, other retailers known as "category-killers" have used Toys "R" Us as their own analogy: Staples, Office Max, Home Depot, and Lowes.

4. *how representative:* The decision maker may generalize from a vivid example that a single number or a small sample is inappropriate. The statistical law of large numbers states that with repeated trials the sample mean will tend to approach the expected mean. In terms of business, what you might expect to happen is only clear when you have seen something happen many times.

   During the dot-com boom of the late 1990s many young people and investors looked at the success of Amazon and Yahoo! and assumed they could achieve the same level of success. This produced a massive wave of start-ups working with the internet as individuals sought to capitalize on the perceived opportunities. The dot-com crash in 2000 showed that the market was able to sustain far fewer companies than founders and investors thought.

5. *illusion of control:* This is the tendency of the decision makers to overestimate their ability to control events. People tend to attribute their success to good decision making and their failures to bad luck or what others have done to them. Continued success can lead to hubris—arrogance or overbearing pride.

   Top managers seem particularly prone to such overconfidence because they have been successful many times; otherwise they would not be at the top of the organization. In mergers and acquisitions, overconfidence leads to paying too much for an acquisition, as we saw with Campeau. Given that only one-third of mergers are successful according to movements in prices of shares, this appears to be a common problem. At Motorola, CEO Robert Galvin blamed the company's failure to shift to digital technology on arrogance. Management thought it had the answer and the customer was wrong.[23]

POWER AND POLITICS

A second influence on strategic leadership stems from the desires and interests of individuals engaged in the process. Sometimes they are trying to make their contribution to the business and feel that they have the right understanding and greater needs than other contributors. Other times they are trying to benefit at the expense of the business. This produces conflict that must be resolved using power that, when used, produces politics. Both "using power" and "playing politics" carry negative connotations, but they are essential to managing an organization.

Individuals use power to get others to do things they want done the way they want them done. In other words, managers are able to get people to do what they want done and to resist being forced to do what they do not want to do.

Politics deals with the complex or aggregate relationships between people in an organization, especially those involving power and authority. All organizations are political systems with rivalries and contests, pressure groups and lobbies, cliques and cabals, and bonds of alliance. They are inevitably involved in finding compromises and reconciling differences so that they can get done what they could not do alone. This is why individuals, groups, and organizations fail to reach goals that have been agreed upon. Politics cannot be avoided, but they can be anticipated and decisions can be made about how to control the more pernicious aspects of them.

When politics are in play, strategic decision making looks less rational. Centralized decision making seems to be orderly and rational, but this is only so because differences have been submerged through the use of concentrated power and influence. When power is dispersed, political tactics surface, making decision making appear less rational. The political process, however, is a way of dealing with disagreements and uncertainty in an organization.

Various tactics are used in playing politics. Ethical questions can be raised about how the tactics are used, but, given the inevitability of politics, there is no way to avoid using political tactics. And an effective tactic is not more morally correct than an ineffective tactic. These tactics include withholding information, providing erroneous information, taking personal credit for work done by others, and driving a personal agenda at the expense of the business.

Groupthink

The group context is important when determining whether cognitive biases will adversely affect the strategic process. Psychologist Irving Janis argued that many groups make poor decisions because of a phenomenon called groupthink.[24] This occurs when a group of decision makers coalesces around a person or a position without proper rational analysis. Failures committed under groupthink can include not questioning underlying assumptions, ignoring or filtering out information that questions the person or position, and developing after-the-fact rationalizations for its position. Commitments to the decision are thus based on emotional rather than "objective" analysis.

Mandates

While it is easy for us to think that business leaders can choose to do what they think is appropriate, this is not the case. Even leaders are answerable to others. Often, the board of directors hires the new CEO on the basis that he or she will produce specific results. This expression of the board's authoritative power becomes the leader's mandate. The board of directors expects the CEO to produce the results in line with the mandate in a timely manner. To help ensure that this happens, directors prefer to choose a person who has accomplished similar results in prior jobs.

VALUES AND ETHICS

Decisions are affected by the judgments we all make about what is desirable and undesirable in a given situation. Our judgments are based in part on values—relatively enduring beliefs that we hold about how one should act and what results matter. Strategic leaders find themselves influenced the same way.

At the personal level, the values held by leaders influence decisions about strategy. When leaders value being market-focused, they will focus actions on serving customers in the selected arena. A leader who values rapid growth is more likely to see acquisitions and alliances as attractive ways to grow a business. A leader who sees technology as a good differentiator is likely to be always looking for ways for the business to be on the leading edge of new technologies; whereas a leader who values being price-competitive is likely to select well-understood production technology to keep costs competitive. A leader who sees common technology as the basis for multiple product lines is likely to develop integrated product lines. A leader who is risk averse will likely choose "conservative" strategies that minimize downside risk and provide payoffs in the short run. This can mean choosing to imitate competitors and using defensive moves to protect the status quo. A leader who is a risk taker will choose "opportunistic" strategies that involve considerable risk but high rewards in the long run. This can mean bold offensive strategies that require innovative actions. What is striking is that the values of the individual can contradict the conclusions of logical analysis, producing what seems to be irrational behaviour.

Values of the leader can be good for the organization. Many successful entrepreneurial start-ups have had leaders whose values played an important role in setting the culture of the business. But leaders' values can also produce disasters. Garth Drabinsky was founder and CEO of Livent, a company that produced theatrical entertainment in the 1990s. Drabinsky, through Livent, was a driving force in the development of the theatre district in downtown Toronto. But the company did things on such a grand scale that its costs exceeded its revenues. To keep Drabinsky's dream alive, top management at Livent boosted revenues by selling the rights to present certain Livent shows. What remained unstated was that Livent had also signed side agreements to return these fees to the buyers. The business went bankrupt in 1998, and when the fraud came to light, top managers were sued by the U.S. Securities and Exchange Commission because the company was listed on the NASDAQ stock market in the United States.

In recent years, leaders of most businesses have created statements of values that have been called the corporate credo, corporate values, or corporate principles. These statements serve as a framework that guides the conduct of all those in the business. They tell all employed there is a right way to do things and expect people "to do things right." They are used as a benchmark for judging individual behaviour and company performance. In doing so, they give management indirect control over people's behaviour. The individual can judge personal performance against the criteria provided by the statement. This comparison influences the individual's self-esteem and motivation. When individuals identify with the organization's values, they are induced to identify with the organization's objectives. These objectives become part of their personal goals, and their behaviour is aimed at accomplishing them.

At Xerox, CEO Anne Mulcahy said that corporate values "helped save Xerox during the worst crisis in our history," and that "living our values" was one of Xerox's five performance objectives for the past several years. "These values—which include customer satisfaction, quality and excellence, premium return on assets, use of technology for market leadership, valuing employees, and corporate citizenship—are far from words on paper. These are accompanied by specific objectives and hard measures."[25]

Lisa Colnett, former senior vice-president, human resources, at Celestica, a Canadian electronics manufacturing company said, "We've developed a set of values that everyone understands and that have real meaning. They are prescriptive and explicit and, at the same time, cover a wide range of stakeholders, including customers, employees, and shareholders. The point is, we are a global company and we want everyone to work together by the same set of ethics and values to achieve the company's goals."[26]

The challenge with ethics is determining which set of values is "right." Values vary by company and by where one is in the world. For example, Asian and European companies are more likely to emphasize values related to the corporation's broader role in society, such as social and environmental responsibility.[27] This raises a fundamental question: Should ethical standards reflect universal principles or are they to be determined locally? If they are not universal, who defines them? Does it have to be the majority of members in the group or can they be defined by a provocative fringe group? The issue of what is right continues to be increasingly complex as businesses become global and populations more diverse economically, ethnically, and religiously.

We often judge the values of corporations using generally accepted standards of rights and wrongs. What is seen as right is called "ethical." This goes beyond the law, which is based on compliance to what society defines as duty based on integrity. Ethics both drive decisions by what they say is right and constrain decisions by what they say is wrong. Ethics shape the values of all those working in the business because all live in a society within which the business operates. Businesses that violate ethical standards can experience serious repercussions as stakeholders object to what has happened by exhibiting their displeasure through various mechanisms, including refusal to cooperate in future lawsuits.

In the end, the level of ethical behaviour in the business is set by the leaders of the business and not simply by ethical codes. Leaders must demonstrate through their behaviour that these codes apply to all. The best thing that leaders can do to make values meaningful is to provide explicit support of them. If they do not make a conscious effort to enforce values and ethics, standards simply become irrelevant.

Summary of Challenges

1. *Explain how strategic leadership is essential to strategy formulation and implementation.* Strategic leadership can be characterized by strategic decision making and the actions in which it results. It is concerned with the management of an overall enterprise and the ways in which top executives influence key organizational outcomes such as performance, competitive superiority, innovation, strategic change, and survival.

2. *Understand the planned process to strategic leadership.* The planned process has management formulate a strategy based on its analysis of the situation and then produce an accompanying plan of implementation. When the business has a vision, the specifics of the strategy will fulfill the vision. This new strategy is likely to involve bold moves away from existing strategy as it makes the most of the competitive environment and the resources and capabilities of the business. With a full sense for the changes needed, management is able to describe the specific changes it needs to implement. Management can find that strategy requires substantial commitments and so uses the planning process to ensure that commitments that have to be made now make strategic sense.

3. *Understand the visioned process to strategic leadership.* The visioned process has top management provide a vision, a creative view of what the business is trying to achieve and where management is trying to take the business. The destination is intended but the route to that destination is unknown because management does not have a comprehensive understanding of what needs to be achieved. The vision allows flexibility, as each person in the organization contributes in a personal way to pursuing the vision. This does not mean that evolution is piecemeal or haphazard. Management works to ensure that people understand the scope of their contribution, and these are vetted against the vision as introduced to ensure that they are productive contributions.

4. *Understand the discovered process to strategic leadership.* In the discovered process, management is open-minded about unanticipated innovations and responses to the uncertain and ambiguous environment in which the business operates. Innovations can be made lower down in the organization as small, incremental, opportunistic steps. They emerge from the interaction between different groupings of people in the organization, different groupings with different amounts of power, different requirements for and access to information, different time spans and parochial interest. Management learns opportunistically from these innovations. It also guides the evolution by continually reassessing, integrating, and organizing the incremental actions. Over time these innovations accumulate and create a pattern of behaviour.

5. *Understand the relationship among the three processes of strategic leadership.* Planning is good for efficiency. Management recognizes, however, that a plan can quickly be outdated by events. Tight control to a plan may be inappropriate. To allow flexibility so that changes are made as events occur and information improves, management also uses the visioned and discovered processes. The visioned process works from the top down through the organizational hierarchy while the discovered process works from the bottom up. Given the complexity of organizations, all three processes are typically found in the organization, but the relative importance of each varies from one organization to the next.

6. *Understand the importance of fit and misfit.* Ideally all decisions made within the business are mutually reinforcing. The implicit assumption of strategic management is that decisions are likely to produce the best results. When they do not fit together, performance is likely suffering and management needs to focus its attention on bringing decisions into harmony with the situation the business is in. However, at times through its "strategic intent" management will have created temporary misfits knowing that it will be taking further actions to close the gaps created.

7. *Explain how cognition, power, and values affect strategic decision making.* Guidance in making decisions is important because there's only so much complexity in a given problem with which any individual or group can reasonably cope.

   Decision-making biases, or threats to rational decision making in general, result from theories about oneself, theories about other people, and theories about one's world. They may impair both rational and ethical decision making and even an organization's ability to realize its vision and mission.

   The effectiveness of strategic decision making is threatened when managers act unethically or without being fully aware of the biases influencing their judgment. Ethical lapses may reflect an individual shortcoming, but they can often be traced to a lack of clear organizational mechanisms for making individuals accountable for their actions.

Review Questions

1. What is top management's most important task?
2. Describe the planned processes of strategic leadership.
3. Describe the visioned processes of strategic leadership.
4. Describe the discovered processes of strategic leadership.
5. What is the relationship between the three different processes of leadership?
6. Why is the fit of various decisions so important?
7. How do you know when decisions do not fit? What needs to be done when this situation occurs?
8. What are the three sources of human influence of the processes of strategic leadership?
9. Why do cognitive biases enter into decision making?
10. What is the relationship between power and politics?
11. How do values and ethics influence decision making?
12. It has been said that, "All businesses are built on the ideas or visions of individuals." Is this statement correct, and how did you reach your conclusion?

Experiential Activities

Group Activities

1. Find codes of ethics for two different companies and compare them. A good source is www.sedar.com. How are the codes of the two companies similar? How are they different? Which do you think is the better statement and why?

2. Find examples in which management describes how it is formulating its strategy. These examples are found in company annual reports, speeches by senior executives, and the popular business press. Using the examples, describe which type of process the company appears to be using.

Ethical Debates

1. You are the CEO of the company and have an exciting new strategy for the company. No one else in the company appreciates your vision unfortunately. Do you use your power as CEO to force people in the company to put the new strategy in place?

2. You are a middle manager in the company and see the current strategy of the company as the road to ruin. Top management has just announced a major program that will help put that strategy in place. The department you manage is key to implementing this program. Do you do what top management asks you to do or do you stall the implementation so that they have time to come to their senses?

Endnotes

1. Lisa Vollmer, "Mulcahy Took a No-Nonsense Approach to Turn Around Xerox," Report on a Speech by Anne Mulcahy in the Top Speaker Series at Stanford Business School, Stanford, California, December 2004. Accessed September 9, 2009, at www.gsb.stanford.edu/news/headlines/vftt_mulcahy.shtml. Stanford Graduate School of Business, Standford Knowledgebase.

2. Elaine Quayle, "From VPHR to CEO—Xerox's Anne Mulcahy," White Paper, HR.BLR.com, October 19, 2006. Accessed September 9, 2009, at http://hr.blr.com/whitepapers.aspx?id=19280.

3. Quayle, "From VPHR to CEO—Xerox's Anne Mulcahy."

4. Keith H. Hammonds, "Not-So-Quick Fix," *Fast Company*, December 19, 2007, Web Exclusive accessed September 9, 2009, at www.fastcompany.com/articles/archive/mulcahy.html.

5. Anne Mulcahy, Remarks at the World Investment Conference, La Baule, France, May 27, 2004. Accessed September 9, 2009, at www.europeplus.org/documents/pressarea/pressreview/remarksamulcahy2004.pdf.

6. Further articles of interest on Mulcahy's actions at Xerox are Keith H. Hammonds, "Copy This," *Fast Company* 92 (March 2005): 96. Accessed September 9, 2009, at www.fastcompany.com/magazine/92/wikn.html; Stephen Hoover, "Customer Driven Innovation at Xerox," Presentation at the Product Development and Management Association (PDMA) International Conference, Atlanta Georgia, October 21–25, 2006; Knowledge@Wharton, "Crisis Helped to Reshape Xerox in Positive Ways," November 16, 2005. Accessed September 9, 2009, at http://knowledge.wharton.upenn.edu/article.cfm?articleid=1319; and Knowledge@Wharton, "The Cow in the Ditch: How Anne Mulcahy Rescued Xerox," November 16, 2005. Accessed September 9, 2009, at http://knowledge.wharton.upenn.edu/article.cfm?articleid=1318.

7. About Panasonic: Vision. Accessed January 11, 2005, at panasonic.co.jp/global/about/vision/index.html.

8. The visioned process is well described in James. C. Collins and Jerry I. Porras, "Building Your Company's Vision," *Harvard Business Review* (September/October 1996): 65–77, and James M. Kouzes and Barry Z. Posner, *The Leadership Challenge* (San Francisco: Jossey-Bass Publishers, 1995).

9. Andrew S. Grove, *Only the Paranoid Survive* (New York: Doubleday, 1999), p. 140.

10. Ibid.

11. Husky Injection Molding Systems Ltd. Issues Fiscal 2006 First Quarter Results, for release December 7, 2005. Accessed September 3, 2009, at www.husky.ca/news/release.aspx?id=192.

12. This approach to strategy builds on work by Bower and Mintzberg. See J. L. Bower and C. G. Gilbert (eds.), *From Resource Allocation to Strategy* (New York: Oxford University Press, 2005); R. A. Burgleman "Corporate Entrepreneurship and Strategic Management: Insights from a Process Study," *Management Science* 19 (1983): 1349–1364; and H. Mintzberg, "Patterns in Strategy Formulation," *Management Science* 24 (1978): 934–948; H. Mintzberg and J. Waters, "Of Strategies Deliberate and Emergent," *Strategic Management Journal* 6:3 (1985): 257–272; T. Noda and J. Bower,

"Strategy Making as Iterated Processes of Resource Allocation," *Strategic Management Journal* 17 (Special Summer Issue 1996): 159–192; R. T. Pascale, "Perspectives on Strategy: The Real Story Behind Honda's Success," *California Management Review* 26 (Spring 1984): 47–72. What we do in our description of the approach is channel the process so that it produces a coherent strategy. This approach is similar to that of R. E. Johnson Jr. and J. D. Bate, *Power of Strategic Innovation* (New York: AMACOM, 2003) and R. K. Lester and M. J. Piore, *Innovation—The Missing Dimension* (Cambridge, MA: Harvard University Press, 2004).

13. Richard T. Pascale, "Perspectives on Strategy: The Real Story Behind Honda's Success," *California Management Review* 26 (1984): 47–72.

14. Giddens, Anthony, *The Constitution of Society. Outline of the Theory of Structuration.* (Cambridge, UK: Polity Publisher, 1984).

15. Jane M. Howell, "The Right Stuff: Identifying and Developing Effective Champions of Innovation," *Academy of Management Executive* 19:2 (2005): 108–119.

16. R. A. Burgelman and A. S. Grove, "Strategic Dissonance," *California Management Review* (Winter 1996): 8–28.

17. Ian MacMillan and Rita McGrath are cited by Chuck Frey and Hitendra Patel, "How Do You Build and Sustain a Culture and Climate for Innovation and Entrepreneurship?" Accessed September 10, 2009, at www.innovationtools.com/Community/PanelDetails.asp?a=338.

18. David Collinridge, *The Social Control of Technology* (New York: St. Martin's Press; London, 1980).

19. "Don Pether," *U of A Engineering Magazine* (Summer 2005). Accessed September 9, 2009, at www.uofaengineer.engineering.ualberta.ca/article.cfm?article=36233&issue=36224; Don Pether, "Competing in the Global Marketplace," CIM Monthly Meeting, Burlington, Ontario, February 16, 2000. Accessed September 9, 2009, at www.dofasco.ca/bins/content_page.asp?cid=2347-2350-2571.

20. "Don Pether," *U of A Engineering Magazine*.

21. Herbert Simon, *Administrative Behavior* (New York: McGraw-Hill, 1957).

22. C. R. Schwenk, "Cognitive Simplification Processes in Strategic Decision Making," *Strategic Management Journal* 5 (1984); Charles R. Schwenk, *The Essence of Strategic Decision Making* (Lexington, MA: D.C. Heath and Co., 1988).

23. Sydney Finkelstein, *Why Smart Executives Fail* (New York: Portfolio (Penguin Group), 2003): 67.

24. Irvin L. Janis, *Victims of Groupthink*, 2nd ed. (Boston: Houghton Mifflin, 1982). An alternative view is provided by S. R. Fuller and R. J. Aldag, "Organizational Tonypandy: Lessons from a Quarter Century of the Groupthink Phenomenon," *Organizational Behavior and Human Decision Processes* 73 (1998): 163–184.

25. Anne Mulcahy, "Keynote Address," Business for Social Responsibility Annual Conference, New York, November 11, 2004.

26. Reggie Van Lee, Lisa Fabish, and Nancy McGaw, "The Value of Corporate Values," *Strategy + Business* 39 (Summer 2005): 5.

27. Ibid., pp 1–14.

3 The Internal Environment: Resources, Capabilities, and Activities

In this chapter, we challenge you to:

1. Explain the internal context of strategy.

2. Identify a firm's resources and capabilities and explain their role in firm performance.

3. Define dynamic capabilities and explain their role in both strategic change and firm performance.

4. Explain how value-chain activities are related to firm performance and competitive advantage.

5. Explain the role of managers with respect to resources, capabilities, and value-chain activities.

Strategy Inside Canadel

With an endless combination of styles, shapes, colours, and materials, the Canadel Workshop allowed customers to personalize their kitchen and dining room furniture. The Workshop was a unique marketing innovation when introduced in 1992.

Canadel is located in Louiseville, near Trois-Rivières, Quebec.[1] The Deveault family started the company in 1982. By 2004, it was one of Canada's largest furniture manufacturers and dominated the North American market for casual dining furniture. Canadel's success was reflected in a return on capital twice that achieved by other companies in the industry.

Canadel helped create the casual dining segment of the furniture market in the late 1980s when it decided to offer a dining set of a table and four chairs for $2000 in 15 colours, including two-tone pieces. This was more expensive than the "dinette" segment, which featured a table and four chairs for $800, and less expensive than the "high dining" segment, which featured a table and chairs for $6000.

What consumers got from Canadel was high-quality furniture relative to its medium price. The furniture closely fitted their tastes because they received furniture they had "designed." Typically, consumers made significant deposits with retailers when they placed their furniture orders. Hence, Canadel required that the retailers selling its furniture must pay for it within 30 days since they had some of the payment and did not have to hold inventories.

The way that Canadel worked with retailers and consumers was a result of decisions the Deveaults made about how the company worked. These decisions had been influenced in part by history. In the early years, the Deveaults had limited capital so they borrowed money from family and friends. They kept Canadel's investment in equipment and machinery down by relying on suppliers to produce parts and chairs for them. After they created the casual dining segment, competitors soon entered so in 1992 Canadel again differentiated itself with its retail Workshop—a freestanding module that was put in retail stores. That year, Canadel also started selling furniture in the United States.

The decisions that the Deveaults made about how the company worked can be described using a value chain. The primary activities that Canadel harnessed to create value were producing lumber, designing wooden furniture parts, assembling the parts to produce furniture, warehousing and distributing the furniture, marketing the furniture, and servicing customers. A number of secondary activities essential to supporting the primary activities of the value chain included management, human resources, information technology, and finance. The following description lays out how each of these activities was performed so that it contributed to the strategy of the company from 1982 to 2005.

Lumber: Canadel's parts were manufactured from high-quality lumber. In 1993, it bought Bois Kennebec to centralize its sourcing, to control the cost and quality of the lumber it used, and to guarantee a continued supply of lumber. Initially Canadel was able to sell surplus lumber to other companies, but within three years it was using all its output and, along with the rest of the industry, started importing lumber from New York state and Maine.

Design: Canadel designed the parts used in its furniture so that they were interchangeable. This allowed a wide range of products to be made from a limited number of parts as they could be assembled in various configurations.

Parts Manufacture: Canadel subcontracted the manufacture of furniture parts to a network of businesses in the Mauricie region of Quebec, an area known for its many furniture makers. Seventy percent of them made parts for Canadel, which accounted for 80 to 90 percent of their business volume. Each company made a limited number of parts in high volume using specialized machines. This allowed them to be larger and more profitable than they otherwise would be. Canadel eliminated subcontractors' cash flow concerns because it paid them in cash each Friday. For these benefits, the company insisted that subcontractors produce high-quality products that were delivered to assembly just-in-time—one to three days before they were needed. Canadel also influenced the availability of good subcontractors by helping some get into business and helping others sell their companies. Canadel benefited from subcontracting because its capital was not tied up in equipment, and subcontractors were responsible for the quality of parts and timeliness of their delivery.

Assembly: This was performed in Canadel's four plants. Each plant was dedicated to a product line (where that line was assembled, painted, and finished) or warehousing. This streamlined production so that delivery deadlines were met. At any time, more than 3000 tables and chairs were waiting to be assembled, and each piece had from five to 10 parts. Once the process started, work-in-process was moved from work station to work station on conveyor systems. Canadel capital investment was low because assembly required limited equipment, and the buildings were low-cost structures while just-in-time production kept inventories low. Quality was maintained by having parts on site only when needed and by using conveyor belts to move product.

Warehousing and Distribution: Orders were put together in the sole warehouse and then shipped. Finished goods inventory was low since the products had been made to order. This made managing inventories easier and also kept down the investment in inventory.

Marketing: A key component of Canadel's marketing starting in 1992 was its Workshop module, which presented styles of tables, chairs, and buffets (including different table and chair legs), colours, wood types, and finishes. Consumers used the Workshop to visualize their options as they "designed" the furniture for themselves. The Workshop let the consumers specify what they wanted, relieving the retailers of much of the selling work. In addition, since the furniture was custom the retailers did not need to carry an inventory of furniture. The success of the Workshop allowed Canadel to choose the retailers it worked with and it gave each retailer an exclusive territory. Retailers bought each Workshop for $4000, so those who had them were serious about selling Canadel's furniture. Canadel's penetration of the U.S. market was facilitated by hiring the experienced sales force of a troubled American company in 1992.

Service: Canadel's furniture was guaranteed for one year after purchase. Returns and repairs for Canadel were less than 1 percent of sales, mostly due to transportation damage. Other North American manufacturers experienced rates from 3 to 7 percent, and Asian manufacturers selling in North America had rates of around 20 percent.

Management: As a family business, three brothers managed the company jointly, with each assuming top responsibility for specific functions. The brothers, along with other members of the management team, had worked in the company for 10 years or more. Management's style was informal with each brother managing his own agenda. There was an "open door" policy. Each brother could walk into another's office unannounced to get comments and to resolve issues immediately. Other employees could also walk in, but this did not happen often; yet the policy maintained a sense of openness and closeness among all. The brothers also felt that they were a part of the community and were committed to keeping their business there. Each Friday they ate lunch together at a local restaurant. At this meeting the past week and plans for the next week were reviewed, and ideas were brainstormed and discussed. One or two key suppliers were regularly invited to join these lunches.

Human Resources: The philosophy of the brothers was to promote from within. They preferred to have employees work their way up through the organization, gaining skills as necessary, rather than hire MBAs who might not stay. This approach kept wages and salaries in line with local conditions while employees, in return, were loyal and diligent.

Information Technology: The complex communication needs between consumer orders, parts manufacturing, assembly, warehousing, and distribution were managed by a computer system. Integration was crucial because the company operated on a just-in-time basis. The software used was proprietary and had been developed at low cost largely by a local programmer. The hardware was a combination of UNIX and Windows NT, so it was low cost and could be maintained locally.

Finance: The outsourcing of manufacturing and just-in-time production required limited investment in the company. Keeping accounts receivable low with the stringent enforcement of its credit policy also helped keep investment down. As a result, Canadel had much higher sales to total assets than competitors did.

From 1982 to 2005, this system served Canadel well and the company grew quickly. With its success, others sought to copy it. The easiest features to copy were tacit; that is, they could be seen: the furniture and the choices possible, the brochures, the work centre. The hardest features to copy were either less available or less tangible: the availability of subcontractors (Canadel had tied up most in the Mauricie region) and of the best retailers for its concept (by being first in the market, Canadel had been able to tie up the best). Even less tangible was the relationship with satisfied consumers, loyal workers, and an appreciative community in Louiseville. The result was that no other furniture manufacturer in the region was able to build a system that matched Canadel's.

Eventually, international challenges limited Canadel's success. In 1998, low-cost Chinese product started entering the North American market, and, as that product got better, the perception of Canadel's value declined because the Chinese product was so much cheaper. This situation was worsened by the rising value of the Canadian dollar. Finally, the U.S. market, which accounted for 80 percent of Canadel's sales, declined dramatically as home sales started slowing in 2006.

Canadel responded in various ways. It replaced the Workshop with a web-based tool called Canadel UD (you design) that allows retailers and consumers to see every product in its line in every possible style, colour, and finish combination (http://udesign.canadel.ca). Canadel also introduced etailing and brought out cheaper product lines, bedroom furniture, and kitchen cabinetry. None of these actions, however, brought sales back to their peak of $174 million in 2004. Sales in 2009 were only $80 million. The rest of the Quebec furniture industry shared a similar fate.

Every company tries to please its customers better than any competitors subject to what it is able to do. How it does this is the topic of Chapter 3: the company's internal environment, where resources and capabilities are examined. Then, Chapter 4 deals with the company's external environment, where macro environment and industry dynamics are considered. Having established this foundation, Chapters 5 and 6 deal with strategic alternatives. Chapter 7 looks at how the performance of the strategic alternatives is examined. ∎

The Internal Environment: Resources, Capabilities, and Activities

A company's resources and capabilities reflect the choices managers make when configuring the activities they choose to perform internally (versus outsourcing). The role of managers is to allocate, reconfigure, and exploit the company's resources and capabilities. The example of Canadel provided us with a sense of what we mean by resources and capabilities.

In this chapter, models and theories are introduced that explain why some companies outperform their rivals and others lag behind. Two rigorous models that help analyze and formulate competitive strategies are the VRINE model and value-chain analysis. The VRINE model focuses on the resources and capabilities the company uses in pursuit of its strategy. Value-chain analysis focuses on activities that use the resources and create capabilities. These models suggest that differences in capabilities and resources account for differences in long-term performance among businesses in the same industry. The models differ, however, in that each has its own explanation for where the source of competitive advantage lies. The VRINE

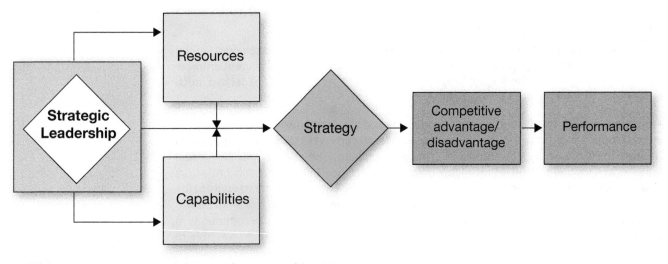

Exhibit 3.1   Resources, Capabilities, and Managerial Decisions

model attributes success to fundamental differences in a company's resources and capabilities. Value-chain analysis attributes success to the activities companies choose to engage in. Yet the two are complementary in that activities draw on resources and capabilities, and capabilities and resources are used to deliver the strategy that accounts for the business's superior performance, which indicates a competitive advantage.

STRATEGIC LEADERSHIP

We must always consider the role played by the managers of the business, irrespective of whether we trace a company's competitive advantage to its resources and capabilities or its value-chain activities. Senior and mid-level managers make key decisions about how to acquire, allocate, and discard resources, and they organize the business's value-chain activities. This is why managers' strategic decision-making capabilities are included as a valuable input into strategy. Exhibit 3.1 provides an overview of how resources, capabilities, and managerial decision making are interdependent; all are necessary to understand how and why companies perform differently within similar industry environments. Notice how the role of management is both to use the resources and capabilities to devise strategies and to make decisions about reconfiguring resources and capabilities. Indeed, managers play the unique role of being both resources and capabilities and making choices about the stewardship and deployment of other resources and capabilities (our opening vignette on Canadel is a case in point here).

Resources and Capabilities

Resources and capabilities are the fundamental building blocks of a company's strategy. The choices made by the company's managers relative to the five elements of a strategy, as organized by the strategy diamond (see Chapter 1), require resources and capabilities. For instance, if a company is to enter new arenas, it will need appropriate resources and capabilities in order to compete. It needs the right resources and capabilities to differentiate its products— whether on quality, image, or price. Likewise, it needs the right resources and capabilities to be considered when deciding to enter a new geographic or product market. Sometimes a company will acquire the resources or capabilities needed using a vehicle such as an acquisition or an alliance.[2] Not surprisingly, successful strategies are built on exploiting the resources and capabilities that a company has, upgrading them as needed, and acquiring the ones it needs. Unsuccessful strategies often reflect the fact that critical resources and capabilities are lacking. We will now clarify specifically what resources and capabilities are to prepare us to examine the two models.

RESOURCES

Resources are the inputs that companies use to create goods or services that customers demand. Resources have financial, physical, individual, and organizational attributes. Some resources are relatively undifferentiated inputs and can be acquired by any company. For instance, land, unskilled labour, debt financing, and commodity-like raw materials are generally available to most companies. Other resources that are more company-specific in nature are difficult to purchase through normal supply chains.[3] For instance, managerial judgment, intellectual property, trade secrets, and brand equity are not easily purchased or transferred. Those resources with physical attributes are referred to as *tangible* resources while those that cannot be precisely measured or assessed (such as knowledge, organizational culture, location, patents, trademarks, and reputation) are referred to as *intangible* resources. Tangible resources are easier to identify and value so they may be less likely to be a source of competitive advantage than intangible resources. Their tangible nature gives competitors a clear sense of what they need to imitate or substitute.

Some resources have both tangible and intangible characteristics. Land, for instance, has physical properties and satisfies certain functional needs. At the same time, some land, by virtue of its unique proximity to customers or suppliers, has an intangible benefit. The intangible aspects of resources can be instrumental in helping companies achieve favourable competitive positions. Wal-Mart, for example, enjoys near-monopoly status in many rural locations. Likewise, McDonald's controls much more than a valuable brand name (an intangible resource that does in fact convey a significant advantage). Like Wal-Mart, it also controls a great deal of valuable real estate by virtue of its location near high-traffic centres. Indeed, without its prime real estate locations, McDonald's would have a less valuable brand name. Obviously, the pace at which McDonald's grew required a certain capability in finding the needed real estate.

resources Inputs used by companies to create products and services.

CAPABILITIES

Capabilities are skills that make the business able to coordinate and exploit its resources (both tangible and intangible) as it creates goods and services. A synonym that is often used to describe the same concept is *competences*. Capabilities may be possessed by individuals as well as embedded in company-wide rules and routines, processes, and systems.[4] Examples of companies and their capabilities are listed in Exhibit 3.2.[5] For instance, Wal-Mart is widely regarded as having excellent capabilities related to the management of logistics, which it uses to exploit resources such as large stores, store locations, its trucking fleet, and massive distribution centres.

Capabilities range from simple tasks that people perform in their daily business, such as taking and fulfilling orders, to complex tasks, such as designing sophisticated systems, creative marketing, and manufacturing processes. Collectively, these capabilities are embedded in the

capabilities A company's skill at using its resources to create goods and services; combination of procedures and expertise on which a company relies to produce goods and services.

Company	Capability	Result
Wal-Mart	Logistics—distributing vast amounts of goods quickly and efficiently to remote locations.	200 000 percent return to shareholders during first 30 years since IPO.
The Vanguard Group	Extraordinarily frugal system using both technological leadership and economies of scale for delivering the lowest cost structure in the mutual-fund industry.	25 000 percent return to shareholders during the 30+ year tenure of CEO John Connelly. Shareholders in Vanguard equity funds pay, on average, $30 per $10 000 versus a $159 industry average. With bond funds, the bite is just $17 per $10 000.
3M	Generating new ideas and turning them into innovative and profitable products.	30 percent of revenue from products introduced within the past four years.

Exhibit 3.2 A Few Extraordinary Capabilities

value chain Total of primary and support activities through which the company adds value.

outsourcing Activity performed for a company by people other than its full-time employees.

distinctive competence Capability that sets a company apart from other companies; something that a company can do that competitors cannot duplicate easily.

core competence Capability that is central to a corporation's main business operations and allows it to generate new products and services.

activities that constitute a company's **value chain**. Not all capabilities are of equal value to the company—a fact that has, in turn, given rise to the rapid growth of outsourcing. **Outsourcing** is contracting with external suppliers to perform certain parts of a company's normal value chain of activities. Two special classes of capabilities with which you should be familiar are distinctive competences and core competences. **Distinctive competences** set a company apart from other companies. **Core competences** are central to the main business operations of the corporation; they are common to the corporation's principle businesses and are what the corporation uses to generate new products and services in the various businesses it owns. A core competence at General Electric (GE), which operates in many unrelated businesses, is the capability of its general managers; GE is able to manage a portfolio of businesses based on sound business principles when most companies have difficulty managing unrelated business simultaneously.

The relationship between resources and capabilities can be illustrated by a few more examples. Intel's manufacturing capacity (that is, its plants, equipment, and production engineers), its patented microprocessor designs, and its well-established brand name are among its key resources. Intel has also demonstrated the organizational capability to design new generations of leading-edge microprocessors and to do so rapidly. Intel demonstrated marketing adroitness by creating the "Intel Inside" campaign, which stimulated greater demand and higher switching costs among end-users—the customers of Intel's customers. This clearly suggests a marketing capability. The combination of Intel's resources and capabilities enables its managers to execute a value-creating strategy and achieve a formidable competitive advantage in the microprocessor industry.

In the oil industry, resources and capabilities have not developed uniformly by all competitors. Some companies, for example, are highly integrated. Integrated companies are involved in every stage of the value chain, including exploration and extraction, refining, distribution, and marketing. The largest integrated operator in Canada is Imperial Oil, which is majority owned by ExxonMobil. Other integrated companies are Husky Energy, Petro-Canada, and Shell Canada. In contrast, the upstream sector focuses solely on exploration and production. Independents include Adda Resources Ltd., Nexen Inc., Talisman Energy, Connacher Oil and Gas Limited, and Ivanhoe Energy. The downstream sector focuses on operating refineries and retail establishments. Companies in this sector include Ultramar and Irving Oil. The resources and capabilities in the three different sectors are very different. Those in upstream activities are petroleum reserves and have capabilities in exploration and extraction. Those engaged in downstream activities have refineries and distribution networks and capabilities in refining, distribution, and marketing. Those in both, the integrated companies, have both sets of resources and capabilities.

Resources and capabilities can be complementary. In the fast-food industry, location is important because most fast-food purchases are impulse buys. McDonald's had excellent site-location capabilities, and the company's real estate holdings (which are tangible resources) consist of prime sites located using this capability—the difference between the cost of a prime location and a mediocre site could be three times the price per square foot.[6] The quality of this capability has also improved over time. At one time, McDonald's used helicopters to assess the growth of residential areas: Basically, planners looked for cheap land alongside thoroughfares that would one day run through well-populated suburbs. This capability evolved as technology evolved. In the 1980s, McDonald's turned to satellite photography to predict urban sprawl. Since then the company developed a software package called Quintillion, which integrates information from satellite images, detailed maps, demographic information, CAD drawings, and sales data from existing stores. This evolving capability has made McDonald's a leader in site location.

The VRINE Model

The VRINE model is based on the perception that competitors in a given industry have different resources and capabilities and that changing these is not done quickly or easily. Also called the Resource Based View (RBV) of strategy, this approach assesses resources and capabilities using their attributes to determine which provide the basis for a competitive

Exhibit 3.3   Applying the VRINE Model

	The Test	The Competitive Implication	The Performance Implication
Is it valuable?	Does the resource or capability allow the firm to meet a market demand or protect the firm from market uncertainties?	If so, the company is able to compete in an industry, but value by itself does not convey an advantage.	Valuable resources and capabilities have the *potential* to contribute to *normal profits* (profits that cover the cost of all inputs, including capital).
Is it rare?	Assuming that the resource or capability is valuable, is it scarce relative to demand or is it widely possessed by competitors?	Valuable resources that are also rare contribute to a *competitive advantage*, but that advantage may be only temporary.	A *temporary competitive advantage* can contribute to *above-normal profits*, at least until the advantage is nullified by other firms.
Is it inimitable and/or non-substitutable?	Assuming that the resource is both valuable and rare, how difficult is it for competitors either to imitate it or substitute other resources and capabilities that yield similar benefits?	Valuable and rare resources and capabilities that are also difficult to imitate or substitute can contribute to *sustained competitive advantage*.	A sustained competitive advantage can contribute to *above-normal profits for extended periods of time* (until competitors find ways to imitate or substitute or environmental changes nullify the advantage).
Is it exploitable?	If the resource or capability satisfied any or all of the preceding VRINE criteria, can the firm actually exploit it?	Resources and capabilities that satisfy the first four VRINE criteria but that cannot be exploited do not convey competitive advantage. In fact, they may increase opportunity costs.	Firms that control but don't exploit their VRINE resources and capabilities (even after they satisfy the V, R, I, and N criteria) generally suffer from lower levels of financial performance and depressed market valuations *relative to what they would enjoy if they could in fact exploit them* (although they won't be in as bad a shape as competitors who don't control any VRINE-certified resources and capabilities).

Source: Adapted from J. B. Barney, "Looking Inside for Competitive Advantage," *Academy of Management Executive* 9:4 (1995): 49–61.

advantage. The specific attributes considered in the model are Value, Rarity, Inimitability, Non-substitutability, and Exploitability, hence the acronym VRINE.[7] Exhibit 3.3 summarizes five basic characteristics that determine whether a resource or capability can help a company compete and, indeed, achieve superior performance. Only those resources with all five attributes have the potential to provide a competitive advantage. This is tested systematically by examining each resource or capability. Whenever the resource or capability does not have an attribute, it is dropped from further consideration as a source of competitive advantage. The resource or capability may still be required, but it is not a source of competitive advantage. Few pass these five tests.

The VRINE model makes use of specific attributes to determine which resources provide the source of competitive advantage so we will leave consideration of these attributes to the model.

VALUE

A resource or capability is valuable if it enables a company to take advantage of opportunities or to fend off threats in its environment.[8] In other words, the resource or capability either allows the business to pursue opportunities that create value or allows the business to address a threat

FOCUS ON SUSTAINABILITY 3.1

The Mining Industry Thinks in Terms of Sustainability

The mining industry extracts minerals from the ground and once the rich deposits are gone it moves to the next richest deposits elsewhere. Thus, it might seem odd that the mining industry would think in terms of sustainability, but it does. In 2002, the International Institute for Sustainable Development issued a report that helped the industry address sustainability. To accomplish this, the meaning of sustainability had to be clarified. Behind the concept of sustainability is a fundamental, immutable value set that is best stated as "parallel care and respect for the ecosystem and for the people within." The goal of sustainability emerges from this value set: to achieve human and ecosystem well-being together. Seen in this way, sustainability has as much to do with achieving well-being for people and ecosystems as it has to do with reducing stress or impacts. It suggests that mining needs to achieve a net environmental and human benefit to contribute positively to sustainability. Conversely, a given mining/mineral project or operation that leads to a net degradation of human and ecosystem well-being is non-sustainable. When deciding whether to proceed with a mine, decision makers, other interests, and the public should understand the implications from this perspective.

The institute proposed that seven questions be addressed when examining sustainability:

1. Engagement: Are engagement processes in place and working effectively?

2. People: Will people's well-being be maintained or improved?

3. Environment: Is the integrity of the environment assured over the long term?

4. Economy: Is the economic viability of the project or operation assured, and will the economy of the community and beyond be better off as a result?

5. Traditional and Non-Market Activities: Are traditional and non-market activities in place in the community and surrounding area?

6. Institutional Arrangements and Governance: Are rules, incentives, programs, and capacity in place to address project and operational consequences?

7. Synthesis and Continuous Learning. Does a full synthesis show that the net result will be positive or negative in the long term, and will there be periodic reassessments?

For each question, the institute offered an "ideal" answer from the perspective of sustainability. By stating the ideal, a direction of progress is presented. And the ideal provides the basis for developing criteria that can be used to judge whether progress is being made over time.

Do you agree with the definition of sustainability as presented for the mining industry? If not, can mining ever be considered a sustainable activity? And if it is not, should we stop mining?

Source: International Institute for Sustainable Development, "Seven Questions to Sustainability: How to Assess the Contribution of Mining and Minerals Activities," Winnipeg, Manitoba, Canada, 2002.

and thereby hold on to the value it is able to create. For any resource to create value, the return on capital tied up in the resource should exceed the required rate of return on the business's capital. When it does not, investors would be better off if the capital were given back to them so they could reinvest it somewhere else.[9]

The Deveaults, described in the opening vignette, created an opportunity for Canadel when they saw a market for casual dining furniture. They put together the resources and capabilities needed to design and market casual dining furniture for which consumers were willing to pay a premium price. Over time Canadel was able to produce this furniture at lower cost than competitors because it had efficient subcontractors making furniture parts for it. It also had lower wood costs because it had bought a lumber mill before prices for wood went up due to shortages.

Some resources, though a source of value, can become less valuable over time. This is most evident with gas, oil, and mineral deposits. Businesses using these deposits make a profit by extracting and selling their content, running down the value of the remaining deposit. These businesses can only survive over the long run by finding or buying additional deposits.

RARITY

Rarity is scarcity relative to demand. An otherwise valuable resource that isn't rare won't necessarily contribute to competitive advantage: Valuable resources that are available to most competitors simply enable a company to achieve parity with everyone else. Sometimes such resources may be called *table stakes,* as in poker, because they are required to compete in the first place. But when a company controls a valuable resource that's also rare in its industry, it's in a position to gain a competitive advantage. When Canadel started up, it relied on subcontractors for parts. Early on, Canadel only subcontracted a few woodworkers in the Mauricie region, but as the company grew it subcontracted more and more of them. By 2004, it had 70 percent of the local woodworking companies working with it. Our judgment is that by this point subcontractors had become rare, since there were not enough for any local start-up to acquire sufficient contractors to match Canadel in size. Another consideration in this judgment is that Canadel was able to secure superior resources. Canadel selected subcontractors whom the company helped to start businesses, in addition to helping owners of existing businesses sell their businesses to others. With its retailers, Canadel was the first company selling casual dining furniture in the United States, so it was able to pick those retailers that would be the most profit-

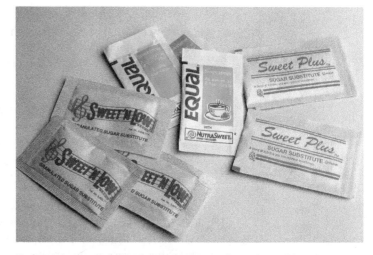

Monsanto enjoyed a competitive advantage for many years because it owned the patent to aspartame, the chemical compound in NutraSweet. The patent on aspartame ran out in 1992, and in 2000 Monsanto sold NutraSweet to private investors. NutraSweet now faces fierce competition from other aspartame-containing products, and newer and more popular non-aspartame-based sweeteners.

able. Once Canadel had their business, they were no longer available to competitors. This same principle of superior locations applies to numerous forms of retailing.

A company that controls a valuable and scarce resource or capability may create a competitive advantage, but there is no assurance that the advantage will persist. We now turn to the two criteria that must be satisfied if the advantage is to be sustained.

INIMITABILITY

That which cannot be imitated is inimitable. But imitation is typically a matter of time as aspiring competitors can eventually imitate most resources. This can be done in various ways, including internal investment, acquisitions, and alliances.[10] One deals with this by determining how long it will take competitors to imitate the resources and capabilities. For Canadel, since only 30 percent of the subcontractors in the Mauricie region did not work for the company and those who did were heavily committed to it, potential competitors were limited in their ability to acquire subcontractors. But inimitability is a two-sided coin. What makes it hard for competitors to copy may also have detrimental consequences for the company. Cirque du Soleil—a Canadian entertainment company that offers a mix of circus arts and street theatre—searches the world for performers who perform implausible physical feats. It then builds shows around these "unusual acts." This creates a problem when someone who is truly unique is either difficult to work with or impossible to replace. At times, acts have been cut from shows because certain performers were no longer able to work. Cirque du Soleil has also addressed the problem of the rarity of its performers by having various troupes perform different shows.[11]

Several factors can limit the ability of competitors to imitate resources or capabilities: high cost, property rights, time, and causal ambiguity.

The Role of High Cost

If, as an old cliché goes, "Everything is said to be available for a price," then competitors will be able to buy the resources they want. The disadvantage that later buyers face is that those selling these resources have a new appreciation of how much they are worth. The consequence is that those who buy assets later have to pay higher prices for them. Canadel was able to buy Bois Kennebec for much less than later companies because demand for lumber was low at the time. As wood became scarce, the cost of lumber mills rose. Sometimes whole companies are bought simply for their resources. At times in the oil industry buying companies with proven reserves has been cheaper than searching for new reserves. Typically, however, acquisition is an expensive approach because the buyer pays a substantial premium over the market value of the company.[12]

The Role of Property Rights

Property rights are assigned through government regulations. For instance, patented items or processes cannot be directly copied during the term of the patent. DALSA in Waterloo, Ontario, owns dozens of patents for the design of CCD and CMOS image sensor chips and digital cameras that have helped it develop a worldwide market for its high-performance digital cameras.[13]

To discourage infringement on patents, imitators are subject to severe legal repercussions, including heavy fines. This requires that the patent holder be prepared to defend them in court—a lengthy and expensive legal process. In the late 1990s, Research In Motion (RIM) in Waterloo, Ontario, introduced the BlackBerry to the market. Before then, NTP, a company based in Arlington, Virginia, received a patent that allowed emails to be sent to mobile devices. In January 2000, when NTP noticed similarities between the BlackBerry and NTP's technology, it sent a letter to RIM pointing out patent infringement and offered to license the technology for a fee. NTP then sued RIM and was awarded damages and fees amounting to US$210 million. RIM, after appealing the fine, sought to reach a settlement with NTP. In 2006, RIM finally agreed to pay US$612.5 million for a licence to NTP's patents going forward.[14]

Other government regulations can limit a business's entry to the market. In Canada, regulation of telecommunications and broadcasting through the Canadian Radio-Television Telecommunications Commission (CRTC) strongly influences the determination of who can compete and how they compete. In 2009, a pressing issue was the throttling practice of Bell Canada on internet traffic using its system. Bell, which has a persistent 95 percent share in residential services in major cities in Ontario and Quebec, claimed that the practice was necessary to prevent congestion of the Bell network, but internet service providers found that throttling limited the attractiveness of certain services such as online video available over the internet.[15]

The Role of Time

Unique historical conditions surrounding the development of resources and the passage of time before an acquisition provides its benefits mean that time has an influence on inimitability.[16]

Coca-Cola was given unique resources due to a set of historical events. During the Second World War, General Dwight D. Eisenhower requested that Coca-Cola be available for five cents a bottle to all U.S. servicemen and servicewomen anywhere in the world. Eisenhower saw this as a way of building troop morale. To make this possible, the U.S. government financed the construction of 64 bottling plants around the world. At war's end, these plants were incorporated into Coca-Cola's company structure without cost. This provided Coca-Cola with a global presence in both bottling capacity and brand recognition.[17] While Coca-Cola's internationalization was subsidized by the government, Pepsi faced considerable cost disadvantages as it expanded internationally. Coke's global advantage over Pepsi remains even today. Of Coke's US$31 billion sales in 2009, fully 75 percent were from outside North America.[18]

The passage of time creates inimitability as well because the situation facing competitors changes over time. The first business faces limited competition when it starts with its strategy. Over time this business builds the resources and capabilities that produce its success. When competitors start building their resources and capabilities to pursue the same strategy as the successful business, they face a well-established competitor with significant resources and capabilities in the areas needed. If the original business continues to build its resources and capabilities, the competitors chasing it may never catch up. RIM with its Blackberry is attempting to do this as it continually invests in new technologies, though these are bringing it into convergence with other mobile devices.

The Role of Causal Ambiguity

Identifying or understanding the causal factors of a resource or capability can be difficult, in part because a complex combination of factors make it valuable.[19] Management itself may not understand the relationship between the resources and capabilities they control and the business's competitive advantage. And when it has ideas about which resources and capabilities matter it may still be unable to sort out what really matters. And even when it does know what matters, the complex network of interrelationships between individuals, groups, and technology are hard to sort out and burdensome to duplicate. If the management of the company faces these challenges in knowing what matters, then the competitor trying to determine what matters from the outside faces an enormous challenge.

NON-SUBSTITUTABILITY

The non-substitutability criterion is satisfied if a competitor cannot achieve the same results using a different combination of resources and capabilities. Some companies find alternative resources or capabilities that "mimic" the benefits of the original resources. This is true in terms of "disruptive technologies." For many years large bookstore chains enjoyed formidable advantages in the retail-book industry because their size gave them greater buying power than smaller retailers. With the development of the internet, Amazon.com was able to capture similar customer volume by selling books online without the need to establish stores.

Canadel cleverly used technology to imitate what custom furniture manufacturers did through custom manufacture and what large furniture manufacturers did by having very broad product lines. It achieved the low cost of volume by standardizing parts so that each part was manufactured in volume, and it achieved customization by assembling these parts in various combinations and then painting and finishing them in accordance with consumer desires. Critical to the customization was the consumer's ability to make the selection using Canadel's Workshop.

EXPLOITABILITY

The business can be organized to exploit the full potential of the resource or capability. The organizational capabilities include organizational structure, systems, and processes. These organizational factors are complementary in that they do not generate competitive advantage in isolation but work in combination with the resources and capabilities to enable the business to attain the full potential of its competitive advantage.

Canadel's success came from its ability to use a strong control system that collected orders from the retailers, created work orders that went to each of the subcontractors, had the subcontractors deliver the parts as needed, assembled the parts in specialized plants, and then consolidated the output of the specialized plants into orders that were shipped to customers. Throughout this process quality was tightly controlled so that quality was reflected in the final products. High levels of performance were facilitated by the open-door policy of management, which allowed issues to be addressed quickly. The interests of the business were furthered by the warm relationship management maintained with employees, subcontractors, and the community. And management's nurturing of Canadel's subcontractors meant that they were reliable and efficient. These organizational aspects pulled together the various resources and capabilities to produce a business with a strong competitive advantage.

Many companies have valuable and rare resources that they fail to exploit. For many years, Novell's core NetWare product gave it a significant advantage in the computer networking market. In high-tech industries, however, staying on top requires continuous innovation, and according to many observers, Novell's decline in the 1990s reflected an inability to produce innovations that met the demands of changing markets and technology. Shortly after Novell's new CEO, Eric Schmidt, was hired in 1997 from Sun Microsystems, he concluded, "I walk down the Novell hallway and marvel at the incredible potential for innovation here. But Novell has had a difficult time in the past turning innovation into products in the marketplace."[20] The company, Schmidt confided to a few key executives, was suffering from "organizational constipation."[21] Schmidt saw that Novell had the resources and capabilities needed to innovate, but it lacked the exploitative capability, especially in its product development and marketing processes, needed to get innovative products to market in a timely manner.

Xerox, too, was unable to exploit its resources to innovate products. It established a successful research team at Xerox PARC in Palo Alto, California—PARC is the acronym for Palo Alto Research Center. Scientists in this group invented an impressive list of innovative products, including laser printers, ethernet, graphical-interface software, bit mapping, and the computer mouse. Unfortunately, Xerox corporate managers at headquarters on the east coast failed to recognize the opportunities that researchers at PARC had created. Innovations slipped away to other companies that captured much of the value of PARC's innovations: Apple, Microsoft, 3Com. Three reasons have been given for Xerox's failure to capitalize on its innovations. First was the disparity between the relaxed and flexible culture that prevailed at PARC and the formal and rigid culture at Xerox headquarters. Second was the distance between PARC and its corporate headquarters—4800 kilometres—which cut it off from the attention of top managers. Third was the disparity between the goals of PARC researchers, who were allowed to pursue ventures of interest to them, with no concern for commercial importance, and the goals of corporate headquarters, where profitability was all important.[22]

Any resource or capability can be assessed using the VRINE model to determine if it is a potential source of competitive advantage. To illustrate how this is done, we use the VRINE model in Exhibit 3.4 to analyze Pfizer's ownership of the patents for Zoloft as a possible source of competitive advantage.[23]

Exhibit 3.4   Applying the VRINE Model to Pfizer's Drug Patents

Putting Pfizer's Drug Patents up to the VRINE test		Answers
	Let's walk through the VRINE model as applied to Pfizer's patents for Zoloft (sertraline HCl), an antidepressant known as a selective serotonin reuptake inhibitor (SSRI). If you were studying Pfizer and the pharmaceutical industry using the VRINE model, you would probably identify a number of resources and capabilities that may be the source of competitive advantage. You would probably identify patents, R&D capabilities, and marketing as key resources and capabilities that drive the differentiator facet of its strategy.	
Value: Do Pfizer's two patents on Zoloft provide value?	In any given year, about (xx) percent of the Canadian population (approximately (xx) million people) will experience a depressive disorder. Approximately (xx) percent of adults will experience depression at some point in their lives. Women are twice as likely as men to experience depression. Thus, it appears that having a patent for a treatment for depression would enable a pharmaceutical company to take advantage of a large market opportunity.	Yes
Rarity: Are they rare?	Pfizer's patents on Zoloft gave it the exclusive right to use the chemical compound sertraline HCl to treat depression (the patents expired in June 2006). When the patents expired, generic drug makers were able to sell copied versions of the drug. The patents for Zoloft were definitely rare during the term of the patents, but are not since they expired (assuming that several generic companies make the drug, its scarcity relative to demand will decline).	Yes, but not since they expired.
Inimitability?	Pfizer is certainly not the only large pharmaceutical company that desires to profit from therapies for depression. However, a patent makes direct imitation illegal until the patent expires.	
Non-substitutability: Is there protection against ready substitutes?	Competitors can and do attempt to find substitute compounds that have similar effects. Indeed, Zoloft itself was a Pfizer innovation in the face of Eli Lilly's patent for Prozac. Zoloft is not the only treatment for depression; other SSRIs include Prozac, Paxil, and others. The patents for Zoloft may convey temporary advantage, but Pfizer's value from them will probably erode over time as others invent substitute compounds and as the patents expire, resulting in direct imitation.	Not completely.
Exploitability: Is there evidence these are exploitable?	To satisfy this VRINE criterion, Pfizer needs to be able to move drugs from successful clinical trial to market distribution. Fortunately for Pfizer, marketing and distribution are two of its core competences. Indeed, Pfizer has more drug representatives than any other pharmaceutical company. Pfizer also has large cash reserves that can be used to bring sufficient quantities of the product quickly to market prior to the lapsing of the patents.	Yes
The verdict?	As you may have guessed by now, Pfizer's patents on Zoloft largely stand up to the VRINE framework, suggesting that patents are a resource that can generate competitive advantage. The expiration of those patents could largely diminish the VRINE advantages they provided. Note, however, that Zoloft is such a resource not just because of patents. Pfizer also possesses the complementary VRINE resources and capabilities underlying its exploitability.	Yes

Once the resource or capability has been identified as a source of advantage, two questions have to be considered. The first question is how long the business can keep on using that resource. The answer is based on the durability of the resource or capability. Some will decline over time while others can be maintained through continued investment. The second question is how long will it be before others can do what the business does. The answer is based on matters of the ability of competitors to imitate or to substitute the resources and capabilities key to competitive advantage, and to exploit them once acquired. In the case of Canadel, duplicating the workshop and the plant would be easy; designing the products and information systems would take longer; and building up the subcontractors, relationships with the community, and sales through desirable retailers would take a long time.

WHERE DO RESOURCES COME FROM?

Our definitions of resources and capabilities describe them as something the company may own or possess. However, in the VRINE model, the resources and capabilities that matter most are not easily purchased. This is the situation for intangible resources such as brand equity, reputation, and innovative capability. Brand equity, for example, takes years to build. The brand equity of Coca-Cola, for example, has been developed through decades of marketing efforts with investments in the hundreds of millions per year; Toyota's reputation for quality automobiles has been developed through stringent quality-control methods developed over decades; and Intel's R&D capability is the result of years of investment. This leaves the business with two options: either it buys out the owner of the brand, which would represent a high cost, or it spends years developing its own brand by implementing policies and strategies that will be maintained over extended periods of time.

Dynamic Capabilities

From the discussion so far, you might conclude that a business's success depends simply on having a set of resources and capabilities that satisfy the VRINE model's five tests. The environment within which a business operates, however, is in a continual state of change, as you will see in Chapter 4. Markets are dynamic as broader forces lead customers and competitors to change. Continuing success of the business then depends on change in its strategy and, in support of the strategy, change in some of the resources and capabilities the company relies on for a competitive advantage. Only by redefining the strategy and altering resources and capabilities will the company have the potential for sustaining a competitive advantage. Recognition of this has led to a distinction that sees two types of capabilities: organizational and dynamic. Organizational capabilities are used on a daily basis to produce goods and services that the company sells. **Dynamic capabilities** are used to renew and change the company's stock of organizational capabilities so that it can deliver a constant stream of new and innovative products and services to customers.[24]

Dynamic capabilities are manifest in several ways. One form of dynamic capability is the ability to integrate different resources and capabilities to create new revenue-producing products and services.[25] Disney, for instance, recently launched its Princess Line, which brings together merchandise based on famous female Disney characters. The effort required that Disney integrate development and marketing campaigns geared toward groups of characters that had before been developed and marketed separately.[26] Another form of a dynamic capability is reconfiguring or transferring resources and capabilities from one division to another. Mail Boxes Etc. (MBE), the postal centre that was recently purchased by UPS, illustrates this fact. By encoding its knowledge of how to start up a master-area franchise, MBE created "templates" for future franchisees. New master-area franchisees are required to duplicate the template exactly prior to making any adjustments to meet local market needs. This is done because their internal research shows that master-area franchisees that duplicate the template significantly outperform those that first customize the model.[27]

The rebundling of resources and capabilities is also accomplished through alliances and acquisitions. Resources and capabilities can both be acquired and lost through these vehicles. Cisco has been able to launch many new products by strategically acquiring companies that had

dynamic capabilities A company's ability to modify, reconfigure, and upgrade resources and capabilities in order to strategically respond to or generate environmental changes.

bits and pieces of network architecture.[28] Nortel, a major Canadian competitor to Cisco, also modified its resources and capabilities through acquisitions. In the 1990s the phone industry relied on Asynchronous Transfer Mode (ATM) technology, which was reliable though expensive. Only Cisco had the expertise to make equipment based on Internet Protocol (IP), which was much cheaper to operate. In order to compete in the new technology, Nortel went on a massive buying spree from 1998 to 2001, spending US$32 billion to acquire 18 companies that had the technology it needed. Its first significant buy was of Bay Networks, Cisco's primary competitor in the router and switching business, for US$7 billion in June 1998. John Roth, Nortel's CEO during this period, said, "It doesn't matter whether you develop or acquire leading technology. Our job is to provide the technology and products our customers need." By buying the resources and capabilities Nortel needed, it was able to capture nearly 40 percent of the optical networking market that Cisco dominated.[29]

The dynamic view of resources and capabilities emphasizes the need to renew resources and capabilities, either in order to keep pace with a changing environment or to reconfigure the organization proactively (that is, to change the environment). One or both of these capabilities—the ability to adapt to change and the ability to initiate change—are particularly important in industries in which time to market is critical, technological change is rapid, and future competition is difficult to forecast.[30] When even strong, incumbent companies do not have such capabilities, they are likely to be outmanoeuvred by new competitors that introduce new industry standards.[31] Consequently, the value of a company's portfolio of resources and capabilities is directly affected by its dynamic capability to reconfigure resources and capabilities to the evolving requirements of the competitive environment. More complex forms of dynamic capabilities are typically associated with dynamic or turbulent environments.

Value-Chain Analysis

The VRINE model is a method of considering why companies in the same industry had different levels of performance due to differences in their resources, capabilities, and dynamic capabilities. Value-chain analysis takes the view that the business's margin or profit depends on the activities it performs. The approach complements the VRINE model because activities are performed using the resources and capabilities of the company. Activities matter because they determine what the customer gets, and this determines the price the customer is willing to pay. Performing these activities produces the cost of the company. The difference between the price paid for the product and the cost of all the activities associated with it is the profit margin of the company or, in economic terms, the value created by the company. This is why the analysis is said to focus on value. The value created by the company can be increased by getting the customer to pay more by providing the customer with more desirable products and services. Value can also be increased by lowering the cost of providing the same products and services to the customer.

Value-chain analysis can be used for four different purposes. First, it can help management determine how changing activities can increase the value created by the company. Second, it can explain why companies in the same industry and with the same activities create different amounts of value. Third, it can determine which activities to outsource. And fourth, it can help corporate management find synergies generated by sharing or combining activities across business units.

The starting point of all value-chain analysis is identifying the activities and the linkages between them. Bestselling business author Michael Porter produced a generic diagram of the activities that can be considered (see Exhibit 3.5).[32] He sorted activities into two types: primary and support. The primary activities deal with the flow of the product or service through the business, such as:

- **inbound logistics**, which include receiving, warehousing, and inventory control of input materials.
- **operations,** which include machining, assembling, and all other activities that transform inputs into the final product.
- **outbound logistics,** which include warehousing, order fulfillment, and other activities required to get the finished product to the customer.

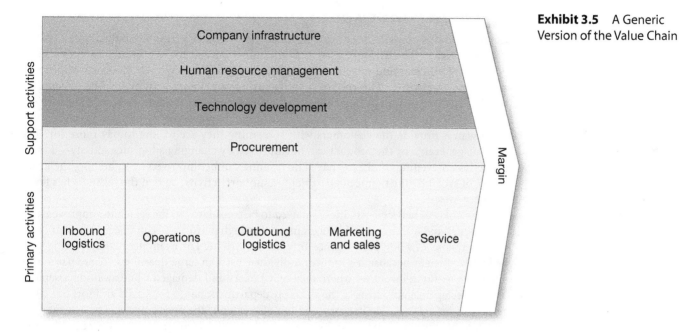

Exhibit 3.5 A Generic Version of the Value Chain

- **marketing and sales**, which include channel selection, advertising, pricing, and other activities associated with getting buyers to purchase the product.
- **service,** which includes customer support, repair services, and other activities that maintain and enhance the product's value to the customer.

The support activities are the activities that support the primary value-chain activities, such as:

- **procurement**, which includes purchasing raw materials, components, supplies, and equipment.
- **technology development**, which includes research and development, process automation, and other technology development.
- **human resources management**, which includes recruiting, hiring, training, development, and compensating employees.
- **company infrastructure**, which includes finance, legal, quality management, information systems, organizational structure, control systems, company culture, and so on.

The description of the activities listed above is generic, and actual analysis of a company's value chain requires that they be specified according to what the business does. Slavishly following the generic example will mean that your analysis may well miss the reality of the situation. One way to identify the relevant activities is using process maps.

Having identified activities clearly, the linkages between them need to be identified. A linkage exists if the performance or cost of one activity affects that of another activity. Linkages between the primary activities are readily apparent because they are all tied to producing the product or service, which is the primary focus of the business. For example, at Canadel the design of standard parts that could be assembled in various ways to produce "custom" furniture both decreased the cost of manufacturing and also increased what consumers were willing to pay because they received a product that was more to their liking. In other businesses, improvements in design reduce manufacturing costs and improve product reliability so that service costs are also reduced. Linkages between support and primary activities are more subtle, but they are there. At Canadel, managing human resources through a policy of "open doors," internal promotion, and hiring people who grew with the business produced a motivated workforce engaged in the primary activities. The information system was another support activity that was crucial to primary activities because it controlled the orders and product flows.

Armed with a clear understanding of the activities performed by the company and how they are linked, we are ready to consider the alternative purposes of analysis.

IMPROVING VALUE ADDED

Greater margins come from improving what the customer gets while reducing the cost of producing what the customer gets. Activities are analyzed to determine how they can be made more efficient and effective. Improvements in efficiency lower the costs of primary and support activities. The cost of manufacturing, a primary activity, can be lowered by installing a more productive machine. The cost of labour per unit of product can be lowered if human resources, a support activity, alters the compensation system. Improvements in effectiveness provide the customers with something they are willing to pay more for. The revenue generated by the product can be improved by changing a logistics activity—adding deliveries on evenings and Saturday. The revenue can be improved by tightening the availability of credit by the finance department, a support activity, so that the business has fewer bad debt losses.

The linkages between activities also need to be considered in the search for improvements in efficiency and effectiveness. Linkages mean that high performance in one activity can come at the expense of poor performance in another activity. For example, manufacturing may be highly efficient because it produces individual parts in large quantities. These parts then pile up in working inventory where they may be lost and damaged while awaiting assembly. This drives up assembly costs as the assembly department has to find parts and sort out damaged parts before it can do its work, and this also extends the operating cycle so that the time between the customer's order and delivery of that order is longer. What is needed is better coordination between the two activities so that they work in harmony with each other. This means that, when making changes in specific activities, linkages among them need to be recognized so that the change in one is not detrimental to another.

The issue of value creation by the company is explored further in Chapters 5 and 6.

COMPARING COMPETING BUSINESSES

Different companies in the same industry can have different margins. This happens because the activities in their value chain differ due to different histories, strategies, and success in implementation. Consider the oil industry, which we discussed earlier. Irving Oil and Talisman Energy are both in the oil business, but the two made very different choices about the activities they engage in. Irving Oil performs refining and distribution while Talisman Energy performs exploration. Even when two companies possess similar resources and capabilities, one company can still gain the upper hand and achieve a competitive advantage by configuring value-adding activities in a different way.[33]

IKEA, a Swedish furniture company, has built a hugely successful business by reconfiguring the value-chain activities of the furniture industry. IKEA does not deal with assembled furniture—flat-packed boxes are all it needs to handle. The boxes arrive at IKEA's stores, which double as warehouses. There, customers shop among display models and then take the boxed, unassembled furniture off the shelves and assemble it at home. By dealing with flat furniture IKEA's shipping costs are low. IKEA also kept down costs early on by having customers do their own transport and assembly of purchased goods. These services are now available but at a charge. Similarly, Dell's success for a long time was based on a radical departure from the prevailing business models in its industry. Its configuration of manufacturing, sales, distribution, and customer-service activities in the personal-computer industry exploited the growing base of knowledgeable PC consumers around the world. Dell PCs use components manufactured entirely by suppliers. In addition, its marketing and distribution rest on a direct-sales model that avoids retailers. This combination of outsourcing component manufacturing and distributing finished products directly to consumers was radically different from its competitors when it started up.

So how does a successful company avoid competition that will limit its success? By making imitation by competitors difficult. It does this by organizing the value-chain activities in unique and specific ways. Competitive advantage based on value-chain configuration usually involves a complex system of interdependent activities. Canadel, for example, relies on subcontractors to provide its parts. For a furniture company that makes its own parts, switching to having subcontractors make parts would require finding them then developing processes to coordinate their work with assembly by the company. And unless the company redesigned its products, it would not be able to achieve the economies and finished product flexibility that Canadel now achieves through subcontracting. Rivals found it very difficult to imitate Canadel's system of activities because the complex system had to work together in an integrated manner, and recreating some aspects such as positive relations with workers and the community were challenging. Hence, competitors balk at imitating successful rivals. The one competitor who did try was eventually affected by the same forces as Canadel and had to declare bankruptcy.[34]

WestJet, another example, introduced a radically different approach to the airline industry, which allowed it to achieve unrivalled cost advantages over Air Canada. Founded in 1996, WestJet performed far fewer activities and in non-traditional ways. For example, it chose to fly point to point using only one type of aircraft, Boeing 737s—a strategy that reduces maintenance and training costs. In addition, the chosen aircraft is more efficient for these shorter routes. WestJet also chose not to perform many of the services normally provided by major carriers such as baggage transfers, meals, and assigned seats. This produced a configuration of activities fundamentally different from those of most other airlines, including Air Canada, which used a hub-and-spokes system for flights. This system had all the airline's flights arrive at its hub at the same time. The advantage was that passengers stayed with the airline as they switched to another flight. This approach also required that hubs be at large airports that could handle surges in traffic and the transfer of massive numbers of bags among various flights. Air Canada and other big airlines have made some changes such as discontinuing meal service to save costs, but they can't stop transferring luggage, abandon the hub-and-spokes system, or convert exclusively to Boeing 737s. The major airlines would put themselves at great risk if they moved to copy WestJet directly because of their many existing commitments to the way they do their business. For this reason Air Canada has stayed with the hub-and-spokes system while gradually lowering the cost difference with WestJet by attempting to copy it through a separate airline subsidiary called Jazz.

The development of Jazz shows that the danger of competition comes from new businesses that have not made prior commitments to which activities they will do and how they will perform them. The business model that WestJet uses was not new but rather copied from Southwest Airlines, based in Dallas, Texas. Ryanair, a discount airline in Europe, has also copied Southwest's model. Even in the United States, Southwest's model has been copied with a few modifications by JetBlue, which was founded by David Neeleman, a former Southwest executive and an adviser to WestJet.

A further example of a new entrant copying an established competitor occurred in the United States. The success of IKEA there led to a copycat retailer setting up operations in California in the 1980s before IKEA was well-established in that country. STOR copied IKEA in virtually every respect: its furniture, furniture names, signs, testing machines, price tags, department names, colour schemes, ball room, checkout areas, shopping carts, general store layout and design, and catalogues. IKEA sued STOR over copyright in 1988, saying it was not against a similar retail concept but was against direct copying of its concept. STOR settled the suit by dropping its catalogue and making some store changes. Then in 1992, IKEA removed the competition by buying STOR for US$20 million.[35]

The message in each of these examples is much the same: Competitive advantage requires value-chain activities that differ from those of rivals and cannot be easily imitated. The way to limit imitation is by having a set of activities that fit so well together that competitors can only compete by doing all the same things in the same way and equally well. Michael Porter reminds us that it locks out imitators by "creating a chain of activities that is as strong as its strongest link."[36]

OUTSOURCING AND OFFSHORING VALUE-CHAIN ACTIVITIES

Outsourcing and offshoring have become prevalent because globalization of economies has provided a broad number of choices; managers are able to outsource or offshore nearly every activity. We often commingle the two concepts but they are different. **Outsourcing** is sourcing the function, product, or service of a value-chain activity from another company. **Offshoring** is taking that activity from a high-cost country to a low-cost country. These are separate decisions and a "yes" to one could be a "no" to the other.

Company examples illustrate the two. Canadel, the company in our opening vignette, outsources the production of furniture parts to subcontractors. IKEA is a business that outsources the assembly and retail distribution of furniture—customers take the furniture home in flat boxes and assemble it themselves. IKEA also outsources some of the production of its furniture to a few joint ventures in Sweden and offshores some production to plants it owns in the United States and Eastern Europe, but it outsources and offshores most of the production to suppliers in 50 countries.

Although outsourcing or offshoring a value-chain activity may be feasible and lower a company's direct costs and overhead, caution must be exercised. The company may risk losing access to the knowledge of customer preferences that inspired its early product breakthroughs in the first place. This in part explains why IKEA, Nike, and Pacific Cycle have held on to marketing and distribution. Boeing learned that outsourcing to suppliers can also be dangerous. It outsourced 70 percent of the inputs into its new 787 airplane, the Dreamliner, to its commercial airframe partners. Boeing turned to its suppliers much earlier in the development process than usual to tap in to foreign ingenuity and cut costs. Suppliers helped Boeing create and understand technologies and provided additional development, design, and manufacturing funding of their own. But Boeing ran into production and design snafus with its partners that required the company to send staffers out to suppliers to iron out difficulties.[37] After repeated delays that have caused much of a nearly two-year holdup, Boeing plans to bring more work in-house.[38]

Value-chain analysis provides a means of identifying activities and capabilities the company must possess itself and those that can be performed outside of the company. Management may consider the following when selecting activities to outsource:

- Would outsourcing an activity improve results such as reduced lead time, higher flexibility, reduced inventory, and/or lower cost?
- Would outsourcing reduce the risk associated with performing the activity in-house? If the activity relies on fast-changing technology or the product is sold in a rapidly changing market, it may be advantageous to outsource the activity in order to maintain flexibility and avoid the risk of investing in specialized assets.
- Is the activity a source of competitive advantage that stems from a cost advantage or product differentiation?

The general advice is that an activity which is a source of competitive advantage is "strategic" and should not be outsourced.[39] But caution should be taken even when outsourcing non-strategic activities. A company may be better served by improving technologies or shaking up existing operations instead of outsourcing the broken parts to lower-cost overseas locales because of interrelationships among activities.

The decision to outsource and offshore is part art and part science. Three criteria appear to be common among successful arrangements.

Commit Time and Effort

Companies typically choose outsourcing and/or offshoring to lower costs. While the supplier does the work for lower cost, it must be committed to invest in quality control and training to keep the outsourced or offshored activity competitive and efficient.

Treat Outsourcing Partners as Partners

Many outsourced operations are run by a third party. There is a temptation to treat such suppliers as order-takers instead of taking advantage of the relationship to learn new things about product and process innovations.

Involve Middle Management

Middle managers are the lifeblood of strategy execution, as you will learn in the following section. Middle managers play the role of bridging the offshored activities with the internal ones and putting additional outsourcing arrangements into place as opportunities arise.

Outsourcing is closely tied to the use of alliances, which is explored further in Chapter 10. Offshoring should be considered as businesses go international, which is discussed further in Chapter 8.

ANALYZING BUSINESS UNIT INTERRELATIONSHIPS

Interrelationships among business units form the basis of a corporation's horizontal strategy. Value-chain analysis can identify opportunities to create a synergy among business units. For example, if multiple business units require a particular raw material, the procurement of that material can be shared among the business units. This sharing of the procurement activity can result in cost reduction. Similar interrelationships may exist simultaneously in multiple value-chain activities.

The cost of coordination, the cost of reduced flexibility, and organizational practicalities should be analyzed when devising a strategy to reap the benefits of synergies. Failure to consider these factors can mean that hoped-for synergy falls short of expectations.

The issue of business interrelationships is explored further in Chapter 9, which deals with corporate strategy.

SEEKING CLUES TO THE VALUE CHAIN THROUGH FINANCIAL ANALYSIS

How might you intuit, at least in a rough way, if a company is exploiting value-chain advantage or particular resources or capabilities to create competitive advantage? Remembering that companies compete based on lower costs, an ability to gain higher prices for comparable products, or a combination of both, one tool you can use is the basic DuPont financial analysis. This analytical tool used in accounting and finance is also a useful tool for strategic analysis. The DuPont formula helps you break down determinants of a company's profitability based on the equation where Return on Assets = Net Profit Margin X Asset Turnover. The basic formula is presented in Exhibit 3.6 and applied in a more detailed version in How Would You Do That? 3.1.

Beyond the math, what does the formula tell you? The DuPont formula integrates the income statement and balance sheet to show how a company's return on assets can be disaggregated into two components—profit margin and asset turnover. Profit margin measures the company's ability to garner higher prices for a given cost while asset turnover measures the company's efficiency at generating revenues from its assets.

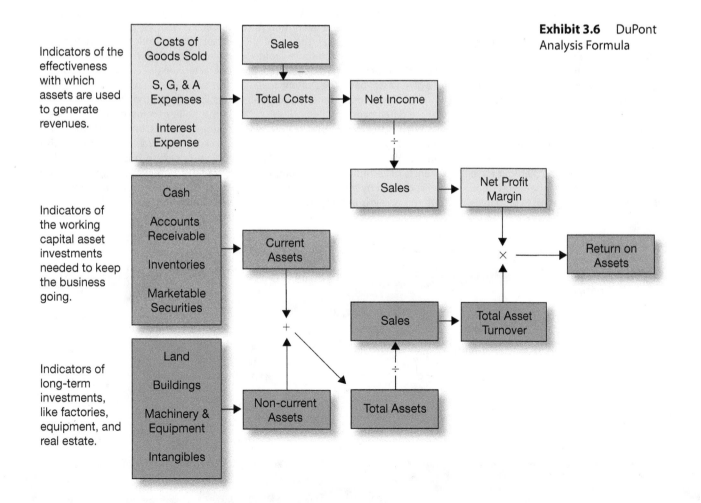

Exhibit 3.6   DuPont Analysis Formula

Applying DuPont Analysis to Understand Competitive Advantage in Retailing

et us apply the DuPont formula to some big-box retailers—Wal-Mart, Sears, and Kohl's—to better understand where they might be gaining their competitive advantage. We start by going to their company websites or sites such as Yahoo! Finance, Google Finance, or Hoover's that provide balance sheet and income statement information on public companies.

In Exhibit 3.7, notice how straightforward the information-gathering is. We simply put together a small grid and transferred a few pieces of financial information for each company. Since we were already gathering data, we decided to look at each company's total equity as well—and we will show you how this small piece of information can add further depth to your DuPont analysis. Also, we picked a single recent year for the data, but you could take an average of several years if you prefer. The important thing is that you have chosen a time period where you think that the differences across companies

are fairly reflective of what they might be doing in the future.

When we look at the information in Exhibit 3.7, we see that Wal-Mart is the largest company of the three in terms of assets and sales. It also has the greatest amount of profits. The problem, though, is that this information does not tell us much about how efficiently or effectively each company is managing its sales or assets. For example, Wal-Mart's sales are 23 times greater than those of Kohl's but only 12 times greater profit. And even though Wal-Mart is so much bigger than Kohl's, it looks like Kohl's is much more profitable in terms of the returns it generates for a given asset base. The DuPont analysis will help us understand the source of these differences.

With the data compiled in Exhibit 3.7, you can calculate the components of the DuPont formula. For instance, net profit margin is simply net profits divided by total sales and so on. With this analysis in hand, we are now

able to better understand the underlying determinants of these companies' performance. That is, you can explain why Kohl's has a higher return on assets than does Wal-Mart, despite the obvious size differences. This information, in turn, should provide you with clues as to the resources, capabilities, and value-chain choices that might be part and parcel to each company's strategy.

DuPont analysis shows that Kohl's has a very high net profit margin—7.1 percent, or $7.10 for every $100 of sales—relative to the others. This means that it is able to sell products for higher prices than competitors, or manage a higher-priced mix of products. This suggests that one of its differentiators, in terms of the strategy diamond, is the ability to merchandise higher-margin products. In contrast, you probably know that Wal-Mart competes with its low prices, so it is willing to make a tradeoff between greater sales and lower relative margins. Thus, Kohl's and Wal-Mart, which are both "discount"

Exhibit 3.7 Comparative Financial Information

Company	Total Assets ($ millions)	Total Sales ($ millions)	Net Profit ($ millions)	Total Equity ($ millions)
Wal-Mart	94 685	244 524	8039	39 337
Sears	50 409	41 366	1584	6753
Kohl's	6315	9120	643	3511

retailers, are using different differentiators to arrive at net profits. You can further see this with asset turns, where Wal-Mart has nearly twice the asset turns as Kohl's. Wal-Mart is very efficient with its assets, as for every $1 in assets it is generating $2.60 in sales. Indeed, it has made unique choices in terms of how it manages its value chain, and through DuPont analysis we can see where it is clearly the low-cost leader. And what about Sears? Well, Sears appears to be stuck in the middle with reasonable net profit margins but very low asset turns at 0.38 times. The combination leaves Sears with the lowest relative ROA of the three.

Finally, recall that we recorded total equity when collecting the financial data on our sample of discount retailers. If you divide total assets by total equity, you arrive at an equity multiplier—in other words, for every $1 of equity, this is the dollar amount of assets it supports. Multiplying ROA by this number produces the company's return on equity, or ROE. This is called the extended DuPont analysis (Exhibit 3.8). Higher equity multipliers mean that a company is using a greater amount of debt to finance its productive assets. One explanation is that management has a greater appetite for debt, and risk, and is perhaps good at

managing this type of risk. However, debt requires fixed payments of principal and interest and when these payments are not made, the company can be forced into bankruptcy. Therefore, extremely high levels of debt (and a correspondingly high equity multiplier) represent poor management of capital structure. Only by comparing one company's multiplier against others in its industry, as well as its own cash flow, can you judge whether debt is excessive.

The DuPont framework supports considerable financial analysis that is a useful starting point when seeking the company's advantages based on identifiable resources and capabilities. But the analysis based on this framework only provides a snapshot of what a company is doing. Ratios vary from year to year as well as by industry, so it is important to calculate them across several years for each company and compare them to other companies in the industry or industry averages to get a sense of their consistency and trends. Also, if you have applied the VRINE model and concluded that the company has resources and capabilities that are valuable, rare, and difficult to imitate but that it is still performing worse than its competitors, then poor exploitation of its resources may be the problem.

HOW WOULD YOU DO THAT?
QUESTIONS

1. This financial analysis helps uncover differences in the way businesses work. Pick two competing companies and develop a DuPont analysis for each. Then compare the ratios of the different organizations to determine how they differ in resources they have and how they are using them.

2. The opening story for the chapter dealt with Canadel and its value chain. Now examine the value chain for another business. Start by picking a business and defining its products, services, or target markets. Then identify why customers buy from it rather than competitors. Next identify its value chain and compare it with those of other rivals. Does it perform its activities differently than its rivals? Likewise, examine the programs of a few leading rivals. Do any of the companies' value-chain activities give them a competitive advantage? If so, why don't others imitate these activities?

Exhibit 3.8   Extended DuPont Analysis

Company	Net Profit Margin	×	Total Asset Turn	=	ROA	×	Equity Multiplier	=	ROE
Wal-Mart	3.3%		2.6		8.5%		241.1%		20.4%
Sears	3.8%		0.8		3.1%		175.4%		23.5%
Kohl's	7.1%		1.4		10.2%		179.4%		18.3%

Strategic Leadership: Linking Resources and Capabilities to Strategy

The Deveault family played a central role in building the resources and capabilities to support a value chain that made Canadel a successful business. They made these decisions in light of their assessment of the external environment. As they saw changes in the environment, they responded by making changes in the company. Initially their changes involved many decisions that supported expansion of the business, but in the last several years their decisions have reflected a struggle to maintain the size of the business by finding additional products that will support the current level of business. The role of managers in this process of guiding resource allocation is so critical that some experts include managerial human capital among a company's resources; others include management among a company's dynamic capabilities.[40] A recent McKinsey consulting report concluded that "companies that overlook the role of leadership in the early phases of strategic planning often find themselves scrambling when it's time to execute. No matter how thorough the plan, without the right leaders it is unlikely to succeed."[41] To incorporate these views, we regard managers as decision agents—the people who put into motion the processes that use the company's resources and capabilities.

SENIOR MANAGERS

In addition to deciding how to use resources and capabilities and configuring a company's value-chain activities, senior managers also set the context that determines how front-line and middle managers can add value. Strategy research has shown that senior managers in the most effective companies around the globe view their organizations as portfolios of processes—specifically, entrepreneurial, capability-building, and renewal processes—and key people, such as those who comprise the firm's middle and frontline managerial ranks.[42]

Engaging middle managers in decision making encourages them to be externally oriented—to seek out opportunities and run their part of the business as if they owned it. Senior managers who foster this process are stepping back from the notion that they are the sole visionaries and saviours of the company and instead seek to share this responsibility with the managers on the front lines. The capability-building process also looks to middle managers to identify, grow, and protect new ways to create value for the organization and its key stakeholders. In many ways, this process is the internal side of the externally oriented entrepreneurial process. Finally, the renewal process is the senior manager's way of shaking up the firm and challenging its historic ways of operating; however, this process is based on information learned through current business activities performed elsewhere in the firm.

In the opening vignette about Canadel, senior management had in place processes and a culture that motivated workers. It also played a major role in the development and management of its subcontractors, who were a crucial component of Canadel's value chain.

Of course, not all senior managers are equipped equally to act effectively. Obviously, basic managerial talent is not bestowed equally on all managers, even if they have risen to the highest levels in the organization. Moreover, specific experiences and backgrounds will make some managers better qualified to work with a specific bundle of resources. Researchers have discovered, for instance, that multinational companies (those with operations in several countries) achieve higher levels of performance when their CEOs have had some experience in foreign operations.[43] In addition, entrepreneurial operations must often rely on few or no valuable or rare resources. Managers of these enterprises generally start with ideas and goals and not much more. In such situations, the positive influence of managers is even more important.[44] Likewise, in companies facing financial or competitive turmoil, the galvanizing and enabling effects of superior senior management are also more pronounced.

MIDDLE MANAGERS

Middle managers are responsible for executing what senior managers want done. They play a key role in what the firm is doing and what it may be adept at doing in the future. This is why senior management considers the firm's leadership pool as they shape strategy and align their leadership-development programs with long-term aspirations. Particularly in large companies, the effect of senior executives on firm performance is a function of the choices they make about the context in which front-line managers work and the appointment of particular managers themselves.

Research has identified four areas where middle managers are better positioned to contribute to competitive advantage and corporate success than are senior executives:[45]

- **Entrepreneur.** Middle managers are close enough to the front lines to spot fires yet far enough away to understand the bigger picture. Because middle management ranks are typically more diverse in terms of ethnicity, gender, experience, and geography, this group has the potential to contribute richer ideas than the senior management team.
- **Communicator.** Middle managers are typically long tenured and have very broad social networks. This gives them great credibility with employees, and they are therefore better able to move change initiatives in non-threatening ways. Their tenure also gives them deep knowledge about how to get things done in the organization.
- **Psychoanalyst.** Internal credibility also enables middle managers to be more effective in quelling alienation and chaos, as seen by high productivity among anxious employees during times of great change. Because they know their troops, front-line managers also know when and how to provide one-on-one support and problem solving.
- **Tightrope walker.** Particularly in the case of dynamic capabilities and environments, companies are faced with the need to balance continuity and radical change. Middle managers are well poised to accomplish this balancing act. With the right process in place courtesy of senior executives, middle managers can help the firm avoid inertia and too little change or slow change and also avoid the paralyzing chaos accompanying too much change too quickly.

In many ways, it's the central role of upper and middle management that distinguishes the internal perspective on strategy from the external perspective that we'll discuss in Chapter 4. After all, if competitive advantage results from the different characteristics of companies, then the key task in the role of management is to identify resources and capabilities, specify the resources that will create competitive advantage, locate an attractive industry in which to deploy them, and then select the strategy to get the most out of them. Finally, it's the job of managers to choose when to change a firm's mix of resources, capabilities, and targeted markets. As you learned in Chapter 2, the management of smaller companies typically differs from that of larger companies in terms of the overall number, not the roles that are played. This means that in smaller companies senior leaders, often the owners or company founders, may wear many if not all of the middle and front-line manager hats described.

Summary of Challenges

1. *Explain the internal context of strategy.* Companies facing similar industry conditions achieve different levels of competitive advantage and performance based on their internal characteristics and managerial choices. Although companies must always take the external context into account when formulating and implementing strategy, the internal perspectives stress the differences among firms in terms of the unique resources and capabilities that they own or control. These perspectives offer important models and analytical tools that will help you to analyze and formulate competitive strategies.

2. *Identify a firm's resources and capabilities and explain their role in its performance.* Resources are either tangible or intangible. Resources and capabilities that help companies establish a competitive advantage and secure higher levels of performance are those that are valuable, rare, and costly to imitate. The VRINE model helps you analyze resources and capabilities. A resource or capability is said to be valuable if it enables the firm to exploit opportunities or negate threats in the environment. In addition, the firm must have complementary organizational capabilities to exploit resources and capabilities that meet these three conditions. Rare resources enable companies to exploit opportunities or negate threats in ways that those lacking the resource cannot. Competitors will try to find ways to imitate valuable and rare resources; a firm can generate an enduring competitive advantage if competitors face a cost disadvantage in acquiring or substituting the resource that is lacking. Unique historical conditions that have led to resource or capability development, time-compression diseconomies, and causal ambiguity all make imitation more difficult. Companies often use alliances, acquisitions, and substitution with less costly resources as mechanisms to gain access to difficult-to-imitate resources.

3. *Define dynamic capabilities and explain their role in both strategic change and a firm's performance.* The process of development, accumulation, and possible loss of resources and capabilities is inherently dynamic. The resource-accumulation process and dynamic capabilities are fundamentally different from the static possession of a stock of resources and capabilities. Dynamic capabilities are processes that integrate, reconfigure, acquire,

or divest resources in order to use the companies' stocks of resources and capabilities in new ways. The ability to adapt to changing conditions or to initiate proactively a change in the competitive environment is particularly important in industries in which time-to-market is critical, technological change is rapid, and future competition is difficult to forecast.

4. *Explain how value-chain activities are related to firm performance and competitive advantage.* Companies produce products or offer services by engaging in many activities. The basic structure of firm activities is illustrated by the firm's value chain. The value chain is divided into primary and support activities. One way a company can outperform rivals is to find ways to perform some value-chain activities better than its rivals or to find different ways to perform the activities altogether. Selective outsourcing of some value-chain activities is one way to perform activities differently. Competitive advantage through strategic configuration of value-chain activities only comes

about if the firm can either deliver greater value than rivals or deliver comparable value at lower cost. The essence of the activity-based value-chain perspective of competitive advantage is to choose value-chain activities that are different from those of rivals and to configure these activities in a way that are internally consistent and that require significant tradeoffs should a competitor want to imitate them.

5. *Explain the role of managers with respect to resources, capabilities, and value-chain activities.* Managers make decisions about how to employ resources in the formulation and implementation of strategy. Managers are the decision agents that put into motion the use of all other firm resources and capabilities; they are key to the success of a firm's strategy. Managers with specific experiences and backgrounds may be more qualified to work with a specific bundle of resources owned by a firm. The influence of managers is more pronounced in contexts such as entrepreneurial phases, turnarounds, and competitive turmoil.

Review Questions

1. What are resources? How do different types of resources differ?
2. What is a capability?
3. What are the five components of the VRINE model?
4. How do time and causal ambiguity relate to the value, rarity, and inimitability of a resource or capability?
5. What is the difference between a stock of resources and capabilities and a flow of resources and capabilities?

6. What are dynamic capabilities? How do they differ from general capabilities?
7. What is a firm's value chain? How does it figure into a firm's competitive advantage?
8. What is your role as a manager in linking resources and capabilities to strategy and competitive advantage?

Experiential Activities

Group Activities

1. What is the role of luck in gaining possession of a particular resource or capability? Can a firm manage luck? Give an example of a resource or capability that a firm garnered through luck and determine whether it was subsequently well managed.
2. Some companies' products are so well known that the entire category of products offered in the industry (including rivals' products) is often referred to by the leading firm's brand name (which is called an eponym). Identify one such product and discuss whether its brand recognition gives the leading firm a competitive advantage. Why or why not?

Ethical Debates

1. The company has spent $200 million over many years developing a new product that solves a serious problem customers have had. Research and development wants to spend millions more dollars to work on improving product safety. In spite of the risks, the product will likely have sales of $1 billion a year. An engineer in the company has estimated that the dangers associated with using the product annually will produce lawsuits costing $10 million per year and will kill two to five of the customers' workers. As CEO, do you put the product on the market now? And do you give Research & Development more money for its activities?
2. Describe ethical issues associated with outsourcing and offshoring. What balance should management strike so that it is as ethically correct as possible with respect to these issues?

Endnotes

1. Ken Mark, "Meubles Canadel: Looking Toward the Future," Ivey Case 9B01M019, Richard Ivey School of Business, 2001; Various issues of *Furniture Today* accessed September 1, 2009, at www.furnituretoday.com; and Deborah Leslie and Suzanne Reimer, "Situating Design in the Canadian Household Furniture Industry," *The Canadian Geographer/Le Geographe canadien* 50:3 (2006): 319–341.

2. J. Haleblian and S. Finkelstein, "The Influence of Organizational Acquisition Experience on Acquisition Performance: A Behavioral Learning

Perspective," *Administrative Science Quarterly* 44:1 (1999): 29–56; F. Vermeulen and H. Barkema, "Learning Through Acquisitions," *Academy of Management Journal* 44:3 (2001): 457–476.

3. D. J. Teece, G. Pisano, and A. Shuen, "Dynamic Capabilities and Strategic Management," *Strategic Management Journal* 18 (1997): 509–529.

4. R. R. Nelson and S. G. Winter, *An Evolutionary Theory of Economic Change* (Cambridge, MA: Belknap Press of Harvard University Press, 1982).

5. G. Stalk, P. Evans, and L. E. Shulman, "Competing on Capabilities: The New Rules of Corporate Strategy," *Harvard Business Review* 70:2 (1992): 54–65; R. Makadok, "Doing the Right Thing and Knowing the Right Thing to Do: Why the Whole Is Greater Than the Sum of the Parts," *Strategic Management Journal* 24:10 (2003): 1043–1054.

6. english.pravda.ru/usa/2001/11/03/20045.html and www.restaurantreport.com/qa/location.html (accessed June 28, 2005).

7. This framework is consistent with the larger literature on the resource-based view of the firm. For another helpful discussion, see J. B. Barney, "Looking Inside for Competitive Advantage," *Academy of Management Executive* 9:4 (1995): 49–61.

8. J. B. Barney, "Firm Resources and Sustained Competitive Advantage," *Journal of Management* 17:1 (1991): 99–120.

9. Ibid.

10. C. K. Prahalad and G. Hamel, "The Core Competence of the Corporation," *Harvard Business Review* 68:3 (1990): 79–92.

11. Douglas Belkin, "Talent Scouts for Cirque du Soleil Walk a Tightrope," *Wall Street Journal*, September 8, 2007, p. A1.

12. P. R. Haunschild, "How Much Is That Company Worth? Inter-organizational Relationships, Uncertainty, and Acquisition Premiums," *Administrative Science Quarterly* 39:3 (1994): 391–414.

13. DALSA corporate profile. Accessed September 20. 2009, at www.dalsa.com/corp/profile.asp.

14. Rhys Blakely and Agencies, "US BlackBerry Service Faces Shutdown," *Times* Online, December 16, 2005, http://business.timesonline.co.uk/tol/business/industry_sectors/technology/article766959.ece.

15. Peter Nowak, "Bell Sued for Throttling Internet Speeds," CBC News, June 2, 2008. Accessed September 22, 2009, at www.cbc.ca/technology/story/2008/06/02/tech-quebec.html; and letter from Édouard G. Trépanier, vice-president, regulatory affairs, Quebecor Media, to Mr. Alex Himelfarb, clerk of the Privy Council and secretary to the Cabinet, on November 14, 2005, regarding petitions to the Governor in Council requesting a review of Telecom Decision CRTC 2005-28, Regulatory framework for voice communication services using Internet Protocol, May 12, 2005. Accessed September 23, 2009, at www.ic.gc.ca/eic/site/smt-gst.nsf/vwapj/dgtp-007-05-quebecor.pdf/$FILE/dgtp-007-05-quebecor.pdf.

16. J. B. Barney, "Looking Inside for Competitive Advantage," *Academy of Management Executive* 9:4 (1995): 49–61; I. Dierickx and K. Cool, "Asset Stock Accumulation and Sustainability of Competitive Advantage," *Management Science* 35:12 (1989): 1504–1511.

17. M. Pendergrast, *For God, Country and Coca-Cola* (New York: Basic Books, 1993).

18. Emily Fredrix, "Coca-Cola's 1st-Quarter Profit Climbs 19 Percent as International Sales Continue to Make Gains," April 20, 2010. Accessed April 20, 2010, at www.canadianbusiness.com/markets/market_news/article.jsp?content=D9F6Q1NG0. Specific international sales are no longer broken down in annual and 10K reports.

19. Dierickx and Cool, "Asset Stock Accumulation and Sustainability of Competitive Advantage."

20. Author's personal communication with Margaret Haddox, Novell corporate librarian, October 2003.

21. Author's personal communication with former Novell executives, September 2003.

22. D. T. Kearns and D. A. Nadler, *Prophets in the Dark* (New York: HarperCollins, 1992); Barney, "Looking Inside for Competitive Advantage"; http://en.wikipedia.org/wiki/Xerox_PARC and http://management-case-studies.blogspot.com/2005/03/managing-innovation-profitably-xerox.html; Leslie Goff, "1972: Xerox Parc and the Alto," July 8, 1999, www.cnn.com/TECH/computing/9907/08/1972.idg; and John Seely Brown and Paul Duguid, *The Social Life of Information* (Boston: Harvard Business School Press, 2000).

23. "Could Cymbalta Bring Cheer for Lilly?" IMS Health.com, August 23, 2004. Accessed August 4, 2005, at open.imshealth.com; C. Baysden, "Report: Blockbuster Drug Marketing Costs Average $239M," *Triangle Business Journal* (February 24, 2005). Accessed August 4, 2005, at www.triangle.bizjournals.com; "Medication for Depression: Antidepressant Medications," Psychology Information Online. Accessed August 4, 2005, at www.psychologyinfo.com.

24. Eisenhardt and Martin, "Dynamic Capabilities."

25. Ibid.

26. B. Orwall, "In Disney Row, an Aging Heir Who's Won Boardroom Bouts," *Wall Street Journal*, December 5, 2003, p. A1.

27. G. Szulanski and R. J. Jensen, "Overcoming Stickiness: An Empirical Investigation of the Role of the Template," *Managerial Decision Economics*, forthcoming.

28. Eisenhardt and Martin, "Dynamic Capabilities."

29. Joel Kurtzman and Glenn Rifkin, *Radical E: From GE to Enron* (New York: John Wiley & Sons, 2001) p. 85.

30. Teece, Pisano, and Shuen, "Dynamic Capabilities and Strategic Management."

31. C. Christensen, *The Innovator's Dilemma* (New York: Harper Business Press, 1997).

32. M. E. Porter, *Competitive Advantage* (New York: Free Press, 1985) p. 37.

33. M. E. Porter, "What Is Strategy?" *Harvard Business Review* 74:6 (1996): 61–78.

34. Ibid.

35. Pamela Krein, "IKEA Suit Forces STOR to Shelve Catalog; Home Furnishings Retailer Claims Copyright Infringement," *Discount Store News*, June 6, 1988; and Kara Glover, "Observers Hail STOR–IKEA Merger: Stor Furnishings International Inc.; Ikea Svenska AB," *Los Angeles Business Journal*, January 6, 1992.

36. Porter, "What Is Strategy?"

37. Kyle Peterson, "Boeing 787 Delays Cast Hard Light on Outsourcing," September 22, 2009. Accessed September 24, 2009, at www.reuters.com/article/ousivMolt/idUSTRE58L4CS20090922.

38. Joseph Weber, "Boeing to Rein in Dreamliner Outsourcing," *Business Week*, January 16, 2009. Accessed September 20, 2009, at www.businessweek.com/bwdaily/dnflash/content/jan2009/db20090116_971202.htm?campaign_id=rss_daily.

39. Richard C. Insinga and Michael J. Werle, "Linking Outsourcing to Business Strategy," *Academy of Management Executive* 14:4 (November 2000): 58–70.

40. Barney, "Firm Resources and Sustained Competitive Advantage."

41. T. Hseih and S. Yik, "Leadership as the Starting Point of Strategy," *McKinsey Quarterly* 1 (2005): 11–26.

42. S. Ghoshal and C. A. Bartlett, "Changing the Role of Top Management: Beyond Structure to Processes," *Harvard Business Review* 73:3 (1995): 86–96; C. A. Bartlett and S. Ghoshal, "Changing the Role of Top Management: Beyond Systems to People," *Harvard Business Review* 73:3 (1995): 132–134.

43. M. A. Carpenter, W. Sanders, and H. Gregersen, "Bundling Human Capital with Organizational Context: The Impact of International Assignment Experience on Multinational Firm Performance and CEO Pay," *Academy of Management Journal* 44:3 (2001): 493–512.

44. M. A. Carpenter, T. G. Pollock, and M. M. Leary, "Testing a Model of Reasoned Risk-Taking: Governance, the Experience of Principals and Agents, and Global Strategy in High-Technology IPO Companies," *Strategic Management Journal* 24:9 (2003): 803–820.

45. Q. Huy, "In Praise of Middle Managers," *Harvard Business Review* 79:8 (2001): 72–79.

4 Exploring the External Environment: Macro and Industry Dynamics

A Chronicle of the Cola War

Coca-Cola sells a billion servings [of Coke]—in cans, bottles, and glasses—every day. You can grab a Coke in almost 200 countries. Its archrival, Pepsi, is not too far behind. Like Ford versus Chevy, theirs is a battle not just for customer dollars but for their hearts and minds as well.

—History Channel, *Empires of Industry: Cola Wars*[1]

As the environment changes, companies are forced to change. Often, the change is challenging. PepsiCo, for example, saw its sales growth slowing in the mid-1990s. Pepsi's leaders needed to transform the company to meet the new industry realities. As Indra Nooyi, an architect of the transformation strategy who later became PepsiCo's chairman and CEO, said, "In a perfect world, I'd be able to tell you we executed this restructuring flawlessly. Naturally, that's not the case. The process was neither smooth nor seamless. Many times it felt like baptism by fire."[2]

The stakes in the century-old soft-drink industry are enormous. The average American consumes 201 litres of carbonated beverages per year and the average Canadian 110 litres. For generations, the soft-drink industry has been one of the most profitable. Experts estimate that gross margins in soft-drink concentrate are approximately 83 percent and net margins about 35 percent.

During the battle, Coca-Cola dominated the fountain market with a strategic partnership with McDonald's, which accounted for 2.8 million to 3.8 million hectolitres of Coke sold each year in the United States alone. Pepsi entered the restaurant business—buying Taco Bell, Pizza Hut, and KFC—to ensure that those restaurant chains sold only Pepsi products and it shared in the industry's rapid growth. Although this seemed a good strategic move at the time, it brought Pepsi into an unfamiliar industry. And when restaurant industry growth began slowing, the venture started sapping Pepsi's profits. Nooyi and her colleagues realized that the restaurant business had to go. As Roger Enrico, Pepsi's CEO at the time, explained, "The central part of Indra Nooyi's, [who later became CEO] proposition was that we weren't retailers ourselves, and we didn't have the expertise to run them the way they could and should be run." Nooyi then put Pepsi's three restaurant chains together in a new company, now called Yum Brands, and spun it off. "You have to think of a business like any investment. You have to know when to get in but, more important, when to get out. Getting out can be a lot tougher, especially if you develop an emotional tie to the business. But the world changes, and so should the models we apply to our companies."[3]

The core carbonated soft-drink business started changing too. Both Coke and Pepsi faced challenges as consumers became more health conscious and substituted juice and water for soda. In order to appeal to investors and stay relevant, Coca-Cola Chairman-CEO Neville Isdell switched from using the word *carbonated* to using the term *sparkling* and *still* in place of *non-carbonated.* "Sparkling beverages," he said, "are what we simply define as non-alcoholic, ready-to-drink consumer beverages with carbonation."[4] Coke's press releases have been changed to say that Coke "markets four of the world's top five non-alcoholic sparkling brands." Industry expert Gary Hemphill, managing director of the Beverage Marketing Group, saw the change in nomenclature as a shift: "It signals a changing marketplace," he said. "'Sparkling' spans multiple categories like carbonated soft drinks, energy drinks, sparkling water, and sparkling juice; whereas the term 'carbonated' is associated solely with carbonated soft drinks."[5] In fact, Pepsi recently acquired Izze Beverage, known for its all-natural, sparkling fruit juices, and both Coke and Pepsi began marketing some sodas as sparkling, including Coke's Fresca and Enviga and Pepsi's Tava.

In another move to stay relevant, Pepsi's Nooyi is shifting Pepsi's strategy to address health issues. Born in India, Nooyi understands the concerns over nutrition, and she has promised that at least half of all new Pepsi products will include "essentially healthy" ingredients or offer "improved health benefits." Under her new strategy, Pepsi's North American drinks business is led by non-carbonated, "healthier" options: waters, "enhanced" waters, teas, and energy drinks, which all show double-digit growth. Pepsi's Aquafina brand is the number-one bottled water in the United States and has so-called functional variants that include B-Power, Calcium+, Daily C, and Multi-V in 20-ounce (0.6-litre) bottles.

Despite the new strategy, Nooyi is aware that strategic wins are a moving target. "The minute you've developed a new business model, it's extinct because somebody is going to copy it," she said.[6]

Coca-Cola did not sit by idly while Pepsi sought higher sales. In 2005, Coke vowed to invest an additional US$400 million annually in innovation. One result was Andina, a fortified fruit drink and energy-enhanced diet drink. It also invested heavily in growing sales in emerging markets including Brazil, India, and Russia. Meanwhile demand in its traditional markets has been nearly flat. In recent years demand for carbonated soft drinks has been declining,

Exhibit 4.1   Annual Per Capita Consumption of Coca-Cola's Products in Selected Markets (in litres per capita)

Source: Accessed May 2, 2010, at www.thecoca-colacompany.com/ourcompany/ar/pdf/perCapitaConsumption2008.pdf.

	1988	1998	2008
United States	65.1	96.1	97.5
Canada	39.7	54.9	56.1
Brazil	19.9	31.2	47.1
India	0.0	0.7	1.7
Russia	0.3	5.0	16.3
World Average	9.2	15.4	20.1

in part due to growing concerns about soft drinks being a major contributor to childhood obesity. The annual per capita consumption of Coke's products in selected markets shows the challenges facing not only Coke but Pepsi (see Exhibit 4.1).

Trading Punches

Although Coke has long been dominant, Pepsi has worked hard to weaken Coke's position. In 1950, for example, Pepsi recruited a former Coke marketing manager and proclaimed the battle cry "Beat Coke." In the 1960s, Pepsi launched its "Pepsi Generation" campaign to target younger buyers. In the mid-1970s, spurred by the success of blind taste tests in Texas, Pepsi launched a nationwide offensive called the "Pepsi Challenge." Coke, however, refused to retreat, countering with such tactics as retail price cuts and aggressive advertising.

Coke's tactics intensified after Roberto Goizueta became CEO in 1981. Once in command, Goizueta more than doubled advertising, switched to lower-priced sweeteners, sold off non-carbonated beverage companies, and introduced new flavours and diet versions of existing brands. Coke's victories included Diet Coke, the most successful new product introduction of the 1980s. Then, however, Coke made a serious tactical error: It tried to reformulate the 100-year-old recipe for Coke. When consumers rebelled, Coke was forced to retreat to the original formula. Pepsi proclaimed the effort to reformulate Coke as an admission that Pepsi had a superior taste.

In the 1980s, Coke and Pepsi had a history on maintaining the health of their independent bottlers by buying up loss-making or inefficient bottlers, reorganizing them, and then reselling them to profitable franchisees. Eventually, they merged many bottling franchisees and took these larger companies public. In 1986, Coke established CCE, and Pepsi established Pepsi Bottling Group. Both of these bottling companies handled the majority of their respective parent companies' U.S. distribution.

Then in 2010 the two companies again copied each other as North American demand was flat and retailers were resistant to price increases. The only way of increasing margins was by decreasing costs. First Pepsi agreed to buy the stakes it did not already own in Pepsi Bottling Group and PepsiAmericas. Coke soon followed, acquiring the 66 percent that it did not own in the North American operations of its largest bottler, Coca-Cola Enterprises.

A New Age

An outside observer might think that such a fierce battle for market share would demonstrate that the two companies had poor performance. In 2009, Coke held 42 percent of the U.S. market while Pepsi held 30 percent and the only other large player, Dr. Pepper Snapple, held 16 percent. Coke's (KO) operating profit was 23 percent, Pepsi's (PEP) was 14 percent, and Dr. Pepper Snapple's (DPS) was 10 percent. But Coke's return on equity was 31 percent,

Pepsi's was 38 percent, and Dr. Pepper Snapple's was 19 percent. The strong rivalry between the two major players had produced their superior performance by maintaining entry barriers in the form of brand equity and control of distribution channels through the ownership or control of regional bottlers. ■

Exploring the External Environment: Macro and Industry Dynamics

Formulating an effective strategy—one that has a good chance of helping the company achieve its objectives—requires an understanding of the external environment. In the broadest sense, the external environment consists of a wide array of economic and sociopolitical factors. In the narrowest sense, the external environment is the specific market arenas that the company has chosen in its strategy. ◆ The opportunities and the threats to its success are both found in the external environment, which is why the external environment exerts a strong influence on the company's profitability.

◆ **Strategy**

In this chapter, you'll learn how to identify the external opportunities and threats that affect a company's strategy. Taken together with Chapter 3, this chapter provides the tools that will enable you to perform a rigorous analysis of the company's competitive environment and its capabilities to implement a strategy.

The long-term profitability of both Coke and Pepsi has been influenced by the structure of the soft-drink industry. Many enterprising entrepreneurs have seen this long-term propensity produce profit in the soft-drink industry and have desired to share in that wealth. Many small, profitable companies have emerged, yet none has succeeded in becoming a major player alongside Coke and Pepsi. In this chapter, you will begin to understand why some industries are more profitable than others, why some industries are easier to enter than others, and what companies can do to influence these environmental factors in their favour.

INDUSTRY- AND COMPANY-SPECIFIC FACTORS

This chapter provides the analytical tools that help explain why some industries are more profitable than others. Using these tools, you can analyze the company's external environment in a systematic way. This chapter starts with methods for analyzing the macro environment and companies' industries. Then it turns to the dynamic facets of the external environment.

FUNDAMENTAL CHARACTERISTICS OF THE EXTERNAL ENVIRONMENT

The external environment has two major components: the macro environment and the industry environment. The various levels of analysis necessary to examine a company's external environment are summarized in Exhibit 4.2. This analysis starts with the macro environment, which is most removed from the company, and works toward the micro analysis, which the company feels almost daily. Included is the industry in which the company competes. Each industry has fundamental characteristics that stand out and, in total, set it apart from other industries. Industry analysis includes many, but not all, of a company's key external stakeholders. Hence, it needs to be supplemented with broader stakeholder analysis such as discussed in Chapter 7 in order to avoid blind spots. Within the industry are strategic groups—groupings of companies pursuing similar strategies.

Exhibit 4.2   The External Environment of the Organization

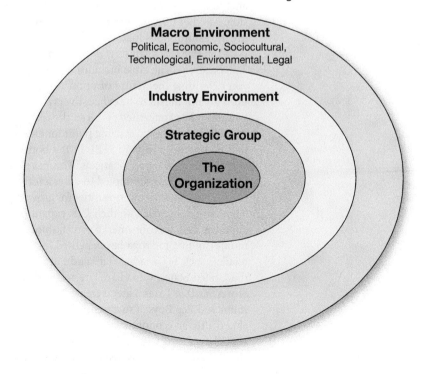

When analyzing the company's external environment, managers ask themselves key questions such as: What macro environmental conditions will have a material effect on our ability to implement our strategy successfully? What appear to be unstoppable trends? What is the company's industry? What are the characteristics of the industry? and How stable are these characteristics?

By addressing questions focused on the industry, managers gain a better sense of a company's strategic options and challenges. Focusing on a particular company operating within an industry such as Coca-Cola alone does not provide much information on the general characteristics of the soft-drink industry, especially since Coke is far from average in terms of resources and capabilities. So industry analysis seeks to understand the external environment in which *all* companies in an industry operate. This goes well beyond only examining the competitors in the industry.

Macro Environment

The macro environment refers to the larger political, economic, social, technical, environmental, and legal issues that confront the company. To analyze the macro environment, we introduce the PESTEL model and present the determinants and consequences of globalization.

PESTEL ANALYSIS

PESTEL analysis Tool for assessing the political, economic, sociocultural, technological, environmental, and legal contexts in which a company operates.

PESTEL analysis is used widely to structure analysis of a company's external environment. PESTEL is an acronym for the *p*olitical, *e*conomic, *s*ociocultural, *t*echnological, *e*nvironmental, and *l*egal context(s) in which a company operates.[7] When applying the analysis, only factors that could have a potential impact on the company in the future are considered. This analysis helps managers better understand the opportunities and threats they face and consequently aids them in building a perception of the future business landscape and how the business might compete profitably.

Management uses its understanding of the macro environment to align strategy with the powerful forces of change that affect the company's landscape. It tries to exploit changes in the environment since this is more likely to be successful than simply trying to survive or oppose change. A good understanding of PESTEL also helps management avoid strategies that may be doomed to failure for reasons beyond their control.

A PESTEL analysis involves three steps. First, the relevance of each of the PESTEL factors is considered. Second, the data for each factor is identified and categorized. Third, the data are analyzed and conclusions are drawn. A common student mistake is to stop after the second step. Another mistake is to assume that initial analysis and conclusions are correct without testing the assumptions made.

The PESTEL analysis is detailed in Exhibit 4.3. It has six sections, one for each of the PESTEL headings. The table includes sample questions or prompts, the answers to which will help you determine the nature of opportunities and threats in the macro environment. The questions are not meant to be exhaustive; rather, they are merely examples of the types of issues that you should be concerned about in the macro environment.

PESTEL is a good starting point for entering into a new country or region because a strategy that is congruent with PESTEL in the home environment gives no assurance that it will be so aligned in new geographic arenas. This has been discovered time and again as retailers successful in one market have attempted to enter another market. Canadian retailers have always looked to the United States for opportunities for growth, and companies such as ALDO and lululemon athletica have done well with their U.S. expansion. The "Cheap Chic" of ALDO shoes has had broad appeal as it allows consumers to buy fashionable shoes at modest prices. The fit and style of lululemon's clothing for yoga has benefited from the North American boom in yoga exercises. Other retailers such as Canadian Tire and Future Shop were forced to pull back after opening stores in the United States. Canadian Tire misread the transferability of its retailing approach to White Stores based in Texas. Later it created a chain of franchise stores in Indiana called Auto Source that mimicked Pep Boys, a successful U.S. chain that sold automotive parts to consumers. The chain closed after an economic recession and increasing competitive pressures from new entrants prevented it from increasing the number of outlets fast enough to carry the cost of running the chain. And Future Shop discovered that it was not able to compete with U.S. electronics retailers.

Political
- How stable is the political environment?
- What are local taxation policies and how do these affect your business?
- Is the government involved in trading agreements such as EU, NAFTA, ASEAN, or others?
- What are the foreign-trade regulations?
- What are the social-welfare policies?

Economic
- What are current and projected interest rates?
- What is the level of inflation, what is it projected to be, and how does this projection reflect the growth of your market?
- What are local employment levels per capita and how are they changing?
- What are the long-term prospects for gross domestic product (GDP) per capita and so on?
- What are exchange rates between critical markets and how will they affect production and distribution of your goods?

Sociocultural
- What are local lifestyle trends?
- What are the current demographics and how are they changing?
- What is the level and distribution of education and income?
- What are the dominant local religions and what influence do they have on consumer attitudes and opinions?
- What is the level of consumerism and what are popular attitudes toward it?
- What pending legislation affects corporate social policies (e.g., domestic-partner benefits or maternity/paternity leave)?
- What are the attitudes toward work and leisure?

Technological
- What is the level of research funding in government and industry and are those levels changing?
- What is the government and industry's level of interest and focus on technology?
- How mature is the technology?
- What is the status of intellectual-property issues in the local environment?
- Are potentially disruptive technologies in adjacent industries creeping in at the edges of the focal industry?

Environmental
- What are local environmental issues?
- Are there any pending ecological or environmental issues relevant to your industry?
- How do the activities of international pressure groups (e.g., Greenpeace, Earth First, PETA) affect your business?
- Are there environmental-protection laws?
- What are the regulations regarding waste disposal and energy consumption?

Legal
- What are the regulations regarding monopolies and private property?
- Does intellectual property have legal protections?
- Are there relevant consumer laws?
- What is the status of employment, health-and-safety, and product-safety laws?

Exhibit 4.3 The Dimensions of PESTEL Analysis

Political Factors

The political environment can have a significant influence on companies as well as affect consumer confidence and consumer and business spending. Managers need to consider numerous types of political factors. For instance, the stability of the political environment is particularly important for companies entering new markets. In addition, government policies with respect to regulation and taxation vary across provincial and national boundaries. Political considerations also encompass trade treaties such as the North American Free Trade Agreement (NAFTA) and regional trading blocs such as the Association of Southeast Asian Nations (ASEAN) and the European Union (EU). Such treaties and trading blocs tend to favour trade among the member countries and to impose penalties or less favourable trade terms on non-members.

Economic Factors

Managers also need to consider the macroeconomic factors that will have near- and long-term effects on the success of their strategies. Factors such as inflation rates, interest rates, tariffs, the growth of the local and foreign national economies, and exchange rates are critical. Unemployment rates, the availability of critical labour, and local labour costs also have a strong bearing on strategy, particularly as it relates to where to locate disparate company functions and facilities.

Sociocultural Factors

The social and cultural influences on a company vary from country to country. Depending on the type of business a company operates, factors such as the local languages, the dominant religions, and leisure time, as well as age and lifespan demographics, may be critical. Local sociocultural characteristics also vary with respect to attitudes toward consumerism, environmentalism, and the roles of men and women in local society. Making assumptions about local sociocultural norms derived from your experience in your home market is a common cause of early failure when entering new markets. However, even home-market norms can change over time, often caused by shifting demographics due to immigration or aging populations. For example, Coca-Cola and Pepsi have grown in international markets due to increasing levels of consumerism outside of the United States.

Technological Factors

Technological factors have a major bearing on the threats and opportunities that companies encounter. Does technology enable products and services to be made more cheaply and to a better standard of quality? Do technologies provide the opportunity for more innovative products and services, such as online stock trading, reduction in communications costs, and increased remote working? How might distribution of products or services be affected by new technologies? All of these factors have the potential to change the face of the business landscape.

Environmental Factors

The environment is always a factor in company strategy, primarily from the standpoint of access to raw materials. Increasingly, however, this factor is best viewed as a direct and indirect operating cost for the company, as well as from the lens of the footprint left by a company on its ecological environment including air pollution, water pollution, and waste. For consumer product companies such as Pepsi, this can require including waste management and farming practices in the countries providing raw materials. In consumer markets, the biodegradable or recyclable nature of packaging can be considered.

Legal Factors

Legal factors reflect the laws and regulations relevant to the region and the organization. Legal factors may include whether the rule of law is well established and how easily or quickly laws and regulations may change. It may also include the costs of regulatory compliance. For instance, Coca-Cola's market share in Europe is greater than 50 percent, and as a result regulators have asked that Coke give up shelf space to competitors' products in order to provide greater consumer choice.

Governments regulate who can operate in many industries. Utilities are typically local monopolies because governments do not allow additional competitors. The reason for this is that building a distribution system is very expensive, so the more users this system can service, the lower the average cost of that service. To offset the pricing power of the utility, the government usually limits the profitability of the utility through price controls.

As you can see, many of the PESTEL factors are interrelated. For instance, the legal environment is often related to the political environment in that laws and regulations will change only when politicians decide that such changes are needed.

GLOBALIZATION

Over the past decade, globalization has become a fact of life in almost every industry; as new markets have opened to foreign competitors, whole industries have been deregulated and

Pressures Favouring Industry Globalization			
Markets	**Costs**	**Governments**	**Competition**
• Homogeneous customer needs • Global customer needs • Global channels • Transferable marketing approaches	• Large scale and scope economies • Learning and experience • Sourcing efficiencies • Favourable logistics • Arbitrage opportunities • High R&D costs	• Favourable trade policies • Common technological standards • Common manufacturing and marketing regulations	• Interdependent countries • Global competitors

Exhibit 4.4 Factors in Globalization

Source: Adapted from M. E. Porter, *Competition in Global Industries* (Boston: Harvard Business School Press, 1986) and G. Yip, "Global Strategy in a World of Nations," *Sloan Management Review* 31:1 (1989): 29–40.

government-run enterprises have been privatized.[8] We define **globalization** as the evolution of distinct geographic product markets into a state of globally interdependent product markets. Because of this, the topic of globalization spans both the subjects of PESTEL analysis and industry analysis in both stable and dynamic contexts.

Globalization entails much more than simply exporting products to another country. Few industries now have simply domestic competitors. Most industries have domestic companies that compete with companies having operations in many countries, and in many cases both sets of companies are doing equally well. In contrast, a truly global industry has a standardized core product, a uniform marketing approach, and integrated competitive strategies for international markets.[9] In these industries, competitive advantage clearly belongs to the companies that can compete globally. The chocolate confectionery industry is such an industry, as the dominant competitors are all global: Hershey, Kraft, Mars, and Nestlé.

Factors that reveal whether an industry has globalized or is in the process of globalizing can be grouped into four categories: *market, cost, government,* and *competition*[10] (see Exhibit 4.4). Globalization makes sense when any form of advantage is applicable across markets.

globalization Evolution of distinct geographic product markets into a state of globally interdependent product markets.

Markets

The more similar markets in different regions are, the greater the pressure for an industry to globalize. Coke and Pepsi, for example, are fairly uniform around the world because the demand for soft drinks is largely the same in every country. The airframe-manufacturing industry, dominated by Boeing and Airbus, also has a highly uniform market for its products because airlines all over the world have the same needs when it comes to large commercial jets.

The cellphone industry offers a more recent example. Although cellphones provide similar basic features and services to end-users (such as voicemail, text messaging, and data services), the systems they operate on vary technically. Companies in the European Union (EU) have mobilized around one GSM (Global System for Mobile Communications) standard, whereas most North American companies adhere to another GSM standard or the CDMA (Code Division Multiple Access) standard that originally dominated most of the U.S. market. The differences in technology make GSM phones completely incompatible with CDMA networks, though, with recent breakthroughs, multi-standard phones are possible.

These differences create fragmented markets for cellphone manufacturers such as Motorola and Nokia. Moreover, the interdependence of the European and North American markets means that manufacturers must maintain a strong regional presence. Finally, recent entrants into the industry, including Samsung and NEC, already engage in other global operations. Thus, the problems of multiple standards and the entry of large global competitors both spur globalization in the industry.

Costs

Any time fixed costs are high, there will be pressure to globalize so that fixed costs are spread across more customers. In both the automobile and airframe-manufacturing industries, costs also favour globalization. For instance, Boeing and Airbus can invest millions in new-product

R&D only because the global market for their products is so large. Coke and Pepsi make huge investments in marketing and promotion, and because they're promoting coherent images and brands, they can leverage their marketing dollars around the world. Pharmaceuticals spend billions of dollars researching and developing new therapies and applications. Consequently, again, there is tremendous pressure to sell products in any economy that might have demand for the drug to help recoup this investment.

Beyond leveraging fixed costs, several other cost pressures to globalization exist. For instance, in many industries the only way to have competitive manufacturing costs is to move operations to locations outside the home country, typically to one of the emerging economies that offers significantly lower wages. Finally, the improvement in logistics and transportation capabilities within companies and in the logistics service industry generally make it very easy to enter new markets. Thus, the cost to globalize has been reduced significantly over the past several decades. This means that competitors seeking growth will globalize; failing to do so in your own company could negatively affect your competitive position.

Governments and Competition

Government policy can both encourage and discourage competition. National governments have encouraged globalization by negotiating reduced trade restriction and subsidizing exports. Trade restrictions take various forms, including tariffs on imported goods, quotas limiting the amount that can be imported, health and safety requirements, and many other laws. The World Trade Organization (WTO) has been remarkably successful in lowering tariffs and other direct trade barriers around the world, but sticky issues such as subsidies and discriminatory local laws, which provide indirect trade barriers, remain. In 2007, the United States challenged Chinese law, which contained a series of measures that reduced taxes and other payments owed to the government by exporters. The measures violated a number of WTO rules, including the explicit prohibition of export subsidies. Chinese companies that qualified for these subsidies accounted for nearly 60 percent of China's exports of factory goods in 2005, including steel, wood, and paper. That year, China agreed to terminate some of these measures.[11]

In the transportation industries, countries have cabotage laws, which dictate the terms that carriers must follow when transporting people or materials within their borders. Many of these laws are designed to promote the development of domestic transport companies and protect national security, but some cabotage laws have been criticized because they can restrict free trade. In September 2009, the United States ended an eight-year exemption that had allowed charter flights for sports teams and celebrities that originated in Canada to make several stops in American cities. This had an immediate impact on Air Canada charters flying under the Jetz label. Each Jetz charter came with its own onboard mechanic to ensure that each flight met its destinations without fail and had exclusive access to private terminals that regular airlines could not use. The ruling also left Canada's six National Hockey League teams scrambling to find alternative travel arrangements south of the border one month before the season started.[12]

Now that you understand how to characterize the general conditions of the macro environment PESTEL analysis and the special issue of globalization, you are prepared to delve deeper into industry analysis. The next two sections provide a framework for analyzing the structure of an industry and better understanding competitors.

Value System Analysis

The company's value chain, which we examined in Chapter 3, is embedded in a larger system that bestselling business writer and professor Michael Porter calls the "value system." The system is a chain of companies, each with its own value chain. That part of the system that creates and delivers the inputs used by the company is "upstream," while that part of the system that takes the company's output to the final consumer is "downstream." What the value system ultimately delivers to the consumer determines what the consumer is willing to pay. How each of the companies in the chain operates influences the value added by each company and how it adds that value. An overall implication is that management wants to be fully aware of the

Past Strategy

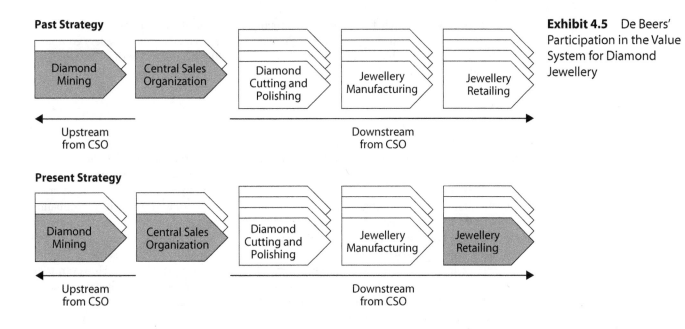

Exhibit 4.5 De Beers' Participation in the Value System for Diamond Jewellery

value system in which it participates and seeks to utilize the system that affords it the best performance.

An example from De Beers demonstrates the value system at work (see Exhibit 4.5).[13] The value system started with the mining value chain (raw diamonds are stones), which moved to the value chain marketing stones, the cutting and polishing value chain, the jewellery manufacture value chain, and finally the jewellery retailing value chain. De Beers had mines that produced a significant share of world production. In 1930, it started generic promotion of diamond jewellery to final consumers and developed the Central Selling Organization (CSO) as the sole buyer and seller of stones. The CSO achieved control over 90 percent of the supply of stones by buying diamonds produced by others and then selling them along with its own. The CSO chose what to sell, whom to sell to, and for how much. It also set grading standards that ensured the quality of the stones sold. De Beers' generic promotion raised diamond sales and increased the profit pool available in the value system. The CSO allowed De Beers to capture a considerable share of the profit in the system by charging 10 to 15 percent on the price of the stones passing through it.

The CSO maintained its market power by disciplining others in the value system. When a mine sold directly to cutters and polishers, De Beers would kill the price of the types of stones that mine sold by flooding the market with stones of equivalent quality. When mines were overproducing, De Beers discouraged production by cutting back on purchases. When cutters and polishers went directly to mines of others to buy stones, De Beers would no longer sell to these buyers. These buyers were also at risk because De Beers periodically bought independent mines so those buying stones from these mines would lose their source of supply. The CSO's activities maintained stability for all participants in the value system and all participants benefited to varying degrees.

De Beers' management of the supply of stones no longer worked by the end of the 1990s for several reasons. The CSO's cost of holding its inventory of stones was quickly escalating, topping US$5 billion, as new mines around the world added to world production and growth in consumer demand for diamonds slowed down, in part due to concern that they were buying blood diamonds sold to finance guerrilla wars in Africa. Meanwhile, new mines were selling directly to cutters and polishers. Finally, the CSO was being prosecuted for acting as a cartel that was constraining trade. All these pressures called for a new strategy. In response, De Beers reconfigured its participation in the value system. It continued in mining activities and formed more joint ventures. But it stopped trying to control the supply of stones and focused on selling high-quality diamonds that would carry the De Beers brand. The CSO reduced the amount it charged but also focused on selling high-quality stones to those manufacturers that it thought would add the greatest value. And it entered the jewellery retailing value chain through a retail joint venture with French luxury goods company LVMH Moët Hennessy • Louis Vuitton (LVMH), which established an independently managed De Beers diamond jewellery company. De Beers is more profitable today with the CSO having a 40 percent market share than when it had an 80 percent market share.

Industry Analysis

Neoclassical microeconomics holds that under perfect competition companies will earn only "normal" profits; that is, enough profit to cover the cost of capital. Assumptions for perfect competition to hold in an industry are numerous sellers and buyers (no monopolies), perfect information, relatively homogenous products, and no barriers to entry or exit. If companies in the industry earn greater-than-normal profits (as most managers and shareholders are trying hard to accomplish), new companies will enter the industry until the increased competition drives profits down to normal levels. If profits fall *below* normal levels, some companies will exit, easing competition and allowing profits to increase to normal levels. However, even a casual examination of industries finds industries with long-run average profits far exceeding normal levels and others with profits way below such levels, suggesting that most industries do not meet the assumptions of perfect competition.

In this book, we are pursuing the goal of managers and shareholders. We assert that their goal to earn above-normal returns is possible. The goal of the strategist is to produce this, and when it has been done, the company has developed an inherent advantage over other companies in its industry. We acknowledge this by saying that the company has a *competitive advantage* over its rivals. To help achieve this advantage, the strategist looks for situations where conditions deviate from pure competition, including few competitors, numerous suppliers and buyers, asymmetric information, heterogeneous products, and barriers that make entry of new companies into an industry difficult. Alternatively, the strategist looks for ways to create and continue imperfect competition. For this reason we will now look at causes of imperfect competition.

I/O ECONOMICS AND KEY SUCCESS FACTORS

Many concepts that managers use when analyzing an industry come from *industrial organization (I/O) economics*. Fortunately, the basic tools of industry analysis are easily described. In practice, management makes strategic decisions by coupling the insights provided by external environment analysis with those provided by internal environmental analysis. The strategy that performs best is one that fits best with both environments.

key success factor (KSF)
Key asset or requisite skill that all companies in an industry must possess in order to be a viable competitor.

Researchers often argue that the goal of managers should be to acquire the necessary skills and resources, often called the **key success factors (KSFs)**, to compete in their industry.[14] For example, Cinram, the world's largest producer of DVDs, sees its key success factors in the home video, audio replication, distribution, and printing industries as including (1) capacity, which is critical to securing contracts with major studios and achieving economies of scale to lower costs and achieving higher margins; (2) exclusive contracts with prominent studios because market share is dependent upon strong relationships and arrangements with large studios; (3) full service offering, in which replicators must offer a complete package of services, including high value-added distribution services, often in multiple territories; (4) access to financing, which is essential for investment in capacity, technological improvements, and product offering; and (5) low cost of production because customers are cost-conscious and will make purchase decisions based on price.[15] In the soft-drink industry, KSFs include (1) the ability to meet competitive pricing; (2) extensive distribution capabilities, including ownership of vending machines and cold-storage cases; (3) marketing skills that raise consumer brand awareness in a highly crowded marketplace; (4) a broad mix of products, including diet and non-caffeinated beverages; (5) global presence; and (6) well-positioned bottlers and bottling capacity.

According to the KSF approach, all companies in an industry must possess the KSFs in order to be viable. What these are is dictated by industry characteristics and has implications for the strategy and the resources and capabilities needed. KSFs satisfy the *value* criteria from the VRINE model introduced in Chapter 3 because they are essential to participating in this industry that is producing excess profits, but they do not satisfy the *rareness* criterion because all companies in the industry have them. Thus, possessing KSFs will not grant a company a competitive advantage over other key players in the industry, but it will permit a company to compete against similar companies. KSFs provide barriers to entry because companies seeking to enter the industry require them but find them complex and costly to put in place.

While I/O researchers focus on the industry as a whole to understand the factors that determine its profitability, the strategist seeks to avoid the factors that limit profitability and take advantage of the factors that enhance profitability. Doing these things differently than the rest of the industry enhances the competitive advantage of the company.

WHAT IS AN INDUSTRY?

In theory, an industry is a group of companies that produce or sell the same product in a market. The number of companies in the market can range from one to many. Most industries have several dominant companies and many smaller companies. In practice, governments have developed a system for classifying economic activity into categories that are designated with numerical codes. The governments of Canada, Mexico, and the United States have all agreed on a common system of codes [the North American Industry Classification System (NAICS)] at the industry level, the five-digit level, but each country uses the sixth digit to define national industries, which differ among countries due to differences in economic and organizational structures. The classification system is a production-oriented system in which each establishment (this is a location at which the activity is performed and can be only part of a company) is classified according to the code. The coding structure is illustrated in Exhibit 4.6.[16]

Defining Industry Boundaries

The generalizations by economists about each industry using NAICS data provide insight into important characteristics of industries but do not allow the specificity of analysis that the strategist needs. The result is that practitioners have chosen to define industries in ways that are meaningful for their own analysis. Sometimes they define industries broadly, including many related industries, and other times they simply include direct competitors. In our analysis, we start by defining industry boundaries in terms of the products, type of customers served, and the geographic coverage of the business of interest. The boundaries can be expanded until important differences among the companies emerge to suggest that the companies no longer directly compete with one another.

Another complication when delineating boundaries is that companies themselves change what they do. In the midst of the Cola War, both Coca-Cola and Pepsi were looking for ways to grow. Growth by taking market share away from the other was difficult, so both redefined the industry they were in as non-alcoholic beverages, which included juices, teas, and water. Coke bought Minute Maid in 1960 and Odwalla (juices) in 2001. Pepsi purchased Tropicana (juices) in 1999 and South Beach Beverage in 2000. As Coke and Pepsi expanded the boundaries of the industry, their competitors changed as well. Nestlé, a Swiss company, controls nearly

Code	Description
321	Wood Product Manufacturing
3211	Sawmills and Wood Preservation
32111	Sawmills and Wood Preservation (sub-group of 3211)
321111	Sawmills (except Shingle and Shake Mills) MEX
321112	Shingle and Shake Mills MEX
321114	Wood Preservation US

Exhibit 4.6 An Example of the North American Industry Classification System (NAICS)

Source: North American Industry Classification (NAICS) 2007, Statistics Canada. Accessed October 2, 2009, at http://stds.statcan.gc.ca/naics-scian/2007/ts-rt-eng.asp?criteria=31-33.

one-third of the market for bottled water, with 70 brands in 160 countries. In North America alone, Nestlé sells nine domestic brands, including Arrowhead, Poland Spring, and Deer Park, and five imported brands, including San Pellegrino and Perrier.

At least one thing should be clear by now: Before entering an industry, the company's managers must know the type of customer, the geographic market, and the type of product that they're considering.

A MODEL OF INDUSTRY STRUCTURE

five-forces model Framework for evaluating industry structure according to the effects of rivalry, threat of entry, supplier power, buyer power, and the threat of substitutes.

Once the boundaries of the "industry" have been identified, the next step is to examine the industry's fundamental characteristics and structure. The model shown in Exhibit 4.7 identifies six forces that determine the profitability of an industry.[17] This is Michael Porter's **five-forces model** with the addition of complementors.[18] On the horizontal axis, the industry purchases inputs or supplies from other industries, transforms them, then sells its products or services to buyers, who can be other industries and/or consumers. The industry faces the threat of potential competitors who will enter if they see the potential for generating profits in excess of their cost of capital. The industry also has to keep in mind that buyers will turn to substitute products and services if they consider the industry's prices too high. These four surrounding forces are

Exhibit 4.7   The Five Forces Determining Industry Profitability

Source: Adapted from M. E. Porter, *Competitive Strategy: Techniques for Analyzing Industries and Competitors* (New York: Free Press, 1980).

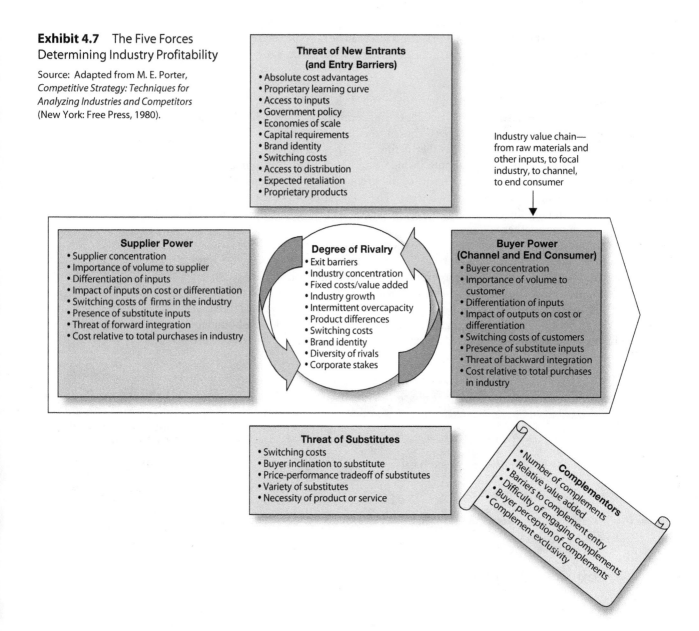

countervailing powers that are all trying to take some of the industry's profits for themselves. A key reason that profitability varies across industries is that the power of these forces differs across the industries.

Rivalry

Economists refer to the tactics that companies use when they compete with each other as **rivalry**. The most critical determinants of rivalry are the number of companies in the industry and their relative sizes. The *concentration ratio* is a measure used to assess the significance of these two determinants. This ratio represents the combined revenues of the largest industry participants expressed as a ratio of total industry sales. For example, the CR4 indicates the percentage of industry sales accounted for by the largest four companies in the industry, CR8 the largest eight, and so on. In Exhibit 4.8, concentration ratios are given for various food industries within the food sector of the Canadian economy. The ratios vary dramatically across the sector, with sales much more concentrated among the top four dairy companies than they are among the top four seafood companies. Also note that concentration ratios change from 1999 to 2003 as successful companies grow in importance and less successful companies decline in importance.

rivalry The act of companies in an industry competing for profit.

The more concentrated the industry, the more aware each of the competitors is about the impact of its actions on the other competitors. This encourages competitors to avoid price competition and compete in other ways. Coke and Pepsi, for example, compete strenuously with each other, but their tactics focus on aspects other than price. Both spend heavily on advertising and improving the availability of their products. The prices they are then able to charge more than cover these costs, improving their profitability.

Rivalry is more likely when certain conditions hold. First, when competitors are numerous, rivalry will be greater. Then the individual competitor thinks that it can lower price without others realizing and retaliating. Second, when companies are similar in size and resources, they are more likely to fight one another and have the resources needed for sustained and rigorous retaliation, as we see with Coke and Pepsi. Third, when a company is strategically important to its owner, that rivalry is more likely to be an aggressive competitor. The owner is relying on the success of this company and so will support its activities and has expectations that it will generate superior results. Fourth, when an industry is growing slowly, more rivalry is likely because the only way for a company to grow sales is by taking customers away from its competitors.

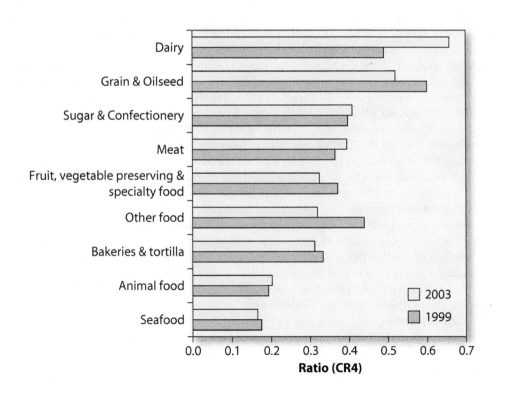

Exhibit 4.8 Concentration in Selected Canadian Food Industries

Source: Chart C3.8, Share of Industry Shipments Accounted for by the Four Largest Companies (CR4), 1999 and 2003, in "An Overview of the Canadian Agriculture and Agri-Food System, 2007," Agriculture and Agri-Food Canada, 2007. Accessed September 28, 2009, at www4.agr.gc.ca/AAFC-AAC/display-afficher.do?id=1205852178020&lang=eng.

exit barriers Barriers that impose a high cost on the abandonment of a market or product.

Fifth, when products and services are difficult to differentiate, companies compete largely on price and service. These are easily identified and copied. Sixth, when buyers can switch from one company's offerings to another's at low cost, competitors have to offer more incentive for the buyer to stay. Seventh, and finally, when **exit barriers** are high, rivalry will be greater. When the profitability of a company is less than the cost of its capital, it is best leaving the industry and redeploying its capital elsewhere.

Leaving is not possible if the company is unable to sell off assets that it has invested in, so the company stays in the industry because it is earning more than if it sold its assets. This was the issue facing north Atlantic fisheries when stocks of northern cod off the coast of Newfoundland declined dramatically. In 1992, the federal government closed down the industry in the hope that this would allow stocks to recover. It assisted exit from the industry by funding the early retirement of older fishermen and retraining of younger fishermen, as well as purchasing fishing boats. Those who remained were given licences to catch species other than cod.

Companies try to avoid price competition because prices are easily recognized and matched. When rivalry turns to price competition, profitability is at risk. At the extreme, price competition sets off a price war. Price wars involve a series of escalating price reductions. One competitor lowers price, then another lowers its price even further and so on, causing ever-falling prices. Price wars drive those companies that were marginally profitable into bankruptcy. The remaining companies in the industry absorb the market share of those that have closed and eventually, with fewer competitors, are able to raise prices and become more profitable.

threat of new entry Degree to which new competitors can enter an industry and intensify rivalry.

barriers to entry Conditions under which it is more difficult to join or compete in an industry.

Threat of New Entry

Industries that have higher than average profitability attract the attention of companies looking for promising new arenas in which to compete. Paradoxically, industries with consistently high average profitability also tend to be the most difficult to enter. This goes back to the economists' argument that as new companies enter an industry, they lower the industry's profitability to normal profits. What keeps new entrants out are **barriers to entry**; and high barriers to entry have the effect of reducing potential competition by limiting supply and reducing rivalry. This results in higher prices and higher profitability in industries with high barriers to entry.

Several industry characteristics contribute to high barriers to entry. First, when economies of scale are found in the industry, those companies that have greater volume have much lower cost per unit than new entrants that have much smaller companies. Second, when products are differentiated, new entrants have to overcome existing competitors' brands and consumer loyalty to them. Third, when the capital required to enter is high, especially when it is high risk because the investment is in advertising and research and development, the new entrants find raising capital difficult. In the microelectronics industry, building a semiconductor fabrication plant (commonly called a fab) in order to manufacture integrated circuits costs more than US$1 billion, with values as high as US$3 billion to US$4 billion not being uncommon. Fourth, when customers consider the cost of switching from existing products and services to the entrant's product and services, the new entrant will have difficulty attracting new customers. Established cellphone carriers try to dissuade customers from switching to a competitor's services by charging very high cancellation fees in the hopes that the costs involved will discourage their customers from leaving. Vendors of IT software also face a great challenge getting customers to switch from their current IT to the vendor's new IT because of the high cost of switching. Fifth, when access to the distribution channels is restricted, with the best channels already filled, the new entrant finds distribution to come at a high cost and not particularly effective. Canadel was able to lock up the best retailers to sell its casual dining furniture, forcing later entrants to settle for the retailers who were still available. Sixth, and finally, when there are cost disadvantages independent of scale, such as location, learning curve, and proprietary technology, the established companies have an advantage. Certain technologies, for instance, give their owners cost advantages that new entrants can't readily match or compensate for. Cellphone technology requires its own network of towers, and this system can bind the customer to a particular phone company.

Consider the soft-drink industry from our opening vignette as an illustration. The soft-drink industry has several barriers making it difficult for new entrants to compete nationally with Coke and Pepsi. Both companies created such strong brand preference that they dominated distribution through fast-food franchises and supermarkets. Any entrant to the soft-drink industry must establish a strong consumer brand preference and have distribution so its product is available to consumers. Putting both of these in place at the same time is nearly impossible. Then along came Gerry Pencer, CEO of Cott Corporation, who saw a way to compete by doing things differently. In 1987, Dave Nichol of Loblaw Merchandising was looking for a private label cola that could compete with Coke and Pepsi[19] because over half the soft drinks sold in Canada were cola flavoured and 72 percent of Canadian households bought their cola at the supermarket. Pencer presented Nichol with a sample made from Royal Crown concentrate—Royal Crown had never had much success in the United States because of poor marketing. Following Nichol's demands, the formula was modified with Royal Crown's approval. In negotiating the modification with Royal Crown, Pencer got a 20-year agreement with Royal Crown that provided Cott with both the concentrate and access to Royal Crown's U.S. bottling network. The new cola was sold under Loblaw's President's Choice brand, so Cott benefited from an effective brand and obtained shelf space. It was a good product and Loblaw always priced it under Coke and Pepsi, even when they cut their prices. Cott's success grew private labels' share of the US$1 billion soft-drink market from 1 percent of the market in 1987 to 20 percent in 1992. Cott controlled 90 percent of the private label volume, and in 1993 Loblaw sold 10 million cases of Cott's cola. The lesson from Cott's experience is that barriers have the potential to limit entry, but a clever competitor can figure ways around them.

Supplier Power

Industry participants also compete with companies in supply industries. Companies in the industry want to earn more by paying as little as possible for what they buy, while companies supplying the industry want to earn as much as possible for what they sell to it by charging as much as they can. The terms of the deals between the industry and its suppliers are determined by the relative bargaining power of each side. The supplier has power when it can dictate contract terms dealing with such things as prices, delivery lead times, minimum orders, post-purchase service, and payment terms that are favourable to it. Then the supplier earns more at the expense of the industry.

Supplier power arises when the suppliers are relatively concentrated, when they control a scarce input, or when they are simply bigger than their customers. In some cases, companies in a focal industry need a unique product or service and have only a few alternative suppliers to which to turn. In these instances, of course, suppliers can demand higher prices. For instance, two-thirds of the iron ore market is dominated by only three companies—Australian-owned BHP Billiton Iron Ore (BHPBIO or BHP), Rio Tinto Hamersley Iron Unit (RTHI), and the world's biggest iron ore producer, Brazilian-owned Companhia Vale do Rio Doce SA (CVRD). Each year the three sit down separately with the key steel makers across the world and hammer out new prices. Remarkably, they all come up with the same price for iron ore. That price has been rising with the dramatic expansion of the Chinese steel industry—in 2005, China bought 43 percent of global iron ore shipments. With the increased demand for ore, reference prices rose each year. In 2005 it rose by 72 percent, in 2006 by 19 percent, in 2007 by 10 percent, and in 2008 by 65 percent. Starting in 2009 pricing became erratic, but the trend was higher, with prices expected to hold for years since building a new mine takes five to six years.[20]

Returning to the opening vignette, it is easy to see that the soft-drink industry is dominated by two major players. They purchase most of their inputs in commodity markets where sweetener and food colouring suppliers have no leverage over soft-drink manufacturers. In contrast, the many bottlers are franchise operations that have to buy soft-drink concentrate from Coke and Pepsi and cans and bottles from canning companies. Under their contracts with Coke and Pepsi, the bottlers cannot buy cola products from any other concentrate maker. Thus, soft-drink bottlers face considerable supplier power.

Even when an industry is sourcing products that may be considered commodities, such as textiles or wood, suppliers can impose payment terms that implicitly raise the cost of the resource for the focal industry. Such is the case when the supplier industry is more consolidated than the focal industry. Because the furniture industry, for example, is highly fragmented, no

supplier power Degree to which companies in the supply industry are able to dictate terms to contracts and thereby extract some of the profit that would otherwise be available to competitors in the focal industry.

single manufacturer has much power when bargaining with the larger wood and fabric suppliers who provide the industry's primary raw materials. Suppliers of wood have many possible companies to which to sell.

Supplier power is also high when companies in the supply industry present a threat of forward integration; that is, if it is possible for them to manufacture finished products rather than just sell components to manufacturers. Coke and Pepsi, for example, could easily integrate forward into bottling instead of just supplying bottlers with concentrate. They have demonstrated this by purchasing bottlers in the past. This potential gives them significant power in negotiating prices with their bottling networks.

Finally, suppliers are powerful when companies in the focal industry face significant switching costs when changing suppliers. For instance, companies purchasing enterprise resource planning (ERP) software have several supplier choices, including SAP, Oracle, and PeopleSoft. However, once a company purchases from one supplier and incurs the significant implementation costs associated with adopting the ERP software, it will be reluctant to switch to another supplier because the costs of doing so are significant. Because of the high costs involved in switching ERP systems, companies switch suppliers less frequently than one would expect in a market with many sellers.

In summary, in transactions between industry participants and companies in supply industries, the relative power of each party affects both the pricing and profitability of each industry. When focal-industry participants have negotiating strength, suppliers have limited bargaining power, and the focal industry acts to reduce the supplier-industry performance rather than the other way around.

Buyer Power

buyer power Degree to which companies in the buying industry are able to dictate terms on purchase agreements that extract some of the profit that would otherwise go to competitors in the focal industry.

The industry also competes with its buyers or customers. This relationship is exactly the opposite of the supplier–industry relationship. The industry wants to earn more by charging as much as possible for what it sells while buyers want to earn as much as possible for what they buy from the industry by paying as little as they can. The terms of the deals between the industry and its buyers are determined by the relative bargaining power of each side. The buyers have power when they are able to dictate terms favourable to them on purchase agreements. Then the buyers pay less and so earn more at the expense of the industry, which receives less for its products or services.

Several factors lead to buyers having high degrees of relative power over their suppliers. First, when the buyers are prestigious, and when their purchases represent a significant portion of the sellers' sales, buyers have power. Second, when a product has little value for the buyer group, buyers are more powerful. Third, when buyers have numerous product choices, and prices of multiple competitors are easy to compare, buyers are powerful. Tire makers, for instance, have little power over carmakers because tires are standardized and there are many competitors in the industry. If a tire maker tried to raise prices, large automobile manufacturers would turn to one of several other companies that could fill their needs. Conversely, when buyers have few alternatives, their power is minimal, and industry prices increase, resulting in higher-than-average industry profitability.

Consider the extreme case of the Toronto Maple Leafs of the National Hockey League. The team last won the Stanley Cup in 1966–67 and in the more than four decades since then has won fewer regular season games than it has lost. Yet Maple Leafs home games have long been one of the toughest tickets to acquire in Canada, even during lean periods. The Leafs have sold out almost every game since 1946. While scalping is technically illegal in Toronto, there are numerous scalpers around the Air Canada Centre. The only ways to get into a game are to buy tickets months in advance or to deal with scalpers at a mark-up considerably above face value. Obviously the team is under no pressure to discount tickets in spite of its poor performance. Still, the owners are delighted with the club. At present the Leafs are the most valuable franchise in the league, worth US$470 million in 2009 while the league average is US$223 million. The franchise is also the most profitable in the National Hockey League, with an operating income of US$78.9 million versus the league average of US$6.1 million.[21]

Information also provides buyers with power, particularly when they have choices, when the products are relatively inexpensive, or when products are not heavily regulated. New-car buyers, for example, are relatively powerful not only because there are numerous makes and models in every category, but because they can now use the internet to compare products and prices online. In contrast, dealers don't have a corresponding advantage when negotiating with carmakers because operating agreements require them to sell certain manufacturers' products.

Finally, buyers are powerful to the extent that they pose a threat of backward integration. Large brewers, for instance, could conceivably make their own beer cans (in fact, some do). The implicit threat that these buyers of aluminium cans have is that they could move backward into a supplier's industry. This naturally diminishes the supplier's price-setting power.

What About Retail Consumers?

Let's make a final—and critical—point about the role of buyer power in any definition of an industry. Note that the industry is the unit that we're analyzing: The focal point of our assessment of rivalry in an industry is the industry segment that we've chosen to analyze. Consequently, when we talk about buyers, we don't mean end retail consumers (unless, of course, we're analyzing an industry that does retailing: grocery stores, new-car dealers, department stores, etc.). Japan's Matsushita Electric Industrial, for example, markets many well-known electronics brands, including Panasonic, Quasar, and JVC. When Matsushita markets Panasonic TVs, its target customers are not household consumers but, rather, large retail chains and electronics wholesalers. Certainly, retail consumers are important, but they don't negotiate directly with manufacturers, and they don't wield any direct power in non-retail segments. Consumers affect industry profits indirectly when they exercise power as the last link in an industry value chain. An analysis of Panasonic's industry segment would examine the relative power of Matsushita and its rivals in negotiating with retailers, such as Best Buy and Future Shop, which carry their products.

Threat of Substitutes

Sometimes products and services provided by other industries can satisfy the same buyer needs as the products of the industry being considered. Then the industry faces the **threat of substitutes**. For example, orange juice and soft drinks are products produced by different industries that can substitute for one another in satisfying the thirst of some customers. Coke and Pepsi are not substitutes in terms of industry analysis because they are in the same industry. Yet products that are not closely related may still be substitutes. For instance, the desire for leisure can be satisfied with either gambling at a casino or taking a cruise. In the airline industry, substitutes for shorter distance trips are car, bus, and rail.

threat of substitutes Degree to which products of one industry can satisfy the same demand as those of another.

The prevalence of viable substitute products from other industries places pressures on the prices that the industry can charge, limiting industry profits. When there are no viable substitutes, there is less pressure on price.

Complementors

As noted earlier, the five forces comprise a framework for organizing one's analysis of industry structure. The profitability of an industry tends to be lower when the competitive forces are stronger. More recently, some have argued that the players outlined in the five-forces model do not always compete exclusively in zero-sum games that simply determine how much each gets of a value set by consumers. By working together, the industry with its suppliers or its buyers creates additional value in the consumer's mind. When this happens the players are **complementors** because the product provided by one industry tends to increase the sales in another industry.[22]

complementor An industry that provides products or services which tend to increase sales in another industry.

The characteristics of complementors are shown in Exhibit 4.7. Companies in the music and electronics industries, for example, sell products that must be used together. Each benefits from the other's presence. Music players such as MP3s sell because they allow people to carry their preferred music with them, while sales of music are higher because people buy digital files to put on their music players. Likewise, the sale of hot dogs increases the sales of hot dog buns, condiments, and beverages. These three products are marketed by complementary industry segments (which is why grocers can sell buns below cost to stimulate sales of higher-margin hot dogs). Sometimes relationships among companies in an industry are complex. For instance, United Airlines and Delta Airlines compete fiercely in trying to attract customers to fill their seats. However, when upgrading their fleets to a newer plane, both airlines are better off when they order a new model airplane from the same manufacturer because the manufacturer is able to produce the plane for less as it achieves greater economies of scale with more orders. Turning to the car business, more new cars are sold when affordable financing is easier to get or when dealers offer extended service warranties. Thus, financing and warranty arrangements can be regarded as complementors to the retail new-car market.

Customers, in addition, are likely to put a higher value on the products of one industry segment when they already have access to complementary products from another segment.[23] The value of computer peripherals obviously increases as the number of personal computers increases. Likewise, the value of a commercial real-estate development is enhanced if there are neighbouring amenities valued by business tenants, such as restaurants, entertainment venues, and transportation facilities.

Industries that complement each other will still compete with each other to determine their share of the value they create together. Looking at the music players again, consumers are willing to spend a limited amount of money satisfying their musical desires. If the music player is more expensive, then they are likely to be willing to spend less on the music. Alternatively, it the music player is cheap, they are willing to spend more buying music to play on it. The relationship between complementors thus has elements of bargaining power akin to supplier-and-buyer relationships; one party to a complementor relationship may receive more of the benefit than the other, even though both are better off.

An important difference between complementors and the other five forces in this model of industry analysis is that the five forces typically work to *decrease* industry profitability while the strong complementors may *increase* profits by increasing demand for an industry's products.

Using the Industry-Structure Model

Understanding the five industry forces and complementors helps managers evaluate the general attractiveness of an industry as well as the specific opportunities and threats facing companies in the industry. The pressure on industry operating margins will be significantly lower in industries where suppliers or buyers exercise high levels of power, where entry barriers are low, and where substitute products are readily available. An industry has high profit potential and is most attractive when the effects of the five forces are minimal and complementors furnish positive externalities.

How does industry analysis affect strategy formulation? Good industry analysis answers a few basic questions that have a significant bearing on potential profitability of the company: Does the company's current strategy fit with current industry conditions—specifically, the industry conditions relevant to the company's chosen industry arenas? What changes in the industry may result in misalignment? Which elements of the company's strategy will need to be altered to exploit future industry conditions? Second, a high-quality strategy will be one that helps the company adapt to the five forces so that they are more in the favour of the company. Specifically, a successful strategy will help minimize buyer power, offset supplier power, avoid excessive rivalry, raise the barriers to entry, and reduce the threat of substitution. A company might minimize buyer power by building customer loyalty through specific differentiators. Supplier power can be offset by assuring that there are multiple sources of key inputs. Excessive rivalry can be avoided by attempting to grow in emerging segments rather than attacking competitors in mature markets. Barriers to entry might be built by making pre-emptive investments that raise costs for new entrants. Finally, the threat of substitutes can be reduced by understanding the benefits that substitutes offer and then incorporating those in your own products or services.

When using the five-forces model to formulate strategy, remember that these forces are not static. The actions of various industry players keep industry conditions in an almost constant state of flux. Consequently, unattractive industry structure is not necessarily an omen that profitability is destined to be marginal. Wise strategists use information gleaned from the study of industry structure to formulate strategies for pursuing opportunities for and dealing with threats to industry profitability. Remember, too, that industry analysis views forces from an overall industry perspective and not from that of a particular company. The industry-wide effect of these forces will determine whether an industry is attractive. We walk through the use of Michael Porter's five-forces analysis in How Would You Do That? 4.1.

Competitor Analysis

The industry analysis that we've discussed so far has focused on the broad industry definition. Another purpose of an industry analysis is to develop a clear understanding of who the company's competitors are and what their behaviours are likely to be in the future in the company's chosen arena or arenas. Consequently, after completing a five-forces analysis, the strategies and behaviours of the company's competitors need to be investigated in detail. We now present a model for mapping out who the competitors are and what their strategies are. This analysis will then be used when formulating the company's strategy, which will be discussed in detail in Chapters 5 and 6. This tool, which is the *value curve,* offers an intuitive way to map competitors' strategies using the industry KSFs discussed earlier in the chapter. Its use is illustrated in How Would You Do That? 4.2.

MAPPING COMPETITORS

Mapping competitors within an industry starts by identifying the primary competitors. Companies generally know who they compete against directly for sales so this is usually the easiest step. But when the company only currently competes in a niche market and doesn't encounter all the competitors with regularity, identifying competitors is more difficult. Then data sources that list the companies in specific industries can be used to identify them. Once the primary competitors are identified, how these companies compete within the industry is documented. Typically groups of similar competitors that form strategic groups are observed. Each group is a set of competitors that follow similar strategies so will have similar KSFs. Companies with similar strategies are more likely to be mutual threats than are groups with significantly different characteristics. For instance, in the beer industry, Anheuser-Busch, Inbev, SABMiller, and Molson Coors have more in common with one another than any of them has in common with micro breweries such as Granville Island Brewing, Great Western Brewing Company, Moosehead Breweries Limited, and Wellington Brewery Inc. Analysis is more useful when it focuses on similar competitors rather than the industry as a whole. This idea is the counterpoint of breaking customers into segments. Instead, we are breaking competitors into segments. In the bicycle industry, Trek manufactures high-quality performance bicycles that are sold through independent dealers. It experiences some competition with Schwinn, which sells its bikes through both mass merchants and independent bicycle dealers. It faces little competition from Huffy, which is made with lower-end components and sold through mass merchandisers such as Wal-Mart and Target.

THE VALUE CURVE

Now that we have described why companies need to have a deep understanding of their competitors, we'll describe the **value curve**. In How Would You Do That? 4.2, we examine the U.S. wine industry. The differentiators of the company's closest competitors can be compared using the value curve—most decision makers can usually produce a value curve intuitively. Describing competitors in this way also helps us identify where the company is using its strengths to create its unique market position. Growth opportunities are those competitive positions that are compatible with a company's unique set of resources and capabilities. The probable *future competition* can also be included in the analysis so that it is not ignored or underestimated.

value curve A graphical depiction of how a company and major groups of its competitors are competing across its industry's factors of completion.

The first step in creating a value curve is determining the criteria (or KSFs) used to describe what the incumbents offer their customers. List these factors along the horizontal axis. The vertical axis is used to rate the level of delivery according to the criteria. For instance, if room comfort were one of the key success factors when evaluating the hotel industry, then establishments like Hyatt and Marriott would rate much higher than hotels like Comfort Inn and Best Western. The scale is not as important as separating the various competitors into **strategic groups** based on similar performance on certain criteria of KSFs. For illustrative purposes, we use a scale of 1 to 5.

strategic group Subset of companies that, because of similar strategies, resources, and capabilities, compete against one another more intensely than with other companies in an industry.

After ranking the companies or groups according to each criteria, the performance level of companies or groups by criteria can be connected with a line. This produces the value curve for that respective company or group. This provides a visual representation of the various ways rivals compete in the industry. For instance, if you were mapping the airline industry, even

A Five-Forces—Plus Complementors—Analysis of the U.S. Airline Industry[24]

Let's apply Porter's five-forces model to the U.S. airline industry to illustrate how it is used in practice. Examination of data maintained by the U.S. Department of Transportation reveals that the department categorizes the airline industry into four groups: international, national, regional, and cargo. This analysis focuses on national airlines (with sales of at least US$1 billion) but includes U.S. international airlines because they are also large, national airlines.

When performing an industry analysis using the Porter model, quantifying the impact of the forces helps you appreciate the relative impact on industry profitability. One way to do this is to assign points to each sub-factor of the five forces. Using a scale of 1 to 5, a 5 is given to a sub-factor that has a strong impact, meaning that that sub-force depresses the profitability of the airline industry. A zero is given to a sub-factor that has no impact on the airline industry's profitability. Points in between can be used for various gradations. After quantifying each relevant sub-factor for a particular force, the "power" for that force is calculated by the *average* score for sub-factors associated with that force. This provides a crude measure of the impact on that force on industry profitability. The results of using this approach for the U.S. airline industry are found in the lists in this section.

A word of caution: The validity of your analysis is only as good as (1) your identification of sub-factors associated with each particular force and (2) your subjective evaluation of each sub-factor. Exhibit 4.7 is intended to be a guide for determining the sub-factors to consider in any analysis but is not necessarily an exhaustive list (relevant sub-forces are industry-specific in many cases).

Rivalry

The first step is to identify the key players in the national passenger-airline market. Who are the rivals? You could turn to numerous available data sources to identify the key players. Using hoovers.com, we identify the top three competitors as United, American, and Delta; other competitors include AirTran, Alaska Air, America West, Continental Airlines, Hawaiian Air, JetBlue, Northwest Airlines, Southwest Airlines, and US Airways. How competitive is this industry? Is competition based on price or non-price competition? It would not take a lot of research to discover that this is a highly competitive industry. Most airlines make extremely low returns; indeed, many are currently losing money. Let's assume that, after studying the industry data, you evaluate the sub-factors as outlined below. A score of 3.6 leads you to determine that this industry has an above average level of rivalry, which will hurt margins for most players.

Exit barriers:	4
Industry concentration:	3
Fixed costs:	5
Industry growth:	4
Overcapacity:	4
Product differences:	3
Switching costs:	3
Brand identity:	2
Diversity of rivals:	4
Corporate stakes:	3
Average:	3.6

Power of Suppliers

Who are the suppliers to national airlines? Most, such as caterers, airports, airplane manufacturers, and security companies, are oligopolies, meaning that the airlines are in a less advantageous position. Key suppliers include makers of aircraft; two companies, Boeing and Airbus, dominate that market and are able to garner significant profits at the airlines' expense by virtue of their specialized positions and government subsidies. The other key supply for airlines is fuel. Due to oil shortages, the price of fuel is currently proving a very problematic issue for airlines. However, this is not a function of supplier power but, rather, conditions in the oil market.

After studying the industry data, you evaluate the sub-factors as outlined below. A score of 2.4 indicates that this force is relatively neutral. Airlines and their suppliers have points of bargaining power that just about cancels out the other.

Supplier concentration:	5
Importance of volume:	1
Input differentiation:	3
Input effect on company differentiation:	1
Switching costs of companies in industry:	2
Presence of substitute inputs:	5
Threat of forward integration:	1
Cost relative to total purchases in supplier industry:	1
Average:	2.4

Power of Buyers

To whom do national airlines sell their services? Buyers can be categorized into three primary groups: business travellers, leisure travellers, and consolidators who buy excess seat inventory at large discounts. What bargaining power do these customers have? Switching costs are very low, though airlines have increased them somewhat through frequent flyer programs. Buyers are price sensitive, but they have very little individual buyer power.

Again, you study the industry data and you evaluate the sub-factors as outlined below. A score of 2.5 indicates that this force is neutral. Each party (companies in your industry and customers) has points of bargaining power that just about cancels out the other.

Buyer concentration:	1
Importance of volume:	1
Differentiation in airline industry:	3
Switching costs of customers:	4
Presence of substitute inputs:	1
Threat of backward integration:	1
Price sensitivity:	4
Buyer information:	4
Average:	2.5

Threat of Substitutes

What is the likelihood that airline customers will use alternative means of transportation? When it comes to business travellers, this would seem minimal. However, communication technology has proven to be a viable substitute for some forms of business travel. For leisure travellers, the threat of substitutes is mainly for shorter flights. Thus, alternatives such as car and bus transportation are more viable substitutes for regional airlines and national airlines that specialize in shorter flights (e.g., Southwest).

After studying the industry data and evaluating the sub-factors, you determine the ratings outlined below. A score of 1.8 indicates that this force is

relatively in the industry's favour—substitutes exist, but they don't seem to be a major threat.

Switching costs:	4
Buyer inclination to substitute:	1
Price–performance tradeoff of substitute:	2
Variety of substitutes:	1
Necessity of product or service:	2
Average:	1.8

Threat of New Entrants

The capital intensity of the airline industry appears to pose an entry barrier. However, JetBlue, AirTran, and other entrants have proven that financing is available when there is a convincing business plan and when economic conditions are conducive to the business model proposed. Brand name and frequent flyer plans also seem to be deterrents to entry. However, JetBlue's success demonstrates that customers are willing to switch airlines if the price is right.

On balance, in this analysis you rate the threat of new entry as only moderate. The structural factors make it unlikely the industry will attract many profitable new entrants.

Average profitability of incumbents:	1
Incumbents have a cost advantage:	5
Learning curve advantage for incumbents:	3
Access to inputs:	5
Government policy (regulation):	2
Economies of scale:	3
Capital requirements:	2
Brand identity:	2
Switching costs:	3
Access to distribution (gates):	2
Expected retaliation:	1
Proprietary products:	5
Average:	2.8

Complementors

Your analysis of complementors suggests that complementors such as credit cards and rental cars are unlikely to become direct competitors, but that it is hard to tie up these complementors in exclusive relationships that competitors can't duplicate with the same or comparable complementor.

Number of complementors:	2
Relative value added:	3
Barriers to complement entry:	2
Difficulty of engaging complements:	1
Buyer perception of complements:	2
Complement exclusivity:	5
Average:	2.5

In summary, it appears that supplier power, buyer power, and substitutes do not pose ominous threats to the airline industry. Complementors, while present, do not make the industry overly attractive. The only two forces that seem to account for the poor performance of the industry are moderately low entry barriers and intense competitive rivalry.

HOW WOULD YOU DO THAT? QUESTIONS

1. Use this analysis as an example and perform a five-forces analysis for one of the following industries: soft drinks, cable television, or cellphone service providers. What are the one or two most important issues from your analysis that managers in that industry must take into account when they revisit their strategies?

Evaluating the Value Curve in the U.S. Wine Industry[25]

Let's uncork an example of the value curve in action. Retail sales of wine in 2009 were valued at US$27.6 billion and imports were valued at US$4 billion. That same year, the United States produced 26.8 million hectolitres of wine and imported 9.5 million hectolitres. Imports had risen by 10 percent from the previous year with greater demand for less expensive bulk wine from Australia (valued at US$639 million) and Chile, which were then bottled in the United States. This market is intensely competitive with wines produced and imported from almost every continent, and new entrants increasingly sell their wines at very low prices.

The threat of new entrants to the wine industry is very high; suppliers (wine-grape growers) are powerful; wineries are concentrated (the CR8 is 75 percent); sales channels are powerful because of consolidation; consumers are powerful because of the breadth of choices; and substitutes (any beverage) are many. Moreover, complements, such as the *Wine Spectator* and wine experts such as Robert Parker, are also powerful because they rank wines based on taste and price, potentially swaying channel and consumer purchases. These factors suggest that the industry is not very attractive to new entrants. In fact, an old saying in the wine industry is that if you want to make US$$5 million, you need to start with US$40 million!

The value curve maps the characteristics considered essential to success by the dominant players. Exhibit 4.9 captures the dominant

Exhibit 4.9 Value Curve for the U.S. Wine Industry

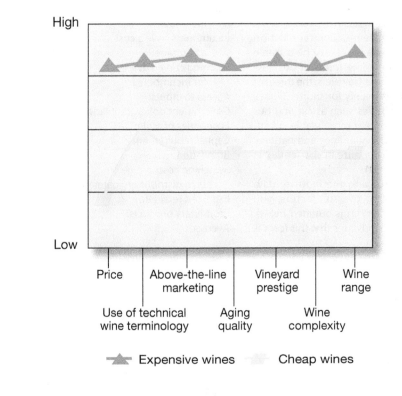

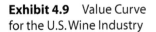

strategic groups—wineries competing in the budget or high-price segments. A new entrant could fight it out in the already hypercompetitive and overcapacity high-price or budget wine segments, or it could try to have a presence in both segments and use the resulting scale to its advantage. The value curve provides a visual image of how incumbents are competing. Mapping the curves of the strategic groups in an industry suggests how a new entrant might reconfigure the way it defines being a winery. In Chapter 6 you will learn how to use the value curve tool to craft a truly revolutionary strategy, and see such application in action by a wine company known as [yellow tail].

1. Using the value curve model illustrated above, map the strategic groups in the soft-drink industry. What groups are there other than the two dominant companies? How do they compete relative to Coke and Pepsi?

without plotting them, you would assume that most of the major airlines would have very similar value curves and, therefore, constitute one strategic group. Plotting Southwest Airlines and its imitators—JetBlue, WestJet, or Air Tran (or Ryanair in Europe)—would reveal a strikingly different value curve. It is often convenient to consolidate similar competitors into a single value curve.

PREDICTING COMPETITORS' BEHAVIOURS

Once competitors have been identified, anticipating what they will be doing helps management prepare the company to compete with its rivals in the future. The specific rivals that are most pertinent to the analysis are those in the company's strategic group, those likely to move into the group, and those operating in groups that the company may enter in the future. In the opening vignette on the Cola War, it is clear that Coke and Pepsi care deeply about what the other is doing. Neither wants to be caught off guard by a move the other may make in the future. Likewise, as new strategic groups have emerged in the beverage industry, such as in the flavoured iced teas or premium sodas, Coke and Pepsi have had to pay more attention to these upstarts.

Several goals can be achieved by closely analyzing the company's closest competitors. For instance, you may gain a better understanding of the competitors' future strategies. Similarly, you may gain a better appreciation for how competitors will respond to your strategic initiatives. Finally, you may also conclude that your company's actions may influence competitors' behaviours, and some of these reactions may be to your benefit (or detriment). Although the company's strategy should not be *determined* by competitors' behaviours, it should be *influenced* by what one thinks that the competitors' behaviours are likely to be.

Porter suggests a four-step approach for making predictions about competitors. The first step in predicting the behaviours of competitors is to understand their objectives. These objectives are often surprisingly easy to determine when the company is, or is part of, a publicly held company because objectives are usually communicated regularly to shareholders through disclosure documents. The second step is to determine the competitors' current strategies. If you have already completed a value curve, you probably have a good idea of those strategies. Further insight can be gained by using public documents to see what competitors are doing in terms of the strategy diamond: arenas, vehicles, differentiators, staging, and economic logic. The third step is more difficult but critical because it is about the future. Seek to understand the competitors' future behaviours by considering what assumptions each competitor holds about the industry and about itself. People's behaviours are strongly influenced by the assumptions they make about themselves and the world. Again, public communications between top executives and shareholders often provide insights into what these assumptions are. Finally, the competitors' future behaviours will likely be related to the resources and capabilities they possess. What are the competitors' key strengths and weaknesses?

After addressing these four primary questions, you are in a position to make reasonable predictions about what your competitors are likely to do in the future. For instance, are they about to change their strategy? You may also gain insights into their likely reaction to any initiatives you are pondering.

Dynamic Characteristics of the External Environment

The various models and analytical tools presented so far provide a snapshot of a company's external environment. In some industries, such a view gives a fairly accurate portrayal of the business landscape in the foreseeable future. In other cases, however, a snapshot captures little more than a first impression: The essential features of many industries are often undergoing gradual or rapid change. What's worse, a snapshot view may overstate a company's competitive advantage: All we see is a company that has staked out a nice position in an attractive market, reaps enormous profits, and regularly makes large deposits in the bank. But if you reflect on Chapter 1's opening vignette on Tim Hortons and Krispy Kreme, you know that competitors do not typically stand still and that overconfidence in the strength of one's competitive position is often a prelude to organizational decline.

Research increasingly shows that the durability of competitive advantages varies by industry or market.[26] In the first category are industries such as utilities and transportation in which the structural characteristics shift very little in the absence of significant regulatory changes. In a second category are industries or markets that may be undergoing gradual changes. This is typically the case in the consumer-products industry. As a rule, the relatively static analysis afforded by the five-forces model plus the complementors dimension applies best to industries in these two categories.

Industries in a third category are those undergoing substantial change, whether because of the scale and scope of environmental changes, because of the rapid pace of such changes, or because of a combination of both. Dramatic change can result from deregulation, which may bring about significant changes in key success factors and completely redesign the competitive playing field. Deregulation in the airline industry, the railroad industry, and the telecommunications industry gave rise to dramatic change in all three Canadian industries.

Changes in technology can dramatically alter the business landscape and the nature of competitive advantage within an industry. What was a relatively stable industry can be thrown into disarray until a new equilibrium is reached. Up until the mid-1980s, for example, the pineapple industry was relatively sleepy and fragmented. Then, Fresh Del Monte (a Cayman Island company separate from the U.S. Del Monte) introduced a new strain developed by scientists at the Pineapple Research Institute.[27] This Extra Sweet Gold pineapple is superior to the pale yellow of the traditional pineapple. It has a bright gold colour; it is sweeter, less acidic, and highly resistant to parasites and rotting. Early introductions into the U.S. market were limited to a few cities on the east coast. The pineapple was so well received that Fresh Del Monte quickly raised prices and exported the pineapple to all major U.S. markets. Despite higher prices, the Extra Sweet Gold captured 70 percent of the market.

What propelled Fresh Del Monte to the top of the market and allowed it to maintain the lion's share of what one would normally consider to be a commodity market? Fresh Del Monte successfully exploited a technological development that other companies ignored. Once it proved successful, Fresh Del Monte claimed proprietary rights to this particular strain of pineapple and was able to forestall other producers from planting the same variety. Eventually, the courts ruled that Fresh Del Monte did not have exclusive legal rights to this strain of pineapple, and companies such as Chiquita and Dole are now converting much of their production to this particular strain. Once again, dominance in the pineapple industry is up for grabs.

We now examine some tools for analyzing industries and formulating strategy in a dynamic context. We start by reviewing the most fundamental reason why some industries are more dynamic than others—the fact that the five forces or essential complementors are changing rather than static. We then discuss two macro-level drivers of industry change: the *industry life cycle* and *discontinuities*. Although globalization itself is a profoundly important driver of change, it often goes hand in hand with the changes that accompany industry evolution and technological discontinuities.

DRIVERS OF CHANGE: MAKING THE FIVE-FORCES MODEL DYNAMIC

While applying the various facets of industry analysis, you have probably thought that your conclusions about industry profitability vary depending on your conclusions about changes occurring in any one of the five forces. These changes reflect the dynamic nature of the environment with some industries being dynamic simply because of the *rapid pace* of change. Think about the almost daily releases of new products in such markets as cellphone handsets, laser printers, and digital cameras. One way to focus on the dynamic nature of the external environment is to start thinking of it in terms of a "storybook" that shows how an industry structure is changing or may change. Any of the five forces can change significantly, upsetting the balance of power and altering the industry's profitability.

Exhibit 4.10 lists selected sources of change and their effects on industry structure and profitability. Entry barriers, for instance, may be weakened, perhaps because of changes in technology.[28] The industry may be in its early stages, with many companies jockeying for position. Some will go out of business or be acquired as the industry matures. As the industry becomes more dynamic, such factors as substitutes and complementors may become more important.

Exhibit 4.10 Dynamics of Industry Structure

Industry Rivalry
- *Increase in industry growth* → Reduced rivalry and less pressure on prices
- *Globalization of industry* → Increased rivalry as new foreign players enter the market, pressure for scale economies leading to consolidation, and market domination by fewer but larger competitors
- *Change in mix between fixed and variable costs* → Shift to greater fixed costs creating more pressure to maintain sales levels and leading to greater propensity to compete on price

Threat of New Entrants
- *Decline in scale necessary to compete effectively* → Increased rivalry because it's easier for start-ups to enter and effectively compete
- *Increases in customer heterogeneity* → Easier entry because some customer segments are likely to be underserved plus increased ability to protect those segments that the firm serves well
- *Increased customer concentration* → Reduces threat of new entry, leading to less pressure to compete on price

Bargaining Power of Suppliers
- *Increasing concentration of firms in supply industries* → Greater supplier power and likelihood of reduced profitability in focal industry
- *Forward-integration by some key suppliers* → Loss of power in focal industry because of reduction in number of viable suppliers
- *Emergence of substitute inputs that are good enough to satisfy basic needs* → Reduction of supplier power and increased profits for focal industry

Bargaining Power of Buyers
- *Increased fragmentation of buyers' industry* → Reduction in buyer power as the number of potential buyers increases and size of buyer industry declines relative to size of focal industry
- *Improvement in buyer information* → Increased buyer power because of ability to compare
- *Emergence of new distribution channels* → Reduction in buyer power because focal industry has more options

Threat of Substitutes
- *Emergence of a new substitute* → Reduced ability to maintain high prices due to more buyer alternatives
- *Decline in the relative price performance of a substitute* → Reduction in the threat of substitutes and pressure to maintain lower prices

Role of Complementors
- *Emergence of new complementors* → Increased demand and less pressure on prices in focal industry
- *Higher barriers to entry in complementor industry* → Greater complementor leverage and ability to profit from complementary relationship
- *Lower barriers to entry in complementor industry* → Reduction in leverage of individual complementors leading to net increase of possible firms who can serve as complementors and increased demand

Source: Adapted from M. E. Porter, *Competitive Strategy: Techniques for Analyzing Industries and Competitors* (New York: Free Press, 1980).

Finally, as an industry matures, buyers become more knowledgeable about product features and costs. We'll start our discussion of industry-change drivers by examining how industries often evolve over time—the industry life cycle.

Industry Life Cycle

Where do new industries come from? A new industry emerges when entirely new products are developed that satisfy customer demands in ways that existing products and technologies could not. The automobile industry emerged after Karl Benz developed an automobile powered by an Otto gasoline engine in 1885 and was granted a patent in the following year.[29] Prior to that time, personal transportation was largely accomplished by means of horse and carriage, or trains for longer trips. Much like living organisms, industries evolve over time. The **industry life cycle** is a model that describes this evolution from inception through to its current state and possible future states. You have probably learned of a similar concept in your studies of marketing relating to the product life cycle. It so happens that competitive dynamics often follow a similar evolution at the industry level—from the point at which an industry emerges to the point at which it matures

industry life cycle   Pattern of evolution followed by an industry inception to current and future states.

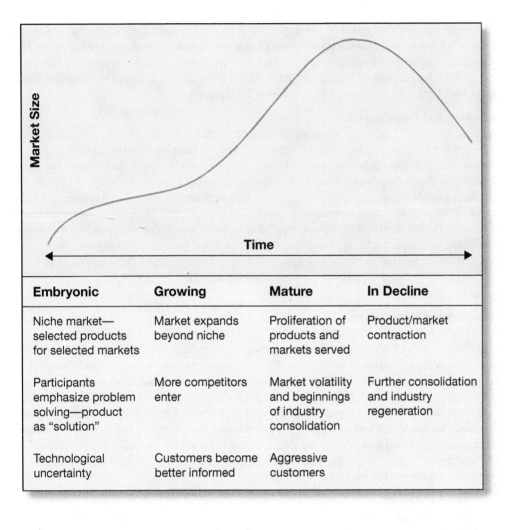

Exhibit 4.11 Industry Life Cycle Curve

Embryonic	Growing	Mature	In Decline
Niche market—selected products for selected markets	Market expands beyond niche	Proliferation of products and markets served	Product/market contraction
Participants emphasize problem solving—product as "solution"	More competitors enter	Market volatility and beginnings of industry consolidation	Further consolidation and industry regeneration
Technological uncertainty	Customers become better informed	Aggressive customers	

or perhaps even stagnates. The industry life cycle is a powerful driver of industry dynamics because it's a phenomenon characterized by change. Exhibit 4.11 illustrates the basic trajectory of the industry life cycle as well as numerous examples of industries at different stages of evolution.[30]

Evolution and Commoditization

One common result of evolution is that an industry tends to become characterized by price competition, partly because many or most of its incumbents acquire similar resources and capabilities and so offer fairly similar products. This trend is called **commoditization**—the process by which sales eventually come to depend less on unique product features and more on price.[31] Commoditization even affects technologically sophisticated products. Take the cellphone industry, for example. Sales of handsets are booming thanks to the addition of cameras, music players, and fancy software. A cellphone that simply provides voice services is becoming a basic commodity distinguished primarily by price. This pattern is found in other industries, from airlines to personal computers, that have followed one-time technological breakthroughs that became widely available.

Some cellphone service providers are introducing new services, such as picture messaging and video downloads, but the revenue they generate is minuscule alongside the vast sums spent on voice calls, and their growth is expected to be slow. In Canada, the commoditization of cellphone service has been limited by heavy regulation of the phone industry. In the U.S. market, although still growing, cellphone service has become more commodity-like, with prices plunging and companies locked in fierce competition for new customers. A marked slowdown in revenue growth could exacerbate the long-running price war in the United States, where competition has pushed the average per-minute cost of a call down more than 65 percent in the past four years, according to Yankee Group, a consulting company.[32] In Europe, there has been an influx of so-called no-frills service providers that basically use a model similar to that

commoditization Process during industry evolution by which sales eventually come to depend less on unique product features and more on price.

of low-cost airlines. One effect of the slowdown is increasing globalization and consolidation in the cellphone industry, as some of Europe's big service providers look for revenue growth by expanding outside their home markets. Demand for cellphone services is growing much faster than analysts had expected in Southeast Asia, Africa, Latin America, and other emerging markets, which tend to be dominated by a couple of local players.

Evolution and Reinvigoration

As some industries mature, certain segments emerge to reinvigorate them, sometimes even restoring their status as growth industries; it is hard to imagine any industry that doesn't have at least one growth segment. The bicycle industry, for example, has existed for more than 200 years, during which time technological advances have periodically increased the product's popularity and given rise to growth segments in an otherwise stagnant industry. In the 1960s, the emergence of children's bike designs and the 10-speed accelerated sales. More recently, the mountain bike has spurred sales growth and also has spawned many new specialized bike manufacturing companies. Now there is a growing interest in adult bicycles that can be ridden for personal transportation. In response, manufacturers such as Ezee, Heinzman, Sparta, and Wisper have introduced ebikes, which include electric motors driven by lightweight batteries.

Evolution and Information

The role of information and customer learning has only recently begun to attract the attention of researchers.[33] We're beginning to see that learning, information, and competition enable newer entrants to replace industry leaders, especially in the later stages of industry-wide change. The emergence of computer retailer Dell is an excellent example. Originally, because Dell targeted sophisticated buyers—buyers who were technologically savvy and who needed little education on the uses of a personal computer—it was able to invest less money in pre- and post-sales activities. Dell could sell leading-edge PCs at a relatively low price and still make a profit, and as the market matured and price competition became more intense, Dell was able to leapfrog IBM and other, larger companies. The effect of customer learning and information often isn't apparent until later in the life cycle.

Evolution and Tactics

In the early stages, customers usually lack knowledge and information about new products. This leads them to look to industry incumbents both as a source of education and as a form of insurance in the way of more extensive product support. The industry moves from introduction to growth once new products establish themselves. Incumbents often add extra services, such as shipping, training, or extended warranties, at little or no cost, in order to retain sales momentum through the growth phase. Taken together, these factors usually mean higher *average* margins in the early stages of growth because high and increasing operating costs are usually offset by relatively high prices. This was the case in the early years of the PC market, when it was dominated by such players as IBM and Compaq. Discounters such as Dell were considered fringe players while they occupied a small, specialized market niche.

Technological Discontinuities

The link between technological discontinuities and industry change should be readily apparent from our discussion of industry evolution as a driver of change.[34] Moreover, technology is one of the key factors in the PESTEL framework: Discontinuities are a special, intensive case of technological change in action. Technological changes can have traumatic effects on industries and companies.[35] Indeed, major technological changes often alter company environments and industry structures significantly. Of course, not all technological changes affect competitors and industries equally. Some, for example, work to the advantage of incumbents, others to that of new entrants. It is to your benefit to get in the habit of thinking broadly about the nature of the changes that create technological discontinuities, given the increasing rate of technological change.

To examine these extreme forms of change, understand first that technological discontinuities include changes in both science-based technologies (such as innovations) and business-process technologies (such as new business models). Needless to say, the two major forms of technology are *process technology* and *product technology*. Process technology refers to the devices, tools, and knowledge used to transform inputs into outputs. Product technology creates new products.[36]

Disruptive Product-Related Change

Technological change is often evolutionary, reflected in a pattern of gradual or *incremental* change. However, periodically episodic change punctuates industry evolution. Such revolutionary change is called *discontinuous* change.[37] Discontinuous technological change occurs when breakthrough technologies appear. Sometimes these breakthroughs sustain the competencies of incumbent companies and sometimes they destroy them. Competency-sustaining technologies are typically introduced by incumbents. Those that destroy incumbents' competencies are called **disruptive technologies**. In many instances, these disruptions are introduced by new companies.[38] A disruptive change introduced by a new technology also alters the industry life cycle. The industry is reinvigorated and, rather than proceeding into decline, accelerates into new phases of growth, as illustrated by Exhibit 4.12.

As an illustration of this process, consider the minicomputer industry. Out of 116 major innovations introduced in the minicomputer industry (the precursor to the personal computer), 111 were incremental, sustaining technological improvements, and only five were disruptive. All 111 sustaining technologies were introduced by incumbents, whereas all five disruptive technologies were introduced by outsiders—companies specializing in new personal computers. In the disk drive industry, virtually every new generation of technology led to the demise of the market leader. Meanwhile, the arrival of the personal computer heralded the downfall of every major competitor in the minicomputer industry.[39]

A challenge, known as the **innovator's dilemma**, unfolds in established industries when incumbents continue to develop competency-enhancing innovations while new entrants develop disruptive innovations.[40] Specifically, the *dilemma* for incumbents is that their economic incentives are to continue developing evolutionary improvements in their existing technology and to avoid sponsoring disruptive innovations, even when the disruptive technology may eventually supplant the existing technology.

Incumbents maintain a course of incremental, sustaining innovations rather than adopting the disruptive innovation for several reasons. The sustaining innovations are introduced to satisfy the needs of companies' best customers, those who demand the most from their products and who pay the highest margins to receive such service. In the case of minicomputers, companies such as DEC were satisfying their largest business customers by continually improving the speed and power of their top-of-the-line minicomputers. These units would sell for tens of thousands of dollars and have profit margins of 25 percent or more. The personal computers that new entrants were producing would sell for only a few thousand dollars, and the margins were ten percentage points or more less. Thus, you could say that DEC was being entirely rational in avoiding this market. However, that calculus ignores the new business landscape that disruptive innovations will create in the not-too-distant future.◆

disruptive technology Breakthrough product- or process-related technology that destroys the competencies of incumbent companies in an industry.

innovator's dilemma When incumbents avoid investing in innovative and disruptive technologies because those innovations do not satisfy the needs of their mainstream and most profitable clients.

 Arenas

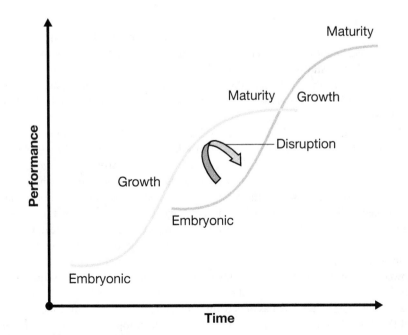

Exhibit 4.12 Discontinuity in the Industry Life Cycle

Exhibit 4.13 The Innovator's Dilemma

Adapted from C. M. Christensen, *The Innovator's Dilemma* (Cambridge, MA: Harvard Business Press, 1997).

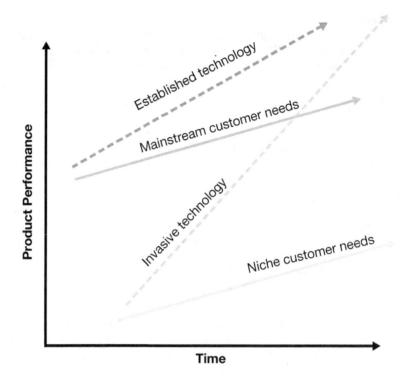

The interplay between incumbents' innovation and new entrants' innovation based on invasive technology is demonstrated in Exhibit 4.13. Notice how established companies follow an innovation trajectory that leads them to overshoot the majority of their mainstream customers' needs. The invasive technology, however, which initially targets lower-end customers, migrates upstream, eventually meeting the basic needs of many mainstream customers. At this point, those using the invasive technology are producing products that satisfy the needs of most customers at a fraction of the cost of those products based on the old technology. The result is that those using the new technology steal customers from those using the established technology. This process, while not universal, has been documented as the source of dynamic change in many industries. A few examples include notebook computers and handheld digital appliances, full-service stock brokerage and online stock brokerage, printed greeting cards and free online greeting cards, classroom- and campus-based higher education and distance education, offset printing and digital printing, and cardiac surgery and angioplasty, just to name a few.[41]

Disruptive Process-Related Change

Disruptive technologies can be process-related as well as product-related. The development of total quality management (TQM) methods, for instance, eventually elevated the Japanese auto industry to world-class status. TQM programs such as *six sigma* and *lean* are process innovations. No automaker in the world can now ignore the competitive threat posed by companies such as Toyota and Honda. Many who did are now struggling to emulate the TQM methods pioneered by these one-time fringe players.

Southwest Airlines radically changed the business model that had long dominated the industry, while established full-service airlines took little notice. Why? Because Southwest's new process couldn't help them meet the needs of their most profitable customers. In time, however, the number and length of Southwest's flights reached the point at which the services provided by its model could satisfy the demands of customers who normally used larger airlines. The success of Southwest's model led new entrants elsewhere to copy it in other markets.

A similar pattern unfolded in the North American steel industry. Co-Steel, which became part of Gerdau AmeriSteel in 2002, pioneered the production of steel using electric arc furnaces in North America—the so-called mini-mill technology. The low cost of these operations allowed mini-mill operators to quickly capture the market for the low-quality products they manufactured, such as steel bar used to reinforce concrete (rebar) in construction projects. At first, large steel companies such as Stelco and Dofasco ignored mini-mills because they only produced the least profitable products. But as mini-mill technology improved, new companies entered the more profitable segments of the industry. In the end, large steel companies found they had to adopt mini-mill technology themselves to hold on to business. Likewise, Wal-Mart's business model was originally of little threat to K-Mart and Sears because it focused on rural areas that they were happy to ignore. Eventually, Wal-Mart took its model into larger markets, but it was too late for its competitors to respond because Wal-Mart had developed its assets and capabilities to the point that it was a superior operator.

WHEN INDUSTRIES DIVIDE

The industry life cycle model is too simplistic to describe the evolution of many industries. In some cases, one industry becomes two or more distinct but related industries. The creation of separate industries can occur when companies start to specialize in subsets of the activities of the value chain that all companies in the industry used to perform. Another reason for division is that technology has made new industries possible. Finally, industries may divide when the market for a particular product becomes large enough that companies can economically justify dedicating a distribution channel to it. This type of division typically results in new industry *segments* or *subindustries* rather than in new industries. A good example is the emergence of so-called *category killers* in various retail industries—industry segments composed of large, highly specialized retail chains, such as PetSmart or Home Depot and Lowe's. These are called "category killers" because they aim to dominate whatever category they participate in by offering the broadest possible assortment of goods at the lowest possible prices. The internet has spawned a number of such segments and some well-known companies, including Amazon.com and BarnesandNoble.com in books and Travelocity.com and Expedia.com in travel.

WHEN INDUSTRIES COLLIDE

Although some changes lead to industry division, others result in new industry definitions that consolidate two or more separate industries into one. As you read this section, note the distinction between industry *consolidation* and industry *concentration*. Whereas *concentration* results in an industry with fewer players, *consolidation* results in fewer industries.[42]

FOCUS ON ETHICS 4.1
Something Fishy Is Going On

Salmon farmed in Canada has been sold in New York as wild salmon at four times the price of farmed salmon. Such mislabelling is only part of the problem. Fish species have also been completely renamed.[43] This breakdown in ethical behaviour results in higher prices for distributors, retailers, and restaurants that buy fish of lesser value, then illegally sell these fish as their higher-value relatives. Both mislabelling and renaming represent significant issues as the market for seafood has grown and is increasingly satisfied by global trade. Factors encouraging this include resource scarcity, the potential for greater profits, and weak legislation.

While companies profit, this behaviour causes consumer losses, subverts eco-marketing, leads to further degradation of fisheries resources, and even causes adverse effects on human health. Consumer losses come from paying more than they should for what they have bought. This behaviour also prevents eco-aware consumers from making effective purchasing decisions on behalf of conservation and has led them to believe that species are more common than they really are. This behaviour renders any boycott of a threatened species meaningless as the boycotted species is hidden through mislabelling. It also contributes to the further erosion of fisheries, not only because consumers cannot make informed decisions on behalf of conservation, but also because mislabelling undermines import/export seafood regulations. Finally, consumer health is at risk. Oilfishes (common names include oilfish, escolar, rudderfish, butterfish, ruddercod, and snake mackerel), which are indigestible by about half of all people, are sold as other species. Certain species, particularly predatory fish like tuna, that are high in the contaminant mercury and Chinese shellfish with high pesticide residuals have been sold to unknowing consumers, as have farmed salmon, which have higher concentrations of contaminants than wild salmon, and salmon farmed in European countries, which have significantly higher levels of contamination than those raised in North and South America.

Part of the recommended solution is that governments support a global mandate to label species, identifying the country of origin and the catching or production method of all seafood, with high penalties for infractions. This has to be accompanied by a worldwide chain of custody standards, such as those recently implemented by the Marine Stewardship Council (MSC) to monitor the value system for infractions. Consumers need to become better acquainted and concerned with their seafood and its origins so that they will support this legislation.

Does it matter that customers do not get what they think they are buying when they cannot tell the difference? If they got what they really asked for, they would likely have to pay more.

Today, for example, both the media and entertainment industries seem to be agglomerations of many once-distinct industries. The definition of the media industry now includes companies with a significant presence in both program distribution (they own or control television networks) and program content (they own or develop new shows). The largest incumbents are often called media and entertainment *conglomerates* (which suggests organizations composed of unrelated divisions), but in reality the dominant players, including Fox, Disney, Viacom, and Vivendi Universal, have consolidated a broad range of functions that were once performed by suppliers, substitutes, complementors, or even customers.

Industry convergence and division happen over time. Opportunities to create significant value tend to be greatest for companies that lead the charge in convergence and division of industries. However, when companies define their industries very broadly, performing external analysis becomes much more complicated. For instance, defining FedEx/Kinko's as a simple printer versus a marketing-communications company connotes a broadly different set of industry conditions.

A final point to make about change is that the *rate* of change varies from one industry to the next. The rate of change in the electronics industry, for example, has been much faster than in the steel industry.

Changes in both industries have prompted complete reconfigurations of industry structure and the competitive positions of various players. The idea that all industries change over time and that business environments are in a state of constant state of flux is readily apparent. As a strategic decision maker, you need to keep asking yourself, How accurately does current structure (which is relatively easy to identify) represent future industry conditions?

FOCUS ON SUSTAINABILITY 4.1
Growing One Fisheries Industry Kills Another

Farmed salmon has been British Columbia's largest agricultural export for the past five years. The B.C. Salmon Farmers Association (BCSFA), established in 1984 and recognized as the voice for "British Columbia's environmentally sustainable farmed salmon industry," is based in Campbell River, a coastal community on north central Vancouver Island. It is committed to sustainable farming, which is the only kind of farming practised in British Columbia. "We believe that a sustainable organization seeks to participate within its community to balance economy, society, and environment within its operations. By seeking balance, we believe an organization will be better able to take into account the needs of future generations and will be a better steward of natural and economic resources. We believe coastal economies, such as our coastal communities, must protect and nurture their ecological roots to support long term growth."[44]

The economic activity of fish farms provides employment and requires supplies and services from secondary industries in coastal communities. These jobs create social benefits: allowing people to build careers and invest in their home communities. Operational success depends on a clean environment, so farms are sited in areas where water currents provide optimal conditions for fish well-being and environmental sustainability. This includes avoiding sensitive wild salmon habitat such as coastal fish spawning and nursery areas. Once salmon farms are in operation, the environment in and around them is monitored continuously. All farm siting and operations are subject to provincial and federal regulation.

Yet while the salmon farming industry promotes its own sustainability, researchers think that wild salmon stocks are at risk, and the danger stems from fish farms. Canadian researchers collected records from 1970 on and found that salmon populations in the areas with many salmon farms were collapsing while those in areas without farms were not.[45] In addition, researchers found that when salmon farms were temporarily closed or allowed to lie fallow, the wild salmon populations from those rivers rebounded and sea lice infestations declined. The agent of destruction is thought to be sea lice living on penned salmon. As wild salmon smolts (baby salmon) pass through the bays on their way from rivers to the sea, they go by the salmon pens, where they are infested by sea lice. Smolts are especially vulnerable to the parasites because they lack scales. Prominent scientists and researchers believe that sea lice from fish farms are lethal to wild salmon. "These young salmon wouldn't be dying if it wasn't for the salmon farms and all those sea lice," said Martin Krkosek, a fisheries ecologist at the University of Alberta. "The wild population is dropping so fast that there isn't much time left to act."[46]

Aquaculture has been seen as a way of protecting wild stocks of fish from unsustainable harvesting. Yet as practised in the salmon industry it is damaging wild population. How do we find a balance when the environmental conditions needed by both wild and farmed stock bring them in close proximity to each other? Or are we only able to have one or the other?

Summary of Challenges

1. *Explain the importance of the external environment for strategy and company performance.* In order to understand the threats and opportunities facing an organization, you need a thorough understanding of its external environment, including not only its industry but also the larger environment in which it operates. The proper analysis of the external environment, together with the company-level analysis you learned in Chapter 3 (e.g., VRINE, value-chain), allows you to complete a rigorous analysis of a company and its options.

2. *Use PESTEL to identify the macro characteristics of the external environment.* PESTEL analysis and an understanding of the drivers of globalization can be used to characterize the macro characteristics of the company's external environment. PESTEL is an acronym for the *p*olitical, *e*conomic, *s*ociocultural, *t*echnological, *e*nvironmental, and *l*egal contexts in which a company operates. Managers can use the PESTEL analysis to gain a better understanding of the opportunities and threats faced by the company. By knowing the company's opportunities and threats, managers can build a better vision of the future business landscape and identify how the company may compete profitably. By examining the drivers of globalization, managers can identify how market, cost, governments, and competition work to favour the globalization of an industry.

3. *Identify the major features of an industry and the forces that affect industry profitability.* The major factors to be analyzed when examining an industry are rivalry, the power of suppliers, the power of buyers, the threat of substitutes, and the threat of new entrants. When suppliers and buyers have significant power, they tend to be able to negotiate away some of the profit that would otherwise be available to industry rivals. Thus, profits tend to be lower than average in industries that face high levels of supplier and buyer power. Likewise, as the threat of new entrants and the availability of substitutes increases, the

ability of rivals in the industry to keep prices high is reduced. Rivalry within an industry decreases profitability. High levels of rivalry result in heavy emphasis on price-based competition. Rivalry is reduced when products are differentiated. Strategic-group analysis is used to gain a better understanding of the nature of rivalry. Whereas industry profits tend to be reduced when any of the five forces are strong, the presence of complementors results in the opposite; they increase the ability of companies to generate profits. Finally, an analysis of competitors' objectives, current strategies, assumptions, and resources and capabilities can help managers predict the future behaviours of their competitors.

4. *Understand the dynamic characteristics of the external environment.* The various models and analytical tools presented can provide an excellent snapshot of a company's external environment. In some industries, such a snapshot view gives an accurate portrayal of the look of the business landscape for the foreseeable future. The five forces of industry structure change, and very rapidly in some industries; other drivers of change to which managers must be attuned include the stage and pace of transition in the industry life cycle and technological discontinuities.

5. *Show how industry dynamics may redefine industries.* In some cases, one industry becomes two or more distinct, but often related, industries. Industries may also divide when the market for a particular product becomes large enough that companies can economically justify dedicating a distribution channel to it. Whereas some changes lead to industry division, others result in new industry definitions that consolidate two or more separate industries into one. Industry convergence and division happen over time, and companies that identify such changes and initiate early changes have a better opportunity to create value.

Review Questions

1. What constitutes the external environment of strategy?
2. What are the five forces affecting industry structure?
3. What are complementors?
4. What is a key success factor (KSF)?
5. What are strategic groups?
6. What factors increase industry dynamics?
7. What is the industry life cycle?
8. What is a technological discontinuity?
9. What is the innovator's dilemma?
10. How does globalization affect the external environment of strategy?
11. What is industry redefinition?

Experiential Activities

Group Exercises

1. Pick two of the industries identified by five digits from the North American Industrial Classification System (NAICS) at www.statcan.gc.ca/subjects-sujets/standard-norme/naics-scian/2007/list-liste-eng.htm or www.census.gov/eos/www/naics/. Next, prepare an analysis for each of these industries. What are the boundaries of these industries? What are their market and geographic segments? Who are the key players? Draw up a five-forces model of each industry and compare and contrast their industry structure. Now shift your analysis to the dynamic five-forces model. For both 5 and 10 years into the future, answer the following questions: Which dimensions of the five-forces model are most likely to change in the near future? Which are most likely to stay relatively stable?

Ethical Debates

1. Genetically modified organisms (GMOs) include food products in which genetics have been used to extend product shelf life, deter pests, and create other product innovations. Much of the food consumed in the United States is genetically modified, while many other developing countries prohibit GMO foods for ethical and other reasons. Ethical objections to GMO foods typically centre on the possibility of harm to persons or other living things. What do you believe explains this striking difference in ethical views about GMO food between the U.S. and other global markets?

2. Despite the pharmaceutical industry's notable contributions to human progress, including the development of miracle drugs for treating cancer, AIDS, and heart disease, tension is growing between the industry and the public. What are some of the key ethical questions, and how does that affect your analysis of the pharmaceutical industry?

Endnotes

1. History Channel, *Empires of Industry: Cola Wars*, DVD, 2000.

2. "How Pepsi Got Its Fizz Back," Knowledge@Wharton, October 22, 2003, Accessed November 6, 2010, at http://knowledge.wharton.upenn.edu/article.cfm?articleid=865. All rights reserved. Used by permission and protected by the Copyright Laws of the United States. The printing, copying, redistribution, or retransmission of this Content without express written permission is prohibited.

3. Ibid.

4. "Coca-Cola Q4 2006 Earnings Call Transcript," Seeking Alpha, February 17, 2007. Accessed November 6, 2010, at seekingalpha.com/article/27072-coca-cola-q4-2006-earnings-call-transcript.

5. K. Macarthur, "Looks Who's Calling Itself 'Sparkling,'" *Advertising Age*, February 19, 2007. Accessed November 6, 2010, at adage.com/article?article_id=115074.

6. L. Garikina, "Indra Nooyi Among the Most Powerful Women," NRI Today, November 2007. Accessed November 6, 2010, at www.nri-today.com/money-business/190-nov-07-indra-nooyi-among-the-most-powerful-women.

7. PESTEL analysis is an acronym built out of the items included in the analysis. This approach to analyzing the external environment was earlier know as PEST analysis (for *p*olitics, *e*conomic, *s*ocial, and *t*echnological) and as STEEP (for *s*ocial, *t*echnology, *e*conomic, *e*cological, and *p*olitical). In principle, each approach is the same.

8. G. Yip, "Global Strategy in a World of Nations," *Sloan Management Review* 31:1 (1989): 29–40.

9. M. E. Porter, *Competition in Global Industries* (Boston: Harvard Business School Press, 1986); Yip, "Global Strategy in a World of Nations."

10. Adapted from Porter, *Competition in Global Industries,* and Yip, "Global Strategy in a World of Nations."

11. G. Robb, "U.S. Files WTO Case against China's Export Subsidies," *Market Watch*, February 2, 2007. Accessed September 30, 2009, at www.marketwatch.com/story/us-files-wto-case-against-china-over-export-subsidies, and S. Weisman, "China Agrees to Remove Certain Export Subsidies," *New York Times*, November 29, 2007. Accessed September 30, 2009, at www.nytimes.com/2007/11/30/business/worldbusiness/30trade.html.

12. D. Martin, "Canadian Teams Scramble as U.S. Bans NHL Charter Flights," CanWest News Service, September 4, 2009. Accessed October 1, 2009, at www.nationalpost.com/sports/story.html?id=1964153.

13. J. Nocera, "Diamonds Are Forever in Botswana," *New York Times*, August 8, 2008. Accessed September 25, 2009, at www.nytimes.com/2008/08/09/business/worldbusiness/09nocera.html?ref=business; N. Stein, "The De Beers Story: A New Cut on an Old Monopoly," *Fortune*, February 19, 2001. Accessed September 25, 2009, at money.cnn.com/magazines/fortune/fortune_archive/2001/02/19/296863/index.htm; and P. O'Connell, "De Beers' Multifaceted Strategy Shift," *Business Week*, January 6, 2009. Accessed September 25, 2009, at www.businessweek.com/managing/content/jan2009/ca2009016_644338.htm.

14. R. Amit and P. J. H. Schoemaker, "Strategic Assets and Organizational Rent," *Strategic Management Journal* 14 (1993): 33–46; J. A. Vasconcellos and D. C. Hambrick, "Key Success Factors: Test of a General Framework in the Mature Industrial-Product Sector," *Strategic Management Journal* 10 (1989): 367–382.

15. Cinram International, Annual Information Form for the Year Ended December 31, 2006, p.13. Released March 30, 2007, www.sedar.com.

16. Further information is found on Statistics Canada's website at www.statcan.gc.ca/concepts/industry-industrie-eng.htm.

17. Adapted from M. E. Porter, *Competitive Strategy: Techniques for Analyzing Industries and Competitors* (New York: Free Press, 1980).

18. Porter, *Competitive Strategy.*

19. A. Kingston, *The Edible Man* (Toronto, MacFarlane Walter and Ross, 1994).

20. A. Kohler, "Benchmark System Dictates Iron Ore Price." Accessed November 6, 2006, at www.abc.net.au/insidebusiess/content/2006/s1660292.htm.

21. Wikipedia, "Toronto Maple Leafs." Accessed November 6, 2006, at http://en.wikipedia.org/wiki/Toronto_Maple_Leafs; K. Badenhausen, M. K Ozanian and C. Settimi, "The Business of Hockey," *Forbes.com*, November 11, 2009, p. 103. Accessed November 06, 2010, at www.forbes.com/2009/11/11/nhl-team-values-business-sports-hockey-values-09-intro.html; and N. Vardi, "Winning Isn't Everything" *Forbes* 180:11, (November 26, 2007): 96–100.

22. A. Brandenburger and B. Nalebuff, *Co-Opetition* (New York: Currency Doubleday, 1996).

23. Much of this section is adapted from important studies in the field of game theory, and we'll return to the topic when we discuss strategic alliances and other cooperative strategies. At this point, we offer merely an overview. See A. Dixit and B. Nalebuff, *Thinking Strategically: The Competitive Edge*

in Business and Politics and Everyday Life (New York: W. W. Norton, 1992), and A. Brandenburger and B. Nalebuff, *Co-Opetition*.

24. J. E. Ellis, "The Law of Gravity Doesn't Apply: Inefficiency, Overcapacity, Huge Debt. . .What Keeps U.S. Carriers Up in the Air?" *BusinessWeek*, September 26, 2005, p. 49; H. Tully, "Airlines: Why the Big Boys Won't Come Back," *Fortune* (June 14, 2004): 101.

25. M. Geisler, "Wine Industry Profile," Agricultural Marketing Resource Center, Iowa State University. Revised September 2010. Accessed November 6, 2010, at www.agmrc.org/commodities__products/fruits/wine/wine_industry_profile.cfm; B. Katz, "Wine Sales Resume in 2009 After Earlier Dip," Reuters Life!, December 2, 2009. Accessed November 6, 2010, at www.reuters.com/article/idUSTRE5B15NH20091202; W. C. Kim and R. Mauborgne, "Blue Ocean Strategy," *California Management Review* 47:3 (2005): 105–121; and "Wine: World Markets and Trade," Foreign Agricultural Service, United States Department of Agriculture, April 2010. Accessed November 6, 2010, at www.fas.usda.gov/htp/horticulture/Wine/3-10WineArticle.pdf.

26. R. Wiggins and T. Ruefli, "Competitive Advantage: Temporal Dynamics and the Incidence and Persistence of Superior Economic Performance," *Organization Science* 13 (2002): 82–105.

27. "A Fruit Revolution," *Convenience Store News* 41:4 (2005): 20; J. Cioletti, "Flavoring the Market," *Beverage World* 124:3 (2005): 6.

28. Adapted from Porter, *Competitive Strategy*.

29. R. Stein, *The Automobile Book* (London: Paul Hamlyn Ltd, 1967).

30. Adapted from K. Rangan and G. Bowman, "Beating the Commodity Magnet," *Industrial Marketing Management* 21 (1992): 215–224; P. Kotler, "Managing Products Through Their Product Life Cycle," in *Marketing Management: Planning, Implementation, and Control*, 7th ed. (Upper Saddle River, NJ: Prentice Hall, 1991).

31. L. Argote, *Organizational Learning: Creating, Retaining, and Transferring Knowledge* (Boston: Kluwer Academic Publishers, 1999); A. S. Miner and P. Haunschild, "Population Level Learning," *Research in Organizational Behavior* 17 (1995): 115–166.

32. D. Pringle, "Slower Growth Hits Cellphone Services Overseas in EU, Japan, Saturation Leads to Some Contraction; Looking Beyond Voice," *Wall Street Journal*, May 23, 2005, A1.

33. See G. Moore, *Crossing the Chasm* (New York: Harper Business Essentials, 2002); C. Shapiro and H. R. Varian, *Information Rules: A Strategic Guide to the Network Economy* (Boston: Harvard Business School Press, 1998).

34. N. Rosenberg, *Technology and American Economic Growth* (New York: Harper & Row, 1986); M. L. Tushman and P. Anderson, "Technological Discontinuities and Organizational Environments," *Administrative Science Quarterly* 31 (1986): 439–465.

35. Tushman and Anderson, "Technological Discontinuities and Organizational Environments."

36. W. P. Barnett, "The Organizational Ecology of a Technological System," *Administrative Science Quarterly* 35 (1990): 31–60; R. M. Henderson and K. B. Clark, "Architectural Innovation: The Reconfiguration of Existing Product Technologies and the Failure of Established Companies," *Administrative Science Quarterly* 35 (1990): 9–30.

37. Tushman and Anderson, "Technological Discontinuities and Organizational Environments."

38. C. M. Christensen, *The Innovator's Dilemma* (Cambridge, M.A.: Harvard Business Press, 1997).

39. Ibid.

40. Ibid.

41. Ibid.

42. Consolidation may result from increased concentration when bigger players in an industry absorb the functions of suppliers, substitutes, complements, or customers (a process under way in the global media and entertainment industries). By getting bigger, these companies broaden the definition of their operations, but successfully managing all the components of a broader operation is a separate matter. Concentration often results in division when players that have grown too big can no longer give adequate attention to some segment of their market or some facet of their operations. Division also occurs when, because of increased concentration, a new market emerges to attract large companies.

43. J. L. Jacquet and D. Pauly, "Trade Secrets: Renaming and Mislabelling of Seafood," *Marine Policy* 32 (2008): 309–318.

44. B.C. Salmon Farmers Association, "Sustainable Aquaculture." Accessed October 3, 2009, at www.salmonfarmers.org/attachments/110508_SustainableAquaculture.pdf; B.C. Salmon Farmers Association, "BCSFA Commitment to Sustainability." Accessed October 3, 2009, at www.salmonfarmers.org/commitment-to-sustainability.php.

45. J. Eilperin and M. Kaufman, "Salmon Farming May Doom Wild Populations, Study Says," *Washington Post*, December 14, 2007. Accessed October 4, 2009, at www.washingtonpost.com/wp-dyn/content/article/2007/12/13/AR2007121301190.html; M. Krkosek and M. Wonham, "Wild Salmon Mortality Caused by Fish-Farm Sea Lice." Accessed October 3, 2009, at www.davidsuzuki.org/publications/downloads/2006/Wild_Salmon_Mortality_Caused_by_Fish-Farm_Sea_Lice.pdf.

46. J. Eilperin and M. Kaufman, "Salmon Farming May Doom Wild Populations, Study Says."

5 Creating Business Strategies

In this chapter, we challenge you to:

1. Define *generic strategies* and explain how they relate to a company's strategic position.

2. Describe the drivers of low-cost, differentiation, and focused strategic positions.

3. Identify and explain the risks associated with each generic strategic position.

4. Show how different strategic positions fit with stages of the industry life cycle.

5. Evaluate the quality of a company's strategy.

A Tale of Three Wheels in the Bicycle Industry

In 2007, 1.4 million bicycles were sold in Canada for Cdn$160 million, and 17.5 million bicycles were sold in the United States for US$2.5 billion.[1] Who sold all of these bicycles? There are literally hundreds of bicycle manufacturers in North America, but most are small, specialized companies.

Among them, one company—Pacific Cycle—continues to sell more bicycles than any other company in North America. It grabbed the lion's share of the U.S. bicycle market in the early 1980s by buying well-known brands and crafting distribution deals with America's largest retailers. Pacific Cycle designs, imports, and markets a full range of bikes and recreation products under such familiar brand names as Schwinn, GT, Mongoose, Kustom Kruiser, Roadmaster, Pacific, Dyno, Powerlite, InSTEP, and Pacific Outdoors. Its powerful brand portfolio serves virtually all consumer demographics, price categories, and product categories (e.g., children's, mountain, and racing bikes).

Cervélo's bicycles are the choice of many champion cyclists.

Chris Hornung, its founder and first CEO, started the company at age 22 as a modest bike import business. He pioneered the concept of sourcing bicycles from Asia for distribution in the United States. While on a buying trip to Taiwan in 1983, he met buyers from Target Corp. and Toys "R" Us, which provided him an entryway into the mass-market retailers.

Pacific Cycle's success came from combining an aggressive acquisition of power brands with low-cost outsourcing, efficient supply-chain management, and multichannel retail distribution. In December 2000, the company acquired the bicycle division of Brunswick Corp. for US$60 million, which included the Mongoose, Mongoose Pro, and Roadmaster brands. In the deal, Brunswick's biggest account, Wal-Mart, also came with the business. This purchase nearly doubled Pacific's sales. A year later, the company bought the assets of Schwinn/GT Corp. out of bankruptcy for US$86 million, a move that added an American icon to the company's portfolio.

The growth of its retail customers, both leading mass-market retailers and independent dealers, has facilitated the growth of Pacific Cycle. The company's brands appeal to the full spectrum of demographics, price preferences, and image and usage criteria that are critical to targeting the key consumer segments served by each channel. This broad-based marketing strategy enables Pacific to provide retailers with one-stop shopping and to respond efficiently to changes in the marketplace. For example, Pacific bought the Schwinn brand, which historically was only sold through specialty bike shops, and sold it to mass merchandisers. "We didn't want to limit the Schwinn brand to just specialty dealers," Hornung said. "The major retailers were anxious to carry a brand that has 107 years of history behind it." The public wanted it too: "Cycling is a family sport, and our move into the mass-market channel simply recognizes that Schwinn—the premium bike brand—must be available where most families shop today," Hornung said. Moving the brand into mass retailers broadened access to Schwinn bicycles to greater numbers of consumers and helped lower the price. The average price of a Schwinn at a mass retailer is US$65, compared to US$387 at a specialty store, according to the U.S. National Bicycle Dealers Association. Overall, the average retail price of bikes has declined steadily, at about 15 percent per year. That decline made it important for Pacific to control costs, Hornung said.

Pacific's strategy has been simple. Import quality bikes from China and Taiwan, distribute them to mass merchants such as Wal-Mart, and keep payrolls to an absolute minimum. Since Pacific has applied this approach to Schwinn, the brand has lost the support of most independent dealers but has been a hit among mass merchants. Consumers now pay less for the new Stingray under Pacific's ownership. It may not be the engineering marvel that was the old Schwinn, but it retails at Wal-Mart for about one-third of the original's price.

In 2004, Pacific Cycle was acquired by Dorel Industries Inc. of Montreal, which set it up as a separate business unit. Dorel continued Pacific Cycle's aggressive growth, buying Cannondale Bicycle Corp. in 2008 so that it could serve the higher-end market segments. Dorel is now one of the largest bicycle suppliers in the world, selling products in more than 60 countries via more than 50 international distributors.

Another successful bike maker, Trek Bicycle, had revenues of about US$600 million in 2007. Richard Burke and Bevil Hogg founded Trek in 1976 as a wholly owned subsidiary of the Roth Corp., an appliance distributor based in Milwaukee, Wisconsin. Trek started with five employees building bikes by hand in a Wisconsin barn. From the beginning, it targeted higher-end users who wanted quality and innovation. One of those users is Lance Armstrong, who won seven consecutive Tour de France cycling races on Trek bicycles. Today, customers pay top dollar for smooth suspensions, custom paint jobs, and innovations in racing geometry. Trek, now a leading supplier of high-quality bikes in the United States, overcame European resistance to American-made cycles by focusing on quality and innovation.

The company extended its product range over time, introducing its first mountain bike line in 1983, the first bonded-aluminum road bike in 1985, a carbon-fibre road bike in 1986, and its first moulded carbon-fibre frame in 1989. Although most of Trek's growth has been fuelled by internally developed products, Trek has made a few strategic acquisitions, including Gary Fisher Mountain Bikes in 1993 and two mountain bike competitors—Bontrager and Klein—in 1995.

Trek's range of products now includes mountain, road, children's, recumbent, police, and BMX bikes. Trek designs and engineers all of its bikes at its Wisconsin headquarters and manufactures a quarter of them in the United States while the rest are manufactured in China and Taiwan. They are sold through wholly owned subsidiaries in seven countries and through distributors in 65 others. End-users in Canada and the United States buy Trek's bikes from more than 1700 independent bicycle dealers.

Whereas Pacific Cycle and Trek represent the larger players in the North American market, Cervélo Cycles is a small Canadian company serving a market niche—time-trial and triathlon bikes. Cervélo's success has made it the largest manufacturer of these bikes in the world. Gérard Vroomen started the company after a top-ranked Italian professional cyclist asked Vroomen, then a student at McGill University, to design the fastest possible time-trial bike for him. Together with Phil White, Vroomen designed and then built a radical bike (in his basement!) that tested extremely well. While cyclists were enthusiastic about the design, bicycle sponsors were not, so Vroomen and White decided to start their own bicycle company in 1995 to produce designs "to help our customers win races." Vroomen sees this commitment to performance as the key to Cervélo's success in an industry that has come to be dominated by China's manufacturing. "Manufacturing in Canada will always be more expensive than manufacturing in China. So you have to figure out the best way to compete. In our case it's pushing the envelope [of] bicycle design."[2] While they are designed in Canada, the business does only what it has to and outsources all other activities, including outsourcing the manufacture of its carbon-fibre frames to Chinese manufacturers.

Cervélo's carbon-fibre bikes cost anywhere from Cdn$2 000 to Cdn$11 000. Yet the company, now located in Toronto, has been successful. By 2004 it had sales of Cdn$11 million and 29 employees, of whom nine were engineers. Building upon its early success, the private company expanded its line to five families of bike models, each with characteristics suited to their use such as road-racing, triathlon, and time trials. Today, Cervélo is the world's largest manufacturer of time-trial and triathlon bikes and they have been ridden to many successes: Carlos Sastre won the 2008 Tour de France on a Cervélo and more than 40 athletes at the Beijing Olympic Games captured three gold, five silver, and two bronze medals riding Cervélo's bicycles. The models that regular customers buy in specialty stores across Canada are the same as those used by the professional cyclists.

Pacific Cycle, Trek, and Cervélo may be in the same industry, but each pursues a very different strategy in an attempt to meet the needs of customers and in so doing create value. In this chapter, you will be introduced to the basics of business strategy—the tools and models that will help you formulate coherent strategies for competing within an industry context. ■

Creating Business Strategies

This chapter builds on Chapters 3 and 4 by discussing ways in which companies formulate business strategies that capitalize on their resources and capabilities to exploit opportunities in their competitive environments. At the same time, it sets the stage for Chapter 6, which explores strategy in dynamic contexts. As we saw in Chapter 1, *business strategy* refers to the choices that a company makes about its competitive posture within a particular line of business. These choices can be summarized by the *strategy diamond* and its *five elements of strategy*.

The chapter's opening vignette about three bicycle companies shows that there is more than one economic logic or way to compete in an industry. ◆ Pacific Cycle markets a product for virtually every segment, offers a range of quality in its product mix, and keeps costs down by outsourcing all of its production to China and Taiwan. Trek, meanwhile, though also a large company with a broad product mix, focuses on specialized and innovative product attributes to target specific customer segments and one channel—independent bike distributors. Cervélo is an entirely different company, marketing a highly specialized product targeted at a narrow range of potential customers.

◆ Economic Logic

As a rule, competitive positions can be established in many different ways, and the task of selecting a configuration is the subject of this chapter. The chapter starts with business strategist and professor Michael Porter's framework for strategic positioning and then describes the conditions under which particular strategic positions are viable. Alternative strategic positions compatible with different stages of the industry life cycle are also examined. The chapter concludes with a process for testing the quality of a strategy because a successful strategy needs to be consistent with both a company's resources and its competitive environment.

Types of Strategies—Finding a Position That Works

Given all the choices that can be made relative to the strategy diamond, the potential strategies available to a company are almost endless. The range of choices can be simplified using a typology that sorts them into types of strategies. A classic framework in the field of strategic management is Michael Porter's *generic strategy model*. This typology is based on how a company positions itself in the market relative to its competitors. Recall that rivalry among companies in an industry was a key force in the industry structure model that we introduced in Chapter 4. The generic strategies are alternative market positions that *reduce the effects of rivalry and so improve profitability*.

Strategic positioning fits within the strategy diamond model that we explored in Chapter 1. The generic strategy typology starts with the intended *economic logic* of the company's strategy and the *arenas* in which it will compete. Underlying the choice of economic logic is the idea of what *differentiators* the company might employ. First, the strategist has to decide whether the company will compete by being a low-cost leader (that is, a competitor that will achieve higher margins due to a lower cost basis than rivals) or by being a differentiator (that is, a competitor that will achieve higher prices and margins because of superior quality). For instance, Trek attempts to position its brands as possessing superior quality, and therefore warranting higher prices, through endorsements by industry superstars such as Lance Armstrong and exclusive distribution through independent bike dealers. Second, the strategist has to decide whether the company intends to serve the broad market or more specialized niches. Those selling bicycles, for example, must decide whether to compete in all geographic markets and all product lines with everything from high-performance to economy-priced bicycles—as you might see when contrasting Cervélo with Dorel.

strategic positioning
Means by which managers situate a company relative to its rivals.

This model also helps decision makers deal with questions about a company's tactics for motivating customers to choose its products. Consider the market for luxury cars. Will customers buy from a company because it offers the lowest-priced luxury sedan (such as the Buick Park Avenue), because it's known for its quality (say, Lexus), or because it offers the most valuable brand image (perhaps Mercedes-Benz)?

A company's choice of position is primarily influenced by two factors: (1) company resources and capabilities and (2) industry structure. Formulating a strategy means deciding how and where to compete—that is, how to position a company relative to its rivals. In addition, if a company hopes to exploit opportunities while withstanding competitive threats from within its industry, its strategy should be built on its unique resources and capabilities.

GENERIC STRATEGIES

generic strategies
Strategic position designed to reduce the effects of rivalry, including *low-cost, differentiation, focused cost leadership, focused differentiation,* and *integrated* positions.

Michael Porter's concept of the **generic strategies** has companies develop defensible strategic positions that are a function of two sets of choices—economic logic (low-cost leadership versus differentiation) and scope of arenas (broad versus niche market arenas). What follows will explain the logic of the resulting four positions—*low-cost leadership, differentiation, focused cost leadership,* and *focused differentiation*—and show how a successfully implemented generic strategic position can reduce the negative effects of industry rivalry. A simple two-by-two matrix, shown in Exhibit 5.1, helps you visualize the four alternative competitive positions; the alternative positions suggested by this model are what we mean by generic strategies.[3] The integrated position, shown in the middle of the exhibit, is discussed at the end of the section.

Porter's generic strategies are not *strategies* in the way we define them using the strategy diamond presented in Chapter 1. Porter's strategies are referred to here as *strategic positions* to avoid confusing them with our more general concept of strategy. Each of these strategic positions still requires a carefully formulated set of choices regarding the five elements of the strategy diamond. However, selecting an intended generic strategic position first gives you a head start and guidance in making specific choices regarding the five elements of the strategy diamond.

Cost or Differentiation

In 1980, Michael Porter introduced an approach to strategy that considered the structure of an industry and its effect on the performance of companies within it (an idea discussed in Chapter 4). Porter also demonstrated the economic logic behind some prescriptions for choosing among viable means of gaining competitive advantage. As you see in Exhibit 5.1, the model hinges on two dimensions: the economic logic and the breadth of the target market.

Exhibit 5.1 The Strategic Positioning Model

Source: The positioning model is adapted from M. E. Porter, *Competitive Strategy: Techniques for Analyzing Industries and Competitors* (New York: Free Press, 1980). The examples used in the model are the authors' analysis.

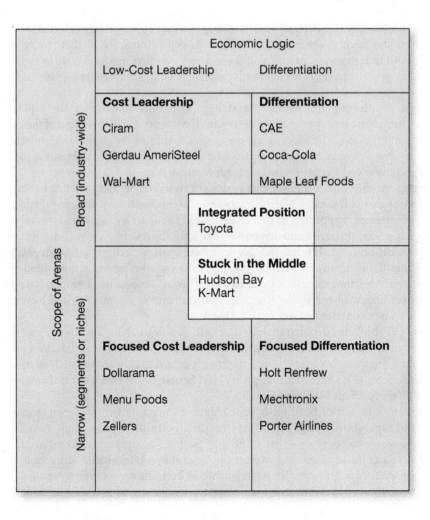

According to Porter, there are two essential economic logics (or the source) of competitive advantage. These are (1) having a lower cost structure than industry competitors or (2) having a product or service that customers perceive as differentiated from other products in the industry—to the point that they will pay higher prices than what is charged for other products in the industry.

Along the horizontal dimension of Exhibit 5.1, companies choose the underlying economic logic by which they intend to establish a competitive advantage—that is, whether to compete on differentiation or cost. *Differentiation* refers to a general condition of perceived product "uniqueness" that causes customers to be willing to pay premium prices. When are customers willing to pay more for a product? Generally, premium prices for otherwise similar products are paid when a company is uniquely able to satisfy a customer's needs. This satisfaction could be along the dimensions of quality, image, speed, access, or other identifiable dimensions of perceived need. However, companies can gain advantage in other ways as well. As shown in Exhibit 5.1, companies may decide to seek higher returns and a competitive advantage by keeping costs lower than those of competitors. This is typically done by offering a product that is good enough to meet the basic needs of many consumers, thereby allowing companies to cut down on production costs.

Scope of Arenas

Companies also make choices about the number and breadth of arenas in which they will compete when they decide how broadly they will compete for customers—a decision known as *scope of arenas*. In other words, companies make choices about which customers to pursue. Some companies compete broadly by trying to offer something for virtually everyone; others focus their efforts on narrower segments of the market. The vertical dimension in Exhibit 5.1 measures the scope of the market arenas in which a company chooses to compete.

Importantly, even though a narrow market scope implies some form of market niche, this does not mean that every niche market is small. For example, Porsche AG has focused on the high-performance sports car market, a niche market in the auto industry, but Porsche still commanded more than US$10.5 billion in revenues in 2010.[4] Indeed, when you think of category killers such as Staples (office supplies) or Home Depot (home and garden supplies), they pursue well-defined, large, and attractive market niches.

Low-Cost Leadership

A strategic position that enables a company to produce a good or offer a service while maintaining total costs that are lower than what it takes competitors to offer the same product or

To avoid head-to-head competition, Pacific Cycle positions itself differently than Trek. Pacific makes many different brands, selling them at various prices in numerous retail outlets.

low-cost leadership Strategic position based on producing a good or offering a service while maintaining total costs that are lower than what it takes competitors to offer the same product or service.

service is known as **low-cost leadership**. Not surprisingly, a company that can provide substantially similar products at a lower cost has a significant competitive advantage. With a cost advantage, a company can gain market share by selling for lower prices than rivals yet maintain the same profit margins. Pacific Cycle has low-cost manufacturers in China and Taiwan make bicycles for it and then passes on some of its cost savings to retailers through lower prices while maintaining retail marketing power through strong brand equity provided by its Schwinn and Mongoose brands. However, a low-cost leader does not necessarily pass on all the cost savings to customers through lower prices. When it keeps its prices close to those of its competitors, it reaps higher margins that it can either distribute to shareholders or use to finance future strategic initiatives. And when a low-cost competitor enters a market served by high-cost competitors, the high-cost competitors either have to get their costs down or go out of business. When Wal-Mart entered Canada, traditional retailers including Canadian Tire, Dollarama, Loblaw, and Zellers had to find new ways to cut costs in order to compete.

As a general rule, a low-cost position requires sacrificing some features or services. Companies that stake out this position try to satisfy basic customer needs rather than highly specialized ones. Dollarama, the largest Canadian discount chain, competes by offering the best products it can for a dollar. Dollarama has excelled for three reasons. First, location costs are kept low by staying out of expensive prime retail areas. Second, it buys directly from Asian manufacturers, rather than through importers. Both of these tactics have lowered cost. And third, Larry Rossy, the CEO, ensures that buyers focus on providing customers with value found in creative products and not simply with products that can be sold cheaply. In 2009, Dollarama had more than Cdn$1.25 billion in sales through its 603 stores located primarily in Ontario and Quebec.[5]

The low-cost strategy works in many industries, though the companies pursuing it are not readily apparent because they have little public visibility. One reason that they are not visible is that they leave the marketing of their products to others. They are simply contract manufacturers so consumers do not associate the companies with the products they have made. An example of such a company is Menu Foods of Streetsville, Ontario, which is a leading North American manufacturer of wet pet food products. It has low-cost, state-of-the-art manufacturing facilities that produce pet food for many other companies. Few people had heard of the company until 2007 when it had to recall more than 100 brands of pet food it had made including Menu Foods, Hill's Pet Nutrition, P&G Pet Care, Nestle Purina PetCare, Del Monte Pet Products, and Sunshine Mills. The recall was necessary because the Chinese feed ingredients it had used were contaminated with chemicals that caused serious health problems in pets.[6] Another strategy is to produce products that become ingredients or components in the products of other companies. An example of the second type is the auto parts manufacturers. There are 450 parts manufacturers in Ontario's auto corridor but only a few giants such as Magna, Linamar, and The Woodbridge Group are well known.

FOCUS ON SUSTAINABILITY BOX 5.1
Following a Smaller Environmental Footprint to Economic Advantage

Some manufacturers of automotive parts recognize that reducing their ecological footprint will make them preferred suppliers to manufacturers of motor vehicles. These parts manufacturers also want to reduce their dependence on oil-based parts as oil becomes ever more expensive. Both needs are being satisfied by developing new products based on using renewable materials.

Initiatives in Ontario involve using renewable materials to make auto parts ranging from mirror casings and bumpers, to door panels, seat foams, and upholstery.

The Woodbridge Group and Cargill Inc. have partnered to produce plant-based polyurethane parts used in interior applications. BioFoam, manufactured by Woodbridge, is currently made with up to 25 percent bio-based materials. BioFoam feels and performs the same as conventional polyurethane foams but is produced using a Cargill polyol called BiOH. Soybeans are crushed and refined to form the BiOH polyol, which is combined with other agents to mould foam for seats, arm-rests, and overhead systems.

More bio-based auto parts are coming from DuPont. Fabrics, carpets, and automotive interiors that are derivatives of DuPont's Sorona Polymer provide superior durability and stain resistance. Another DuPont bioproduct named Cerenol is poised to give automotive coatings greater chip resistance and flexibility.

What are the key strategic questions involved in reducing a company's environmental footprint?

In summary, with the low-cost position, companies attempt to deliver an acceptable product that satisfies basic needs at the lowest possible cost. In doing so, the company attempts to create a sustainable cost gap over other companies. Successfully following this path results in above-industry-average profits. However, cost leaders must maintain parity or proximity in satisfying the basic needs of buyers. Doing so is a challenge because it generally requires tradeoffs—eliminating some features or services in order to drive costs down.

Differentiation

If a company markets products whose quality, reliability, or prestige is discernibly higher than its competitors', and if its customers are willing to pay for this uniqueness, the company has a competitive advantage based on **differentiation**. Successful differentiation enables companies to do one of two things:

differentiation Strategic position based on products or offers services with quality, reliability, or prestige that is discernibly higher than that of competitors and for which customers are willing to pay.

1. Set prices at the industry average (and gain market share because consumers will choose higher quality at the same price).
2. Raise prices over those of competitors (and reap the benefits of higher margins).

A successful broad differentiator is Maple Leaf Foods. Although it is the largest Canadian pork processor and one of the country's largest poultry producers, it is a small player in these meats by North American standards. To avoid commodity competition. Maple Leaf Foods differentiated its product by offering pork and poultry fed an all-vegetable grain diet rather than a diet containing animal by-products. With the societal shift toward healthy eating and concern over all-natural foods, the strategy allowed Maple Leaf to achieve strong sales figures while offering its products at prices slightly higher than competitors. Maple Leaf's basis for differentiation was seriously threatened in the summer of 2008 when an outbreak of listeriosis, a potentially deadly bacterial infection, was traced back to two lines in the company's Bartor Road plant in North York, Ontario. Maple Leaf instituted a voluntary recall before the outbreak was linked to the plant, expanding the recall to all products from the Bartor Road facility once the link was confirmed. In a press conference, Michael McCain, president and CEO of Maple Leaf Foods, stated, "Tragically, our products have been linked to illness and loss of life. To those people who are ill, and to the families who have lost loved ones, I offer my deepest and sincerest sympathies. Words cannot begin to express our sadness for their pain." These actions were important in showing customers that the company cared about its customers.[7]

Differentiation is not cheap. Coca-Cola and Pepsi spend billions on brand promotion and comprehensive coverage by making product available nearly everywhere that people are found. Or consider Mercedes-Benz, perhaps the world's leading manufacturer of premium passenger cars. It has invested heavily in building a reputation for innovative engineering, safety, and comfort, along with product design aimed at buyers who will pay premium prices for the image that goes along with a Mercedes.[8] Interestingly, although most North Americans regard Mercedes as a focused differentiator because only affluent customers can afford its products, Europeans have a different view. In Europe, Mercedes markets a wide line of products that appeal to a wide market, ranging from tiny Smart cars to more familiar luxury sedans.

A successful differentiation position requires that a company satisfy a few basic criteria. First, it must uniquely satisfy one or more needs that are valued by buyers and do so in a manner superior to that available from most competitors. However, doing so will *typically* result in higher costs in some value-chain activities. Thus, the second requirement that must be satisfied is that customers must be willing to pay higher prices for the added points of differentiation. Consequently, companies successful at a differentiation position pick cost-effective forms of differentiation. The result is above-average industry profits.

Focused Low-Cost Leadership

A strategic position that enables a company to be a low-cost leader in a narrow segment of the market is known as focused cost leadership. WestJet was originally a focused low-cost leader, specifically targeting regional air travel in Western Canada. Its strategy was closely modelled on that of Southwest Airlines, which is headquartered in Dallas, Texas. In order to keep its costs low, WestJet only flew out of secondary airports, had only one type of plane (Boeing 737), and had limited in-flight service. The success of WestJet has been driven by this commitment to keeping prices low; however, other factors such as customer service and successful marketing

focused low-cost leadership Strategic position based on being a low-cost leader in a narrow market segment.

transformed WestJet into a major competitor in the Canadian airline market. In 2008 it was exploring a strategic alliance with Southwest that would expand its arena. The challenge of creating an alliance was demonstrated in the spring of 2010 when both companies announced that they were withdrawing from negotiations as they pursued other potential partners.[9]

For many years in the steel industry, mini-mills using electric-arc furnaces were focused low-cost producers of long products (structural steel, rod and bar, wire, and fasteners). One of the world's largest mini-mill steel producers was the Canadian company Co-Steel. It was an early entrant and in 2002 merged with the Brazilian steelmaker Gerdau to become Gerdau AmeriSteel, an international steel company with annual production of 11.8 million tonnes of finished steel and revenue of about US$1.7 billion. Low cost was attributed to two factors associated with the technology mini-mills used. First, they required much less capital investment. The capital cost per tonne of annual installed capacity was US$140 to US$200 per ton for a mini-mill compared with US$1 000 for an integrated steel mill. Mini-mills required less capital investment in equipment because they started with scrap iron and steel, which was nearly the finished product, while traditional integrated steel mills started with coke, iron ore, and limestone. Second, the operating costs were much lower because scrap was close to the finished form of the product. Integrated mills found themselves unable to compete on price for any products made by mini-mills. However, the technology was such that the mini-mills were unable to make flat products (sheet steel and heavier steel plate), so mini-mills took over the markets for long products while integrated mills focused on flat products.

Even high-tech companies can pursue a focused low-cost strategy successfully. Montreal-based Mechtronix World Corp. was founded in 1987 and is now the world's third-largest and fastest-growing provider of flight simulation equipment and training. In 2008 it had revenues of Cdn$55 million. This success has to be measured against that of Montreal-based CAE, which was founded in 1947. CAE is the world leader in this same business, has annual revenues exceeding US$1.4 billion, and employs approximately 7 000 people at more than 75 sites and training locations in 20 countries. So how did Mechtronix take on CAE? Mechtronix produces simulators that are based on different technology so they are cheaper to buy and less expensive to maintain than those of CAE. This has produced a value curve that appeals to smaller customers such as the "Tier 2" regional airline (with about 20 aircraft and 200 pilots)—a market niche not well served by CAE.[10]

Focused Differentiation

focused differentiation
Strategic position based on targeting products to relatively small segments.

When unique products are targeted to a particular market segment or arena, the positioning strategy is called **focused differentiation**. Porter Airlines, an upstart regional airline, is a focused differentiator. It started operating out of the Toronto City Centre Airport, a local airport located on the Toronto Islands, in 2006. It has been able to differentiate itself against established competitors. Porter's prices are competitive with Air Canada, which flies out of Toronto Pearson International Airport on the outskirts of the city. But Porter differentiates what it offers its customers in terms of convenience, upscale amenities, and comfortable flights. Convenience comes from using a small airport that is right next to downtown Toronto. This provides easy access, quick check-in and security, and short taxi to and from the runway. All this cuts total travel time considerably. Upscale amenities are provided in a new passenger lounge and on flights. The lounge features free wireless internet access, complimentary coffee/tea/soft drinks, and free use of a business centre with workstations for Porter's passengers. On all flights, beer and wine are complimentary and passengers receive snack boxes. Comfortable flights are provided on Porter's propeller-driven Bombardier Q400 airplanes, which are fast and quiet and offer custom leather seats with two to three inches more legroom than typical economy-class seating. The appeal of Porter's offer has supported its growth from the initial route to Ottawa to routes to elsewhere in Canada (Halifax, Montreal, Quebec City, and Thunder Bay) as well as to the United States (Boston, Chicago, and New York).

In the bicycle industry, Cervélo focuses on a small, specialized segment of the market that demands unique product features. Trek Bicycles, which also started as a focused differentiator, is moving toward being a broad-based differentiator by offering products in numerous market segments. Trek can still be classified as a focused differentiator, however, because its products boast high quality and demand price premiums over products from Pacific Cycle and because it only sells products through independent bicycle dealers.

Porter Airlines has developed a successful and rapidly growing business by providing premium service on flights in and out of Toronto.

Companies that are successful as focused differentiators find themselves in niche markets. And by definition, the greater the differentiation, the smaller the market segment to which a product will appeal. In the motorcycle industry, Harley-Davidson is a focused differentiator when compared with Honda because it makes larger models targeted at specific market segments. Its lowest-priced motorcycle begins at around US$6500. This does not mean that the focused differentiator is without competition. Orange County Choppers has entered Harley's market space and has tried to outfocus it by selling only made-to-order motorcycles—a very small segment of the motorcycle market.

Some companies are successful in broadening their focus beyond their original niche. Research In Motion Ltd. (RIM) started as a focused differentiator by designing the BlackBerry to meet the specific needs of business users, and this set RIM apart from competitors. The BlackBerry included features such as a full QWERTY keyboard and push email so that the device was always available for incoming emails, and RIM provided security for all communication by encrypting it and routing it through RIM's in-house servers rather than third-party carriers. The differentiated offer is always subject to erosion, however. Encryption created a problem for RIM as it expanded into overseas markets. The United Arab Emirates, home to Middle East business hub of Dubai, and India threatened to suspend BlackBerry email services because their governments were unable to eavesdrop on potential criminals and terrorists using secure devices.[11]

Harley-Davidson has successfully focused its business strategy on the large, high-priced end of the motorcycle market. Other manufacturers, such as Orange County Choppers, have tried to muscle into Harley's well-defined market space with bikes such as the Fire Bike shown here.

Some companies are not able to grow successfully beyond their niche. In the bicycle industry, Cannondale built a strong reputation producing high-end mountain bikes. It then sought to transfer this reputation to the motocross motorcycle market. Unfortunately the ability to make sturdy, high-performance bicycle frames did not transfer into the ability to make high-performance engines and drive trains used in motorcycles. Moreover, the dealers for mountain bikes did not sell motorcycles. The failure of Cannondale's strategy led to bankruptcy, and Cannondale was bought by Pegasus Partners in 2003. In 2007, Dorel bought Cannondale and reorganized its bicycle business so that Cannondale became part of its CSG unit, which sells premium brand bikes to independent bicycle dealers, while Pacific Cycle is part of its PCG unit, which sells regular brand bikes to mass merchandisers such as Canadian Tire and Wal-Mart.

Integrated Positions

Initially it is very difficult for any company to offer both a differentiated product demanding higher prices and still maintain a lower cost structure than competitors. In fact, companies that attempt to exploit both low-cost and differentiation strategies are often described as "stuck in the middle"—meaning they aim to do both but do neither very well. Chrysler, for instance, suffered from attempting to lower costs while simultaneously trying to deliver differentiated products. This resulted in a lineup of cars that did not command premium prices (because of some of the quality problems associated with cost-control initiatives) and higher than average costs (because of the increased costs of design efforts to differentiate the product). It is hard to escape the fact that the tradeoffs required to achieve superiority on one dimension make it hard to succeed on the other. However, as companies perfect their initial position, the tradeoffs may not be as stark. Some companies eventually are able to achieve an **integrated position**—one in which elements of one position support a strong standing in the other. And while it is typically unwise for a company to aim to excel at both low cost and differentiation, the competitive reality is that if a company excels on one dimension, it must still be good on the other dimension. For instance, a company that sells very unique products must also have good cost controls in place. Similarly, a company that competes on price (or low cost) is wise to develop additional attributes that differentiate its products beyond price alone.

integrated position Strategic position in which elements of one position support strong standing in another.

Low-cost competitors can adopt some elements of a differentiation position. NOVA Chemicals is North America's largest producer of polystyrene and has the highest value-added products. It accomplishes this by focusing on being the most efficient producer while selling higher priced products such as ARCEL, an expandable, resilient, mouldable foam resin, used in high-price, high-margin packaging for personal computers, televisions, and other electronic products. Alternatively some low-cost companies develop strong brand images even though branding typically supports a differentiation strategy. Heavy reliance on branding enables McDonald's to position itself as a reliable, high-quality provider of low-cost fast food. Whether the company has achieved an integrated position, however, is judged by whether it achieves higher prices than its competitors for similar products.

Toyota is an excellent example of a company that has achieved an integrated position. Toyota first entered the North American market as a low-cost leader because it was able to manufacture small cars at a much lower cost than North American automobile manufacturers. Over time, Toyota invested heavily in quality control, design, and marketing that allowed it to sell cars at higher prices. The consequence was that it earned much larger margins than most automobile manufacturers.

IKEA Svenska AB is an example of a business that has become the world's largest home furnishings retailer by specializing in stylish but inexpensive furniture. IKEA's success can be traced back to its product differentiation and cost leadership. IKEA outlets are essentially warehouses stacked with boxes of unassembled furniture. The company operates under a fairly unique premise: namely, that value-conscious buyers will perform some of the tasks that other retailers normally perform for them, such as transporting and assembling their own furniture. By transferring these functions to the customer, IKEA drives costs down and, therefore, can offer prices low enough to fit most budgets. Thus, IKEA targets a large segment of the market, ranging from young low- to middle-income families. At the same time, the company has established a highly differentiated image with its enormous selection of self-assembly home furnishings and fun in-store experiences.

Companies that have integrated low-cost and differentiation positions can be found in most industries. So can companies whose products don't seem to fall into either category.

As Exhibit 5.2 shows, integrated—and enviable—positions have in fact been forged in the auto industry. For instance, Toyota is a successful company with an integrated position that generates better profit margins on comparable models than Chevrolet, Hyundai, or Ford. In this model class, Chevrolet appears to be a successful low-cost leader while Ford is attempting to be a differentiator, yet their margins are significantly less than Toyota. Notice that Chevrolet's margins are even greater than Ford's. Hyundai seems to be stuck in the middle. Its stated strategy is to be a low-cost leader. However, operational problems have resulted in costs greater than all but Ford in this example. Yet the quality and image of the brand does not permit them to charge prices consistent with a differentiator.

The financial results of successful low-cost, differentiation, and integrated positions in either the broad or narrow arena are illustrated in Exhibit 5.3, which demonstrates that what matters when defining strategy is the relative position of price and costs. The successful differentiated competitor receives substantially higher prices while costs are only moderately higher. The successful low-cost competitor, on the other hand, has substantially lower cost yet receives only moderately lower prices. Achieving each of these positions is predicated on the effective implementation of a cost or differentiation advantage, or both. In the next section, we explore the drivers of cost and differentiation in detail.

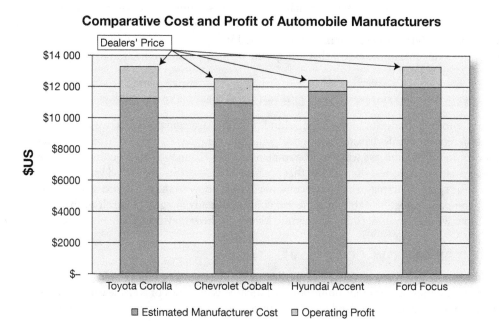
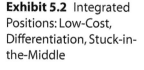

Exhibit 5.2 Integrated Positions: Low-Cost, Differentiation, Stuck-in-the-Middle

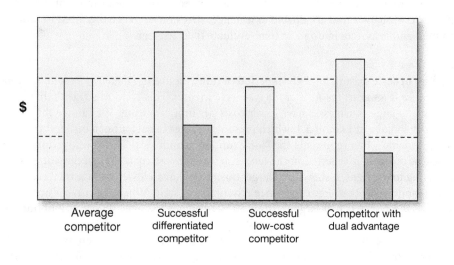
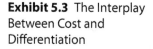

Exhibit 5.3 The Interplay Between Cost and Differentiation

Strategic Position, Company Resources, and the Strategy Diamond

The appropriate strategic position for any company depends on two factors: (1) its resources and capabilities and (2) the condition of its industry environment. A company with strong innovative capabilities, for example, will generally favour differentiation strategies. Why? Because the ability to make product improvements, whether incremental or radical, enables a company to offer newer and more unique products directed at specific customer needs. Intel favours heavy investment in product innovation so that it can remain on the leading edge of new-product introductions in the microprocessor industry. Notice, however, that Intel's differentiators (innovation and product development speed) are particularly valuable in the arenas where computer manufacturers such as Dell want to be able to provide the latest and greatest technologies to their customers. This strategy enables Intel to charge higher prices during the early stages of the product life cycle, generating increased cash flows that it can, in turn, invest in building its brand and further differentiating its products.

Alternatively, capabilities in large-scale manufacturing and distribution generally favour low-cost strategies. Cooper Industries, for example, is a leading worldwide manufacturer with four plants in Canada. It has skills in acquiring and consolidating companies in mature tool, hardware, or electrical-product industries, infusing them with modern manufacturing technology and increasing supplier power over critical customer segments. In particular, Cooper's ability to modernize manufacturing processes (the company calls it Cooperizing) gives the company a cost advantage over many competitors. Thus, it uses differentiators that are cost-effective and give it an advantage in arenas where customers look at price as a key decision criterion. The point we are making here with the Intel and Cooper examples is that a strategic position is valuable to the extent that it helps the company position itself in a desirable market.

Economic Drivers of Strategic Positioning

In order to fully understand the logic behind different strategic positions, we need to identify the different economic drivers that support and facilitate each strategic position and foster their success. In this section, we will describe some of the key economic drivers of both low-cost and differentiation strategies. (Remember that because *focus* strategies are special variations on these two basic types of strategy, the same economic drivers apply to them.) In order to comprehend how companies might be able to achieve a competitive advantage as a result of their strategic position, we need to understand economic drivers and how they function.

DRIVERS OF LOW-COST ADVANTAGE

Product costs that must be recovered in the market vary across companies for several reasons. Some of the more common (and important) include economies of scale, learning, production technology, product design, and location advantages for sourcing inputs. In this section, we'll review some of these more important sources of potential cost advantage. A successful low-cost strategy requires that a company is proficient at exploiting one or more of these drivers. Conversely, companies that are unable to leverage these cost drivers either need to acquire the capabilities and resources to do so or to re-evaluate their strategy.

Economies of Scale

economy of scale Condition under which average total cost for a unit of production is lower at higher levels of output.

Economies of scale exist if, for a given period of time, *the average total cost for a unit of production or service is lower as the scale of the business increases.* This concept suggests that bigger is better because larger businesses have lower costs per unit of output. We can see this diagrammatically by looking at Exhibit 5.4, which presents the cost behaviour of a business in which all costs are variable—this represents the "long run" to economists. The lowest possible cost for every size of business is reflected in the long-run average cost curve. When this curve is downward sloping to the right, it shows that larger businesses have a lower average total cost per unit of output, and we say that they experience economies of scale. When the curve is upward sloping to the right, it shows that larger businesses have higher average cost per unit of output and we say that they experience diseconomies of scale.

In Exhibit 5.4, the curves labelled SAC 1 through 4 are the short-run average total cost curves for four different scales or sizes of business going from small to large. The curve for each size is U-shaped. The curve labelled LAC is the long-run average cost curve. It is an

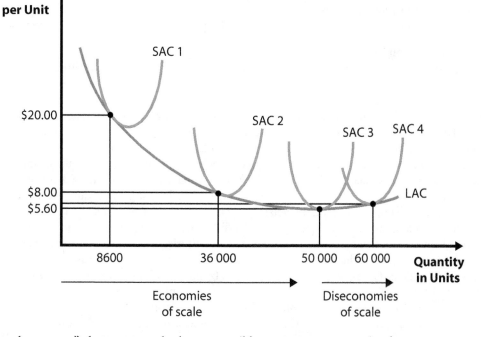

Exhibit 5.4 Economies and Diseconomies of Scale

"envelope curve" that presents the lowest possible average cost per unit of output at every possible scale of business. In the diagram, the lowest average costs drops as the scale gets larger until the third largest, which is the most efficient scale, is producing 50 000 units per period at a cost of $5.60 per unit. Above 50 000 units the average cost per unit rises, indicating that a further increase in scale causes the average cost per unit to rise.

Economies of scale may be found in any one of the business's activities performed at various sites or plants of the business or for the business as a whole. Taken together, these produce the overall cost curve for the business. Some of the main sources of economies of scale include the following:

Specialization
Larger size allows increased specialization as work is divided into distinctive tasks that enhance productivity, which lowers cost per unit. For example, in a small business each employee has to do many tasks and so never develops the skills and knowledge that an employee in large companies develops as he/she focuses on specific tasks.

Spreading Fixed Costs
The cost of research and development, marketing, and licences are fixed charges that are independent of scale. The business that has higher volume can spread these costs over the larger volume, lowering the contribution of each to average total cost per unit. In addition, the cost of performing a transaction, whether buying or selling, is similar, whether the business is large or small. Large businesses are able to spread these costs across more units of production.

Technological Scale
Sometimes the cost of production is less on large-scale equipment because the cost of making the equipment goes up at a slower rate than the volume of output produced by the equipment. This is the case in many processing industries, including chemicals, petroleum refining, and iron ore reduction. In other cases, the equipment is very efficient but large scale. A smaller company could buy this equipment but would still have higher costs because it would not be running the equipment at full capacity. Many small companies get in trouble with this. They reach a size where they need to adopt the technologies used by large companies but cannot carry the cost on buying, installing, and then running the equipment at inefficient volumes of production.

Better Use of Joint Products
Larger plants that produce by-products in sufficient volume can use what was once considered waste as the input to an additional business, eliminating a cost of disposal and gaining a new source of revenue. This happens in many industries that produce joint products such as in the

meat packing business. Small plants have to pay disposal costs for getting rid of fat, but large plants can supply a local plant that renders this into non-edible oil that is then sold to other manufacturers. This type of expansion when performed by a corporation is called vertical integration.

Pursuing Economies of Scale

A business pursues economies of scale though growth, either organically or through acquisition. Organic pursuit of scale is achieved by increasing the size of the business over time. As it gets larger, its cost per unit fall. Pursuit through acquisition involves buying similar businesses and then consolidating their activities so the same amount of work is done but at a lower cost. The cost savings due to consolidation come from the elimination of employees, facilities, and increasing bargaining power when buying inputs. In February 2002, Newmont Mining Corporation completed the acquisition of Normandy Mining Limited, an Australian company, along with its largest shareholder, Franco-Nevada Mining Corporation Limited, a Canadian company, for US$5.2 billion, making Newmont the world's largest gold producer at that time. This yielded both operational and financial benefits. Then there is Coca-Cola, which had to deal with a more complex situation. It had created a distribution system in which individual franchisees held exclusive rights to specified geographic territories. In each territory, the operation was the optimal size for the territory served, but the size of the territories was suboptimal for serving its markets. Coca-Cola solved this problem by buying back many franchises during the 1980s and 1990s and consolidating them into larger geographic territories. It then built larger bottling plants that had greater economies of scale in the enlarged territories. This lowered the overall delivered cost when serving Coca-Cola's customers. Another example comes from the beer industry. In 2005, Molson Inc. and Adolph Coors Company merged to form Molson Coors Brewing Company. The new entity expected to achieve US$175 million in cost reductions. CEO Leo Kiely stated, "It is consistent with the company's plans to structure its U.S. and Canadian brewery network to optimize brewing and packaging operations, leverage the facilities' proximity to customers and reduce related distribution and overhead costs." Analyst Mike Van Aelst of CIBC World Markets said Molson Coors was likely to shut down some of its production at its main plant in Colorado, although it could not move its core brands because their brand image is associated with the Rocky Mountains.[12]

The possibility of economies of scale typically increases over time as technology evolves and industries mature. Part of the reason is that machinery companies build highly specialized machines that produce larger volumes at a lower cost per unit. An example is Husky Injection Molding Systems of Bolton, Ontario, which builds machines that produce PET containers used to bottle water and soft drinks. It has been a leader, creating new moulding machines that produce large volumes of containers at lower cost than existing technology. Another example is the development of the steel industry. In the middle of the last century, the technology used in the industry by integrated manufacturers was basic oxygen steelmaking. This involved putting molten iron produced in a blast furnace into a Basic Oxygen Furnace (BOF) and then casting it into steel products. In the steel industry, however, technology then evolved in the other direction. The development of Electric Arc Furnace (EAF) technology allowed steel to be made from scrap in the mini-mills—so-called because they were much smaller than the integrated mills. An early adopter of this new technology, Co-Steel based in Whitby, Ontario, quickly took over market share in certain products (initially reinforcing bar, or REBAR) because they could still make a profit at lower prices. Eventually the integrated manufacturers adopted the mini-mill technology so they could recapture markets in these same products. Of note, EAF technology not only reduced costs but also reduced the point at which economies were achieved. It supported the emergence of specialist producers, which lead to the reconfiguration of the industry.

Expansion in pursuit of economies of scale can be limited by the constraints of market demand and the company's market share. A small market limits the advantages of larger scale while a small market share can prevent the business from achieving greater size. But getting bigger is not always beneficial because of diseconomies of scale.

diseconomy of scale Condition under which average total costs per unit of production increases as the volume of output increases.

Diseconomies of Scale

Costs per unit do not continue to decline as a business expands. If they did, industries would become dominated by a single business. And if mergers and acquisitions produced the cost savings that they were based on, many more of them would be considered successful.

In reality, almost all operations processes are subject to the diseconomies of scale that occur when average total cost *increases* at higher levels of output. Diseconomies of scale can be due to growing bureaucracy, the increasing costs of labour, and differences in efficiency between interdependent operations. Moreover, a company can have economies of scale in some value-chain activities and diseconomies of scale in other activities.

Minimum Efficient Scale

Industries with businesses of many different sizes call into question the idea that there is an optimal size of business for an industry as suggested by the U-shaped average total cost curve. Empirical studies have determined that the long-run average total cost curve per unit is closer to L-shaped than U-shaped. The average total cost per unit of output drops as scale increases and then reaches a point where increasing scale further has no appreciable effect on total average cost. This produces an L-shaped long run average cost curve. This means that there are no apparent diseconomies of scale once the business reaches a particular size. The point at which the curve flattens is called the **Minimum Efficient Scale (MES)**. A business larger than this scale will not have appreciably lower average cost per unit of output as the volume of output increases.

> **Minimum Efficient Scale (MES)** The minimum scale at which the business fully exploits the economies of scale.

The MES is shown diagrammatically in Exhibit 5.5. The curve labelled SAC 1 shows the short-run average cost curves for a business that, at 20 000 units of output, is too small to achieve all the economies of scale. But the business producing 50 000 units has achieved a scale that captures all economies of scale and getting any larger will not lower its average cost per unit. This is why the long-run average cost curve is flat.

The shape of the long-run average cost curve is a significant determinant of how many companies populate the market. When the MES is either small in absolute volume or small relative to the output of the industry serving the market, the number of competitors is greater. Returning to Exhibit 5.5, if the MES is 50 000 units, then a new company that only sells 20 000 units will have costs twice as high as the current competitor. It can only survive if companies producing 50 000 units per period allow a price high enough for the entrant to cover its costs. When the MES is so great that even one company cannot exploit all the economies of scale, the market is said to support a "natural monopoly."

The Learning Curve

In addition to scale economies, other factors can contribute to lower operating costs. Two companies of the same size, for example, may have significantly different operating costs because one has progressed farther down the learning curve—in other words, it has excelled at the process of learning by doing. The principle is that *incremental production costs decline at a constant rate as production experience is gained;* the steeper the learning curve, the more rapidly costs decline. This idea is attributed to T. P. Wright, who proposed a theory for basing cost estimates on the repetitive operations of airplane assembly processes in 1936.[13] In the 1970s, the U.S. Department of Defense commissioned research to refine learning-curve mathematics so that it could make more precise cost estimates. Although both economies of scale and the learning curve

> **learning curve** Incremental production costs decline at a constant rate as production experience is gained; the steeper the learning curve, the more rapidly costs decline.

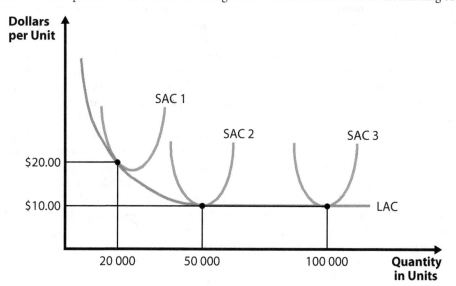

Exhibit 5.5 The Minimum Efficient Scale for the Business

are related to the quantity produced, the underlying mechanisms are quite different. Economies of scale reflect the scale of the operation *during any given period of time*—the volume of current production. Cost decreases attributable to the learning curve reflect *the cumulative level of production since the production of the first unit.*

The learning curve has strategic significance when cost savings of 20 percent to 30 percent are possible as cumulative output doubles. Then the company with greater experience is able to use its lower cost position to discourage competitors. By lowering price as the company's costs decline, it is able to maintain a market price that keeps itself profitable and limits the profitability of its less experienced competitors who have higher costs. Texas Instrument (TI) employed this tactic early in the history of semiconductor manufacture. At the start it priced its semiconductors below the cost of production on the assumption that its costs would drop quickly with cumulative experience. Its low prices caused sales to surge and average costs were even lower than anticipated. TI drove industry prices down so quickly that dozens of competitors were unable to make profits because they had less experience than TI and so were driven out of industry. Part of TI's success with the learning curve is attributable to its tight control of costs and its search for sources of increased efficiency.

Learning is more important in industries when products and processes are new, so much is yet to be learned. The effects of learning are likely modest in mature industries. Then other attributes such as quality and customer service play a greater role in the company's success.

Multiunit Organizations and the Learning Curve

A related effect of the learning curve occurs when a multiunit organization transfers learning from one unit to another. Franchise systems, for instance, can codify their knowledge about the most effective way to operate a store.[14] Technically, therefore, each new franchise doesn't have to start from scratch. Rather, every unit benefits from corporate training programs that give new franchisees a head start at tackling the learning curve. Because units can share new knowledge about effective practices, multiunit companies can make faster progress in mastering learning curves than single-unit operations.

Other Sources of Cost Advantage

Other potential sources of cost advantage include *economies of scope, production technology,* and *product design.*

economy of scope Condition under which lower total average costs result from sharing resources to produce more than one product or service.

Economies of Scope

As the term suggests, *economies of scope* are similar to economies of scale in that both are volume related. Economies of scope refer to potential cost savings associated with *multiproduct* production. When a company produces two or more products, it has greater scope of operations than a company that produces only one. If such a company can share a resource among one or more of its products—thereby lowering the costs of each product—it benefits from economies of scope. We discuss this concept more fully in Chapter 8 because it's fundamental to diversification as a corporate strategy. Economies of scope, however, are available not only to large diversified companies but also to small privately held enterprises that are just beginning to expand their product offerings.

In 1999, Grocery Gateway, a Toronto-based web grocer, started delivering groceries directly to consumers who had ordered them over the internet around Toronto. Its infrastructure included an ordering system, a warehouse, and a fleet of trucks. Management levered its infrastructure and made the company less dependent on the success of online grocery buying by providing third-party consumer-direct fulfillment for companies that included the Liquor Control Board of Ontario, Staples Business Depot, and Starbucks Inc. Unfortunately, Grocery Gateway was still unable to achieve the profitability needed to survive so in 2004 Longo Brothers Fruit Markets Inc. (Longo's), an Ontario, family-run independent grocer, took it over.

Another example of scope is provided by Frito Lay Canada, which manufactures several different types of potato chips: regular cut, ripple, and thick cut. These products are produced using the same type of potatoes, cooking process, flavouring process, and packaging. The only difference is that the potatoes are cut differently to make each product. By sharing cooking and flavouring facilities among different varieties of potato chips, the average cost to produce each type of potato chip is greatly reduced.

Production Technology

Naturally, different production technologies entail different costs. Often, a new entrant who wants to compete against industry incumbents with significant scale and experience advantages tries to match or beat incumbents' costs by introducing a production technology that is subject to different economics. Earlier Co-Steel's development of mini-mill technology was described under low-cost leadership. That technology was able to produce certain steel products at considerably lower cost than the integrated mills owned by Hamilton, Ontario–based Dofasco and Stelco could.

EarthRenew Organics Ltd. of Calgary, Alberta, is another company that has lowered costs by developing a technology that combines two separate activities: processing the waste generated by livestock production and generating electricity. The company has developed and patented a technology that cooks organic wastes such as farm manure using the heat created as turbines generate electricity. The exhaust from the gas-driven turbines is then used in place of separate burners to dry organic waste. By coupling the two processes together, up to 85 percent of the energy in natural gas is used. This is much more efficient than running two separate processes, and the sale of the electricity offsets the cost of gas. EarthRenew's technology has been proven in full-scale production at a 25 000-head feedlot in Alberta and in 2009 was installed in California.[15]

Product Design

Similarly, product design can sometimes be altered to lower a company's production costs.[16] When Canon decided to enter the photocopier industry, incumbents such as Xerox had formidable advantages in scale and experience. Canon, however, redesigned the photocopier so that it required fewer parts and allowed for simpler assembly. The new design dropped Canon's costs below those of Xerox and enabled the new entrant to gain significant market share at Xerox's expense.

Sourcing

Finally, different sourcing practices result in different cost structures. Some companies try to attain lower production costs by locating their operations in cheaper labour markets. Others outsource manufacturing altogether. Pacific Cycle initially had a cost advantage over Trek because Pacific Cycle outsourced production to China and Taiwan while Trek produced its bicycles in the United States.

As with diseconomies of scale, there are also diseconomies of scope. Sometimes businesses diversify into additional products or locations that do lower costs. The challenges and complexities of managing the additional business proves difficult and costs go up. The classic cases of turning around money-losing businesses involve cutting the businesses down in size to a core that is profitable. In the process, fewer selections of products are offered, plants are closed, and markets are abandoned.

How you might analyze the opportunities for lowering costs by pursuing economies of scope and scale is described in How Would You Do That? 5.1.

DRIVERS OF DIFFERENTIATION ADVANTAGE

To sell products at premium prices, companies must make their uniqueness and value apparent to customers. This section lays out the economic logic and some common drivers of a successful differentiation strategy. While companies that pursue differentiation advantages must still be cost conscious and good at managing tangible aspects of their products and services, they must typically also excel at managing the intangibles such as "a sense of loyalty to the company," "customer brand awareness," "close relationships with customers," and "close cooperation among managers." As a rule, differentiation involves one or more of the following differentiators among product offerings: *premium brand image, customization and convenience, unique styling, speed,* and *unusually high quality.* And though these differentiators have much about them that is intangible, these intangibles need to be expressly managed and developed.

When the strategist decides that the company wants to appeal only to a subset of buyers, marketers need to identify what those buyers are interested in by segmenting the market—a process known as *market segmentation*. They must identify the unique needs of these buyers, and then the company must satisfy them in ways that competitors do not and preferably cannot.

How to Assess the Impact of Scale and Scope on Cost[17]

Often the scale and scope economies are apparent to all competitors in an industry. For example, the benefits of size are well understood in Canadian banking.[18] But even then, new sources of scale and scope economies arise as economic and technological conditions change. This means that management needs to continually re-examine the sources of and the company's ability to exploit these opportunities. When they are not apparent or are not exploited, the first to recognize and exploit them are able to develop competitive advantage and dramatically alter the structure of an industry.

Evaluating the potential for scale and scope economies requires a systematic process such as value-chain analysis (described in Chapter 3). A useful starting point for such analysis is by defining the value chain. Then you can determine whether there are economies of scale by considering the evidence that shows whether increasing the scale reduces cost. You can determine whether there are economies of scope by identifying similar activities in related businesses, matching them up, and determining whether engaging in them jointly reduces cost. In this process you need to take care that you have strong arguments for cost reductions based on specific qualitative and quantitative evidence. General statements of lower costs due to scale and size do not have much meaning unless they are disassembled and quantified.

Furthermore, the potential for scale and scope differs among various activities of the business, so your analysis needs to identify those activities where the effects are of the greatest importance. These are activities where a large percent of the cost structure lies and/or where the magnitude of scale or scope is large.

An illustration of such analysis is found in the home appliance manufacturing industry. Exhibit 5.6 shows the activities performed in manufacturing appliances, beginning with research and development and extending through customer service. Upstream in the chain there are few benefits from being a broad-line producer except for the possibility of sharing some more generic elements of research and

Exhibit 5.6 Relative Importance of Scale and Scope Economics in the Major Appliance Industry

	Research & Development	Purchasing	Manufacturing	Distribution	Advertising	Sales	Service	Contract Market
Percentage of cost structure	3%	30%	25%	6%	2%	7%	3%	
Scale economies within a line	+	+	+++	+	+			
Scope economies across lines		+		+++	++	+++	+++	+++

design. However, in manufacturing individual appliances, scale effects are considerable as is the size of the minimum efficient scale plant—500 000 units a year. Scope effects are therefore modest at this end of the chain as all appliances are produced on separate lines. Downstream scope effects are significant. Distribution, branding, sales, and service are all more efficient when done on a large scale across a full line of products.

Looking now at the strategy of major players in the appliance business in the mid-1980s, Exhibit 5.7 shows that each was pursuing a different strategy given its arena. Design and Manufacture (D&M) was a focused private-label producer of dishwashers. It offered no other product and had no downstream capabilities in distribution, sales, or service. Maytag followed a focused differentiated strategy as a narrow-line producer of laundry equipment. Sears, which commanded the largest market share in the industry, did no manufacturing but sold and serviced a wide range of products under the Kenmore brand. General Electric (GE) and Whirlpool manufactured, distributed, and serviced a full line of appliances, although they did no retailing.

These companies with different arenas and different activities were able to exist simultaneously in the appliance industry because each had access to the necessary scope and scale economies throughout the chain although not always within the boundary of their own organizations. D&M was large enough to realize significant scale effects in manufacturing dishwashers but following manufacture, it handed its products off to large retailers that had access to downstream scope economies. Sears realized significant scope economies in distribution, sales, and services while buying appliances in large-enough quantities to sustain its suppliers. GE and Whirlpool manufactured multiple product lines, with scale effects in each, and realized economies in distribution, branding, and service.

The history of Maytag illustrates the vulnerability of pursuing a single-business strategy in a dynamic industry. For many years Maytag followed a focused differentiated strategy. It built its differentiation when the industry was fragmented. The company enjoyed a reputation as a quality leader in the home appliance industry. Its reputation for quality was reflected in the durability and reliability of its washers and dryers. Quality was also reflected in its promotion of the "Ol' Lonely" Maytag repairman. The strategy required that the company engage in activities throughout the value chain that preserved its high-quality image.

As the industry matured Maytag was slow to see the downstream economies that were emerging. Its management recognized too late that Maytag's narrow product line and extensive vertical scope would not produce success. At this point it acquired a handful of marginal producers to fill out its product line. This produced a host of quality problems that directly threatened the basis of Maytag's differentiation— quality. Maytag was eventually bought by the Whirlpool Corp. in 2005.

The above example shows that scale and scope economies can translate into material advantages for the company. But the competitive environment is dynamic so one needs to be continually re-evaluating the sources of scale and scope advantages and pursuing them as appropriate.

In recent years the competitive pressures on the appliance industry have increased tremendously with the entry of low-cost manufacturers from Asia and the consolidation of retailers selling appliances. Manufacturers have responded by focusing on those components that account for the greatest share of costs. They consolidated production in larger, low-cost plants and lowered the costs of purchasing. Consolidating production often involved buying out the competitors and then moving production to lower cost

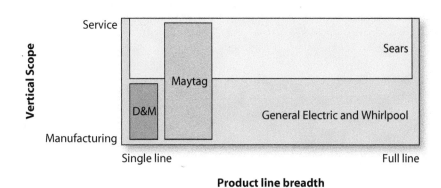

Exhibit 5.7 The Strategy of Major Players in the Appliance Business

locations. In this process much of the North American production was moved to Mexico by GE, which owns 48 percent of Controladora Mabe S.A., Mexico's largest appliance manufacturer, and by Whirlpool, which bought Vitromatic S.A. de C.V., Mexico's second-largest appliance manufacturer. Meanwhile, Samsung and LG have built plants in Mexico and Haier has built a plant in South Carolina. Canada now has only three appliance plants left.[19] In addition, the major manufacturers developed global purchasing programs through which they buy key components, parts, and materials anywhere in the world for delivery anywhere in the world based on best delivered value in meeting product specifications. Many key components and parts come from a well-known set of suppliers in low-cost countries and are common to all appliance manufacturers.

1. Let's revisit the activity analysis described in this feature. Pick an industry that has several competitors for which you can find operational details. Describe the value chain for this industry. Then pick two competitors that have different strategic positions and describe the value-chain activity of each. Finally, explain how the differences in the activities performed support the position each has chosen.

2. Pick two industries that are at different stages in the industry life cycle. Describe the major activities in the value chain for each industry. Then compare the activities performed by each, noting the relative importance of each activity and how it is performed.

Premium Brand Image

When Toyota introduced its premium Lexus line in 1989, its strategy was based on extensive analysis of the U.S. market for luxury cars and product development efforts—the project was called Luxury Export United States, or Lexus, and became the name of the car. Relying on its ability to manufacture high-quality automobiles, Toyota was confident that it could penetrate the highly profitable luxury car segment. To support this entirely new brand, it developed a separate dealer network. When introduced into North America, the car won many technical awards that used targeted marketing to create customer awareness.

Convenience and Customization

Some companies have emphasized a particular aspect that sets them apart from the competition. Grocery Gateway, the online grocer, took the hassle and inconvenience out of grocery shopping by picking and then delivering groceries to the customer's home.[20] Curves International customized its gyms to appeal to older, less fit women who feel more comfortable with their peers. The small, local gyms are open only to women and the 10 to 12 hydraulic-resistance machines in each gym are easy to use. And it billed its exercise program as providing a 90-minute workout in 30 minutes. Curves was started in 1992 by an entrepreneur in Harlingen, Texas, and in 2008 had opened more than 10 000 locations around the world, with 669 across Canada.[21] In the past three years more than 2 500 U.S. franchisees have closed, in part due to cheaper competition and a depressed economy.[22]

Unique Styling

Some companies use style, fashion, and design as key ingredients in creating an advantage through differentiation. Ironically, this can result in premium prices even when product quality is not particularly high. For instance, Harley-Davidson generates prices for motorcycles that exceed those of the competition even though its quality is measurably lower. Why would a potential motorcycle customer pay more for a Harley when it breaks down more often and requires more regular trips to the repair shop? Because many customers for large motorcycles are looking for the image that a Harley-Davidson motorcycle portrays. At a technical level, Honda motorcycles are superior and their quality is higher. Yet, for many enthusiasts, the styling, sound, and image offered by a Harley is worth every penny (or every US$7 000 to US$20 000, as the case may be) that they cost.

Speed

Speed comes in many different ways; for instance, it can mean how fast the customer is served or how fast products are updated. Intel is a company that has relied on its capacity to innovate to produce ever more complex integrated circuits that have greater power. Its speed of innovation is expressed in Moore's Law, a prediction attributed to Intel's co-founder Gordon Moore, that the number of transistors on an integrated circuit (a microchip) double every 18 to 24 months. Intel has used its innovative capacity to develop new products before competitors. Apple, Dell, and related product developers such as Microsoft have engineered their leading-edge products around Intel microchips, helping create a high demand for Intel's product.

Unusually High Quality

Apple's computers cost, on average, 10 percent more than comparably equipped Dell computers. The reason cited most often by Apple users who pay this premium is the quality of the hardware and software. Its operating system is demonstrably more reliable and less susceptible to crashing than the Windows operating system installed on Dell computers. Similarly, in the fast-food industry, quality makes a difference. Customers willingly pay four times more for gourmet hamburgers at Red Robin locations in Alberta and British Columbia and Fuddruckers restaurants in Saskatchewan than they do at McDonald's, Wendy's, or Burger King because the product is of significantly higher quality.

Creating Value and Promoting Willingness to Pay

Differentiation works when the business can charge a price that more than recovers the extra costs of delivering the value-added features. The more successful the business is with this

willingness to pay Principle of differentiation strategy by which customers are willing to pay more for certain product features.

strategy, the greater the difference between price and its costs, and so the greater its profit margin when compared to competitors.

Threats to Successful Competitive Positioning

For a company using any of the generic strategies that we've discussed in this chapter, success hinges on a number of factors. Does the company have the right resources, such as those that may accrue from scale or learning, for implementing a low-cost strategy? Will the marketplace reward a differentiation strategy? In some markets (those that, like steel, are more commodity-like), customers' purchase decisions are driven much more strongly by price than by product features, and in these cases there's not much that companies can do to justify higher prices. A summary of the common drivers of differentiation and low-cost advantage, along with the threats to those positions, is listed in Exhibit 5.8. Under most circumstances, a successful strategic position must satisfy two requirements: (1) It must be based on the company's resources and capabilities and (2) it must achieve some level of consistency with the conditions that prevail in the industry.

THREATS TO LOW-COST POSITIONS

In terms of these two critical requirements, let's look first at the numerous threats facing companies aiming for a low-cost competitive position. First, the company may face threats on the technological front. In particular, the resource that makes it possible for a company to compete on the basis of cost—often a certain technology—can be imitated. Efficient production and process technologies can move from company to company by any number of means, such as consultants with clients throughout the industry and the movement of key personnel from company to company.

Granted, even though an imitator may acquire comparable technology, the original company may still enjoy the benefits of greater experience and the learning curve. A more serious threat to low-cost competitors is the possibility that another company may introduce a new technology—one that, like mini-mill technology in the steel industry, supports a different scale and a more efficient learning process. In such cases, even small latecomers can establish cost positions significantly lower than those of larger, more experienced low-cost leaders.

Second, low-cost leadership means offering an acceptable combination of price and quality. A real threat to an intended low-cost position is the failure to offer sufficient quality to satisfy buyers' basic needs. As described earlier, Dollarama's success is not simply due to its low prices. It has been able to compete with Wal-Mart by coupling lower prices with creative and quality products. While low cost is a driver in the customer buying process, quality leads them to return and buy again.

Recently, the treatment of labour in low-cost competitors has become an issue. Some businesses in developing countries where labour is plentiful have struggled to stay competitive by

Exhibit 5.8 Low Cost and Differentiation: Drivers and Threats

	Drivers	Threats
Low Cost	• Economies of scale • Learning • Economies of scope • Superior technology • Superior product design	• New technology • Inferior quality • Social, political, and economic risk of outsourcing
Differentiation	• Premium brand image • Customization • Unique styling • Speed • Convenient access • Unusually high quality	• Failing to increase buyers' willingness to pay higher prices • Underestimating costs of differentiation • Overfulfilling buyers' needs • Lower-cost imitation

keeping labour costs as low as possible. Practices they have used include extended working hours, limited or no basic employee services, employing children, and violating safety and health standards in the workplace. Watchdog groups regularly publicize such cases, and the reforms they demand push up costs.[23] Increased public awareness in countries where protection of labour is stronger has led consumers in these countries to demand better treatment of labour in the low-cost countries. Many multinational companies buying from low-cost suppliers have established codes of ethical conduct for their suppliers, but enforcing these standards—inspecting and auditing overseas suppliers—also increases costs.

THREATS TO DIFFERENTIATION POSITIONS

The intent to provide a differentiated product does not necessarily result in competitive advantage and enhanced profitability. Three situations can sabotage a differentiation strategy. First is that customers are not willing to pay for the differentiating feature although including it is costly. Until recently, Audi had manufacturing costs comparable to those of BMW and Mercedes, but it could not get customers to pay comparable prices so its profit margin suffered. Several years ago John Deere incorporated expensive IT technologies in their farm tractors. While farmers liked the technologies, they were unwilling to pay its price. Deere now introduces new features gradually, at a pace that keeps them ahead of competitors but only as quickly as farmers demonstrate their willingness to pay.

Second is the failure of management to recognize the cost of differentiation. Jaguar in the early 1980s had highly differentiated cars for which buyers paid premium prices. Unfortunately, hands-on manufacturing processes meant that costs were so high that the company lost money. Ironically, Jaguar's managers were proud of its antiquated processes in part because managers believed that customers appreciated them. Ford purchased Jaguar in 1990 and attempted to address costs by partially automating assembly plants so that the best aspects of both traditional and modern methods were combined.[24] But even with these changes Ford could not cut costs enough to be profitable so it sold the troubled brand to Tata of India in 2008.

Third is the easy imitation of the differentiating feature. When competitors have matched a product's unique feature, it is no longer unique and so loses its ability to command premium prices. For example, in Southern Ontario, Exclusively Women's Fitness Centres has pursued the same demographic audience as Curves—older, less active females. But it has also sought to differentiate itself by adding additional services that appeal especially to women such as child care, weight loss and nutrition centres, and spas. Coca-Cola and Pepsi have discouraged imitation by exercising bargaining power over suppliers and buyers and conducting aggressive marketing campaigns to sustain brand image.

THREATS TO FOCUS POSITIONS

Focused low-cost or focused differentiation positions are specialized cases of low cost leadership and broad differentiation so are subject to all the same threats as those just reviewed. But they face one additional threat because they are focused. Competitors can come along that take away their customers by being more focused than the original company with the focused strategy. This can happen because the original company diffuses its focus as it expands to meet the needs of ever more customers. Alternatively, a competitor can come along that has a more finely segmented understanding of the market place and so is able to craft a strategy that has greater appeal to a subset of customers served by the original focused competitor. For instance, Harley-Davidson faces the threat that custom chopper shops will pull away customers because they can more uniquely satisfy the needs of a segment of Harley's market.

THREATS TO INTEGRATED POSITIONS

Michael Porter argues that a good strategy is one that competitors have difficulty copying without doing everything the same way. Competitors that try to pursue several generic strategies are said to be **straddling**, and they can get "stuck in the middle" and so perform neither strategy well. Porter dealt with this by pointing out that the generic strategies were mutually

straddling Unsuccessful attempt to integrate both low-cost and differentiation positions.

exclusive. He warned against the temptation to straddle positions: Companies that try both to differentiate and to achieve a low-cost position will end up straddling two inconsistent positions.[25]

All companies, Porter suggested, must make decisions about their positioning in the market and will consequently choose one strategy over another. Developing a low-cost strategy means that a company must forego subsequent opportunities to enhance product uniqueness or quality (that is, to develop a position based on differentiation). In this respect, selected strategies and foregone opportunities must be regarded as tradeoffs. H&R Block, for example, can't enter the field of high-level estate and tax planning because such services require the high-cost specialists that a low-cost competitor cannot afford. Thus, H&R Block trades off the advantages of high-margin services for the advantages of a low-cost tax preparation business. By the same token, a "pure" differentiator trades off the cost-saving advantages of producing standardized products for the advantages of satisfying a demand for customized products.

Although many companies have succeeded in pursuing integrated strategies, it is still critical for managers to understand the tradeoffs they make when they opt for one position over the other. Virtually no company can succeed in being all things to all customers. For one, companies need to know exactly what opportunities they're foregoing.

Second, knowing what tradeoffs can be made in an industry helps managers recognize what competitors can and can't do in attempts to juggle strategies. WestJet's rise in popularity and success in the late 1990s pushed Air Canada to try to compete with the low-cost provider. In 2001, Air Canada combined its various regional carriers (Air BC, Air Nova, Air Ontario, and Canadian Regional Airlines) to form Air Canada Jazz, which was modelled along the lines of WestJet and directly with it by focusing on low-cost regional flights. In 2006, Air Canada Jazz became an independent company known as Jazz Air Income Fund. In 2007, Air Canada Jazz's total sales of $881 million were still well short of WestJet's $2.1 billion and its profit margin of 1.6 percent heavily trailed WestJet's almost 9 percent profit margin The likely explanation for this is that Jazz had to combine practices, planes, personnel, and routes of existing airlines so was unable to copy WestJet's model.[26]

In the United States, Southwest Airlines, after which WestJet was modelled, was protected from straddling by the larger airlines such as United, American, and Delta because its lower cost position reflected many decisions they were unable to copy. United, Delta, and American do not have the option of flying just one type of aircraft, even if this practice saves on training and maintenance costs. Nor can they abandon their expensive hub facilities, which are integral to the logistics of their flight systems, even though the hub system and its accompanying gate fees are much more costly than Southwest's, which uses secondary airports in smaller destination cities.

Strategy and Fit with Industry Conditions

 Economic Logic

In Chapter 1, we introduced the strategy-diamond model of strategy formulation. Recall that an important input into this model is a company's objectives. Earlier in the chapter we detailed generic strategies *by type*, but in order to show how the strategy-diamond and generic-strategy models are compatible, we need to remind ourselves that when managers decide on generic competitive positions, they aren't deciding on strategies themselves: ◆ Rather, they are stating *objectives* with respect to several elements of their overall strategy—indicating precisely how they intend the company to deal systematically with differentiators, economic logic, and certain aspects of arenas.

Industry conditions have an important effect on strategy formulation. This is evident from the opportunities and threats presented to a company during each phase of the industry life cycle. In this section, each phase of the life cycle will be treated as if conditions are not likely to change in the short term. Industry analysis can be used to take a snapshot view of the industry at that point. In reality, many industries are changing rapidly. This will be recognized in Chapter 6, where strategies are considered that take advantage of changes such as when an industry moves from one stage into the next. For now, the appropriateness of particular strategies is described given the life-cycle stage.

STRATEGIES FOR DIFFERENT INDUSTRY LIFE-CYCLE CONDITIONS

Industry conditions should inform strategic leaders and have an influence on the strategies their companies formulate. Of course, not all companies will respond similarly to different industry conditions, but conditions at different phases of an industry life cycle provide differential opportunities and constraints. Consequently, companies' strategies tend to vary across these different phases. Exhibit 5.9 summarizes some of the more common effects of the industry life cycle on the elements of companies' strategies.

Embryonic Stage

During an industry's *embryonic* phase, business models are unproven, no standardized technology has been established, capital needs generally outstrip the resources and capabilities of start-ups, and uncertainty is high. Early movers—those who succeed in establishing solid competitive positions during this stage—can set themselves up to be in a strong position during later phases of the industry life cycle.[27] Because primary demand is just being established and customers lack

Exhibit 5.9 Strategies Tailored to Industry Life Cycle

Phase of Industry Life Cycle	Arenas	Vehicles	Differentiators	Staging	Economic Logic
Embryonic	Staying local	Internal development Alliances to secure missing inputs or distribution access	Target basic needs, minimal differentiation	Tactics to gain early footholds	Prices tend to be high Costs are high; focus is on securing additional capital to fund growth phase
Growth	Penetrating adjacent markets	Alliances for cooperation Acquisitions in targeted markets	Increase efforts toward differentiation Low-cost leaders emerge through experience and scale advantages	Integrated positions require choice of focusing first on cost or differentiation	Margins can improve rapidly because of experience and scale Price premiums accrue to successful differentiators
Mature	Globalizing Diversifying	Mergers and acquisitions for consolidation	More stable positions emerge across competitors	Choices of international markets and new industry diversification need rational sequencing	Consolidation results in fewer competitors (favouring higher margins), but declining growth demands cost containment and rationalization of operations
Decline	Abandoning some arenas if decline is severe Focusing on segments that provide the most profitability	Acquisitions for diversifying Divestitures enable some competitors to exit and others to consolidate larger shares of the market	Fewer competitors result in less pressure for differentiation, but declining sales results in greater pressure for cost savings	Timing of exit from selected segments or businesses	Rationalizing cost

good information on the relative quality of products, successful tactics during this phase include getting a strong foothold and building capacity to meet growing demand.

One industry in the embryonic stage is the industry producing alternative sources of power. The demand for alternatives has produced many companies focused on developing fuel cell technology. At present, the combination of fuels and oxidants that will produce the most commercially viable products is unclear. Hence, many companies are developing alternative technologies that are currently in demonstration projects. One of the leading companies in this research is Burnaby, B.C.–based Ballard Power Systems. Its technology uses hydrogen as its fuel and oxygen as its oxidant. The company has had considerable success but has found developing the advanced technologies needed both difficult and expensive. The company, which never made a profit between 1998 and 2007, sold its automotive fuel cell technology to Daimler and Ford in 2007. Its failure to commercialize that technology pushed down its U.S. market capitalization from a peak of US$8.4 billion in 2000 to US$616.5 million in 2007. The sale, valued at US$100 million, saw about 20 percent of Ballard's workforce move to the new company. This gave Ballard cash for additional research and narrowed its focus on the fuel cells it is seeking to commercialize.

Growth Stage

As industries enter periods of rapid growth, incumbent companies increase market share by taking advantage of footholds established earlier. Rapid growth increases speed down the learning curve and presents leaders with an opportunity to establish low-cost positions that are difficult to imitate, at least in the short term. During this phase, however, technologies can change as new entrants learn from and improve on the work of early movers.

After introducing the PalmPilot, for example, Palm enjoyed an apparently formidable advantage in the personal digital assistant (PDA) industry. The PalmPilot was hailed as the most successful consumer-product launch in history, reaching sales of 2 million units within three years and surpassing the adoption rates of camcorders, colour TVs, VCRs, and cellphones.[28] As the PDA industry grew in size, new companies entered the high-potential market, including Research In Motion (RIM). Like Palm, RIM created its own software for the BlackBerry, its PDA device. Originally targeted at the business customer, RIM's BlackBerry gained popularity in the mainstream consumer market as well and in 2005 moved ahead of the PalmPilot as the market leader in PDA devices. Even Palm's new webOS smartphone platform, while well received by analysts and reviewers, never caught on with consumers as the firm made critical mistakes in its rollout, marketing, and planning.[29] This shows that moving early and quickly along the learning curve doesn't necessarily constitute an impenetrable competitive barrier to competition. New technologies and changing industry competitive structure remain threats.[30, 31]

During the growth phase of an industry, companies make important decisions about how they intend to grow: They determine the strategic vehicles that they'll use to implement their preferred strategies. High-tech companies, for example, may seek alliances with established companies in adjacent industries, similar to the embryonic stage, in order to fill in gaps in their own range of competencies. Such is the case in the biotechnology industry; virtually all of the pure biotech companies have established alliances with large pharmaceutical companies in order to access clinical trial expertise and marketing capabilities.[32] During the growth stage, too, companies with desirable resources become attractive acquisition targets, both for incumbents wanting to grow rapidly and for companies in related industries seeking to enter the market.

Maturity Stage

As industries mature and growth slows, products become more familiar to the vast majority of potential customers. Product information is more widely available, and quality becomes a more important factor in consumer choice. A mature market, therefore, increases the ability of companies to reap premium prices from differentiation strategies.

Mature industries often undergo *consolidation*—the combination of competitors through merger or acquisition. Consolidation is often motivated by the twofold objective of exploiting economies of scale and increasing market power. For example, the North American bicycle industry profiled through the examples of Pacific Cycle, Trek, and Cervélo has experienced a virtual cascade of mergers and acquisitions for the better part of a decade. Although each new combination promises cost savings through greater economies of scale, evidence of significant savings remains inconclusive at best. Market power is a factor because many bicycle companies want to stay large enough to serve the needs of big-box retailers.

The pharmaceutical industry is a mature industry in which the large companies selling ethical or prescription-only drugs are finding it increasingly difficult to sustain performance. Their problem is that, as patents on older drugs expire, they have trouble developing new blockbuster drugs. They have tried to address this by massive consolidation to achieve greater economies of scale and a rapid scale up in sales and marketing activity to broaden reach. From 1988 to 2003, industry consolidation through merger and acquisition increased the market share of the top 10 pharmaceutical companies from 26 percent to 47 percent. Companies that are more successful with mergers have acquired companies providing new products. Roche, which bought a majority holding in U.S.–based biotech Genentech in 1990, has enjoyed great success, as has Johnson and Johnson (J&J), which adopted a strategy of smaller, "bolt-on" acquisitions. For example, in 2009 J&J agreed to pay US$1 billion for an 18.4 percent stake in Irish drugmaker Elan Corporation plc and US$500 million for a majority stake in its pipeline of experimental Alzheimer disease drugs. In addition, J&J has an option to help finance Elan's purchase of Biogen Idec's rights to Tysabri in the event that Biogen is acquired. This drug is expected to generate US$1 billion a year.

Decline Stage

In declining industries, products can take on the attributes of quasi commodities. Because price competition can be intense, containing costs is critical, and companies with low-cost positions have an advantage. Although customers don't entirely ignore differentiated products, declining sales discourage companies from investing in significant innovations.

During this stage, many companies consider the strategy of exiting the industry. Generally, the decision to exit means selling the company or certain divisions to competing companies. Because demand is declining, the industry probably suffers from overcapacity. Thus, reducing the number of competitors can enhance the profitability of those companies that remain. But this fact doesn't mean that exit signifies failure. In many cases, exit can be the best use of shareholders' resources.

The apparel industry in high-wage countries has been in decline since 2001. Canadian production, employment, and export levels in Canada are half of what they were at the beginning of the decade. This decline does not mean that demand is decreasing but rather that demand in Canada and in the United States, which was its main export market, are being increasingly satisfied by imports from low-wage countries. While many Canadian companies have gone out of business, some have been successful because they have dealt with the challenging environment.

Winnipeg-based Western Glove Works Ltd. designs, manufactures, and sells denim shorts, capris, and jeans—five million pair in 2008. The company makes its own brands, including Silver and 1921, and is the private-label manufacturer for Victoria Beckham's dVb line and Sheryl Crow's Bootheel Trading Co. as well as a number of retailers including Wal-Mart and Mark's Work Warehouse. Its products are sold through stores as well as online. Starting in 2001, it gradually shifted its manufacture of jeans in Canada to contract factories in China, Bangladesh, India, Hong Kong, and elsewhere. In 2008, it stopped manufacturing jeans in Winnipeg. Although production has ceased, Western Glove still has a staff of about 125 doing the company's distribution, marketing, merchandising, and design in Winnipeg. Bob Silver, the CEO of the private company, said, "Over the last three to five years I have tried everything I could think of to justify continuation of production. ... But it is just no longer possible."[33]

Montreal-based Gildan Activewear is another Canadian company that has moved production offshore. Gildan manufactures and sells blank T-shirts to major screen printers that add designs and logos for resale to companies or event organizers for advertising purposes. It has become a low-cost leader in the North American market for T-shirts. Gildan achieved its low-cost position by relocating its manufacturing facilities in low-wage countries such as Honduras. There, its 15 000 employees are engaged in Gildan's vertical integrated activities of yarn spinning, knitting, dyeing, finishing, cutting, and sewing operations. The company continues to invest significant capital in new facilities that house the latest state-of-the-art manufacturing equipment and technology. In 2009, Gildan recorded sales of US$1.0 billion and net earnings of US$95 million.

An alternative approach has been taken by Vancouver-based Arc'teryx, named after the first dinosaur to fly, which was founded in 1991. Its strategy relied on isolating itself from the threat of imports from low-wage countries by producing high-end outdoor gear such as mountain climbing jackets, backpacks, gloves, and other clothing. Arc'teryx is now widely recognized as the leading North American specialist in outdoor apparel, climbing equipment, and high-end protective shells. It has accomplished this using a team of outdoor enthusiasts who understand the market and are constantly finding better ways to meet its customers' needs. The company has produced more than 40 product innovations in its 16-year history, which include new construction technology, paradigm-shifting designs, and major fabric technology developments. Its highly complex products are manufactured at its Vancouver facility. In 2001 Arc'teryx was acquired by Adidas-Salomon AG, which retained the management team and let it operate with minimal intervention from the new parent company.

Testing the Quality of a Strategy

Now that you have command of an adequate repertoire of strategy formulation tools—namely, the strategy diamond, VRINE model, industry structure, and the strategic positioning models—you should be able to use them to test the quality of a company's strategy. Clearly, developing a successful business strategy is a complex task. Although we've focused in this chapter on decisions regarding competitive position and strategic interactions, we must also stress that evaluating the effectiveness of a strategy requires that you apply all the tools and models that we've discussed in the first five chapters of this book. In this section, we'll lay out a simple five-step process that makes use of all of these tools and models to evaluate the quality of a company's strategy. These steps are summarized in Exhibit 5.10.[34]

Exhibit 5.10 Testing the Quality of Your Strategy

Adapted from D. C. Hambrick and J. W. Fredrickson, "Are You Sure You Have a Strategy?" *Academy of Management Executive* 15:4 (2001): 48–59.

Key Evaluation Criteria	
1. Does your strategy exploit your key resources?	With your particular mix of resources, does this strategy give you an advantageous position relative to your competitors?
	Can you pursue this strategy more economically than your competitors?
	Do you have the capital and managerial talent to do all you plan to do?
	Are you spread too thin?
2. Does your strategy fit with current industry conditions?	Is there healthy profit potential where you're headed?
	Are you aligned with the key success factors of your industry?
3. Will your differentiators be sustainable?	Will competitors have difficulty imitating you?
	If imitation can't be foreclosed, does your strategy include a ceaseless regimen of innovation and opportunity creation to keep distance between you and the competition?
4. Are the elements of your strategy consistent and aligned with your strategic position?	Have you made choices of arenas, vehicles, differentiators, staging, and economic logic?
	Do they all fit and mutually reinforce each other?
5. Can your strategy be implemented?	Will your stakeholders allow you to pursue this strategy?
	Do you have the proper complement of implementation levers in place?
	Is the management team able and willing to lead the required changes?

DOES YOUR STRATEGY EXPLOIT YOUR COMPANY'S RESOURCES AND CAPABILITIES?

Your first step in testing the quality of a strategy is determining whether your strategy and competitive position exploit your company's resources and capabilities. Low-cost strategic positions require manufacturing resources and capabilities that are likely to contribute to a cost advantage. For instance, Pacific Cycle is the lowest cost bike distributor in North America by virtue of its lean operations and the complete outsourcing of bike manufacturing to Taiwan and China. Likewise, a differentiation position depends on your ability to produce quality products and to project the necessary image of quality. In Trek's case, it has been careful to cultivate its high-performance image by sponsoring bike luminaries such as Lance Armstrong and selling only through the exclusive independent dealer channel. When two companies follow similar strategies, you must determine whether you can use your resources to implement your strategy more economically than your competitors can. Finally, you need to be sure that you have the capital resources—financial and human—necessary to pull off your strategy.

DOES YOUR STRATEGY FIT WITH CURRENT INDUSTRY CONDITIONS?

Next, you must ask whether your strategy fits with the current conditions in your competitive environment. You need to know whether that environment is hostile, benign, or somewhere in between. Essentially, you want to be sure that you understand the profit *potential* of both your current position and the position toward which your strategy is taking you. Pacific Cycle viewed the big-box retailers and consolidation of the bike industry as opportunities for profitable growth. Ironically, Trek viewed the same environment with an eye toward shoring up relationships with independent bike dealers as a way to combat the influx of sales through low-cost, big-box retail channels. Thus, you need to determine whether your strategy aligns with the key success factors favoured by your competitive environment.

ARE YOUR DIFFERENTIATORS SUSTAINABLE?

If competitors can imitate your differentiators, can you protect your current relationship with your customers? Imitation can erode competitive advantage, but some forms of imitation can reinforce brand loyalty to individual companies. Frequent flyer programs, for example, are very easy to imitate, but customers who have accumulated many points with one carrier are harder to steal than those who do not have very many points. Ironically, then, imitation in this case actually serves to increase existing brand loyalty and, potentially, to benefit both companies. Frequent flyer programs put up barriers to customer mobility, and without some kind of barrier that increases the cost of switching brands, a company with easily imitated differentiators will have to rely on a continual stream of innovative offerings in order to sustain revenues.

ARE THE ELEMENTS OF YOUR STRATEGY CONSISTENT AND ALIGNED WITH YOUR STRATEGIC POSITION?

Your next step in testing the quality of a strategy is determining whether all of the elements of your strategy diamond are not only internally consistent but that they are also aligned with your strategic position, whether it is the one you occupy currently or the one toward which your strategy may direct you in the future. The challenge is to ensure that your choices of arenas, vehicles, differentiators, staging, and economic logic are mutually reinforcing and consistent with your objective, whether it's to be a low-cost leader, a differentiator, or a focused company. For instance, to be poised for the growth phase, your strategy will need to accommodate rapid growth through the use of acquisitions or significant internal development of additional products and services. If you do not do so, your company will be marginalized. This may be an acceptable outcome if the intended strategic position is one of focus. Alternatively, if your industry is approaching the end of the growth phase, have you implemented appropriate cost containment measures that will be required when additional price competition increases? The key is to make clear and explicit links between the vision of the company, your strategy, and industry conditions. When these factors are aligned, the likelihood of achieving your objectives is maximized. When one of these features is not in alignment with the others, lack of coherence almost always causes the company to slip behind competitors.

CAN YOUR STRATEGY BE IMPLEMENTED?

Concocting a brilliant strategy within the safe confines of your office at headquarters does you no good if your company can't implement it. To test whether your strategy can be implemented, you need to make sure that it's aligned with the appropriate implementation levers. For instance, do you have the appropriate people, the necessary systems and processes, and incentives that are congruent with your objectives? If not, can you make these modifications within the organization in time to execute the strategy? Do you have the sufficient managerial talent and interest to pursue the strategy? One of the biggest obstacles to company growth is insufficient managerial resources (e.g., time, people, interest) to focus on the details of execution. As a start-up, WestJet offered low-cost flying with people who care. It consistently advertised that all its employees were owners and provided the best service possible. To provide what it advertised, WestJet had to hire staff, pilots, and flight attendants who fit the corporate culture and desired and accepted part-ownership in the company as part of their compensation. The most successful companies routinely discuss the integration of strategy and leadership. For instance, all discussions of new strategic initiatives will include answers to the question of "who exactly will get this done?" If there is no clear answer to this question, or if those individuals are likely to be spread too thin as a consequence, even attractive plans should not be given a green light.

Summary of Challenges

1. *Define generic strategies and explain how they relate to a company's strategic position.* Strategic positioning is the concept of how executives situate or locate their company relative to rivals along important competitive dimensions. The strategic positioning model—Michael Porter's generic strategy model—is an enduring classic in the field of strategic management. Porter's strategy model uses two dimensions: the potential source of strategic advantage and the breadth of the strategic target market. The four generic strategies are low-cost leader, differentiation, focused low-cost, and focused differentiation.

2. *Describe the drivers of low-cost, differentiation, and focused strategic positions.* Low-cost leaders must have resources or capabilities that enable them to produce a product at a significantly lower cost than rivals. Successful low-cost leaders generally have superior economies of scale, are farther down the learning curve, or have superior production or process technologies than their rivals. However, to substantially reduce costs over rivals, low-cost leaders generally have to be willing to make tradeoffs—they cannot offer all the features, attributes, and quality that a successful differentiator can. Like-

wise, successful differentiators will normally have to accept higher costs than low-cost leaders. To make a differentiation strategy pay off, companies must segment the market so that customer needs are well understood, products are designed to satisfy uniquely those needs, and the products offered increase a customer's willingness to pay. Companies that attempt to straddle both positions generally do not perform well along either dimension. However, some companies have been successful at integrating basic features of both low-cost and differentiation. Those that do typically perfect one set of economic drivers before trying to complement those with the seemingly inconsistent drivers associated with the other economic logic. A focused strategy is generally the application of a low-cost or differentiation approach to a narrowly defined arena.

3. *Identify and explain the risks associated with each generic strategic position.* Successful strategic positions are still vulnerable. Threats to low-cost leadership include not having the resources necessary to implement the position, having low-cost drivers imitated by companies with better products, and not having sufficient quality to attract buyers. Threats to a

differentiation strategy include increasing costs significantly to differentiate a product only to misperceive customer preferences, excessive cost to provide the targeted differentiation, and differentiating in ways that are easily imitated. A company relying on a focus strategy risks growing too large, trying to meet too many needs, and then being outfocused by a more specialized company. An integrated position runs the risk of unsuccessfully straddling the logic of seemingly inconsistent economic drivers, resulting in neither a low-cost position nor a differentiated one.

4. *Show how different strategic positions fit with stages of the industry life cycle.* During embryonic stages, primary demand is just beginning, and customers lack good information on the relative quality of products. Thus, building a strong foothold and the capacity to meet growing demand are more important than aggressively differentiating products. During growth stages, building on early footholds provides incumbents with an opportunity to gain market share and move down the learning curve and establish low-cost positions. Maturity stages bring lower levels of growth, and information is widely available to customers. Differentiation can reduce competitive

threats and result in higher prices. During industry decline, price competition intensifies and cost containment becomes more important.

5. *Evaluate the quality of the company's strategy.* The quality of a company's strategy can be assessed by answering a few questions that can be answered by the basic tools of strategy, including the strategy diamond, VRINE model, industry structure, and the strategic positioning models. First, you must determine whether the strategy and competitive position exploit the company's resources and capabilities. Strategic positions such as low-cost leadership and differentiation have economic assumptions that cannot be satisfied in the absence of complementary resources and capabilities. Second, a quality strategy will also fit with the external environment—the current environment and the anticipated environment in dynamic contexts. Third, a company's differentiators must be sustainable. Fourth, all of the elements of the strategy diamond must be internally consistent and aligned with the current or desired strategic position. Finally, a quality strategy is one that can be implemented by the company. Brilliant plans are of little value if the company is unable to execute them.

Review Questions

1. What do we mean by *generic strategies*?
2. What criteria must be met in order for differentiators and low-cost leaders to be successful?
3. What is the relationship between economies of scale and minimum efficient scale?
4. What are economies of scope?
5. How does the learning curve work?

6. What is market segmentation? What role does it play in strategic positioning?
7. What is willingness to pay? How does it relate to strategic positioning?
8. How does the industry life cycle affect business strategy?
9. What are the steps in testing the quality of a strategy?

Experiential Activities

Group Exercises

1. Review the opening vignette about the three bicycle manufacturers. Use the strategy-diamond and the generic-strategy model to describe the positioning strategy of each company. Based on what you know about the bicycle industry, can you identify any underserved (or overserved) segments?
2. Go back to Exhibit 5.1 in Chapter 5. Identify low-cost leaders from two of these industries. What seem to be the drivers of their cost-leadership positioning strategies? Are they the same? If not, why?

Debates

1. Among the global trends facing business, it is increasingly unclear who should provide basic social services (e.g., pensions, public health services, school infrastructure), regulate business and personal behaviour (e.g., self-regulation versus government oversight), and be accountable for protecting rights, public goods, and resources. In developing a business strategy, where should a company's leaders draw the line between what is acceptable from a purely legal standpoint and what would be dictated by the ethics of different generations or demographic segments of consumers?

2. Environmental issues, including climate change, are increasingly discussed in the executive suite as it relates to strategy formulation and implementation. How "green" should a company be that is pursuing a low-cost strategy in an increasingly environmentally conscious society? And if following a differentiation strategy, would customers pay extra for being "green?" Is "green" a viable differentiator in either low cost or differentiation?

Endnotes

1. Personal interview with Trek executives, Fall 2004; "Trek Bicycle Corporation Hoover's Company In-Depth Records," *Hoover's*, www. hoovers.com. Accessed September 28, 2005; S. Silcoff, "Dorel Buys Biggest U.S. Cycle Maker: Gains 27% of U.S. Market Share with US$310M Purchase of Schwinn, GT Brands," *Financial Post*, January 14, 2004, p. 1; www.montaguebikes.com/montague_history.html. Accessed October 20, 2005; B. Mader, "Shifting into High Gear," *The Business Journal of Milwaukee*, May 16, 2003; B. Mader, "Company to Launch Schwinn Line for Mass Retailers," *The Business Journal of Milwaukee*, August 7, 2002; Z. Olijnyk, "Beat China on Quality," *Canadian Business* 78:22 (November 7–20, 2005); G. Witte, "Schwinn's Bard Bump in the Road," *Washington Post*, December 9, 2004; www.pacific-cycle.com/ourstory/timeline.php. Accessed April 27, 2007. Industry volumes provided by Dorel Distribution, Canada; Cervélo's website at www.cervelo.com/en_us/company/history. Accessed July 7, 2009.

2. Z. Olijnyk, "Beat China on Quality," *Canadian Business* 78:22 (November 7–20, 2005).

3. Exhibit adapted from M. E. Porter, *Competitive Strategy: Techniques for Analyzing Industries and Competitors* (New York: Free Press, 1980).

4. C. Whitbread, "Germany: Porsche AG Revenue Rises 18% in 2009/ 10,"AutomotiveWorld.com, September 29, 2010. Accessed November 7, 2010, at www.automotiveworld.com/news/oems-and-markets/ 84022-germany-porsche-ag-revenue-rises-18-in-2009-10.

5. S. Silcoff, "A Loonie Business Plan That Worked," *Financial Post*, March 22, 2008; "Annual Report," Dollarama 2009.

6. K. Byron, "Animal Feed Provider Recalls Ingredient," CNNMoney.com; April 19 2007, http://money.cnn.com/2007/04/19/news/companies/pet_ food/index.htm.

7. D. Burn, "Canadian Powerhouse," www.foodincanada.com (January/ February 2004): 30–37, www.bizlink.com/foodfiles/PDFs/jan-feb/ janfeb-processoroftheyear.pdf. Accessed August 1, 2009; and "Maple Leaf CEO Michael H. McCain Responds to Determination of Link to Plant," CNW Group, August 23, 2008, www.newswire.ca/en/releases/archive/ August2008/23/c6402.html. Accessed August 1, 2009.

8. www.autointell.net. Accessed July 15, 2005.

9. B. Jang, "WestJet, Southwest Union Hits a Rough Patch," *Globe and Mail*, April 2, 2010. Accessed November 8, 2010, at www.theglobeandmail. com/globe-investor/westjet-southwest-union-hits-a-rough-patch/ article1521292/.

10. C. McCormick, "A Revolution in Cockpit Simulator Technology," www.wingsmagazine.com/content/view/2883/60/. Accessed August 1, 2009; and Z. Olijnyk, "Plane and Simple: Flight Simulation," *Canadian Business*, February 27–March 12, 2006.

11. The issue of RIM encryption methods is complex. A good explanation is by I. Austen, "BlackBerry Secure for Company but Not Employee," *Seattle Times*, August 8, 2010. Accessed November 8, 2010, at seattletimes. nwsource.com/html/personaltechnology/2012573084_encrypt09.html.

12. "Molson, Coors Merger Complete, Job Cuts Announced," Prepared Foods newsletter, February 14, 2005, www.preparedfoods.com/Articles/ e_newsletter_food/53d3279255788010VgnVCM100000f932a8c0____. Accessed August 1, 2009.

13. See S. S. Liao, "The Learning Curve: Wright's Model vs. Crawford's Model," *Issues in Accounting Education* 3 (1988): 302–315.

14. E. D. Darr, L. Argote, and D. Epple, "The Acquisition, Transfer, and Depreciation of Knowledge in Service Organizations: Productivity in Franchises," *Management Science* 41 (1995): 1750–1762.

15. Company website for EarthRenew Organics: www.theorganicpages. com/topo/companylisting.html?CompanyId=29175. Accessed August 1, 2009.

16. C. K. Prahalad and G. Hamel, "The Core Competence of the Corporation," *Harvard Business Review* 68:3 (1990): 79–91.

17. This section draws heavily on D. J. Collis and C. A. Montgomery, *Corporate Strategy* (Chicago: R.D. Irwin, 1997), pp. 69–73.

18. Examples are J. Allen and Y. Liu, "Efficiency and Economies of Scale of Large Canadian Banks" Bank of Canada Working Paper 2005-13, May 2005; and, J. D. Murray and R. W. White, "Economies of Scale and Scope in Multiproduct Financial Institutions: A study of British Columbia Credit Unions," *Journal of Finance* 38:3 (June 1983). In addition, decision making can be driven by the perception that they exist though they may not be present. See A. Bourdeau De Fontenay, J. Liebenau, and B. Savin, "A New View of Scale and Scope in the Telecommunications Industry: Implications for Competition and Innovation," *Communications & Strategies* 60 (Fourth Quarter 2005): 85.

19. Competition Bureau, Technical Background, "Acquisition of Maytag by Whirlpool," modified March 9, 2009, www.cb-bc.gc.ca/eic/site/cb-bc.nsf/ eng/02113.html. Accessed August 1, 2009.

20. "Canada's Grocery Gateway Delivers for Home Depot, Starbucks, Staples," Internet Retailer, November 22, 2002, www.internetretailer. com/internet/marketing-conference/62258-canadas-grocery-gateway- delivers-home-depot-starbucks-staple.html. Accessed August 1, 2009.

21. D. Gehman, "Curves International Corporate Spotlight," April 30, 2004, www.americanexecutive.com/content/view/5367/79/index. php?option=com_content&task=view&id=5367&Itemid=102. Accessed August 1, 2009.

22. R. Gibson, "Curves Loses Stamina, Closing Fitness Clubs," *Wall Street Journal*, July 7, 2010. Accessed November 7, 2010, at online.wsj.com/article/ SB10001424052748704862404575351293938715632.html.

23. See www.sweatshops.org, www.behindthelabel.org, and www.business- humanrights.org/Home. Accessed August 1, 2009.

24. Personal interview with Jaguar executives, June 2003.

25. M. E. Porter, "What Is Strategy," *Harvard Business Review*, November/ December 1996.

26. See www.flyjazz.ca/en/home/aboutjazz/history.aspx, finance. google.com/finance?q=TSE%3AWJA, and finance.google.com/ finance?q=TSE%3AJAZ.UN. Accessed July 7, 2009.

27. D. C. Hambrick, I. A. MacMillan, and D. L. Day, "Strategic Attributes and Performance in the BCG Matrix: A PIMS-Based Analysis of Industrial Product Businesses," *Academy of Management Journal* 25 (1982): 510–531.

28. D. B. Yoffie and M. Kwak, "Mastering Strategic Movement at Palm," *Sloan Management Review* 43:1 (2001): 55–63.

29. M. Santo, "Palm Purchased by HP For $1.2 Billion," HULIQ, April 28, 2010. Accessed November 8, 2010, at www.huliq.com/3257/palm-purchased-hp-12-billion.

30. Hambrick, MacMillan, and Day, "Strategic Attributes and Performance in the BCG Matrix."

31. R. Shaw, "Gartner: BlackBerry Now World PDA Market Leader," BB Hub: The BlackBerry Weblog, February 14, 2006, www.bbhub.com/2006/02/14/gartner-blackberry-now-world-pda-market-leader. Accessed August 1, 2009.

32. F. T. Rothaermel and D. L. Deeds, "Exploration and Exploitation Alliances in Biotechnology: A System of New Product Development," *Strategic Management Journal* 25:3 (2004): 201–221.

33. M. Cash, "Western Glove Ends 'Peg Era of Making Jeans: Loonie Forces Production to Asia," *Winnipeg Free Press*, October 20, 2007, www.winnipegfreepress.com/subscriber/business/local/story/4061556p-4665087c.html. Accessed August 1, 2009.

34. This adapted exhibit and section draws heavily on D. C. Hambrick and J. W. Fredrickson, "Are You Sure You Have a Strategy?" *Academy of Management Executive* 15:4 (2001): 48–59.

6

Crafting Business Strategy for Dynamic Contexts

The Evolving Wine Industry in Ontario

Ontario's Wine Industry Facts

- 146 grape wineries and approximately 30 fruit and other types of wineries

- more than 13 million grape vines on 17 000 acres in southern Ontario

- 7000 jobs are linked to the province's wine and grape industry

- 1 million tourists visit Ontario wineries each year

- VQA wines are increasingly popular in Ontario and abroad

For the year ending March 31, 2009:

- total domestic wine sales in Ontario (blended and VQA) reached a high of 55 million litres, valued at $533 million

- VQA wine sales reached a high of 11.4 million litres, valued at $173 million

Source: Ontario Ministry of Consumer Services, "Supporting Ontario's Wine and Grape Industry: McGuinty Government Strengthens VQA Wines," Ministry News, April 28, 2010. Accessed November 9, 2010, at www.sse.gov.on.ca/mcs/en/Pages/News_28Apr2010.aspx.

Ontario's wine industry has experienced periods of revolutionary change interspersed by periods of evolutionary change. After the first commercial operations started in 1866 on Pelee Island in Lake Erie, the industry grew gradually, moderated by a societal "temperance" movement, whose members chose to be temperate in the use of alcohol, or to abstain entirely, and by sporadic restrictive legislation. Wine could be sold but liquor was illegal until 1927, when a compromise was reached. Thereafter wine could only be sold through Liquor Control Board of Ontario (LCBO) stores and the store of the winery where the wine was produced. All marketing, including pricing, was controlled by the LCBO no matter where the wine was sold.

Allowing the sale of liquor, which substituted for wines, starting in 1927 had cataclysmic consequences for the wine industry. Wineries found themselves holding large inventories of unsalable wine. In turn, the government stopped issuing licences for new wineries, and consequently grape prices dropped dramatically. This provoked revolutionary change in the government's rules regarding the wine industry and the grape growers who supplied it, producing a new regulatory regime.

The new regulatory regime was based on an institutional structure that raised the price of grapes to farmers and raised the prices of wine so that Ontario wineries could make money using expensive grapes grown in Ontario. Grape prices were set through mandatory negotiations between the Ontario grape growers and wineries. Wine prices were kept high because the LCBO controlled the sale of most wine and favoured Ontario wines through its retail mark-up policy. Prices of Ontario wines were made competitive by having low mark-ups on Ontario wines and high mark-ups on imported wines. Under these new rules, the wine industry gradually consolidated as existing companies bought up other companies. By 1980, the six remaining large wineries sold an average of 2 million cases a year. They carried a broad range of blended wines that were of lower quality, were packed in multiple sizes of containers, and were sold widely through the LCBO as well as their own stores. Their product mix was favourably priced relative to imports, so 75 percent of the wine sold in Ontario was produced in the province.

The grape growers continued to use varieties of grapes that grew well in Ontario, such as *Vitis labrusca* (a native species that was good for making grape jelly!) and French hybrids (native species crossbred with *Vitis vinifera*). Grape growers received high prices, so they had little incentive to change their vines, though consumers wanted wines made with *Vitis vinifera*, the species of grape that produces more than 99 percent of the world's wine today. In the mid-1960s, researchers established that *vinifera* vines could be grown in the province and innovative growers started experimenting with them. In 1976, the first new winery licence in nearly four decades was issued to Inniskillin Winery, which was making wine using *Vitis vinifera* grapes. Thereafter other growers planted *vinifera* vines as they became available from local nurseries. In 1980, 800 tonnes of *Vitis vinifera* grapes, including Chardonnay, Riesling, Gamay, the Cabernets, and Merlots, were harvested. Other new boutique wineries established around the time included Château des Charmes (1978), Colio Wines (1981), Hillebrand Estates (1980), and Pelee Island Winery (1983). These wineries produced a narrow range of products focusing on medium-priced still wines, often vintaged (dated by year of production) varietals (made from a specified grape), sold in 750 ml bottles. The next shock that produced revolutionary change came in the late 1980s when Ontario's differential mark-ups on imported wines (at the time 62 percent on U.S. wines and 75 percent on European wines versus 13 percent on all-Canadian wines and 23 percent on blends of Canadian-imported wine) were challenged. The outcome was that Ontario agreed to remove the differential by raising the mark-up on domestic wines to 66 percent by 1998. This set off a significant increase in the price of Ontario wines, and Ontario wineries lost 24 percent of their market share over the next five years.

Donald Triggs of Vincor International said, "You had two choices as a Canadian wine producer. Go to higher price points if you wanted to stay small. Or get bigger fast if you were in the popular-priced segment."[1] Vincor International took the latter path as it consolidated the traditional wineries. Vincor started as a management buyout of Labatt's wine operations for Cdn$30 million in 1989. In 1992, it acquired Inniskillin Winery, and then in 1993 it acquired T. G. Bright, the largest winery in Ontario. Afterward it acquired another winery in Ontario and in Quebec and two in British Columbia. It pursued economies of scale by integrating their sales, marketing, production, and accounting. Another winery that grew to national prominence was Andrew Peller Ltd. (formerly Andrés Wines), which started in British Columbia and extended its operations into Ontario and Quebec. Each winery increased its volume and the amount of high-quality viniferous wines as grapes became available. In 2002, Vincor was the largest winery in Canada, with sales of Cdn$377 million, and Andrew Peller was the second largest with sales of Cdn$139 million. In 2006, after expanding internationally, Vincor was bought by Constellation Brands for US$1.09 billion.

The boutique wineries were destined to be small so they worked on producing wines that were good value at mid-prices. The success of the earlier entrants encouraged more boutique start-ups—almost 40 wineries established from 2005 to 2009. By 2008, there were approximately 125 wineries in Ontario, visited by 1 million tourists. To ensure that consumers felt justified paying higher prices, Ontario's wineries formed a voluntary association, the Vintners Quality Alliance (VQA). Its role was to administer an appellation system for Ontario wines and to set various standards, including that all VQA wines contain 100 percent Ontario-grown grapes and that they pass taste tests before they could carry the VQA label. In 2009, 97 of Ontario's wineries were producing VQA table wines.

As good grapes are needed to produce good wines, vines of traditional grape varieties needed to be replaced. This was encouraged by the government under the Grape Adjustment Program. Grape growers received subsidies for replacing 3 318 hectares (about half the vines planted) with the *vinifera* demanded by wineries. In addition, *labrusca* grapes were banned from all table wines made in Ontario. With these actions the *vinifera* grape harvest increased to 4000 tonnes in 1990, 20 400 tonnes in 2000, and 32 000 tonnes in 2007. In 2009, there were more grapes than the wineries wanted to buy.

The history of the wine industry in Ontario shows that change was not a steady process, but rather a series of evolutionary periods punctuated by revolutionary periods. During each phase, the environment was different and the companies that were successful through one period were not necessarily those that were successful during another. ∎

Crafting Business Strategy for Dynamic Contexts

This chapter shows how companies develop competitive advantage in the face of dynamic competition and market conditions. In Chapter 5, the industry life cycle implied that environmental change is evolutionary, though sometimes it is revolutionary in that it is rapid and even unpredictable. The dynamic environment makes strategic change essential if strategy is to fit with the environment. In some cases, the business is able to alter the environment with the strategy it chooses to pursue. Then business might even rewrite the rules of competition in its favour. Given that change is needed, the strategist has to decide when and where to change strategy and what to change.

This chapter sets the stage with a description of what a dynamic environment is. Given this description, we look at the decision of when to change strategy. The choices are whether to be proactive or reactive. Businesses taking proactive stances are first movers and second movers (otherwise know as fast followers). Having decided to move, they have to decide where to attack the market: at the high end, the low end, or somewhere else. They also have to decide how they will attack the market (i.e., decide which offensive moves they will use). Businesses that are reactive do not determine when and where the competitive battle will be fought. They let competitors make those decisions, and all they have to decide is what defensive moves they will use to fight back. The chapter concludes by integrating the formulation of strategy with the implementation of strategy, since these need to fit together seamlessly.

THE CHALLENGES TO SUSTAINING A COMPETITIVE ADVANTAGE

A competitive advantage can be eroded by environmental change, as was demonstrated in the opening vignette. The source change often comes from a combination of drivers, which you read about in Chapter 4. Recall that a company has a competitive advantage when it creates value in ways that rivals cannot duplicate. Possessing resources and capabilities that meet the VRINE criteria improves the likelihood of developing a competitive advantage. Such resources and capabilities facilitate the creation of strategic positions having low cost and/or differentiation that companies cannot match because they lack such resources and capabilities. A competitive advantage is threatened by anything that causes resources and capabilities to no longer satisfy the VRINE criteria: something that causes them to lose their ability to create value; that makes them more common; that makes them easily imitated or substituted; or that weakens the company's ability to exploit them.

The source of many of the threats to the VRINE resources and capabilities comes from the dynamic environment within which the business operates. This environment can be separated into four facets: *competitive interaction, industry evolution, technological disruption,* and *global issues.* The first three dimensions are explored in this chapter, while global issues are examined separately in Chapter 9. All four categories are interrelated and need to be considered when addressing the need to change strategy. We start this chapter by examining the ways in which the first three dimensions can undermine competitive strategy.

Competitive Interaction

Research on competitive interaction has identified four underlying phases, which are summarized in Exhibit 6.1.[2] To illustrate these phases, consider a regional title insurance company that has a strategy designed to make it a premier national company. The strategy involves a sequence of actions: initial entry into adjacent regional markets, followed by increased focus on differentiators that build brand awareness, followed by rapid expansion using acquisitions that are funded by stock that is increasing in price.[3] In phase 1, the business's activities, even competitively aggressive moves, go unnoticed or ignored by competitors. In phase 2, customer reactions

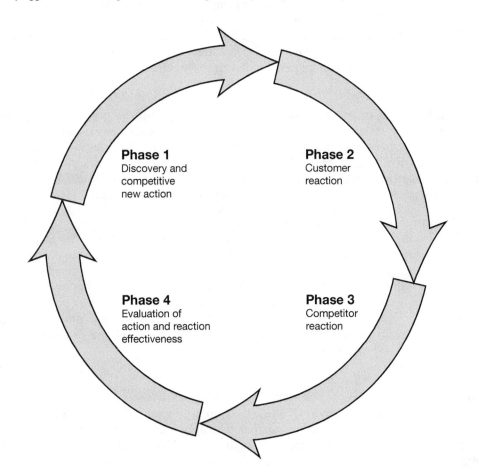

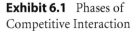

Exhibit 6.1 Phases of Competitive Interaction

are positive. In phase 3, competing companies respond to the first business-competitive moves. Finally, in phase 4, competitors evaluate the results of their interactions, and the cycle recommences. Competitive moves initiated in phase 1 can be characterized along four dimensions: aggressiveness, complexity of moves, unpredictability, and tactics that delay the competitors' reactions. The nature of the moves in terms of these aspects can influence the response of competitors. Competitive responses can also range widely.[4] *Competitive interaction theory* suggests that managers are wise to predict how competitors might react to possible actions by the business and, in light of this, determine the best course of action.[5]

When the competitors are all established in the industry, a challenger can erode the leader's position by rapidly launching many assaults on the leader in a short period of time. Such interaction explains how, in 2005, SABMiller regained market-share-growth leadership from Anheuser-Busch in the light-beer segment by using aggressive advertising. SABMiller's advertising suggested that Anheuser-Busch's beers lacked flavour and backed it up with consumer surveys saying that the SABMiller's beers had more and better taste. The attacker is more likely to succeed in improving its market position when the moves are complex and unpredictable. Such an attack confuses the industry leader, causing it to lose focus as scarce resources are used to defend on multiple competitive fronts. Finally, the attacker can gain competitive market position when competitors find it difficult to respond quickly. Nike's competitive success against Reebok in the late 1980s can be partially attributed to the fact that Nike initiated competitive moves such as promotions, new product launches, and endorsements. Nike also responded to Reebok's actions much faster than Reebok responded to Nike's.[6] These tactics hold true in industries ranging from telecommunications and personal computers to airlines and brewing.

When the competitor is a new entrant, that entrant can change the dynamics of competitive behaviour, especially when the entrant's business model or strategy varies significantly from those of the established competitors. The reason is that the business models have different incentives and different value-chain activities. A new entrant typically emphasizes different product attributes and starts out as a lower-margin business. In this way the new entrant changes the rules of competition within the industry and, in doing so, takes market share away from the incumbents. Disruptive entrants are found in many industries, such as airlines (Southwest and WestJet), banking (ING Canada and PC Financial), retail (Amazon.com), and retail brokerage (Disnat, eNorthern, and Questrade). The vexing dilemma for established competitors facing a new entrant is, Should we respond to the new entrant and, if so, how? Incumbents typically have great difficulty devising strategies to deal with a new entrant.

Industry Evolution

The nature of rivalry changes as an industry evolves over the industry life cycle and as competitors redefine segments of the market. These changes cause competitive advantage to shift from companies with obsolete resources and capabilities to those with resources and capabilities better suited to the new form of rivalry. The implication is that management needs to anticipate how strategy must be changed in order to provide a sustained competitive advantage. Of course, the best case is for the business to set a direction for change that favours its own resources and capabilities.

The Pressures of Commoditization

With *commoditization,* products and services are no longer perceived as differentiated. This undoes the basis for segmentation of the market so competitors are drawn into industry-wide competition using price as the dominant method of increasing sales. Tactics have been identified to deal with the pressures of commoditization, but the strategist still has to decide when to use them.[7] If the business changes its strategy too soon, it risks losing extra profits, but if it moves after others, it may never be able to regain the market lost to them. And all the tactics have clear implications for the five elements in the strategy diamond (arenas, differentiators, vehicles, pacing, and economic logic).

Technological Change

New technology improves the business's efficiency in terms of processes and its effectiveness in terms of new products and services it offers the customer. Products due to new technology that readily come to mind include laptop computers, cellphones, and music players. The process changes are harder to identify, but they are significant and include the migration by Canada's Big Five banks to online banking and online discount brokerages (RBC Direct Investing, BMO

Investor Online, TD Ameritrade, CIBC Investor's Edge, and Scotia Online) and Amazon.com's move from online bookselling to being a logistics provider for countless retailers.[8]

The impact of technological change depends on who introduces the change and how fast adoption of the new technology occurs. When a leading business in the industry introduces the change, that business is ready for it and so is likely to continue to dominate the industry. For instance, Boeing is a leading manufacturer of airframes—the bodies of aircraft. It has held on to this position by introducing innovative new designs such as the Dreamliner and, although it is having difficulty producing this aircraft, Boeing is managing to stay ahead of Airbus. When an entrant to the industry introduces the change, established competitors can be marginalized or eliminated. For instance, the introduction of the personal computer decimated the major manufacturers of minicomputers, including Data General, Digital Equipment, and Wang Laboratories. The new technologies introduced by entrants are often referred to as *disruptive technologies* because they alter who the leaders of the industry are.

The speed at which the technological change occurs also has an impact. Physicist Thomas Kuhn showed that this change tends to cycle through two phases: evolutionary and revolutionary.[9] During the evolutionary phase, the fundamentals of the technology are relatively constant and change is slight. During the revolutionary phase, change is dramatic as the fundamentals change; hence, it has been called *discontinuous change*. Discontinuities that affect *product* technology often favour differentiation strategies.

Technological change is inevitable so the strategist has several decisions. Which technologies are to be used and how is the technology to be used? Use of technology can be either proactive or reactive. Apple was proactive in creating its iPod to take advantage of the digitalization of music. Then Apple went on to release its iPhone in 2007, which had a touch screen and was easy to use because of the integration of software and hardware. Apple capitalized on this with its App Store, which provided new applications for its iPhone, from games to social networking programs, news services, or travel widgets. Makers of mobile phone handsets were reacting in early 2009, trying to emulate Apple by producing their own smart phones and stores providing applications. Imitation of Apple carried a risk for these followers, as customers could see the imitators as no longer leaders in technology.[10]

Speed of Change

The speed of change is a critical factor in keeping up with the basis of competition in an industry. Speed tends to compound the effects of every driver of change, whether industry evolution, technological discontinuities, or other causes. As the pace of change increases, the basis of competitive advantage changes. Success and even survival of the business depends on the management's ability to anticipate and to react swiftly to these changes.

First Movers and Second Movers (or Fast Followers)

The first question that a strategist has to ask when thinking about changing strategy is, When should I do it? **First movers** are businesses that make important strategic and technological decisions early in the development of an industry. First movers can sometimes establish the rules of the game and create an industry structure that is beneficial to them. In many cases, the most profitable avenue is the one that those *leading* industry change travel on.[11] They are followed by **second movers**. Their actions also have an impact on the industry's rules and structure. Later followers travel a well-trodden avenue.

first mover The company that is first to offer a new product or service in a market.

second mover (often *fast follower*) Second significant company to move into a market, quickly following the first mover.

Not all managers think being the first to market with a new product matters. A study of 72 400 businesses in the United States reported that 31 percent of all companies considered being first to market with a new product of great importance. Of these companies, 44 percent of IT companies and 29 percent of non-IT companies saw this as being of great importance.[12]

THE PROS AND CONS OF FIRST-MOVER POSITIONING

Intuitively, first movers appear to have a distinct advantage. After all, many races are won by the first contestant out of the starting blocks. The history of the internet offers a wealth of first-mover success stories. Amazon.com started retailing books over the internet in 1995 and by 2008 dominated this segment, which accounted for 21 percent to 30 percent of all book retailing.[13] However, first movers do not always attain dominant positions (see Exhibit 6.2[14]).

Exhibit 6.2 A Gallery of First Movers and Fast Followers

Product	Pioneer(s)	Imitators/Fast Followers	Comments
Automated teller machines (ATMs)	DeLaRue (1967) Docutel (1969)	Diebold (1971) IBM (1973) NCR (1974)	The first movers were small entrepreneurial upstarts that faced two types of competitors: (1) larger firms with experience selling to banks and (2) the computer giants. The first movers did not survive.
Ballpoint pens	Reynolds (1945) Eversharp (1946)	Parker (1954) Bic (1960)	The pioneers disappeared when the fad first ended in the late 1940s. Parker entered eight years later. Bic entered last and sold pens as cheap disposables.
Commercial jets	deHaviland (1952)	Boeing (1958) Douglas (1958)	The pioneer rushed to market with a jet that crashed frequently. Boeing and Douglas (later known as McDonnel-Douglas) followed with safer, larger, and more powerful jets unsullied by tragic crashes.
Credit cards	Diners Club (1950)	Visa/Mastercard (1966) American Express (1968)	The first mover was undercapitalized in a business in which money is the key resource. American Express entered last with funds and name recognition from its traveller's cheque business.
Diet soda	Kirsch's No-Cal (1952) Royal Crown's Diet Rite Cola (1962)	Pepsi's Patio Cola (1963) Coke's Tab (1964) Diet Pepsi (1964) Diet Coke (1982)	The first mover could not match the distribution advantages of Coke and Pepsi. Nor did it have the money or marketing expertise needed for massive promotional campaigns.
Light beer	Rheingold's & Gablinger's (1968) Meister Brau Lite (1967)	Miller Lite (1975) Natural Light (1977) Coors Light (1978) Bud Light (1982)	The first movers entered nine years before Miller and 16 years before Budweiser, but financial problems drove both out of business. Marketing and distribution determined the outcome. Costly legal battles, again requiring access to capital, were commonplace.
PC operating systems	CP/M (1974)	Microsoft DOS (1981) Microsoft Windows (1985)	The first mover set the early industry standard but did not upgrade for the IBM PC. Microsoft bought an imitative upgrade and became the new standard. Windows entered later and borrowed heavily from predecessors (and competitor Apple), then emerged as the leading interface.
Video games	Magnavox's Odyssey (1972) Atari's Pong (1972)	Nintendo (1985) Sega (1989) Microsoft (1998)	The market went from boom to bust to boom. The bust occurred when home computers seemed likely to make video games obsolete. Kids lost interest when games lacked challenge. Price competition ruled. Nintendo rekindled interest with better games and restored market order with managed competition. Microsoft entered with its Xbox when they perceived gaming to be a possible component of its wired world.

Apple introduced Newton, the first PDA, in 1993, but PalmPilot became the dominant company. And de Havilland introduced the first commercial jets although the industry is now dominated by Boeing and Airbus. In some cases, the first mover is not able to exploit the advantages of being first, and in other cases, a first-mover strategy can even be a liability.

Being a first mover is valuable if the business

- Achieves an absolute cost advantage in terms of scale or scope,
- Develops an image and reputation that are hard to imitate at a later date,
- Locks customers' preferences into its products or services, or
- Achieves a scale that makes imitation unlikely.[15]

First movers bear significant risks, including the costs not only of designing, producing, and distributing new products, but also of developing the market for them. Developing a market can take a lot of time, money, and effort. Larger competitors sometimes stand by watching a smaller competitor develop the market and, once the market is developed to a volume they find attractive, they either enter with a similar product, perhaps of higher quality or with added features, or simply buy the business that developed the market.

The value of being a first mover diminishes—and that of being a fast follower increases—when

- The first mover's new product or service is leapfrogged by a follower using a new technology.
- The first mover's product or service strikes a positive chord with customers but is flawed.
- The first mover lacks a key complement, such as channel access, that a follower possesses.
- The first mover's costs outweigh the benefits of its first-mover position. Followers, for example, do not have to pay the cost of developing the market.

The history of first movers and followers on various innovations is described in Exhibit 6.2. Successful first movers tend to have unique resources and know how to extend their advantage by defending their position. They also exploit the complementary assets needed to bring a new product to market. The difference between leading change and responding to it is often determined based on the relative strength of the resources in the company.

SECOND MOVERS

Being a second mover does not necessarily mean that a company is a *late* mover. Effective second movers can be characterized as *fast followers*—even if the elapsed time between first and second moves is several years. The lag is not necessarily detrimental because new products take time to develop a market. The rapid growth and huge sales increases—known as the **takeoff** period—starts, *on average,* within six years of the new-product introduction.[16]

takeoff Period during which a new product generates rapid growth and huge sales increases.

The industry life cycle suggests that the drivers of demand evolve over time, but it does not predict how *quickly* they will evolve. Indeed, it may take some new products a decade or more to reach the growth stage, and only then will they attract competitors. Mechtronix recognizes that flight simulators similar to its own may well be launched by larger companies within several years. But there is an upside: Copycats validate Mechtronix's technology, helping convince customers to take a chance on a tiny Canadian company that has managed to open a market where none existed.

In the Ontario wine industry, the fact that there were many fast followers into the production of viniferous wines was beneficial for the industry. This allowed the establishment of the Vintners Quality Alliance (VQA), which indicated wine of higher quality. Because many wineries were involved in the VQA, consumers were interested in their wines and the wineries had sufficient quantity to satisfy that interest.

Typically, survivors are either first movers or relatively fast followers. Those businesses that are *habitually* late movers eventually fail as businesses unless they are protected by government regulation, monopolistic or oligopolistic industry positions, or extensive cash reserves. Increasingly, however, competitive advantage results from the ability to manage change and harness the resources and capabilities consistent with first- or second-mover strategies.

FIRST MOVERS AND COMPLEMENTARY ASSETS

Exhibit 6.3 provides an additional framework for assessing whether a business should pursue a first-mover or fast-follower strategy by incorporating the factor of *complementary assets.* The framework shows that any company contemplating a first-mover strategy should consider the protection from imitation against the strength of its complementary assets. Within the framework are explanations for why a number of notable first movers fared poorly despite apparently advantageous positions one would expect them to extract by virtue of being a first mover.[17]

Using the framework, we can see that the developer of an exciting new game played on a game console can protect its game by patent. But the game has to be compatible with the game player. This requires that the creator of the game be told by the manufacturer how the player works so that the game can be coded correctly. This means that the manufacturer of the player has control over the essential complementary asset. It wants more games that play on the machine so the machine will sell, but it makes more profit when the game makers have to pay it a license fee for each game they sell for the player. The game manufacturer seeks to maximize its profits by trading off the licensing fee against the incentive for game creators to make additional games for the player.

Exhibit 6.3 First-Mover
Dependencies

Status of Complementary Assets

	Freely available or unimportant	Tightly held and important
Weak protection from imitation	It is difficult for anyone to make money: Industry incumbents may simply give new product or service away as part of its larger bundle of offerings	Value-creation opportunities favour the holder of complementary assets, who will probably pursue a fast-follower strategy
Strong protection from imitation	First mover can do well depending on the execution of its strategy	Value will go either to first mover or to party with the most bargaining power

Bases of First Mover Advantages

Where to Assert Change

The second question the strategist has to answer is, Where will I target change? Will the business disrupt the market at the high end, at the low end, or somewhere else?

HIGH-END DISRUPTION

high-end disruption Disruption that provides a product for a new or emerging segment not being served by existing businesses in the industry.

A high-end disruption occurs when a product fits a new or emerging market segment that is not being served by existing incumbents. With a vastly improved product, customers' expectations are raised and a new market is created. Even the largest incumbents can be unseated by the business providing this product because it sets a new value curve. The boutique wineries that have sprung up in Ontario since the 1970s have chosen to serve a higher end market that wanted vintaged (aged) wines and varietals (specific types of grapes) and which traditional wineries in Ontario had not produced.

Cirque du Soleil significantly disrupted the circus industry by incorporating many features more common in Broadway theatre than in traditional circuses, generating significant new growth and higher profits than any traditional circus. Incumbents can also use a high-end disruption to move away from head-to-head competition as competitors converge on common value curves, in particular with commoditization, but undertaking high-end disruption doesn't necessarily mean that the disrupter will become, or even intends to become, the industry leader. High-end disruption comes at a price as the disruptor, when an incumbent must change the way it does things. Hence, the incumbent must redefine its business model.

LOW-END DISRUPTION

low-end disruption Disruption that targets customers who do not need the full product performance provided by existing businesses in the industry.

Low-end disruption targets customers who do not need the full performance that customers at the high end of the market require. These customers only want limited functionality in the product and are not willing to pay for enhancements. This approach allows an entrant to the industry time to gain a foothold in the market because the incumbents do not respond to its actions—they do not value the customers it attracts. Once the foothold is established, the entrant improves the value curve and starts satisfying customers in the middle of the market. This is possible when the incumbents provide improvements that satisfy their most profitable customers and in so doing produce features that the middle-market customer values. Mechtronix is a low-end disruptor as its flight simulators are low-priced and so appeal to smaller airlines. Four graduate engineering students at Concordia University in Montreal developed the first prototype in the 1980s, but it was not ready for commercial application. They revisited the idea in 1995 when smaller regional airlines and low-cost carriers, such as Dallas-based Southwest Airlines, started becoming significant players in the airline industry. Mechtronix is able to produce highly effective training hardware at a fraction of the cost of custom-built machines made by CAE because its product is based on a different technology. Mechtronix simulators are based on electronics and computer software built into surplus cockpits that are tailored to match the desired aircraft. Meanwhile, CAE Inc.'s simulators are based on the hydraulic systems and avionics of real planes. The result is that Mechtronix's simulators are cheaper to buy and less expensive to maintain. This fits well with the cost structure of low-cost airlines.[18]

HYBRID DISRUPTION STRATEGIES

Most newcomers adopt some combination of low-end disruption and new market strategies. Amazon.com pursued a single-minded low-end disruption strategy at the start by offering books at lower prices, but it also created high-end disruption by creating a community as it provided reviews of books by other readers and recommended other books of interest to the reader based on what others had bought. WestJet Airlines has also pursued a hybrid strategy.[19] WestJet's focused low-cost strategy has been able to achieve the lowest-cost position in the industry by eliminating many services (a business model it borrowed from Southwest) but also by adding services that increased customer loyalty. In addition, it has targeted overpriced but underserved markets, thereby stimulating new demand—both taking a portion of the existing market from incumbent competitors *and* creating a new market by attracting consumers who could not ordinarily afford air travel.

Offensive Moves That Lead Industry Change

The third question the strategist has to answer is, What changes will I make? Disruption that initiates change can be introduced in five ways: *reconceiving a product/service, reconfiguring the value chain, redefining the arenas, rescaling the industry,* and *reconsidering the competitive mindset*. They are summarized in Exhibit 6.4 and described in greater detail below.

Exhibit 6.4 Offensive Moves

Type of Industry Disruption	Reconceiving a Product/Service	Reconfiguring the Value Chain	Redefining the Arenas	Rescaling the Industry	Reconsidering the Competitive Mindset
Definition	Breaking away from existing industry conceptions of what products and services look like	Changing elements of the industry value chain	Changing when and where you compete	Using a business model that relies on different economics relative to scale	Avoid direct competition
Example	• Creating a new value curve (e.g., Cirque du Soleil) • Separate function from form (e.g., electronic hotel keys)	• Use a new value chain (e.g., Amazon) • Compress the value chain (e.g., IKEA)	• Changing temporal and geographical availability (e.g., Redbox) • Total imagined market versus served market (e.g., disposable cameras)	• Increase scale for greater economies of scale (e.g., waste disposal) • Downscale in search of higher prices in niche markets (e.g., microbreweries)	• Look to make competitors complementors (e.g., American and Delta defraying costs from Boeing) • Avoid head-to-head competition by moving into areas where there is little competition (e.g., [yellow tail])

RECONCEIVE A PRODUCT OR SERVICE

Creating a New Value Curve

Creating a new value curve requires that management look for better ways for satisfying customers. New ideas can come from building on the best of the existing industry, importing ideas from other industries, and eliminating features that incumbents take for granted but are not critical to key customers. This approach has worked in both fast-paced and seemingly stagnant industries—both situations are ripe for significant changes. Fast-paced industries are dynamic by definition. Stagnant industries are often ripe for new technologies that will send the industry on a new growth trajectory, or through shakeout. A shakeout is a dynamic process but usually negative for many incumbents.

Cirque du Soleil created a new value curve, which is summarized in Exhibit 6.5. Cirque's value curve illustrates that a number of features common in other circuses were dropped but other features unheard of before in the circus industry were added. These novel ideas appear to have been borrowed from another form of entertainment—Broadway. The combination of changes was so dramatic that Cirque produced a revolutionary strategy that redefined circus entertainment. Inniskillin was also an innovator in that it started commercial production of viniferous wines in Ontario in 1975.

Most companies focus on their existing rivals and actively attempt to match or beat their rivals' offerings to the customer. The result of this is that their strategies often converge, and convergence is closer when those in the industry share common industry wisdom about how to compete. Convergence is often associated with incremental innovation that rarely results in breakthroughs that create new markets.

Mapping the value curves reveals the market positioning by competitors along key buying criteria. Competitors can have different value curves or a similar value curve when their strategies have converged to the point of creating a strategic group. The value curve is a source of hypotheses about the assumptions being made by the industry about what matters. Discovering a new-market space can be achieved by answering four questions as illustrated in the Four-Actions Framework shown in Exhibit 6.6.[20] First, what product or service attributes that rivals take for granted should be *reduced* well below the industry standard? Second, what factors that the industry has taken for granted should be *eliminated*? Third, what product or service attributes should be *raised* well above the industry standard? And fourth, what factors that the industry has never offered should be *created*? The answers will define a new value curve for an industry, or at least a segment of an industry. Meeting the new curve means modifying the business's strategy

Exhibit 6.5 Cirque du Soleil at the Nexus of Circus and Broadway

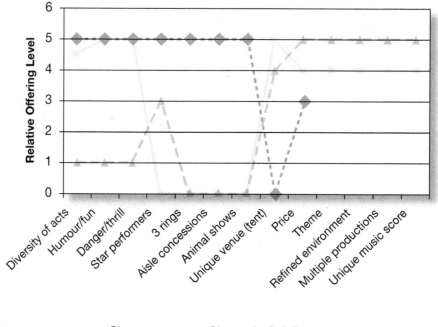

----◆---- Circus   ———— Cirque du Soleil   --▲-- Broadway

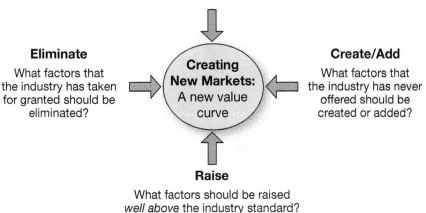

The key to discovering a new value curve lies in answering four basic questions.

Reduce
What factors should be reduced *well below* the industry standard?

Eliminate
What factors that the industry has taken for granted should be eliminated?

Creating New Markets: A new value curve

Create/Add
What factors that the industry has never offered should be created or added?

Raise
What factors should be raised *well above* the industry standard?

Exhibit 6.6 The Four-Actions Framework of New Market Creation

so that either its products are further differentiated from competitors', its cost structure is driven significantly below that of competitors, or both. In addition, following this new curve often goes beyond stealing customers from competitors to generating new customers for the industry or industry segment. How Would You Do That? 6.1 illustrates the application of the value-curve tool, in conjunction with the four-actions framework, to the wine industry using [yellow tail].[21] While we introduce the four-actions framework in the creation of a new value curve, the framework translates well to all the revolutionary strategies covered in this section.

Separating Function and Form

Another way to bring about change is to adopt a form used in one industry to serve functions in other industries. The difference between function and form is that *function* is the benefits provided by the product while *form* is the embodiment of the product. The history of credit cards provides an example of what we mean. Credit cards first emerged at the beginning of the 20th century. The function of a credit card includes the identification of cardholders and their accounts, along with permission to charge a purchase. The form of the card is a slim piece of plastic. The form was modified when a magnetic strip was added to the card to encode data about customers and their accounts. This made the card more secure and sped up the payment to merchants. Other businesses then saw the potential benefit of the form for other functions, including employee identification badges, hotel keys, debit cards, membership cards, and discount cards. All these uses were conceived of by businesses in other industries that were attempting to provide customers with better products and services.

RECONFIGURE THE VALUE CHAIN

The value chain is the sequential steps of value-adding activities needed to create a product or service bought by the customer. Some businesses have reconfigured the value chain in new ways. Two ways of improving the customer's value equation are by creating a *new* value chain and by *compressing* the existing value chain.

Radically New Value Chain

Sometimes making completely new assumptions about the value chain can be successful. When Jeff Bezos started Amazon.com, he saw that the internet could be used to provide a radically new value chain for a number of industries. Amazon started with books and has since branched out into many products. Beyond eliminating the costly physical infrastructure of retail stores, the Amazon model cut other significant costs from the value chain. For instance, large book retailers return, on average, about 30 percent of their orders each year to wholesalers and publishers, but Amazon returns a slim 3 percent.

HOW WOULD YOU DO THAT? 6.1

[yellow tail] Creates a New Value Curve in the Wine Industry[22]

The Casellas, the family that owns [yellow tail], an Australian winery, began crafting wine in Italy in the 1820s. The family moved to Australia in 1951 and, after years of growing and selling grapes to local wineries, decided to use their own winemaking skills. In 1969, the family started a new winery and in 1994 a new generation of Casellas entered the family business. They embarked on an ambitious vision of blending Old World heritage with New World technology in a new winery. Today, Casella Wines is run by fifth- and sixth-generation Casella family members. In 2000, Casella Wines joined forces with W. J. Deutsch & Sons, another family-run company, to bring Casella wines and [yellow tail] to the North America.

The intensely competitive U.S. wine industry was mapped in Chapter 4 in How Would You Do That? 4.2. It had two dominant strategic groups—wineries competing in the budget segment or high-price segments (or often both). This creates a major challenge for any potential entrant. How should it position itself so it has something that is of interest to buyers? [yellow tail] designed a value curve for entering North America through a process of moves over many years. Exhibits 6.7 and 6.8 show the Casellas reconfigured the way [yellow tail] was defined as a winery: offering wines at a moderate price; avoiding wine lingo; encouraging impulse purchases with its catchy labels; and targeting only two high-demand wines, Chardonnay and Shiraz. New features were added that incumbents did not offer—easy drinking, ease of selection (again, only two varieties), and a spirit of fun and adventure.[23] The four-actions framework was

Exhibit 6.7 A Value Curve for [yellow tail]

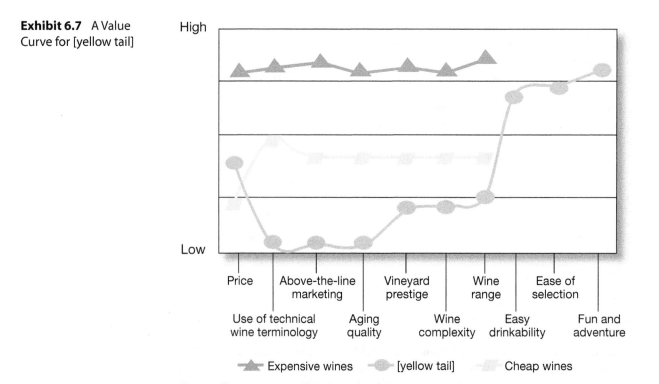

Exhibit 6.8 The Four-Actions Framework and [yellow tail]

Reduce	Eliminate	Create/Add	Raise
Wine complexity Wine range Vineyard prestige	Enological terminology and distinctions Aging qualities Above-the-line marketing	Easy drinking Ease of selection Fun and adventure	Price versus budget wines Retail store involvement

used to create a new value curve. It created alternatives instead of competing head-on with the major players. It converted non-customers to customers by luring traditional beer and cocktail drinkers with its catchy labels and easy-drinking wines. [yellow tail] is sold in Canada for around $11 a bottle and in the United States for around US$7 a bottle. The wine has sold very well in both countries.

Ultimately, the choice between low-end disruption and new market strategies depends on a company's resources and capabilities, and the ability to then execute the chosen strategy. The Casellas conceived of a new approach to the wine industry, and did so with the knowledge that [yellow tail] possessed the resources and capabilities needed to deliver the value curve.

HOW WOULD YOU DO THAT?
QUESTIONS

1. Pick an industry and use this How Would *You* Do That? box as a template to map its value curve. What are the key success factors that define industry participation? Does there appear to be more than one strategic group in this industry operating with different value curves? Can you come up with a new value curve that would change the industry?

2. Identify a company that you believe is pursuing a revolutionary strategy. How do its actions map onto the Four-Actions Framework?

Skype Technologies' popular web-based phone service is another example of a radically new value chain. Skype allows users to make phone calls using the internet. To use Skype, customers download its free software onto a PC equipped with a microphone and speakers or a USB phone. Initially, all calls had to be made PC-to-PC, but Skype service now allows PC-to-phone calling, and these calls are at much lower rates than traditional phone service. After eBay purchased Skype in 2005, Skype added new services, including content distribution (users can send and receive pictures and ringtones, for example) and a call-forwarding service. The only portion of the traditional telecommunications value chain that Skype required was the local land line for customers who use dial-up internet. By allowing PC-to-phone calling it further encroached on the market of phone companies.

Compress the Value Chain

A simpler way to reconfigure the value chain is to simply compress it, typically by eliminating a wholesaler or distributor. Dell and IKEA are examples of this. Dell eliminated retail stores by selling computers directly over the internet and outsourcing the manufacture of components and assembly of computers. IKEA lowered the cost of Scandinavian-style home furnishings and other housewares significantly by compressing several value chain activities. By designing furniture in pieces that can be easily assembled, it eliminates two costly steps from the value chain. First, it cut transportation costs because unassembled furniture is shipped to its retail stores in flat packaging, allowing it to ship more product in much smaller spaces. Second, it leaves the cost of assembly to its customers, who buy the product still in the box and then assemble it at home. So, IKEA passes some of the savings on to customers and keeps the rest in the form of higher margins.

REDEFINE YOUR ARENAS

Managers generally know who their customers are and in what arenas they compete. Finding potential customers expands the potential sales of the company's products.

Changing the Temporal or Geographic Availability

Potential customers can be found in places or at times different than those conventionally served by the industry. Coca-Cola and Pepsi have been open-minded about this. Given the location of soft-drink machines, they must think that someone is thirsty wherever people are found. Other businesses have been catching on to this. Catalogue shopping has been added by placing magazines featuring more exotic goods in the seat pockets of planes. Coffee shops have put outlets inside bookstores such as Chapters Indigo. Credit cards are being offered by grocery chains including Loblaw and Sobeys. DVDs are being rented from vending machines in grocery stores. Fast-food chains have put outlets inside large retailers such as Wal-Mart. And many retailers, distributors, and wholesalers have created websites so that customers can buy from them anywhere and at any time.

Imagining the Total Possible Market Rather than the Served Market

One way to redefine the business's arena is to imagine all the *possible* buyers of the product rather than who currently buys it. In the mid-1980s, the makers of disposable cameras stepped beyond the regular photography store to sell to children and in many new places, including grocery and convenience stores. This opened up an entirely new market for makers of photographic film.

New technologies can facilitate the reconceptualization of the total possible market. Copeland Corporation, owned by Emerson Electric, is illustrative. Copeland produces compressors that it sells to manufacturers of refrigerators and air conditioners. In 1987, it started producing innovative but more expensive scroll compressors that were more efficient, reliable, and quieter than the semi-hermetic compressors they replaced. Japanese competitors also made scroll processors, and analysts predicted that they would increase production of them dramatically in the future. Copeland's management determined that a major expansion in production would lower unit costs so much that it would be price-competitive in a broad market that included the price-sensitive home air conditioning market as well as developing economies. It chose to invest in a major expansion and, by doing so, forestalled Japanese expansion and held on to Copeland's market leadership. Management's decision paid off as Copeland has sold more than 23 million scroll compressors made in plants around the world.[24]

Spearheading Industry Convergence

Industry convergence occurs when two distinct industries evolve toward a single point where old industry boundaries no longer exist. Professor Nils Stieglitz distinguishes four different types of industry convergence, of which two are associated with production and two with product. First is technological convergence in upstream markets. Then production of dissimilar products starts to depend on the same assets. An example is that multipurpose semiconductors have replaced many electronic components that used to be produced by different industries. Second is technological convergence in downstream markets. Then production assets of different industries are brought together in an industry producing a single product. An example is the single device that can copy documents, print computer files, scan documents to produce electronic images, and fax (send and receive) electronic replicates of documents. Third is a product convergence of substitutes. Then products of different industries rapidly evolve into close substitutes as features of one industry's product are incorporated in the other industry's product. For example, the original personal digital assistants (PDAs) were used for managing contacts, appointments, and tasks. RIM added email capacity and then phone capacity to PDAs. Meanwhile, manufacturers of cellphones added the features of PDAs to their phones. Fourth and final is a product convergence of complementarities. Then existing products and services become complementary to one another. For example, internet standards and technology made computers (data processors) and telephone services (data communications) mutually complementary.[25]

Industries will converge over time, and revolutionary companies are the ones that will discover and lead this convergence. Opportunities to create significant value are often found in the convergence of two or more industries because this is where new value is being created for customers.

RESCALE THE INDUSTRY

Strategy can be built as the cost structure of businesses change. Opportunities can be found by exploring whether industry conventions about minimum efficient scale are correct. Change can favour either larger or smaller scales of operation.

Increase Scale

The financial services industry is currently in the middle of a major rescaling from national to international. Canada's five big banks have grown larger by adding operations abroad, mostly through mergers and acquisitions. Increased scale has also occurred in the funeral business. Both Loewen Group Inc. and its major competitor, Service Corporation International (SCI), worked on "rolling up" the funeral business by buying local funeral homes and cemeteries and then consolidating their operations. Purchase of such items as embalming fluid, coffins, advertising, and other essential ingredients was centralized. Furthermore, economies of scale were pursued by sharing embalming and hearses among groups of homes. However, Loewen was tripped up in 1995 following a court ruling in Mississippi for US$500 million and filed for bankruptcy protection in 1999. It was revived in 2002 as a much smaller company called Alderwoods Group. In 2006, SCI continued to pursue its strategy by buying Alderwoods for US$1.2 billion.

There is no clear guide as to when to grow or how. Some companies increase scale in ways that are revolutionary. Examples include such disparate industries as waste management services and adult education. SCI and Waste Management, did so through acquisitions, but others, such as Athabasca University, which offers adult education, did so through internal growth.

Downscaling to Serve Narrow or Local Customers

In some industries, downscaling the size of the business presents the opportunity to generate significant margins. Downscaling necessarily implies going after a smaller segment of the market. While the market volume is smaller, focusing on fewer customers allows the business to add significant value for those it serves.

Local microbreweries provide an excellent example of this. Traditionally beer companies have produced beer using inoffensive, indistinctive recipes that satisfy a wide range of tastes. They have then used their marketing talent to position different brands based on lifestyles associated with the brands. Beer consumers interested in taste have been dissatisfied with these beers, creating an opportunity for microbreweries interested in producing distinct beers. Examples of successful microbreweries can be found across Canada: Granville Island Brewing Co. and Vancouver Island Brewery in British Columbia; Big Rock Brewery and Wild Rose Brewery in Alberta; Creemore Springs Brewery Ltd., Kawartha Lakes Brewing Co., Steam Whistle Brewing, and Wellington Brewery in Ontario; Boréale and McAuslan Brewery in Quebec; Garrison Brewing Co. and Propeller Brewing Co. in Nova Scotia; and Quidi Vidi Brewing Co. in Newfoundland.

Bed and breakfast inns (B&Bs) are another example of how a small business can compete against large national chains in the lodging industry. B&Bs have only a few rooms. At one level of analysis, the cost structure would seem very inefficient compared to the scale economies available to national chains. However, when B&Bs provide high levels of personal service and properties are unique and charming, they can charge prices that well exceed those of the chain hotels.

RECONSIDERING THE COMPETITIVE MINDSET

Creating Complementors out of Suppliers, Buyers, and Competitors

The five forces in Michael Porter's five-force model (*suppliers, buyers, substitutes, new entrants,* and *rivals*) to which *complementors* have been added, all compete for a share of industry's profits.[26] Complementors do not themselves compete in the industry and they do not buy from or sell to it. When their products and services are used with the industry's product or service, the industry's product or service becomes more valuable to customers. This means that complementors help to increase the total profits of the industry. Captive finance companies such as General Motors Acceptance Corp. (popularly known as GMAC until its name changed to Ally Financial in 2010) and GE Capital have been complementors for those companies selling large assets such as cars and homes. The companies extended credit to customers who did not have the cash needed to buy the products. Similarly, parcel delivery companies such as FedEx, Purolator, and UPS are complementors for online retailers as their ability to ship product quickly and reliably increases online sales. And novel software that allows gaming and storage and transfer of music on personal computers increases the sales of such computers.

The value net model is a framework that represents all the players in the market and the interdependencies between industries. This model is summarized in Exhibit 6.9. Within the model, the product of Industry B is a complementor if customers value the product of Industry A more when they also have Industry B's product than when they have only the product of Industry A. Alternatively, the product of Industry B is a competitor if customers value the product of Industry A less when they also have Industry B's product.

Technical standards for new technology are a key area of competitive and cooperative behaviour. Examples over time include Apple versus open standards for personal computers

Exhibit 6.9 The Value Net

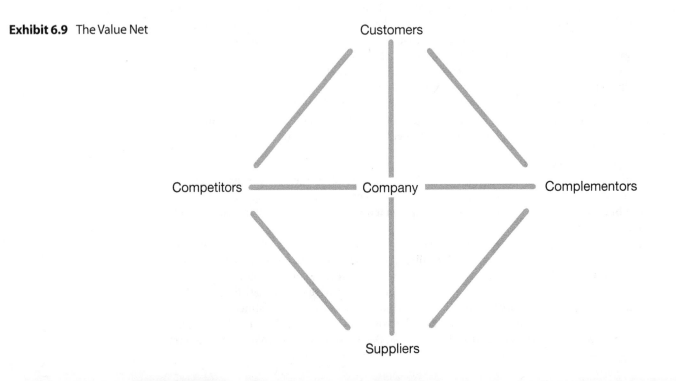

and, more recently, HD-DVD versus Blu-ray. A personal computer is of little value without applications that run on it. In 1977, Apple introduced the Apple II, a personal computer that was more advanced than anything made by competitors, in large part because the company produced both the hardware and software. It kept its system "closed" so that it was able to appropriate all profits from sales of both hardware and software. IBM was anxious to catch up with Apple. To do so it chose to build a personal computer that used off-the-shelf technology from outside suppliers, including Intel's 8080 CPU and Microsoft's disc operating system (DOS), and released the IBM PC in 1981. IBM announced its standards so that third parties could provide compatible hardware and software. This design decision gave other companies the information they needed to produce clones of IBM computers. As they did so, the price of personal computers dropped and the sales of all DOS-based computers soared. The large number of DOS-based personal computers led many software designers to write applications for the DOS machines. The combination of low prices of IBM-compatible computers and the availability of software to run on them meant that DOS-based hardware and software soon dominated both markets.

Since 2003, two incompatible formats have been fighting to become the industry standard for high-definition video players: Blu-ray, which was developed by Sony, and HD-DVD, which was developed by Toshiba. The success of either format relies on having manufacturers prepared to make equipment and studios prepared to record media based on the standard. Proponents of each standard set about convincing various complementors to adopt the standards they were promoting. Companies that agreed to adopt each standard are identified in Exhibit 6.10. Data in the table show that, although the companies are competitors, they are willing to adopt a common standard so that they have access to the market that is being created. Over time, support of Blu-ray increased, and in February 2008 Toshiba, the holdout for HD-DVD, announced that it would no longer manufacture HD-DVD products.

This example leads us to two observations about competitors and complementors.

1. A company is your *competitor* if customers value your product *less* when they have the other company's product. Here there are two levels of competition. The first is between companies providing competing technology based on different standards: Blu-ray versus HD-DVD products. The second is competition among all those who produce competing products based on the same standard: players, storage devices, and movies.

2. A company is your *complementor* if customers value your product *more* when they have the other company's product than when they have your product alone. Here there are two levels of complementarity. The first is across product classes. Customers prefer being able to buy a full range of products that are compatible, such as movies, home theatres, and storage devices. The second is within a product class. Customers prefer the standard that has the greatest amount of product associated with it because then they have more choice.

Complementor Type	Blu-ray	HD-DVD
Manufacturer support (home theatre)	Hitachi, Mitsubishi, LG, Sharp, Sony, Panasonic, Samsung, Philips, Thomson/RCA	Toshiba, LG, Thomson/RCA, Onkyo, Samsung
Manufacturer support (PC storage)	Apple, Dell, BenQ, HP, LG, Panasonic, Philips, Pioneer, Samsung, Sony, TDK	Microsoft, Intel, HP, NEC, Toshiba
Media support	Sony Pictures (including MGM/Columbia TriStar), Disney (including Touchstone, Miramax), Fox, Warner, Lions Gate	Paramount, Studio Canal, Universal, Warner (until end of May 2008), the Weinstein Company, DreamWorks Animation

Exhibit 6.10 Various Complementors Lined up Behind Blu-ray and HD-DVD Formats[27]

Exhibit 6.11 Creation of New Markets through Offensive Moves

Dimensions of Competition	Head-to-Head Competition	New-Market Creation
Industry	Emphasizes rivalry	Emphasizes substitutes across industries
Strategic group and industry segments	Emphasizes competitive position within group and segments	Looks across groups and segments
Buyers	Emphasizes better buyer service	Emphasizes redefinition of the buyer and buyer's preferences
Product and service offerings	Emphasizes product or service value and offerings within industry definition	Emphasizes complementary products and services within and across industries and segments
Business model	Emphasizes efficient operation of the model	Emphasizes rethinking of the industry business model
Time	Emphasizes adaptation and capabilities that support competitive retaliation	Emphasizes strategic intent— seeking to shape the external environment over time

Complementary thinking can be beneficial for a business. This has been recognized by the makers of mobile platforms as each seeks to have the best and broadest collection of applications. To give developers a little extra financial motivation, manufacturers have funds to invest in developers making compatible applications. Google has a US$10 million fund to support its Android, Kleiner Perkins has a US$100 million iFund to support iPhone-only start-ups, and Research In Motion has a Cdn$150 million BlackBerry Partners Fund for its mobile device. This approach helps encourage complementors and increases the opportunities available.

SHIFTING THE FOCUS OF STRATEGIC THINKING

Several of the offensive moves just reviewed suggest the benefit of shifting the focus of strategic thinking away from conventional head-to-head rivalry to creating new markets. This altered thinking requires different assumptions, which are summarized in Exhibit 6.11. New-market creation emphasizes *actions and capabilities that eclipse the competition rather than meet it head-on,* whereas the traditional view emphasizes actions and capabilities that are determined by competitors' moves. [yellow tail], the company discussed in How Would You Do That? 6.1, provides a good example of how a set of moves produced a successful strategy.

Defensive Moves for Incumbents Caught Off Guard

Offensive moves take a business into new areas, but oftentimes an existing business is set upon by new competitors entering its market space. Sometimes management of the existing business does not see the new competitors coming, and other times it is slow reacting to them. In either case, the business has to take defensive action to deal with the new competitors if it hopes to survive. We lay out seven strategic options that management can use, but before doing this we want to make two points. First, the success of any move depends on the company's strengths and weaknesses, and sometimes a wise choice can strengthen the business's resources. Second, the moves are not mutually exclusive. A business can pursue several moves at the same time because it does not know which move, if any, will be successful. The seven moves for dealing with a dynamic industry are absorbing, avoiding, containing, countering, countervailing, locking out, and shaping.

1. ABSORBING

The most direct way to deal with the new competitor is to buy it. This is what Rogers Communications did in the cellphone business. Rogers got into wireless communication in 1985 with the founding of Rogers Cantel. In 1996, Microcell Telecommunications became Canada's first cellular telecom carrier with a GSM-based network that used the same standard the iPhone uses. In 2001, Rogers adopted GSM technology, and in 2004 it bought Microcell for an estimated Cdn$1.4 billion and changed the company's name to Fido Solutions. This made Rogers the only GSM-based network in Canada. In the United States, IKEA also bought out STOR in 1992, a competitive entrant, after STOR opened stores on the west coast of the United States that virtually replicated its retail format.[28]

2. AVOIDING

Another way to deal with a competitive entrant is to avoid it by moving on, as IBM did.[29] In the early 1990s, IBM's core PC and minicomputer business was flagging. Its first strategic move was to become a PC- and networking-software powerhouse, second behind Microsoft. Its second move was into IT and internet consulting markets, where it emerged as the largest company among such competitors as Accenture. Its third move was into business associated with the trend toward outsourcing IT and service solutions, where it became the market leader in competition with companies such as EDS. In 2008, it added Business Analytics and Optimization Services through its acquisition of Cognos. Throughout this transition process, IBM drew on its resources, capabilities, and dynamic capabilities in services and software. In many ways, IBM, though ostensibly on the defensive, was pursuing an offensive strategy, effectively combining improvisation and experimentation with deft staging and pacing. IBM not only emerged as a leader in information technology but also avoided the commoditization pressures that affected PC companies such as HP. Eventually IBM completely exited its core PC manufacturing business by selling its operations to China-based Lenovo.

3. CONTAINING

When the competitor is already present in the market, the business can work to contain the competitor, as Loblaw, Canada's largest food chain, tried to contain Wal-Mart's entry into its market. Wal-Mart entered Canada in 1994 through the purchase of 122 Woolco stores. It converted these stores to the Wal-Mart name and sold general merchandise in them. Then Wal-Mart added a limited line of groceries to these stores. Wal-Mart had food retailing experience, having developed Super Centers in the United States by coupling a supermarket with each general merchandise store. Loblaw anticipated that Wal-Mart would create Super Centers in Canada, so it moved to deny Wal-Mart market space. It did so by expanding its stores under the Great Canadian Superstore banner, a banner with a retail value curve very similar to Wal-Mart's. By tying up the market space before Wal-Mart entered, Loblaw hoped that Wal-Mart would decide not to enter. But if Wal-Mart did, Loblaw hoped that it would buy Loblaw—in England Wal-Mart bought ASDA, a food chain that occupied Wal-Mart's market position after Archie Norman revived the English company using Wal-Mart's business model. Allan Leighton, Norman's second-in-command at ASDA and later an executive with Wal-Mart, was an adviser to Loblaw as it built its containment strategy. Unfortunately Loblaw had great difficulty executing the strategic change necessary. The chain lost many of its general merchandise buyers because they were unwilling to move to Brampton, Ontario, when distribution centres were consolidated to make the supply chain more efficient. Working with general merchandise also challenged Loblaw's logistics system, which was reflected in poorly stocked store shelves. For many consumers the changes produced a value curve that was below what they had come to expect from the grocery chain.

4. COUNTERING

A company can counter the new entrant's offer by improving its own offer. Air Canada tried to contain the impact of WestJet by creating the regional carrier Jazz, by offering Aeroplan Miles, and by continuing to use its bargaining power within the major airports as WestJet started to move into primary locations, such as Toronto's Pearson International Airport. WestJet responded by offering AirMiles as part of their incentive program. Then in 2006 Air Canada "unbundled" its fares, creating a fare package called Tango that had a bare-bones service package with prices that matched WestJet and three higher fare levels that offered extra amenities.

When the new entrant bases the contest on a new technology, the businesses using old technology can improve the old technology for some time while the entrant continues to develop the new technology. The risk for the businesses using the old technology is that, when the new technology becomes irrefutably superior, they will not be able to catch up. In the automotive industry, plastics and nonferrous metals have been replacing steel. The steel companies have fought back by cooperating to develop ways of making cars. Dofasco and 34 other international steelmakers joined with Porsche Engineering Services Inc., a North American unit of Porsche AG, to design and build an Ultra Light Steel Auto Body (ULSAB) that reduced vehicle weight by more than 25 percent and cost by 14 percent while improving safety and fuel efficiency. As a result of ULSAB, Dofasco was the first Canadian steelmaker to produce tubular steel specifically targeted at automotive components manufactured using a revolutionary hydroforming manufacturing process.[30]

When the incumbent is successful at defending its market, the entrant can be discouraged completely or, if it still chooses to enter, it can seek out the incumbent as a partner or acquirer. Microsoft, for example, is so aggressive at adding free software features to its popular Windows platform that new software companies routinely include partnership with Microsoft as part of their entry strategies.

5. COUNTERVAILING

Countering an entrant already in business elsewhere is challenging because the entrant can draw on the resources it generates in the other market. One way to counter this is for the business under attack to enter the attacker's other market. This has several possible outcomes. If the entrant continues aggressive entry, the business being attacked can be equally aggressive in the entrant's original market, weakening its performance and limiting the resources the entrant has to devote to the new market. If the entrant is sensitive to competitive pressures, the entrant could condition its behaviour and become less aggressive because it does not want to be under threat in its original market. The market for photographic supplies provides an example. Kodak alleged that Fujifilm made virtually all of its profits in Japan, Fujifilm's profit sanctuary, so Kodak tried to enter Japan. Unfortunately, the businesses in Fujifilm's marketing channels prevented Kodak from successfully penetrating the Japanese market—Kodak was locked out.[31] Sometimes simply the threat of retaliation reduces the likelihood of cutthroat competition. The frequent use of countervailing power in this way has been called the "exchange-of-hostage theory" in international business. It has been observed among competing oligopolistic companies from different countries, especially European and U.S. companies.

6. LOCKING OUT

The business can keep potential entrants out through such activities as patenting, behaviour channel control, and government regulations. A common practice among drug companies is patenting whole families of chemicals so that competitors cannot patent a chemical similar to the one their drug is based on. Lock outs have also occurred in distribution industries. Canada Pipe controlled the behaviour of customers through its Stocking Distributor Program, which offered distributors quarterly and annual rebates, as well as point-of-purchase discounts if they purchased all of their cast iron pipe from Canada Pipe.[32] Amazon moved to lock in publishers selling Print-on-Demand (POD) books to it by requiring that they use Amazon as the POD printer.[33] In the case of IKEA, before it bought STOR, it brought a lawsuit in which it argued that STOR's replication of IKEA's catalogues, checkout areas, colour schemes, department names, furniture, furniture names, price tags, shopping carts, signs, and store layout and design constituted unfair competition and copyright infringement.[34]

7. SHAPING

Sometimes denying the market to the entrant is impossible. Then the threatened business seeks to channel the direction in which the entrant develops and so remove the direct threat. This is what the Canadian Medical Association (CMA) did to chiropractics. Founded in 1895, chiropractics was a relatively new form of medical treatment that was characterized by the CMA as quackery. But today the Canadian Medical Association (CMA) and chiropractics show mutual respect, although not all doctors and chiropractors agree on all issues. This was achieved by regulators and educators as they shaped the evolution of the chiropractic practice so that it complemented conventional health care.

THE PITFALLS OF THE DEFENSIVE MINDSET

A word of caution is in order about the seven defensive moves for dealing with a dynamic industry. Although they are viable strategies for dynamic markets, they are nonetheless purely defensive. Relying on them exclusively will lead to purely defensive strategizing: *Any company that invests in resources and capabilities that support retaliation to the exclusion of innovation and change may only be prolonging the inevitable demise of the business.*

Ralston Purina lost its way because it became trapped in its retaliatory mindset. Ralston was long considered one of the most efficient and competitively aggressive pet-food companies in the world. Every time a competitor made a move or a new entrant set foot in its market, Ralston responded with a two-pronged defence: undermining prices in the competitor's stronghold markets while simultaneously attacking its weaker markets. This defensive posture, which secured Ralston's market leadership for more than 20 years, also ensured that the company lagged behind the industry in terms of innovation. In 2003, Ralston sold out to Nestlé, whose constant attention to innovative products allowed it to take over Ralston's position as industry leader.

Taking an Option on Revolutionary Move

Instead of retaliating, businesses may decide that waiting for uncertainty to clear is the best course of action. While it is waiting, the business can make a small investment that will allow it to have an option on making a bolder move later. This type of investment is generally referred to as a **real option**. One example of this comes from BCE during the 1990s. At the time, various industries had been defined and regulated in the Canadian communications industry: local and long distance telephone services; wireless (mobile) and land wired service; and cable television, which used network technology but could not transmit voice. Top management at BCE saw that the barriers between these industries were crumbling due to technological innovation. But it was not clear what operating assets would be needed when the industries converged. So BCE invested in the partial ownership of a number of businesses. This gave it strategic control

real options Process of maximizing the upside or limiting the downside of an investment opportunity by uncovering and quantifying the options and discussion points embedded within it.

For more than 20 years, Ralston Purina fiercely—and successfully— defended its position as top dog in the pet-food industry. Unfortunately, the company put so much energy into its defensive strategy that it had little left for innovation. Ralston sold out to Nestlé in 2003.

so that the companies remained viable integration partners later when BCE saw the potential for meaningful synergies. BCE's initial investments created options for future investment and takeover of these businesses.[35]

Another example is provided by Intel, which invested heavily in internal research and development. It determined that it was unlikely to be the source of most innovations that could change how processing technology was used. Consequently, Intel made a conscious decision to invest in start-ups. Being a partial owner in start-ups gave Intel inside information on new technologies being developed elsewhere. Intel had no obligation to increase its investment in these operations or to buy the products or internalize these innovations. However, making these small investments gave it the ability to do so in the future.

Where greater uncertainty and flexibility exist, the potential value in having options to manage it is greater. Increasingly, managers in industries characterized by large capital investments and high degrees of uncertainty and flexibility (such as oil and gas, mining, pharmaceuticals, and biotechnology) are thinking in terms of real options. These companies typically have plenty of the market and R&D data needed to make confident assumptions about uncertain outcomes. They also have the sort of engineering-oriented corporate culture that isn't averse to using complex mathematical tools to assess risk.

Although real-options analysis is not a cure-all for strategic uncertainty, the technique is getting much more attention among companies and industries. Intel, for example, now trains finance employees in real-options valuation and has used the technique to analyze a number of capital projects. As a starting point, we suggest that you introduce yourself to real options by considering the following five categories:[36]

1. Waiting-to-invest options. The value of waiting to build a factory until better market information comes along may exceed the value of immediate expansion.
2. Growth options. An entry investment may create opportunities to pursue valuable follow-up projects.
3. Flexibility options. Serving markets on two continents by building two plants instead of one gives a company the option of switching production from one plant to the other as conditions dictate.
4. Exit (or abandonment) options. The option to sell (or walk away from) a project in response to new information increases its value.
5. Learning options. An initial investment may generate further information about a market opportunity and may help to determine whether the company should add more capacity.

FOCUS ON ETHICS 6.1
Kiva Microfunds[37]

Microfinance in general is disruptive because it reaches new groups of customers who were not previously served by traditional bank-lending practices. Kiva Microfunds was founded in 2005 to lend money to small businesses in the developing world and, since 2009, in the developed world, starting with the United States. Kiva allows microfinance institutions, called field partners, to post profiles of qualified local entrepreneurs on its website at www.kiva.org. Lenders browse the site and choose an entrepreneur they wish to fund. Kiva aggregates loan capital from individual lenders and transfers it to the appropriate field partners, who then disburse the capital to the entrepreneur chosen by the lender. As entrepreneurs repay their loans, the field partners remit funds back to Kiva. As the loan is repaid, the Kiva lenders can withdraw their principal or reloan it to another entrepreneur.

Even in a disruptive industry, Kiva is a disruptive player because of the way it acquires the funds it lends. The individuals acting as lenders are less likely to demand market rates of return on their loans. This allows Kiva to offer loans at lower costs than other microfinance vendors while still being economically sustainable (low-cost disruption).

Mixing mission and market with the scale and collaborative nature of the web makes it unique and (presumably) disruptive. Using the web to solicit funds from individual lenders/donors and to communicate with lenders is cheaper than traditional means (direct mail, face-to-face solicitation, etc.). However, Kiva still relies on the field partners to oversee borrowers and collect payments.

What are the consequences of this activity on others than those giving and receiving the money?

Formulating and Implementing Dynamic Strategies

In this final section we focus on the ways in which dynamic strategies should be reflected in your application of both the strategy diamond and the strategy implementation models. We devote Chapter 8 to a more detailed discussion of implementation levers and organizational structure, so the remarks in this section provide just a basic introduction. Arenas and staging, in conjunction with the implementation levers, are key decision areas as you move forward to put your strategy into place.

FOCUSING ON ARENAS AND STAGING

The model of strategy formulation is critical because it establishes a set of simple rules for describing the business and showing how it creates value. Of course, all five elements of strategy are important and must be managed in concert, but the *arenas* and *staging* diamonds are especially important. In addition to recognizing the need for dynamic capabilities, focusing on these facets of strategy is what differentiates a dynamic strategy from a strategy developed for more stable contexts.

The Role of Arenas

Arenas designate the customers to be served and the products to be provided. ◆ In each section of this chapter—sections dealing with industry and product evolution, technological discontinuity, and turbulence—we have emphasized that the strategist is always making important and reasoned choices about the company's mix of customers, products, and services. The remaining four diamonds of strategy—vehicles, differentiators, staging, and economic logic—tell the strategist whether the mix of arenas fit together.

The role of arenas in the company's strategy will vary according to the factor being considered in the dynamic environment. In the context of *industry evolution,* for example, arenas must fit with a company's resources, capabilities, and dynamic capabilities. With regard to *technological discontinuities*, the role of arenas, though overlapping with its role in low-end disruption strategies, was broadened to include potential customers, particularly when the strategy is designed to create new markets. *Globalization*, introduced in Chapter 10, adds yet another dimension to the role of arenas: If a company is going global, managers need to apply what they have learned about competing in one geographic arena to the task of competing in others. Finally, in navigating *turbulent and hypercompetitive markets*, managers must think of arenas as laboratories—sites in which to conduct experiments or launch probes into the possible future of the business and its strategy.

The Role of Staging

Competing in turbulent environments requires finesse in addressing the staging element of the strategy diamond. ◆ In many ways, conducting strategy in a turbulent environment requires the regular deployment and testing of options—options for new growth initiatives, new businesses, and new ways of doing business.

Recent research on how businesses manage the staging of strategy in order to succeed in turbulent or hypercompetitive environments is anchored in so-called *systems, chaos,* or *complexity theories.* Studies are peppered with such biological terms as *self-organizing systems* and *co-adaptation,* and they're concerned with the same phenomenon—adaptation to a changing external environment in which change may be rapid and its direction uncertain.[38] By and large, they all share a basic premise: Companies need to adapt in order to survive in chaotic environments. In one study of several companies competing on the edge of chaos, researchers encountered the following three levels of activity, summarized by the curves in Exhibit 6.12:[39]

1. Activities designed to test today's competitive strategy (defending today's business).
2. Activities designed to lead to tomorrow's competitive strategy (drive growth in emerging businesses).
3. Activities designed to influence the pacing and timing of change (seeding options for future new businesses and growth initiatives).

Exhibit 6.12 Creating Options for Future Competitive Advantage

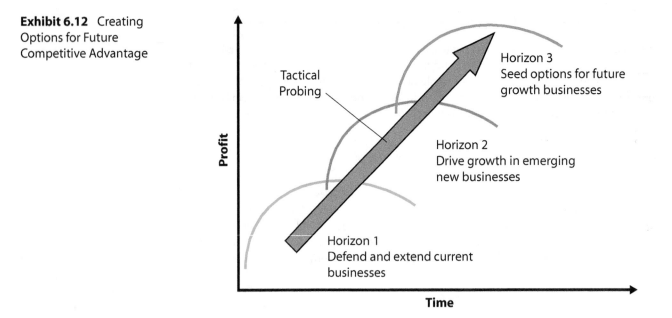

The lower left-hand curve depicted in Exhibit 6.12 is the defence of existing businesses. The middle and upper right-hand curves represent activities focused on the future—the conditions toward which the change-oriented activities at the foundation of the strategy are aimed. At the same time, however, future products will embody indelible links to the past. In this model of business strategy, the bridge between past activities and future conditions is built on a substructure of experimentation and learning. For instance, S. C. Johnson found that one of its innovative home pesticide products in Europe could not pass U.S. regulatory hurdles, preventing its introduction in that country. However, through experimentation with its fragrances division, a key technology in the product gave rise to Glade PlugIns, introduced in 1993. S. C. Johnson effectively joined knowledge embedded in previously disconnected and geographically removed operating units (pesticides and fragrances divisions) to create an entirely new product category in the home air-freshener industry.

Successful businesses are those that have adjusted their strategies to the prevailing business conditions. Managers use their understanding of the competitive environment to jettison or modify ineffective aspects of strategy as customers migrate toward businesses that offer the most attractive value curve. Dell, for example, developed its direct-sales model for the consumer and small-business PC market. Then in 2002 Dell launched Dell Direct Stores, kiosks mostly in malls and shopping centres, where customers could see products first-hand before ordering online or by phone. This was followed in 2008 by Dell's abrupt abandonment of all 140 of its U.S. Dell Direct Stores as it moved its products into a number of retailers, most notably Best Buy but also Wal-Mart and Staples.

Experimentation

A striking feature of this model of dynamic strategy is the close relationship between operating decisions and the evolution of strategy. A clear strategy enables the company to excel in a given business, but it also gives rise to experimentation that produces options for the future—Horizons 2 and 3 in Exhibit 6.12. Often, we don't think of the operating decisions as *strategic* activities because, in and of themselves, they're fairly inconsequential in affecting cost or competitive impact. In dynamic markets, however, many of these decisions are in effect low-cost experiments that test the current strategy and seek to improve on it.

Consider the discount broker Charles Schwab. The company found itself being squeezed on one side by deep-discount internet start-ups such as E*Trade and on the other side by discount initiatives by full-service brokers such as Merrill Lynch. Schwab experimented with new ways of reinforcing customer relationships and identifying new markets. It developed futures-trading programs, simplified its mutual-fund offerings, and launched internet-based products and services. Some of these experiments went nowhere—Schwab aborted a line of credit cards and a foray into online mortgages. But those that succeeded enabled Schwab both to further differentiate itself from bare-bones discounters and to gain ground in markets dominated by full-service brokers.

Setting Pace and Rhythm

Finally, as managers move from one horizon to another they must think about the speed and pace of change. Many managers do not appreciate fully the role played by time and timing in formulating and executing strategy. Consider the various approaches to staging and pacing described in Exhibit 6.13.[40] Obviously, attention to pacing and staging can prompt a company to think more seriously about the need for constant experimentation and probing. The way that 3M encourages innovation by giving its scientists time and resources to work on their own pet projects partially explains why that company is consistently able to generate new and innovative products.

The Role of Implementation Levers

The previous discussion provides some perspective on various approaches to strategy. The formulation of strategy is closely allied with the implementation of strategy as the organizational structures, systems, and processes determine what people are able to accomplish. This means that the formulation of strategy must reflect the current capabilities of the organizational structure, systems, and processes and that these meet the needs of a business operating in a dynamic environment. In addition, the strategic leadership and the culture of the organization must reflect a commitment to reasoned risk taking, learning, and responding to change. Pursuit of a dynamic strategy is also beneficial when top management practises and promotes core values that support it.

In moving to a new strategy, the organizational aspects of the business must be adjusted to meet the requirements of the new strategy. The staging element of strategy bridges formulation and implementation because it specifies how certain levers will move along the way.

British Airways	"Five years is the maximum that you can go without refreshing the brand. . . We did it [relaunched Club Europe Service] because we wanted to stay ahead so that we could continue to win customers."
Emerson Electric	"In each of the last three years we've introduced more than 100 major new products, which is about 70 percent above our pace of the early 1990s. We plan to maintain this rate and, overall, have targeted increasing new products to [equal] 35 percent of total sales."
Intel	The inventor of Moore's Law stated that the power of the computer chip would double every 18 months. IBM builds a new manufacturing facility every nine months. "We build factories two years in advance of needing them, before we have the products to run in them, and before we know the industry is going to grow."
Gillette	Forty percent of Gillette's sales every five years must come from entirely new products (prior to its acquisition by P&G). Gillette raises prices at a pace set to match price increases in a basket of market goods (which includes items such as a newspaper, a candy bar, and a can of soda). Gillette prices are never raised faster than the price of the market basket.
3M	Thirty percent of sales must come from products that are fewer than four years old.

Exhibit 6.13 Staging and Pacing in the Real World

FOCUS ON SUSTAINABILITY 6.1
Sustainable Waterloo

Concern over rising temperatures across the globe is increasing due in large part to the continued use of carbon-based fuels. Many believe that carbon dioxide production has to be drastically reduced. One of the most straightforward solutions is to introduce government regulations on carbon emissions, including Ontario's commitment to a cap-and-trade carbon market by 2012.

In 2008, Mike Morrice and Chris DePaul decided that a more productive approach would be to help businesses rather than force businesses to address the carbon issue. They created a not-for-profit organization called Sustainable Waterloo that will lead others in the Waterloo Region of Southern Ontario toward a sustainable future. The organization's initial project is The Regional Carbon Initiative. The group provides participating organizations with an online tool to measure their carbon emissions, educational forums to learn from their peers about how to reduce emissions, and as much public recognition as possible for those companies that are successful in reducing emissions. Pledging partners include Athena Software, Enermodal Engineering, VeriForm Inc., and XCG Consultants. Each of these companies has made a public commitment to reduce carbon emissions.

Morag Carter, director of the Climate Change Program at the David Suzuki Foundation, said, "The David Suzuki Foundation believes that Sustainable Waterloo can play an integral role in reducing carbon emissions amongst high-tech companies in the Waterloo Region and set an example for other Canadian regions and organizations to follow."[41]

Sustainable Waterloo is disruptive as a not-for-profit because it is helping businesses adjust to a changing environment. Those businesses that are not proactive in making changes will find that they have to react to changing governmental regulations.

Which do you think is the better way to go? Move ahead on one's own or wait and then respond to government regulations?

Summary of Challenges

1. *Distinguish the ways in which companies' strategies are related to dynamic contexts.* Dynamism can have dramatic effects on the quality of a company's strategy and it can undermine competitive advantage—sometimes with blinding speed but more typically over some extended period of time. Indeed, as noted in the opening vignette, the winery industry in Ontario had periods of gradual change interspersed with periods of dramatic change—evolution and revolution. The speed of change in an industry can either complement or compound the effects of industry evolution, technological discontinuities, and globalization.

2. *Identify, compare, and contrast the various routes to revolutionary strategies.* Offensive strategies are ones that do not take the existing rules of competition in the industry for granted but rather attempt to create value by approaching competition by violating some of these taken-for-granted rules. Reconceiving products and services, either by creating a new value curve or by separate function and form, can result in new offerings with high added value for customers. Companies can also reconfigure the value chain, either by developing a new value chain or by compressing the existing value chain. Value can be created by redefining the arenas, either through focusing on the total possible market, rather than current customers served, or by spearheading industry convergence. Opportunities to increase margins are also found in rescaling the industry, either by consolidating the industry in search of greater economies of scale or by downscaling the industry in search of profitable niche markets. Finally, revolutionary strategies can be found in reconsidering the competitive mindset, both by focusing on complementors and by shifting the competitive focus away from head-to-head competition and searching for areas where the competition has not yet ventured.

3. *Evaluate the advantages and disadvantages of choosing a first-mover strategy.* First movers are companies that initiate a strategic action before rivals, such as the introduction of a new product or service or a new process that provides a traditional product or service of dramatically higher quality or at a lower price, or both. Second movers are relatively early movers (because they are still not last movers) but delayed enough to learn from first movers. Effective second movers are sometimes referred to as *fast followers*. They are distinguished from late movers, whose tardiness penalizes them when the market grows. First movers do not always have an advantage because there are significant risks associated with being the first to introduce new products, services, and business models.

4. *Recognize when an incumbent is caught off guard by an offensive strategy and identify defensive tactics reducing the effects of this competition.* Most established companies find it difficult to revolutionize an industry and are caught off guard when other

businesses do so. In such cases, companies can resort to defensive tactics such as absorbing, avoiding, containing, countering, countervailing, locking out, and shaping. They can also attempt to avoid surprise by taking out options on new businesses and technologies early in their life cycle (such as through investments in start-ups) that will give them the opportunity to acquire the new business at a later time on favourable terms should it prove to be a revolutionary idea.

5. *Explain the difficulties and solutions to implementing revolutionary strategies.* Vision is critical in that it serves as a set of simple rules that describe the business and how it creates value. Although all five elements of strategy are important and must be managed in concert, the arenas and staging diamonds are perhaps most important in dynamic markets. And, like the five elements of strategy, a balance among the implementation levers is critical. These levers must accommodate environmental turbulence and hypercompetitive environments. The strategic flexibility demanded of these environments requires that organization structure and systems can be easily decoupled and recombined as circumstances change. Rigid bureaucracy is generally incompatible with turbulent environments. Strategic leadership must further support the company's ability to identify the need for and undertake strategic change.

Review Questions

1. What are four sets of challenges to sustained competitive advantage outlined in this chapter?
2. What is the relationship between first and second movers?
3. What is industry commoditization? What are two strategies a company may undertake to combat industry commoditization?
4. What is a new-market-creation strategy?
5. What is a low-end disruption strategy?
6. What are the three levels of activity that underlie strategies for turbulent and hypercompetitive markets?
7. What is the role of timing and pacing in revolutionary strategies?
8. What seven defensive strategies might industry incumbents pursue in dynamic markets?
9. How might you apply real-options analysis, financially and conceptually, in the context of revolutionary strategies for turbulent and hypercompetitive markets?
10. What are the implications of dynamic strategies for strategy formulation and implementation?

Experiential Activities

Group Exercises

1. If you were the CEO of Research In Motion (RIM), what material from this chapter would be most relevant to you? How would this material help you to formulate a strategy? What might key components of that strategy be? Now put yourself in Nokia's position. Would you see either RIM or Apple as a threat? If so, what strategy would you formulate in response?
2. Review the list of first- and second-mover companies in Exhibit 6.2. What specific resources and capabilities do you think successful first movers must possess? What specific resources and capabilities do you think successful second movers and fast followers must possess? Do you think that a company could be both a first mover and fast follower if it wanted to be?

Ethical Debates

1. Some companies manage disruptive strategy threats by investing in the companies that bring them to market so that if the threat turns out to be wildly successful they can still benefit from it financially. Is this a purely business decision or are there ethical concerns as well?
2. You learned how incumbents can be blindsided by disruptive strategies. Litigation appears to be a prominent tool that incumbents can use to at least slow new entrants' growth. What might be some of your ethical concerns when using litigation to manage competition? Do you think that a company's size will affect its ability to use this tactic? Does this matter?

Endnotes

1. The quote is cited by M. Ryval, "Glass Half Full," *Globe and Mail*, September 28, 2001. Accessed October 14, 2009, at http://v1.theglobeandmail.com/series/wine/glass.html. Additional information on the industry can be found in K. F. Harling, "Business Strategies as Markets Open: A Case Study of Ontario Wines," *Agribusiness* 10:3 (May/June 1994): 259–273; and "Vincor International Inc.—Company Profile, Information, Business Description, History, Background Information on Vincor International Inc." Accessed October 13, 2009, at www.referenceforbusiness.com/history2/75/Vincor-International-Inc.html. Specific information on VQA is "VQA Wineries Overview." Accessed October 13, 2009, at www.vqaontario.com/Wineries; and "VQA Wineries in the Niagara Region." Accessed October 13, 2009, at www.vqaontario.com/Wineries/NiagaraPeninsula.

2. Adapted from K. G. Smith, W. J. Ferrier, and C. M. Grimm, "King of the Hill: Dethroning the Industry Leader," *Academy of Management Executive* 15:2 (2001): 59–70.

3. D. C. Hambrick and J. W. Fredrickson, "Are You Sure You Have a Strategy?" *Academy of Management Executive* 15:4 (2001): 48–59.

4. M. Chen, "Competitor Analysis and Interfirm Rivalry: Toward a Theoretical Integration," *Academy of Management Review* 21 (1996): 100–134; M. Chen and D. C. Hambrick, "Speed, Stealth, and Selective Attack: How Small Firms Differ from Large Firms in Competitive Behavior," *Academy of Management Journal* 38 (1995): 453–482.

5. A. M. Brandenburger and B. J. Nalebuff, *Co-Opetition* (New York: Currency Doubleday, 1996).

6. K. G. Smith, W. J. Ferrier, and C. M. Grimm, "King of the Hill: Dethroning the Industry Leader."

7. K. Rangan and G. Bowman, "Beating the Commodity Magnet," *Industrial Marketing Management* 21 (1992): 215–224; P. Kotler, "Managing Products through Their Product Life Cycle," in *Marketing Management: Planning, Implementation, and Control,* 7th ed. (Upper Saddle River, N.J.: Prentice Hall, 1991); P. Kotler, "Product Life-Cycle Marketing Strategies," in *Marketing Management,* 11th ed. (Upper Saddle River, N.J.: Prentice Hall, 2003), 328–339.

8. S. Brown and K. Eisenhardt, *Competing on the Edge* (Boston: Harvard Business School Press, 1998).

9. P. Anderson and M. L. Tushman, "Technological Discontinuities and Dominant Designs: A Cyclical Model of Technological Change," *Administrative Science Quarterly* 35 (1990): 604–633.

10. A. Plowright, "Rivals Play Catch-up with Apple," *Mail & Guardian Online,* February 17, 2009. Accessed October 13, 2009, at www.mg.co.za/article/2009-02-17-rivals-play-catchup-with-apple.

11. J. Barney, *Gaining and Sustaining Competitive Advantage,* 3rd ed. (Upper Saddle River, N.J.: Pearson/Prentice Hall, 2007), p. 90.

12. L. M. Rausch "Information Technology Innovation Survey: Fall 2001," Division of Science Resources Statistics; Directorate for Social, Behavioral, and Economic Sciences; National Science Foundation, February 2004, Table 11a: Strategic Importance of Being First to Market New Products. Accessed October 15, 2009, at www.nsf.gov/statistics/nsf04305/pdf/nsf04305.pdf.

13. J. Milliot, "As Amazon Soars, Bookstores Creep," *Publishers Weekly,* April 4, 2008. Accessed October 15, 2009, at www.publishersweekly.com/article/CA6550867.html.

14. Adapted from S. Schnaars, *Managing Imitation Strategies* (New York: Free Press, 1994), pp. 37–43.

15. Schnaars, *Managing Imitation Strategies,* 37–43; J. Covin, D. Slevin, and M. Heeley, "Pioneers and Followers: Competitive Tactics, Environment, and Growth," *Journal of Business Venturing* 15:2 (1999): 175–210.

16. G. Tellis, S. Stremersch, and E. Yin, "The International Takeoff of New Products: Economics, Culture, and Country Innovativeness," *Marketing Science* 22:2 (2003): 161–187.

17. This framework is adapted from A. Afuah, *Innovation Management: Strategies, Implementation, and Profits,* 2nd ed. (New York: Oxford University Press, 2003). An earlier version appears in Schnaars, *Managing Imitation Strategies,* 12–14.

18. Z. Olijnyk, "Plane and Simple: Flight Simulation," *Canadian Business,* February 27–March 12, 2006.

19. These examples are drawn from an extensive and detailed list provided by C. Christensen and M. Raynor, *The Innovator's Solution* (Boston: Harvard Business School Press, 2003).

20. Adapted from W. C. Kim and R. Mauborgne, "Blue Ocean Strategy," *California Management Review* 47:3 (2005): 105–121.

21. W. C. Kim and R. Mauborgne, "Value Innovation: The Strategic Logic of High Growth," *Harvard Business Review* 75:1 (1997): 102–113; Kim and Mauborgne, "Charting Your Company's Future," *Harvard Business Review* 80:6 (2002): 76–82.

22. W. C. Kim and R. Mauborgne, "Blue Ocean Strategy."; Wine Institute, "Strong Sales Growth in 2004 for California Wine as Shipments Reached New High," April 5, 2005. Accessed July 12, 2005, at www.wineinstitute.org; www.elitewine.com/site/index.php?lang=en&cat=news&art=159.

23. Adapted from W. C. Kim and R. Mauborgne, "Blue Ocean Strategy."

24. The scroll compressor is explained at www2.mat.dtu.dk/info/experiencing/scroll (accessed October 15, 2009) and illustrated at www2.mat.dtu.dk/info/experiencing/scroll/model.html (accessed October 15, 2009).

25. N. Stieglitz, "Digital Dynamics and Types of Industry Convergence: The Evolution of the Handheld Computers Market," in J. F. Christensen and P. Maskell (Eds.), *The Industrial Dynamics of the New Digital Economy* (Cheltenham, U.K.: Edward Elgar, 2003), pp. 179–208.

26. The concept of the value net is common among game theorists but was popularized by A. Brandenburger & B. Nalebuff in *Co-Opetition: A Revolutionary Mindset that Combines Competition and Cooperation* (New York: Currency Doubleday, 1997).

27. J. P. Falcone and M. Moskovciak, "HD DVD vs. Blu-ray," March 21, 2006, updated February 19, 2008. Accessed October 15, 2009, at http://reviews.cnet.com/hd-dvd-vs-blu-ray-guide.

28. P. Krein, "IKEA Suit Forces STOR to Shelve Catalog; Home Furnishings Retailer Claims Copyright Infringement," *Discount Store News,* June 6, 1988.

29. R. D'Aveni, "The Empire Strikes Back: Counterrevolutionary Strategies for Industry Leaders," *Harvard Business Review* 80:11 (November 2002): 5–12.

30. American Iron and Steel Institute, "New Steels Can Help Vehicles Achieve Five-Star Crash Rating, Double Fuel Economy at No Additional Cost," January 30, 2002. Accessed October 15, 2009, at www.autosteel.org/AM/Template.cfm?Section=Media_Center1&CONTENTID=7761&TEMPLATE=/CM/ContentDisplay.cfm.

31. Y. Tsurumi and H. Tsurumi, "Fujifilm-Kodak Duopolistic Competition in Japan and the United States," *Journal of International Business Studies* 30:4 (Fourth Quarter 1999): 821–822.

32. Canada Pipe's Stocking Distributor Program policy was challenged by the Canadian Competition Commission in 2002, but on appeal the wrong test had been used to determine if it was predatory pricing. J. A. Campion and M. Warner, "Commissioner of Competition v. Canada Pipe Company Ltd.—New Life for the Abuse of Dominance Provisions of the Competition Act," *Toronto Law Journal* 1:10 (November 2006).

33. A. Savikas, "Amazon Ups the Ante on Platform Lock-In," March 28, 2008. Accessed October 10, 2009, at http://toc.oreilly.com/2008/03/amazon-ups-the-ante-on-platform-lock-in.html.

34. Krein, "IKEA Suit Forces STOR to Shelve Catalog . . ."

35. From M. E. Raynor, "Strategic Flexibility," in J. L. Bower and C. G. G. Gilbert, *From Resource Allocation to Strategy*, (New York: Oxford University Press, 2007).

36. M. Amram and N. Kulatilaka, *Real Options: Managing Strategic Investment in an Uncertain World* (New York: Oxford University Press, 1998); E. Teach, "Will Real Options Take Root? Why Companies Have Been Slow to Adopt the Valuation Technique," *CFO Magazine* (July 1, 2003): 73.

37. Based on a story by F. Hecker, "Hybrid Organizations as Market Disruptors," April 23, 2009. Accessed October 10, 2009, at http://blog.hecker.org/2009/04/23/hybrid-organizations-as-market-disruptors.

38. See, for example, S. Kauffman, *At Home in the Universe: The Search for the Laws of Self-Organization and Complexity* (New York: Oxford University Press, 1995); M. Gell-Mann, *The Quark and the Jaguar* (New York: W. H. Freeman, 1994); J. Casti, *Complexification: Explaining a Paradoxical World through the Science of Surprise* (New York: HarperCollins, 1994).

39. R. Lewin, *Complexity: Life at the Edge of Chaos* (New York: Macmillan, 1992). Examples drawn from S. Brown and K. Eisenhardt, *Competing on the Edge: Strategy as Structured Chaos* (Boston: Harvard Business School Press, 1998).

40. Brown and Eisenhardt, *Competing on the Edge*.

41. Quoted in "Sustainable Waterloo: Organizational Background," Accessed November 9, 2010, at www.sustainablewaterloo.org/files/downloads/2009/SustainableWaterlooOverview.pdf.

7 Performance of the Strategy

In this chapter, we challenge you to:

1. Recognize how owners evaluate the performance of a company.

2. Appreciate the role of instrumental objectives when managing performance.

3. Know why performance management is needed and how it is done.

4. Understand the five approaches to corporate social responsibility.

5. Explain the importance of stakeholder analysis and the five-step process used to analyze it.

Talisman Energy Inc.

Jim Buckee, former CEO of Talisman Energy.

Oil derrick in desert.

Talisman Energy Inc. of Calgary, Alberta, is one of Canada's largest independent oil and gas companies. Originally known as BP Canada when it was part of British Petroleum plc, it became an independent company in 1992. Until 2007, Talisman was led by its CEO, Jim Buckee, who was known for taking unpopular assets and making them profitable. Through a string of acquisitions costing billions, he created an international company focused on conventional oil and gas discoveries.

One of the most controversial moves under Buckee's leadership was Talisman's purchase of Arakis Energy in 1998. Arakis was a small Canadian oil exploration company, but one of the largest companies in the Sudanese oil industry. Talisman purchased Arakis when it was unable to finance its obligations in the Greater Nile Oil Project in Sudan. Though U.S. financiers would not lend money to a company doing business in Sudan, Buckee was confident that support for the project would develop.

The purchase of Arakis gave Talisman a 25 percent stake in the Greater Nile Petroleum Operating Company (GNPOC) and put 10 percent to 15 percent of Talisman's business in Sudan. The other partners in the project were the China National Petroleum Company (40 percent), the National Petroleum Company of Malaysia (30 percent), and the Sudan National Petroleum Corporation (5 percent). Talisman, the only publicly owned company in the partnership, was the lead partner in charge of operations. Significant production of oil started in 1999 and Sudan became a significant exporter of oil.

Since 1955, Sudan had engaged in a bitter civil war: north versus south, Arabs versus Africans, and Muslims versus Christians and animists.[1] The upper hand in this war was held by the northern Arab Muslims, who controlled the national government. The discovery of oil by Chevron in the 1970s changed the complexion of the war as fighting shifted focus to control of the oil fields in southern Sudan. Air and ground attacks on civilians by the government and allied forces increased significantly, appearing to be part of a strategy to clear oil fields of populations threatening oil exploration and exploitation. This action led to international calls accusing the Sudanese government of human rights abuses, war crimes, and genocide.

Talisman was concerned about the situation but saw the revenues its activity generated as supporting the country's social and political development. Through its presence there, it was able to lead by example, providing jobs and training and undertaking community development projects such as schools and hospitals. The company also encouraged the Sudanese government to show tolerance, protect human rights, and continue the peace process. The company believed that its voice would be lost if it abandoned its investment in Sudan.

Non-governmental organizations (NGOs) and other stakeholders argued that Talisman was indirectly making the war worse and was complicit in human rights abuses and in crimes against humanity. The oil it produced generated revenue for the Sudanese government, who then used that revenue to purchase weapons and invest in the production of armaments. And the security that government forces provided in the areas that Talisman operated in exposed the locals to abuse by these forces. Those concerned with Talisman's presence in the Sudan pressured it to leave.

Various NGOs, including church groups, organized protests and letter-writing campaigns that gained widespread public recognition. They also pressured governments to take action. The Canadian federal government pledged to consider sanctions while the U.S. government, which had already declared Sudan to be a state sponsoring terrorism, forbade U.S. companies from doing business in Sudan. The NGOs also pressured public sector pensions and mutual funds to take action against the company. The drive was successful as major investors such as the Ontario Teachers' Pension Plan threatened to sell their shares if Talisman did not pull out of Sudan.

Talisman tried to satisfy those who were complaining. It created a corporate responsibility and government affairs group and began issuing an annual corporate responsibility report. It also engaged in initiatives including the Extractive Industries Transparency Initiative and the Global Compact. And it cited the codes of conduct and international principles that it was implementing: the International Code of Ethics for Canadian Business and Amnesty International's Human Rights Principles for Companies. Talisman's view was that it was improving human rights through "constructive engagement" such as building a hospital and schools, repairing waterworks, and providing free vaccinations. It asked for its critics to recognize that it had limited influence on the actions of the government because it only owned 25 percent of the GNPOC.

The external parties were not mollified. In June 2001, the U.S. House of Representatives passed the Sudan Peace Act, which if turned into law would have led to the delisting of Talisman shares on the New York Stock Exchange. Also in 2001, the Presbyterian Church of Sudan sued Talisman in a U.S. court for genocide. In the suit Talisman was alleged to have cooperated with and assisted the Sudanese government in a campaign of genocide and forced displacement of Christian and animist African Sudanese living in an area granted to Talisman as an oil concession.

In October 2002, Talisman had had enough. It announced that it was selling its Sudanese assets to ONGC Videsh Limited, the international subsidiary of India's Oil and Natural Gas Corporation Limited (ONGC), which was primarily government-owned. Talisman said that the decision to sell was based on shareholder fatigue and a concern that shares were being discounted based on perceived political risk. The estimated price was Cdn$1.2 billion, producing a 30 percent after-tax return for Talisman. Ram Naik, India's oil minister, was blunt about the role of human rights on the purchase. "I know in the U.S.A. or Canada these feelings are there. But we in India don't have such feelings on this issue. We feel the investments are safe and, since it's a producing field, we are keen to have it. My greatest interest is to have equity in oil as soon as possible."[2]

Observations

We can see from Talisman's experience that human rights have become a significant international issue and many feel a responsibility for them. This has important consequences for multinational corporations that were traditionally beyond the reach of international institutions or public international law. They are now being asked to address concerns that used to be considered issues of the sovereign governments.

Another example of a corporation adjusting to the changing pressures is Glencore International AG. This privately owned Swiss company has a history of trading with pariah nations such as the Congo and Iraq. Its relationships with these isolated and unstable regimes gave it access to resources at low prices because many others chose not to deal with these nations. As a result, Glencore "has a stronger grip over more individual markets for the earth's riches than almost any other single company."[3]

Glencore started to bolster its compliance with international strictures as it sought to finance its increasing acquisitions and to allow the affiliated public companies that it had an interest in to perform well. Its revised policy was that "it requires that its companies and their employees comply with any economic sanction in force in countries where they do business."[4]

Still another example is the China National Offshore Oil Corporation (CNOOC) Ltd., one of the largest state-owned oil producers in China. It announced in October 2007 that it would not be pulling out of Myanmar (formerly Burma) and might increase its presence in the gas-rich country, although the United States and other Western countries wanted to tighten sanctions on the government of Myanmar after a bloody crackdown on democracy protesters. Yang Hua, chief financial officer of CNOOC, said the company's presence in Myanmar was "making people's lives better" by developing resources that would otherwise go untapped. He also pointed to simple commercial reasons to stay. "If we pull out, then we can't successfully invest our money in terms of exploration success." Other energy giants with a presence in Myanmar are Total SA and Chevron Corp.[5]

The very different stances taken by the various companies to working with less democratic regimes leaves one wondering what the right approach is. What do you think it should be? ■

Performance of the Strategy

We examined designing a strategy in Chapter 5 and changing a strategy in Chapter 6. We are now ready to consider how to determine whether a particular strategic choice, or changing an existing one, is a good decision. This depends on being able to select one strategy from several alternatives and, at a minimum, compare a change in strategy with the existing strategy. Our approach will assume that management has fully appraised the alternatives in terms of being able to marshal the resources needed to put the strategic alternatives in place and that each alternative provides a sustainable competitive advantage. Keep in mind that, even when the strategy looks good according to this analysis, management has to make it happen. So in this chapter we first consider how to identify a good strategy based on performance and then describe various approaches to managing performance. Further requirements for implementation of a strategy are described in Chapter 8.

Selecting a Strategy

The selection of a strategy is heavily influenced by the metric used to evaluate the performance of the business. Many different metrics have been used over time (financial measures, stakeholder measures, and corporate social responsibility measures), but in our opinion the correct measure is value of the business since the purpose of strategy is to direct the company so that it produces as much value as possible.[6] Stakeholder analysis and corporate social responsibility, while important, reflect constraints that limit the value that can be produced, so we present them after we have considered how value is measured.

Use of value as the right measure is supported by business leaders. Jean-Yves Monette, president and CEO of Montreal-based international coffee supplier Van Houtte Inc., explains that, "A few years ago we implemented a development plan that calls for broad-based growth, deployment of the Van Houtte brand across Canada and the U.S. and optimal use of our Coffee Services network, the only one of its kind in North America. While this strategy is solid and we have the financial means to execute it, it behooves us to examine all possible ways to maximize shareholder value."[7] Executives at Loblaw Companies are also focused on value. In the company's 2006 annual report, management reported that, "The Company believes that if it successfully implements and executes its various strategic imperatives in support of its long term operating and financial strategies, it will be well positioned to pursue its vision of providing sustainable superior returns to its shareholders."[8]

The estimation of value draws directly on financial management in that the business is simply an aggregation of investments. Since each investment is appraised on the basis of cash flow, then a business is simply an aggregation of investment that can be assessed in the same way. This means that the value of the business can be determined using discounted cash flow. Another reason for focusing on cash flow is that the business is only able to pay the owner or investor a return when it generates cash. Furthermore, cash flow is especially important in businesses whose activities are constrained by the availability of cash, such as smaller businesses, high-growth businesses, and businesses with heavy debt loads.

Calculating the value of the business under a given strategy has three components: the cash flow it generates into the future, the terminal value of the business at a point in the future, and the cost of capital invested in the business.

CASH FLOW

Cash flow is the net flow of dollars into and out of a business within a period. The calculation of cash flow for a particular strategic alternative uses data taken from the projected financial statements for the business over time. These statements are assumed to provide an accurate portrayal of what management will be able to accomplish as it pursues a particular strategy. Each strategic alternative will have its own projected statements that reflect the cash flows of that alternative.

The projected financial statements need to capture the period over which the business expects to generate excess returns on its incremental investments. Two features of these are

Calculating the Value of the Business

A nand and Palatty Chowdhury had run a successful Indian restaurant in Scarborough, Ontario, for four years and reached a point where they were looking for a new challenge. They had two ideas in mind:

1. Opening a second restaurant in downtown Toronto.

2. Opening a deli to sell their sauces and various ethnic foods in Mississauga.

But they were at a loss as to how to decide which to pursue. Their friend Brian, who was an accountant, offered to help. He asked them to forecast the revenues, costs, and investments for each of the business ideas over time. When they had done this, they went to see him. Brian sat down with them and asked them to describe the two business ideas.

Anand, who was interested in developing a second restaurant, had already found a location. Once it was established, sales would be $800 000 a year and the gross margin would be 40 percent. The rent would only be $10 000 a quarter, but the kitchen would have to be refurbished and the restaurant furnished for $200 000. Once established, about $1000 would have to be spent each quarter replacing damaged equipment. Working with these estimates and a few more assumptions, Brian and the Chowdhurys came up with a spreadsheet that specified the future for the restaurant (see Exhibit 7.1). Brian used a 25 percent tax rate and assumed that the growth rate of the business after the second quarter of 2011 was zero, so the formula for the terminal value was the annual cash flow in the second quarter of 2011 divided by 2.4 percent, which represented an

Exhibit 7.1   The Net Present Value of a Second Restaurant

	2008 3	4	2009 1	2	3	4	2010 1	2	3	4	2011 1	2	
Sales		20 000	40 000	80 000	100 000	120 000	140 000	170 000	200 000	210 000	220 000	230 000	
COGS		12 000	24 000	48 000	60 000	72 000	84 000	102 000	120 000	126 000	132 000	138 000	
Gross Margin		8000	16 000	32 000	40 000	48 000	56 000	68 000	80 000	84 000	88 000	92 000	
		40%	40%	40%	40%	40%	40%	40%	40%	40%	40%	40%	
Rent	10 000	10 000	10 000	10 000	10 000	10 000	10 000	10 000	10 000	10 000	10 000	10 000	
Insurance	7000	7000	7000	7000	7000	7000	7000	7000	7000	7000	7000	7000	
Advertising	50	0	0	0	200	300	300	400	400	400	400	400	
Other (Utilities/Credit Card/etc.)	1000	2600	4200	7400	9000	10 600	12 200	14 600	17 000	17 800	18 600	19 400	
Total OPEX	18 050	19 600	21 200	24 400	26 200	29 500	29 500	32 000	34 400	35 200	36 000	36 800	
EBIT (1-t)	-13 538	-8700	-3900	5700	10 350	15 075	19 875	27 000	34 200	36 600	39 000	41 400	
Cash Flow from Ops	**-13 538**	**-8700**	**-3900**	**5700**	**10 350**	**15 075**	**19 875**	**27 000**	**34 200**	**36 600**	**39 000**	**41 400**	
Change in Working Capital	-5000	0	0	0	-2000	0	0	0	-2000	0	0	0	
CapEx	-200 000	-1000	-1000	-1000	-1000	-1000	-1000	-1000	-1000	-1000	-1000	-1000	
Sales of PPE	0	0	0	0	0	0	0	0	0	0	0	0	
Cash Flow from Investments	**-205 000**	**-1000**	**-1000**	**-1000**	**-3000**	**-1000**	**-1000**	**-1000**	**-3000**	**-1000**	**-1000**	**-1000**	**Terminal Value**
Total Cash Flow	-218 538	-9700	-4900	4700	7350	14 075	18 875	26 000	31 200	35 600	38 000	40 400	1 675 375
Discount rate 10%	0.9765	0.9535	0.9310	0.9091	0.8877	0.8668	0.8464	0.8264	0.8070	0.7880	0.7694	0.7513	0.7336
	-213 392	-9472	-4672	4376	6682	12 494	16 361	22 006	25 785	28 729	29 943	31 085	1 258 729
Net Present Value	**1 208 654**												

effective annual rate at 10 percent. Brian discounted all the cash flows at an annual rate of 10 percent to a net present value of $1 675 375.

Palatty was more interested in developing a deli. She calculated that annual sales would reach around $600 000, but the gross margin would only be 25 percent. It was attractive to her because it would require less investment than starting a new restaurant. Only $40 000 would be needed to stock the store and shelving, and equipment would cost $10 000. Each year $1000 would go into capital improvements, and the stock in the store would increase as sales grew. Working with this and a few more assumptions, Brian and the Chowdhurys came up with a spreadsheet for the deli (see Exhibit 7.2). Brian discounted all the cash flows at an annual rate of 15 percent because the risk was higher given the lack of experience in this business. Brian again used a 25 percent tax rate and assumed no growth in the business after the second quarter of 2011. He calculated the terminal value by dividing $4950 by 3.6 percent, representing an equivalent annual rate of 15 percent. The net present value discounted at an annual rate of 15 percent was $25 917.

As they looked over the results, Palatty expressed her disappointment that the deli had not fared well under the analysis. She said, "I still really like the idea of the deli because it would be close to our home. I think we will have trouble running two restaurants because that will mean one of us has to be at each to run things. And when you look at the numbers, most of the value of the new restaurant is in the terminal value." Brian responded, "These are calculations and other things have to be taken into account as well. But the deli will be a lot of work and the rewards are small relative to a second restaurant. Still, the choices made in a family business are often decided by the preferences of the family rather than what the numbers show."

Exhibit 7.2 The Net Present Value of a Deli

| | 2008 | | 2009 | | | | 2010 | | | | 2011 | | |
	3	4	1	2	3	4	1	2	3	4	1	2	
Sales		32 000	64 000	80 000	100 000	120 000	130 000	140 000	145 000	150 000	155 000	160 000	
COGS		24 000	48 000	60 000	75 000	90 000	97 500	105 000	108 750	112 500	116 250	120 000	
Gross Margin		8000	16 000	20 000	25 000	30 000	32 500	35 000	36 250	37 500	38 750	40 000	
		25%	25%	25%	25%	25%	25%	25%	25%	25%	25%	25%	
Rent	9000	9000	9000	9000	9000	9000	9000	9000	9000	9000	9000	9000	
Insurance	7000	7000	7000	7000	7000	7000	7000	7000	7000	7000	7000	7000	
Advertising	50	0	0	0	200	200	200	200	200	200	200	200	
Other (Utilities/Credit Card/etc.)	2000	4560	7120	8400	10 000	11 600	12 400	13 200	13 600	14 000	14 400	14 800	
Total OPEX	18 050	20 560	23 120	24 400	26 200	27 800	28 600	29 400	29 800	30 200	30 600	31 000	
EBIT* (1-t)	-13 538	-9420	-5340	3300	-900	1650	2925	4200	4838	5475	6113	6750	
Cash Flow from Ops	**-13 538**	**-9420**	**-5340**	**3300**	**-900**	**1650**	**2925**	**4200**	**4838**	**5475**	**6113**	**6750**	
Change in Working Capital	-40 000	0	0	-400	-500	-600	-650	-700	-725	-750	-775	-800	
CapEx	-10 000	0	0	-1000	0	0	0	-1000	0	0	0	-1000	
Sales of PPE	0	0	0	0	0	0	0	0	0	0	0	0	
Cash Flow from Investments	**-50 000**	**0**	**0**	**-1400**	**-500**	**-600**	**-650**	**-1700**	**-725**	**-750**	**-775**	**-1800**	**Terminal Value**
Total Cash Flow	-63 538	-9420	-5340	4700	-1400	1050	2275	2500	4113	4725	5338	4950	139 201
Discount rate 15%/Year	0.9657	0.9325	0.9005	0.8696	0.8397	0.8109	0.7830	0.7561	0.7302	0.7051	0.6809	0.6575	0.6349
	-61 356	-8784	-4809	-4087	-1176	851	1781	1890	3003	3332	3634	3255	88 382
Net Present Value	**25 917**												

important from a strategic perspective. The first is how high the excess return will be and the justification for such a return. The second is how long the excess return will last. This has been called the competitive advantage period (CAP) and lasts as long as the business is able to earn above-normal returns. Generally, cash flow models span five to 10 years because that is the period over which the competitive advantage is economically sound. The CAP is likely to be shorter in a dynamic industry where things are changing quickly and where barriers to entry are lower.

The simplest calculation of cash flow is the operating cash flow (OCF) or earnings before interest, tax, depreciation, and amortization (EBITDA). It is calculated from the income statement as:

$$
\begin{aligned}
\text{Operating Cash Flow} &= \text{Earnings Before Interest and Taxes (EBIT)} \\
&\quad + \text{Depreciation and Amortization (DA)} \\
&= \text{Earnings Before Interest, Taxes, Depreciation,} \\
&\quad \text{and Amortization (EBITDA)}
\end{aligned}
$$

Interest charges are added back to the cash flow so the effect of how the business is financed is removed. Taxes are added back because they depend on the vagaries of the laws in a given year and can fluctuate dramatically in earnings power. Finally, depreciation and amortization are added back because they are non-cash charges. EBITDA is widely used in financial circles because it relates enterprise value to cash flow though it fails to consider the future investment requirements of the business.

The free cash flow (FCF) is the amount of cash available after the strategic investment needs of the business have been considered and taxes have been paid. It is calculated as follows using data from projected income statements and balance sheets:

$$
\begin{aligned}
\text{Free Cash Flow} &= \text{Earnings Before Interest and Taxes (EBIT)} * (1 - t) \\
&\quad + \text{Depreciation and Amortization (DA)} \\
&\quad - \text{Capital Spending (CapEx)} \\
&\quad - \text{Change in Working Capital (NWC)},
\end{aligned}
$$

in which t is the tax rate. Capital spending (CapEx or CX) and change in working capital are included to reflect the reinvestment of cash flow in new equipment, new facilities, and additional working capital to support the business's growth in sales. Calculated in this way, the measure excludes financing costs.

TERMINAL VALUE

The terminal value is the present value of a perpetual stream of future cash flows growing at a specific constant rate, g. The terminal value is used because it is unrealistic to think that one can accurately forecast cash flows in the distant future.[9]

COST OF CAPITAL

The discount rate used when bringing future cash flows to the present is the weighted average cost of capital (WACC) for the business. It is the weighted after-tax cost of equity and interest-bearing debt, so it reflects the cost of money invested in the business. The cost of money can be adjusted to account for the greater or lesser risk associated with a particular strategic alternative.

VALUE

The value of each alternative can be calculated with the three sets of values for each strategic alternative. The most desirable one is the alternative that has the highest net present value, all other things being equal. How this is done is illustrated in How Would You Do That? 7.1.

Performance Management

We have established that the ultimate goal of management is to maximize the value that the business creates. So why, if the success of a business is based on the single goal of maximizing value, do businesses have many goals? The reason is that a single goal for a business is too general for many people in the business to relate to. What they need are specific goals that they can work toward in their jobs. Such goals are instrumental goals because they are not ends in their own right but rather contribute to the achievement of higher goals and ultimately to the overall performance of the business. Looking at Loblaw Companies, while management's overall concern was providing sustainable superior returns to its shareholders, it identified and developed specific key performance indicators to measure the progress of short- and long-term strategies. These indicators measured format (i.e., same-store sales, fresh perception, penetration of controlled label sales, and Joe Fresh Style percentage share of total general merchandise sales); specific comparative sales for Health and Beauty; Natural Value and President's Choice Organics; index pricing targets; targeted on-shelf availability; and employee satisfaction. In 2007, targets were implemented across the company to enable management to assess progress made on each imperative as well as the effectiveness of implementation of the company's strategy.[10]

Management ensures that the instrumental goals contribute to the overall performance of the business by developing a system of goals. This is done within the company's high-level strategic and financial control process, its performance management system. The principal activities in the system are defining the strategy, setting overall goals, setting targets, monitoring performance, and responding to differences between expected and actual results. The names given to these systems have varied, though they follow the same general principles. Traditional systems include the DuPont analysis and management by objectives (MBO). Recent approaches are value-based management (VBM) and the balanced scorecard (BSC). Each has its own rationale for managing performance, and this is reflected in the metrics used.

Before discussing the uniqueness of each of these, we want to point out that an outsider looking at the goals needs to discriminate between goals of the business as a whole and instrumental goals. At times management will focus its attention on achieving certain instrumental goals because these are particularly problematic for the business. Failure to determine which goals are most important, however, leaves one confused about what matters and unable to make sensible tradeoffs because one does not understand the relative priority of goals.

Associated with all approaches to managing performance is the adoption of dashboards, which are reporting tools that consolidate and arrange numbers, metrics, text, and sometimes scorecards on computer screens. They provide relevant information to decision makers, helping them make better decisions more quickly. Information technology has made possible the display of real-time data on screens that are tailored to specific roles and departments. Dashboards do not have to conform to a specific management methodology. The dashboard in Exhibit 7.3 shows key indicators that the executive it was designed for is interested in. Before the dashboard

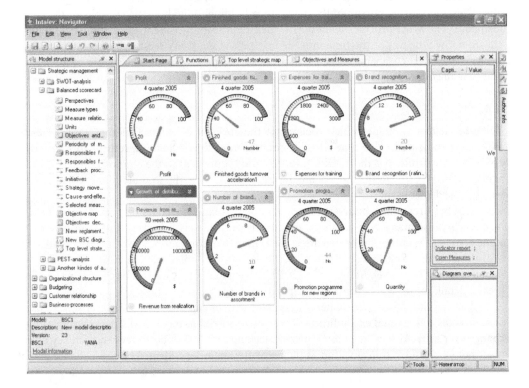

Exhibit 7.3 One Example of a Dashboard[11]

existed, providing information to managers was a much slower process as support staff had to collect data, analyze it, and produce reports that were then given to managers. At its best the report was a single sheet of paper that included key data from the previous day.

DUPONT ANALYSIS

DuPont analysis, illustrated in Chapter 5, was created by Donaldson Brown, who served as the chief financial officer at General Motors in 1919. He realized that the return on assets (ROA, a common corporate goal at the time) was affected by both profitability and efficiency. Based on this insight, he developed a system that tied together the balance sheet and income statement. This system was later modified to focus on return on equity (ROE) rather than ROA.[12]

DuPont analysis is still used today because it is a powerful tool for measuring performance using data available in financial statements. Many of the standard financial ratios are incorporated in the system. As a management tool, however, it suffers from focusing on "line items" that are hard to isolate and control (such as revenue growth of 10 percent, gross margins of 35 percent, and turning working capital four times). It also deals with aggregate data so has little significance except to top managers who look at the business or division of the corporation as a whole.

MANAGEMENT BY OBJECTIVES (MBO)

Management by objectives was first outlined in 1954 by Peter Drucker, who has been called the father of management.[13] MBO seeks to achieve alignment between individual goals and the goals of the business. The method uses the organizational hierarchy of the business to structure goals, providing everyone in the organization with specific objectives that, if achieved, contri-bute to the overall success of the business. MBO involves a process that starts at the top of the organizational structure with the chief executive officer setting the objectives for the business as a whole. The CEO then negotiates with his/her subordinates what they will accomplish so that their efforts further the achievement of the CEO's objectives. These negotiations produce objectives for the subordinates. The subordinates in turn negotiate objectives with their own subordinates and so on down the organizational hierarchy. In this way, the construction of objectives cascades down the organizational hierarchy. The validity of the objectives is checked with the SMART method. Every objective is to be Specific, Measurable, Achievable, Realistic, and Time-specific.

MBO relies on self-control and clear responsibilities for every position in the organizational structure. Moreover, the method requires considerable interpersonal activity in setting objectives, monitoring pursuit of them, and then holding individuals responsible for their performance. The MBO process breaks down when responsibilities are unclear and when managers are not willing to put the time into the interpersonal activity required to make the system work. While fewer companies now use MBO today, its principles are reflected in other performance management techniques.

VALUE-BASED MANAGEMENT (VBM)

Value-based management (VBM) focuses on the creation of value. Different approaches to VBM have measured value four ways: discounted cash flow valuation, returns to shareholders, economic profit, and the market-to-book ratio (equivalent to the q ratio and market value added (MVA)). Though the metrics are different, in practice, the four are highly correlated so which is used is not crucial.[14]

VBM requires a deep understanding of the performance variables that create value for the business because management cannot act directly on value. This leads to the identification of value drivers (i.e., any variables that affect the value of the company). The value drivers are then organized so that they are consistent with the decision variables that are under control of the management at each level. At higher levels, the drivers tend to be generic, but as one moves into greater detail, the drivers become more operational (see Exhibit 7.4).

The key value drivers are elements that management can influence such as customer satisfaction, costs, and capital expenditures. These drivers need to be reviewed periodically as they change over time. Also, when management is seeking to improve performance, each key driver must not be considered in isolation as they are often interdependent. The consequence is that

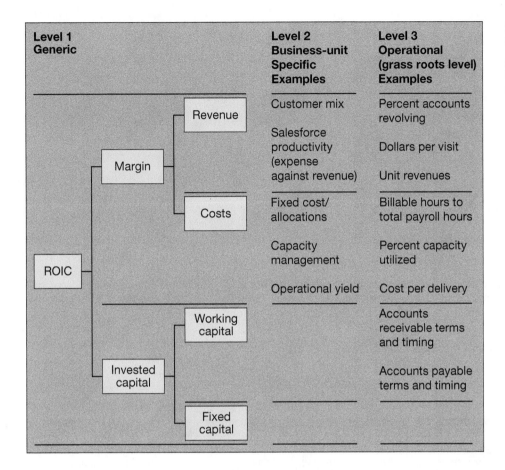

Exhibit 7.4 Levels of Value Drivers

Source: Timothy Koller, "What Is Value-Based Management?" *The McKinsey Quarterly* 3 (1994): 91.

bringing about a positive change in one can have an adverse effect on another. Finally, working with value drivers requires that management think in terms of processes rather than financial statements.

The continuing adoption of VBM by businesses indicates that it is an attractive way to manage performance. At this time, the challenges of the approach are largely related to its adoption: it has to be adopted by the full organization, possibly including change of multiple systems; top management has to champion the adoption; and people throughout the organization have to be trained. One also has to be careful not to use measurement methods that are overly complex.

BALANCED SCORECARD (BSC)

The balanced scorecard was developed and popularized by Harvard professor Robert Kaplan and Palladium Group founder David Norton in the past decade.[15] It is called a scorecard because it is a combination of metrics that reflect the strategy of the business. The metrics relate to four different facets of the business:

1. **Finance:** *How do we look to the owners?* Examples of metrics are operating income and ROE.
2. **Customer:** *How do we look to customers?* Examples of metrics are on-time delivery and percent of sales from new products.
3. **Internal:** *What must we excel at?* Examples of metrics are cycle time, yield, and efficiency.
4. **Innovation and learning:** *Can we continue to improve and create value?* Examples of metrics are time to develop the next generation of products and new product introductions relative to competitors.

The first perspective is short-term and deals with financial performance that is a lagging indicator. The other three perspectives deal with leading indicators that determine future financial performance of the business. The BSC approach assumes that the combination of measures in the BSC gives managers more sense of what needs to be done to create value.

Implementing a Balanced Scorecard at Agri-Chem[16]

Agri-Chem is a manufacturer of agricultural chemicals. It blends active ingredients into packaged products that are sold to distributors who supply farmers around the country. Management adopted the balanced scorecard and created the set of metrics shown in Exhibit 7.5.

Exhibit 7.5 The Four Elements of Agri-Chem's Balanced Scorecard

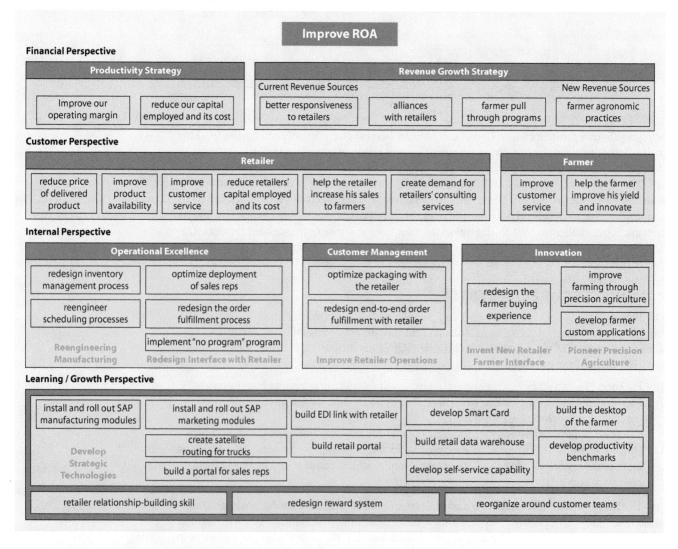

Management observed strong relationships among specific metrics in the scorecard (see Exhibit 7.6).

Building on this data, management formulated a strategic map that linked the various metrics together (see Exhibit 7.7). Within the map, management then tied together specific metrics into five complementary strategic themes:

1. Reengineering manufacturing
   a. redesign scheduling procedures in the plants
   b. redefine inventory management processes across the logistics chain
   c. implement SAP's ERP module in manufacturing

2. Redesigning the interface with distributors
   a. implement SAP's ERP module in marketing
   b. deploy sales representatives better, give them better data, and develop their customer service skills
   c. make product available during the planting season using "floating" inventory
   d. simplify the backroom of retailers by implementing a "no program" program

3. Improving distributor operations
   a. provide retailers with customer packaging in their name
   b. help distributors manage their inventory as an extension of Agri-Chem's
   c. use a retail portal so retailers have the same information as Agri-Chem

4. Inventing a new distributor-farmer interface
   a. provide farmers with a "Safe" buying experience
   b. provide farmers with a convenient buying experience by giving them "Smart" cards

Exhibit 7.6 Agri-Chem's Specific Metrics

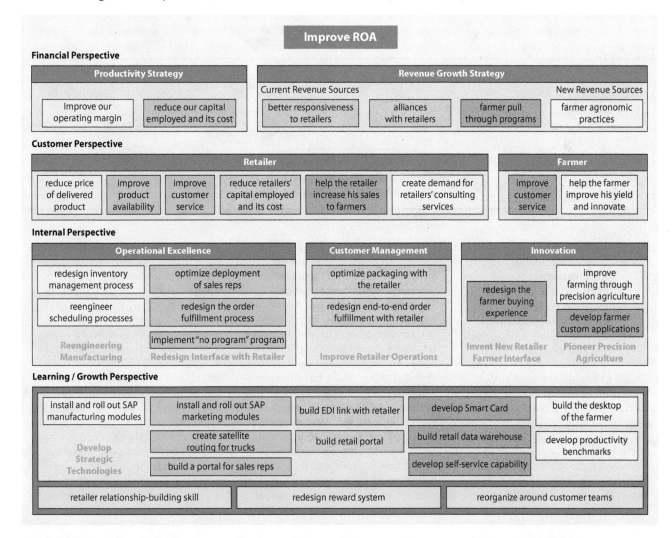

Exhibit 7.7 Agri-Chem's Strategic Map

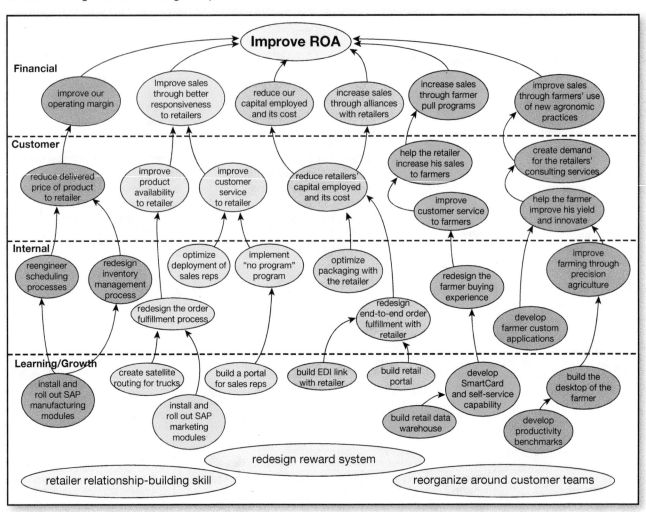

5. Pioneering precision agriculture
   a. develop precision agriculture tools for farmers to use in the field
   b. make farming a science that improves farm economics
   c. provide farmers with productivity benchmarks

At its foundations were employee-focused programs to develop relationship-building skills, incentive programs, and customer focus.

By having separate themes, Agri-Chem was able to put together an aggressive three-year program to transform the value chain to its end use customer, the farmer. It did so by focusing on one theme at a time in a phased process moving from left to right. For each initiative it had a specific scorecard to drive successful implementation.

Looking at the second initiative, to redesign the interface with the retailer, note that this initiative was to be started after manufacturing had been re-engineered because then manufacturing would have the capability to better support sales. In this initiative SAP's ERP marketing module would be installed. Marketing could then feed better information to manufacturing, allowing a breakthrough in operations. Historically, Agri-Chem's salespeople forecast how much of each product each retailer would demand and then encouraged retailers to stock product early using programs that gave price discounts. Even with good forecasting routines, the process led to costly overstocks and understocks each year as farmers' fertilizer purchases differed from inventories the retailers had put in. By encouraging dealers to stock less by ending discounting to retailers, Agri-Chem could meet retailers' sales needs by holding a "floating" inventory from which product could be moved quickly to where it was needed. Ending the program selling would change the job of representatives from placing stocks with retailers during the winter to responding to retailer needs during the spring planting season.

This would allow the redeployment of sales representatives who would now have to be more responsive to retailer needs. Success in serving the customer would increase sales and improve the retailer's return on net assets (RONA) and in turn improve Agri-Chem's ROA.

Each initiative had its own balanced scorecard. The one for redesigning the interface with the retailer is presented in Exhibit 7.8. The elements in the strategic map have various measures associated with them. For each measure there is a specific target that has to be achieved.

With this done, Agri-Chem had an overlay that could be used to ensure that systematic actions were being taken that would implement the strategy of the business and improve the value it added.

Exhibit 7.8 Agri-Chem's Balanced Scorecard for the "Redesign Interface with Retailer" Initiative

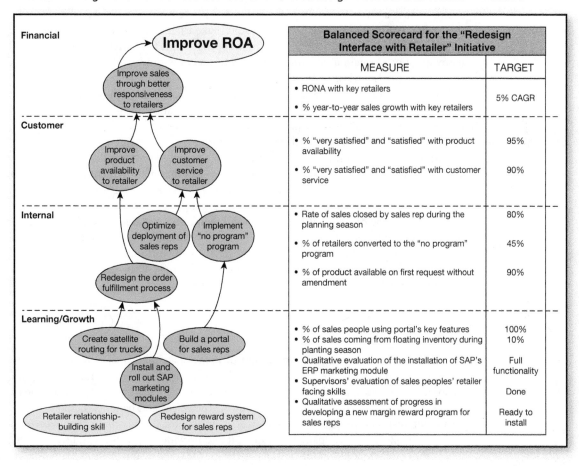

In 2008, Kaplan and Norton incorporated the balanced scorecard into a previously identified complete performance management system.[17] This system is a closed loop that consists of five stages, starting with formulating a strategy and describing it. The second stage is translating the strategy into strategic objectives, measures, and strategic initiatives. The output of this stage is a strategic plan, a strategy map, and a balanced scorecard. The third stage is planning operations in terms of sales plans, resource plans, and key processes to improve. The output of this stage is an operating plan, dashboards, budgets, and pro forma profit-and-loss statements. After executing the processes and initiatives according to the plan, the fourth stage is monitoring what is and is not accomplished and learning from this through strategic and operational reviews. The fifth and final stage is testing the strategy and adjusting it to improve on it and redirect it as appropriate.

A unique component of this approach is the balanced scorecard. At present the rule of thumb is that a business needs 23 to 25 metrics in the overall scorecard. This many captures the essence of the business while more would make each metric less important and cause loss of focus. As the BSC is still a relatively new approach and the variety of metrics used is large, many questions remain about which metrics to use, how to weigh them, and how to measure the value of the metrics. Because the financial metrics are more readily available and better understood, there is a tendency to have more of them and to weigh them more heavily when constructing the scorecard. Another issue is that the relationships among the metrics are not necessarily linear. As with the value drivers, the metrics are interdependent so management needs to make tradeoffs when setting targets for them.

An example of a company's development of a balanced scorecard is found in How Would You Do That? 7.2. Building such a scorecard requires that management start with a complete understanding of how the business works and the interrelationships among the various aspects of the business. Only with a thorough understanding can they identify the key performance indicators and the causal relationships among them. This has not stopped management from adopting this approach. By 2007, Bain, a consulting company, reported that 66 percent of the companies it surveyed had adopted the BSC while David Norton, one of the BSC's creators, put the number at 60 percent in the United States and Europe, 40 percent in Latin America, and 33 percent in Asia.[18]

Stakeholders

The owners of the business are one group of many stakeholders that the company relies on as it goes about its activities. The company also relies on the efforts of many others including customers, workers, bankers, and communities. Customers pay the company for the products and services it sells. Workers provide labour for the wages and benefits. Bankers provide debt for the interest they are paid. Suppliers provide inputs for the payments they receive. And the community allows the company to locate in it and provides the utilities and services needed in return for employment of its citizens, payment for the utilities and services provided, and taxes paid to the community so it can provide general amenities to its citizens. Each of these receives a direct benefit for cooperating with the company. Hence each has a "stake" in the company and so is a called a **stakeholder**.

stakeholder An individual or group whom the business seeks to cooperate with because they have or control something the business needs as it pursues its strategy.

Many mistakenly believe that satisfying stakeholders is an objective that drives thinking about strategy. In fact, it is a constraint, not an objective.[19] Stakeholders make demands of the company that the company must meet to obtain their cooperation. When the "payments" made to the various stakeholders are determined in an open arm's-length transaction, stakeholders are able to protect their own interests. And they will only continue to cooperate with the company so long as they are satisfied with what the company does for them. The cost of satisfying stakeholders is reflected in the income statement and so has an impact on what is left for owners. Only the company that has a sustained competitive advantage is able to provide these payments and still produce an above-normal profit for the owners, the residual claimants on the company.

STAKEHOLDER ANALYSIS

Satisfying stakeholders' expectations about what they should receive is not easy. Each stakeholder has different expectations about what the company should do for it and the ability to

Exhibit 7.9   Stakeholder Expectations and Methods of Influence

Stakeholder	Expectations	Methods of influence
Community	– employment – employee participation in the community – financial support of the community's welfare – environmental effects	– awards from community organizations – boycotts, demonstration, protests – lobbying politicians – interacting with regulators of business activities
Customers	– business practices (customer service, warranties) – products and services bought – value curve that appeals – quantities needed	– quantity purchased – amount and timing of payment – new product ideas – product liability suits – claims, complaints, returns
Employees	– compensation – opportunities for advancement – healthy work place – work place participation – long term employment	– join/leave the firm – productivity – attention to quality – absenteeism – union activity – work place grievances
Financiers	– payment of principal and interest – opportunities for further lending – timely disclosure of pertinent business information	– availability of loans – covenants on loans – enforcement of covenants – interest rate charged
Government	– employment – tax revenues – environmental effects – legislated business practices	– licences and permits – regulations and standards – enforcement of regulations and standards – subsidies, grants, and tax relief
Managers	– compensation – opportunities for advancement – authority and power – workplace participation	– join/leave the firm – productivity – attention to quality
Shareholders	– value of the stock – dividends – corporate social responsibility	– buy/sell shares – elect directors – vote with/against management – public expression of feelings
Suppliers	– business practices (payments reliable) – prices paid for products and services – quantities bought – quality accepted	– prices and credit terms – quality and quantity delivered – willingness to meet special demands – technical assistance

Source: After a table in Mark C. Baetz and Paul W. Beamish, *Strategic Management: Canadian Cases* (Chicago: Irwin Professional Publishing, 1987).

exert influence, as can be seen in Exhibit 7.9. Management is often caught in the crossfire of stakeholders who have competing expectations. This is what happened to management at Talisman Energy. Management has to determine how far it can and will go to satisfy each and, in so doing, determine the balance among these competing interests. Moreover, management has to change what it provides stakeholders over time both as changes occur in stakeholders' expectations and the company's ability to provide "payments" to them.

STAKEHOLDERS AND STRATEGY

Top management's challenge when crafting deals with various stakeholders is doing so without losing sight of the company's strategy. Management has to negotiate a deal with each stakeholder that satisfies that stakeholder while still allowing the company to create value when pursuing its chosen strategy. A process for working with stakeholders starts with the identification of the value chain associated with the strategy, the critical stakeholders tied to that chain, what their short- and long-term interests are, how the strategy will affect them, and their potential influence on strategy. Then a deal is negotiated to obtain the stakeholders' support, or action is considered to alter the value chain so they are removed from the chain. We will now work through this process in detail. It is divided into five steps illustrated in Exhibit 7.10.

Step 1: Identify the Value Chain

When setting strategy, decisions made about the arena of the company determine where it comes in contact with the environment. The company takes in inputs from the environment, converts them through the activities found in the value chain, and then puts them back into the environment with the selling and servicing of the products.

Step 2: Identify the Stakeholders

The stakeholders who interact with the value chain are identified. These intersections run the gamut from employees who work for the company, to suppliers who sell raw materials and equipment to the company, to customers who buy from the company, to competitors who compete for the company's customers, to governments that impose taxes and rules of conduct on companies. If there are subgroups within the broader groups, they need to be identified specifically. This will produce a long list, but the point of this step is to recognize who the stakeholders are because they may have demands that the business has to meet. The list can be pruned by cutting those who may have interests but have little power over the company.

Step 3: Determine the Stakeholders' Expectations

Stakeholders have expectations about what they will receive from cooperating with the company. Their expectations for the present and in the future need to be assessed. The best indicator of what stakeholders want is what they have been satisfied with in the past. When they say they are dissatisfied with what they receive, you need to decide whether this will produce resistance in the future or is simply setting their position for future negotiations. Future expectations matter because strategy involves commitments into the future. The company does not want to commit itself to a strategy now and then have the stakeholder "hold it up" in future by refusing to cooperate. Then the company will be committed to a course of action that it can only sustain by satisfying stakeholders' greater demands.

At this point in the process, the number of stakeholders considered in the analysis can be reduced to those who appear to have expectations that are outside the "normal" expectations of business practice. Management has to consider only how it will deal with those with inflated expectations.

Step 4: Determine Stakeholders' Power and Influence over Decisions

How hard the stakeholder bargains depends on two factors: how important a deal is to it and how much power it has. Not all stakeholders are affected equally by the strategy. Some stakeholders are easily dealt with because effects are mild, and any positive or negative effects associated with the company are secondary or have minimal impact on them. At the other end of the spectrum, some stakeholders are demanding because they bear the brunt of the company's decisions, good or bad. There are also variations in power. Some stakeholders feel powerful because the company does not have an alternative. If the government insists that the company meet its regulations, then the company must meet them. Alternatively, the company in a single-plant town has considerable power with local stakeholders because it provides much of the local employment and tax revenue. A company has much less power in a large, diversified municipality because if the company does not succeed, others may move in to take its place.

The framework in Exhibit 7.11 will help you categorize stakeholders according to their influence in determining strategy versus their importance to strategy execution. This distinction may help you identify major omissions in strategy formulation and implementation.

Step 1: Identify the Value Chain
Step 2: Identify the Stakeholders
Step 3: Determine the Stakeholders' Expectations
Step 4: Determine Stakeholders' Power and Influence over Decisions
Step 5: Determine Which Stakeholders Will Be Satisfied and How

Exhibit 7.10 Five Steps in Stakeholder Analysis

The exercise of power can take many forms, as can be seen in Exhibit 7.11. It ranges from the formal power (boards of directors and owners), to economic power (suppliers, financial institutions, and unions), to political power (dissident stockholders, political action groups, and governmental bodies). It can be exercised through direct control over what is decided, through veto power over decisions, or through nuisance influence. This calls for your sensitivity to the many forms it can take.

Step 5: Determine Which Stakeholders Will Be Satisfied and How

Now the relevant issues need to be prioritized according to their impact on the company in the present and in the future. In this way management determines where it will focus its attention and resources. Then management decides which stakeholders' expectations will be met. This depends in part on how critical the stakeholder is to the business. If it is not critical but the stakeholder is unwilling to settle for lower "payments," then management can seek out stakeholders who are satisfied with what the company has to offer. If this is not possible, then the company can go to the extreme of reconfiguring the value chain so the stakeholder is no longer relevant to the business.

The effective application of stakeholder analysis for a newly appointed manager is described in How Would You Do That? 7.3. From this example, you can see why stakeholder analysis can be an important input into both strategy formulation and implementation. You can also see how the roles of certain stakeholders create important interdependencies between formulation and implementation.

Remember that at the end of this process, the company's ability to generate value is determined by its ability to get cooperation from its stakeholders. This cooperation has greater value to the company than the cost of gaining that cooperation. In other words, if all the value created by the business is distributed to stakeholders other than the owners, the owners have no monetary incentive for investing in the business.

		Power of the Stakeholder over Strategic Decisions			
		Unknown	Little/no power	Moderate degree of power	Significant power
Effect of Strategy on the Stakeholder	Unknown				
	Little/no effect				
	Moderate effect				
	Significant effect				

Exhibit 7.11 A Stakeholder-Analysis Grid

Driving Stakeholder Analysis at Tritec Motors

Two of the challenges of performing stakeholder analysis are determining how stakeholders are affected by a firm's decisions and how much influence they have over the implementation of the decisions that are made. Not all stakeholders are affected in the same way, and not all stakeholders have the same level of influence in determining what a firm does. When stakeholder analysis is executed well, as you will see from the following example of the Tritec joint venture in Curitiba, Brazil, the resulting strategy has a better chance of succeeding because the entities you might rely on in the implementation phase also helped to formulate the strategy.

The Stalled Motor Maker

Formed in 2001, the Tritec joint venture between Daimler-Chrysler and BMW represented a US$400 million state-of-the-art engine manufacturing facility in Curitiba, Brazil. From the start, however, production problems with the new motors were wreaking havoc with BMW's newly minted line of wildly successful Mini Coopers. On the Chrysler side, Daimler's acquisition of the U.S. firm resulted in the triage of the main line of vehicles that would receive engines from the Curitiba plant. In sum, the Curitiba plant was producing poor-quality engines for BMW, and Daimler was paying for half of a factory that it was not even using.

In stepped Bob Harbin, a 25-year employee of Chrysler. Bob was given 90 days to come up with a plan to fix Tritec's problems. This was a make-or-break assignment for Harbin. Fortunately, Harbin knew how to apply stakeholder analysis, and he knew that the key players he involved in designing the turnaround strategy would likely be instrumental in executing it as well. In some cases, even if they did not have a role in implementation, certain stakeholders, such as the Brazilian government, could actually hurt Tritec's turnaround chances.

The Discovery Process

Bob Harbin spent the first five days of his assignment meeting with top executives at Daimler and BMW. These corporate partners were Tritec's financial backers and its only customers so Harbin needed both to understand their needs and expectations and to determine how much discretion they would afford him if drastic changes were needed. Next, he spent two weeks in Curitiba. There he met with everyone from the shop-floor employees to his future management team. He also spent time with key local parts suppliers as well as members of the newly installed Brazilian government. The government was particularly important because it had put tax incentives and export credits into place to entice Tritec to Brazil. A change in government meant that those credits were now in danger of being annulled. Throughout this discovery process, Harbin reiterated a common vision: "If we can't produce quality engines and get them to BMW on time, the plant will likely be closed. No job, no tax revenues, no engines. Period." This quickly captured the stakeholders' attention and fostered a sense of urgency and cooperation among the key stakeholders.

Sending Messages and Implementing a Plan

After the first 30 days, Harbin assembled his leadership team based on impressions gained during his early interviews. Most of his team consisted of Brazilians. This sent a strong message of confidence to the Brazilian workforce as well as to the Brazilian government. Together, Harbin and his team put together a rescue plan for the engine-manufacturing process. When the plan was prepared, he took it back to Germany for the endorsement by both BMW and Daimler. Upon receiving their approval, he had a plan backed by the most important stakeholders: the alliance partners, the Brazilian government, Tritec's employees, and the new Tritec management team.

Harbin began the steady process of turning around Tritec. Although there were minor setbacks along the way, within one year the factory was a world benchmark plant in many areas for both Daimler and BMW. By 2005, Toyota executives considered it one of the world's best-run auto-engine plants because its production quality and efficiency were so high.

Plotting Roles

Although every firm has multiple stakeholders, in this situation the major stakeholders were BMW, Daimler-Chrysler, local employees, suppliers, the Brazilian government, and the leadership team. What roles did these stakeholders play in the tough decisions faced by Harbin? Plot each stakeholder individually on the stakeholder-analysis grid (see Exhibit 7.12).

BMW is located in two places on the stakeholder analysis grid. First, it is an owner/investor in the Tritec joint venture so it has voting and veto rights over all major decisions; thus on the power dimension BMW is plotted in the far-right column. Second, BMW is also the customer buying the engines made in this factory. Thus, BMW simultaneously has an economic interest apart from its ownership stake.

Daimler's position is more straightforward: it is an equity investor in the plant—thus it has an equity interest—and it has voting rights over all major decisions.

Suppliers have a non-ownership economic interest in the health of the plant. If the plant were to close, they would lose a major buyer. What influence/power do they have over decisions? They do not have major decisional power, but they do wield economic power.

Employees do not directly influence factory decisions, but they do have an economic, non-equity stake in the factory.

The Brazilian government clearly has a stake in ensuring that local businesses are prosperous. However, that stake is not as direct nor as significant as an equity stake or employees' or suppliers' economic interest.

What does this analysis suggest? It suggests that if BMW does not get on board, all bets are off. Moreover, although the government is a critical stakeholder, at this stage of the game it is not as critical as making sure suppliers, employees, and management implement a plan that keeps BMW and Daimler-Chrysler satisfied.

HOW WOULD YOU DO THAT? QUESTIONS

1. Based on the framework applied to Tritec Motors here, use the opening vignette in Chapter 2 on Anne Mulcahy at Xerox to map out the key stakeholders in her turnaround effort. Which stakeholders would you expect to be most resistant to change? Which would be most supportive? Create a 90-day action plan for Mulcahy, following the example laid out by Bob Harbin above.

Exhibit 7.12 Stakeholder-Analysis Grid

		Power of the Stakeholder over Strategic Decisions			
		Unknown	Little/no power	Moderate degree of power	Significant power
Effect of Strategy on the Stakeholder	Unknown				
	Little/no effect			Brazilian Government	
	Moderate effect				Tritec Leadership Team
	Significant effect		Tritec Suppliers Employees		BMW Daimler-Chrysler

Corporate Social Responsibility (CSR)

The company today finds itself operating in a society that has greater demands than simply those of stakeholders. Society includes those who do not have a direct relationship with the business but are interested in it creating social good. How far a company should go to satisfy the demands of society has been debated over time. While Milton Friedman was an economics professor at the University of Chicago, he expressed the view that a company is an economic unit and its purpose is to make money and nothing else. It makes money because it creates something that society values. A company that does not show a profit at least equal to its cost of capital is irresponsible because it is wasting society's resources. The profit a company makes can be turned back to the shareholders and they can do what they want with it. Peter Drucker, a consultant and leader in management thought, saw the situation differently. He recognized that producing economic profit is a key but not the only responsibility of the business. With profit, the company is able to discharge other responsibilities, be a good employer, be a good citizen, and be a good neighbour. "Every organization must assume responsibility for its impact on employees, the environment, customers, and whomever and whatever it touches. That is social responsibility."[20] Then there are others who argue that business should address social ills because it is the institution with the money to do so.

Management of many companies think that CSR is the "right thing to do." In some cases, CSR is very much a part of the corporate identity. Husky Injection Molding has positioned itself as a leader in social responsibility and wants to maintain this position. Being a good corporate citizen was also a personal value of Robert Schad, the company's founder and CEO for many years. At Home Depot, CSR had its origins in the values of its founders, Bernie Marcus and Arthur Blank, who came from modest backgrounds and believed that a company should give back to the communities that supported it. At Weyerhaeuser, a strong internal driver from the outset was that the company carried the family's name so Frederick Weyerhaeuser wanted it to reflect well on the family. And for VanCity Savings Credit Union in Vancouver, CSR is strongly rooted in its origins as a cooperative committed to working for the sustained development of communities.[21]

ALTERNATIVE PERSPECTIVES

When a company acts in ways that are socially responsible, it has justifiable pride in its positive involvement in the community and on society. But no company can solve all of society's problems or bear the cost of doing so. This means that management needs to define what its stand will be on social issues and have a process for proceeding on satisfying those needs. Over time, various approaches to corporate social responsibility have been offered. Here we consider five of them: moral obligation, sustainability, licence to operate, reputation, and mutual interest.[22]

Perspective 1: Moral Obligation

A moral obligation requires that the company take actions based on a code of conduct that defines right or wrong. Doing the "right thing" makes the company a good "citizen" of society. Commercial success, the argument goes, will come from honouring ethical values and respecting people, communities, and the natural environment. This is the perspective that the church groups and others had when they were challenging Talisman's participation in the Sudanese oil fields.

Over time, various codes of conduct have been developed by business associations and governmental organizations. In 2004, the Organisation for Economic Co-operation and Development (OECD) issued a revised version of its Principles of Corporate Governance first issued in 1999.[23] The revisions added recommendations that would help rebuild and maintain public trust in companies and stock markets. The revised principles called on governments to ensure genuinely effective regulatory frameworks, on companies themselves to be truly accountable, on strengthened transparency and disclosure to counter conflicts of interest, and for institutional investors to take a more prominent role in governance and for shareholders to have an effective role in helping set executive compensation.

The challenge of relying on moral obligation implied by codes is that absolute mandates are not always easily fitted to complex business situations where competing values, interests, and costs are involved. What is moral is prescribed by one's values, and these vary within a society and vary even more so between societie. This calls into question *who* is to determine the values by which the companies operate. This problem is partially relieved by the view that there are universal human rights that all should observe. But in general, moral principles tend to constrain business action rather than drive it.

Perspective 2: Sustainability

Sustainability is a characteristic of a process or a state that can be maintained indefinitely at a certain level. For companies, sustainability means operating in ways that meet their present needs without compromising the ability of future generations to meet their own needs. This emphasis on avoiding short-term behaviour that is environmentally wasteful or socially detrimental appeals to enlightened self-interest. And it addresses the concern that modern industrial society, which continues to grow in scale and complexity, might also collapse, as have prior societies due to the impact of their own growth on ecological support systems.

One of the most trumpeted concerns in recent years is that human activity is generating gases that are causing global warming. In response to this, the Canadian Council of Chief Executives (CCCE) issued a report addressing climate change and sustainable development. It includes five propositions to move forward as a country: 1) a national plan of action that has governments, industry, and consumers working together; 2) investment in the new technologies that achieve a rising standard of living with a reduced environmental impact; 3) targets that spur environmental progress while keeping companies healthy and profitable; 4) using price signals such as emissions trading and environmental taxation to encourage appropriate behaviour; and 5) Canadian leadership in addressing climate change globally.[24]

A challenge with the concept of sustainability is that it is so far-reaching as to become meaningless to a specific company. In becoming so broad, it raises questions about how management makes tradeoffs without saying how it can address them.

Perspective 3: Licence to Operate

A "licence to operate" is an informal licence that goes beyond what is legally permissible to what is socially acceptable both today and tomorrow. A company with a licence has continued access to those demanding its products and services and those supplying the inputs it needs. Society also accepts what it does and how it does what it does. Finally, society has to find the level of profit it makes acceptable. A company that does things that are socially unacceptable, although not illegal, may lose its licence to operate as some stakeholders create conditions such that the company cannot conduct its activities profitably. Moreover its behaviour can precipitate laws and regulations that limit the actions of many companies in the future.

A company maintains its licence by two sets of actions. First, it must meet all societal standards: national standards and rules of commerce, international agreements, codes of conduct, and standards of civil society. And second, it must meet societal expectations regarding such things as product development, supporting democracy, share information of relevance to others, open itself to scrutiny of others, and accept input from civil society. Meeting the first set is easier because the standards are relatively clear. Meeting the second set requires that the company discuss with others what it needs to do to meet their demands.

The recent development of wind farms in Canada has been rich with businesses seeking licences to operate. Electricity generated by turbines on wind farms is attractive because it is a pollution-free and an infinitely sustainable form of energy, and it does not create greenhouse gases. Ninety-eight percent of the land used in wind farms can be used for regular agriculture and the sale of electricity generated can supplement the income of farmers. Although wind power has so many positive features, wind-farm projects often meet with strong resistance from local residents concerned about the destruction of natural vistas—thirty-storey-tall wind turbines set in clusters are unsightly; they cause noise and vibrations; they create shadows, the possibility of falling ice, threats to bird safety; and they are less reliable and efficient in their production of electricity.

Developers of wind farms have had to obtain all necessary municipal, provincial, and federal permits so the projects can go ahead. They have also had to deal with the concerns of people near the farms. Schneider Power Inc., the first private wind developer based in Ontario, has its own approach to community relations:

> The Schneiders say they make a point of bringing local people and other stakeholders onside early, knocking on doors and meeting people face-to-face. "We want to make sure our communities are happy—and that's not just some outsourced communication strategy," Thomas [Schneider, CEO and president,] says.
>
> Ruth Frawley, clerk-treasurer of the Township of Manitoulin, where the company's Providence Bay/Spring Bay farm is located, can attest to the Schneiders' skills in community relations. "Right from day one, they came and introduced themselves, and made presentations," she recalls. A zoning amendment was involved, because the development is on farmland, and the Schneiders "made a concerted effort to hold public meetings on their own. I think they were an excellent company to do that, and the locals appreciated it."
>
> The Spring Bay wind turbines are painted green on the bottom and fade to white at the top, an attempt to blend in with the surrounding landscape. "I can see them from miles and miles away . . . and I don't have a problem with them. I like them," Ms. Frawley says.
>
> Thomas says many communities oppose wind power because they don't feel developers listen to them. "It only takes one wind project that sours community relations and it will affect the rest of the province," he says, citing projects in Shelburne, Orangeville, and Collingwood that have been controversial.
>
> Schneider Power makes a point of avoiding communities where there's strong opposition to wind farming. So far, the strategy seems to be paying off when it comes to investor support: it has raised Cdn $6-million through private placements, and now has 27 investors on its roster. And its 10,900 hectares of land under development represent agreements and continuing relationships with 40 to 50 landowners, Thomas says.[25]

Three challenges face the company that seeks to maintain a licence to operate. First, by seeking to satisfy stakeholders, the company cedes primary control over its agenda to outsiders. Second, societal expectations are in continual evolution so the company has to be continuously engaged and change what it does. And third, societal expectations vary from location to location so what the company needs to do varies. Variations are most evident in differences in laws. Then the business has to decide whether it will satisfy the most restrictive laws or deal with each set as required.

Perspective 4: Reputation

A good reputation is thought to improve a company's image, strengthen its brand, enliven morale, and even raise the value of its stock. It is also seen as a form of insurance that can buffer the company from negative perceptions of their industry. This is particularly prevalent for firms involved with natural resources (mining, energy) or environmentally sensitive operations (chemicals). They hope that a good reputation for social consciousness will temper public criticism in the event of a crisis.

Achieving a good reputation is built on society having a positive perception of the company. According to Stephanie Bertels and John Peloza, a firm's reputation is built on both its own actions and the status of its actions relative to those of others in the company's industry. Expectations of performance are set by the actions of those in the industry. The company with a "good" reputation is one that demonstrates "superior" performance in relation to these expectations.[26]

The fundamental concern with relying on reputation is that quantitative evidence of the impact of reputation on consumer purchases and stock market value is inconclusive and the relationship between good deeds and stakeholder attitudes is difficult to measure. There is also a risk that high-profile, cause-related marketing campaigns become ends in themselves with sight lost of the social and business results they are intended to produce. An interesting twist is that reputational activities create their own demand. This leads those who benefit to pressure the company to continue to provide them with benefits. If the company stops doing so, they will speak out about the loss and hence damage the company's reputation. This causes the company to become locked into activities that may not benefit its performance except if they are discontinued. Finally, reputational activities can escalate as competitors match the company, forcing it to do more so that it stands out as superior.

Perspective 5: Mutual Interest

In this approach, a company focuses on actions that have the most significant social impact while providing the greatest business benefits. Doing this advances social conditions while reinforcing the company's strategy.

Whole Foods Market Inc. is one of the largest retailers of natural and organic foods in the world. Started in Austin, Texas, in 1980, its sales in 2006 were US$5.6 billion from 177 stores in the United States, 3 in Canada, and 6 in the United Kingdom. Whole Foods targets shoppers who are affluent, well educated, health-oriented, and passionate about their food and the environment. It has made decisions about sourcing and operations that reinforces the social dimension of its value proposition.

In sourcing, it has a buying program called Whole Trade Guarantee that ensures that products imported from the developing world have been sourced and produced ethically, sustainably, and transparently. It supports sustainable production in seafood by offering shoppers environmentally sound seafood options certified by the Marine Stewardship Council and in agriculture by seeking out organically and biodynamically grown foods. And it has advanced animal welfare by creating the Animal Compassion Foundation to develop more natural and humane ways of raising animals and by no longer selling live lobsters and crabs because it considered its handling of these creatures inhumane.

In operations, it has committed to reusable packaging, giving away or selling reusable tote bags for groceries. It has committed to energy conservation by using solar cells, installing skylights, and purchasing wind energy credits to offset its use of electricity—credits are used because wind power does not flow directly through grids to stores. It has committed to recycling glass, plastic, aluminum, and cardboard and composting inedible food and organic waste. It has committed to using a minimum of virgin raw materials when constructing stores, relying instead on recycled and sustainable building materials. It also uses environmentally friendly cleaning products in its stores.

With the mutual interest perspective, management faces two challenges when determining what issues to focus on. First, the issues that matter vary considerably from one company to another. Management needs to understand thoroughly the value chain of the company and then be able to see how the chain interacts with the environment. Second, social issues change over time. This means that management has to periodically reassess what issues matter. For example, for Whole Foods to remain competitive given its methods of operation, it might be forced to adjust its policies with regard to energy and the environment.

Given five different perspectives, which one is best? Both Kenneth Andrews and Michael Porter believe that the mutual interest perspective is the best because it is an integrated, affirmative approach. The other approaches to CSR attack the issue from the perspective of mitigating harm and provide a fragmented, defensive posture.[27]

To pursue the mutual interest perspective, Porter presents a systematic five-step approach for identifying, prioritizing, and addressing social issues while keeping the strategy and activities of the business in mind. This approach is a variant on the process we have already covered under stakeholder analysis.

First, the value chain of the business is laid out. This helps identify the social issues that affect its value chain directly—they are issues in the environment that intersect directly with the activities of the business.

Second, the relevant issues are determined. These intersections include quantity and quality of available inputs (human resources, transportation), rules and incentives that govern competition (intellectual property rights, safeguards against corruption, encouragement of investment), the size and sophistication of local demand (product standards, fairness in governmental purchasing), and the local availability of supporting industry (service and machine producers). Those that matter either affect the company's operations or influence its long-term competitiveness.

These issues present an opportunity to create shared value for the company and society. Issues that do not affect these but are important to society are best left to other companies to address.

Third, the relevant issues are prioritized according to their impact on the company now and in the future. In this way management determines where it will focus its attention and resources.

Fourth, management determines how to perform activities in the value chain in ways that improve social dimensions. There may be standard approaches to dealing with the issue. Alternatively, the company can reconfigure the activities in the value chain.

Fifth and finally, clear, measurable goals need to be set that measure how well the social issues are met and results need to be tracked over time.

While we have presented five perspectives, the distinctions among them are not as clear in reality because they are not mutually exclusive. For example, meeting societal expectations can build a reputation as a good corporate citizen. This is an overlap of the licence to operate and the reputational approaches. Among other things, a good reputation affords resource companies their social licence to operate and improves relations with regulators, which helps companies obtain the required permits for their operations with fewer hold-ups. Failing to obtain community support or attracting the ire of the non-governmental community can increase costs by holding up approvals in lengthy public hearings.

Cominco built trust and relations with communities living near its Pend Oreille mine development in the state of Washington, reducing the level of conflict to "just about zero." A nearby mine that failed to develop relations with its local communities and non-governmental organizations saw its project challenged in court, even after permits had been issued by the relevant regulatory authorities. The company ended up investing seven years and $30 million in a mine that never opened.[28]

THE TRIPLE BOTTOM LINE

Ever increasing concern about the sustainability of the ecological environment and society has led some to argue that each business is accountable for its impact on the ecological environment and society as well as for producing a profit. This has been captured with the concept of the triple bottom line (TBL, 3BL, or "people, planet, profit"), which considers the economic, ecological, and social impacts of business. The triple bottom line is an explicit way of recognizing what economists call "externalities" associated with a company's activities and what systems analysts call interdependencies. When using the triple bottom line approach, the company sets goals with respect to each dimension to ensure that it is creating a profit for its shareholders while protecting the environment and improving the lives of those with whom it interacts. An example of various measures that business can consider is found in Exhibit 7.13.

Companies that have recognized these interdependencies have taken action that they might not have had they only been focusing on the economics. McDonald's has moved to address obesity issues in its customers by changing portions and offering healthy alternatives. Toyota has produced the gas-electric hybrid car while P&G and Unilever have been developing products that can be sold to the desperately poor in ways that will lift them out of poverty.

Exhibit 7.13 The Triple Bottom Line[29]

	Economic	Environmental	Social
Typical Measures	Sales, profits, ROI	Air quality	Labour practices
	Taxes paid	Water quality	Community impacts
	Monetary flows	Energy usage	Human rights
	Jobs created	Waste produced	Product responsibility
	Total	Total	Total

FOCUS ON ETHICS 7.1
Resource Towns[30]

Approximately 1000 communities across Canada have been built to house the workers for an industrial enterprises that are extracting or processing resources such as minerals, fish, forest products, and hydroelectric power. Examples include Grand Falls-Windsor, Newfoundland (pulp and paper); Glace Bay, Nova Scotia (coal); Black's Harbour, New Brunswick (fish packing); Murdochville, Quebec (copper); Elliot Lake, Ontario (uranium); Copper Cliff, Ontario (nickel); Snow Lake, Manitoba (copper, zinc); Drayton Valley, Alberta (oil); Kitimat, British Columbia (aluminum); and Tumbler Ridge, British Columbia (coal).

These developments are the most precarious and unstable communities in Canada. Their economies depend on decisions that outside corporations or governments make about the nature and extent of the extractive or processing activity while the vagaries of international markets for resources create booms and busts. Much of the economic benefit derived from the resources is added elsewhere. Finally, those based on mining know that their resource base will be exhausted eventually.

A fundamental issue is what do the companies that give rise to these communities owe to them in order to help them survive if not thrive? Many companies have a poor record for sustaining these communities over time, and the towns have little prospect for doing it themselves, especially in Ontario and Western Canada where the towns are remote. The influx of secondary industry is prevented by the isolation of the community from major markets, the relatively high wages paid by resource industries, and high development costs.

A good example is Sturgeon Falls, Ontario, which is 5 kilometres north of Lake Nipissing and 35 kilometres west of North Bay. In 2001, it had a population of 5978. A paper mill was constructed in 1898 by the Sturgeon Falls Pulp Company. The mill was the largest and oldest employer in the one-industry town, and had been the mainstay of the economy. Throughout its life, the mill slipped in and out of receivership and had many owners, including Abitibi Paper and then MacMillan Bloedel, which

was bought by Weyerhaeuser in 1999. At its peak the plant employed 600. In October 2002, Weyerhaeuser announced that it was closing the corrugated cardboard producer due to overcapacity in the market and the inefficiency and age of the plant.

In explaining the closure, a Weyerhaeuser spokesperson cited an excess of product on the market and a lack of customers. From 1999 through 2002, 22 plant and machine closures in this product line occurred in North America. This was Weyerhaeuser's fourth closure in the last two years in this product line. The spokesperson also stated that the plant only produced 100 000 tonnes a year versus the standard for a world-class machine row of between 200 000 and 400 000 tonnes, and that it could build a new plant for the $200 million that it would cost to repair the existing plant. The Weyerhaeuser spokesperson said, "If we as a company do not adapt, then we will not survive and none of our employees will have jobs." Weyerhaeuser did not look for a buyer for the mill, but it did commit $80 000 toward an industrial adjustment committee for the community.

"It translates into a major financial loss to the municipality," said Gary O'Connor, mayor of Sturgeon Falls. "Federal Economic Development Initiative of Northern Ontario (FedNor), Northern Development and Mines, Human Resources and Development Canada (HRDC), and our own economic partners here in West Nipissing and Sudbury East have been at the table drafting a recovery plan ever since."[31] Sturgeon Falls created its own economic development commission while the Northern Ontario Heritage Fund stood ready to provide loans of up to $5 million per economic development project with no limit on the number of projects. The major concern was that skilled labour would leave before the jobs were created.

The paper mill was demolished in 2004. The power dam that had been owned by the mill remains and sells its power to Ontario Power Generation.

Did Weyerhaeuser fulfill its obligation to its employees and to the town? Should it have kept the plant open?

Summary of Challenges

1. *Recognize how owners evaluate the performance of a company.* Evaluating the performance of a business depends on who is looking at its performance. Business owners receive the profits the business generates so they are its residual claimants. All other stakeholders have been paid before the business is able to pay the owners. Owners have several different ways of assessing the business's performance. They can use several different financial ratios based on numbers found in the income statement, earnings per share, cash flow for each period, and value that is really the present value of the estimated cash flow generated by the business in future. From a strategic perspective,

value is the best measure since it is able to reflect the overall impact of strategy on performance.

2. *Appreciate the role of instrumental objectives when managing performance.* Performance, as we refer to it from the perspective of strategy, deals with the overall performance of the business because this is the measure that reflects the impact of strategic choices. But there are cases where certain objectives other than overall performance are of significant importance. These are instrumental objectives because achieving them is required to produce the desired overall performance. When achieving these objectives is critical but very difficult, management may

emphasize them so that they get the attention, effort, and resources needed to achieve them.

3. *Know why performance management is needed and how it is done.* The idea of focusing on overall performance of the business is too general for the many employees in the business to relate to as they perform work that is supposed to improve business performance. A mechanism is needed to direct individuals as they do their work so that each contributes to the performance of the business. Several different approaches have been developed over time to accomplish this. They go under the name *performance management*. Earlier approaches that are still used by some companies are DuPont analysis and management by objectives. More recent processes are value-based management and the balanced scorecard.

4. *Understand the five approaches to corporate social responsibility (CSR).* The five approaches are moral obligation, sustainability, licence to operate, reputation, and mutual interest. Moral obligation has the weaknesses of being indeterminate as to whose morals should count and inflexibility as morals are expressed in terms of rights and wrongs. Sustainability is not a natural order so there are questions as to where the limits are set. Licence to operate cedes primary control of the business strategy to others who then decide what the business can and cannot do. Reputation is not clearly related to profitability, and some actions that bolster reputation can work against it. Mutual interest requires that the business understand its value chain and adjust the interactions between the value chain and the environment over time as social issues change. While using every approach presents managerial challenges we favour the mutual interest approach because it clearly reflects strategy in the decisions made.

5. *Explain the importance of stakeholder analysis and the five-step process used to analyze it.* Stakeholder analysis identifies the variety of parties who have a vested interest in the formulation and implementation of a company's strategy or some influence on company performance. Having identified them, management can decide what it is prepared to give them to gain their cooperation. The *first step* in stakeholder analysis is identifying the value chain so that the relevant stakeholders can be identified. The *second step* is identifying those stakeholders who intersect with the value chain. The *third step* is determining shareholder expectations. The *fourth step* is determining each stakeholder's power or influence over decisions that strategy depends on. The *fifth step* is determining which stakeholders will be satisfied and how.

Review Questions

1. Is management doing the right thing for owners when it pushes for the highest value possible?
2. Why is cash flow a better measure of performance than profit?
3. What is the difference between operating cash flow and free cash flow? Why does it matter?
4. Identify three stakeholders in a business, their expectations, and how they try to influence management to meet their expectations of what they might receive from a business?
5. What two factors determine how hard the stakeholder bargains with management of the business?

6. What is the difference between serving stakeholders and being socially responsible?
7. Describe the five approaches to corporate social responsibility. Which approach do you think is best? Why?
8. What is the common process of a performance management system?
9. Describe how the four alternative approaches to performance management differ.
10. What is the difference between a dashboard and a balanced scorecard?

Experiential Activities

Group Exercises

1. Using the financial statements from a public company of your choice, calculate the operating and free cash flows.
2. For a fast-food restaurant chain and for a mining company, identify the stakeholders and what they want. Who is the most powerful stakeholder in each business?

Ethical Debates

1. Of the three companies cited in the opening vignette about Talisman Energy, which do you think took the correct stance as a business: Talisman, Glencore, or CNOOC? Why do you think that? And what implications did their decision have on the performance of the business?

Endnotes

1. Extensive explanation of the situation is found in Stephen J. Kobrin, "Oil & Politics: Talisman Energy and Sudan," *International Law and Politics* 36 (2004): 425–456. Additional information is provided by Sudan Update, in "Raising the Stakes: Oil and Conflict in Sudan." Accessed December 5, 2010, at www.sudanupdate.org.

2. Anon., "Politics Trump Human Rights in Sudan," June 24, 2002. Accessed July 20, 2007, at www.sudanembassy.org/default.asp?page=viewstory&id=59.

3. Ann, "Aggressive Swiss Giant Rides Resource Boom," *Wall Street Journal*, July 31, 2007, pp. A1, A12.

4. Ibid.

5. Unknown, "Chinese Oil Giant Won't Leave Myanmar, Executive Says," *Wall Street Journal*, October 15, 2007, p. A4.

6. Many companies now use the corporate valuation model to make decisions about alternative strategies. Specific work on strategy that supports this view is: Daniel F. Spulber, *Management Strategy* (Boston: McGraw-Hill, 2004); Robert Grant, *Contemporary Strategy Analysis*, 5th ed. (Malden, M.A.: Blackwell Publishing, 2005), and George S. Day, "Evaluating Strategic Alternatives," in Liam Fahey and Robert M. Randall, *The Portable MBA in Strategy* (New York: John Wiley and Sons, 1994). Financial valuation in which the linkage between strategy and finance is emphasized is: Tim Koller, Marc Goedhart, David Wessels, *Valuation: Measuring and Managing the Value of Companies*, 4th ed. (McKinsey & Company Inc., 2005), and James M. McTaggart, Peter W. Kontes, and Michael C. Mankins, *The Value Imperative* (New York: Free Press, 1994).

7. "Van Houtte Reviewing Strategic Options to Enhance Shareholder Value," News Release for Van Houtte Inc. via CNW Telbec, Montreal; www.sedar.com: News Release January 12, 2007.

8. Loblaw Companies Ltd., Annual Report for 2006, p. 6.

9. Skepticism about the ability of a business to sustain its earning into the future has led to broader measures of performance than simply value. In the past, financial analysis dealt with this concern by considering the "quality of earnings." More recently analysis of performance has been assessed more strategically. At Accenture, it has been measured in five dimensions: growth in revenue, profitability, positioning, longevity, and consistency. See Tim Breene and Paul F. Nunes, "Going the Distance: How the World's Best Companies Achieve High Performance," *Outlook* 3 (2006) Accenture.

10. Loblaw Companies Ltd., Annual Report for 2006, p. 6.

11. www.intalevnavigator.com/index.php?id=4204 and www.intalevnavigator.com/fileadmin/images_products/navi/es4.gif.

12. Thomas J. Liesz, "Really Modified Du Pont Analysis: Five Ways to Improve on Return on Equity," presented at the SBIDA 2002 Conference, San Diego, California, and retrieved from the SBANC Research Archive, Small Business Advancement National Center, University of Central Arkansas, February 7–9, 2002. Accessed October 30, 2009, at www.sbaer.uca.edu/research/sbida/2002/Papers/19.pdf.

13. Peter Drucker, *The Practice of Management* (1954).

14. Samuel C. Weaver and J. Fred Weston, "A Unifying Theory of Value Based Management," Working Paper 4-03, Finance Dept., Anderson Graduate School of Management, University of California, Los Angeles, 2003.

15. Kaplan and Norton have been prolific authors on the subject: R. S. Kaplan and D. P. Norton, "The Balanced Scorecard: Measures That Drive Performance," *Harvard Business Review* (January/February 1992): 71–80; R. S. Kaplan and D. P. Norton, "Putting the Balanced Scorecard to Work." *Harvard Business Review* (September/October 1993): 2–16; R. S. Kaplan and D. P. Norton, "Using the Balanced Scorecard as a Strategic Management System," *Harvard Business Review* (January/February 1996): 75–85; R. S. Kaplan and D. P. Norton, *Balanced Scorecard: Translating Strategy into Action* (Boston, M.A.: Harvard Business School Press, 1996); R. S. Kaplan and D. P. Norton, *Strategy Maps* (Boston, M.A.: Harvard Business School Press, 2004); and R. S. Kaplan and D. P. Norton, *Alignment* (Boston, M.A.: Harvard Business School Press, 2006).

16. After an example provided by Francis Gouillart, president of Emergence Consulting, which is described in Robert Kaplan and David P. Norton, *The Strategy-Focused Organization* (Boston, M.A.: Harvard Business School Press, 2001), pp. 123–130.

17. Robert S. Kaplan and David P. Norton, "Mastering the Management System," *Harvard Business Review* (January 2008).

18. Darrell Rigby and Barbara Bilodeau, "Bain's Global 2007 Management Tools and Trends Survey," *Strategy & Leadership* 35:5 (2007): 9–16, and Stuart Crainer, "Keeping Score," *Business Strategy Review* (London Business School, Autumn 2006): 45–50.

19. Andrew Campbell and Marcus Alexander, "What's Wrong with Strategy?" *Harvard Business Review* (November/December 1997): 42–51.

20. Peter Drucker, *The Daily Drucker* (New York: HarperBusiness, 2004), p. 126.

21. In 2002, Natural Resources Canada (Corporate Policy and Portfolio Coordination Branch) sponsored a series of reports on companies and their CSR policies. Companies included were CP Railway, DuPont Canada, Home Depot Canada, Husky Injection Molding, Marine Harvest, Nutreco Canada, Syncrude, Teck Cominco, Telus, Vancity Credit Union, and Weyerhaeuser Canada. The final report, titled *Corporate Social Responsibility: Lessons Learned,* was accessed October 30, 2009, at www.fivewinds.com/uploadedfiles_shared/CSRlessons.pdf.

22. These approaches are identified and discussed by Michael E. Porter and Mark R. Kramer, "Strategy and Society: The Link Between Competitive Advantage and Corporate Social Responsibility," *Harvard Business Review* (December 2006): 78–92. An excellent source for illustrations of CSR is: Natural Resources Canada, *Corporate Social Responsibility: Lessons Learned, Final Summary Report, Sustainable Development and International Affairs,* Corporate Policy and Portfolio Coordination Branch, Ottawa, Ontario, 2002. Accessed October 30, 2009, at www.fivewinds.com/uploadedfiles_shared/CSRlessons.pdf.

23. OECD, *OECD Principles of Corporate Governance*, OECD Publication Service, Paris, France, 2004. Accessed October 30, 2009, at www.oecd.org/dataoecd/32/18/31557724.pdf.

24. Canadian Council of Chief Executives (CCCE), *Clean Growth: Building a Canadian Environmental Superpower*, A Policy Declaration of the Canadian Council of Chief Executives, prepared by the Council Task Force on Environmental Leadership, October 1, 2007. Accessed October 30, 2009, at www.ceocouncil.ca/publications/pdf/test_14a7f87d43da18e574aa830d322a9cbe/Clean_Growth_ELI_Policy_Declaration_October_1_2007.pdf.

25. Paulette Peirol, "Father and Son Feel the Breeze at Their Backs," *Globe and Mail,* April 20, 2007. Accessed October 30, 2009, at www.theglobeandmail.com/servlet/story/RTGAM.20070420.wsrearthwind20/BNStory/robAgenda/.

26. Stephanie Bertels and John Peloza, "Running to Stand Still: Managing CSR Reputation in an Era of Ratcheting Expectations," Working Paper 2006-8, Centre for Corporate Governance and Risk Management, Segal Graduate School of Business, Simon Fraser University, Winter 2006.

27. The mutual interest perspective was first presented by Kenneth Andrews in his text, *The Concept of Corporate Strategy*, 3rd ed. (Homewood, Ill.: Richard D. Irwin; 1987). Recently Porter assessed this perspective in relation to alternative perspectives that are presented in the literature on corporate social responsibility (CSR). See M. E. Porter and M. R. Kramer, "Strategy & Society" *Harvard Business Review* (December 2006): 78–9.

28. Industry Canada has a website for corporate social responsibility. Accessed October 30, 2009, at www.ic.gc.ca/eic/site/csr-rse.nsf/eng/home.

29. Andrew W. Savitz, *The Triple Bottom Line* (Jossey-Bass/Wiley, 2006): p. xiii.

30. Saarinen Oiva, "Single Sector Communities in Northern Ontario," in Gilbert A. Stelter and Alan F.J. Arbitise, eds., *Power and Place: Canadian Urban Development in a North American Context* (Vancouver: University of British Columbia, 1986), p. 228; Steven High, "Oral History and Deindustrialization: The Plant Shutdown Stories of Displaced Sturgeon Falls (Ontario) Paper Workers," Concordia University, Montreal, 2006. Accessed October 22, 2009, at http://elenarazlogova.org/hist306f06/stevehigh.pdf; and "Gripped by Uncertainty: Sturgeon Falls Springs into Action Following the Closure of Its Primary Employer," *Northern Ontario Business* (January 1, 2003). Accessed October 23, 2009, at www.thefreelibrary.com/Gripped+by+uncertainty:+Sturgeon+Falls+springs+into+action+.

31. Gripped by Uncertainty following...-a096627815.

8 Implementing Strategy

In this chapter, we challenge you to:

1. Outline the interdependence between strategy formulation and implementation.

2. Demonstrate how organizational structure serves as a lever when implementing strategy.

3. Illustrate the use of systems as levers when implementing strategy.

4. Describe why managers need to be prepared to hold their subordinates accountable.

5. Explain the dual roles that top management plays in strategy implementation.

6. Explain how implementation produces a strategy that was not as intended.

7-Eleven: The Convenience Store That Out-Competed the Competition[1]

7-Eleven Corporation is one of the world's largest retailers with a chain of convenience stores, including 5800 stores in Canada and the United States and 23 200 licences in 17 countries throughout the world. In 2004, the company's total revenues were US$12.2 billion just before Japanese retailer Seven & i Holdings Co. took it private.

The pressure for change in the convenience business increased as other retailers started invading its market niche. Other retailers tried to get consumers into their stores by charging loss-leading prices for many of the core products of convenience stores. In spite of this, 7-Eleven held on to its dominance of the industry because its management transformed the company between the mid-1990s and 2005. Under the leadership of James Keyes, the company focused on improving a small set of strategically vital retailing functions: in-store merchandising, pricing, ordering, and customer data analysis. Many of the ideas used in making improvements came from its Japanese franchise, which was run by Hirofumi Suzuki. Keyes designed 7-Eleven's organization so that it was able to execute the strategy and keep its franchisees on target. "I'm trying to establish a winning strategy, one that allows the organization to clear competitive hurdles [. . .] the coach can't throw the ball. He can't execute the plan. The coach has to be able to teach the players to do that [. . .]. Before, they didn't even know why the score was important; they were just out playing."[2]

Structure

The structure of 7-Eleven reflects two sets of activities: (1) those due to the size of the company and that are the corporation's responsibility: information technology, large suppliers, distribution, overall store layout, product placement and pricing, and support services for stores, such as accounting and payroll, and (2) those that come from being close to the customer and that are the responsibility of store employees: ordering, stocking products that are locally appealing, and providing customers with a pleasant shopping experience.

This simple structure requires only seven layers and promotes the fast flow of information and efficient execution. It also reduces the chances of messages being garbled.

1. President /Chief Executive Officer
2. Chief Operating Officer
3. VP Operations
4. Division Managers
5. Market Managers
6. Field Consultants
7. Store Managers

The only potential change in structure comes each quarter when 200 stores are reviewed using an eight-category performance framework to determine whether any should be closed.

Systems

7-Eleven utilizes both a sophisticated information system and face-to-face meetings. Heavy investment in information technology supported the improvement of its capabilities and functions. The company's proprietary retail information system now contains an integrated set of tools designed around the economic model. Features of the system include: category management, item-level sales analysis, handheld terminals for ordering and recording, point-of-sale terminals with centralized pricing, integrated credit and debit card authorization, integrated gasoline and pay-at-the-pump functionality, automated back office functions connected directly with the company's accounting system (cash and sales reporting, payroll, gasoline pricing, inventory control), and market information, including weather forecasts, merchandising messages, and sales history.

7-Eleven gathers enormous amounts of retail data from every sale at point-of-sale (POS) terminals in each store. The data go to corporate headquarters and are then distributed to those making decisions. For top management the data are converted into easy-to-use graphs and charts that show how 7-Eleven's 2500 products are selling every hour of every day and anticipate inventory needs. Top management also tracks the performance of the 30 to 40 new items added every week to verify whether they are in tune with the continually changing retail environment. Store operators use the information when making ordering decisions and stocking decisions on the 15 percent to 25 percent of their inventory they

Exhibit 8.1 A Sample Planogram for Retail Shelf Space[3]

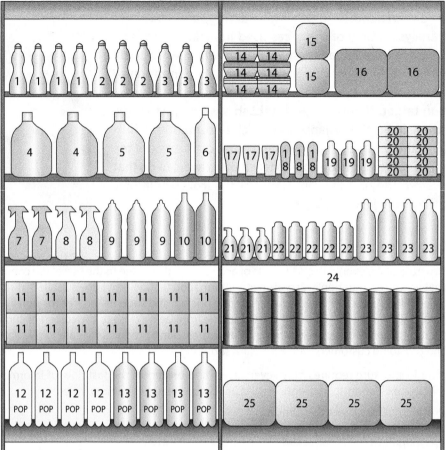

Household & Beauty Shelf Display

Item	Product
1	Dish Soap with Bleach
2	Dish Soap - Antibacterial
3	Dish Soap - Fruit
4	Laundry Detergent
5	Laundry Detergent
6	Fabric Softener
7	Shower Cleaner
8	Window Cleaner
9	Easy Scrub
10	Pine Cleaner
11	Square Tissues
12	2 Litre Pop
13	2 Litre Pop - Diet
14	Baby wipes
15	Diapers - Tissue Pack
16	Diapers
17	Face Wash
18	Sunscreen
19	Baby Lotion
20	Toothpaste
21	Hand Soap
22	Talcum Powder
23	Baby Wash
24	Toilet Paper
25	Diapers

select that tailors their stores to the customers at their location. The other 75 percent of inventory is sourced from company-approved vendors and is placed according to centrally designed and controlled planograms, such as that illustrated in Exhibit 8.1.

The two key metrics that drive the business are store sales per day and inventory turns. Improving these rests on having an assortment of products and services in each store that make the store more attractive than the competitors. Top management recognizes that those who are closest to the customers can best gauge what will work, so it has promoted the Retailer Initiative, in which store managers and sales associates are expected to continually seek new and better ways to serve customers. The people in the store select some of the items and make sure the store has the appropriate inventory. Without these expectations, people wait to be told what to do by top management and would tend to do the bare minimum.

To motivate hourly sales associates, they are asked to manage a section of the store. Ordering inventory is a critical part of this job. To help them decide how much to order the associate can access past sales levels, inventory data, new merchandise information, weather information, events in the local area, and trends in local competing stores on a graphic order terminal—a handheld terminal that the operator can carry to store shelves. The sales associate uses all this information to develop a hypothesis about which products, how many products, and what time the products will sell the next day. Based on this, the associate orders inventory. Afterward, actual sales are compared with hypothesized sales to determine the accuracy of the hypothesis. By repeating the process of hypothesis, order, and inspect, the accuracy of order placement is improved while also spotting trends.

Person-to-person communication is also an important part of the management system. This communication is channelled into two sets of structured and scheduled meetings at which real-time information is exchanged so that the relevant decision makers understand current priorities and have timely customer data.

The sequence of meetings starts early Monday morning with eight members of the executive team and their guests. They survey the prior week using the data found in the Friday book—a data book that identifies what is and is not moving in their inventory of 2500 products through 5800 stores across North America—and exhaustive information on new products and promotions. They also discuss priorities and tactics for the upcoming week and any strategic issues that have come up. Just before noon the second meeting starts. It is a two-hour national video conference divided into two parts. The first hour is for divisional vice-presidents and higher executives. They go over the updated forecast for the month and the quarter and strategic topics. In the second hour, department heads, product managers, category managers, and sales and marketing managers join the discussion for the Leadership Meeting. This meeting starts with a financial review so those lower in the organization see a direct link between what they do and the earnings per share. This is followed by the Obstacles Meeting, in which store issues that need corporate resolution are escalated to higher levels. Issues are identified and accountability for their resolution is assigned. Progress on the issues and their resolution is tracked and discussed in later meetings. The end of this meeting leads to further staff meetings and divisional communications.

Before noon each Tuesday, the chief operating officer holds an hour-long conference with 7-Eleven's 800 field consultants to give them messages that they need to deliver to stores from Wednesday through Friday. The meeting starts with a message of the week from the COO. Then the consultants are told everything they need to know to educate store owners and associates about the week's priorities. This includes case studies, new merchandising issues, featured products, and lessons from test markets. The meeting closes with the CEO providing a closing message. He often references a visit to a store or an upcoming special promotion or tie-in.

Field consultants oversee a group of stores. The consultants ensure compliance with corporate standards and guide the stores on how to make themselves more attractive. The consultants also collect information from the stores on marketing and store trends so headquarters can build a coherent strategy.

The result of all this coordination is that everyone has a common understanding of the situation and knows how to do their work so that it contributes to pursuit of the company's strategy.

Staff

7-Eleven needs people who understand what their responsibilities are and who are able to execute them. Systematization of processes and automation of the support work has dramatically lowered execution costs and improved productivity. It has also allowed the company to draw from a broader labour pool because fewer skills are required. But having employees who are simply robots makes it harder to attract capable people. Already 7-Eleven finds attracting and retaining capable employees challenging, as retail jobs pay modest wages and opportunities for advancement are not obvious.

To deal with this 7-Eleven has created an interesting work environment at several levels. Franchising stores allows the operators have incentive to run the stores well. Meanwhile, empowering front-line managers and associates by giving them authority and decision rights has motivated employees and reduced turnover.

To ensure that employees are capable, 7-Eleven has intense and thorough training programs. Candidates are certified to take on increasing levels of responsibility that start with writing an order. They are taught how to use 7-Eleven's proprietary system to determine what consumers are buying in the store each day. Managers and hourly associates are taught how to analyze trends, develop hypotheses, and make considered choices. All get a pay raise once they have completed training.

Overall

When Larry Keyes resigned in 2005, 7-Eleven's stock appreciation over the prior five years had outpaced all major competitors, including Casey's General Stores, the Pantry, and Uni-Mart. It dominated the industry's vital statistics in the prior two years with same-store merchandise growth at almost twice the industry average, revenue per employee at just about two-and-a-half times higher, and inventory turns at 72 percent more than the industry average. Same-store sales grew in four of the five previous years. Furthermore, its acquisition of two regional U.S. chains helped grow sales by more than 30 percent and increased gross profit margins by 2 percentage points. ■

Implementing Strategy

To this point we have been working through the analytical process of creating and selecting a strategy. But even the perfect strategy is of little value unless the business has implemented it. So when strategy fails, three questions come to mind:

1. Is the strategy flawed?
2. Is the implementation of the strategy flawed?
3. Are both the strategy and implementation flawed?

It should come as no surprise that, more often than not, implementation problems are the source of performance problems.[4] Obviously, no strategy can be effective if it's implemented poorly. By the same token, although we tend to attribute success to effective strategies, some of the most stellar performers achieve competitive advantage because of *how* well they execute their strategies. This creates a dual interdependency between the two, as shown in Exhibit 8.2. When selecting a strategic alternative, the viable ones are those that can be implemented. And once a strategy is chosen, it needs to be implemented.

Executives responsible for formulating strategy are often prone to downplaying the obstacles to implementation. Consider the number of hardware and software firms that have attempted to become IT solution providers by adding a consulting arm to their existing business. Most have failed because they lacked the organization needed to execute the strategy.[5] SAP, a provider of ERP software, demonstrated this. The company grew quickly at first because of high customer demand for its unique product. Management, in its zeal for growth, however, neglected to develop the organizational structure, retain employees, and balance rewards for sales with rewards for profitability. Consequently the performance of SAP declined though eventually it recovered (as you will see in Exhibit 8.3), after a new CEO dramatically revamped the firm's infrastructure, human resource policies, and cost controls.[6] The interrelationship among organizational levers means that a change in one aspect likely requires changes in others.[7]

In this chapter, we focus on issues concerning strategy implementation. We break this discussion into two parts: managing administration of the business and managing change. The distinction is that managing administration deals with organizational levers that management can pull (structure, systems, and processes), as well as managing the culture and

Exhibit 8.2 Formulation and Implementation

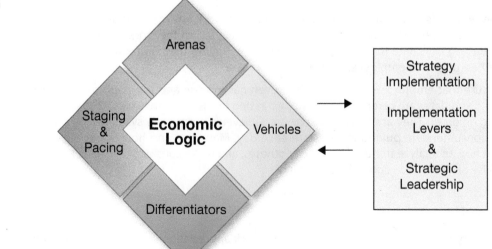

Exhibit 8.3 Picking Up the Pieces at SAP

The enterprise software company SAP dodged a bullet, but just barely. It did so not by overhauling its strategy but rather by dramatically changing its leadership and implementation approach. We will focus on SAP America, one of the largest subsidiaries of the German firm SAP, because it characterizes much of what took place globally in this firm. From 1992 through most of 1996, SAP America's revenues grew at an astounding triple-digit annual rate, from $49 million to an annualized $818 million. The number of employees over that same period grew from 284 to 1621. This rapid growth was spurred by two things. First, SAP had what many U.S. multinationals perceived to be the best ERP product on the market. The product was highly profitable due to its relatively standardized design and high market demand. Second, SAP was a fairly decentralized organization, with functional emphasis primarily in sales and on an incentive system that rewarded sales and sales growth. Career paths were unclear and focused on regions, but because the compensation was so lucrative, employees could earn huge salaries based on sales and then jump ship to a firm where their career and mobility might be more clearly laid out. As a result, SAP America was built for speed (though not efficiency), and its rocket-like sales growth reflected the levers and leadership that were in place.

Coming into late 1995, however, the rocket seemed to be running out of fuel. The combination of growing competition from the likes of Oracle and Siebel systems, market saturation, and a lack of organizational accountability that was a by-product of the growth focus was beginning to undermine SAP's profitability, customer service, and reputation. SAP Germany's kick in the pants to SAP America started with the promotion of then-CFO Kevin McKay to the position of CEO (and the departure of the old CEO, Paul Wahl, to competitor Siebel Systems). McKay moved quickly to increase cultural sensitivity to costs and cost management, implement an administrative structure to bolster the organization's overall professionalism, and formalize human resource policies. This latter step took the form of hiring an HR director (no one had held that role at SAP America before, despite all of the hiring that had gone on), who put a formal HR system in place. These decisions were complemented by increased R&D funding to explore the Internet applications of SAP software, a platform that the software giant had ignored up to that point. At the same time, McKay subtly shifted SAP's strategy from one of pure growth through new accounts to account "farming"—an increased focus on garnering a greater share of each existing customer's IS business needs, coupled with the modification of the firm's reward system to reward such behaviours.

While these changes caused many people to leave SAP, this loss was more than offset by the hiring of new executives and workers who bought into the new organizational arrangements and SAP's vision. By 2000, the firm had successfully launched a Web-based version of its software, called MySAP, and regained its position of industry leadership.

setting performance criteria. Managing change is more comprehensive and looks at how leadership of the business programs the implementation of strategy, beginning with creating urgency for change. By the end of this chapter, you should be able to identify the organizational levers that management uses and specify the steps of a change process used to implement the strategy.

Managing the Company

Leading the company is different from managing it. Leading involves giving direction to and energizing the people in the business. Meanwhile managing the administration involves designing the organizational structure and processes, hiring the people, then managing the people within the business so that they pursue the strategy. The opening vignette on 7-Eleven illustrated all the aspects that management had to put together to support pursuit of the strategy:

- 7-Eleven's organizational dimensions work in unison to support a strategy focused on providing customers with convenience.
- The relatively flat organizational structure facilitates both the flow of information and quick decision making.
- The systems in place coordinate operations and allow rapid adjustment to what the customer wants. In part, this comes from allowing stores to stock items local managers think will satisfy the unique desires of their customers.
- People are selected and trained so that they function well in the systems that the company uses to coordinate activities.

Strategic success requires that companies have both good leadership and good management, though the emphasis in recent decades has been on leadership at the expense of management. With the role of strategic leadership covered in Chapter 2, this chapter deals with managing the business around a strategy.

Managing the organization starts with the strategy itself. The strategy will only deliver superior performance if certain things are achieved, primarily offering the value curve that will appeal to consumers for less than the cost of doing so. Accomplishing this requires that certain tasks be performed very well. These are the key tasks of the organization and the people are placed in organizational units such that these tasks are performed very well. Processes or systems are used to engage people within and across the organizational units so that they cooperate in a coordinated manner. As people do the work, culture is created—that is an overall reflection of "how things are done around here." These aspects of managing will now be considered in greater detail.

This chapter first deals with the management controls under organization, then it addresses the culture of the business.

ORGANIZATIONAL ELEMENTS

Every strategy has an economic model that explains how it is going to make money. Associated with the model are decisions concerning which activities are in the value chain and how they are performed so that they produce the desired value curve for customers. People then have to be organized so that the business performs the necessary work.

A business that has a low cost strategy must take prices as given. The fixed-price nature of the industry means that additional profits only come from lowered costs. The preferred structure in these cases is centralized, functional units. It favours efficiency and economies of scale. Efficiency comes from standardization, which allows repetition over large volume. This lowers the cost per unit. Costs are also reduced by having little duplication of resources. The weakness of this design is that for many people in it, it is bureaucratic and few see the big picture as each functional group gets wrapped up in its own process.

A business that has a differentiation strategy must support differentiation of the product or service. The structure needed allows differences and encourages innovation so that new products are found or developed quickly. Decision making is decentralized and economies of scale are not the driving factor. People working in this design have to work effectively in a dynamic situation. The weakness of this design is that it has higher costs so it has to be able to deliver products that customers are willing to pay more for.

A business that has a focused strategy usually organizes around customers, geographies, or product lines. A decentralized structure has operating units built around each dimension of the focus. The weakness of this design is the duplication of resources and the loss of efficiency as each unit requires dedicated resources.

Looking at the retail industry, the two critical tasks are getting merchandise sold to stores and getting people to come and buy in stores. A specialty retailer wants its buyers to provide a selection of merchandise that consumers will pay a premium for because they are "special." A large retailer wants its buyers to provide a broad array of merchandise at low cost that many consumers will buy. Each situation requires that the buyer focus on getting the required merchandise. Merchandising is so critical that it is a separate organizational unit responsible for buying merchandise and telling the stores how to sell it. The other critical task is running a store that consumers are attracted to. In a specialty store, this includes providing knowledgeable sales staff and an ambiance that sets the store apart from other retailers. In a large retailer, this means keeping shelves stocked and providing fast checkouts. Store management is so important that it is also set up as a separate organizational unit that is focused on providing an attractive retail environment so that customers prefer to shop at the company's stores.

Identifying what the key tasks are is of particular importance when a business is changing its strategy. A new strategy will change the importance of particular work and perhaps even the way work is done. If this is not explicitly recognized, then the work required by the new strategy may not get done because people are more comfortable doing things the way they always have. For example, E. D. Smith and Sons in Winona, Ontario, shifted from producing its own branded jams and other products to make private-label products for food retailers, including Loblaw Companies. This shift meant that marketing became much less important to the company while manufacturing and new product development became much more important. The marketing department was virtually eliminated because E. D. Smith no longer had to create demand for its own brands. Money was invested in manufacturing as it was modernized and rationalized so that it was a lower cost processor while R&D was expanded so that E. D. Smith could provide customers with a range of novel and unique products.

Management has a very powerful influence through its design of the organization. Many elements of the organization fall under this influence, and decisions are not easily made as the organization is a system of mutually interdependent elements. This means that a decision about one element has an impact on other elements of the organization. And the relationships among the elements become more complex as the size of the organization increases. The interdependence means that the decisions have to be made to complement other decisions. There is not necessarily a right decision in many cases, but the need to complement other decisions is always necessary.

Organizational design revolves around decisions about structure, systems, and staff. Management designs the structure and systems and makes certain that they are working. And with respect to staff, it ensures that positions in the organizational structure are filled by people with the appropriate competencies. We will now consider each of these levers by itself and then consider the fit among them.

Organizational Structure

Most new businesses start small, with an owner/manager and a few employees. Once a business grows beyond this size, those in charge have to decide how the work will be organized and controlled. There is no automatic system for assigning decision rights or motivating individuals to use information to promote firm objectives. What those in charge have to do is create an organizational design in which responsibility is allocated, roles are defined, control and accountability are established, and decision-making authority is delegated.

Those in charge organize the people in the company so that the work gets done. They do so by delegating some decisions and make some themselves. When they delegate, they assume those they delegate to will have the perspective, the information, and the personal capabilities, including expertise needed to make good decisions. People are given authority and resources to act on the decisions they make.

Organizational structure is the formal configuration of individuals and groups with specific tasks, responsibilities, and authority within the organization. The organizational chart provides a representation of the basic elements of structure. The diagrammed structure typically forms a pyramid-like hierarchy with those below reporting to those above. Even with teams, hierarchy exists as each team has a leader. Hierarchy is efficient for setting goals, making decisions, assigning tasks, allocating resources, managing people who cannot direct themselves, and holding people accountable. Where there is greater task specialization, the chart will show this by having more boxes.

Power originates at the top of the structure. Centralized organizations have power concentrated at the top in the hands of a few people. These organizations tend to be more bureaucratic and are less responsive to a changing environment. Decentralized organizations distribute power throughout the organization, so decisions can be made by lower-level employees as opposed to higher-ranking managers. This allows more flexibility in decision making so the organization can be more responsive to a changing environment. Associated with structure is decision rights. Decision makers can only be effective when they have information needed to make decisions, authority to act on their decisions, and the resources required to carry out their decisions.

Most structures have discrete subunits that report to the top management. Breaking the organization into coherent units is known as departmentalization. Various forms of departmentalization include by function, product, market, customers, and geographic regions. The predominant form of structure for a business is the functional form. The matrix organization is more complex, since it combines both functional and product departmentalization so that people within the matrix have two reporting relationships. Conflict can be reduced by going to a pseudo-matrix structure in which those within the matrix have reporting relationships to one set of departments and simply informational relationships to the other. Often the informational lines are excluded from the organizational chart so what is going on is not readily evident from the organizational chart. In many food companies, product managers report to a marketing manager but are responsible for coordinating the contributions of diverse functional groups and managing the flow of information among contributing personnel. Many corporations have strategic business units (SBUs), each of which is an autonomous division or organizational unit that is responsible for its profit—Hint: think of it as a company. Each SBU has its own strategy, customer, and competitors. Maintaining separate units provides the corporation with greater flexibility as it can buy and sell units according to how well they fit with the overall corporate strategy.

Texts on organizational behaviour describe the strengths and weaknesses of various forms of departmentalization, so they will not be described here. The structural forms found in them are idealized so that the differences in structure are clear and the arguments telling. In reality organizational charts rarely copy the forms presented in the textbooks because structure evolves over time and so accumulate various organizational features like barnacles attached to a ship. Management adds and subtracts units and modifies existing structures rather than radically redesigning the whole structure. Sometimes this happens because units are divided as they develop greater specialization. Other times an organizational problem is dealt with by restructuring a part of the organization while leaving the rest of the organization unchanged. Still, the principles associated with the idealized forms are valuable because they can be used to determine how to resolve structural issues.

More complex organizational structures are those associated with joint ventures (intra-organizational design), franchisors, corporations (operating versus holding companies—countless variations for multi-business corporations that capitalize on the benefits of discrete subunits), and global corporations. These will be described in later chapters as appropriate.

Evidence of the breakdown in structure includes people who do not know what they are responsible for, people who do not act on their responsibilities, people who have far more work than they can do effectively or efficiently, and individuals who act on issues beyond the sphere of their responsibilities. These problems can often be clarified using linear responsibility charting. A breakdown occurs when units are interdependent, but each acts according to its own interests, such as when R&D designs products that customers do not want, and when one person makes all the major decisions in a structure that has a top management team.

Organizational Systems

Organizational systems and their component subsystems or "processes" are essential because they help people with different responsibilities work together. They tell people what to expect and what is expected from them and when. Within every functional area there are specific systems that help the functional activities add value. Wal-Mart, for example, has systems that are designed to ensure that its logistics and purchasing operate flawlessly. Daily co-ordination of logistics and purchasing produces efficiencies that allow Wal-Mart to sell at retail prices that are the same prices that many merchandisers buy at yet continue to operate profitably. These systems deal with the technical side of the business and are of significance to the capabilities of resources as described in Chapter 3. Here we are interested in another set of systems—the administrative systems of the business. These are systems associated with the company that are necessary to sustain it as an organization of people. They form what Michael Porter referred to as secondary activities in his description of a business' value chain. As a business grows, greater effort has to go into designing administrative systems because direction and control of the organization becomes ever more complex.

When a system has a problem, a critical event usually highlights it. Often the immediate diagnosis is that the person associated with the problem is at fault, but more careful examination shows that what the person is doing is rational in light of what the system encourages. The critical event simply highlights that the system is not working as intended. If not acted upon, those affected may be able to create their own "workarounds" so they are not adversely affected by the poor system. Once this has happened, identifying the problem usually requires an audit, which finds that the system is not working as described. With this in mind, we turn to describing the principle systems and sources of breakdowns.

We focus on the systems that address measurement, rewards, and staffing. Although each is described separately, each system is closely intertwined with the others, so they need to be compatible with one another; that is, they have to fit together.

Measurement Systems

Measurement systems enable managers to gather, aggregate, disseminate, and evaluate information on activities of the business, departments, and individuals. Measurement systems can use quantitative and/or qualitative data. Related measurement subsystems are planning, management control, and performance management.

Planning provides anticipatory control by setting metrics (objectives and goals) that reflect expectations about future performance. Plans for longer periods are strategic, for the medium term operational, and for the next year budgetary. Breakdowns in planning systems can occur when plans are not converted into actionable steps, plans are unachievable because they are out of touch with reality, and the objectives of plans are not well specified.

Management control measures actual performance against expected performance, highlighting matters that require special attention by management. Control is reactive in that it deals with failures to perform as planned. Management control is generally the responsibility of the accounting system. Breakdowns in management control are evidenced by failure to provide feedback in a timely and detailed manner, excessive controls that are costly and reduce management's flexibility, and an accounting system that cannot provide reliable information.

Performance management, as described in Chapter 6, measures individual employee contributions toward goal achievement. Breakdown in performance management is evidenced by failure to hold people accountable for results that do not meet planned objectives.

Rewards System

The reward system provides incentives that induce people to join the organization and to make value-enhancing decisions. Rewards are tied to measurement systems since the reward is based on some measured result, but other criteria such as seniority and loyalty may also be included when determining rewards. We typically think of money as "the" reward, but satisfying work and promotion are also rewards. Negative rewards are possible, such as being placed in a dead-end position in an out-of-the-way location, like being sent to a corporate Siberia.

The reward equation helps define the mix of rewards that are used to motivate behaviour (see Exhibit 8.4). The first step is to determine the total reward that will be payable. This can be separated into monetary rewards and non-monetary rewards. The relative size of the two components depends on what people see as important and the availability of non-monetary rewards, such as advancement and recognition. The second step is to take the monetary reward and determine how much will be fixed compensation and how much will be results-based. The results-based component can be larger when the results are readily observed and measured in the pay period. This component needs to be smaller when results are less certain and show up over a longer period of time. The third step is to take the results-based component and separate it into individual performance and group performance. The individual component can be larger when superior results come from individual efforts. The group component can be larger when group cooperation and integration is critical to producing results. The fourth step is to take the group component and determine at which level this cooperation occurs: team, unit, or company as a whole. At all points the results achieved are measured in

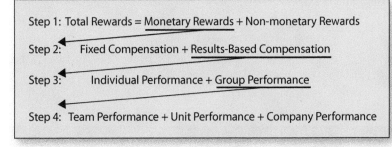

Exhibit 8.4 The Reward Equation

In 2010, Steve Filby, assistant vice-president of financial planning and analysis at Sun Life Financial, described how Sun Life had revised its planning process around Donald Hambrick and James Fredrickson's diamond strategy model.

"Sun Life Financial adopted the diamond model in 2008. That year, it was introduced in a new leadership development training program. Then in 2009 the model was formally incorporated in the company's strategic planning process.

"The model was adopted for several reasons. First, it encouraged sound logic when developing strategy. Second, it helped develop consistency among the elements. Third, it provided a common language among all when discussing strategy. For example, at a planning review meeting when someone says, 'I think we've got a staging problem here,' everyone knows what is meant. Fourth and finally, using the diamond model got more people thinking about business unit strategy and thinking about it in different ways. People started challenging previously held beliefs and assumptions about the markets, what Sun Life was doing, and how it competed.

"As with any new process, initial results using a new approach to planning were mixed. Some understood the tool and its concepts and adopted them immediately, while others were slower in appreciating and then using them. Another problem was that some concepts required deeper analysis. For example, arenas and vehicles were descriptive so they were easy to identify while differentiators and economic logic proved more challenging because analysis was required to determine what they were. And in the process some managers learned that what they thought were differentiators were not recognized as such by customers.

"As Sun Life enters its second cycle of strategic planning based on the diamond model, the strategies of the business units are becoming clearer, more concise, and descriptions of them more consistent. Now top management is focusing on extending the use of the diamond model to the Business Group and Enterprise level. Each Business Group has several business units within it. For example, the Asia Business Group operates a number of businesses within each of five countries. The challenge that top management faces is crafting a statement at the enterprise level that captures the essence of all the group's strategies—the corporate strategy. Management at the Business Group and Enterprise levels have started working on their statements and this is where most work still has to be done in adopting the diamond model."[8]

HOW WOULD YOU DO THAT?
QUESTIONS

1. How long do you think it will take to get everyone engaged in the new strategic planning process?

2. Why will it take the amount of time that you estimate?

terms of the goals set. Individual rewards have to fit with individual goals and so, too, with group rewards.

Evidence of breakdowns in the reward systems are rewards unrelated to performance or, worse still, rewards for short-run performance that has little to do with strategic performance. For example, SAP found that its compensation system rewarded people for generating new sales regardless of whether SAP product packages were priced to yield a profit for the firm. In terms of sales, the firm grew quickly, but SAP eventually realized that many of its customer relationships were costing it more money than it was making. Another breakdown is paying individual "stars" well while success of the business depends on people cooperating with one another.

A common feature of executive compensation packages in recent years has been the use of stock options, commonly referred to simply as options. An option is the right to buy a number of shares at or after a given date in the future (an exercise date) at a price agreed upon when the option is granted. The benefit of options is that they direct the manager's energy toward the longer term because the manager gains if the stock is sold at a price higher than the price the manager paid for it. Many stock options are for restricted stock—managers are not allowed to sell the shares for a specified period after they were acquired. An option loses its motivational influence when the option is said to be "underwater"—the company's share price has fallen below the price of the option.

Staffing

Having set the structure, the structure has to be filled with the right people. These are people with the right skills, knowledge, and attitudes for the positions they fill. Staffing is increasingly important in every business because people are an important but intangible resource. A business is less likely to be successful today unless it has the right people filling the jobs in the organizational structure. In a recent study, management researcher Jim Collins examined 11 firms that went from good to excellent performance and sustained it over a 15-year period. He then compared these firms with peer companies that had similar performance prior to the study but never reached the level of great performance. In all 11 cases of good-to-great companies, making sure they had the right people working was a major priority for CEOs early in their tenures. Collins reports that many executives believe the people lever is the most crucial to the successful implementation of strategy. Successful CEOs, according to Collins, "attended to people first [and] strategy second. They got the right people on the bus, moved the wrong people off, ushered the right people to the right seats—and then they figured out where to drive it."[9]

In many organizations, of course, the skills of their people make it possible for them to do what they do best.[10] That's why the VRINE framework regards such expertise as an important part of a company's bundle of strategic capabilities. Some consultants and scholars think that these bundles of skills, all the way down to the level of those possessed by specific individuals, are the key factor in a firm's long-term viability and its ability to innovate new products.[11] People decisions are critical to performance because decisions about which and how many people to employ hinge on the desire either to improve efficiency or generate new revenues.[12]

Staffing includes the activities connected with the recruitment, selection, development, and compensation of people. It is a continuous function as people are always on the move in the business: being hired, being promoted, being fired, resigning, and retiring. In a small company, top management performs staffing, while in large companies the human resources or personnel department works with management to draw up job specifications, provide training programs, and design processes for managing people, but management maintains control because it decides who is promoted, who is trained, and what experiences people are given. It also determines who is replaced. A specific aspect of staffing that is important to strategic management is getting an effective CEO, one who is sympathetic to the strategy and has the skills needed to pursue it. The selection process is extensive and much is spent on it because the decision is so critical to the business.

A breakdown in staffing is evident when the wrong people fill critical positions. "Wrong" staffing decisions come in many forms, including people unsuited by temperament or personality to fill a position, people too emotionally devoted to the old structure and old culture, and people lacking experience and knowledge. This may happen for a variety of reasons, including selecting the person on the basis of seniority, loyalty, or sentiment or avoiding a highly unpleasant personal

FOCUS ON SUSTAINABILITY 8.1

Sustainability: Developing Future Corporate Leaders[13]

Developing leaders is seen of crucial importance to the success of companies in future. Factors motivating this are the view that human capital is becoming a source of competitive advantage and a growing concern about having sufficient leaders as baby boomers retire. There are not enough natural leaders to fill the needs so larger corporations have started training their own leaders to meet their needs for the next two generations. Companies known for developing great leaders include General Electric, IBM, Kraft, Microsoft, and Procter & Gamble.

Beginning in 2002, *Chief Executive*, in conjunction with Hewitt Associates, began publishing its annual Top 20 Companies for Leaders based on selecting companies recognized for their leadership brand: companies that develop and produce great leaders. The best practices of these businesses were defined by *Chief Executive*. In 2006 its Best Practices List included the following seven criteria:

1. Having leaders at all levels who focus on creating a work climate that motivates employees to perform at their best.

2. Ensuring that the company and its senior management make leadership development a top priority.
3. Providing training and coaching to help intact leadership teams, as well as the individual leaders, work together more effectively.
4. Rotational job assignments for high potentials.
5. External leadership development programs for mid-level managers.
6. Web-based, self-study leadership modules for mid-level managers.
7. Executive MBA programs for mid-level managers.

An issue is whether success of the large companies is attributable to the capabilities of their leadership in place or to the organization systems that foster capable leadership. What do you think? What does this imply about the value of leader training?

confrontation by a person who is not promoted. Even someone who has performed superbly in one position may be unsuitable for another position, so the decision to hire and promote needs to be taken seriously.

Fit of the Organizational Elements

While we have described the three elements of organizational architecture separately, they are highly interdependent in operation. The way one element is designed has implications for how the others are designed. This means that they have to be designed to fit together so that they reinforce one another. Creating organizational fit takes years of sustained effort but pays off by creating capabilities that rivals cannot copy easily. Strategically minded executives are like captains; they may not be able to control the weather, but they can design a ship and equip it with a crew that can navigate the ocean under all weather conditions.

The example of 7-Eleven Corporation demonstrated good fit among the administrative elements. But even the best fit is only reasonably good and is never perfect. Delegating decision making to discrete and differentiated subunits produces inherent conflicts that cannot be overcome through more complex design. People need to be prepared for some degree of conflict and discomfort with the design and adjust to whatever currently seems to be the best choice, and then make the design work. The time for redesign is reached when an alternative design will require less energy to perform the necessary work.

A structure that employs decentralized decision making needs to have systems that mitigate the negative effects of having delegated decision-making rights. This is done through planning and control systems that give direction to decision making and coordinate what is done through the business. The importance of following the procedures is especially important in franchise operations because that is their strength—a business model that works. Follow the rules and the sales and profits will follow. Unfortunately the human resources department of a North American coffee chain was not sensitive to this. In the search for future franchisees, it advertised that it was looking for people who wanted to be their own boss. It attracted entrepreneurial types who wanted to run things their own way. These people did not follow the franchisor's procedures and profitability was dismal wherever new entrepreneurial recruits ran things. Product quality was inconsistent, as was service and in-store ambiance. All of this occurred because selection of staff was not aligned with how the business needed to be run.

Exhibit 8.5 Common Follies Found in Reward Systems

We Hope For . . .	But We Reward For . . .
Long-term growth, environmental responsibility	Quarterly earnings
Teamwork	Individual effort
Setting challenging "stretch" objectives	Achieving goals, "making the numbers"
Downsizing, rightsizing, delayering, restructuring	Adding staff, adding budget, adding Hay points
Commitment to total quality	Shipping on schedule, even with defects
Candour, surfacing bad news early	Reporting good news, whether it's true or not; agreeing with the boss, whether or not (s)he's right

When people are rewarded for achieving certain results, the structure has to give them the rights to make the decisions that allow them to produce these results. Conversely, if people are rewarded for particular results, expecting them to produce other results is naive. This is characterized as "expecting A while rewarding B." An example of such a misalignment is a high-tech company that emphasized proudly its "pay-for-performance" policy. Examination of the compensation data by an outside consulting company found that only 5 percent of pay was directly linked to individual performance. And the people in the lowest quartile of performance were getting almost as much from the annual bonus pool as the company's top quartile. Other examples are found in Exhibit 8.5.[14]

Hiring people who are motivated by what the reward system offers them is important. If a person is not interested in the rewards on offer, then there is little reason to expect that they will be encouraged by the rewards to do what is required. In other words, motivation lies within people and rewards only fuel and guide it.

Of particular importance is that every manager is responsible for making certain that those who report to him or her have been given the resources and authority they need and are held accountable for both the results they have achieved and how they have achieved them. When individuals deviate from either, top management has to make sure that the problem does not lie in the structure or systems. If it does, management has to fix them. If the problem lies with employees, they have to be dealt with, possibly by replacing them with people who can produce the necessary results.

If management does not make the hard decisions about administration, the business is likely doomed to failure because it will not be able to keep up with competitors that have leaders who do make these decisions.

Changing Organization Elements

A particular organizational design is appropriate at a point in time, and as things change both in the business and around the business, periodic restructuring makes sense. But changing structure or any other element requires compensating change in the other elements because they are interdependent. For example, a change in organizational structure will require a change in both measurement and rewards systems, while a change in strategy will require large-scale changes in organizational elements. For example, IBM CEO Louis Gerstner, who was responsible for turning around IBM from 1993 through 2002, wanted to move the company to a customer-oriented perspective. When it stopped issuing profit-and-loss statements by geographic units, the geographic managers were furious because they needed the statements "to manage their businesses." Gerstner replied, "Sorry, you no longer manage a business. You now serve as a critical support function to our integrated worldwide customer organization."

Change is often pursued in an evolutionary fashion. With a partial change of one element, other elements of the organization are brought into synchronization with it. This can involve addressing problems created by the changes. As they occur, alterations are made to eliminate the cause of the problem. For example, a new control system was installed in a company. The executive who had designed the system watched the behaviour of people as they operated within the new system. He gave the system a chance to affect behaviour. After observing peoples' dysfunctional behaviours, he was able to determine the cause of the problem and alter the system so the cause was eliminated.

Major changes are best made infrequently. If they are frequent, people have limited incentive to learn the new jobs, to devise more efficient processes, and to develop relationships with fellow workers. Frequent change also promotes more focus on short-term payoffs and less on long-term investment. Change is also disruptive, though it is essential as the strategy is adjusted to the changing times. This creates a constant tension between initiating change and maintaining the equilibrium of the organization.

Making meaningful change is costly, time consuming, and often difficult. The organizational levers have to be redesigned such that they are compatible with one another. The greatest difficulties when making change are often associated with people. A change in structure, for example, changes peoples' jobs. The consequence is that some people lose power and prestige, their compensation changes, and they must learn how to do new jobs. In 2004, CEO Gordon Nixon of the Royal Bank of Canada moved the wealth management division into a broader department called consumer banking.[15] A bank spokesperson explained that the old structure had five global businesses aligned in silos. The new consumer business, which broadened its coverage to banking investments and insurance, reduced inefficiencies in how the bank operated. Three senior executives retired and another quit. Juliette John, portfolio manager with Bissett Investment Management in Calgary, commented that some people are always disappointed in such a process and structural change provides a good chance to clean house.

Even the potential for change produces difficult personnel issues and encourages corporate politics. Those who think they will suffer resist change, while those who think they will benefit push for change. When the structure changes higher up in the organization, those lower down in the organization are affected as they see the career track they were working on to move up the organization disappears. Hence, even though not affected directly, they will resist change.

Leadership has to decide what tasks are strategically critical because they need to be given prominence in the structure. These are separated into self-contained units and serve as the central building blocks for the organizational structure. The rest of the structure is designed to ensure timely integration with these parts of the structure.

Having "disintegrated" the work by dividing it into various units and jobs within units, systems are needed to "integrate" the work, pulling it together so that the business acts as if one all-knowing person is doing the work. This is accomplished by creating various systems that people participate in as they do their work.

CULTURE

While the levers of structure, systems, and staffing have a profound effect on the behaviour of people, management cannot fully specify all behaviour in the company. Culture is an outgrowth that management does not have direct control over though management works to influence it. Culture is created when people in the business become bound together by common attitudes, beliefs, and values. These are influenced by the way that management puts into effect the decisions that it has made about the formal organization. Characteristics of the formal organization associated with the culture are:

- **the extent of individual initiative:** the degree of responsibility, freedom, and independence that individuals have,
- **the extent of risk tolerance:** the degree to which employees are encouraged to be aggressive, innovative, and risk-taking,
- **the clarity of direction:** the degree to which the organization has clear objectives and performance expectations for individuals,
- **the degree of integration:** the degree to which the units within the organization are encouraged to operate in a coordinated manner,

- **the extent of management support:** the degree to which managers communicate clearly with subordinates and provide them with assistance and support,
- **the extent of control:** the number of rules and regulations and the amount of direct supervision used overseeing and controlling employee behaviour,
- **the granting of rewards:** the degree to which reward allocations (that is, salary increase and promotions) are influenced by the personal judgment of managers based on employee performance against expectations in contrast to seniority, favouritism, and so on,
- **the tolerance of conflict:** the degree to which employees are encouraged to air openly conflicts and criticisms, and
- **communication patterns:** the degree to which communications are restricted to flowing through the formal hierarchy of authority.

Employees who have common experiences in these matters have a similar perspective on the organization and how they should behave in it. They come to understand that "this is the way things work around here." The corporate culture reflects what they think is good and bad behaviour. Of note is that within the corporation, groups can have their own subcultures that bring them into conflict with other groups that have different subcultures in the corporation.

The culture is stronger when there is a greater sense of commonality among the people in the company. A strong culture in which all embrace the same values and beliefs can be beneficial for a business when it supports the business strategy. Stories about Wal-Mart's cost controls are legion. Managers share hotel rooms to save money. Associates are asked to bring home pens and pads from conferences they attend. Wal-Mart buyers call suppliers collect. Shrinkage incentives are directed toward employees, motivating them not to steal. All of this has created a culture that frugality is good. This emphasis on cost control supports the company's low-cost strategy.

The culture is reinforced when it attracts new members to the corporation who agree with the existing culture. The culture is also reinforced when those more in tune with it progress to senior positions in the company. Once there, they sustain the culture and so it continues. The challenge for an organization with a special culture is finding enough recruits who fit with the culture. This became a problem at Ben & Jerry's as the U.S. ice cream company increased in size. Surveys of members showed less agreement on the beliefs that the original founders preached. As Ben Cohen, the active founder, constrained structure and systems to reflect his beliefs, the company struggled and was unable to recruit talented management. Eventually Cohen allowed the company to adopt standard management practices of large companies and Ben & Jerry's performance recovered.

Dysfunctional behaviour is caused when strategy changes but culture remains rooted in the past. Management moves the company to the new culture through what it can control: strategy and structure, process and people. One way of starting this process of change is by analyzing what prevents the company from achieving its desired vision, mission, and goals. Another way is to define the missing links, be they in resources, the leadership style, or the behaviour of people that is required. This gap analysis provides input into the development of change programs to influence and shape the culture of the company.

The core of cultural change is changing the mindset of employees. They need to adopt new ways of thinking, and new ways of working and interacting with one another. This means acquiring new attitudes and new skills in the workplace. To do this, the beliefs, assumptions, and values of people in the workplace need to be influenced and shaped. There are many ways to do this, and the more they are used, the more likely that change will be achieved. Company structure, systems, policies, and procedures are aligned to support the new culture. In particular the reward system needs to recognize, encourage, and reinforce the practice of the desired culture. Any practices not aligned to the desired patterns of behaviour need to be abandoned.

The change agents who lead the cultural change need to be role models for the new culture. They have to have the desired attitudes, beliefs, and skills and replace those who have not. Their consistent behaviour will encourage others to emulate their behaviour. Albert Schweitzer said it best when he remarked, "Setting an example is not the main thing in influencing others. It is the only thing."

Employees also need to be changed. Existing employees are trained in the new belief systems, core values, and desired patterns of behaviour. New employees are recruited who have attitudes and values that fit with the desired culture and then put through orientation programs that reinforce this.

Management capitalizes on every channel possible to publicize and communicate the new corporate culture. Newsletters, emails, department meetings, branch managers' meetings, management meetings, family day gatherings, sports club activities, and company anniversary events can be used to promote and reinforce the new culture within organizations.

Changing culture is difficult and takes time, often years. For example, Louis Gerstner said, "I always viewed culture as one of those things you talked about, like marketing and advertising. It was one of the tools that a manager had at his or her disposal when you think about an enterprise." He added, "The thing I have learned at IBM is that culture is everything."[16] And while management can create the conditions for change, in the end all management can do is invite the workforce to change the culture. Inability to change culture dooms the potential of a new strategy as the trials of North America's Big 3 automotive manufacturers demonstrated so strongly. Change was resisted by both management and workers for decades while foreign manufacturers made large gains in market share.

PERFORMANCE CRITERIA

Leadership also sets the goals for the business. These provide the criteria that measure the aggressiveness and pace at which the business pursues its vision. Leadership can set goals that require big changes quickly or small changes gradually. Leadership also determines the criteria that must be satisfied to get resources. These criteria help ensure that resources are channelled to the activities that support the strategy. This is all part of performance management as described in Chapter 7. Finally, leadership determines what it takes to get rewarded, which focuses people on achieving the right results.

Managing Change[17]

The company's strategy must change as times change, but change does not just happen. Someone has to make sure change happens and the person with the ultimate responsibility for that is the leader of the organization, who is usually the chief executive officer. The change process the leader uses can be broken into a set of steps that are performed in sequence. The amount of work required in each step will vary from situation to situation, but following the sequence of steps is important because each establishes the foundation for the next step. The first four steps deal with building the climate for change, while also building energy for change and setting out new directions. The remaining steps are the action phase, putting changes in place, and making sure they are maintained.

STEP 1: CREATING A SENSE OF URGENCY

Before change can start, people have to feel change is necessary. So the first step is to build a sense of urgency that change has to start NOW. This means thawing the view that the status quo is fine. People realize this when the company is losing money and its very survival is in doubt. They have likely seen if not personally experienced the impacts of the company's decline failing business. Getting people to recognize the need to change when there is no visible crisis is much harder because people are complacent. Complacency can be bred by internal factors (a relaxing work schedule, lavish headquarters, lavish celebrations and functions, always receiving performance bonuses, "happy talk" by senior managers) and the failure to see the bigger picture (staff focusing only on unit goals, no comparison with competitors, no assessment of customer satisfaction, denigrating outsiders who are critical of the business).

Driving people out of their comfort zones is not easy. Time permitting, the surest way is to let the leadership group educate itself about the seriousness of the challenge facing the company in future. This requires a frank discussion of facts such as the new competition and projected earnings and market share or other relevant indicators. Outsiders who can share the "big picture" from a different perspective can also help broaden the awareness of organization members. When time is short, necessity can require that those in the leadership group replace those who do not appreciate the need for change. The goal is to achieve a critical mass of at least 75 percent of the people in the leadership group who believe that "business as usual" is no longer acceptable. People must see urgent need to change resulting from a crisis, a potential crisis, or a great opportunity.

STEP 2: BUILDING COALITIONS

The term *leadership* immediately conjures up the concept of the heroic leader, someone who gives orders and makes sure that people obey. But today's companies have allowed decision rights to migrate to those of specific knowledge so that leadership is more collaborative.[18] The consequence is that one strong leader alone cannot make change happen. What the leadership group seeks to do is build a coalition with others through the organization who are like minded in that they share a sense of the problems, opportunities, and commitment to change. By building a coalition, the leadership group is able to extend its power through the hierarchy of the company. The requirements for this guiding coalition are that those in it have enough legitimate power that they can make meaningful changes; are diverse and of sufficient expertise that they can produce intelligent, informed decisions; are credible with those it seeks to influence and get to change; are trusted and respected by others in the organization; and are sufficient in number that they can dominate any struggle for power. The number involved in the coalition depends on the size of the organization.

STEP 3: DETERMINE DIRECTION

People need a sense of where change will be taking them and the organization. As described in Chapter 2, management uses different mechanisms to achieve this. The leadership team in cooperation with the coalition can help in this by creating a clear, concise vision that can be explained in five minutes and elicits understanding and interest with the stakeholders. If it does not meet either condition, it needs to be reworked.

The vision functions in many different ways: it provides a spark to motivate people, it provides a filter to evaluate how the organization is doing, it provides a rationale for the changes the organization will have to weather, and it helps keep all the projects and changes focused. Without focus, change effort can dissolve into a series of incompatible projects that start to look like they are being done simply for change's sake. Failed change efforts are often littered with plans and directives but no vision.

STEP 4: COMMUNICATE DIRECTION

The direction, once established, only serves the business when people throughout the business know what it is, understand it, appreciate it, and are ready to commit to achieving it. This requires extensive, persuasive communication. The guiding principle is simple. Use every existing communication channel and opportunity because some people take a longer time before they hear and understand. From this step onward, communication has to continue so that people stay focused on actively working toward making the change needed. Communication takes many forms: speeches, interviews, newsletters, and even in day-to-day activities. For example, when presenting an award, a leader can take a moment to explain how the employee's performance fits into the vision and how the performance is a contribution to something much larger than the act being rewarded.

All communications need to be consistent in the message sent and demonstrate their commitment to it by acting in ways that fit with the vision—they need to "walk the talk." Deeds along with words are powerful communicators of the new ways, and nothing will kill a change effort quicker than an executive saying one thing and doing another. This is especially so during a time of change when the spotlight is on them. Everyone is watching what they say and do.

A results-oriented leader may want to skip one or more of these first four steps in order to get right on with making things happen. Doing so imperils, perhaps even condemns, the change effort. Without the solid foundation established by all of these steps, any change action is unlikely to take hold and survive for the long term. We now turn to the action steps.

Mary Horton at The Source Book

In 2001, Mary Horton became The Source Book Inc.'s (TSB) third CEO in 12 months. TSB was an electronic photography/illustrator database that brought together buyers and sellers in the advertising, design, and publishing worlds. Essentially it functioned as the "Facebook" distributor of photography, showcasing the company's talents to secure high-visibility assignments and to recognize outstanding work in addition to a cataloguing system.

Horton was familiar with the business because she had worked there the prior summer while studying for her M.B.A. On arriving at the business she talked with various people in the company and mixed this with her views to produce a vision for the company. At a Friday meeting she shared this with all the staff. She identified three tasks that had to be performed well for the book to be a success: they had to have the right artists in the book, they had to produce a beautiful book, and they had to distribute the book to the right people. Her plan gave people hope because it ran counter to the strategy of cost cutting in the past. But she told them that it would mean that TBS would have to focus on activity that produced profits.

Horton took direct responsibility for those aspects that she believed would determine the success of the business. She focused on restructuring the sales and marketing organization, hiring/firing, and strategy formulation. She divided up her schedule to make sure that all her tasks got attention. She spent 20 percent of her time with clients, generating sales and promoting her vision of the business, 10 percent on strategic analysis, 50 percent managing employees, and 20 percent performing tasks. Over the long run she saw herself as being less of a doer and more of a manager and strategist.

Horton worked on building credibility with others. She developed it with the board by drawing up a plan that she kept in her top drawer. She referred to it from time to time to ensure that she was consistent and on time with her activities and kept the board informed of how well she was doing in comparison to the plan. She developed credibility with customers by going on the road and meeting with many artists and advertising agents. She first visited the less important clients and worked up to the more important ones. Finally, Horton gained the respect of people in the company by taking Sally Nanwen, the top sales representative, along with her. Nanwen was impressed with Horton's performance in sales, and Nanwen's opinion was soon known throughout the company.

The sales department had been downsized by the previous CEO. Horton focused on rebuilding it. One issue was who should manage it. It had two managers, one for photography and one for illustrations, who were very close to their clients. Both were thoroughly opposed to the sales quotas and active management of their staff that Horton had proposed when announcing her vision. The manager of photography had quit immediately but made it clear that she could be talked into resuming her old position. Horton chose not to bargain with this person because Horton was not prepared to accept anything less than the behaviour she believed necessary to achieve the necessary performance. Horton fired the manager of illustration because he had become moody and unpredictable in his work habits. He would come in late, take long lunches, and leave early. "I had to either lure them into staying or nudge them out of the organization. If they stayed, their cynical attitudes would continue to erode company morale. If they left, we would lose industry contacts and I would have to manage the sales force myself." Horton promoted Sally Nanwen to management of the sales department after building both sales capabilities and a performance management system.

Horton contributed to sales capabilities when she completely redesigned the media kit, which, while a critical sales tool, was also a forum for communicating her vision. She also created a sales support group in the office of the president that was handled by an executive assistant who responded to sales reps' questions and customers' concerns. This kept her apprised of any sales rep or customer issues.

Horton established a periodic performance review process. Every three months sales figures were evaluated, as well as the timing of sales and overall attitude of the representative. When the system was first put in place targets were easily achieved so individuals did not feel threatened. In later periods they were gradually raised. Some of the representatives left because they thought the job should focus on artistry rather than making money. The replacement representatives hired were highly motivated by making money. Horton reasoned that it was easier to teach the industry to motivated employees than it was to teach drive and ambition to employees who focused on artistic qualities of the clients' work.

Horton placed production, finance, administration, and legal under the direction of Laura Maroni, the chief operating officer, whom Horton had promoted from the CFO position at TBS. Horton replaced the production manager after determining that the main production problem was cost and not quality. Several products were 30 percent over budget. Horton also had a habit of walking through the office and plant when she arrived at work and when she left. She would ask people what could be done to make their jobs run easily and smoothly. And when she saw people working late she asked them how their jobs could be made easier and more manageable. This behaviour suggested that although Maroni had been given the authority for production, in reality Horton was making the decisions.

Horton started experiencing conflicts with Maroni because their responsibilities overlapped. Horton felt that Maroni was strictly a numbers person, having worked in various financial and accounting positions before becoming the COO of TBS. One aspect dealt with collections. Horton discovered from clients that the billing department sent impolite letters and hounded them. Maroni felt that late payment of bills freed TBS from having to be pleasant with clients. Horton felt that Maroni's treatment of clients hurt business. She said, "Values and norms are important to me. Laura is often yelling at people. I don't like managers who yell at co-workers." A causal factor was likely that Maroni was under stress with her broad workload that she was not prepared for. If so, this was really a poor promotion decision by Horton.

Horton did not know how to deal with Maroni. Maroni had provided Horton with insights into troubles at TBS and had been key to Horton being appointed CEO—Maroni had close relationships with several members of the board. Horton had promoted Maroni, thinking that she could handle Maroni because one of her greatest strengths was being able to work with various people in trying situations. Now she was not so sure. This was just another example of how trying "people problems" can be in managing a business.

1. In this How Would You Do That?, you learned how Mary Horton turned around The Source Book. Going through what she did, identify the administrative breakdowns that she fixed in the business.

STEP 5: EMPOWER EMPLOYEES

For this step the leadership group has to make the changes to structure, systems, and staffing. These administrative changes will remove most barriers to change and allow employees to develop new ideas, approaches, and the required behaviours that support the new strategy. The worst problem can be bosses who make demands contrary to the vision, who criticize change, and worst, who passively resist change. People deserve the chance to get on board and when they do not they need to be removed. To support the new way of doing things, resources will likely need to be reallocated as well.

STEP 6: GENERATE SMALL WINS

The argument for generating short-term wins comes from putting together two features of change. First, achieving the full organizational changes needed to support the strategy takes a long time. Second, successful change creates excitement, certainty, and momentum, and it also serves to answer critics. By achieving short-run wins within 12 to 24 months, the effort put into making change is validated and the level of urgency is maintained. This helps keep people pursuing the vision.

Thus, leaders need to plan the short-term successes rather than leave them to chance. This means creating projects that produce unambiguous contributions to the change effort. The chances of success are greater when the projects are relatively independent of other activities, well resourced, and reasonably achievable. More complex and harder changes are best left until after a record of earlier successes. A caution is that the production of short-term results should not threaten long-term results.

Short-term successes need to be celebrated and those producing them rewarded so people see that change is working and is appreciated. This needs to be kept in proportion, however, as much more work needs to be done. Too much celebration can lead people to think the work is done or that the rest of the work will be easily accomplished.

STEP 7: CONSOLIDATE GAINS

Continuing short-term wins add up to a long-term win. The sequencing of the actions that produce short-term wins is determined by management as it makes staging decisions. Producing the string of short-term wins necessary requires the perseverance and persistence of leadership as it continues to communicate the vision, to plan further projects, to make adjustments to the administrative systems, and to deal with those who resist change. Fortunately, the earlier wins provide credibility that can be used to get buy-in for further changes. At times, new people can be brought in as change agents to reinvigorate the team.

The various activities mentioned are things that management can control and over time will alter the behaviour of people. As people's behaviour changes, so, too, do their values. This is a slow process and leaders need to measure the change made against where the business needs to be. They can change the aspects of the business they have direct control over and talk about the behavioural and value changes needed. In the end, though, the people are the ones who decide whether to make the changes needed. Changing a strong culture can take strong leadership from five to 10 years to achieve.

STEP 8: INSTITUTIONALIZE THE NEW DESIGN

Having achieved the changes necessary to have an organization that supports the strategy being pursued, leaders must ensure that the changes are permanent. Old habits die hard, and left alone, many of the successes will be undone as people revert to the old ways.

The following actions can help solidify the organization around the changes. First, show people how the new approaches, behaviours, and attitudes account for the business's success. People have to be helped to make the connections between the effort and the outcome. And second, the next generation of leaders has to believe in and embody the new ways. What happens in the organization is driven by its leadership, and leadership that bends back to the old ways can undo all that has been accomplished.

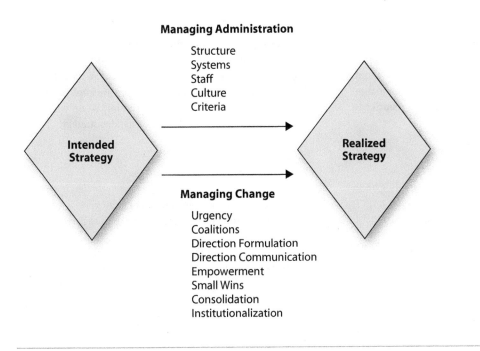

Managing Administration

Structure
Systems
Staff
Culture
Criteria

Intended Strategy

Realized Strategy

Managing Change

Urgency
Coalitions
Direction Formulation
Direction Communication
Empowerment
Small Wins
Consolidation
Institutionalization

Exhibit 8.6 Sources of Deviation When Implementing Strategy

Intended and Realized Strategy

Neither managing administration nor managing change is a precise process that produces the intended results. Intended results cannot be achieved while things happen that were not intended. The consequence of challenges in implementation is that the realized strategy is never quite what was intended. Potential sources of challenge are all the items illustrated in Exhibit 8.6.

Summary of Challenges

1. *Outline the interdependence between strategy formulation and implementation.* For a business to have superior performance, management needs to have both formulated a good strategy and implemented the strategy. Failure to do either and both will result in poor performance. Formulating the strategy is more of an analytical process while implementation of the strategy is very much a job of managing the situation.

2. *Demonstrate how organizational structure serves as a lever when implementing strategy.* Organizational structure is the formal configuration between individuals and groups with respect to the allocation of tasks, responsibilities, and authority within the organization. Within the organization, groups of people can be combined into departments in various ways. Departmentalization by function is the most popular approach as people are organized into common functions such as procurement, assembly, marketing, finance, and accounting. Alternative ways are by product, customer, or geographic region. A more complex approach to organization is the matrix in which many people have two bosses; they have to report to superiors in charge of two different things. Of course, all employees have to answer to higher ranking people responsible for the organization as a whole.

3. *Illustrate the use of systems as levers when implementing strategy.* Systems that are crucial to implementing strategy deal with measurement, reward, and staffing. Measurement systems provide the metrics that are used to gauge what is happening in the business. For example, performance management involves setting goals and then seeing whether the goals were achieved. Reward systems provide the incentive for people to achieve the goals that have been set. Finally, staffing makes sure that people with the necessary capabilities to produce the desired results are in the various jobs throughout the structure of the business.

4. *Describe why managers need to be prepared to hold their subordinates accountable.* Using structure, managerial responsibility is allocated down through the organization. Systems are used to coordinate and control what is happening, but this is done on a moving-forward basis. Success is predicated on people producing the results as agreed upon. When managers are not held accountable for producing the result, they will not necessarily strive to achieve the results they are accountable for. This destabilizes the organization and is very costly for the business.

5. *Explain the dual roles that top management plays in strategy implementation.* Top management is responsible both for managing administration and managing change. Administration is

needed in an organization of nearly any size to organize the activities of and relationships among people. Change is needed because every business operates in a changing environment. Managing change involves moving the business from one strategy to another. Managing administration is a subset on managing change because altering administration is only a small part of putting a new strategy in place.

6. *Explain how implementation produces a strategy that was not as intended.* Assuming that the strategy was a viable strategy, it has to be put in place. This involves getting people lined up in support of many different decisions that must be made. What the decisions are and whether they are implemented and how they are implemented all have an impact on whether the implementation fully supports the intended strategy.

Review Questions

1. What is strategy implementation?
2. How are formulation and implementation related?
3. What systems are relevant to strategy implementation?
4. How are people relevant to strategy formulation and implementation?

5. How can rewards affect the pursuit of strategy?
6. What are the roles of strategic leadership in successful strategy implementation?
7. What component of the strategy diamond maps most closely to issues related to strategy implementation?

Experiential Activities

Group Exercises

1. Use your library's resources to a company that has poor performance. Search on the web for materials that explain the poor performance of the company and determine whether the problem is one of poor strategy, poor implementation, or both.
2. Refer to the chapter opening vignette outlining 7-Eleven. If you were a competitor, how easy would it be for you to copy 7-Eleven and beat it at its own game?
3. Use your library's resources to find a chief executive officer who has stepped down from this position. What was the explanation for why this happened?

Ethical Debates

1. As part of a corporate restructuring, your analysis helps you conclude that you have rather extensive redundancy in corporate finance and accounting positions. Management concludes that through consolidation, cross-training, and other shifts in responsibility, you could do the same work with 30 percent fewer staff. How do you downsize these jobs in the next 12 months without damaging the morale of the surviving employees and while trying to treat the terminated employees in a fair manner?
2. Your corporation has promoted you to the position of general manager for its newly acquired manufacturing subsidiary company in China that will be producing units for the North American market, which has proven very cyclical over time. When you get there, your first activity is planning future sales. You ask the existing managers how they estimate sales and they tell you that they manufacture as many units as needed to keep all the workers employed. You then ask, "Well, who buys them?" You are told that in the past the government has told the plant where to ship the units manufactured. What do you do?

Endnotes

1. Mark Gottfredson, Rudy Puryear, and Stephen Phillips, "Strategic Sourcing: From Periphery to the Core," *Harvard Business Review* 83:2 (February 2005); Erica Grieder, "Confidence, Simplicity and Openness to Change: Keyes for Leadership," November 10, 2003. Accessed November 17, 2009, at www.mccombs.utexas.edu/news/pressreleases/keyes_wrap.asp; A.Ishikawa and T.Nejo, *The Success of 7 Eleven Japan* (World Scientific Pub. Co., 2002); Steven Marlin, "The 24-Hour Supply Chain," *InformationWeek* (January 26, 2004). Accessed November 17, 2009, at www.informationweek.com/story/showArticle.jhtml?articleID=17500779; Gary. L Neilson and Bruce A. Pasternack, *Results* (New York: Crown Business Books, 2005); Sonja Sherwood, "7-Eleven's Lessons from Japan—Strategies of the Fittest," *The Chief Executive*, November 2002.

2. Neilson and Pasternack, *Results*, pp 192–193.

3. Accessed November 17, 2009, at www.dmsretail.com/retailplanograms.htm.

4. D. Hambrick and A. Cannella, "Strategy Implementation as Substance and Selling," *Academy of Management Executive* 3:4 (1989): 278–285.

5. A. Slywotzky and D. Nadler, "The Strategy Is the Structure," *Harvard Business Review* 82:2 (2004): 16.

6. SAP Harvard Business School Case, SAP America 9-397-067, December 3, 1996.

7. SAP Annual General Shareholders' Meeting, Mannheim, Germany, May 3, 1997; SAP 1997–2003 Financial Reports. Accessed July 15, 2005, at www.sap.com/company/investor/reports/pastfinancials/index.epx; Harvard Business School Case 9-397-067, SAP America, December 3, 1996; N. Boudette, "How a German Software Titan Missed the Internet Revolution," *Wall Street Journal*, January 18, 2000, p. A1.

8. Personal communication with Stephen Filby, assistant vice-president, financial planning and analysis, Sun Life Financial, September 22, 2010.

9. J. Collins, "Level 5 Leadership," *Harvard Business Review* (July/August 2001): 66–76.

10. J. Bradach, *Organizational Alignment: The 7-S Model* (Boston: Harvard Business School Publishing, 1996).

11. C. K. Prahalad and G. Hamel, "The Core Competence of the Corporation," *Harvard Business Review* 79:1 (1990): 1–14; R. Nelson and S. Winter, *An Evolutionary Theory of Economic Change* (Cambridge, M.A.: Harvard University Press, 1982); D. J. Teece, G. Pisano, and A. Shuen, "Dynamic Capabilities and Strategic Management," *Strategic Management Journal* 18 (1997): 509–534; K. M. Eisenhardt and J. A. Martin, "Dynamic Capabilities: What Are They?" *Strategic Management Journal* 21 (2000): 1105–1121.

12. B. Becker and B. Gerhart, "The Impact of Human Resource Management on Organizational Performance: Progress and Prospects," *Academy of Management Journal* 39 (1996): 779–802.

13. G. Filbeck, R.F. Gorman and X. Zhao, "Identifying the Best Companies for Leaders: Does it Lead to Higher Returns?" *Managerial and Decision Economics* 31(2010): 19–31.

14. S. Kerr, "On the Folly of Rewarding for A while Hoping for B," *Academy of Management Journal* 18:4 (December 1975): 769–83.

15. Stuart Laidlaw, "Executive Shakeup Continues at Royal," *Toronto Star,* September 23, 2004, p. C01.

16. Martha Lagace "Gerstner: Changing Culture at IBM—Lou Gerstner Discusses Changing the Culture at IBM," HBS Working Knowledge, December 9, 2002. Accessed November 14, 2009, at http://hbswk.hbs.edu/archive/3209.html; and Louis V. Gerstner, *Who Says Elephants Can't Dance? Inside IBM's Historic Turnaround* (New York: HarperBusiness, 2002), p. 187.

17. This follows the well-received book by John P. Kotter, *Leading Change* (Boston, M.A.: Harvard Business School Press, 1996). Richness of the change process is found in Andrew Pettigrew and Richard Whipp, *Managing Change for Competitive Success* (Oxford, U.K.: Blackwell Publishers, 1991).

18. Dean Roger Martin, "The Death of the Heroic Leader," *Rotman Management* (Fall 2000): 5–7. Accessed December 5, 2010, at www.rotman.utoronto.ca/rogermartin/Death_of_Heroic_Leadership.pdf. Derived from "On the Clock: Are Retail Sales People Getting a Raw Deal?" Knowledge@Wharton: October 1, 2008. Accessed November 14, 2009, at http://knowledge.wharton.upenn.edu/article.cfm?articleid=2066.

9 Corporate Strategy

In this chapter, we challenge you to:

1. Define corporate strategy.

2. Understand the special challenge of corporate strategy.

3. Identify the different types of diversification.

4. Explain how companies can successfully enter attractive industries when those industries have the greatest barriers to entry.

5. Describe the relationship between corporate strategy and competitive advantage.

6. Explain the differences between corporate strategy in stable and dynamic contexts.

BCE Inc.[1,2]

BCE Inc., Canada's largest communications company, provides an interesting perspective on corporate strategy. Created by an act of Parliament in 1880 as Bell Telephone, for decades the company developed local telephone businesses in Ontario and Quebec and, under the monopoly rights granted it, maintained long distance calls across Canada. Over time it built on its telecommunications expertise. In 1964, it owned 100 percent of Northern Electric, a manufacturer of telephone equipment. In 1970, Bell bought an interest in Telesat Canada, a communications satellite monopoly. In 1976, it created Bell Canada International Management, Research and Consulting Ltd. (BCI).

Conglomeration

By 1982, Bell Canada controlled nearly 80 other companies. That year it was reorganized with Bell Canada Enterprises (BCE), becoming a holding company that owned shares in various operating companies, with Bell Canada becoming one of its many separate divisions. In this way, only Bell Canada remained under the regulatory control of the Canadian Radio-television and Telecommunications Commission (CRTC) while the activities of BCE's other businesses were beyond the CRTC's consideration. This allowed Bell Canada Enterprises to start its first wave of diversification in 1983. BCE acted as a central bank under Jean de Grandpré, who was CEO of Bell Canada and then of BCE between 1976 and 1989, redirecting the cash generated by the telephone business into other businesses. Tele-Direct (Publications) Inc., a subsidiary of BCE, expanded from publishing directories in Canada to publishing operations and investments around the world. Meanwhile, BCE launched a wireless telephone business (Bell Mobile) and acquired ownership of an oil and gas pipeline (TransCanada PipeLines Ltd.) in 1983, of a trust company (Montreal Trust) in 1989, and of a real estate developer (through BCE Development Corporation) in 1985.

Refocusing

Raymond Cyr replaced Jean de Grandpré as CEO following BCE's poor performance as a diversified corporation. Top management determined that the core business was telecommunications and started undoing the diversification. The pipeline was sold in 1989 and the real estate business was dissolved. This left BCE as a holding company with three principal subsidiaries: telecommunications services (Bell Canada), telecommunications equipment manufacturing (Northern Telecom Limited), and financial services (Montreal Trustco Inc.). BCE's performance remained weak, however, as Bell Canada faced increasing competition due to deregulation of the long distance phone industry. Meanwhile Northern Telecom—renamed Nortel in 1995—was also facing increased competition, especially in foreign markets.

Convergence

Lynton Wilson replaced Raymond Cyr as CEO in 1996 until 1998, followed by Jean C. Monty from 1998 to 2002. In the 1990s, dramatic changes in digital technology were creating new means of communication and "convergence" was all the talk, though which players would dominate was unclear. BCE attempted to extend and combine both content creation and distribution through this period. The overall objective was to achieve balanced corporate performance that would lead to profitable growth, positive free cash flow, and improving returns.

BCE continued extending its distribution network as it acquired a majority ownership in Aliant Inc., a telephone carrier serving Canada's four Atlantic provinces; Telesat Canada, Canada's commercial satellite communications system; and Teleglobe Inc., Canada's overseas communications carrier. In addition, it extended itself into the new technologies, creating Bell Nexxia, a national IP-broadband company, and changing Tele-Direct (Publications) Inc. into Bell ActiMedia Inc. and repositioning it as a multimedia company. Bell ActiMedia became the business incubator for Sympatico, Canada's largest consumer internet portal, and negotiated a partnership with American internet giant Lycos Inc.

BCE also worked on developing content. It acquired CTV Inc., Canada's leading private 18-channel television network, and created BCE Emergis, an ecommerce company. However, the big move occurred in 1999 when it joined with the Thomson Corporation to create Bell Globemedia, a corporate structure that included the operations of CTV, the *Globe and Mail*, and two leading web portals: Sympatico-Lycos and Globe Interactive. Bell Globemedia was largely a response to gaining control over content after CanWest Global Communications purchased the Southam newspaper chain.

Meanwhile, the subsidiary Nortel acquired Broadband Networks Inc., a leading manufacturer of fixed broadband wireless communications networks, and then purchased Bay Networks, a leading internet protocol networking company in 1998. Following the second purchase Nortel was renamed Nortel Networks. In 2000, Nortel became an independent global company as BCE distributed 94 percent of its stake in Nortel to shareholders. The distribution helped remove the distraction of Nortel's phenomenal growth (its stock price had gone up 366 percent over 15 months) and left BCE as a communications company.

By 2001, BCE had organized its operations into four principal operating units: a national tele-communications network division (Bell Canada); an ecommerce intermediary (BCE Emergis); a broadcasting, print, and multimedia division (Bell Globemedia); and a venture capital and investments division (BCE Ventures).

Refocusing

In 2002, Michael Sabia replaced Jean Monty as CEO. Sabia viewed BCE as an antiquated relic that would have to deal with growing competition. He saw connectivity as the foundation and the core of BCE's business. To be successful, BCE would focus solely on this and build layers of value-added services that met specific customer needs. Non-core assets would be sold. And so they were. In 2002, Teleglobe Inc. was sold after BCE had lost billions of dollars on financing it. Bell Canada's directories business was also sold, while Bell Canada International (BCI) was liquidated. In 2004, BCE Emergis's U.S. health operations were sold, leaving it with ebusiness solutions to the financial services industry in North America and the health industry in Canada. In 2006, Bell Globemedia was sold. Finally, in 2007, Telesat was sold.

Meanwhile, Bell formed many alliances. In 2004, Bell Canada launched Sympatico.MSN.ca in partnership with Microsoft Corporation. In 2005, Bell Canada became Clearwire's exclusive strategic partner for voice over internet protocol (VoIP) and certain other value-added inter-net protocol (IP) services and applications in the United States. Bell Canada also became Clearwire's preferred provider of these services and applications in markets beyond North America. It also announced an alliance with Rogers Communications Inc. (Rogers) to jointly build and manage a nationwide wireless broadband network through Inukshuk Wireless Inc. Then, in 2006, BCE and Aliant formed Bell Aliant. This combined Bell Canada's regional wireline operations in rural Ontario and Quebec with Aliant's wireline, information techno-logy, and related operations in Atlantic Canada.

Under pressure from investors, BCE announced late in 2006 that it would eliminate BCE Inc.'s holding company operations and convert into an income trust. The new entity would be named Bell Canada Income Fund. As an income trust, shareholder value would be increased because trusts pay most of their cash flows to investors, unlike corporations, which pay divi-dends to shareholders. This would provide huge tax savings for BCE, one of Canada's biggest corporate taxpayers. However, the federal government stood to lose millions of tax dollars from such a move. This provoked an alarmed federal government to impose a 31 percent income tax on trusts and caused BCE to review its options. BCE followed up by announcing that it would not proceed with its planned conversion to an income trust. Instead, it would restructure, eliminating the BCE holding company.

Flirting with Privatization

Due to its stagnant share price, BCE was courted for acquisition by pension funds and private equity groups starting in April 2007. In June, BCE accepted a purchase offer of $42.75 per share in cash, for a total valuation of $51.7 billion, from the group led by the Ontario Teachers' Pension Plan. With tightening credit markets in the spring of 2008, the investment banks financing the deal started negotiating revised terms of their loans with higher interest rates and greater restrictions to protect themselves. In November 2008, KPMG informed BCE that after privatization, the solvency of the company was threatened by the proposed financial structure. As a result, the purchase was cancelled. BCE then announced plans to return value to BCE Inc.'s shareholders with a reinstated common share dividend and a new common share buyback program.

The performance of BCE's price per share from 1984 through 2009 is found in Exhibit 9.1 from the New York Stock Exchange (NYSE). BCE has been called a "blue chip" stock although

Exhibit 9.1 The Price of Common Shares for BCE (BCE on the NYSE) in US$, January 1978 to July 2010

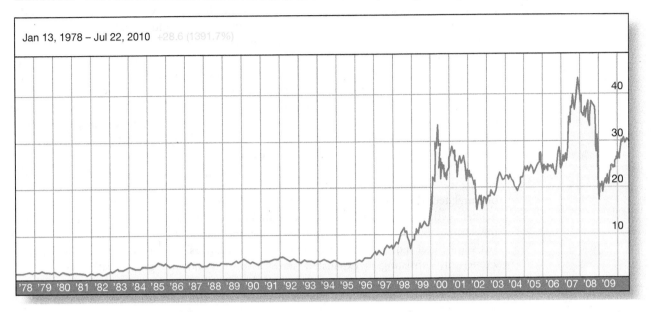

it has underperformed the U.S. market. Only during the run-up to the technology crash in 2000 did it outperform the Dow Jones Index from the NYSE.

BCE's story is just one of many that highlight the dynamic nature of corporate strategy. Business history is full of corporations buying and selling businesses. This chapter will describe a few of them to illustrate the concepts associated with diversification. ■

Corporate Strategy

A successful company generates value for its shareholders. With its success, it does more of the same until it runs into barriers defined by the natural limits of expansion in its chosen domain. At this point, management faces a critical decision: Do we pay the net cash flows out as dividends or do we seek new investment opportunities? Rarely does management decide to give excess capital back to the owners. Instead, it seeks out new investment opportunities that include providing more services, providing more products, or covering a larger geographic space. By doing this, the company is diversifying what it does. Initially these opportunities can be close to what the business is already doing, but eventually they are so different that the company is better off having separate business units conducting different activities.

When the company has more than one business, decision making is altered. Managers at the top of the organization focus on a unique set of strategic issues: which industries to enter, how to enter them, how to produce greater value from the business units that are part of the corporation than if they were independent, and how to allocate resources across the separate businesses.

In this chapter we examine corporate strategy—the strategic management of companies with multiple business units. Each business unit is a separate entity that has its own customers and control over the activities needed to satisfy those customers. A company that has multiple units is said to be diversified and its business units form a corporate portfolio.

Competitive Advantage of a Corporation

The justification for a business to grow is that it has further opportunities to invest in that generate a higher expected return than money invested elsewhere, holding risk constant. In other words, the corporation has a competitive advantage that allows it to provide an above-normal return on money invested in it. As discussed earlier, the competitive advantage is the outcome of a combination of revenues, costs, and investment. Revenues can be enhanced through differentiation, costs can be lowered through superior capabilities and spreading fixed costs, while investment can be lowered using low-cost resources.

Once a company has multiple business units, the management of this company is faced with a peculiar challenge with respect to competitive advantage. While the management of each business works to develop a competitive advantage for that business, the management of the corporation has to create a greater competitive advantage than those of the businesses in it in order to justify the existence of the corporation. In other words, corporate management has to find a way to build shareholder value beyond what shareholders could earn from investing in a portfolio of stock comprised of different businesses.

The competitive advantage of a corporate strategy is closely tied to the relationships among the businesses in the corporate portfolio. At its simplest, businesses are either related or unrelated. Related businesses have activities in their value chains that can be performed better together than if the businesses operated alone. Unrelated businesses have activities in their value chains that are so dissimilar that none can be combined. For Canada, analysis has shown that more than 80 percent of corporate diversification is across industries, with 71 percent consisting of expansion across two-digit industry groups rather than within industry groups, suggesting that most diversification was unrelated. In addition, industry concentration and average company size were both positively associated with the amount of diversification per company. This was consistent with the "constrained optimization" view that large companies in concentrated markets looked to diversification as a means of achieving growth as potential expansion in main product areas approaches exhaustion.[3] The importance of unrelated diversification has been decreasing in the United States, however, and this is a possible trend in future for Canada as more attention is paid to "strategic fit" and profitability rather than growth.[4]

We now examine the source of competitive advantage for the corporation depending on whether businesses are related or unrelated.

Related Diversification

Corporate management can create competitive advantage by capturing benefits from combining activities of related businesses. The combination is *horizontal* when some of the activities in value chains of the businesses are similar, allowing the businesses to exploit complementary resources. Two public software companies that have bought other related companies are Descartes Systems Group Inc. of Waterloo, Ontario, and Enghouse Systems Limited of Markham, Ontario. Descartes has focused on buying up other companies providing similar software solutions used by customers for handling logistics in supply chains. Meanwhile, Enghouse Systems has bought companies making distinct enterprise software and made them profitable by cutting costs. The combination is *vertical* when the value chain of one business is added to one end of another business. For example, J. D. Irving Limited is the largest single landowner in New Brunswick, Nova Scotia, and Maine (and has also been identified as being one of the largest foreign landowners in the United States). These forest lands feed several pulp and paper plants and sawmills, which in turn feed the company's paper, tissue, and diaper factories throughout New Brunswick, Nova Scotia, Maine, New York, Quebec, and Ontario.[5]

HORIZONTAL INTEGRATION

When businesses sharing similar activities are brought together, three relationships among business are important to creating competitive advantage: tangible relationships, intangible relationships, and competitor relationships. Tangible relationships arise from the ability to share activities in the value chain because of common customers, channels, technology, and other factors. Intangible relationships arise from the ability to transfer know-how among separate value chains. Competitive relationships arise from the actual or potential competition with competitors that spill over into other of the corporation's businesses. Each type of relationship matters because it leads to competitive advantage in a different way.

Tangible Relationships

Tangible relationships provide competitive advantage if sharing activities lower costs or enhance differentiation enough to exceed the cost of sharing. This can be achieved when jointly performing one activity, such as sharing a sales force. This can also be achieved by having multiple activities, such as when each business has its own sales force that engages in cross-selling—selling both its own products as well as those of the related business.

The analysis of tangible relationships starts with the value chains of the businesses. Any activity that is performed in the activity chain of both businesses has the potential for being shared. When businesses have so much in common that the only separation is separate sales forces, they are not truly separate businesses in a strategic sense.

Sharing provides both benefits and costs. The benefits come from lowering costs and increasing differentiation. But sharing also creates costs because supporting relationships requires changes in behaviour. This is driven in part by the conflicting "dominant logics" that shape decision making in the different businesses. The three types of costs that arise are the costs of coordination, compromise, and inflexibility. Managers must coordinate the combined activities by setting master schedules, priorities, and resolving conflicts. This takes their time and energy and costs money. Ongoing compromise is needed when sharing requires that the activity be performed in a way that is not performed optimally for either business. Failure to compromise means that the benefits of sharing are not fully achieved. Finally, the cost of inflexibility may be felt in two ways. First, response to competitive actions facing one business may not be possible because that would hurt the other business. Second, the corporation may want to exit a business but doing so would make the shared activity less for the remaining business. These costs must be factored against the benefits from sharing an activity. Only when the benefits exceed the cost of sharing will these relationships add to the competitive advantage of the corporation.

Identifying activities that can be shared is done by first separating activities according to the value chain. Those activities in each business's value chain that share commonalities are candidates for being shared. Let us consider five common activities that might be shared: the primary activities of procurement, manufacturing, marketing and distribution; and the secondary activities of technology and infrastructure.

Procurement

When businesses have common suppliers, joining together can produce greater buying power that provides greater discounts for each. Uniprix, Quebec's second-biggest pharmacy chain, was founded in 1977 by a group of pharmacists who wanted to increase their purchasing power without giving up control of their stores. Other activities that can be combined are warehousing, inventory control, and quality assurance.

Manufacturing

Separate businesses can share common components. Daimler's plan for turning around Chrysler in 2001 involved increasing cooperation with Mercedes-Benz and Mitsubishi to benefit from economies of scale. In part, Daimler planned to use a number of Mercedes-Benz components such as transmissions, steering systems, and diesel engines in Chrysler Group vehicles.[6] Similarly, GM saved considerable cost on Chevrolet's Malibu model that it introduced in 2003. The Malibu and the Saab 9-3 had the same gas tank, which saved 30 percent on the cost of the gas tank. The Malibu and the Opel Vectra shared the same suspension, which saved 30 percent. And the Malibu, Saab 9-3, and Vectra all had seats made by Faurecia, a French company, of more comfortable and durable yet cheaper material.[7] Business can also share assembly plants, maintenance operations, and control systems for inventory, scheduling, and quality. Bombardier was able to turn around the floundering aerospace companies it bought by transferring the Bombardier Manufacturing System and other techniques from its mass transit business. This included rearranging manufacturing layout to improve the flow of information and materials. Just-in-time inventory control and new quality control methods were also introduced. In addition, design and manufacturing engineers were brought together so that designers were more conscious of the cost in the design of their airplanes.[8]

Marketing and Distribution

Numerous marketing activities can be shared. Consolidating the sales force is a common way of lowering cost and increasing sales at the same time. At Dorel of Montreal, senior management coordinate the businesses of all three segments (juvenile, recreation/leisure, and home furnishings) to maximize cross-selling and cross-marketing. In addition, Dorel has permanent, full-service agency account teams established in close proximity to certain major accounts. These teams provide these customers with the assurance that inventory and supply requirements will be met and that problems are immediately addressed.[9]

Kaboose Inc. of Toronto consolidated its advertising activity in New York, where Kaboose had built a hugely experienced sales force. This office sold online advertising and marketing services to the world's leading consumer product brands who wanted to reach parents in Canada, the United Kingdom, and the United States through Kaboose's various websites (AmazingMoms. com, BabyZone.com, Funschool.com, Kaboose.com, ParentZone.com, and Zeeks.com).[10]

Another benefit of shared marketing is selling under a corporate brand. Over time, growers have continued to join Clifford Produce, a company that produces field and greenhouse vegetables around Ruthven, Ontario. Together with these growers it has become one of the largest greenhouse produce marketing operations in North America. The company ships produce under the Paysanne label. Reno Vespa, owner of Vespa Farms and president of the new Clifford Produce, said, "This new group gives us the size and resources to be a major player in the industry."[11] Clifford's size and the reputation of its brand have strengthened its bargaining position with retailers.[12]

Businesses can also share warehousing and delivery activities. In the fast-food industry, "multibrand" facilities are used to promote sales and decrease costs. Both Yum! and Wendy's in cooperation with Tim Hortons have introduced such facilities. Costs are reduced through economies of scope as two brands are placed in a single facility rather than housing each outlet in a separate facility. In addition, physical resources are productive when the combination has two food services with different peak hours. In 2000, Afton Food Group of Burlington, Ontario, acquired Robin's Foods Inc. of Thunder Bay, Ontario, so that it could combine its 241 Pizza locations with Robin's Donuts' 245 locations. The twinned locations were attractive because Robin's prime time was 5 a.m. to 2 p.m, while 241's was 5 p.m. to midnight and oriented toward home delivery.[13] Furthermore, revenues are enhanced at multibrand facilities because each has broader appeal to groups of customers. People with different tastes can satisfy those tastes yet eat together.

Research and Development

Shared research and development (R&D) can reduce costs. By sharing the same automotive platform across three different GM companies, the engineering costs for Chevrolet's Malibu, Opel's Vectra, and Saab's 9-3 were reduced by 33 percent.[14] Meanwhile cooperation on design between Mitsubishi Motors, Chrysler Group, and Mercedes-Benz, particularly in the joint development and use of technologies, components, and vehicle platforms, was seen as reducing costs while improving the quality and design of their vehicles.[15]

Knowledge about technologies in one business can be used in another business to further differentiate its product. For example, the Timken Company took its automotive and industrial sensor technology knowledge into its consumer product designs, giving manufacturers new ways to enhance products and differentiate their brands. It also took designs it pioneered for automotive applications and used them to offer solutions for four-stroke engines, drive trains, and steering.

Administration

Various administrative services can be centralized, such as accounting, finance, human resources, information technology, and legal services. Having a data warehouse provides a distinct *centralized* repository for vital business data from a variety of corporate databases that can then be analyzed and used as a strategic competitive weapon.

Tangible relationships are the most compelling source of competitive advantage because they are easily recognized, quantified, and implemented, but intangible relations also provide benefits.

Intangible Relationships

Intangible relationships provide competitive advantage if sharing know-how lowers the cost of an activity or enhances differentiation enough to exceed the cost of sharing. Businesses can benefit from one another even though they cannot share activities. They can share the skills and know-how generated from their commonalities, such as the type of customer, the type of purchase, and the type of manufacturing process each deals with, following a common strategy and a similar configuration of the value chain (such as many dispersed sites where activities are performed).

Knowledge consists of insights and experience either embodied in individuals or embedded in organizational processes or practice. This know-how can be transferred either through long-term observation of people who have the knowledge or through mentoring and apprenticeship programs that train people in the knowledge.

Co-Steel Inc., a Canadian company that was an early entrant into mini-mill steel technology, saw technology as an important ingredient of the company's success. To encourage the best use of technology, all new technology was owned at the corporate level. The operating divisions were joint ventures that did not compete with one another but each month they received the operating information of all companies. This served to identify superior practices across the mills, and knowing this, the mills learned from one another by sharing their experiences. To encourage the transfer of technology among the companies, regular technical meetings were held. In addition, each CEO spent a week a year at a sister company.

Bombardier's Aerospace division has also benefited from transferring skills and expertise in management from one business unit to another. When developing the 70-seat Canadair Regional Jet, Bombardier's first move was to call together design engineers and staff to build a financial model. They wanted to build the right plane to the right quality at the right cost. John Holding, a Bombardier executive, said, "We are not here to only make a great airplane. The Concorde is a great aircraft, but it does not make money. Bombardier is here to make money."[16]

RONA Inc. developed an intangible relationship with its dealers when, in 2009, it introduced a new succession-planning program designed to make it easier for family members of independent dealers, RONA employees, or aspiring entrepreneurs from outside the company to acquire stores.[17] This helps provide better dealers for the company.

Competitive Relationships

Competitive relationships are present when a company actually or potentially competes with diversified rivals in more than one business unit. Then competitive actions affecting one business unit can have an impact on other businesses in the corporation. For example, corporations tend to be in similar sets of businesses and compete with one another in each of these businesses. The reason for similar portfolios of business is that the diversification of the portfolio was driven in each case to achieve the benefit of relationships among the businesses.

A corporation with other divisions may carry commitments that prevent it from responding to competitive action elsewhere. For example, in the mid-1980s, the Great Atlantic and Pacific Tea Co. (A&P) decided to enter the food retailing market in Kitchener-Waterloo, Ontario. This market was one of the few where A&P did not have stores, although two other major chains were present (Oshawa Foods had stores under the Dutch Boy banner while Loblaws had stores under the Zehrs banner). Rather than simply put in stores under the A&P banner, top management chose to put the stores in under a new banner, Super Fresh, operating as a separate business unit. Being a new banner provided the new stores with a considerable competitive edge. Super Fresh had broad latitude in its merchandising moves because what it did had no competitive implications for the rest of the A&P organization, as A&P did not have any stores in the Kitchener-Waterloo market and Super Fresh was not identified with A&P. Both Dutch Boy and Zehrs had stores in the surrounding towns so any competitive response by them to counter Super Fresh was extremely costly because it affected their stores not only in the Kitchener-Waterloo market but also in the surrounding towns.[18]

Another example showing that competitive behaviour is based on corporate interests rather than responses to rivalry facing a single business comes from the entertainment industry. The current trend within the entertainment industry has been toward the increased concentration of media ownership among a smaller number of corporations. In 2009, CanWest Global was Canada's largest media company. It owned the Global Television Network, operating 18 industry-leading specialty channels and having ownership in five specialty channels. CanWest Global was also Canada's largest publisher of English-language daily newspapers and owned and operated more than 80 online properties. Of particular importance to these media empires are their interests in broadcasting properties (television and radio) because they offer the most extensive channel for communicating brand and efficient cross-promotion and also generate the highest profit margins compared to other media sectors. The result is that broadcasters are highly competitive because success in broadcasting influences the corporation's effectiveness in other markets.[19]

The overall gains that come from diversification into related business are lower costs and better differentiation. But these gains do not happen automatically. Management has to identify opportunities to consolidate their activities and then achieve the benefits possible.

VERTICAL INTEGRATION

Vertical integration is the term applied when a corporation diversifies by extending the activities included in its value chain. Shermag Inc., headquartered in Sherbrooke, Quebec, designs, produces, markets, and distributes high-quality residential furniture. The company is a vertically integrated manufacturer and importer with its own cutting rights, sawmill, veneer facility, manufacturing operations, and global sourcing division. In some cases, a company can create value by moving into suppliers' or buyers' value chains if it can bundle its product with complementary products. Automakers and dealers, for example, have been involved in financing the purchase of cars because it helps sell their cars.

There are two directions when management decides to integrate vertically. Integrating upstream or **backward integration** involves moving toward the sources of supply. This was what Henry Ford did when he created the River Rouge Complex for the Ford Motor Company. The move expanded the company's value chain from making and assembling car parts back into making materials including steel and glass that were used to make the parts. Integrating downstream or **forward integration** involves moving toward end-users. This is what Coca-Cola and PepsiCo have done as they have taken over the bottlers of their soft drinks. With vertical integration, the corporation has two or more connected industries under singular managerial control.

When vertically integrating, management can aim for full integration (then the corporation participates in all industries in the value stream) or partial integration (then the corporation takes positions in only selected industries in the value stream). An example of full integration is a single corporation that owns the oil wells, refines the oil, and sells gasoline at roadside stations. An example of partial integration was the decision at Maple Leaf Foods to only partially integrate into the pork chain. In 2001, corporate strategy was to grow the businesses of animal feed, swine genetics, pork processing, and distribution but to leave hog production to independent livestock producers.

Vertical integration makes sense when it bolsters the competitive advantage of the corporation. Then the stages are more profitable when combined than when separate. Vertical integration has the potential to reduce costs in two ways. First, it lowers the cost of production when there are economies of joint operation. Costs are lower since processes are connected directly. The most obvious example is that of working with steel. Enormous amounts of energy are used to heat steel so that it is malleable. The energy savings are considerable when the various operations of creating and shaping steel are done without the steel cooling down. Second, it overcomes the inefficient coordination of activities between separate companies. Coordination between separate companies requires that contracts be negotiated and enforced. Bargaining and monitoring performance and resolving differences cost money and time. In addition, investments can be made simply to improve bargaining power. These costs are all called "transaction costs," and they can be avoided by bringing businesses under a single management that can resolve differences by fiat.

But vertical integration has four potentially negative consequences. First, putting separate businesses under the control of a corporate management imposes additional administrative costs. The activities of the businesses have to be coordinated and transfer prices for products and services moving between the businesses have to be set. Second, each business may not be able to achieve economies due to size or scope because it just serves the other corporate business. If it is sized to achieve these economies, it has to work with suppliers or customers who may be unwilling to deal with it because they compete with its sister business. They consider dealing with the large company as supporting a value stream that contains a competitor. Third, when the business is vertically integrated, it has to serve the needs of its partner so has less incentive to change how it does things though its competitors may be changing. When the business is separate, it has a greater need to be competitive and so pursues a strategy that is best

---

backward integration
Diversifying into related activities that extend the company's value chain while moving closer to sources of supply.

forward integration
Diversifying into related activities that extend the company's value chain while moving closer to final consumers.

for it and develops distinctive capabilities that let it pursue this strategy. Fourth, risk for the corporation is compounded because the corporation is committed to specific businesses. This means running a business at a level that may be less profitable but is necessary to match the needs of the sister company in the value stream. This interdependence also makes it harder for the corporation to dispose of a business because another business it owns is dependent on the business. The tendency is to run the businesses so they help one another rather than maximize the value that each business could create. The risk then is that the value of the corporation is not maximized.

Deciding whether to vertically integrate is a situation-specific decision, and the rationale is not always to pursue an opportunity but rather to hold on to what one has. For example, in Quebec, McKesson Canada has distributed pharmaceutical products, over-the-counter medications, and consumer products for 100 years. Quebec is a highly coveted market because of the large number of prescriptions dispensed there—90 000 per drugstore annually versus 40 000 elsewhere in Canada. In 2008, McKesson bought Groupe PharmEssor Inc., the owner of the Proxim and ProxiMeds drugstore brands, with about 270 independently owned outlets in Quebec. Then in 2009 it bought Uniprix, which owns and operates the Uniprix, Unipharm, and Uniclinique banners and has 400 independently owned outlets. The independent owners of both companies were being courted by retailing powerhouses such as market leader Jean Coutu and Shoppers Drug Mart, owner of the Pharmaprix brand in Quebec. As the independents purchased more of their drugs from other sources, McKesson's sales were increasingly vulnerable. By owning the banners, McKesson gained first right of refusal to buy independent pharmacies that carried the banner names if they were approached by a competing pharmacy chain. Furthermore, the purchase of the banners signalled to the other pharmacy chains that McKesson intended to stay and protect its business in Quebec from their expansion plans.[20]

Alternatively, in 2008, Irving Oil of Saint John, New Brunswick, leased its 252 Irving-owned and franchised stores (its Mainways Blue Canoe and Big Stop fuel and convenience stores) to Quebec-based Alimentation Couche-Tard Inc. for 20 years. The Irving convenience stores were rebranded while gas pumps retained the Irving brand and Irving continues to supply the fuel. The partners share fuel and convenience store revenues. This deal followed a similar deal in 2001 when 56 of Irving's Mainway stores in Quebec were converted to the Couche-Tard brand.[21] These actions allow both companies to focus on what they do best.

UNRELATED DIVERSIFICATION

A corporation with two or more businesses engaged in entirely unrelated industries is called a **conglomerate**. Capturing benefits when holding such businesses in the corporate portfolio is very difficult. Building competitive advantage rests on the capabilities and skills of corporate managers. These include the abilities:

conglomeration Diversification of the company into activities that are entirely unrelated to its current value chain.

1. to identify new businesses that will provide good and consistent returns on investment,
2. to enter a new industry at low cost, either through an efficient start-up or buying a business at low cost,
3. to leave an industry at high value through negotiating or attracting a high price for the business being sold,
4. to provide management for the businesses acquired that is superior to businesses run separately,
5. to encourage managers of businesses in the portfolio to perform better than businesses run separately,
6. to shift resources within the portfolio more effectively than others in pursuit of superior performance, and
7. to recognize the need to dispose of businesses before they have a detrimental impact on corporate performance.

Onex Corporation of Toronto is one corporation that has been very successful with unrelated diversification. Founded in 1984 by Jerry Schwartz, by 2008 Onex had completed more than 250 acquisitions valued at approximately $43 billion and generated 3.4 times the capital it had invested and managed by earning a 29 percent compound IRR on realized and publicly traded investments. Onex's stock traded on the Toronto Stock Exchange as OCX

Exhibit 9.2　The Price of Common Shares for ONEX (OCX on the TSE) in Cdn$, April 1999 to July 2010

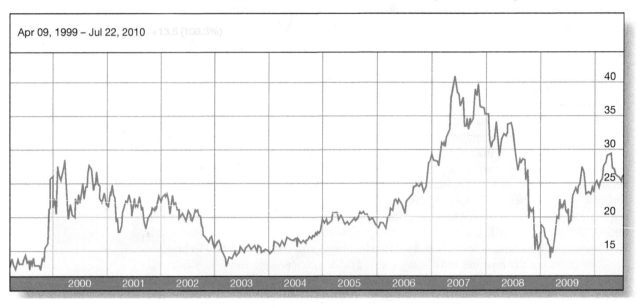

Exhibit 9.3　Companies Onex Has Interests In

| Principal Operating Companies | Organized under the laws of | Percentage of Equity Shares Directly or Indirectly Held by Onex | Percentage Voting Interest of Onex |
		At December 31, 2008[a]	At December 31, 2008
Investments made through Onex			
Celestica	Ontario	13%	79%
Cineplex Entertainment	Ontario	23%	(b)
Sitel Worldwide	Delaware	66%	88%
Investments made through Onex and Onex Partners I			
Center for Diagnostic Imaging	Delaware	19%	100%
Cosmetic Essence	Delaware	21%	100%
Emergency Medical Services	Delaware	29%	97%
ResCare	Kentucky	6%	(b)
Skilled Healthcare	Delaware	9%	89%
Spirit AeroSystems	Delaware	7%	76%
Investments made through Onex and Onex Partners II			
Allison Transmission	Delaware	15%	(b)
Carestream Health	Delaware	39%	100%
Hawker Beechcraft	Delaware	20%	(b)
RSI	Delaware	20%	50%[b]
Tube City IMS	Delaware	35%	100%
Investments made through Onex, Onex Partners I and Onex Partners II			
Husky	Ontario	36%	100%
The Warranty Group	Delaware	29%	100%

Source: Onex Annual Information Form for 2008. Released February 25, 2009, p. 6.

(see Exhibit 9.2). As of December 21, 2009, a share was worth $24.52. In the prior decade, an Onex share had lost 6 percent of its value while the TSX Composite Index had gone up 42 percent.

The range of Onex's investments is outlined in Exhibit 9.3. Although the company has majority control over most of its subsidiaries, rarely does it have total ownership. Onex's

Exhibit 9.4 The Price of Common Shares for Masco Corp. (MAS on the NYSE) in US$, July 2000 to July 2010

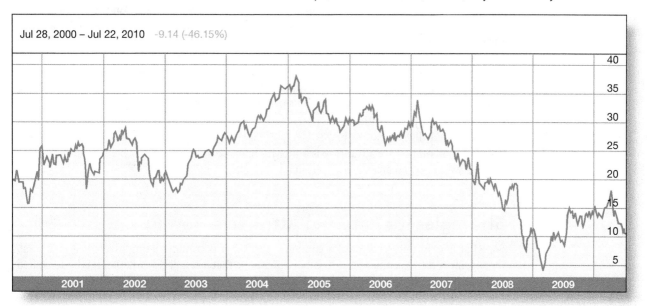

Jul 28, 2000 – Jul 22, 2010   -9.14 (-46.15%)

private equity investment in companies is its biggest activity, but Onex also invests in real estate, including real estate investment trusts, commercial real estate loans and other developments, and debt and credit securities. Onex also has credit securities investments designed to take advantage of the credit shortage after 2008.

A value stated by Onex is to be diversified by industry, geography, and asset type so that the effect of business cycles is smoothed over the long term.[22] This is why Onex holds ownership in companies spanning five continents that are involved in electronics manufacturing services, customer management services, theatre exhibition, automotive products, managed health care, personal care products, and communications infrastructure.

Schwartz's vision for Onex is to acquire undervalued and mismanaged companies, streamline their infrastructures or add to their asset base, and then to sell the companies for a profit. Onex uses debt or other innovative financing to purchase the undervalued companies and then initiates a comprehensive restructuring of the company purchased. Onex strongly values the people of the company it acquires. Almost 99 percent of all employees that went through the Onex acquisition process eventually found themselves with better pay and improved medical and dental plans. In some cases, Onex management personally distributed bonuses in cash to top performers of each organization. Some performers and their families were sent to vacation resorts at the company's expense. Poor performers were encouraged to abstain from drugs and alcohol and were typically sent for training and rehabilitation, if necessary, at the company's expense.[23] Once the performance of the business was boosted, either parts of the company or the whole were sold at a profit.

Another example of a successful conglomerate is Masco Corporation. Founded in 1929 by Alex Manoogian, Masco increased its revenues at an average annual rate of 19 percent between 1957 and 1989, and its net income rocketed at an average of 22 percent each year. Volume peaked in 2006 at US$12.5 billion and by 2008 had dropped to US$9.6 billion following the decline in the U.S. construction industry. This is reflected in the recent decline in its common stock traded on the New York Stock Exchange under MAS that is now worth 48 percent less than a decade earlier (see Exhibit 9.4). In 2008, its businesses were organized into five divisions (see Exhibit 9.5).

Masco Corp. is one of North America's largest manufacturers of brand-name products for the home improvement and new home construction markets. Masco is also a leading provider of a variety of installed products and services, including insulation, for homebuilders. Its products include faucets, kitchen and bath cabinets, paints and stains, bath and shower units, spas, showering and plumbing specialties, windows, and decorative hardware.

Exhibit 9.5 Sales in Masco Corp., 2008 (in millions of US$)

	2008
Cabinets and Related Products	$2.3
Plumbing Products	$3.1
Installation and Other Services	$1.9
Decorative Architectural Products	$1.6
Other Specialty Products	$0.7
Total	$9.6

Source: Masco Corp, 10K filed with the U.S. Securities and Exchange Commission.

Masco's Canadian operations, Masco Canada Ltd., had sales of more than Cdn$50 million, which included hardware branded Delta, Waltec, Laboratory/Institutional, and Cambridge Brass.

Masco's growth came from purchasing a multitude of small and medium-sized manufacturing companies, most of which were leaders in their market niches. Masco was different from Onex in that it purchased healthy, innovative companies. It then allowed the companies to continue doing what they did best. In addition to its hands-off management approach, Masco operated an extremely efficient, streamlined headquarters located in a relatively small, low-profile facility in an industrial park in Taylor, Michigan, west of Detroit. With just a few hundred employees in corporate offices, Masco has a reputation as a lean, well-run corporation.[24]

Unrelated diversification places heavy demands on corporate management because the potential for competitive advantage is limited. There are none of the possible benefits of related businesses and the greater diversification adds greater complexity.

Strategies for Entering Attractive New Businesses

So, what new businesses should a company enter if it is contemplating diversification? First, management has to decide where its capabilities lie so that it can decide whether it is better suited to related or unrelated diversification. The range of businesses to consider is more restricted with related diversification since the businesses must require the same or related resources and must be similar strategically. But there are literally thousands of possible businesses that a corporation might enter, so how else might managers narrow the search? Recall that in Chapter 4 you learned how to analyze the attractiveness of an industry. Among other things, attractive industries tend to benefit from higher levels of profitability. So, a manager might target a high-profit industry that requires related resources and is strategically similar to the company's core business. However, in Chapter 4 you also learned that industries have higher average profits for reasons; one critical reason is that it likely has strong entry barriers. Consequently, the most attractive markets are generally the hardest to enter. This paradox can be addressed in five ways. First, the corporation can leverage existing resources by forming an alliance with another company that has complementary resources. Chapter 10 addresses using alliances as a way of entering a new market. Second, the corporation can circumvent entry barriers by acquiring a company already in the industry. Chapter 11 addresses mergers and acquisitions as a vehicle for entering a new market. Third, the corporation can start a new business that appears non-threatening to current competitors. This can be done by entering a niche market. Fourth, the corporation can start a new business that revolutionizes the industry by altering the cost structure and/or the product offered. This changes the rules of the industry so that competitors have to change the way they play to match the new rules. Fifth and finally, the corporation can draw on its existing resource strengths and use them to enter a closely related industry. We will now outline the last three methods for accomplishing entry using concepts you have already learned. Although we deal with these methods separately, they are not mutually exclusive; they are often used in combination to formulate robust entry moves into attractive industries.

FOCUS ON A NICHE

The generic positions for strategy in Chapter 5 were low-cost leadership, differentiation, focus cost leadership, and focus differentiation. An entry that is focused involves pursuing a niche in the market and appears less threatening to the incumbents because it seems to have modest goals. Consequently, it attracts little attention and is not likely to provoke retaliatory behaviour. One type of niche that is particularly attractive is a segment of the market whose needs are currently underserved. Husky Injection Molding of Bolton, Ontario, is a company that thrived because it focused on a niche market: machinery and moulds for making PET packaging, in particular bottles filled with soft drinks and water. At the time that this niche was developing, the markets for both plastic moulding machinery and moulds had low profitability because there were many competitors and growth was slow. Under Robert Schad, Husky's founder and CEO, the company focused on making machines and moulds for making PET packaging. Initially competitors were unaware of this niche and when they did recognize it, they had trouble competing because Husky had developed a considerable technological advantage in serving this niche. By 2001, Husky held 50 percent of the world market for PET pre-forms, had sales of

Cdn$640 million, and employed 2800 people worldwide. Eventually competitors caught up and in serving this niche and Husky's performance declined. ONEX bought 36 percent ownership of Husky in 2007.

Another example is Red Bull, which entered the soft-drink market with a niche product: a non-alcoholic energy drink that Dietrich Mateschitz, an Austrian, adapted from a drink he discovered while doing business in Thailand.[25] Though the soft-drink market is highly attractive (Coca-Cola and PepsiCo enjoy gross margins of more than 60 percent and return on assets of more than 17 percent), the failure of many entrants shows that both Coca-Cola and PepsiCo are not ready to surrender any of their profitable business to other companies. Red Bull entered the United States in 1997 with little fanfare but, city by city, introduced the product and targeted the young adult market. The drink's popularity grew quickly and eventually captured more than 70 percent of the U.S. market for energy drinks, a rapidly growing industry itself. Even though this was a niche market, that kind of growth grabbed the attention of Coca-Cola, PepsiCo, and many other companies and entrepreneurs. As competitors moved in, Red Bull's market share slipped into the 40 percent range, but the market has grown significantly as well, so Red Bull's sales continue to climb.[26]

USING A REVOLUTIONARY STRATEGY

Another way to enter an industry is with a revolutionary strategy. This affords some protection from competition because such a strategy breaks with the conventional way business practiced by the incumbents. When it is very different, incumbents are predisposed to think such a strategy is inferior, unwise, or risky. Only after such a strategy proves successful will incumbents rally to try to protect their ground, but by then they are often too late.

As you learned in Chapter 6, a strategy can be made revolutionary in several ways. For illustrative purposes, we use reconfiguring the value chain as an example, but a successful new-business entry could be accomplished with any revolutionary strategy. Recall that Skype entered the telecom services industry by avoiding the existing telecom infrastructure. Skype used voice over internet protocol (VOIP) that allowed their customers to utilize their PCs to place calls, thus bypassing the entire value chain of incumbents and giving Skype a totally different (and lower) cost structure. It avoided direct retaliation from incumbents because the service was targeted at price-sensitive customers and the telecom industry was not interested in these customers.

Pixar, part of the Walt Disney Company since its acquisition in 2006, provides another example of diversification. Facets of other revolutionary strategies were mixed with value-chain reconfiguration. Pixar was established as an independent company in 1986 when co-founder and then former CEO of Apple Steve Jobs purchased the computer graphics division of Lucasfilm Ltd., a technology company, for US$10 million. Pixar started out as a high-end graphics hardware developer and began to experiment with film shorts and commercials using new animation technologies that it had developed and controlled. After years of unprofitability, it contracted with Disney to produce a number of computer-animated feature films. Its technology revolutionized the animation used to make cartoons and advertising. Coupling the technology with excellent storytelling, Pixar produced a string of hits of which *Finding Nemo* (2003), *The Incredibles* (2004), *Ratatouille* (2007), and *WALL-E* (2008) each received the Academy Award for Best Animated Feature, an award introduced in 2001. In recognition of Pixar's success, Walt Disney bought Pixar in 2006 for US$7.4 billion.

LEVERAGING EXISTING RESOURCES

The business can take its existing capabilities and pursue businesses that build on these capabilities. This can be encouraged by a *corporate venture unit*, a distinct organization unit controlled by the parent company that is responsible for investing in business opportunities that are new to the corporation. Such units may engage in a variety of forms of investment, from making small investments in independent start-ups, to incubating internal business ideas, to spinning out businesses. A spin-out happens when a business takes assets, intellectual property, technology, and/or existing products from the parent organization to form another independent company, or when an employee or group of employees leaves an existing company to start up an independent company.

Johnson & Johnson (J&J), for example, set up an Internal Ventures Group in 2007 to encourage collaborative ventures among its 230 subsidiaries. The group seeks out and supports the development of internally generated and unexploited early stage technologies and promotes new projects or ventures that currently have a low priority in J&J's strategic priorities. Once identified by the group, ideas are passed on to J&J's Development Corporation, an internal venture capital group, and the Corporate Office of Science. If the ideas are considered worthy of support, J&J's Development Corporation acts as the lead investor for the project and solicits funds and resources, including laboratory space and scientific expertise, from outside partners.

One of J&J's first internal ventures funded in this way was a project to develop a medical device called the Macroflux system, which is a patch that provides a needle-free delivery of therapeutic agents. Launched in 2004, the project was incubated in J&J's subsidiary ALZA Corporation and became a spin-out in October 2006 when Macroflux Corporation raised $75 million in equity financing. Another spin-out was Movetis AV, which was founded in December 2006 by three former managers of Janssen Pharmaceutica, a J&J subsidiary. The company specializes in gastrointestinal disorders and aims to develop eight medicines licensed from Janssen Pharmaceutica and one from Ortho McNeil, another J&J company.[27]

COMBINATION STRATEGIES

In the examples of the entry strategies above, several have elements of two or more of the strategies. For instance, Skype combined its reconfigured value chain with a niche strategy; it specifically targeted price-sensitive customers who would tolerate inferior quality.

The key to entering an attractive business is to do so in an indirect way, such as using an entry strategy that does not directly assault the incumbents and immediately threaten their profitability. Those pursuing niche markets are often ignored initially by incumbents because they represent customers that the incumbents were not previously serving. Reconfiguring the value chain and leveraging existing resources help protect companies entering attractive markets. A reconfigured value chain gives the entrant a cost advantage and leveraging existing resources gives the entrant something to build off that incumbents and other possible new entrants are not likely to have.

Competitive Advantage and Corporate Strategy

At the business level, competitive advantage reflects the relative position of a company compared to positions of industry rivals. At the corporate level, it reflects management's success in creating more value from the company's business units than those units could create as stand-alone enterprises or subsidiaries. Our goal is to identify the conditions under which the strategy of owning a corporate portfolio of businesses creates value for shareholders.

You are already familiar with the element of arenas in business strategy. Sometimes a company chooses a corporate strategy of competing in only one arena. However, the corporate strategy of many companies involves operating in more than one arena. Corporate strategy becomes more complicated if the competitive or operational characteristics of those arenas differ in some way, whether subtly or substantially. Ultimately, it is the combination of arenas, resources (i.e., VRINE), and implementation that determines whether the corporate strategy leads to competitive advantage.

ARENAS

Theoretically, a company can compete in any combination of discrete business arenas. In practice, of course, companies rarely enter arenas randomly but rather select those that are logically connected to the arenas in which they already participate. ◆ The key to logical connection is *relatedness.* Businesses can be related along several different dimensions, including similarity in markets, use of identical resources, and reliance on comparable dominant logic.

Resources provide the basis for corporate competitive advantage. The nature of corporate resources varies along a continuum, and whether the resources are specialized or general dictates the limits of a company's scope, the manner of organizational control and coordination, and the effectiveness of corporate headquarters. Although most companies maintain some degree of relatedness among the various businesses in which they participate, some combinations require greater relatedness than others. Finally, it is not always easy for an outside observer to determine the dimensions along which corporate businesses are related.

Some conglomerates are actually portfolios of strategic business units within which several related businesses are combined for management purposes. GE, for instance, participates in such far-flung enterprises as jet engines, elevators, light bulbs, appliances, and financial services. Each of these businesses, however, is located in a business group with conceptually similar units.

RESOURCES

We saw in Chapter 3 that resources and capabilities are tangible or intangible, and their usefulness in creating a competitive advantage depends on five factors: (1) how valuable they are, (2) whether they are rare in the industry, (3) whether they're costly to imitate, (4) the availability of substitutes, and (5) whether the company has complementary capabilities to exploit them. We need to remember that these factors apply to the usefulness of resources in creating competitive advantage at the *business* level. At the corporate level in the VRINE framework (that is, valuable, rare, inimitable, nonsubstitutable, exploitable), they must be supplemented by an additional factor: namely, how *specialized* or *general* a company's resources are.

Specialized Resources

Specialized resources have a narrow range of applicability. Knowledge about fibre optics, for example, is fairly specialized, whereas managerial know-how and skill are more general in nature. Granted, fibre optics has many uses in multiple contexts (such as telecommunications, electronics, routing and switching equipment), but its utility is more limited than that of a general resource such as general managerial skill.

specialized resources
Resources with a narrow range of applicability.

General Resources

General resources can be exploited across a wide range of activities. In fact, many companies have created significant shareholder value by leveraging expertise in efficient manufacturing and mass-marketing techniques across different businesses engaged in a variety of industries. General resources are not confined to narrow applications, and the extent of resource specialization affects both a company's scope and its organizational structure.

general resources Resources that can be exploited across a wide range of activities.

IMPLEMENTATION

As explained in Chapters 1 and 2 and reaffirmed in Chapter 8, *implementation levers* include organizational structure, systems, and people. Strategic leaders use these levers to implement strategies. The success they have in using these levers to manage their diversified companies has a significant effect on the level of value that can be created through their portfolios. While the levers that are critical for corporate strategy vary from company to company, some of the more important levers to achieve successful diversification include knowledge-transfer mechanisms, coordination mechanisms, rewards, and corporate oversight.

Knowledge transfer enables a diversified company to apply superior performance results observed in one organizational business unit to other units that are not performing as well. Three mechanisms facilitate knowledge transfer. First, just the knowledge that superior results are being achieved in another business unit can be used to reset performance expectations for future performance in other units. In this case, no real knowledge of actual practices is transferred, but the superior performance is used to create stretch goals that motivate learning in other units. Second, underperforming units can study the operational practices of high-performing business units to determine the source of superior performance. Finally, knowledge transfer is perhaps best facilitated when members of lower-performing business units simply seek advice from the higher-performing units. It is often the case that high-performing business units have explicit routines and practices that can be detailed by key employees in those units.[28] In practice, knowledge transfer is difficult because the source of superior performance may not be entirely clear.

Coordination mechanisms are the management systems and processes that facilitate intracompany activity. Coordination depends on a variety of structural mechanisms, including reporting relationships, informal meetings and exchanges, and detailed policies and procedures for such activities as intracompany transfer pricing. Greater relatedness of businesses within a company requires more intense coordination across business units because resources are often shared across business units. For instance, adhesive technology is used in multiple divisions in 3M, and this knowledge sharing requires coordination. Alternatively, at GE knowledge transfer or resource sharing (other than cash) does not occur between GE's jet engine and consumer finance divisions. Consequently, 3M can generate more revenue-enhancement synergy between related units than GE can generate between unrelated businesses, but reaping these possible benefits requires that energy and resources be devoted to coordination.

Successful diversification will likely require adjustments in how managers are compensated and rewarded. Generally speaking, a company with a highly diversified (broad) portfolio of businesses will have a wider range of rewards than a focused or related diversified company of their strategies and they do not share resources or need to cooperate with each other. Conversely, in a corporation with related businesses, business units are likely to have more similar strategies, share resources, and cooperate with each other as they implement their strategies. For the corporation with related businesses, one consequence is that similar strategies in units accommodate similar reward systems. Another is that the reward based overall corporate performance is greater to encourage cooperation.

Unwieldy corporate-level management can be a drag on corporate earnings. What factors should determine the size and organization of corporate-level management? Basically, two factors govern this decision: the company's resources and the scope of its involvement in disparate arenas. When a company's portfolio contains numerous unrelated units that aren't significantly interdependent, it doesn't need heavy corporate-level oversight; there's not much that corporate-level management can do to add value on a day-to-day basis (a good example is Warren Buffett's Berkshire Hathaway Inc.). By contrast, when a company's portfolio consists of highly interdependent businesses, more corporate-level control is needed to facilitate the sharing of resources and to oversee interbusiness transactions (e.g., S. C. Johnson, whose businesses include insect control, home cleaning, and plastic products).

Now that we've identified the ingredients of a good corporate strategy, we need to remind ourselves that it's the alignment of these ingredients in support of a company's mission and vision that makes it possible for its managers to implement the company's corporate strategy and create competitive advantage at the corporate level. Indeed, the configuration of these elements will determine whether a company achieves corporate-level competitive advantage.

Corporate Strategy in Stable and Dynamic Contexts

By this point, you probably have a strong suspicion that corporate strategy is developed according to the relative dynamism of the context in which an organization operates. You are correct, and in this section we'll see how corporate strategy is designed to take dynamic context into account. Moreover, because alliances and acquisitions are vehicles for both business and corporate strategy, we'll elaborate on this theme in subsequent chapters as well. We'll see, for example, that depending on whether a company's context is stable or dynamic, the same vehicles are likely to play different roles. In particular, alliances and acquisitions have different implications for the allocation of a company's resources and capabilities. We'll show that because certain issues arise in both stable and dynamic contexts, differences are often matters of emphasis. At the same time, even if the *content* of strategy is similar in both stable and dynamic contexts, the dynamic context will have an effect on the implementation of strategy.

CORPORATE STRATEGY IN STABLE CONTEXTS

Many ideas of the relationship between diversification and corporate strategy are based on analyses of companies operating in relatively stable contexts. As we've seen, historically a company may have diversified into a high-growth industry because growth prospects in its current industry were unattractive. That's why Canadian Pacific Railway (CPR) got into a host of new businesses ranging from meat packing to insurance. But recall that unrelated diversification often fails and can lead corporations to divest themselves of unrelated businesses.

Stable Arenas and Formal Structures

Creating synergies among its businesses is an important part of a corporation's strategy. Synergies can come from shared know-how, coordination of business-unit strategies, shared tangible resources, vertical integration, and pooled negotiating power.[30] In relatively stable environments, such synergies are typically functions of static business-unit arenas and the formal structural links among them. Corporate-strategy objectives focus primarily on synergies as means of achieving economies of scope and scale. In fact, corporate strategy explicitly defines the form and extent of the coordination and collaboration among business units. Thus, the managers of individual units are often compensated according to a combination of division- and corporate-level performance. Generally, the overarching objective of corporate strategy in a stable environment is ensuring that the company operates as a tightly interwoven whole.

A good example of related diversification in a stable industry is Shawcor Ltd. It started as a pipe-coating specialist in the 1950s and evolved into a global company providing a range of pipe products and services for pipelines and industries. Shawcor has sales of nearly Cdn$1 billion through it six divisions, with 5200 employees in manufacturing and service facilities located in 20 countries. Most recently it acquired Flexpipe Systems of Calgary, which developed corrosionless high-pressure continuous pipeline technology. The acquisition gives Shawcor a new product to sell while helping Flexpipe accelerate its growth by providing access to the United States and other international markets, support and resources for product development and growth programs, and cost efficiencies in material procurement.

What we mean by "stable" is changing as the environment seems to be ever more dynamic because markets change. Masco Corporation, the multibillion-dollar manufacturer and distributor of plumbing fixtures and other homebuilding and home repair supplies, stuck with what it knew and did well until its major market, homebuilding in the United States, collapsed. Moreover, the world is a smaller place due to advances in information technology and lower cost transportation.

CORPORATE STRATEGY IN DYNAMIC CONTEXTS

The same factors described in Chapter 6 that create the need for a dynamic strategy also apply to corporate strategy: competitive interaction, industry evolution, and technological change. The evolution of the Corel Corporation shows how the corporation needs to be flexible when operating in a dynamic context.

Corel Corporation was founded by Dr. Michael Cowpland in 1985 as a systems integration company. Corel soon became a value-added reseller of computers, selling complete systems for desktop publishing tasks. Corel later added optical disk drives to its system line-up and then started marketing local area networks.[31] Cowpland continued to extend the corporation by hiring a development team that worked relatively autonomously to create graphic software that had better design and layout capabilities. The team developed CorelDRAW, which was released in 1989 and was an instant success. It was the first graphics application to incorporate in one package all of the major graphics functions: illustration, charting, editing, painting, and presentation. Sales of CorelDRAW were enhanced because Corel developed and simultaneously sold multiple versions of CorelDRAW, each of which was tailored for a select market niche. Standard practice in the industry was to develop and sell different versions of the program sequentially. Corel captured 55 percent share of the global market for drawing and illustration software products.

Corel was reaching saturation with its single product line so management began looking for new avenues of growth. In 1994, Corel launched an initiative to branch into four new markets: consumer games and educational products on CD-ROM, video-conferencing called CorelVideo, computer-aided design called CorelCAD (CAD), and office suites (or "bundles" of productivity software). This fuelled speculation Corel was trying to reinvent itself but wasn't sure how, and that it was "throwing stuff at the walls and looking to see what would stick."

Corel bolstered its office suite by purchasing Novell Inc.'s PerfectOffice, a suite of Windows applications from Novell that included WordPerfect, Quattro Pro, Presentations, InfoCentral PIM, and Paradox. With this transaction, Novell refocused on networking software, while Corel moved from a niche market to facing Microsoft directly. The challenge that Microsoft presented was that its operating system dominated the market because it came as installed software on personal computers. Corel addressed this challenge by transferring all its programs over to Linux—the only non-Microsoft operating system for computers. Corel's Linux Operating system was made as similar to Windows as possible, with the idea that this would help convert Windows users to Linux. Corel's Linux OS retail market share in the United States increased from 2.3 percent in November 1999 to 19.3 percent in February 2000, though it earned little from Linux.

To build its presence in Linux-based software, Corel proposed a merger with Inprise/Borland in February 2000. The scheme was abandoned when Corel's shares fell in price and the lack of strategic fit became evident. In August of that year, Cowpland stepped down, and Derek Burney, the new president and CEO, focused Corel on Windows and Mac application development. In October, Microsoft invested US$135 million in Corel to pave the way for a Corel contract that could bring Microsoft.Net software to others. The investment helped keep Corel from running out of cash and positioned Microsoft.Net as being based on a neutral technology. By November, Corel was rumoured to be looking for a buyer for its Linux distribution and sold it in 2001.

In early 2003, Corel was struggling as an unprofitable public corporation trading at a deep discount to its peers. Revenue was shrinking and the prospects for success with the new product lines seemed remote. To compound these challenges, Microsoft was seeking to sell off its 20 percent stake in the company, creating additional downward pressure on its stock price.

In March 2003, Vector agreed to buy Microsoft's 20 percent stake through a private transaction, making it Corel's biggest single shareholder, then tendered an offer to buy more shares from the market. In August, the majority of remaining shareholders agreed to tender their shares and in the fall Corel became a private company. Then Corel implemented sweeping changes to refocus on packaged software using an extensive global distribution channel. Speculative R&D projects were scrapped, and non-core businesses were divested. Growth and profitability improved dramatically.

For the fiscal year ending in 2005, Corel's Adjusted EBITDA was Cdn$49 million compared to a pro forma loss of more than Cdn$17 million for the fiscal year ended in 2003. On the strength of these impressive turnaround results, Corel successfully completed an IPO in May 2006 with Morgan Stanley as lead underwriter. And it was back—as a successful company selling packaged software.

Adaptec Inc. is another company that found that it had to adjust to fit in with a changing environment. It was once an integrated maker of both computer hardware and software. The strategy was logical because being integrated allowed it to make complementary products. Adaptec soon discovered that it was unable to keep up in both businesses due to rapid changes in technologies and strong competitors. In 1999, management decided to focus on hardware so it spun off its software side as Roxio through an IPO. Ironically, Adaptec attempted to keep abreast of software developments by buying EZ CD Pro from Incat Systems in 1995 and CD Creator from Corel in 1996. These products provided important contributions to Roxio's current line of products.

Diversification in Dynamic Contexts

Diversification can be a viable strategy in dynamic contexts, especially when it opens up the possibility of pursuing developing opportunities. Corel, Adaptec, and 3Com all pursued opportunities and were able to survive, although in each case the corporation ended up divesting some businesses. This points to the pressure of competition even in dynamic environments. The successful corporation needs strong resources and capabilities, especially in the areas of learning, knowledge transfer, and rapid responsiveness. It also needs a governance structure that allows nimbleness and quick response time. This is often killed when the corporate hierarchy has multiple layers involved in making and approving decisions.

Coevolution

The ebbs and flows of companies' corporate strategies in dynamic contexts are best described as a web of shifting linkages among evolving businesses—a process that some researchers call **coevolution**.[32] Borrowed from biology, the term *coevolution* describes successive changes among two or more ecologically interdependent species that adapt not only to their environment but also to each other. Business units coevolve when senior managers do not target specific synergies across business units but rather allow business-unit managers to determine which linkages

coevolution Process by which diversification causes two or more interdependent businesses to adapt not only to their environment but also to each other.

do and do not work. As business-unit managers search for fresh opportunities for synergies and abandon deteriorating linkages, internal relationships tend to shift. As in the organic world, coevolution can result in competitive interdependence, with one unit eventually absorbing another or rendering it unnecessary. Coevolution means that cross-business synergies are usually temporary, and managers must learn to deal with the fundamental tension that results from the agility afforded by fewer linkages and the efficiency afforded by more. Finally, research suggests that in successful coevolving companies, managers, rather than trying to control, or even predict, cross-business-unit synergies, simply let them emerge in the "natural" course of corporate operations.[33]

Ironically, of course, coevolution means that units owned by the same corporation are potentially both collaborators and competitors. This paradoxical relationship is perhaps easiest to detect when a company operates both traditional and ebusiness units. It's less obvious when it arises because new technologies have emerged to threaten established processes, but the costs of allowing a competitor—even one with which you share a corporate umbrella—to gain a technological advantage are often steep. In dynamic contexts, corporate strategy usually takes the form of temporary networks among businesses, and if strategic alliances are added to the mix, the network may include companies that the corporation doesn't own as well as those it does.

Divestitures and corporate spinoffs can be effective strategic vehicles for dealing with the sort of disruptive innovations that we discussed in Chapters 4 and 6, and they also figure frequently in stories of corporate coevolution.[34] ◆ Because disruptive technologies compete with established technologies, it may not be enough to simply reorganize them as new units under the same corporate umbrella. The resulting problems from retaining ownership of the disruptive part of the business range from the creation of messy internal politics to simply starving the new business of resources so that it eventually fails. We've summarized the key differences between corporate strategies in stable and dynamic contexts in Exhibit 9.6. How Would You Do That? 9.1 demonstrates how you might identify a dynamic corporate strategy at Maple Leaf Foods.

 Arenas

Stable Contexts	Dynamic Contexts
Top management team emphasizes collaboration among the businesses and the form of that collaboration.	Top management team emphasizes the creation of a collaborative context that is rich in terms of content and linkages.
Collaboration is solidified through stable structural arrangement among wholly owned businesses.	Collaboration is fluid, with networks being created, changed, and disassembled between combinations of owned and alliance businesses.
Key objectives are the pursuit of economies of scale and scope.	Key objectives are growth, manoeuvrability, and economies of scope.
The business units' roles are to execute their given strategies.	The business units' roles are to execute their strategies and seek new collaborative opportunities.
Business units' incentives combine business with corporate-level rewards to promote cooperation.	Business units' incentives emphasize business-level rewards to promote aggressive execution and collaborative-search objectives.
Balanced-scorecard objectives emphasize performance against budget and in comparison to within-firm peer unit.	Balanced-scorecard objectives gauge performance relative to competitors in terms of growth, market share, and profitability.

Exhibit 9.6 Comparison of Corporate Strategies in Stable and Dynamic Contexts

Identifying Strategy at Maple Leaf Foods[35]

aple Leaf Foods (MLF) is a leading Canadian food processing company with revenues of Cdn$5.2 billion in fiscal 2008. Its operations are organized into three groups: meat products, agribusiness, and bakery. In 2008, the Meat Products Group comprised value-added packaged meats; chilled meal entrées and lunch kits; and value-added fresh pork, poultry, and turkey products. The Agribusiness Group included hog production and animal by-products recycling. The Bakery Products Group was comprised of Maple Leaf's 89.8 percent ownership in Canada Bread Company, a producer of fresh and frozen value-added bakery products, sandwiches, and specialty pasta and sauces. MLF's mission is described as being "an organization that continuously creates superior shareholder value in the food industry, benefiting all stakeholders."[36] The value of a common share was Cdn$10.85 on

December 21, 2009. Over the previous decade it had fallen 28 percent while the TSE Composite Index had risen 42 percent. The price of its common stock from 1996 through 2009 is shown in Exhibit 9.7.

Overall principles that guided corporate strategic decisions over the last two decades have been:[37]

1. Add value for our customers
2. Add value to our products
3. Invest in leading market shares
4. Build our brands
5. Innovate
6. Drive costs out
7. Diversify globally

Exhibit 9.7 Value of a Common Share of Maple Leaf Foods in Comparison to the Dow-Jones Index, 1999 to 2009

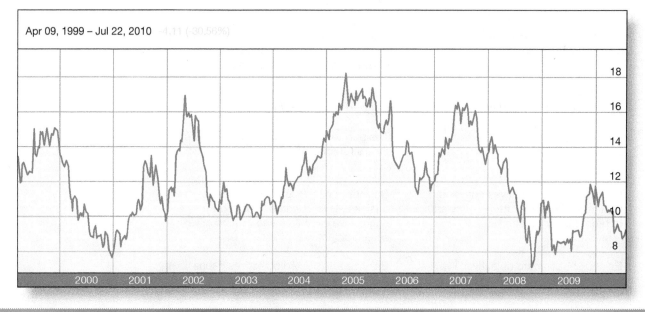

Apr 09, 1999 – Jul 22, 2010

These principles have played out differently in each of the groups. In both the Bakery Products and the Meat Products Groups, MLF has invested heavily in brand development, innovation, and value-added products for markets around the world. In 2002, major organizational changes were made to the Bakery Group, and in 2004 Schneider Foods was acquired and added to the Meat Products Group. In the Agribusiness Group, strategy evolved, going heavily into the overall production of pork in 2000 and then withdrawing starting in 2006.

Around these major strategic events were many smaller moves as individual business units were bought and sold and others were reorganized and sometimes moved from one group to another. These changes are reflected in changes in the organizational structure of the operating companies and groups over time.

Major Strategic Events

Major strategic events are infrequent in business. The history of MLF shows how infrequent they are even in a corporation with many businesses. Four major events in corporate strategy are evident in the sales and employment numbers of MLF (see Exhibit 9.8).

Assembling and Disassembling the Agribusiness Operations (1999 and 2006)

Prior to the creation of Maple Leaf Foods, Canada Packers and Maple Leaf Mills were both vertically integrated in poultry production, starting with producing hatching eggs and ending with processing poultry. After the creation, the agribusiness operations were gradually expanded around the notion that MLF's Meat and Agribusiness combined were in the protein value chain. This chain included the fresh and processed meats, animal nutrition, hog production, and rendering operations.

In 1999, management performed an extensive study of MLF's Protein Value Chain that consisted of businesses in both the Meat Group and the Agribusiness Group. The overall goal was selective expansion in the chain. MLF would own directly 100 percent of certain components of the Protein Value Chain (feed operations, swine genetics, processing, and rendering) but would keep its participation in agricultural production low. In hog production, its target was to have "effective" ownership of only 30 percent of the hogs it slaughtered. In poultry growing, MLF limited direct investment so that it avoided needing the associated poultry quota

required under Canada's supply management system. MLF would vertically coordinate the chain so that it ran as well as if it had been vertically integrated, as some competitors were doing.

Structuring its participation in the value chain in this manner provided Maple Leaf Foods with many advantages. Doing so provided an opportunity for cost synergies, scale economies, and better food safety management. Participating in multiple steps in the chain also provided natural hedging because typically when hog production generates poor returns, processors perform better and vice versa. MLF also required a lower level of capital than a fully integrated production operation because it minimized investment in the low-return production business. And MLF had a secure supply of animals for its meat-processing operations.

Growth would be facilitated because MLF could use the Made in Canada brand image to sell pork and pork products around the world. Many international customers considered Canada a premier producer because of the country's perceived cleanliness and environmental characteristics.

In 2006, management revised the strategy because the sharp rise in the Canadian dollar and depressed global

Exhibit 9.8 Sales and Employment at Maple Leaf Foods, 1996–2008

Sales in Millions of Dollars

| Fiscal Year | Group | | | |
	Meat Products	Agri-business	Bakery Products	Total
1996	1225	1301	684	3210
1997	1612	1398	668	3678
1998	1966	653	663	3282
1999	2113	741	676	3530
2000	2446	846	651	3943
2001	3112	879	784	4775
2002	2900	944	1200	5044
2003	2900	919	1300	5119
2004	4127	925	1313	6365
2005	4102	801	1226	6129
2006	3746	816	1334	5896
2007	3458	241	1511	5210
2008	3304	233	1706	5243

Employment

| Fiscal Year | Group | | | |
	Meat Products	Agri-business	Bakery Products	Total
1996	6352	1700	3992	12 044
1997	5345	1750	4000	11 095
1998	6150	1600	3500	11 250
1999	6276	1817	3473	11 566
2000	8100	1900	3450	13 450
2001	8400	1900	4700	15 000
2002	8600	2100	7300	18 000
2003	8900	2100	7000	18 000
2004	n.a.	n.a.	n.a.	n.a.
2005	14 599	1867	7414	23 880
2006	13 300	2000	8300	23 600
2007	13 300	900	8300	22 500
2008	14 200	900	8500	23 600

prices for pork had seriously eroded the profitability of the protein business in recent years. In October, MLF's management announced the "transformation" strategy aimed at significantly increasing the profitability of protein operations. The new strategy focused on expanding the Meat Group's successful value-added fresh and further processed meat and meals businesses, which attracted high prices so could support a higher cost base. All other operations in the protein value chain, including feed, hog production, and primary processing operations, were sized to support its value-added fresh and further processed meat businesses. At the same time, efforts were made to lower the manufacturing cost base.

The consequences of this new strategy were multiple.

- Hog growing operations shifted from partial ownership to full ownership. This was accompanied by reducing production from 1.5 million hogs annually in 2006 to 820 000 hogs by the end of 2008. As hog production was concentrated in Manitoba, operations in Alberta and Ontario were ended, as was a joint venture in Quebec.

- The animal nutrition business (Shur-gain and Landmark) was sold in 2007 except for two feed mills in Western Canada required to meet internal hog feed requirements.

- The pork processing business focused on supplying raw material needs for processing, reducing the fresh pork produced. This reduced the number of hogs processed from 7.5 million to 4.3 million annually.

- Existing primary pork processing was consolidated into one double-shifted plant in Brandon, Manitoba, and the remaining plants in Lethbridge, Alberta, and Burlington, Ontario, were divested.

- The organizational structure was simplified by integrating five operating companies in the protein value chain into one integrated protein organization.

Restructuring the Bakery Products Group (2002)

MLF had a long-running interest in the baking industry as majority owner of Canada Bread and minority owner of McGavin Foods. Over time, MLF had acquired partial interest in many bakeries and had operations in the United Kingdom and United States.

In 2002, the Baking Group was reorganized. In the previous few years, MLF had taken steps to address the "spaghetti mess" of ownership in its bakery assets, in order to create a cohesive and focused operating unit. This included purchasing the remaining shares of Multi-Marques (2001) and Ben's Bakery (2002). As a final step, in late 2002, Canada Bread, Maple Leaf Bakeries, U.S.A., and Maple Leaf Bakery, U.K., were combined into Canada Bread. In the process, Maple Leaf Foods was given additional shares of Canada Bread, increasing its economic interest to 73.3 percent. The reorganization of the business reflected a North American structure focused on fresh, frozen, and pasta products. Maple Leaf Bakery, U.K., continued to focus on bagels.

Acquisition of Schneider Foods (2004)

The Meat Products Group changed dramatically in 2004 when MLF acquired Schneider Corp. for Cdn$500 million from Smithfield Foods, a hog producer and meat packer in the United States. The acquisition of Schneider Corp. provided MLF with the following advantages:

- Diversified product mix by increasing the amount of processed pork products relative to fresh pork products and increasing market penetration in higher-margin value-added specialty processed meats.

- Enlarged market share at retail outlets in both processed meat and poultry markets.

- Strengthened MLF's leadership position as a low-cost producer by increasing scale economies and improving synergies in production and distribution.

- Strengthened MLF's leadership position in product innovation and development of high-value, high-margin products.

Following the acquisition, Schneider Corp. became the Schneider Food operating division under the leadership of existing Schneider management, including its president, Douglas W. Dodds. Merging of the two operations was completed by 2006.

Changes in Operating Structure

A look at corporate organizational charts over time reveals how the structure of the corporation changed over time as corporate strategy changed and business units were reorganized to bring structure in line with it. While the groups were constant as lines of business, the activities in each of the groups changed considerably over time.

The organizational chart for MLF from 1997 shows the greatest diversity in the range of businesses. Only in 1995 had McCain Capital and the Ontario Teachers' Pension Plan bought control of MLF from Hillsdown Holdings (see Exhibit 9.9).

Following the change in ownership, the management began sharpening focus of MLF by identifying core and non-core operations, as reflected in the organizational chart of 2004 (see Exhibit 9.10). Businesses that were sold included a major real estate development, flour mill, and franchise operations (Country Style Food Services operating under Country Style and Buns Master brand names). Meanwhile, Rendering was shifted from Meat Products to Agribusiness while International Trade moved the other way. In line with the expansion of the protein operations, Pork was now a separate operating unit in Meat Products while Landmark Feeds and Elite Swine had been added to Agribusiness.

Exhibit 9.9 Organization of Maple Leaf Foods Operating Companies, March 1997

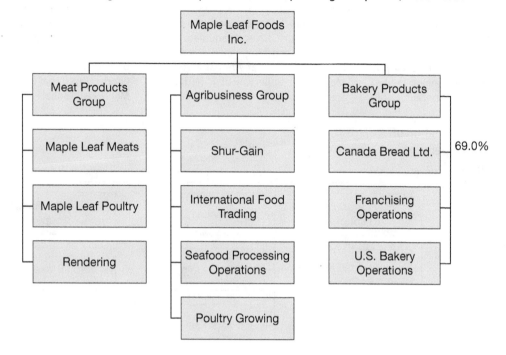

Exhibit 9.10 Organization of Maple Leaf Foods Operating Companies, March 2004

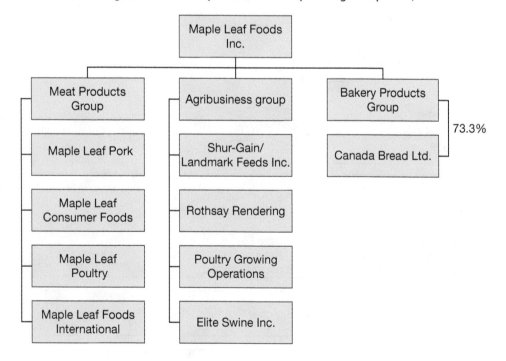

Following the acquisition of Schneider Corporation, it was set up as Schneider Food, a separate operating unit in the Meat Products Group (see Exhibit 9.11).

By 2007, the corporate operating structure was again being revised. In Meat Products, the operating units were no longer by type of meat (poultry and pork) but by form of product (fresh and frozen). In Agribusiness, the operations of Shur-Gain and Landmark Feeds had been combined into a business named Maple Leaf Animal Nutrition. Meanwhile Bakery, which had been steadily growing, had been broken into two operating units based on form (fresh and frozen) (see Exhibit 9.12).

By 2009, MLF focused on producing value-added fresh and further processed meat and meals businesses. Maple Leaf Consumer Foods, Maple Leaf Fresh Foods, and Maple Leaf Global Foods were under

Exhibit 9.11 Organization of Maple Leaf Foods Operating Companies, March 2005

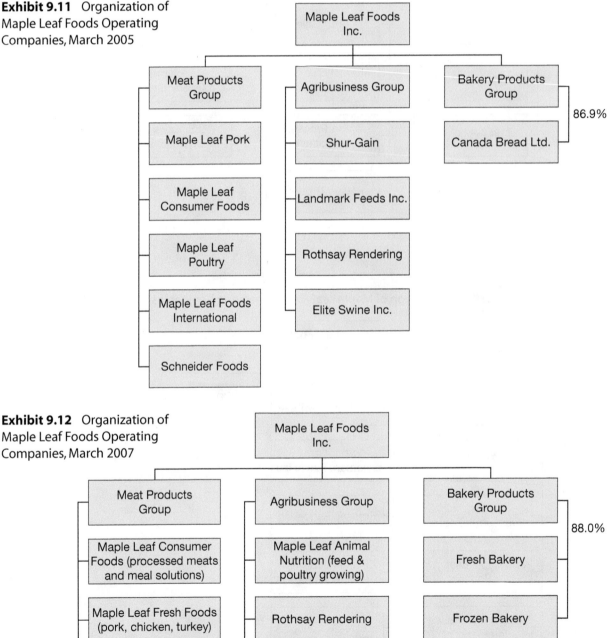

Exhibit 9.12 Organization of Maple Leaf Foods Operating Companies, March 2007

single management as set out in the Transformation Strategy. Furthermore, the poultry operations, from producing hatching eggs to raising chickens and turkeys, had been sold (see Exhibit 9.13).

Changes Along the Way

In a large corporation, many separate businesses are bought and sold over time. These may be operating units but more often they are small businesses that are added to operating units or parts of operating units that are disposed of as operations are rationalized.

The Meat Products Group provides several examples. In 1997, MLF acquired the Burns/Gainers processing facilities in Winnipeg, Edmonton, and Lethbridge. In 1998, MLF commenced construction of a world-class pork processing plant in Brandon, Manitoba. In 2001, MLF purchased two fresh pork operations in Manitoba from Schneider Corporation and then closed one, consolidating primary processing in its Brandon plant. Then in 2000, MLF purchased Hub Meat Packers Ltd. in Moncton, New Brunswick, and Larsen Packers Limited in Berwick, Nova Scotia.

In the Bakery Products Group, following the reorganization in 2002, MLF continued to increase its ownership of Canada Bread, which continued making strategic acquisitions in Canada (Olafson's Baking Company [B.C. in 2002] and Aliments Martel Inc [Quebec in 2008]), in the U.K. (New York Bagel [2002], The French Croissant Company, Avance, UK, and the Harvestime Bakery [2006], and La Fornaia and Bernard Matthews [2007]), and in the U.S. (Grace Baking Company [2002]).

Systems

All businesses, including Canada Bread, operated as a full-fledged operating company in the Maple Leaf group of companies, as complete and equal participants in all MLF's systems, programs, process standards, and business strategies through a common corporate shared service.

HOW WOULD YOU DO THAT?
QUESTIONS

1. Given the continual evolution of the structure of Maple Leaf Foods, how easy would it be for an external observer to determine the performance of particular lines of business? And what are the implications of the continual changes for the managers of lines of business?

Exhibit 9.13 Organization of Maple Leaf Foods Operating Companies, March 2009

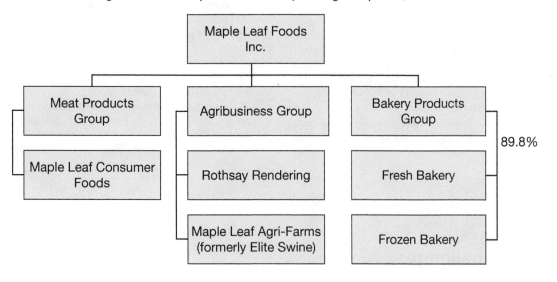

FOCUS ON SUSTAINABILITY 9.1
Husky Injection Molding[38]

Husky has had an honour code since Robert Schad started the company in 1953. This honour code was later supplemented by Husky's *Purpose and Values*. Husky's *Purpose* is "to be a role model of lasting business success based on our core values." The five core *Values* are:

- Make a Contribution;
- Proactive Environmental Responsibility;
- Passion for Excellence;
- Uncompromising Honesty; and
- Bold Goals.

Husky prides itself on "living out" its *Values*, which influence its corporate strategies, form the basis for its business and management practices, and guide the behaviour of employees around the world. Every new employee to the company goes through an extensive orientation, a large part of which deals with understanding the company's *Purpose and Values* and how these translate into company policy and expected behaviour. The company tries to incorporate its *Values* into core business practices wherever possible and is always looking for new opportunities to do this. For example, when Husky draws up plans for a new facility, the environmental and social values of the company are expressed in the design.

Husky participated in one of the first private, public, and First Nations partnerships in Canada, the innovative Moose Deer Point First Nations Community sustainable community project. The project came about because of an experience Schad, Husky's president and majority shareholder, had. Once, when Schad was driving through the Moose Deer Point First Nations reserve on the way to a cottage he owned on the eastern shore of Georgian Bay in Ontario, his car broke down. A young man from the reserve repaired the car. Touched by the young man's generosity, Schad gave thought to what he could do to reach out to this community. He had a vision that the construction of a world-class injection moulding facility on the reserve would help provide economic development and career development opportunities for developing a healthy and prosperous community. Husky could offer valuable insights and expertise to help support this development until the facility could be run independently.

Working with J. Edward Williams, chief of the Moose Deer Point First Nations community, he launched a partnership program with the indigenous peoples through the Schad Foundation (Husky's philanthropy program). With additional funding from both the federal and provincial governments, a state-of-the-art injection moulding facility called Niigon (an Ojibway word meaning "for the future") was constructed on the Moose Deer Point reserve. The facility's design follows Husky's holistic approach to construction and includes a wellness centre, fitness centre, and environmentally sound land use plan. The company is wholly owned by the Moose Deer Point First Nations people, and all employees are residents of the First Nations community. All dividends are reinvested in social, environmental, wellness, and infrastructure projects.

For Husky, the project met all five of the company's values: it makes a contribution, is environmentally proactive, exercises the company's passion for excellence and honesty, and sets bold goals. For the Moose Deer Point First Nations community, Niigon is a win-win situation—it gave a tremendous boost to local economic development by providing close to 70 jobs in the first five years of operation.

If you were a shareholder in Husky, would you approve or disapprove of the way Husky has decided what businesses it is in? Explain your view.

Summary of Challenges

1. *Define corporate strategy.* Corporate strategy encompasses issues related to decisions about entering and exiting businesses. A fundamental part of corporate strategy is the decision about what business *arenas* to enter and exit. However, corporate strategy also encompasses the overall management of the multibusiness enterprise, such as corporate headquarters' efforts to orchestrate the cross-business-unit synergies. Corporate strategy deals with the logic for owning more than one business within a company.

2. *Understand the special challenge of corporate strategy.* The special challenge of corporate strategy is that the management of the corporation has to create a competitive advantage above and beyond that of the businesses in its portfolio in order to justify the existence of the corporation. In other words, corporate management has to find a way to build shareholder value in ways that shareholders cannot by simply owning a portfolio of stock in different businesses.

3. *Identify the different types of diversification.* Companies have several options when expanding the scope of their operations beyond the original business definition. In this chapter, we discussed the concept of related and unrelated diversification. Related diversification could be either horizontal or vertical. Horizontal diversification is increasing the businesses that have similar activities in at least part of their value chain. Vertical integrations is extending the value chain of a business by adding on additional activities in the value stream that the

business participates in. Vertical scope is ownership of business activities along the company's vertical value chain. Horizontal scope, typically called diversification, is the ownership of businesses with value chains that are linked in a value system.

4. *Explain how companies can successfully enter attractive industries when those industries have the greatest barriers to entry.* In the evolution of companies over time, most decide to expand into new businesses. The industries that are the most attractive to entrants are industries that are more profitable on average than others. However, entry barriers make it difficult for companies to enter these industries, so that most new entrants to such industries earn profits far below the industry average, and even below what entrants to unattractive industries earn. To successfully enter an attractive industry, a company needs to orchestrate an indirect assault, not attack the incumbents in their strongholds, such as by entering in a niche segment of the industry. In addition, successful entrants leverage their existing resources and enter with a fundamentally different value chain than incumbents.

5. *Describe the relationship between corporate strategy and competitive advantage.* Competitive advantage at the corporate level is a function of the fit among arenas, resources, and organizational systems, structures, and processes. When these are connected in a coherent fashion, the corporation is more likely to achieve its long-term objectives. When resources are specialized, the company will likely find greater value creation opportunities in a narrow scope of business arenas. Conversely, general resources can be applied across a greater spectrum of businesses. Companies with a broad scope of business activities have different demands for organization structure, systems, and processes than companies that are narrowly focused on a specific set of business arenas.

6. *Explain the differences between corporate strategy in stable and dynamic contexts.* In relatively stable environments, synergies are typically achieved through static definitions of the business-unit arenas and formal structural links among them. Corporate strategy objectives are aimed primarily at using synergies to achieve economies of scope and scale and, in fact, the strategy explicitly defines the form and extent of business units' coordination and collaboration. Companies in dynamic contexts must usually have strong resources and capabilities in the areas of learning, knowledge transfer, and rapid responsiveness for diversification to yield benefits. Otherwise, the nimbleness and responsiveness required of business units in dynamic contexts is dampened as a consequence of corporate ownerships being more of an encumbrance than an advantage. In dynamic environments, allowing managers of business units to pursue a pattern of synergistic relationships that mimics biological coevolution is generally more advantageous than corporate-forced synergistic relationships.

Review Questions

1. How does corporate strategy differ from business strategy?
2. How has the practice of corporate strategy evolved over time?
3. What is a conglomerate?
4. How can managers decide whether they should diversify into a new business?
5. What are the types of diversification and how is value created by each type?
6. What is the difference between economies of scope and synergies?
7. What is the relationship between diversification and company performance?
8. What factors tend to limit the attractiveness of diversification?
9. How does a dynamic industry context affect the possible benefits of diversification?

Experiential Activities

Group Exercises

1. Choose two corporations that have closely diversified strategies—perhaps corporations that you have analyzed as cases in the past. For each corporation, identify its vertical and horizontal scope. Having done this, examine the resources that are necessary for each business arena for the companies. How similar are the resource requirements? Identify the dominant logic in each of their main lines of business (if you picked a very diversified corporation, just deal with the two or three largest business segments). How similar are they across the business divisions?

2. Collect information on the history of Magna Corporation. Using this data, describe over time how the various business units in the company evolved and the strategy of each. Also describe the performance of the corporation as a whole. Then answer whether you would invest in this corporation and justify your reason.

Ethical Debates

1. Textbook publishers face growing competition on numerous fronts, including new models of textbook delivery. One such model provides students with online textbook content for "free" on the condition that students provide personal information about themselves for vendors of credit card, student loan, and cellphone companies. For any publisher that is considering diversification into this new media space, what might be some of the ethical issues?

2. You can imagine that companies in the alcohol, tobacco, or firearms businesses may feel a need to diversify into less scrutinized or regulated businesses. How might ethical issues related to these core businesses affect their ability to enter, or costs of entry, into new businesses? How might these ethical issues affect their ability to exit, or costs of exiting, their traditional businesses?

Endnotes

1. Various years of Annual Reports and Annual Information Forms for BCE Inc. available through System for Electronic Document Analysis and Retrieval (SEDAR) of the Canadian Securities Administrators at www.sedar.com. "Bell Canada." Accessed December 20, 2009, at http://en.wikipedia.org/wiki/Bell_Canada.

2. "Bell Canada." Accessed September 12, 2008, at http://en.wikipedia.org/wiki/Bell_Canada.

3. John R. Baldwin, Desmond Beckstead, Guy Gellatly, and Alice Peters, "Patterns of Corporate Diversification in Canada: An Empirical Analysis," Micro-Economic Analysis Division, Statistics Canada, Ottawa, Paper No. 150, June 2000.

4. Michael Porter, *Competitive Advantage* (New York, Free Press, 1985), p. 320.

5. "K. C. Irving." Accessed December 20, 2009, at http://en.wikipedia.org/wiki/K._C._Irving.

6. "Improving Profitability." Accessed December 20, 2009, at www.daimler.com/Projects/c2c/channel/documents/107950_profitability_e.pdf.

7. "Malibu on a Budget," *BusinessWeek*, February 10, 2003. Accessed December 20, 2009, at www.businessweek.com/magazine/content/03_06/b3819006.htm.

8. Larry MacDonald, *The Bombardier Story* (Toronto: John Wiley and Sons, 2001), p. 156.

9. Dorel Industries Inc., Annual Information Form for the fiscal year ended December 30, 2008, available www.sedar.com.

10. Kaboose Inc., Annual Information Form for fiscal year ended December 31, 2008. Rick Spence, "Krazy Train," *PROFIT* magazine, December 2006. Accessed December 15, 2009, at www.canadianbusiness.com/entrepreneur/managing/article.jsp?content=20061201_143543_5000. In 2009, Disney bought some of the company's assets for US$18.4 million and Barley's Private Equity Ltd. purchased other assets for £54 million in cash less third-party debt outstanding at closing, which was approximately £10 million.

11. "Clifford Produce Poised for More Growth," *Greenhouse Canada*, May 25, 2009. Accessed December 20, 2009, at www.greenhousecanada.com/content/view/1691/67/.

12. Nora Caley, "Stand by Your Brand," *Grocery Headquarters*, October 1, 2009. Accessed December 20, 2009, at http://groceryheadquarters.com/articles/2009-10-01/Stand-by-your-brand.

13. Astrid Van Den Broek, "Merger Will Twin Pizza and Donuts," *Marketing Magazine*, March 20, 2000. Afton went bankrupt in 2004 and Robin's was bought in 2006 by Chairman's Brand Corporation, which owns Coffee Time.

14. "Malibu on a Budget," *BusinessWeek*.

15. "Improving Profitability."

16. MacDonald, *The Bombardier Story*.

17. "RONA unveils new succession-planning program for store ownership," *Hardware and Home Centre Magazine*, November 30, 2009, Accessed December 20, 2009, at www.centremagazine.com/issues/ISArticle.asp?aid=1000349255.

18. Still, the competitors chose to respond at great cost and Super Fresh closed down after several years to be replaced with another concept, Food Basics, that proved very successful and was rolled out across the province. From personal interviews by the author.

19. Sylvia M. Chan-Olmsted, *Competitive Strategy for Media Firms Strategic and Brand Management in Changing Media Markets* (Mahwah, New Jersey: Lawrence Erlbaum Associates 2005), p. 85.

20. Jonathan Ratner, "Shoppers Drug Mart and Jean Coutu May Feel the Heat from U.S." *Financial Post*, June 24, 2008. Canada Press, "McKesson Canada Makes bid for Quebec's Uniprix Pharmacy Group," January 20, 2009. Accessed December 16, 2009, at www.tmcnet.com/usubmit/2009/01/20/3925508.htm. Reuters, "McKesson to Buy Right to Acquire Uniprix Pharmacies." Accessed December 16, 2009, at www.reuters.com/article/idUSN1936779120090119.

21. Dave Shipley, "Irving, Couche-Tard Swing Convenience Stores Deal; Retail Energy Company Handing Over Mainways, Blue Canoes and Big Stops to Que. Firm," *Telegraph-Journal* (Saint John, N.B.), May 9, 2008, p. B.1.

22. Accessed December 20, 2009, at www.onex.com/Principles_and_Values.aspx.

23. Accessed December 20, 2009, at http://forum.prisonplanet.com/index.php?topic=369.130;wap2.

24. "TriMas Corp." Accessed December 20, 2009, at www.fundinguniverse.com/company-histories/TriMas-Corp-Company-History.html.

25. Accessed April 8, 2009, at www.answers.com/topic/red-bull-gmbh.

26. Based on the companies' 10K filings for 2006. The averages over the past decade are consistent with these figures.

27. Silico Research, "Johnson & Johnson Turns to Internal Venturing," July 16, 2007. Accessed December 20, 2009, at http://silico.wordpress.com/2007/07/16/johnson-johnson-turns-to-internal-venturing/.

28. G. Szulanski, R. Cappetta, and R. J. Jensen, "When and How Trustworthiness Matters: Knowledge Transfer and the Moderating Effect of Causal Ambiguity," *Organization Science* 15 (2004): 600–613.

29. C. W. L. Hill, M. A. Hitt, and R. E. Hoskisson, "Cooperative versus Competitive Structures in Related and Unrelated Diversified Firms," *Organization Science* 3 (1992): 501–521.

30. M. Goold and A. Campbell, "Desperately Seeking Synergy," *Harvard Business Review* 76:5 (1998): 131–143.

31. Accessed May 17, 2008, at www.fundinguniverse.com/company-histories/Corel-Corporation-Company-History.html.

32. Kathleen Eisenhardt and Charles Galunic, "Coevolving: At Last, a Way to Make Synergies Work," *Harvard Business Review,* January 1, 2000; S. Brown and K. Eisenhardt, *Competing on the Edge* (Boston: Harvard Business School Press, 1998).

33. Ibid.

34. C. Christensen, *The Innovator's Dilemma* (New York: Harper Collins, 1997).

35. Various Annual Reports and Annual Information Forms for Maple Leaf Foods, 1996–2009, available through System for Electronic Document Analysis and Retrieval (SEDAR) of the Canadian Securities Administrators at www.sedar.com.

36. Annual Information Form for Maple Leaf Foods, 1999, p. 3.

37. Annual Report for Maple Leaf Foods, 2004, p. 8.

38. Husky's story is described in "CSR Case Study: Husky Injection Molding—Determined to Make a Contribution," which is found on the website for the Oil, Gas and Mining Sustainable Community Development Fund. Accessed December 20, 2009, at commdev.org/files/1074_file_husky_e.pdf. Niigon Technologies is found at www.niigon.com/home.htm (accessed December 20, 2009).

10 International Strategy

Dell Goes to China

"Today there are one billion people online worldwide, and many of the world's second billion users are right here in China," said Michael Dell, chairman and chief executive of Dell Inc. "We intend to earn their confidence and their business."[1] Dell was speaking in Shanghai in 2007. At the time, his company was the world's second-biggest PC maker and the third largest in China.

The company entered China in 1995 and by 1999 ranked a distant seventh in PC sales there. This small share bothered Dell executives as China was a growth market with enormous potential while the United States was a maturing market where competition was fierce. Consequently, Dell's executives were eager to expand sales in China. William Bao Bean, an analyst with Deutsche Securities in Hong Kong, said, "Faster sales growth in China could really give Dell a boost because of how big the market is and how much potential it has."[2] By 2005, Lenovo Group held 33 percent of the Chinese market, Founder Technology 12 percent, and Dell, the largest foreign PC vendor, 9 percent.[3] China was Dell's second-largest market in Asia, behind Japan.

Dell had been highly successful since it started in 1984. Much of Dell's success was attributed to its direct sales model, which had customers order computers directly over the internet from Dell. These computers were then made to customer specifications. This approach allowed Dell a just-in-time (JIT) supply chain with lean and cost-effective production facilities. Having direct contact with customers also gave the company better information on what customers wanted, which produced a relationship with customers. Between the low cost of production and the relationship with consumers, Dell grew at a compound annual growth rate (CAGR) of 80 percent for the first eight years, then 60 percent for the next six and was immensely profitable. Even in 2006 Kevin Rollins, then president and CEO of Dell, stressed his company's belief that the direct sales model worked well across the globe, though some critics called it a flop and the president of Dell's Chinese operations had announced his resignation in October 2005.[4]

Dell's approach in the United States had been to build its direct-to-consumer sales using the Dell direct model and to build corporate sales only after it had established a strong, profitable foothold with consumers. Numerous challenges faced Dell in using the direct sales model in a developing country such as China. The first set of challenges related to infrastructure needed to support the model. Few consumers had access to the internet so were not able to order online. Moreover, few consumers had credit cards or credit at all so were unable to pay for orders online. And China lacked a secure, timely, and cost-effective service for delivering goods ordered by customers. A second set of challenges related to cultural differences. Chinese consumers preferred to "see and feel" a product before purchasing it. This is why many of Dell's competitors, such as Lenovo, had retail locations across China. When making a purchase, consumers typically went to a mall or plaza where the electronics merchants had gathered. There, consumers were able to get comparative product information and prices. Chinese consumers were not particularly interested in customization because their culture did not encourage individualism, even if they did appreciate the differences in performance. When making the purchase, Chinese consumers were used to haggling over the price—the price of anything from groceries to properties was negotiable. Given the level of consumer income, price was usually the final deciding factor and consumers favoured low price over superior performance. And by paying in cash, sales taxes were avoided. Third was the business environment. Merchants disliked having to pay fees to credit card companies, and preferred the liquidity provided by cash. Furthermore, a general protectionist attitude favoured local businesses and those that already had an established name in China. In addition the government had influence over purchases while nationalized corporations were favoured through law in "grey areas." It also provided little protection in such areas as copyright infringement. Then in 2008 China phased in higher statutory tax rates for U.S. companies operating in China.

Dell originally used its direct-selling model when it entered China. This worked well with commercial buyers there, but to reach first-time computer consumers, Dell used an Indian distributor. Starting in 2006, Dell opened stores—called "experience stores"—in Chongqing, Nanjing, and Tianjin, which let Chinese consumers touch Dell's products and experience the unique advantages of these products. These stores complemented Dell's direct-selling approach as the markets for PCs changed and customers bought more laptops, which were harder to customize. The stores were only used to display Dell's products; they were not involved in sales. Dell had already opened more than 200 similar stores in the United States, Taiwan, and Japan before opening the stores in China. Michael Dell justified the use of these stores: "The thing I've been saying internally is the direct model is not a religion. It's a great strategy, [and it] works well; there are things we can do with it. But that's not the only thing we can do as a company."

By 2008, Dell was broadening its presence in retail stores in China as well as elsewhere in the world—Dell products were available in more than 12 000 stores around the world. In China it was selling laptop and desktop computers in Suning stores and expanding its relationship with Gome, the number-one consumer electronics retailer in China. Additionally, Dell sold systems in Hontu stores and in several PC chain retailers, including Wuxing, Meicheng, Heng Chang, and Heyong.

The Dell-in-China situation showcases elements of the strategy diamond. In terms of its arena, China was a relatively new market within which Dell targeted certain market segments, or sub-arenas, and used different channels to reach each.

In terms of vehicles, Dell moved beyond its Dell direct sales model—selling computer systems directly to customers through online websites. It showed flexibility by forming alliances with independent distributors, an approach it had learned to use in its earlier entry into India. Dell's plan, as it had been in India, was initially to use local distributors and then to migrate sales to the typical kiosk sales model in which it could employ the Dell direct model. Dell continued using its direct model to reach corporate and government markets in China because this approach provided performance-for-value and maintained a solid relationship with customers.

In terms of staging, Dell's approach in the United States had been to build its direct-to-consumer sales using the direct model and to build corporate sales only after it had established a strong, profitable foothold with consumers. In China, Dell did the opposite, pursuing corporate and government customers with the Dell direct approach and pursuing consumers, at least initially, through distributors.

Finally, Dell's economic logic was that of both scale and scope economies. As a global company, it had the power to buy the best technologies on the best terms. It could use this advantage to compete in China and at the same time further enhance its direct model's footprint on the global computer market.

Dell's experience in China also shows how a company must engage these elements flexibly and entrepreneurially to do business in markets different from their home markets. That is, internationalizing companies face challenges of being global yet local at the same time.

Dell's early success made it the envy of the industry and its low-cost model made it seem invincible. But other companies figured out how to make and sell PCs as cheaply as Dell. The respective market positions of the top five desktop, notebook, and PC makers has HP leading the pack. Dell is no longer the dominant player it once was and is even losing market share in China (see Exhibit 10.1).

The direct selling model was the source of Dell's advantage. It eliminated the need for stocking a physical sales channel and Dell's success with it gave it buying power that it used to squeeze prices down with suppliers. The advantage disappeared as the market for computer equipment changed radically and Dell responded too slowly.

Rivals caught up with Dell's low-price model because Dell's pressure on suppliers for standardization and low costs unintentionally cut costs for its rivals as well. Although Dell was still more efficient by not working through retail outlets, the cost benefits that this

Company	Global Market Share	Annual Sales Growth
Hewlett-Packard	19.90%	7.00%
Acer	13.40%	16.60%
Dell Inc.	12.90%	-5.90%
Lenovo	8.70%	17.20%
Toshiba	9.70%	9.70%
Others	40.00%	-15.80%
Total	100.00%	-7.20%

Exhibit 10.1 Global PC Industry Market Share Comparables as of 2009, Third Quarter[5]

once brought were whittled away. The second factor hurting Dell was that it sold around 85 percent of its machines in the corporate market, but growth in the computer business was coming from the consumer market and emerging countries where Dell's lack of retail presence was a grave disadvantage. The absence of physical stores also limited Dell's attempts to expand beyond PCs into consumer-electronics products such as televisions as other electronics retailers had. Furthermore, rivals such as HP and IBM were able to provide computer equipment as part of a package of services addressing specific business problems. Dell tried to develop a services division to remedy this in part through the acquisition of Perot Systems in 2009. It also cut costs by selling production facilities and laying off staff. ∎

International Strategy

In corporate strategy we concentrated on expanding the company by engaging in various businesses within a country. Now we consider expanding the company's activities into other countries. Entering other countries is challenging because each country presents a different and complex environment making some national markets more attractive than others. Top management has to decide whether the corporation will "go international" and which countries it will enter. Having decided to enter, management then has to select the vehicle of entry. And when the company has activities in multiple countries, top management has to decide how it will integrate and coordinate them. In this chapter we address all these decisions, but before we do this, we need to appreciate the importance of international activity to Canadian business and the pressures that make doing business ever more international.

Internationalization of business activity, more recently called *globalization*, is not new but it has accelerated significantly in recent years as companies take advantage of opportunities created by advances in information and communications technology, substantial decreases in the cost of transportation, the spread of market-based ideologies, and countries' openness to foreign investment and trade. These changes have expanded market boundaries from local, to regional, to national, to international.

Today Canadian companies compete with companies around the world, including foreign-owned companies operating in Canada. This means that management needs to think in terms of **international strategy** even when the Canadian company is simply competing domestically. But there are also many Canadian companies that have chosen to compete internationally and have been very successful at doing so: Bank of Nova Scotia, Bombardier, McCain, Research In Motion (RIM), ShawCor, Talisman Energy, and Toronto Dominion Bank.

international strategy Process by which a company approaches its cross-border activities and those of competitors and plans to approach them in the future.

Many of the largest companies in the world are global companies. Each year *Fortune* magazine provides a snapshot of the largest global behemoths in its list of the top Global 500 based on sales. The top 20 for 2009 are identified in Exhibit 10.2. These companies had revenues greater than many countries' gross domestic product! The top companies are clearly clustered among the oil and gas, automotive, banking, and insurance industries. Wal-Mart and GE stand out as exceptions.[6] But a company does not have to be large to be global. Companies that have become global very early in their lives include Logitech (which was global from inception, starting in Switzerland and California) and Skype (which started in Sweden and went global in a year, and was acquired and then sold by eBay).

Exhibit 10.2 Top 20 Global Companies Based on Revenue[7]

Rank	Company	Primary Industry	Revenues (U.S. $ millions)	Profits (U.S. $ millions)	Country of Head Quarters
1	Royal Dutch Shell	Oil and gas	458 361	26 277	Netherlands/United Kingdom
2	Exxon Mobil	Oil and gas	442 851	45 220	United States
3	Wal-Mart Stores	Retailing	405 607	13 400	United States
4	BP plc	Oil and gas	367 053	21 157	United Kingdom
5	Chevron	Oil and gas	263 159	23 931	United States
6	Total	Oil and gas	234 674	15 500	France
7	ConocoPhillips	Oil and gas	230 764	-16 998	United States
8	ING Group	Financial services	226 577	-1067	Netherlands
9	Sinopec	Oil and gas	207 814	1961	China
10	ToyotaMotor	Automotive	204 352	-4349	Japan
11	Japan Post Holdings	Postal, banking, insurance	198 700	4208	Japan
12	General Electric	Conglomerate	183 207	17 410	United States
13	China National Petroleum	Oil and gas	181 123	10 271	China
14	Volkswagen	Automotive	166 579	6957	Germany
15	State Grid	Electric power transmission	164 136	664	China
16	Dexia Group	Banking	161 269	-4868	Belgium
17	ENI	Oil and gas	159 348	12 917	Italy
18	General Motors	Automotive	148 979	-30 860	United States
19	Ford Motor	Automotive	146 277	-14 672	United States
20	Allianz	Financial services	142 395	-3577	Germany

The example from Dell showed that an international strategy is reflected in all facets of the strategy diamond (see Exhibit 10.3). Notice, for instance, that Dell identified the need to be a global player based on its growth objectives, customer needs, and opportunities to garner new customers. These needs fit with the economic logic of Dell's strategy. They also leveraged Dell's differentiators—relationships with customers and Dell's quality image. Dell then identified China as an important stage for meeting its aspirations to become a global company. Finally, it chose an entry strategy—starting with an alliance with Indian distributors—for staging its entry into China.

Developing a company's international strategy is not a decision taken lightly because competition is fierce. Simply copying what competitors are doing is dangerous because each

Exhibit 10.3 The Five Elements in International Strategy

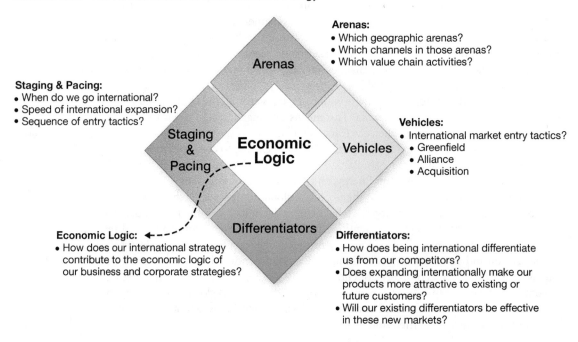

Exhibit 10.4 Your 1-2-3 Model of Internationalization

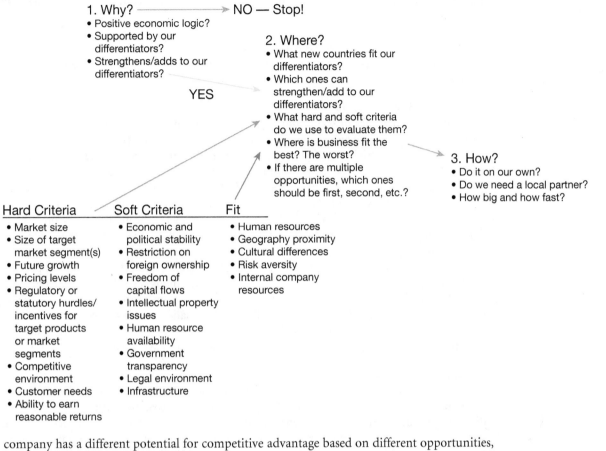

company has a different potential for competitive advantage based on different opportunities, resources, and capabilities. This means that what makes sense for one company may not make sense for another. Careful assessment is needed so that the company pursues those opportunities where it can develop a competitive advantage. This analysis can be structured according to the process in the 1-2-3 model of internationalization presented in Exhibit 10.4. This approach organizes the answers to the strategic questions asked in Exhibit 10.3 into three steps: (1) *Why* should we expand into another geographic arena (is the economic logic compelling and do our differentiators apply)? (2) If so, *where*—which new geographic arena? and (3) If this arena, then *how*—what vehicles will we use, and how should entry be staged and paced? Notice, for instance, that Dell identified the need to be a global player based on its growth objectives, customer needs, and opportunities to garner new customers. These needs fit with the economic logic of Dell's strategy. They also leveraged Dell's differentiators—relationships with customers and Dell's quality image. Dell then identified China as an important stepping stone—or stage—in its global growth aspirations. Finally, it chose an entry strategy—starting with an alliance with Indian distributors—for staging its efforts to do well in the new China market.

Why an International Strategy?

Step 1 of the 1-2-3 model involves deriving the economic logic for considering internationalization. The economic benefit of pursuing internationalization needs to be assessed to validate that it exists and in sufficient amount to more than offset the complexities and risks added by internationalization.

KEY FACTORS IN INTERNATIONAL EXPANSION

The international strategy affects a company's economic logic, found in the strategy diamond. The four most important aspects are *economies of scale and scope, location, multipoint competition,* and *learning.* While most of these aspects are directly related to the economic logic of a company's strategy, they also can contribute to the differentiators. Companies must understand the specific benefits in one or more of these areas before they proceed with international expansion plans.

Global Economies of Scale and Scope

Economic Logic

Being international has implications on both the economies of scale and the economies of scope. ◆

Economies of Global Scale

The potential economies of scale from global expansion include spreading fixed costs over a larger sales and asset base and increasing purchasing power.[8] Attempts to gain scale advantages must be focused on activities and resources that are scale-sensitive. Scale can be achieved when these activities and resources are concentrated in just a few locations.[9] For example, the cost of a semiconductor fabrication plant (more than $1 billion) means that a company with several plants can supply the world market. But the larger scale that accompanies global expansion only creates competitive advantage if the company is able to operate at high levels of production. A large plant operating at half its capacity is unlikely to achieve the economies needed to be competitive.

In some industries, such as pharmaceuticals and aircraft manufacturing, a global presence lets the company generate sufficient sales to spread the enormous cost of new-product development. When the company can amortize those costs across many markets, it lowers its average cost per sale. Companies in these industries that are international have superior performance.[10] Economies of scale can also be realized for intangibles such as a company's brand when it is used in many countries, as Coca-Cola, McDonald's, and RIM have done.

Economies of Global Scope

A specialized form of scope economies is available to companies as they expand globally. Earlier economies of scope were defined as the ability to lower average costs by sharing a resource across different products. Companies operating in several markets are able to pursue economies of scope based on geography. For example, many of the international consumer products companies focus their product development on products to be sold internationally and, when a product proves successful, quickly move to sell in all markets, thereby pre-empting competitors.

Associated with having a global scope is serving customers who have global needs. Many airlines flying international routes want suppliers who can service their needs internationally.

Huge international chains, such as McDonald's, are able to achieve economies of scale through the international appeal of their brands.

LSG Skychefs has operations around the world providing catering for airlines including Alitalia, Alaska, American, Lufthansa, Malaysia, Northwest, SAS, US Airways, United, and Qantas. It is the second-largest airline catering company in the world, behind Gateway Gourmet. LSG Skychefs has also pursued economies of scope in products by extending into other aspects of in-flight service (including the design and sourcing of in-flight equipment, in-flight logistics, in-flight management, onboard retail management) and the management of airport lounges.

Local suppliers may have some advantages over global players in terms of being able to provide more immediate service and greater knowledge of local business practices. These use lower local prices and service levels to force global suppliers to keep prices down and service levels high.

Location

The location of each market (national and regional) that a company operates in has different supply conditions, competitors, demand conditions, and complements. This has implications for the markets that the business wants to participate in.

Some markets are more profitable than others and determining this is done using five-force industry analysis. Knowing which markets are more profitable lets the company focus on these markets. ◆ When products produced in low-cost markets can be sold in a high-priced market, the company is able to practise **arbitrage** between markets. Arbitrage involves buying something in one market at one price and then selling it in another market at a higher price. In current terminology, arbitrage is called "optimizing the supply chain" of international companies. Current practice involves locating production activities where costs are low. Analysis of this requires both an understanding of the value system that the company participates in and information used to perform five-force analysis in the various markets and industries of interest.

◆ **Arenas**

arbitrage Making profit by taking advantage of the price difference between two or more markets.

Gildan Activewear of Montreal is a Canadian company that has optimized its supply chain by moving its production from Canada to Central America, where it uses low labour costs to manufacture fleece, socks, and T-shirts. It has 15 000 production employees in the Dominican Republic, Haiti, Honduras, and Nicaragua with most (60 percent) located at its biggest facility in Rio Nance, Honduras. Selling these products in North America and Europe produced sales of over Cdn$1 billion in 2009—its largest customer was Wal-Mart. Gildan, meanwhile, is seeking to reduce its risk exposure to the U.S. market, which accounts for nearly 90 percent of its sales, by expanding sales into Australia, China, Japan, and New Zealand.

Global steel companies also practice arbitrage as they produce steel slabs where raw materials are cheaper, then shipping the slabs to markets where they will be rolled into steel sheets used to make appliances and cars. For example, in 2003 the cost of making slab steel in Brazil was 40 percent below those of comparable mills in the U.S.[11] In 2006, Dofasco (more recently ArcelorMittal Hamilton) contracted with CST of Brazil (a subsidiary of Arcelor Brazil at the time and more recently ArcelorMittal) to import 800 000 tonnes of steel slabs a year that would be rolled into flat steel for the U.S. automotive industry.[12]

A caveat to building competitive advantage based on arbitrage opportunities is that the benefit is often fleeting. Other companies quickly move into the low-cost location unless the first company has erected barriers to entry. This was evidenced when North American companies moved production to Mexico after the North American Free Trade Agreement came into effect in 1994. Not many years later China became the lowest cost location for production and companies looking for low costs moved there. For example, in 1998 Huffy moved production from a unionized plant in Ohio to a nonunionized plant in Missouri. Then in 1999 it moved production to contracted factories in China and Mexico and in 2001 ended contracts in Mexico and began relying almost entirely on factories in China.[13] Therefore, a company relying on arbitrage as a core part of its competitive strategy must be continually identifying new arbitrage opportunities as well as increasing entry barriers for competitors trying to follow it.

Multipoint Competition

Companies can develop competitive advantages through multipoint competition. **Multipoint competition** occurs when a company competes against another company in multiple product markets or multiple geographic markets (or both). For instance, Procter & Gamble and Unilever not only compete head to head in personal care products around the globe; they also compete in the soaps and detergents markets. When a company competes in multiple markets, a special

multipoint competition When a company competes against another company in multiple product markets or multiple geographic markets (or both).

kind of multipoint tactic, the stronghold assault, becomes possible. A *stronghold assault* refers to the competitive actions a company takes in another company's key markets, particularly when the attacking company has little presence in that market. In the case of international strategy, stronghold assault refers to attacks on the geographic markets that are most important to a competitor's profitability and cash flow. A classic example of international stronghold assault are the actions of French tire manufacturer Michelin and the U.S. tire company Goodyear in the 1970s.[14] Before then, both companies had negligible market presence in each other's respective domestic markets (Europe and the United States). Michelin became aware of Goodyear's intent to expand its presence in Europe, so it shipped tires to the United States, where it sold them at or below its actual cost. Michelin did not care whether it made money on these sales because they were a minuscule part of Michelin's overall sales. Michelin's sales tactic forced Goodyear to drop its prices in the United States, lowering the profitability of its largest market. But Michelin's low-pricing tactic caused its sales to grow in the U.S., forcing it to make its U.S. operations efficient so that it could be profitable in the U.S. market—one of the auto industry's largest markets. Meanwhile Goodyear started selling tires in Michelin's home markets, further eroding the profitability of both companies. Eventually, both ended up in the international courts charging each other with "dumping"—selling goods below cost in a foreign country. The Michelin–Goodyear war left the industry landscape forever changed, and both companies had to adjust their strategies to survive in the new international industry they had helped create.

Assaulting a competitor's stronghold is used both to underprice a product in the other's home market and to eliminate the assaulter's home market monopoly. Even today, these reasons motivate global investment, but as the Michelin case highlights, it must be used with care and can be countered. Companies employing this tactic are wise to have strategies in the staging component of the strategy diamond for shifting from price competition to more sustainable bases of competition.

Knowledge

Participating in foreign markets provides challenges and experiences that can produce new knowledge. This knowledge can be beneficial to the company when it is used to improve existing products and processes and create new products. Michelin, the French tire company, benefited from buying UniRoyal Goodrich. While the purchase gave Michelin considerable market volume, Michelin also learned marketing practices from UniRoyal Goodrich that it has since employed successfully in its tire business elsewhere in the world. Dell learned that its direct selling model was ineffective in China and since then has gone to selling much more product through stores. S.C. Johnson is another company that benefited from what it learned as a result of international operations. Its European operations developed a product that delivered household pesticides using a simple plug-in device. S.C. Johnson took this technology from its European operations and used it in its U.S. fragrance division to produce Glade Plug-Ins, a whole new category of air fresheners.[15]

Sometimes, the company can benefit from simply sharing knowledge that already exists in particular locations. First it identifies best practices, then it makes sure that the businesses in each country adopt them. An example of the benefit of sharing best practices is illustrated by an experience at British Petroleum (BP). The U.S. business that operates convenience stations was looking for ways to reduce costs in BP stores. Operations in the Netherlands and the United Kingdom had developed practices that reduced working-capital requirements (mostly inventory). Copying these practices and implementing them in the United States resulted in a 20 percent reduction in working capital.

Developing knowledge through foreign experiences can be encouraged by locating a business or a particular aspect of company operations in a part of the world where competition is the fiercest, where technology is developing fastest, and where consumer trends are set. Most innovations in technology-driven industries occur overwhelmingly in technology clusters because of unique features of the location such as nearby universities and government incentives as well as the mobility of individuals to move among and communicate with employees in other competitors. By "being there," the company is aware of and likely on the leading edge of new technology. This is why so many companies have located in California's Silicon Valley. Similarly, DuPont and W. L. Gore & Associates have locations in France and Italy, where the leaders in the high-fashion industry are found. By being in such locations, the companies learn about future customer preferences (e.g., touch, feel, colour, etc.) that they need to incorporate in their products (Lycra and Gore-Tex) so that they stay on the leading edge.

From the perspective of knowledge, the most important markets strategically are those that feature an opportunity to learn and innovate in ways that can improve the organization's operations, products, and services around the globe.[16]

THE CONS OF INTERNATIONAL EXPANSION

International expansion is no panacea for corporate-growth needs. It is inherently hazardous even when it promises revenue opportunities. For instance, at the beginning of the 1990s, PepsiCo established an ambitious goal to increase its international sales from US$1.5 billion to US$5 billion in just five years. PepsiCo aggressively pursued this growth, yet Pepsi's international market share actually shrank while Coke's share increased.[17] Wal-Mart had similar experiences. While Wal-Mart is typically at the top of *Fortune*'s list of the largest global companies, its non–U.S. operations have not done well, leading the company to exit Germany and to close 20 stores in Japan. The lesson is that global expansion can detract from profitability just as easily as it can contribute to profitability. This demonstrates that simply participating in international markets is not enough. One also needs to have a competitive advantage in order to exploit international opportunities. When assessing the economic logic of internationalizing, costs must also be considered. These costs include foreignness and governance.

Foreignness Costs

Foreignness has two dimensions: being new to the market and being new in the market. New to the market means that the overall competitive situation is uncertain. This disadvantage may be cultural, in that the company's managers do not understand local market conditions. Swiss Chalet had such an experience when it located restaurants in the northeastern United States. It advertised its rotisserie cooked chicken as barbecued while U.S. customers expected barbecued chicken to be covered with a sweet, tangy sauce. When they tried the chicken, they were highly disappointed because the chicken did not meet their expectations for taste. Meanwhile Tim Hortons' U.S. expansion was slowed down by lack of brand awareness and limited interest in hockey.[18] Management has to make decisions when it has only limited information about the market and so is feeling its way and needs to respond to the unexpected. Over time this cost will diminish as management gains experience with the market.

New in the market means that the business has the typical challenges of revenues and cost. Revenue can be affected as the market is not developed for the product and because competitors react aggressively to the new entrant, limiting the amount of business it can capture. Cost can be affected because entry has high investment costs and operating costs are high due to low initial volume both in terms of scale and experience. Establishing operations in a new country requires developing the logistics of purchasing, installing facilities, hiring and training staff, and establishing internal management systems and building external business networks. The high costs of a new operation can put a new entrant at a serious competitive disadvantage relative to local or more established foreign competitors. Hence the reactions of the established competitors are most serious and most likely to be successful driving the entrant out soon after entry. The cost of being new in the market will diminish as the business gains market share and so has staying power.

Governance Costs

While the disadvantages of newness decline over time, the costs of governance and coordination tend to increase as internationalization increases. The simple requirement of setting up a separate local entity creates cost and adds complexity. This business needs to be coordinated with the rest of the company, even if the only connection is cash flows. More often coordination of various additional activities of the company is needed. Even when the issues are simply technical, this can prove a problem. Airbus, in designing its A380, had teams designing parts of the plane in Germany and Spain using version 4 of CATIA design software, while the French and British offices had upgraded to version 5 of CATIA. This caused overall design problems because while the designers assumed copper conductors, the wiring harnesses (which included 530 kilometres of cables, 100 000 wires and 40 300 connectors) were manufactured using aluminum.

Exhibit 10.5 Costs and Benefits of Internationalization

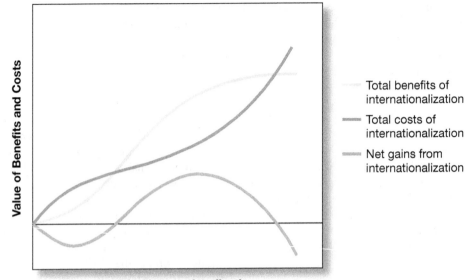

Total benefits of internationalization

Total costs of internationalization

Net gains from internationalization

Level of Internationalization

Design differences were not easily transferred between versions of the software so the failure of parts to fit together only became apparent when components were brought together for assembly. The mismatch caused a production delay of two years.[19] Beyond simple technical issues are human factors. People may not transfer data in a timely manner and may distort it. This creates coordination difficulties and possible misalignment between headquarters and divisional managers. The difficulty and cost of coordinating operations increases as the business enters more countries because every country has a relatively unique business environment.

Maximizing Benefits Subject to Costs

The benefits and costs associated with internationalization are shown in Exhibit 10.5.[20] A company's level of internationalization, shown on the horizontal axis, refers to the degree to which it has tapped foreign markets, particularly for product or service sales. The potential economic benefits of internationalization are modest at first and then grow to become quite significant before the marginal benefits level off. These potential increases in revenue must be balanced with the costs of internationalization. Costs are significant in early efforts to internationalize. After a presence is established, economies of scale and scope kick in, and the incremental costs of further expansion are minimal. However, governance costs can increase with higher levels of internationalization. This increase in costs is similar to diseconomies of scale and scope. The consequence is that performance gains from internationalization come only at moderate to high levels of internationalization; however, at very high levels of internationalization, companies tend to suffer performance declines.[21] The tradeoff between costs and benefits of internationalization results in an S-curve relationship between internationalization and company performance. At a practical level, the goal of managers is to exploit the benefits of economies of scale and scope, location, and knowledge while keeping down the offsetting costs of internationalization.

Where to Grow Internationally

Having thought about why the company will have a competitive advantage as it internationalizes, the second step is determining where the company will put its assets and capabilities to work. The logical place for a Canadian company to first go international is in a market where other Canadian companies already have a market or where it buys inputs because this indicates economic relationships. For most Canadian companies this is the United States. Both countries have a friendly business environment, similar markets, and are in close proximity. Not surprisingly, the United States took 76 percent of Canada's exports and provided 63 percent of Canada's imports in 2008. Canada has been an important source of vehicles and energy to the

United States while the United States has been an important source of vehicles, machinery, and commercial services (see Exhibit 10.6). And cross-border sales of services are also significant. Majority U.S.–owned affiliates in Canada sold services worth Cdn$88.8 billion while majority Canada-owned companies sold services in the United States worth Cdn$53.4 billion in 2006. For the foreseeable future the United States will continue to be a significant market into which Canadian companies will expand. But growing markets in the expanding European Union, South America, and Asia present new opportunities. For example, strong growth is forecast in developing markets, in particular in the so-called BRIC countries (Brazil, Russia, India, and China), where Canada has very limited presence. When these countries are compared to the developed countries, the size of their markets can be appreciated (see Exhibit 10.7). As the economies of the developing countries grow, they are expected to create a vast middle class of many millions of new consumers. These markets are estimated to account for as much as 50 percent of the world economy in the coming generation. As they grow, these developing countries are giving rise to a new breed of savvy global competitor. They are shaking up entire industries, from farm equipment and refrigerators to aircraft and telecom services, and changing the rules of global competition.[22]

Given the opportunities that present themselves, a method is needed to prioritize which markets are the ones that a company should enter. One approach developed by professor and global strategist Pankaj Ghemawat is the CAGE framework (Culture, Administration, Geography, and Economics).[23] The key strength of this tool is that it takes the company's home base and considers the "distance" between that country and other countries the business could enter. Distance is measured in terms of differences and similarities on the four categories of CAGE that are similar to those in the PESTEL model. The greater the distance between different

	Canada's Imports from the United States in Billions	United States' Imports from Canada of U.S.$'s
Total Imports from the Other	$261.1	$339.5
Vehicles	$45.5	$47.5
Machinery	$41.4	$21.7
Electrical Machinery	$24.2	$10.0
Oil and Natural Gas	$16.8	$115.8
Plastic	$11.6	$10.7
Agricultural Products	$16.2	$18.0
Private Commercial Services	$42.9*	$24.7*
* For 2007		

Exhibit 10.6 Trade between Canada and the United States in 2008[24]

Exhibit 10.7 Comparative Country Information of the Top 10 Markets by Population

Country	Est. Population 2007	Labour Force	Internet Users	GDP (in $ millions)	Average GDP Real Growth Rate (%)
China	1 321 851 888	798 000 000	123 000 000	10 000 000	10.50
India	1 129 866 154	509 300 000	60 000 000	4 042 000	8.50
European Union	460 827 146	222 700 000	247 000 000	12 820 000	2.80
United States	301 139 947	151 400 000	205 327 000	12 980 000	3.40
Indonesia	234 693 997	108 200 000	16 000 000	935 000	5.40
Brazil	190 010 647	96 340 000	25 900 000	1 616 000	2.80
Pakistan	164 741 924	48 290 000	10 500 000	427 300	6.50
Bangladesh	150 448 339	68 000 000	300 000	330 800	6.10
Russia	141 377 752	73 880 000	23 700 000	1 723 000	6.60
Nigeria	135 031 164	48 990 000	5 000 000	188 500	5.30

countries, the greater the risk exposure in entering them. Using the CAGE framework makes differences visible, helps one understand the liability of newness, and discounts market size by distance. Ghemawat believes that the framework is most fruitfully applied at the industry level because greater specificity is possible at that level of analysis.

THE CAGE FRAMEWORK

CAGE framework Tool that considers the dimensions of culture, administration, geography, and economics when assessing the distance between different markets.

The **CAGE framework** is demonstrated in Exhibit 10.8.[25] Under each of the categories, certain attributes create distance and in turn distance implies differences in industries and the products they produce and the services they provide. Using the approach, one assesses the degree of differences in various attributes and the implications of these differences for the company moving into each foreign market.

Taking the four dimensions of distance into account can dramatically change one's assessment of foreign markets. Tricon Restaurants International, the company that manages the Pizza Hut, Taco Bell, and KFC chains, had to decide how to reduce its portfolio of operations in 27 countries to something that was more manageable given its limited operating cash flow in the late 1990s after PepsiCo set it up as an independent company. Analysis based on per capita income showed that affluent people were more likely to consume fast food and that they also consumed more of it on a per capita basis. By these criteria countries such as Canada, Germany, Japan, and the United Kingdom appeared very attractive. Applying the CAGE approach, which considered many more factors, changed the attractiveness of particular countries considerably. When fast-food consumption numbers were adjusted for their geographic distance from Tricon's headquarters in Dallas, Canada and Mexico became much more important. The importance of these two markets was further enhanced by the common land borders and the North American Free Trade Agreement. Mexico's use of the Spanish language had a

Exhibit 10.8   The CAGE Framework

Cultural Distance	Administrative Distance	Geographic Distance	Economic Distance
Attributes Creating Distance			
Different languages	Absence of colonial ties	Physical remoteness	Differences in consumer incomes
Different ethnicities: lack of connective ethnic or social networks	Absence of shared monetary or political association	Lack of a common border	Differences in costs and quality of:
Different religions	Political hostility	Lack of sea or river access	• natural resources
Different social norms	Government policies	Size of country	• financial resources
	Institutional weakness	Weak transportation or communication links	• human resources
		Differences in climates	• infrastructure
			• intermediate inputs
			• information or knowledge
Industries or Products Affected by Distance			
Products have high linguistic content (TV)	Government involvement is high in industries that are:	Products have a low value-of-weight or bulk ratio (cement)	Nature of demand varies with income level (cars)
Products affect cultural or national identity of consumers (foods)	• producers of staple goods (electricity)	Products are fragile or perishable (glass, fruit)	Economies of standardization or scale are important (mobile phones)
Product features vary in terms of size (cars), standards (electrical appliances), or packaging	• producers of other "entitlements" (drugs)	Communications and connectivity are important (financial services)	Labour and other factor cost differences are salient (garments)
Products carry country-specific quality associations (wines)	• large employers (farming)	Local supervision and operational requirements are high (many services)	Distribution or business systems are different (insurance)
	• large suppliers to government (mass transportation)		Companies need to be responsive and agile (home appliances)
	• national champions (aerospace)		
	• vital to national security (telecom)		
	• exploiters of natural resources (oil, mining)		
	• subject to high sunk costs (infrastructure)		

negative effect on its overall attractiveness. The overall consequence of considering distance was that Canada was very attractive and Mexico was tied with the United Kingdom for second place. Having analyzed the country attractiveness, Tricon then considered how its own characteristics affected its distance from foreign markets. Many company-specific features made Mexico even more attractive as a market: It already owned more than four-fifths of its Mexican outlets and had a 38 percent share of the local market.[26] Let's now examine each dimension of CAGE so we better appreciate what is considered in each component.

Cultural Distance

Culture, the first facet of CAGE, can be the most perplexing aspect to deal with because it has a sometimes invisible but indelible influence on people's values and behaviours. *Cultural distance*, examines differences in the way individuals from different countries observe certain values and demonstrate certain behaviours.

Researchers have identified significant cultural differences among countries. Among them, for instance, Geert Hofstede drew together distinct cultural differences around the following dimensions:

- **power distance:** the extent to which individuals accept the existence of inequalities between subordinates and superiors within a hierarchical structure),
- **uncertainty avoidance:** individuals' willingness to coexist with uncertainty about the future,
- **individualism:** how the individuals in a society value individualistic behaviours as opposed to collective ones,
- **predominant values:** regarding quantity or quality of life, that is, whether more importance is given to material aspects or a stronger emphasis is laid on interpersonal relationships, and
- **long-term or short-term orientation:** the focus on future rewards or the concern about the maintenance of the stability related to the past and the present.[27]

A cross-section of these cultural dimensions for a sampling of developed and developing countries around the world is presented in Exhibit 10.9.

In Exhibit 10.9, the United States has one of the highest scores for individualism, which its culture encourages. This can be contrasted with China and Korea, where individualism is very low as the interests of society are seen coming ahead of those of the individual. In Germany, culture is not as individualistic as the United States, which is reflected in both the expectation and institutions that protect workers from layoffs.

Exhibit 10.9 Cultural Differences among Countries

Country	Power Distance	Individualism	Masculinity	Uncertainty Avoidance	Long-term Orientation
Arab World*	80	38	52	68	NA
Brazil	69	38	49	76	65
China	80	20	66	30	118
Germany	35	67	66	65	31
India	77	48	56	40	61
Japan	54	46	95	92	80
Philippines	94	32	64	44	19
South Korea	60	18	39	85	75
Sweden	31	71	5	29	33
United Kingdom	35	89	66	35	25
United States	40	91	62	46	29

*Hofstede estimated these values for the region comprised of Egypt, Iraq, Kuwait, Lebanon, Libya, Saudi Arabia, and United Arab Emirates. Long-term orientation was not included in his estimates.

Administrative Distance

Administrative distance reflects the historical and present political and legal associations between trading partners; for example, colonial ties between trading partners, or participation in common trading blocs. To determine administrative distance, historical or current political factors that might favour or impede a business relationship between a company and a new country market are examined. As you can imagine, trade practices between countries can be significantly affected by laws and regulations enacted at the national or international level. Because they affect fundamental business practices, they often affect the competitive position of companies as well. Some of the key legal considerations for Canadian companies include the following:

- **Free Trade Agreements.** The North American Free Trade Agreement (NAFTA) initiated by Canada, Mexico, and the United States in January 1994 formed the world's largest free trade area. Tariffs on goods and services covered under the agreement were fully eliminated on January 1, 2008. As part of NAFTA negotiations, side agreements were reached on environmental and labour cooperation. The environmental agreement requires that each party ensures its laws provide for high levels of environmental protection without lowering standards to attract investment. The labour agreement facilitates greater cooperation on labour and promotes the effective enforcement of each country's labour laws and regulations. In spite of NAFTA, the United States continues to actively use trade policy to protect its national industries, sometimes at the expense of Canadian industry. Since 2001, the United States has been "thickening" the Canada–U.S. border as a result of a U.S. preoccupation with security and international terrorism and this has restricted trade.

- **Import Laws.** The World Trade Organization has worked to reduce barriers to trade but many still exist. Some are quota and tariff-based—note that economists view a quota as having an equivalent tariff. The first type of policy is voluntary export restraint, which generally gives rise to a negotiated import quota that is enforced by the exporting country. Canada, for example, agreed to limit its exports of softwood to the United States. The second type is antidumping and countervailing tariffs. Antidumping tariffs are applied on a country-specific basis when a government finds evidence that exporters from one or more countries may be selling their goods in the home country's domestic market below their average cost. Countervailing tariffs are applied on a country-specific basis when the government finds evidence that a foreign government is giving an exporting industry an unfair advantage, often in the form of subsidies or tax breaks. In addition, numerous laws and standards are set nationally to protect public health, public safety, and national security. These are called non-tariff barriers to the extent that they restrict trade among nations.

- **Foreign Corrupt Practices.** Canadian companies that conduct business with foreign governments or companies are at risk for problems associated with corrupt practices. In force since 1999, Canada's Corruption of Foreign Public Officials Act (CFPOA) contains both anti-bribery and accounting provisions.[28] Its counterpart in the U.S. is the Foreign Corrupt Practices Act (FCPA), which has anti-bribery provisions that apply to U.S. public and private companies, and U.S. and foreign companies registered with the Securities and Exchange Commission (SEC), including Canadian companies. Also covered are foreign persons acting in the United States. There is no materiality test to this act, which makes it illegal to offer even a penny as a bribe. The government focuses on the intent of the bribery more than the amount of it. Violations of the CFPOA and FCPA can result in fines, imprisonment, and regulatory sanctions for companies and their individual officers, directors, employees, and agents acting on their behalf.

- **Accounting Standards.** Canada has accounting standards that companies must adhere to. And when there is any relationship with the United States, its standards may also apply. Hence, Canadian companies that are publicly traded or have a U.S. footprint and that conduct business in foreign jurisdictions seek to comply with both the Canadian and the U.S. legislation as well as with all applicable local legislation in their countries of operation. The overall standards are evolving, however, due to the development of international financial accounting standards.

- **Intellectual Property Protection.** A patent provides the party filing for it the exclusive right to the idea for a limited period of time. A patent is only valid in the country that granted it, so that innovators seeking to protect their invention in other countries must file for a patent in each country. The Patent Cooperation Treaty (PCT) was created to provide an efficient and cost-effective way to enter into the patenting process in up to 127 countries at one time. While the PCT process does not result directly in the issuance of any national patents, an applicant for a patent in any of the signatory countries may file a patent application within one year in any of the other signatory countries and claim the benefit of the filing date in the first county. This also lowers the cost of filing in multiple countries before the market value of the patent is realized. Despite international attention to the importance of intellectual property rights, their protection remains problematic in many developing countries.

  Most Canadian companies first patent inventions in the U.S. and sometimes do not even bother patenting it in Canada. This is understandable given that Canada represents only about 2 percent of the total sales of most technology products while the U.S. is the world's largest market for technology. This "invent here, sell there" approach is very different for U.S. companies, which invent, patent, and sell in the U.S. An implication is that Canadian companies benefit from a stronger global patenting system.

  Several realities put interesting twists on patents for Canadian businesses. First, a patent is only as good as one's willingness to finance legal action to pursue those who are violating the patent. Second, the U.S. showed its willingness to use its patent law to benefit its industries. During court proceedings initiated in 2002 by NTP Research against Research In Motion (RIM) and concluded in 2006, a U.S. court took the unprecedented step of expanding the rights of a U.S. patent owner to cover RIM's activities taking place in Canada. Third, the granting of controversial patents by the U.S. Patent and Trademark Office to companies has led them to seek to extract royalties and licensing fees by alleging that their patents have been infringed upon.

- **Taxation.** When companies operate in more than one country, they often trade products, components, and services back and forth. Companies have an incentive to seek to place their profits in the country where taxes on profits are lowest. They try to accomplish this by requiring operations in the high tax locations to pay high prices for goods they buy from company operations elsewhere and having them receive low prices for what they sell to operations elsewhere. Tax authorities seek to prevent companies from shifting profits in this way by making their own determination of what the company's transfer prices should be across countries. For a company to apply and administer its transfer pricing regime, it has to have special expertise in many areas, including international tax, economics, and the industry.[29]

- **Investment Review.**[30] The Investment Canada Act (ICA) provides for federal government review of foreign investments in Canada. Under the ICA, direct acquisitions by non-Canadians that take control of Canadian businesses are subject to notification to Industry Canada or the Department of Canadian Heritage. Investments are subject to review and require ministerial approval if asset value exceeds a monetary threshold. In 2008, this threshold was Cdn$295 million unless the business acquired was engaged in specific industries (financial services, transportation services [including pipelines], uranium mining, and cultural businesses), in which case the threshold was Cdn$5 million.

  Canada is one of only a few countries (Australia being another) with a formal investment review process for foreign acquisitions that exceed prescribed monetary thresholds. This approach is more explicit and visible than the approach adopted in many other countries that employ informal barriers to foreign investment. These range from state-owned enterprises and special government rights in certain companies to overt political interference in the engineering of "national champions."

  Although from 1985 through 2008 (23 years) not a single acquisition subject to approval had been denied, in 2008 the government denied the proposed US$1.3 billion acquisition of MacDonald, Detwiller and Associates Ltd. (MDA) by Alliant Techsystems. MDA's space division developed the Canadarm, which is used by NASA, and the Radarsat 2 satellite, which scans Canada's Arctic region. The acquisition was denied because it did not pass the "net benefit to Canada" test.

Geographic Distance

Geographic distance deals with how far apart trading partners are in physical terms: the size of the country, differences in climates, and nature of transportation and information networks. You can think of *geographic distance* as absolute, in terms of the miles or kilometres that separate a company from another market or supplier. Technology, however, has shrunk distance in terms of transportation time, most dramatically through the introduction of the shipping container. The first purpose-built ships to carry containers began operation in Denmark in 1951, but it was not until 1956 that U.S. trucking entrepreneur Malcom McLean started using large containers that were never opened in transit between shipper and consignee and that were transferable on an intermodal basis, among trucks, ships, and railroad cars. Today, approximately 90 percent of non-bulk cargo worldwide moves by containers stacked on transport ships in some 18 million total containers that make more than 200 million trips per year.[31]

The technology of digitalization has also reduced the impact of geographic distance as a constraint of trade for some industries. For example, the internet provided W.W. Grainger, a leader in the U.S. maintenance, repair, and overhaul (MRO) industry, with a vehicle for selling into the European markets. Prior to the internet it could not justify an investment in a far-flung European brick-and-mortar presence. With the internet, it was able to provide European customers with a virtual storefront.

Economic Distance

Finally, *economic distance* captures fundamental differences relating to income, the distribution of wealth, and the relative purchasing power of segments of a geographic market. Economic distance has been a major barrier to companies that have been successful selling products in developed markets that then want to sell in emerging markets. What these companies have to do is recognize the economic distance (the 4 billion people who live on less than $2 per day are said to be "at the bottom of the pyramid") and then overcome it by developing products that consumers in emerging markets can afford. An example is of a product marketed by Hindustan Lever (part of the Unilever family of companies): a shampoo that works best with cold water since poor people often lack access to hot water.

In the following How Would You Do That? 10.1, you can see a sample per country per capita income difference for a cross-section of countries. This data will give you a sense of the income that individuals or companies may have to spend on a new product or service. At the same time, you should gain an understanding of the pricing for comparable products or services.

An important economic factor for Canadian companies is the exchange rate with foreign currencies, particularly with respect to the U.S. dollar. The direction of expansion by Canadian companies has been strongly influenced by the exchange rate between Canadian and U.S. dollars (see Exhibit 10.10). From 1958 through 1960, the Canadian dollar was greater than the U.S. dollar, but since then the trend was downward, reaching a low of US$0.64 in 2002. As the Canadian dollar declined, Canadian manufacturing was ever lower cost and Canada enjoyed a large trade surplus as the advantage went to Canadian exporters. Some Canadian companies grew complacent and did not control costs as well as they might have. Meanwhile, U.S. companies found that they could buy Canadian companies for less. Since then the Canadian dollar has rallied to US$0.94 in 2008. This dramatic rise has decreased the cost competitiveness of Canadian products in the United States, making manufacturing in the United States more favourable. The increase in the Canadian dollar relative to the U.S. dollar occurred so quickly that companies struggled to make the necessary adjustments to their operations at the same pace, and some were not able to cope. In 2010, with the exchange rate near parity, the cost advantage is gone and Canada's poor productivity performance is exposed. However, Canadian companies that rely on imported products have benefited from the lower prices of import as determined in Canadian dollars.

Economic distance also includes the economics of supply for comparable or substitute products in a market. For instance, processed cheese (such as Velveeta) tends to cost less than fresh cheese in U.S. supermarkets, and low relative price is a key selling point for processed cheese. A recent U.S. entrant to the Brazilian cheese market assumed this same price relationship. After setting up its factory, however, it found that high-quality fresh cheese was cheap and readily available in Brazilian supermarkets. The company assumed wrongly that it would have a price advantage, when in fact the economics of cheese production in Brazil made processed cheese a higher priced product that consumers found less attractive.

Exhibit 10.10 The Value of the Canadian Dollar Expressed in US Dollars[32]

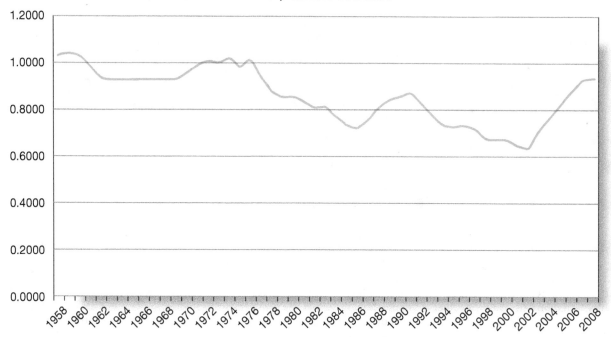

Based on the CAGE-adjusted CAP calculated for Virgin in How Would You Do That? 10.1 (see page 270), for instance, you would probably recommend that Virgin Mobile should think about entering the U.S. market. Beyond this work, a full analysis could consider how a company's own characteristics operate to increase or reduce distance from foreign arenas. ◆ Companies with a large cadre of cosmopolitan managers, for instance, will be less affected by cultural differences than companies whose managers are all from the home country. Other company characteristics can help or hurt as well. In Virgin's case, consideration of company-specific features makes the United States even more attractive. For instance, Virgin's parent company, Virgin Atlantic Airways, has a pretty sexy image in the United States, particularly in the demographic that would be the ideal target market for Virgin Mobile. Despite starting well behind companies such as Orange or Vodafone in the United Kingdom, Virgin has become the fastest-growing cellphone provider in that country, with more than 700 000 customers added in its first 15 months of operation.

Economic Logic

What we have learned by using CAGE in the context of Dell and Virgin Mobile is that the CAGE framework can be used to address the questions of where to expand internationally (which arena) and how to expand (by which vehicle). ◆ It can also help map out the staging and pacing of strategic international expansion moves so as to maximize the strategy's anchoring in the company's VRINE-based resources and capabilities.

Arenas

The CAGE-based logic appears to be at work in recent moves by Indian and Chinese competitors. For instance, Chinese technology-based companies such as Lenovo are offering their products (laptops in Lenovo's case), but outsourcing the service side to English-speaking Indian companies. In contrast, a number of Indian companies have bought third- and fourth-tier U.S. or European manufacturers and used their proximity to China to outsource production to China. The chapter opening vignette about Dell further demonstrates the usefulness of the CAGE framework. As you saw, the vehicles Dell used to enter China were just as important in its China strategy as the choice of geographic arena it entered. For Dell's corporate clients in China, a CAGE framework would reveal relatively little distance on all four dimensions, even geographic, given the fact that many PC components are sourced from China. However, for the consumer segment, the distance is rather great, particularly on the dimensions of culture, administration, and economics. One outcome here could have been Dell's avoidance of the consumer market altogether. Only after disappointing experiences did Dell realize that a different approach was needed.

Putting CAGE to Work at Virgin Mobile

The starting point for your CAGE analysis is something called a country attractiveness portfolio (CAP). A CAP is created using data on a country or region's per capita income, along with data on some aspect of the market's desirability, such as market penetration or per capita spending on a focal product or service. With this information, you would have two reference points that you plot on a grid for each country. For instance, if you were Virgin Mobile, a U.K.–based cellphone company with an interest in entering a new geographic arena outside of its home European Union market, you would want to collect information on the percentage of the population that uses cellphones in other countries, along with country per capita income. By looking at the CIA's *2006*

World Factbook, which is summarized in Exhibit 10.11, you found the following information (you also happened to collect information on each country's population, since that will give you an idea of the percentage of people who have cellphones or the current market penetration for cellphones in each country).

A rank order of the data for cellphones shows that China has the biggest actual market. In some markets you see that the number of cellphones in use actually exceeds the labour force, which means that kids and retired people must be using them as well. Your next step is to plot out some of this data on a grid, so you have a better visual image of the possible market arenas. This is where the population data come in. You simply plot each

country's location on the grid using number of cellphones on the *x* axis and per capita income on the *y* axis—then use the bubble size to give you a rough impression of the relative opportunity presented by each market, in terms of the actual population. We picked population because it maps well to the idea of the potential cellphone market, but you could use other aggregated indicators such as gross domestic product, number of factories, and so on. The best dimension is one that can give you an idea of the country's market size for the particular product or service you are analyzing. Exhibit 10.12 shows you your CAP, using population as an indicator of market size.

Based solely on the information in Exhibit 10.12, you would conclude that you were done with your analysis.

Exhibit 10.11   Market Characteristics

Rank	Country	Cell Phones	Per Capita Income	Population
1	China	334 824 000	$7600	1 321 851 888
2	European Union	314 644 700	$29 400	460 827 146
3	United States	194 479 364	$43 500	301 139 947
4	Japan	91 473 900	$33 100	127 433 494
5	Russia	74 420 000	$12 100	141 377 752
6	India	69 193 321	$3700	1 129 866 154
7	Brazil	65 605 000	$8600	190 010 647
8	Mexico	38 451 100	$10 600	108 700 891
9	South Korea	36 586 100	$24 200	49 044 790

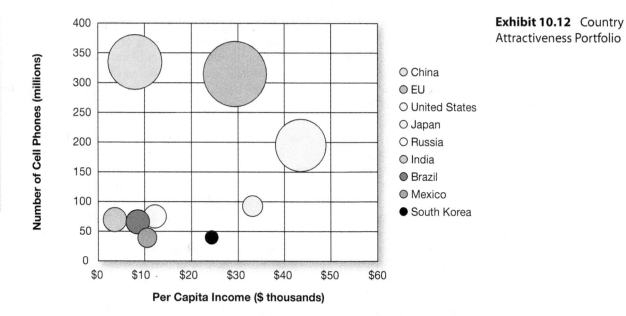

Exhibit 10.12 Country Attractiveness Portfolio

○ China
◉ EU
○ United States
○ Japan
○ Russia
◔ India
◕ Brazil
◕ Mexico
● South Korea

And this is why so many CAPs are fundamentally flawed. The information in Exhibit 10.12 does give you an idea of the relative attractiveness of each country market, and you can see their relative size related to per capita income, and so on. For a company such as Virgin, it would probably like to enter a new country market where income is high and the market is very big. It does fine in Europe, and as can be seen from Exhibit 10.11 (and 10.12), that market is both big and relatively rich. However, these exhibits do not show how well Virgin is prepared to enter those markets—it only shows that they are big, but will they be big (as in a home-run) for Virgin? The third and final step is to adjust the size of the bubbles upward or downward for CAGE-based differences along the dimensions of culture, administration, geography, and economics. This will tell you how attractive each country is, *after adjusting for the critical CAGE differences*. For instance, this would probably lead you to discount all the markets, other than the U.S. market, and you might adjust the U.S. market upward. A CAGE-adjusted CAP is shown in Exhibit 10.13.

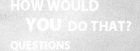

HOW WOULD YOU DO THAT? QUESTIONS

1. Pick another industry that is of interest to you. What did you identify as your indicator of potential market size? What market performance indicator did you use (for instance, in the example we used current cellphone usage)? How different were your CAP and CAGE-adjusted CAPs?

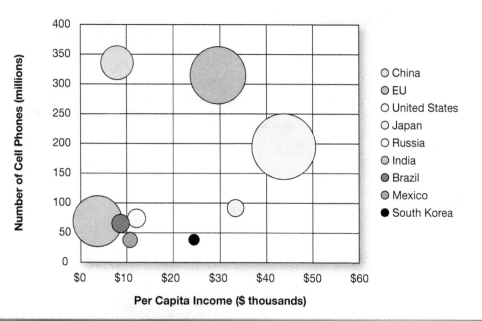

Exhibit 10.13 CAGE-Adjusted CAP for Virgin Mobile

○ China
◉ EU
○ United States
○ Japan
○ Russia
◔ India
◕ Brazil
◕ Mexico
● South Korea

How to Enter Foreign Markets

 **Vehicles**

Now that economic logic and selection of the geographic arena have been addressed, it is time to turn to the third step in the 1-2-3 model: selecting the vehicle of entry to be used in the new arena. The first choice that managers must make is whether to use a vehicle that requires the company to put some, or even considerable, capital at risk. As shown in Exhibit 10.14, companies can choose among a variety of non-equity and equity vehicles for entering a foreign country.[33] Exhibit 10.15 provides examples of the vehicles chosen by different companies around the world.[34]

The second choice that managers must make is the type of the vehicle as each offers different levels of ownership control and local presence. Here the many vehicles have been organized into four overarching classes: *exporting, contractual agreements, alliances and joint ventures,* and *wholly owned subsidiaries.* At the end of this section, the use of importing as a foreign-country entry vehicle will be discussed; it can be seen as a stealth form of internationalization.

Foreign-country entry has been viewed historically as a staged process. Like the industry life cycle, the internationalization life cycle starts with a company importing some of its raw materials or finished product for resale at home, followed perhaps by exporting products or raw materials abroad, and lastly ending in some type of partial or full ownership of plant, equipment, or other more extensive physical presence in a foreign country. These stages can be accomplished using vehicles ranging from simple contracts for purchases or sales on a transaction basis, through alliances, and perhaps even via mergers or wholesale acquisitions. Lincoln Electric, which was discussed in the previous section, offers an example of international growth through acquisition.

Over time, research has suggested that stages are better viewed as being descriptive than predictive. Some companies follow the stages, starting with importing through foreign direct investment, while others jump right to the direct investment stage as their first internationalization effort.[35]

Also of note is that degrees of risk and control vary by entry vehicles. For instance, a company exporting its products abroad is at risk for the payment for the product, and perhaps its reputation depending on what happens in the foreign locale. The exporter has little control over the downstream activities once it has shipped the product even though it can have a legal or distribution agreement with local companies. This section examines alternative entry vehicles.

Exhibit 10.14   Choice of Entry Vehicles

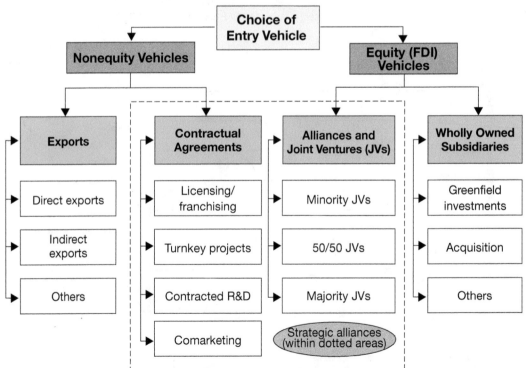

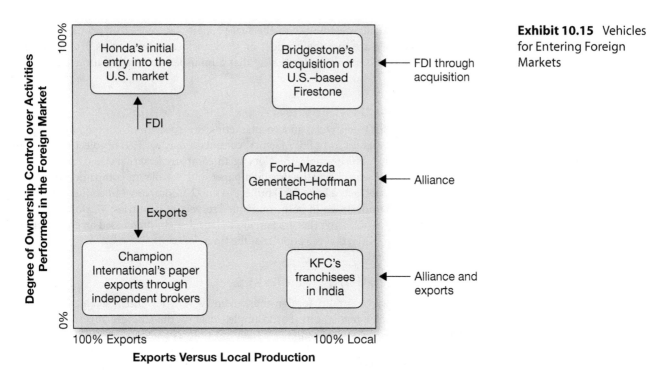

Exhibit 10.15 Vehicles for Entering Foreign Markets

Exporting can take the form of shipping a product overseas and leaving marketing and distribution up to a foreign customer. It can also take the form of licensing or franchising, turnkey projects, R&D contracts, and co-marketing. Due to some of the characteristics of these latter vehicles, such contractual arrangements are sometimes considered a form of strategic alliance.

exporting Foreign-country entry vehicle in which a company uses an intermediary to perform most foreign marketing functions.

DIRECT EXPORT

Direct exporting involves selling inputs or outputs (products and services) to foreign customers. Exporting is popular with small companies because this is a low-cost way of entering new markets. Generally local representatives or distributors retained by the exporter import the product and are responsible for customs, packaging, and other trade requirements as well as selling the product. The main costs associated with exporting are transportation and meeting the packaging, ingredient, and labelling requirements of the target country. Exporting is most common when customers in foreign markets have similar preferences but the local product is more expensive. A large percentage of the "born-global" companies discussed later in the chapter used exporting as a vehicle to go global quickly.[36]

CONTRACTUAL AGREEMENTS

Contractual agreements are used by the exporter, which relies on another company to manage its market presence. The contract can range from a verbal agreement to an extensive legal document, but often relates to one of the following four types of agreements.

contractual agreement An exchange of promises or agreement between parties that is often enforceable by the law.

Licensing and Franchising

Licensing and franchising provide a case in point. When a company licenses its products or technologies in another country, it transfers the risk of actually implementing market entry to another company, which pays the licensor a fee for the right to use its name in the local country. Franchising in a foreign country works similarly to franchising in a domestic market. A company receives a sign-up fee and ongoing franchise royalties in exchange for teaching the franchisee how to open and operate the franchisor's business in the local market.

The risk to the licensor or franchisor is that the licensee or franchisee will violate the terms of the agreement, either to the detriment of the product or service itself, by refusing to pay agreed-upon fees or royalties or simply selling a copy of the product or service under another name (that is, essentially stealing the intellectual property entirely). The primary risks to the franchisee or licensee are that the product or service will not perform as promised, or that the licensor or franchisor will do something that diminishes the market attractiveness of the product or service.

Turnkey Projects, R&D Contracts, and Co-marketing

Turnkey projects, R&D contracts, and co-marketing are specialized contractual agreements whereby a company agrees to build a factory, conduct a specific R&D project, or co-market or co-brand a product. For example, the Norwegian company Kvaerner A/S contracts to build paper mills and deep-sea oil rigs for Brazilian paper and petroleum companies; the German company Bayer AG contracts a large R&D project to the U.S. company Millennium Pharmaceuticals with the work undertaken in both companies' respective countries; McDonald's in Japan packages its kids' meals with toys that are familiar to Japanese children based on characters, such as Pokémon or Hello Kitty, that are popular at the time.

ALLIANCES AND JOINT VENTURES

Alliances are another common foreign-market entry vehicle. Often, alliances are chosen because of government regulations. For example, recently the Chinese government allowed non-Chinese ownership of companies in China but only as partnerships with Chinese companies. Alliances may also be used as an international-strategy vehicle due to management's lack of familiarity with the local culture or institutions or because the complexity of operating internationally requires the company to focus on the activities it does best and to outsource the rest. Some combination of regulations, market familiarity, or operational complexity explains why companies competing internationally use alliances. For instance, Co-steel partnered with Texas Industries when it launched Chaparral Steel in 1973 in Texas because the local partner had market knowledge. CAMI Automotive, originally known as Canadian Automotive Manufacturing Inc. and located in Ingersoll, Ontario, was a joint venture between Suzuki and General Motors of Canada Ltd. that was established in 1986 as part of GM's initiative to capture and practise the Japanese mystique of automotive management. Suzuki withdrew from the joint venture in 2009.

Equity alliances are another way of entering the market. In 1999, Chinfon-Manulife (CMIC) became the first wholly foreign-owned life insurance company authorized to work in the Socialist Republic of Vietnam. It was a joint venture between Manulife Financial of Canada and the Chinfon Global Corp. of Taiwan. CMIC was 60 percent owned by Manulife and 40 percent by Chinfon. In 2002, Manulife chose to buy out Chinfon Global's share. But acquisitions of ongoing businesses can prove difficult. After serious difficulties with acquisitions, Lincoln Electric now engages only in foreign direct investment through alliances with local players. This provides critical knowledge about local market conditions, both in terms of production and market demand. Alliances are sometimes required because national laws require a certain proportion of local content in a product, such as a car or motorcycle, sold in the local market. Brazil and China are two examples of countries that have stringent local-content laws. Minimum efficient scale is another explanation for the use of alliances as an FDI foreign-entry tactic.

For example, the Tritec venture in the early 1990s, an alliance between BMW and DaimlerChrysler, was necessary because neither company had the volume of production needed economically to justify a plant capable of producing 400 000 engines annually—the minimum efficient scale. By joining together, they shared the cost of building a new plant large enough to produce 400 000 engines. BMW got the engines it needed for its line of Mini Coopers assembled in England, and DaimlerChrysler got the engines it needed for the Neon and PT Cruiser lines assembled in Mexico, the United States, and South Africa.[37]

foreign direct investment (FDI) Foreign-country entry vehicle by which a company commits to the direct ownership of a foreign subsidiary or division.

WHOLLY OWNED SUBSIDIARIES

A wholly owned subsidiary is created when the company makes a direct investment in a foreign market to facilitate the entry into that market. The investment, called **foreign direct investment** (FDI) in government statistics, tends to be the most expensive entry tactic because it requires

	By assets	By revenue
Manufacturing	51.3	52.1
Oil and gas	49.1	55.9
Wholesale	35.5	35.1
Administrative services	25.5	18.8
Mining (except oil and gas)	34.5	34.7
Professional, scientific, and technical services	16.5	15.9
Retail	20.3	15.9
Transportation and warehousing	26.9	16.5
Accommodation and food	16.4	11.2
Real estate and leasing	13.7	11.5
Construction	5.0	4.9
Arts and recreation	1.6	1.5
Information and culture	5.7	7.8
Education and health	1.4	1.6
Agriculture and forestry	1.9	1.6
Utilities	6.7	31.1
All non-financial industries	29.3	30.2

Exhibit 10.16 The Percentage of Canadian Business Activity Under Foreign Control, 2003[38]

the greatest commitment of a company's time and resources. Canada has been an attractive place for foreign companies to invest. As a consequence a considerable number of companies in Canada are under foreign control (see Exhibit 10.16). Manufacturing and oil and gas have been most dominated by foreign control. An important implication is that even if one is employed in Canada, one can benefit from understanding international strategy because there is a good chance that one is working for a company that is pursuing an international strategy, albeit a foreign controlled one.

Greenfield Investments

FDI can be implemented in several ways. A **greenfield investment** involves the start-up of a foreign-owned entity from scratch. By starting from scratch, the company has greater latitude as to where the business will be located. This allows it to take into account such factors as the availability and skills of the labour force, transportation costs, utility costs, and local government inducements.

greenfield investment Form of FDI in which a company starts a new foreign business from the ground up.

Acquisitions

Acquisitions provide the company with rapid entry because the company purchases existing businesses that are already staffed and successfully operating. For instance, in 2003 Manulife became the second-largest insurer in North America and number five in the world when it bought U.S. life insurer John Hancock Financial Services. In 2006, Dofasco was acquired by the European steel company Arcelor, and in 2007 Stelco was bought by United States Steel. The ability to use acquisition is determined by the availability of potential acquisitions at competitive prices. But Canadian companies also invest in foreign countries. Two Canadian food companies, Dare and Voortmans, have operations in the United States. From 1997 to 2002, Canadian companies in the electrical and electronic components industry made 86 foreign acquisitions valued at Cdn$53.8 billion.[39]

IMPORTING AND INTERNATIONAL STRATEGY

Importing is a stealth form of internationalization because the company is serving its market with products or services produced outside its home country. Products imported can come in various levels of value added, ranging from inputs such as raw materials to components to finished goods. Companies that import need considerable knowledge related to trade such as customs regulations that imports must comply with, valuation of goods imported, duties assessed, trade finance and insurance, and foreign trade zones.

importing Internationalization strategy by which a company brings a good, service, or capital into the home country from abroad.

Outsourcing and Offshoring

Outsourcing involves buying services and products from others rather than producing them in the business. The outsourcing of services has been facilitated by information technologies (IT) such as telecommunications and the widespread diffusion of the internet. The delegation of one or more IT-intensive business processes, referred to as *business process outsourcing (BPO)*, has an external nondomestic provider own, administer, and manage the selected process based on defined and measurable performance criteria. Companies in such service- and IT-intensive industries as insurance, banking, pharmaceuticals, telecommunications, automobiles, and airlines seem to be the early adopters of BPO. Of the industries just mentioned, insurance and banking are able to generate savings purely because of the large proportion of processes they can outsource, such as claim processing, loan processing, and client servicing through call centres.

When those providing the services and products are in another country, then the term becomes *offshoring*. Offshoring has become prominent in recent years although it is not a new phenomenon. For decades Nike designed shoes and other apparel in the U.S. and manufactured them abroad. Following the North American Free Trade Agreement, Canadian and U.S. companies established *maquiladoras* (assembly plants) in Mexico. Magna, Canada's largest auto-parts manufacturer, has eight plants in Mexico. Hershey has moved production from plants in Canada and the U.S. to Mexico. More recently, offshored activities have moved farther afield. Dorel's Pacific Cycle does not make a bicycle in the United States but instead imports them from Taiwanese and Chinese manufacturers. What has changed in recent years is the prominence of international outsourcing as services, components, and raw materials have been brought into North America from countries such as China, Brazil, and India. GE was instrumental in moving IT activities to India. India is an attractive supplier because its talented workforce is cheap, well educated, and speaks English. Another advantage is that, because it is on the other side of the world, it receives problems from Western companies, works on them overnight, and has the answers back to the Western companies in the morning. Information-technology companies in India earn \$3.75 in exports for every dollar they earn in India. Infosys, the country's most celebrated IT company, collects only 1.2 percent of its income from the domestic market. Ironically, the leading provider of IT services to Indian companies is IBM.[40]

offshoring Moving a value chain activity or set of activities to another country, typically where key costs are lower.

Outsourcing and **offshoring** locations tend to be selected based on the degree of automation of a production process or service, the relative labour costs, and the transportation costs involved. When automation and transportation costs are both high, the knowledge-worker component of the location calculation becomes less important. You can see how you might employ the CAGE framework to evaluate potential outsourcing locations. However, in some cases companies invest in both plant and equipment and the training and development of the local workforce. Brazil is but one case in point, with examples from Ford, BMW, Daimler-Benz, and Cargill. Each of these multinational organizations is making significant investments in the educational infrastructure of this enormous emerging economy.[41]

How to Manage International Strategy Configurations

Once a company has international activities, but preferably before, management has to decide how it will configure activities because this affects interactions between headquarters and country operations. The configuration is as much about strategy formulation as it is about implementation. Management makes choices about which value-chain components to centralize, where to centralize those operations geographically, and the degree to which those decentralized and centralized value-chain activities will be managed and coordinated. The tradeoffs that management makes will likely differentiate the company's products and services from those of its competitors.

RESOLVING THE TENSION BETWEEN LOCAL PREFERENCES AND GLOBAL STANDARDS

Management has to face up to an underlying tension created by the company's attempts to be responsive to the local needs of diverse sets of customers yet remain globally efficient. The tradeoff selected between customizing for local needs and achieving cost efficiencies then requires further tradeoffs with respect to the company's value chain regarding which activities will be standardized and which will be locally tailored. These are issues that management must wrestle with in designing and managing the company's international strategy.

Globalizing companies must reconcile the natural tension that exists between local preferences and global standards. The domination of local preferences over the search for global efficiencies, left unchecked, often leads to what strategy researchers describe as *market fragmentation*.[42] In addition, local adaptation of products and services is significantly more expensive than relying on global standards. Consequently, attempting to achieve high levels of local responsiveness will almost always lead to higher cost structure.[43] A product that is uniform across markets is highly efficient to produce because the company can simply design a factory of the most efficient size in a location that most efficiently balances the costs of inputs with the transportation costs of getting outputs to the desired markets. If this product has the same brand around the world, then marketing and promotion efforts are similarly focused on that single brand. However, even products such as Coca-Cola, which appear to be ubiquitous, have different flavourings, packaging, and promotion constraints in each market. Some of these constraints are a function of local regulatory pressures; others reflect underlying differences in consumers' tastes. Just as important, other constraints are a function of the competitive norms that have prevailed in the industry, either globally or locally. The variations of international strategy configurations that we cover in this section—making tradeoffs between local responsiveness and global efficiency—are summarized in Exhibit 10.17.[44]

Exhibit 10.17   International Strategy Configurations and Local/Global Tradeoffs

	Relatively Few Opportunities to Gain Global Efficiencies	Many Opportunities to Gain Global Efficiencies
Relatively High Local Responsiveness	**Multinational Vision** Build flexibility to respond to national differences through strong, resourceful, entrepreneurial, and somewhat independent national or regional operations. Requires decentralized and relatively self-sufficient units. **Example:** MTV initially adopted an international configuration (using only American programming in foreign markets) but then changed its strategy to a multinational one. It now tailors its Western European programming to each market, offering eight channels, each in a different language.	**Transnational Vision** Develop global efficiency, flexibility, and worldwide learning. Requires dispersed, interdependent, and specialized capabilities simultaneously. **Example:** Nestlé has taken steps to move in this direction, starting first with what might be described as a multinational configuration. Today, Nestlé aims to evolve from a decentralized, profit-centre configuration to one that operates as a single, global company. Firms like Nestlé have taken lessons from leading consulting firms such as McKinsey and Company, which are globally dispersed but have a hard-driving, one-firm culture at their core.
Relatively Low Local Responsiveness	**International Vision** Exploit parent-company knowledge and capabilities through worldwide diffusion, local marketing, and adaptation. The most valuable resources and capabilities are centralized; others, such as local marketing and distribution, are decentralized. **Example:** When Wal-Mart initially set up its operations in Brazil, it used its U.S. stores as a model for international expansion.	**Global Vision** Build cost advantages through centralized, global-scale operations. Requires centralized and globally scaled resources and capabilities. **Example:** Companies such as Merck and Hewlett-Packard give particular subsidiaries a worldwide mandate to leverage and disseminate their unique capabilities and specialized knowledge worldwide.

Each of the four configurations identified in Exhibit 10.17 presents tradeoffs between global efficiency and local responsiveness. Recognize that in reality, most companies' international strategy configurations vary slightly or significantly from those shown in Exhibit 10.17. By definition, strategy must be internally consistent and externally oriented. However, management must make judgments as to what an external orientation means in terms of how the strategy takes competitive pressures and consumer preferences into account. At the same time, management must also make judgments about the company's internal resources and capabilities to support a particular international-strategy configuration. This explains why companies with seemingly very different international-strategy configurations can coexist in the same industry.

International Vision

When Lincoln Electric first embarked on becoming a global company, it had relatively independent operations in many markets around the world. It used its strongest national positions to cross-subsidize market-share battles or growth initiatives in other countries. Such an approach is essentially a portfolio of geographically removed business units that have devoted most of their resources and capabilities to maximizing local responsiveness and uniqueness. Companies that employ this configuration, such as Lincoln Electric, seek a global presence but may not use the same brand names in each market or consolidate their buying power or distribution capabilities.

Multinational Vision

Another configuration centralizes some resources, such as global brand and distribution capabilities, in order to achieve cost savings; but decentralizes others, such as marketing, in order to achieve some level of localization. This strategy is common among companies that have created something in their home market that they wish to replicate in foreign markets, allowing them the economies of scale and scope necessary to create and exploit innovations on a worldwide basis. Heavy R&D companies such as Intel and Pfizer fit this mould: Even though the products that they produce are relatively standardized around the world, local marketing and distribution channels differ.

Global Vision

This configuration focuses only on global efficiency. A tradeoff is made between local responsiveness and the lower costs associated with global efficiency. With this configuration, production and sourcing decisions are designed to achieve the greatest economies of scale. Companies following this configuration potentially sacrifice the higher prices that follow customization, but they are counting on the likelihood that their products or services will meet enough needs to be demanded without finely tuned customization. Companies in commodity industries such as steel and copper, such as BHP-Billeton, fall into this category. Because end customers make purchase decisions based on price alone, the company is organized to realize the lowest possible production costs.

Transnational Vision

cross-subsidizing When a company uses profits from one aspect of a product, service, or region to support its competitive activity.

The final international-strategy configuration that we discuss is one that attempts to capitalize on both local responsiveness and global efficiency. When successfully implemented, this approach enables companies to achieve global economies of scale, **cross-subsidization** across markets, and the ability to engage in retaliatory and responsive competition across markets. This configuration is available to companies with high degrees of internationalization. However, as with any other strategic tradeoff, it is extremely difficult to find the balance between cost efficiencies and the ability to customize to local tastes and standards. McDonald's is often used as an example of a company that fits this configuration because it uses its purchasing power to get the best prices on the global commodities it uses for inputs, yet tries to tailor its menu offerings to fit local tastes and cultural preferences.

Born-Global Companies

Born-global companies deserve special mention because more and more organizations appear to have operations that span national borders early in their existence. These companies employ an amalgam of exporting and FDI, but do so much more rapidly than companies have in the past. In the strategy diamond, exporting and FDI are considered vehicles, and the timing and sequencing of the usage are viewed in the context of staging. Each of these vehicles provides a company and its management with experience and knowledge about cross-border business practices.

One reason that global strategy—and the four international strategy configurations—will become an increasingly important topic is the fact that more and more companies, even very small ones, have operations that bridge national borders very soon after their founding. Perhaps appropriate for the internet age, this new breed of companies that emerged in the 1990s is being dubbed "born global" because their operations often span the globe early in their existence. A common characteristic of such companies is that their offerings complement the products or capabilities of other global players, take advantage of global IT infrastructure, or otherwise tap into a demand for a product or service that at its core is somewhat uniform across national geographic markets. Although many companies may fall into this category by virtue of their products, the operations and customers of born-global companies do actually span the globe. Born-global companies position themselves globally, exploiting a combination of exporting and FDI.

Logitech, the computer-mouse and peripherals company, is perhaps one of the best early examples of a successful born-global company.[45] It was founded by two Italians and a Swiss, with operations and R&D initially split between California and Switzerland. Logitech's primary focus was on the PC mouse, and it rapidly expanded production to Ireland and Taiwan. With its stylish and ergonomic products, Logitech had captured 30 percent of the global mouse business by 1989, garnering the start-up a healthy $140 million in revenues. Today, Logitech is an industry leader in the design and manufacture of computer-peripheral devices. It has manufacturing facilities in Asia and offices in major cities in North America, Europe, and Asia Pacific and employs more than 6000 people worldwide.[46]

HOW TO SUCCEED AS A GLOBAL START-UP

Successful global start-ups must complete two phases. In the first phase, managers ask, "Should my company be a global start-up?" If they can answer "yes" to all or most of the follow-up questions entailed by phase 1, then they need to be sure that they can quickly build the resources and capabilities identified in phase 2. Research has shown that those companies unable to connect the dots in phase 2 were forced to cease operations after short, albeit sometimes lively, adventures.[47]

During phase 1—*and before moving on to phase 2*—managers should consider questions that will help them determine whether the company should be a global start-up:

■ Does the company need human resources from other countries in order to succeed?
■ Does the company need financial capital from other countries in order to succeed?
■ If the company goes global, will target customers prefer its services over those of competitors?
■ Can the company put an international system in place more quickly than domestic competitors?
■ Does the company need global scale and scope to justify the financial and human capital investment in the venture?
■ Will a purely domestic focus now make it harder for the company to go global in the future?

If the answer to all or most of these questions is "yes," managers can commit to moving the company into phase 2 and put together the tools they will need to move the company into the global market:

■ Strong management team with international experience
■ Broad and deep international network among suppliers, customers, and complements
■ Pre-emptive marketing or technology that will provide first-mover advantage with customers and lock out competitors from key suppliers and complements
■ Strong intangible assets (Logitech has style, hipness, and mindshare via its brand)
■ Ability to keep customers locked in by linking new products and services to the core business, while constantly innovating in the core product or service
■ Close worldwide coordination and communication among business units, suppliers, complements, and customers

So why do we introduce the concept of global start-ups at this point in the text? One reason is because of their increasing prevalence, which is driven, in part, by globalizing consumer preferences, mobile consumers, large global companies, and the pervasiveness of the internet and its effects. The second reason, which should become clear after reading the next section, is that dynamic contexts typically give rise to the need for companies to strive for a global presence and to understand global markets early in their evolution.

International Strategy in Stable and Dynamic Contexts

 Arenas

A recent McKinsey study suggests that the creativity that some companies have found in emerging economies, and that has resulted in inexpensive but high-quality products, will now compel incumbents to go down the same road.[48] This assertion gets at the heart—the question of urgency and timing—of how international strategy is approached in relatively stable versus dynamic contexts. ◆ Moreover, it also suggests that industries that might have been considered relatively stable will increasingly take on dynamic characteristics as a result of global competition. In many ways, what you have learned so far about business and corporate strategies in dynamic contexts is equally applicable in purely domestic and already globalizing organizations. The key difference, however, is that cross-border business adds another level of complexity to both strategy formulation and execution and that, unfortunately, such complexity may be unavoidable for companies in dynamic contexts.

GLOBAL CONTEXT AND INDUSTRY LIFE CYCLE

Recall from earlier chapters that we differentiated between external- and internal-based views of strategy. The internal view emphasizes resources, capabilities, and activities as the source of competitive advantage, whereas the external view draws attention to how companies need to adapt or modify their competitive positions and strategies to the external environment to position themselves in a manner conducive to superior returns. These views have implications for the dynamic nature of international strategic action, as well. Taking the external perspective, for instance, typically draws managerial attention to the dynamic nature of the industry life cycle and how that drives decisions to internationalize. Specifically, as an industry matures, the international implications of industry structure—and therefore strategic choices and company behaviour—should change in fundamental ways.[49]

First-Mover Advantage

In the introductory stage of an industry's life cycle, the external perspective would expect companies to engage in few exports, largely because the market for the industry's products is still highly uncertain and there are few accepted quality, service, or technological standards. As you will see, the length of this stage may vary significantly by country. Companies should begin to export during the growth stage of the industry life cycle because new companies enter the market and compete for existing customers. Early movers in the domestic market then have an opportunity to be early movers in foreign markets as well and to continue growth even as domestic competition heats up. As the industry matures, exports gain even more steam in the face of domestic market saturation, and companies start producing products abroad to satisfy foreign demand and to search for global efficiencies. Industry shakeouts and consolidations also tend to follow industry maturity, and consolidation through acquisitions leads to a few large global companies.

Staging and Geographic Markets

Similarly, when discussing international strategy from an external perspective, the fact that geographic markets differ in many legal, cultural, and institutional ways—differences that, in turn, are likely to have implications for product demand—must also be taken into account. Indeed, demand characteristics of geographic markets have been shown to evolve at different rates. For example, the time from new-product introduction to the growth stage (sometimes called market takeoff) in Portugal may occur after a longer period of time than the same transition in Denmark. Indeed, although the average period of time between a new-product or new-service introduction and market takeoff is six years, a new product takes only about four years to take off in Denmark, Norway, and Sweden compared to nine years in Greece and Portugal (the United States averages 5.3 years).[50]

Role of Arenas in Global Strategies

Identification of arenas ensures that the most critical national markets are identified and brought into the plan. Similarly, even with thoughtful treatment of staging and arenas, structures, systems, and processes must be in complete alignment with the company's vision and global intent. A company that strives to execute the most complex global strategy—the transnational strategy—must have enormous investments in its ability to coordinate and integrate activities around the globe, complemented by customer characteristics that enable such a global strategy to create true value.

Resources and Global Strategy

The resource-based perspective has important implications for international strategy in dynamic contexts as well. It is here that the questions of staging and geographic arenas from the strategy diamond model are critically important to effective international strategies. From the resource-based perspective, staging is important because the company's global resources and capabilities do not materialize overnight. Lincoln Electric's experience is a case in point here. Lincoln's pace of international expansion exceeded its organizational capabilities to integrate foreign acquisitions, let alone manage them once they were integrated. Lincoln also attempted to internationalize almost exclusively through acquisitions. However, research on foreign expansion reveals that the companies most successful at internationalizing combine greenfield investments with acquisitions and alliances.[51] Simply expanding through greenfield investment can lead to inertia and lack of learning. Acquisitions help broaden a company's knowledge base. However, exclusive reliance on acquisitions is not only costly but makes knowledge transfer and learning more difficult. Companies that balance greenfield investments and acquisitions seem to transfer more knowledge and create more value than companies that rely on either process exclusively.

Capabilities and Global Strategy

One of the fundamental ideas of having a dynamic view of strategy is to continuously build and renew company capabilities. Many born-global companies fall into this dynamic-context category nearly from inception. By continuously evolving its stock of resources and capabilities, a company maximizes its chances of adapting to changing environmental conditions. Thus, when a company decides to enter a particular new foreign market, it must also embark on developing the resources necessary to make that market-entry decision a success. At the same time, what it learns in those new geographic markets should be evaluated for application or adaptation to existing market positions.

In addition, as a company internationalizes and becomes more dependent on a particular foreign location, the need for high-level capabilities to perform the local activities increases commensurately.[52] For instance, as IKEA expands around the globe, its ability to understand local furniture markets increases. However, these needs are greatest in markets where it faces the most exposure; IKEA's early missteps in the United States have been attributed to lack of market intelligence.[53] This leads us to our closing section on global strategy in dynamic contexts.

DEVELOPING A MINDSET FOR GLOBAL STRATEGY

Dynamic Competitiveness

Given the emphasis on the importance of leadership skills throughout this text, it should come as no surprise that what may make or break the effectiveness of a company's international strategy is the internationally related capabilities and global mindset of the company's executives, particularly in dynamic markets. Moreover, such capabilities and mindset may enable one company to change a once relatively stable competitive context into a dynamic and vibrant one.

Global Perspective

The global mindset has two distinct but related dimensions. The first dimension is something that strategy researchers simply refer to as global perspective.[54] Executives with a global perspective require a combination of specific knowledge and skills. In terms of knowledge, executives with a global mindset have an appreciation for the fact that countries and their peoples differ culturally, socioeconomically, and sociopolitically; view those differences as potential opportunities as opposed to threats; and can link such differences to necessary adaptations in business operations. In addition, they also recognize that the management processes guiding those business operations must also be adapted to cultural, socioeconomic, and sociopolitical differences.

As opposed to conventional and routine cross-country transfers, companies are exposing managers to problem-solving situations in different business environments. An interesting example in this context is Dell Computer. Traditionally, Dell's practice has been to use local managers to run its outfits in different parts of the world. For important functions, Dell uses teams of specialists who move around the world providing expertise in specific areas. One such team that picked up design expertise while setting up Dell's manufacturing facilities in Texas has been spending time in countries such as Ireland, Malaysia, China, and Brazil to set up plants there. In each of these countries, the team spends typically six months to one year.

Learning on a Worldwide Scale

In many ways, the second dimension of a global mindset requires the first dimension as a foundation. The second dimension is the capacity to learn from participation in one geographic market and transfer that knowledge to other operations elsewhere in the world. This means that the company not only has globally savvy executives, but that these executives form an effective network of communication throughout the organization on a worldwide scale. You can tell that a company and its managers possess this second dimension when the company is routinely able

---

FOCUS ON SUSTAINABILITY 10.1
Sustainability and International Business[55]

As global trade has grown, ships have moved many of the goods over oceans. Most ships are scrapped after 30 years when the ships need so much refitting and repair that they are uneconomical. Shipbreaking involves breaking them up so that materials from the ship, especially steel, and other useful equipment and material can be reused; near 95 percent of the vessel's material can be reprocessed. But in addition to the materials for recycling, ships (particularly older vessels) contain many substances such as asbestos, polychlorinated biphenyls (PCBs), and lead that are banned or considered dangerous. The costs associated with dealing with these substances including insurance and health risks have made shipbreaking in developed countries expensive.

This has led to a shift in where shipbreaking is done. Until the late 20th century, it took place in port cities of industrialized countries such as the United Kingdom and the United States. In the 1990s, China was an important player but since then it has been repositioning itself in less environmentally unfriendly industries. Today, most shipbreaking yards are in Pakistan, Bangladesh, and India.

Shipyards in developing countries find shipbreaking economically viable because they are able to operate at low cost. Operating practices involve running ships up on beachheads where they are broken down. Many developing countries have lax or no environmental law, so large quantities of highly toxic materials are allowed to escape into the environment, causing serious health problems among shipbreakers, the local population, and wildlife. Workers involved in this work are exposed to dangerous vapours, chemicals, and substances. Moreover, protective equipment is sometimes inadequate or nonexistent because the companies do not face the risk of personal injury lawsuits or workers' health claims.

In recent years, environmental groups such as Greenpeace have made shipbreaking a high priority for their campaigns. This has led to the development of Green Ship Recycling, which can recover up to 99 percent of the ship's materials and correctly process hazardous waste such as asbestos. In May 2009, the International Maritime Organization's (IMO) Convention on the Safe and Environmentally Sound Recycling of Ships was adopted. This covered approximately 43 000 vessels each over 500 gross tonnes. That same year the International Ship Recycling Association (ISRA) was formed to represent recycling yards at the IMO meetings. Initially it comprised six Turkish, two Chinese, one Dutch, and one U.S. dismantling yard. The chair of the ISRA said, "We want this organization to bring a voice to the IMO. We want to show the world things can be done in a green, high-quality way and there can still be a return and it is a good business."[56] ISRA members were said to be aware that considerable change in the attitude of ship owners and the yards was required.

Should such activities have work and environmental standards more rigorously enforced? And what would this do to world trade?

Up to 130 large ships are dismantled each year at yards operating on beaches at Sitakundu, 30 kilometres (18 miles) north of Chittagong City. Sitakundu's shipbreaking yards have boomed in recent years due to soaring demand for steel.

to take knowledge gained in one market and apply it elsewhere, as was demonstrated in the case of S. C. Johnson's transfer of a plug-in household insect repellent product from Europe to the development of a new category of air-freshener products in the United States—Glade Plug-Ins.

Ironically, many global companies, and even more so with less global ones, are not very effective at retaining their managers once they return from an international assignment. These managers are either *expatriates*—someone from the home country who has moved abroad temporarily—or, increasingly, *inpatriates*—a manager recruited from the "local" market for their local business savvy. This apparent disconnect between a need for globally seasoned executives and their retention by the companies that need them most can be explained by two factors. First, when the managers accept an international work assignment they often lose contact with the elements of the organization where strategy is formulated, such as corporate headquarters. In the case of inpatriates, they may never have had an opportunity to establish a strong network and power base at headquarters. Second, the expatriates' or inpatriates' companies do not have a repatriation plan in place to take advantage of their expertise. Because they have been out-of-sight-and-out-of-mind, there is no ready way to plug them into the top management team.

Obviously, the development of a global mindset is more easily said than done. Our hope is that, given the fact that there are very few industries or markets untouched by global competition (just look around your classroom, for instance, and you will likely see at least one person from another country), you will take it upon yourself to start investing in your own global mindset.

Summary of Challenges

1. *Define international strategy and identify its implications for the strategy diamond.* A company's international strategy is how it approaches the cross-border business activities of its own company and competitors and how it contemplates doing so in the future. International strategy essentially reflects the choices a company's executives make with respect to sourcing and selling its goods in foreign markets. A company's international activities affect both its business strategy and its corporate strategy. Each component of the strategy diamond may be affected by international activities.

2. *Understand why a company would want to expand internationally and explain the relationship between international strategy and competitive advantage.* Companies often expand internationally to fuel growth; however, international expansion does not guarantee profitable growth and should be pursued to help a company build or exploit a competitive advantage. International expansion can exploit four principal drivers of competitive advantage: economies of scale and scope, location, multipoint competition, and learning. However, these benefits can be offset by the costs of international expansion, such as the liabilities of newness and foreignness, and governance and coordination costs.

3. *Use the CAGE framework to identify desirable international arenas.* CAGE stands for cultural distance, administrative distance, geographic distance, and economic distance and is a tool to help you better understand the company-specific implication of a country attractiveness portfolio (CAP). You learned how to identify a portfolio of geographic markets and rank them on their relative attractiveness. The first step involved gathering data on personal income and market performance for a particular segment or industry. The second step involved

creating a CAP by plotting the data on a grid to observe relative differences in attractiveness across countries. The third step asked you to make judgments about relevant CAGE dimensions and apply them to your CAP.

4. *Describe different vehicles for international expansion.* Foreign-country entry vehicles include exporting, alliances, and foreign direct investment (FDI). Exporters generally use local representatives or distributors to sell their products in new international markets. Two specialized forms of exporting are licensing and franchising. Alliances involve partnering with another company to enter a foreign market or undertake an aspect of the value chain in that market. FDI can facilitate entry into a new foreign market and can be accomplished by greenfield investment or acquisition. Although importing is not technically a form of international expansion, it does provide companies with knowledge, experience, and relationships on which future international expansion choices and activities can be based.

5. *Apply different international strategy configurations.* The different forms that international strategies may take are driven by tradeoffs in attempts to customize for local needs and to pursue global cost efficiencies. The first configuration seeks to achieve high levels of local responsiveness while downplaying the search for global efficiencies. The second configuration seeks relatively few global efficiencies and markets relatively standard products across different markets. The third configuration seeks to exploit global economies and efficiencies and accepts less local customer responsiveness (i.e., more standardized products). The fourth configuration attempts to simultaneously achieve global efficiencies and a high degree of local product specialization.

6. *Outline the international strategy implications of the stable and dynamic perspectives.* Cross-border business adds another level of complexity to both strategy formulation and execution, and unfortunately such complexity may be unavoidable for companies in dynamic contexts. As products mature, companies' international strategies evolve, often moving from little global involvement during the introductory phase to high degrees of internationalization in mature markets. Resources need to be renewed more rapidly in dynamic markets. Thus, when a company enters a new foreign market, it must also embark on developing the resources necessary to make that market-entry decision a success. In addition, what is learned in new markets can be leveraged for application in existing markets. Obviously, these objectives can be best achieved when managers with an international mindset are in place.

Review Questions

1. What is meant by international strategy?
2. Which aspects of the strategy diamond are related to international strategy?
3. What are the four most important ways a company's international strategy can be related to its competitive advantage?
4. What three foreign-country entry vehicles are emphasized in this chapter?
5. What is typically the most cost- and time-intensive entry vehicle?
6. What are characteristics of companies that fit the four international strategy configurations discussed in this chapter?
7. On what two dimensions do the four international strategy configurations differ?
8. What does the external perspective tell you about international strategy in dynamic contexts?
9. What does the resource-and-capabilities-based perspective tell you about international strategy in dynamic contexts?
10. What role do managers play in effective international strategies, particularly in dynamic contexts?

Experiential Activities

Group Exercises

1. Why have companies typically followed an international strategy path that started with importing or exporting, followed by alliances, and then FDI? What risks do born-global companies face in trying to do all of these at once? What resources and capabilities must they possess to do all of these effectively?
2. Are all internet companies global by definition? What opportunities and barriers does the internet present to company internationalization?

Ethical Debates

1. You have successfully grown your local pasta company and while travelling in other countries you found that you might be able to produce and sell your product profitably there as well. In exploring these opportunities further, you were surprised to find that one of these countries has much stricter ingredients labelling and contents laws, while the other country much looser ones (in comparison to those of your home country, which you considered to be pretty strict to begin with). All three opportunities look to be profitable, regardless of the differences in regulations. Which regulations do you abide by in each country? The strictest ones, or the respective country standards, even if they are different?
2. As you learned in the section exploring CAGE, Canada's Corruption of Foreign Public Officials Act is a federal law that makes it illegal for a Canadian business person to influence, bribe, or seek an advantage from a public official of another country. You, as an employee of a Canadian company, are bidding for a contract in a foreign country where you understand that bribery is a common practice. Does the Canadian law put your company at a competitive disadvantage? What should you do?

Endnotes

1. "Dell Introduces a Low-Cost PC for China," *New York Times*, March 21, 2007. Accessed December 5, 2010, at www.nytimes.com/2007/03/21/technology/21iht-dell.4984005.html.

2. Ibid.

3. Sumner Lemon, "Dell to Stick with Direct Sales in China," IDG News Service, December 19, 2006. Accessed January 10, 2010, at www.networkworld.com/news/2006/121906-dell-direct-sales-china.html.

4. China Martens, "Dell CEO: We've Had a Few Challenges. We'll Be Back," IDG News Service, January 12, 2006. Accessed January 10, 2010, at www.networkworld.com/news/2006/011206-dell-ceo.html?ap1=rcb.

5. Gina Roos, "PC Market Returns to Annual Growth, says iSuppli," *Electronics Advocate*, December 3, 2009. Accessed January 10, 2010, at www.electronicsadvocate.com/2009/12/03/pc-market-returns-to-annual-growth-says-isuppli/.

6. Information provided on companies' respective websites. General information on the global Fortune 500 can be found at www.fortune.com.

7. "Global 500," *Fortune*. Accessed January 10, 2010, at http://money.cnn.com/magazines/fortune/global500/2009/.

8. A. D. Chandler, *Scale and Scope: The Dynamics of Industrial Capitalism* (Cambridge, M.A.: Harvard University Press, 1990).

9. A. K. Gupta and V. Govindarajan, "Converting Global Presence into Global Competitive Advantage," *Academy of Management Executive* 15 (2001): 45–56.

10. J. W. Lu and P. W. Beamish, "International Diversification and Firm Performance." *Academy of Management Journal* 47 (2004): 598-609.

11. Philip Siekman, "Good Steel Made Cheaply Brazil Does It Amazingly Well. And U.S. Manufacturers Are Reaping the Benefit," *Fortune*, May 12, 2003.

Accessed January 10, 2010, at http://money.cnn.com/magazines/fortune/fortune_archive/2003/05/12/342310/index.htm.

12. Staff reporters, "CST Plans to Ship Steel Slabs to Dofasco – Brazil," *Business News Americas*, March 1, 2006, p.17. Accessed January 10, 2010, at www.bnamericas.com/news/metals/CST_plans_to_ship_steel_slabs_to_Dofasco.

13. "Wal-Mart Imports from China, Exports Ohio Jobs," *AFL-CIO Wal-Mart Campaign, Sept. 2005*, p. 4. Accessed January 10, 2010, at www.aflcio.org/corporatewatch/walmart/upload/report_ohio.pdf.

14. K. Ito and E. L. Rose, "Foreign Direct Investment Location Strategies in the Tire Industry," *Journal of International Business Studies* 33:3 (2002): 593–602.

15. Based on information from a personal interview with Sam Johnson.

16. Adapted from A. Gupta and V. Govindarajan, "Managing Global Expansion: A Conceptual Framework," *Business Horizons* 43:2 (2000): 45–54.

17. R. Tomkins, "Battered PepsiCo Licks Its Wounds," *The Financial Times*, May 30, 1997, p. 26.

18 David Farkas, "HORTONS Hears a 'Who?'(Tim Hortons lacks brand recognition in United States)," *Chain Leader*, September 2000.

19. James Wallace, "Airbus A380 a Bit Too Superjumbo," *Seattle PI*, October 28, 2006. Accessed January 10, 2010, at www.seattlepi.com/business/290276_airbus28.html. "Airbus A380." Accessed January 10, 2010, at http://en.wikipedia.org/wiki/Airbus_A380.

20. J. W. Lu and P. W. Beamish, "International Diversification and Firm Performance: The S-Curve Hypothesis," *Academy of Management Journal* 47 (2004): 598–609.

21. Ibid.

22. Based on surveys reported in *BusinessWeek* and Grant Thornton LLP. See *2007 Grant Thornton International Business Report* at www.gti.org, and "Emerging Giants Multinationals from China, India, Brazil, Russia, and Even Egypt Are Coming on Strong. They're Hungry—and Want Your Customers. They're Changing the Global Game," *BusinessWeek*, July 31, 2006.

23. Pankaj Ghemawat, *Redefining Global Strategy* (Cambridge, M.A.: Harvard Business School Press, 2007).

24. "U.S.–Canada Trade Facts." Office of the United States Trade Representative, Executive Office of the President, Washington, D.C. Accessed January 10, 2010, t www.ustr.gov/countries-regions/americas/canad.

25. P. Ghemawat, "The Forgotten Strategy," *Harvard Business Review* 81:11 (2003): 76–84. Recreated from www.business-standard.com/general/pdf/113004_01.pdf.

26. P. Ghemawat, "Distance Still Matters," *Harvard Business Review* 79:8 (2001): 137–147.

27. G. Hofstede, *Culture's Consequences. International Differences in Work-Related Values* (Newbury Park, CA: Sage Publications, 1980); G. Hofstede, *Culture's and Organizations. Software of the Mind* (London: McGraw-Hill, 1991).

28 The act is described at www.justice.gc.ca/eng/dept-min/pub/cfpoa-lcape/index.html (accessed January 10, 2010).

29. Resources relating to Transfer pricing for Canada are found at www.transferpricing.com/worldtranferpricing_files/world_files/canada/canada.htm (accessed January 10, 2010).

30. Drawn directly from the Competition Policy Review Panel, "Chapter 7. Competitiveness Agenda: The Legal Foundations," of Compete to Win, Industry Canada, June 2008. Accessed January 10, 2010 at www.ic.gc.ca/eic/site/cprp-gepmc.nsf/eng/00059.html.

31. "Containerization." Accessed January 10, 2010, at http://en.wikipedia.org/wiki/Containerization.

32. Statistics Canada, CANSIM table 176-0064; Bank of Canada. Accessed January 10, 2010, at www45.statcan.gc.ca/2009/cgco_2009_014c-eng.htm.

33. Adapted from Y. Pan and D. Tse, "The Hierarchical Model of Market Entry Modes," *Journal of International Business Studies* 31 (2000): 535–554.

34. Examples drawn from A. Gupta and V. Govindarajan, "Managing Global Expansion: A Conceptual Framework," *Business Horizons*, March/April 2002, pp. 45–54.

35. J. Johanson and J. Vahlne, "The Internationalization Process of the Firm," *Journal of International Business Studies* 8 (1977): 23–32; F. Weidersheim-Paul, H. Olson, and L. Welch, "Pre-Export Activity: The First Step in Internationalization," *Journal of International Business Studies* 9

(1978): 47–58; A. Millington and B. Bayliss, "The Process of Internationalization: UK Companies in the EC," *Management International Review* 30 (1990): 151–161; B. Oviatt and P. McDougall, "Toward a Theory of International New Ventures," *Journal of International Business Studies* 25 (1994): 45–64.

36. O. Moen, "The Born Globals: A New Generation of Small European Exporters," *International Marketing Review* 19 (2002): 156–175.

37. BMW sold its ownership in the Tritec Motors plant to DaimlerChrysler in 2007, See "BMW Sells Stake in Tritec Plant (Updated)," Motorfile, Accessed January 9, 2011 at www.motoringfile.com/2007/07/12/bmw-sells-stake-in-tritec-plant/

38. Adapted from G. Gellaty, D. Sabourin, and J. Baldwin, "Changes in Foreign Control under Different Regulatory Climates: Multinationals in Canada," *Canadian Economic Observer*, March 2006, Table 1.

39. Allison Taylor, "Canadians Hold Their Own when Making Foreign Acquisitions," *ITWorldCanada*, June 2, 2004. Accessed January 10, 2010, at www.itworldcanada.com/news/canadians-hold-their-own-when-making-foreign-acquisitions/115068.

40. "Domestic Outsourcing in India: Bittersweet Synergy," *The Economist*, October 22, 2009. Accessed January 10, 2010, at www.economist.com/businessfinance/displaystory.cfm?story_id=14710627.

41. www.fordfound.org, and http://www.cargill.com.br/brazil/pt/home/index.jsp (accessed January 10, 2010).

42. G. Hamel and C. K. Prahalad, "Do You Really Have a Global Strategy?" *Harvard Business Review* 63:4 (1985): 139–148.

43. Gupta and Govindarajan, "Converting Global Presence into Global Competitive Advantage."

44. Adapted from C. Bartlett, S. Ghoshal, and J. Birkenshaw, *Transnational Management* (New York: Irwin, 2004). Note that Bartlett and Ghoshal distinguish among international, multinational, global, and transnational strategies. We have found these distinctions are difficult for students to apply and have chosen to use the underlying dimensions of local responsiveness and global efficiency as the tradeoffs that international strategy emphasizes.

45. B. Oviatt and P. McDougall, "Global Start-Ups: Entrepreneurs on a Worldwide Stage," *Academy of Management Executive* 9:2 (1995): 30–44.

46. www.logitech.com (accessed January 10, 2010).

47. Summarized from Oviatt and McDougall, "Global Start-Ups: Entrepreneurs on a Worldwide Stage," *Academy of Management Executive* 9:2 (1995): 30–44.

48. J. S. Brown and J. Hagel, "Innovation Blowback: Disruptive Management Practices from Asia," *McKinsey Quarterly,* January 2005.

49. M. Porter, *Competitive Advantage* (New York: Free Press, 1998).

50. G. Tellis, S. Stremersch, and E. Yin. "The International Takeoff of New Products: Economics, Culture and Country Innovativeness," *Marketing Science* 22:2 (2003): 161–187.

51. F. Vermeulen and H. Barkema, "Learning Through Acquisitions," *Academy of Management Journal* 44 (2001): 457–476; M. A. Hitt, M. T. Dacin, E. Levitas, and J. Arregle, "Partner Selection in Emerging and Developed Market Contexts: Resource-Based and Organizational Learning Perspectives," *Academy of Management Journal* 43 (2000), 449–467.

52. Gupta and Govindarajan, "Converting Global Presence into Global Competitive Advantage."

53. "Furnishing the World," *The Economist*, November 19, 1994, pp. 79–80.

54. B. Kedia and A. Mukherji, "Global Managers: Developing a Mindset for Global Competitiveness," *Journal of World Business* 34:3 (1999): 230–251.

55. The ship recyclers organization is described by Helen Hill, "Green Ship Recycling Gets New Voice" Accessed January 10, 2010, at www.isra-dis.com/documents/isra_krant.pdf?phpMyAdmin=4bbf5f48c950e07c4aef0b50ba31d75b. Further discussion of the industry's problems is found in Paul J. Bailey, "Is There a Decent Way to Break Up Ships?" International Labour Organization (ILO), Geneva 2000. Accessed January 10, 2010, at www.ilo.org/public/english/dialogue/sector/papers/shpbreak/index.htm,; and "Ship Breaking." Accessed January 10, 2010, at http://en.wikipedia.org/wiki/Ship_breaking. A repudiation of these issues is provided by Anil Sharma, "Ship Recycling In India: Myth vs. Fact." Accessed January 10, 2010, at www.gmsinc.net/gms/news/ship-recycling-in-india.pdf. The standards being developed are described in "The NGO Platform's Green Ship Recycling Standard," Draft 2, June 23, 2008. Accessed January 10, 2010, at www.ban.org/Library/Green_Ship_Recycling_Standard_Draft_2.pdf.

11

Alliances as Vehicles

In this chapter, we challenge you to:

1. Explain why strategic alliances are important and their main features.

2. Describe the process of building and managing alliances.

3. Identify the various forms of strategic alliances.

4. Summarize the considerations when negotiating the alliance.

5. Compare and contrast cooperatives and franchising as strategic vehicles.

6. Understand the characteristics of alliances in stable and dynamic competitive contexts.

The iconic NASDAQ MarketSite Video Wall was upgraded in 2008 with the installation of 96 Christie DLP(r) rear-projection engines produced by Christie in Kitchener, Ontario.

Digital Cinema[1]

The rapid development of digital technology over the last decade was both disruptive and monumental because it required new skills, capabilities, and assets and changed the industries in the value system from making movies to showing movies. Customers shifted to buying digital technology products as the benefits of change became evident. As digital standards improved, companies in the value system had to develop financial plans and capabilities to remain competitive.

Developing Technology

Texas Instruments had been working on digital technology since at least 1988 when it launched its Digital Light Processing (DLP) in 1997. By 2005, DLP was the only one that met the demands of digital cinema. Thus its chips were the kernel for projectors from all major suppliers: BARCO (a Belgian company), Christie (the Ontario-based subsidiary of a Japanese company, Ushio), and NEC (a Japanese company). Examples of digital projectors are shown in Exhibit 11.1.

Developing Standards

Various innovators developed digital devices that best suited their interests, but the lack of comprehensive technical standards for digital technology meant that these devices were sometimes incompatible with other developers' devices.[2] The major movie studios recognized that standards were needed if they were to benefit from digital technology, but U.S. anti-trust laws prevented their coming together to agree on such standards. Therefore, in 1999, Tom McGrath, then COO of Paramount Pictures, petitioned the U.S. Department of Justice for anti-trust waivers so that film studios could form an alliance to develop uniform standards for digital cinema. While the studios waited for the waivers, the Society of Motion Picture and Television Engineers began work in 2001 on standards for digital cinema. In 2002, the studios received their anti-trust waivers and formed the Digital Cinema Initiatives, LLC (DCI). In June 2005, DCI issued technical specifications and recommendations for the resolution of image files (2K), the transmission of data (JPEG 2000 compression), and defined security requirements (encryption). DCI also offered compliance testing for exhibitors and equipment suppliers.

An Early Player

Cinedigm Digital Cinema Corp. (originally known as Access Integrated Technologies Inc. and AccessIT until 2009) was incorporated in 2000 to pursue the opportunity provided by digital cinema. Its management intended to promote digital cinema by providing a full set of technology solutions, software services, electronic delivery, and content distribution services. The company was well ahead of the opportunity because by 2003 only 159 screens showed digital cinema: 89 in America, 16 in Europe, and 54 in Asia.

Alliances Form

DCI's digital standards published in 2005 reduced much of the industry's uncertainty about the technology, but the cost of digital technology was still a barrier to adoption. This barrier

Exhibit 11.1 Christie's P2220 Digital Projector

Exhibit 11.2 The Business Model for a Third-Party Integrator

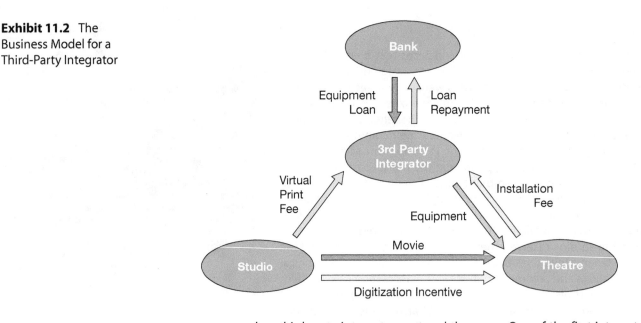

was overcome when third-party integrators entered the scene. One of the first integrators was Christie/AIX, which was an alliance between Cinedigm and Christie. It was 100 percent owned by Cinedigm but was called Christie/AIX to indicate that Christie projectors were being used. Christie/AIX's business model, illustrated in Exhibit 11.2, worked as follows. Using money borrowed from banks, Christie/AIX assembled and then installed all the equipment needed to make a theatre digital. It recouped the cost of digitizing the theatre over 10 to 15 years as each theatre had that time to repay Christie/AIX's installation fees. In addition, the studios paid Christie/AIX a virtual print fee, ranging from $1000 to $1500 for each movie delivered to a theatre. This fee equalled the studio's cost of making a film print and was considerably greater than Christie/AIX's cost of producing a digital print. Some studios also encouraged the adoption of digital technology by subsidizing the theatre's cost of adopting it. The integrators sped up the adoption of digital cinema because they standardized content format, delivery, and presentation while minimizing financial risks of the new technology for studios and exhibitors.

Cinedigm and Christie's original agreement when forming Christie/AIX included a contingency clause, which allowed either partner to terminate the agreement. With Christie/AIX's rapid success, this clause was eliminated and Christie/AIX committed to buying 4000 projectors from Christie at a pre-agreed price.

BARCO and Eastman Kodak also formed a strategic alliance to compete with Christie/AIX. In this alliance BARCO provided the projectors and Kodak provided the computer servers and software, giving the alliance a full menu of products, systems, and services needed for digital cinema systems. The alliance sold, installed, and serviced the systems. As part of the agreement, BARCO adopted Kodak colour science and image management to expand the capability and performance of its cinema projectors.

When these alliances were formed in mid-2005, there were 400 digital screens in the world. BARCO had 80 percent of the European market, 80 percent of the Asian market, and 30 percent of the U.S. market. Christie, however, had the greatest number of projectors being used worldwide.

Adoption of Digital Cinema

Spurred on by the third-party integrators, the theatres quickly adopted digital cinema. The rate of adoption was limited as worldwide production of digital projectors was approximately 5000 units per year. To overcome this limiting factor, Christie increased its manufacturing capacity for its DLP Cinema projector, the Christie CP2000, by 400 percent in one year. In 2008, Christie Digital announced that it alone had manufactured more than 5000 projectors since it started producing them.

This story contains three examples of different forms of alliances: companies coming together as a consortium to set common technical standards, a long-term contract between a company (Cinedigm) and a supplier (Christie), and two companies (BARCO and Eastman Kodak) merging their technology and capabilities to improve the product they can offer. The range of these examples shows the tremendous variation in alliances while the fact that all three are part of this story suggests the frequency with which they occur. ■

Alliances as Vehicles

The business that seeks growth has three alternatives open to it: grow organically, cooperate with other companies, or buy another company. This chapter deals with the second alternative, which is called a *strategic alliance*. This is an agreement between two or more individuals or companies that they will act together to achieve common goals. This chapter starts by developing fuller meaning of a strategic alliance and ways of cooperating. Then you will learn how alliances can increase competitive advantage. From there the chapter turns to consider where partners for alliances can be found and major criteria when selecting a partner. Having learned how to identify a partner, the chapter next considers forming and managing the alliance. **Alliances** are used in several arenas (corporate and international strategy), so these are recognized. The chapter concludes by considering the use of alliances in static and dynamic environments.

alliance A relationship between two or more companies that enhances the effectiveness of the strategy of each.

Strategic Alliance Defined

A strategic alliance is a relationship between two or more companies that enhances the effectiveness of the strategy of each. The major features of strategic alliances are as follows: the alliance is voluntary; it involves the exchange, sharing, or co-development of products, technologies, or services; the companies in it continue to act independently with respect to matters not covered by the alliance; and the arrangement is of limited duration. An alliance can be formed by companies in similar or different positions in the value system.

Various relationships that have been called alliances are identified in Exhibit 11.3. Note that the term *alliance* has become widely used as in "our suppliers are our alliance partner." Many of these relationships are contractually specified, price-driven, financial relationships rather than strategic alliances. An alliance is strategic when it has three distinguishing characteristics:

1. The exchange of knowledge associated with technology, skills, or products takes place.
2. Trust plays a key role in the management of the alliance.
3. Success of the alliance depends on the collaborative efforts among the companies forming the alliance.

Consider, for example, the "alliance" between Nestlé and Mars that allows Nestlé to put Mars-brand M&Ms in its ice creams. The success or failure of this alliance is not going to make or break either company, so it is not strategic.

Mars allows Nestlé to put its M&Ms in Nestlé's ice creams. The success or failure of this "alliance" is not likely to make or break either company.

Exhibit 11.3   Various Alliances

Consortium: A group of individuals or companies formed to undertake an enterprise or activity that would be beyond the capabilities of the individual members.

Cooperative: An enterprise, or business, owned by an association of persons seeking to satisfy common needs (access to products or services, sale of their products or services, employment, etc.).

Countertrade: Any commercial arrangement in which sellers are required to accept, in partial or total settlement of their deliveries, a supply of raw materials, components, or products from the buyer. **Switch trading** is a countertrade transaction involving a third party, which trades the buyer's form of payment into a form of interest to the seller.

Distribution Alliance: An arrangement under which manufacturers of non-competing products who serve the same end users consolidate loads from all manufacturers in the alliance. This permits more frequent shipments of fully loaded vehicles.

Franchising: An agreement under which one company (the franchisor) allows another (the franchisee) the right to sell its products or services.

Joint Venture: An agreement by two or more parties to form a single entity to undertake a certain project. Each of the businesses has an equity stake in the new entity and shares revenues, expenses, and profits.

Licensing: An agreement under which a firm buys the right to use an asset (for example, a particular production process, trademark, or patent) for a particular period of time that is enforced by contract. The licensor receives a fee for little additional investment while the licensee is able to lever its activities.

Cross-licensing: Licensing in which companies get access to the assets of each other. This is used in the drug and technology industries.

Minority Investment: A company invests in another company, becoming a minority shareholder. **Cross shareholding** is when companies make mutual minority investments in each other and is common in Japan, Korea, and Europe.

Network: An arrangement in which two or more companies collaborate without formal relationships but through mechanisms that provide reciprocal advantages, such as code sharing by airlines.

Outsourcing: An arrangement in which one company takes on a particular activity for another company.

Purchasing Alliance: Companies combine their purchase orders for raw materials, components, or products.

Sales Alliance: An arrangement in which two or more companies conduct joint selling of complementary products and services to specific clients.

Solution Alliance: An arrangement in which two or more companies develop and sell a specific marketplace solution. Solutions often combine services with products.

Supplier Alliance: An arrangement in which a supplier agrees to provide a specified type or line of goods or services for a longer term in return for advantageous pricing.

An interesting twist is that an alliance can be strategic to one company but only tactical or operational to the other company in the relationship. This distinction is typically a function of the relative size of the alliance partners and the character of the alliance. Wal-Mart, for example, has only one or a few suppliers for each product it sells. For suppliers the relationship is strategic when Wal-Mart is their dominant customer, but for Wal-Mart, the relationship is tactical because it has alternative suppliers and it readily switches to the suppliers that best meet its requirements. This mismatch was illustrated in 1994 when Rubbermaid sought to offset the cost of resin used to make Rubbermaid products by raising its prices to Wal-Mart, its single largest customer. The giant retailer pulled Rubbermaid products off the shelf and replaced them with products manufactured by Sterilite, a competitor.[3] Wal-Mart only started carrying Rubbermaid products again after Rubbermaid was acquired by Newell in 1999.

One notable way of classifying alliances is by whether the alliance involves equity investment. Equity investment in another company is a strong signal of commitment to the relationship. In joint ventures, equity is invested in a separate, joint-owned organization. In other cases larger companies make minority investments in smaller partners for two possible reasons. First, doing so allows the large company to deal with uncertainty at low cost. When the large company makes the initial investment, it seeks the right to purchase a majority share of the small company later on should it so desire. This type of investment is done often in industries such as biotechnology, computer software, and telecommunications, where the direction of technological change is uncertain. When the smaller company proves to have pursued a valuable technology, the large company exercises its right to invest more in the smaller company. Second, minority investment is done when a national government restricts majority or full investment by foreign companies.

A non-equity alliance involves no exchange of equity and a new company is not formed. Non-equity alliances include licensing, joint research and development, joint product development, and joint distribution. Usually these arrangements are formalized with legal contracts. Non-equity alliances have strategic significance when they extend over a long term, involve the two-way exchange of information, link together business processes, and/or involve the exchange of managers. On the positive side non-equity alliances are easier to form and dissolve, typically involve less governance, and create fewer management issues. On the negative side, non-equity alliances suffer from unclear objectives, possibly because partners have different objectives for the alliance. This, along with the lower commitment to them, means that they are also less permanent.

Use of Alliances

As markets become global and trade barriers drop, companies engage increasingly in strategic alliances to improve their capabilities in light of ever increasing competition. Moreover, innovations, such as digital communications, entertainment, and online services, create the need to include new performance attributes in value curves so that a company's product appeals to customers. Everywhere, companies are discovering that they cannot "go it alone" as they seek to create such curves, so they are looking to collaborate with other companies by using strategic alliances.

Alliances have grown from accounting for 2 percent of company revenues in 1980 to nearly 16 percent in 1995. By 2007, large multinational corporations had more than 20 percent of their total assets tied up in alliances and this percentage would have been much higher if outsourcing arrangements were factored into the calculation.[4]

Alliances are typically a temporary phenomenon lasting six or seven years on average. On average 60 to 70 percent of alliances fail.[5] This hides the fact that some companies have 90 percent success with their alliances, whereas other companies have only 30 percent success.[6] The implication is that the ability to make and manage alliances is a managerial capability that varies among companies.

Successful alliances may be terminated when one partner has learned from its partner what it wanted to know. On terminating the alliance, it speeds up its own organic growth. The alliance may also be terminated when the reason for forming the alliance is no longer strong enough to keep the companies together. Then they agree to go their separate ways. Finally, the alliance can end when one of the companies in the alliance sees the relationship as so beneficial that it buys the other company. This is the topic of the next chapter, Chapter 12.

Unsuccessful alliances are terminated when at least one of the parties is not getting what it expected from the alliance. This can happen when the governance mechanism of the alliance is insufficient to control behaviours of companies relative to their commitments. Another reason the alliance can be unsuccessful is that a company entered the alliance with a poor understanding of what it was committing to or unrealistic expectations of what could be accomplished through an alliance. This situation could have been avoided through well-crafted negotiations in which objectives and expectations were clarified and realistic commitments set.

Building and Managing an Alliance

From a managerial perspective, one needs to know whether to use an alliance and, if so, how to go about building and managing it. These questions can be addressed using a five-stage process: building the case for an alliance, identifying and screening potential partners, negotiating and setting up the alliance, managing the alliance and determining when to terminate the alliance (see Exhibit 11.4). The first stage involves building the case for an alliance and starts with assessing the strategy of the company. Needs and weaknesses are identified and ways of overcoming them are addressed. If an alliance is deemed the best way to address these matters, one proceeds to stage two. The second stage involves identifying possible partners and then screening them to see which one is best. This screening can be done in a staged process with a general screening to reduce the number of candidates to a workable number and then performing detailed due diligence analysis of the most attractive candidate. Stage three deals with negotiating the alliance. These negotiations craft the agreement, which lays out how the alliance will operate. Then the alliance is set up in accordance with the agreement. Stage four involves ongoing management of the alliance. Performance is tracked and adjustments are made to the alliance as necessary. Up to this point, the process has been very similar to that used when performing mergers and acquisitions. In stage five a periodic strategic assessment of the alliance is conducted. Management needs to consider whether the alliance is still necessary and is the best solution. If it is not, then management needs to terminate the alliance. We now consider each of these five stages in more detail.

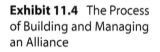

Exhibit 11.4 The Process of Building and Managing an Alliance

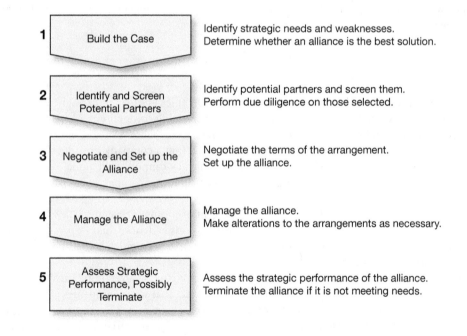

STAGE 1: BUILDING THE CASE FOR AN ALLIANCE

Companies participate in alliances because they enhance their competitive advantage. Building the case for the alliance involves examining various ways in which the value added by the company can be increased. Enhanced competitive advantage is only meaningful, however, if it can be sustained. Sustainability fits with the VRINE framework presented in Chapter 3 in that resources and capabilities must be valuable, rare, difficult to imitate, and exploitable. The alliance itself provides the organizational arrangements needed to fulfill the final requirement of the VRINE framework. If an alliance (or network of alliances) satisfies these criteria, it likely has a collaborative advantage that helps one or more of the member companies achieve a competitive advantage over rivals outside the alliance.

Enhancing Competitive Advantage

Enhancement of competitive advantage can come from three different sources: improving operations, enhancing competitive conditions, and facilitating entry and exit (see Exhibit 11.5).

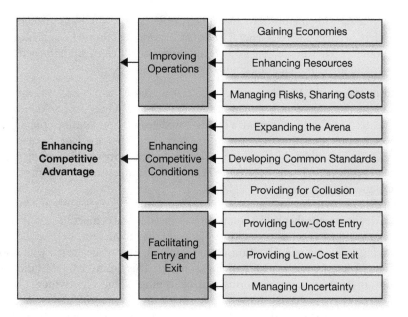

Exhibit 11.5 The Three Sources for Improving Competitive Advantage

All three sources can increase the value of the business. However, these gains must be measured against the cost of creating and operating the alliance. The benefits produced by the alliance have to be greater than the cost or the alliance does not make sense.

Improving Operations

Operations can be improved by achieving economies, expanding resources, and managing operating risks while sharing operating costs.

Achieving economies A company may lack the volume needed in an activity to achieve sufficient economies of scale to be competitive. A possible reason is that the company would need to dominate its industry or market in order to achieve such volume. By cooperating with another company that has similar needs but is in a different industry or market, the two can join together in the activity so that cost is reduced. The oil companies, for example, want to keep their refineries operating at higher levels as this lowers the overall refining costs. The result is that they often produce more fuel than can actually be sold through their own branded facilities within a region. They address this problem by swapping fuel with other oil companies that do not have a refinery within the region. For example, the Shell refinery in the Edmonton area may have an exchange agreement with Husky in Prince George, B.C. This allows Husky in Northern Alberta to "lift product" (fill tanker trucks) at the Shell facility and Shell to "lift product" at the Husky refinery in Prince George.[7]

An alliance can also provide additional products that expand the arena of the business to employ its resources fully. Recall that Toronto-based Grocery Gateway described earlier formed an alliance with Home Depot, Starbucks Inc., the Liquor Control Board of Ontario, and Staples to deliver products for them. This web-based grocery store lowered its distribution cost through greater scale and at the same time earned additional revenue from its distribution fleet.

An alliance between a customer company and its supplier can reduce costs in several ways.[8] The arrangement between them can encourage them to adjust their operations to better meet the needs of the other by improving quality by reducing defects, returns, and warranty work; eliminating inventory through just-in-time delivery; and directing R&D into solving the customer's problems and taking advantage of new technology.

An alliance can spread the cost of investing in a new technology across several companies. For example, the steel companies sought to lower the weight of cars made with steel so that they were weight-competitive with plastics and other metals. Finding a way to make a lighter-weight car was too expensive for an individual steel company so in 1998 Dofasco and 34 steel companies from around the world came together to work with Porsche Engineering on the Ultra Light Steel Auto Body (ULSAB) project. The project produced a high-tech, strong, safe, and cost-efficient auto body that weighed 25 percent less than the benchmarked model made by traditional manufacturing methods. In another example, in 2005 three automakers (the BMW Group, DaimlerChrysler AG, and General Motors Corporation) formed an alliance to develop hybrid drive systems. They pooled their best technologies and thereby strengthened the innovative potential of all three participating companies.[9]

Expanding resources A company that lacks critical resources can access them by forming an alliance with a company that has them. In 2006, O-Two Medical Technologies of Toronto allied with Neotech Medical Equipment, a Dubai-based health-care solution company that represented specialized medical equipment manufacturers in the Middle East. Neotech's role was to distribute O-Two's devices, ranging from emergency respiratory care devices through to CPR and burn relief products.[10] This supplemented O-Two's resources and at the same time allowed O-Two to expand its strategic arena.

In industries where technology is evolving rapidly, alliances give relatively quick access to key technological developments that help a company stay ahead of the competition. Borland Software Corp. writes software that works on multiple platforms, including Java, Net, Oracle, and SAP.[11] DMR Consulting, a division of Fujitsu Consulting (Canada), formed an alliance with Borland that allowed it to build its own software on Borland's software. This meant that DMR did not have to program software for the different platforms, making its programmers much more productive.

When a resource is too expensive to acquire or to maintain, a company can get access to as much of the resource as needed through an alliance. For example, often small companies do not have all the capabilities they need to perform all the jobs they take on. They ally with other small businesses that have the necessary capabilities that then perform the tasks they cannot do themselves.

When another company can perform one of its functional activities for less, the company outsources the activity to the low-cost company, in effect forming an alliance with the other company. A similar argument holds when one company is more expert at an activity. Four Seasons Hotels Inc. manages more than 80 luxury hotels around the world on behalf of real estate owners and developers for 3 percent of the gross income and approximately 5 percent of profits from the properties. Four Seasons typically participates in the design of the property and has nearly total control over every aspect of the operation. Property owners like to have Four Seasons provide the management because its superior skills generate higher revenues, making the properties worth more as an investment.[12]

A final way of improving resources is by learning from the other company in the alliance. Sometimes both companies learn, as do John Deere and Hitachi, which regularly exchange key employees in certain product segments. Other times knowledge goes from a customer to a supplier. Honda and Toyota both have supplier development programs in which they work with the supplier to improve the suppliers' cycle times, inventory, reliability, and quality. The suppliers find that by learning how to satisfy the high performance standards of these customers, they can satisfy many more customers. A study of Toyota's U.S. suppliers found that suppliers for GM and Ford could not match Toyota's suppliers' efficiency.[13]

Managing risks while sharing costs Alliances can be used to manage risks while sharing operating costs with other companies. Banks are able to pursue attractive lending opportunities by forming syndicates that buy corporate bonds. These bonds can be worth billions of dollars. Each bank limits its risk by agreeing to purchase a portion of the loan amount. Oil companies also use alliances when drilling for new wells. Drilling wells is costly and the likelihood of finding oil is not great. The Gulf of Mexico, for example, has been called the "Dead Sea" under the impression that no new oil will be found there, yet BP operating with other partners has found oil there. In 1999, it struck oil 240 kilometres southeast of New Orleans in the Thunder Horse Oil Field. The platform supporting the floating production, drilling, and headquarters cost US$1 billion and is 50 percent larger than the next largest floating semi-submersible rig in the world. Thunder Horse is owned 75 percent by BP and 25 percent by ExxonMobil.[14] In 2009, BP announced that it had struck oil 400 kilometres southeast of Houston in 1259 metres of water. The Tiber Prospect well was drilled to a total depth of approximately 10 685 metres, making it one of the deepest wells ever drilled by the oil and gas industry. Tiber is operated by BP, with a 62 percent working interest with co-owners Petrobras (20 percent) and ConocoPhillips (18 percent). The risk associated with such oil exploration has been demonstrated with the failure of the Thunder Horse platform to ever reach planned production levels and has been

The Thunder Horse platform was a breakthrough in deep-water oil production and features more than 100 technological firsts in the industry. The risk associated with this enterprise became apparent when the platform almost sank during Hurricane Dennis in 2005 while being positioned in the Gulf of Mexico.

emphasized with the blowout, fire, and sinking of the Deepwater Horizon oil drilling platform in April 2010, which produced a major ecological disaster.

Enhancing Competitive Conditions

The alliance can enhance competitive conditions, allowing the companies to earn more than they could without it. It does so by expanding the arena the company competes in, by developing common standards, and by providing for collusion.

Expanding the arena A company does business in its arena, which can be extended by allying with another company to get access to new customers to sell to and new products to sell. The new customers can be in different market segments, served by different market channels, in different industries, and in different countries. The new products can be in growth markets or help provide solutions to problems. Sometimes regulations limit what the company can do in its market. An alliance provides a way of growing both within its current market by doing something different and so redefining its market and expanding beyond its current market by moving into other markets.

Developing common standards Common standards for both technologies and for industries help companies work together. In the entertainment industry the adoption of digital projectors required standards so that complementary technologies could be developed to produce films that could be shown on digital projectors. These standards were used to develop digital cameras, sound equipment, and editing equipment as well. In addition, standards were developed to protect the digital rights of movie studios. Another important alliance in recent years has been the World Wide Web Consortium (W3C), which sets standards for the World Wide Web. The standards are presented as recommendations, but developers must follow if they wish to label their product W3C-compliant. Without common standards the web would be a lot less useful because incompatible versions of HTML (a computer coding language) would produce inconsistent web pages.[15]

Common standards, however, are not always universal standards. Companies sometimes come together to co-develop a network. By working with the same standards, the network creates resources and capabilities that give the players in it a competitive advantage. Then networks themselves take on the characteristics of companies and compete with networks formed by other companies that developed competing standards. Dramatic battles have been fought by alliances over emerging technological standards. As you can see in Exhibit 11.6, Sun, HP, IBM, and MIPS are all placing bets on certain technological standards, and they have a vast array of partners helping them to battle their respective parts of the fray.[16] Importantly, the fortunes of the many small companies in the network are dependent upon the success of the larger

Exhibit 11.6   Alliance Networks of Sun, HP, IBM, and MIPS

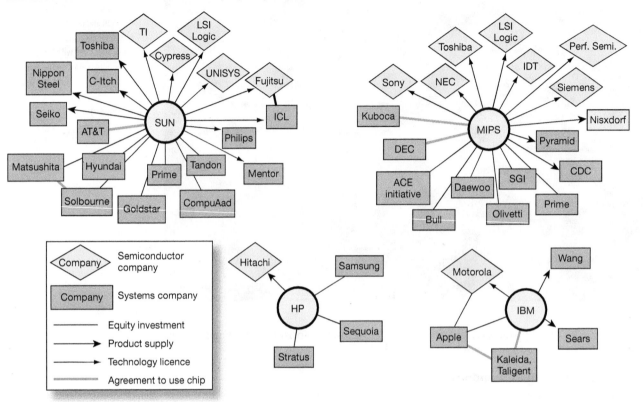

group. For example, in the mid-1970s two networks were created around two different standards for videotape technology. Sony's Betamax technology was technically superior to JVC's VHS format, but VHS machines were simpler and cheaper to manufacture and the tapes could record longer viewing times. Moreover, JVC was aggressive in lining up more manufacturers to produce machines based on its VHS standards. With more VHS video cassette recorders sold than Betamax machines, movie studios converted more of their movies to VHS standards. The consequence was that VHS dominated video screens until the creation of DVD technology. With DVDs the major electronics corporations agreed on a single standard for playback of prerecorded material. This was followed by a minor skirmish over the high-definition successor to DVDs (Memory-Tech and Toshiba had the HD-DVD while Sony had the Blu-ray), which ended in victory for Sony in 2008. Winning the standards war provides the winner with the advantage of being ahead of others in that technology because it has been working with it longer and also the ability to license the use of its technology by others.

Another example of network competition comes from the airline industry where three alliances—Star created in 1997, One World in 1999, and Sky Team in 2000—are battling for passengers.[17] Exhibit 11.7 lists several alliance networks formed in the past, some of which have been dissolved or restructured as the nature of the partners' relationships or the competitive environment has evolved.

Providing for collusion   Collusion occurs when two or more companies coordinate their decisions so that competition in the industry is reduced, with the intent of improving their performance. Collusion can be either explicit or tacit. Explicit collusion occurs when companies communicate directly with each other as they coordinate prices, production, and so on. The Organization of the Petroleum Exporting Countries (OPEC) is a permanent intergovernmental organization of 12 oil-exporting developing nations that coordinates and unifies the petroleum policies of its member countries. This form of collusion is illegal in many countries although it occurs.

Under Canadian law, an alliance can be examined under merger or conspiracy law if the agreement between competitors "prevents or lessens, or is likely to prevent or lessen, competition substantially in a market." This holds when agreements create, maintain, or enhance the ability of the parties to the agreement to exercise market power. For example, an agreement that

Exhibit 11.7 Different Alliance Networks

Business or Industry	Selective Rival Constellations
Hardware and Software for Interactive TV	▶ Motorola, Scientific Atlanta, Kaleida ▶ Time Warner, Silicon Graphics ▶ Intel, Microsoft, General Instruments ▶ H.P., TV Answer
Video CDs	▶ Sony and Philips ▶ Toshiba, Time Warner, Matsushita, others
Global Telecommunications	▶ AT&T Worldpartners (includes 12 partners) ▶ British Telecom and MCI ▶ Sprint, Deutsche Telekom, France Telecom
Automobiles and Trucks	▶ G.M., Toyota, Isuzu, Suzuki, Volvo ▶ Ford, Mazda, Kia, Nissan, Fiat, VW ▶ Chrysler, Mitsubishi, Daimler-Benz
Biotechnology Research	▶ Genentech network ▶ Centocor network
Pharmaceutical Marketing (United States)	▶ Merck and Medco (merger) ▶ SmithKline and DPS (merger) ▶ Eli Lilly and PCS (merger) ▶ Pfizer and Value Health ▶ Pfizer, Rhône-Poulenc, Caremark, others
Global Airline Services	▶ Delta, Swissair, Singapore Airlines, SAS ▶ KLM and Northwest ▶ British Airways and USAir
Global Comercial Real Estate Services	▶ Colliers International (44 companies) ▶ International Commercial (23 companies) ▶ Oncore International (36 companies) ▶ New America Network (150 companies) ▶ Cushman & Wakefield (52 alliances) ▶ CB Commercial (70 affiliates) ▶ Grubb & Ellis (six affiliates)

provides higher prices than without the agreement is viewed as lessening competition. An agreement can also prevent competition by hindering the development of future competition.[18]

Still, under Canadian regulations unusual things happen. In 2000, Ted Rogers and J. R. Shaw, controlling shareholders of Shaw, signed a non-compete agreement that "divided Canada in half—Rogers Communications in Ontario, Quebec, and the Maritimes, and Shaw in Manitoba, Saskatchewan, Alberta, and British Columbia—and agreed not to acquire or start a new broadband wireline cable business outside their territory for 10 years. The purpose was to allow Rogers and Shaw to bid on cable operations in their areas for the lowest possible price without competition from the other."[19] The Canadian Radio-television and Telecommunications Commission (CRTC), which regulates the country's cable television industry, was unaware of the nine-year-old non-compete covenant between Rogers and Shaw. As far as Rogers was concerned, the non-compete agreement was effective at least until 2010. The deal between the companies broke down in 2009 when Shaw acquired Mountain Cablevision and Rogers went to court over it.

Tacit collusion takes place when companies signal to each other with the goal of coordinating their production and pricing decisions. Anti-combines and anti-trust legislation prevent trade associations, a form of alliance, from acting as a coordinator of such activity. Nevertheless, individual companies engage in market signalling through practices such as public announcements about their price increases, capacity changes, and so on. Tacit collusion is hard to prove legally since competitors can chose to ignore these market signals.

Facilitating Entry and Exit

The third benefit of strategic alliances is that they facilitate entry and exit from an industry.

Providing low-cost entry   Entry into a new arena requires resources and products that the company may not possess. An alliance can provide these to the business at less than the cost of acquiring assets and developing new capabilities and products. In 1998, Torstar's new ventures group recognized that ethnic newspapers proved attractive—ethnic communities were growing rapidly and members of these communities still preferred printed newspapers. Torstar entered this market by acquiring a 50 percent interest in the Canadian operations of Sing Tao's media group. *Sing Tao Daily* is the largest Cantonese-language newspaper in Canada, with editions in Toronto, Vancouver, Calgary, and Montreal.[20]

When entering foreign markets, companies often form an alliance or license their products to a local company so they can benefit from its distribution channel. Pharmaceutical companies do this but may also engage in additional joint actions to deal better with domestic regulations. The company that has developed the drug sometimes contracts the marketing and promotion of the drug to a foreign company under the originator's name, and other times it engages jointly in local clinical trial activities, then sells the product together. For example, Novartis developed an HMG-CoA reductase inhibitor, then got it approved in Canada and the U.S. and sold it under the name Lescol. But in Japan, Novartis allied with Mitsubishi–Tanabe Pharma. There, they did joint clinical trials and then sold the drug under the name Lochol.[21]

Low-cost exit   When a company exits a market it likely wants to sell the associated assets but may not have a buyer willing to pay much for them. Allying with a potential buyer allows that buyer to observe directly how valuable the assets are. This encourages it to pay a higher price for the business and also encourages various stakeholders to continue to work with the business. If they thought it was going to "die," they would walk away from it.[22]

Managing uncertainty   The company may not be able to tell which strategy it should pursue. It can reduce the risk of making the wrong choice by waiting until it has better information about which alternative is better. One way management can determine what to do at different points in time is to analyze the situation using real options. Using this approach management makes partial investments in attractive alternatives and, as additional information is produced, determines which alternatives to invest in further. Traditionally the large pharmaceutical companies have taken this approach with respect to new biologically created drugs. They have allied with start-up companies, investing in those with promising drugs, and, as the drugs prove more promising, investing further. When the drug appears to be marketable, they exercise the option under which they provided the investment to buy the start-up and incorporate its drug in their own portfolio of drugs.

In 2007, GE and BP formed an alliance to develop, deploy, and demonstrate the integration of gasification and power generation technology in hydrogen power projects. Initially, the companies will apply GE's proprietary gasification and turbine technology in five hydrogen power plants that use petroleum coke or bituminous coal as feedstock. These projects will demonstrate that low-carbon power can be produced from fossil fuels in a manner that is efficient, reliable, and economical.[23]

Sustaining Competitive Advantage

Recall from the VRINE framework that resources and capabilities are the basis of competitive advantage only when they satisfy certain criteria: The ability to enhance competitive advantage implies that alliances add value and that they are able to design and operate the alliance. For the value added to be sustained, what the alliance does needs to be rare and difficult to imitate.

Rare

The high frequency with which strategic alliances are formed suggests that they are not rare, so the value they create is not sustainable. Closer examination is required, however, since alliances have been created for various reasons. The ultimate question is whether other companies, in alliances or not, are able to match the capabilities of the alliance. If not, then the competitive advantage of the alliance is sustainable.

Costly to Imitate

The alliance also needs to be able to take advantage of the resources it has put together. This requires various organizational aspects including contracts, equity investments, governance, reputation, and trust. While each is important in its own right, there is a dynamic among them. Contracts define the parameters of any business alliance, but ideally the contract is put in the drawer while the alliance is working, and the focus is on building a living relationship with the other partner(s) in the alliance.

STAGE 2: IDENTIFYING AND SCREENING POTENTIAL PARTNERS

Once the rationale for an alliance has been built, the next step is determining whom the company might collaborate with in an alliance. This involves identifying potential partners and then screening them to determine the best partner to strike an alliance with.

Identifying Potential Partners

The search for clients can be an unruly process. Some structure can be given to this using the five-force model of industry structure introduced in Chapter 4. This focuses attention on the companies that are closely related to the company. What follows are examples of alliances between various competitors and complementors that demonstrate the types of alliances that could be created. Using these examples as a guide, one can readily envision the kinds of possibilities that exist.

Rivals

Alliances between companies in the same industry are called *horizontal alliances*. These alliances are particularly important when there is a network effect—a phenomenon in which a service becomes more valuable as more people use it, thereby encouraging ever-increasing numbers of adopters. The network effect applies to banks and their bank machines, cellphone companies and wandering, and airlines and their shared facilities and cross-listed flights.

Rivals can also form alliances as they pool their resources and limit their risks. BP did when it joined with other oil companies (ConocoPhillip, Exxon, and Petrobras) to search for oil in the Gulf of Mexico.

When competitors form an alliance, they must be willing to share resources but each also wants to hold on to those resources that provide its competitive advantage. For example, the two makers of copiers and printers, Fuji Photo and Xerox, agreed to collaborate in the Japanese and Pacific Rim markets in 1962. Fuji agreed because the alliance would not affect its film business in these markets, while Xerox believed that the venture would not endanger its copier business elsewhere in the world.

A more complex situation produces *co-opetition*: a situation in which companies both cooperate and compete. Three situations are possible. First, they can cooperate, then compete. When not ready for competition in a particular area, they cooperate until they build their competence or achieve a common standard. They may even share proprietary knowledge with others to help create the standards. Once the standards exist, then they compete for business. Second, they can cooperate while competing. By allying with each other they can learn from each other how to overcome their own weaknesses. Third, they can cooperate among themselves and compete with others. Such alliances tend to be vertical as companies at different stages of the value system ally together to compete with similar vertical alliances formed by other companies. In each case the business benefits from cooperating with others but is competitive with others.

New entrants

Companies already in the industry can diversify by collaborating with new entrants or limit the impact of a new entrant by co-opting it. Mexican retailer Cifra was not hurt directly by Wal-Mart's entrance into Mexico in 1992 because it entered into a joint venture with Wal-Mart. It benefited from being a co-owner of the joint venture that shared retail, wholesale, and distribution centre operations.[24]

Suppliers

A company can partner with a supplier in a vertical alliance. These alliances can range from sole-sourcing and just-in-time arrangements to more complex forms such as joint ventures.

An alliance can be used to ensure the supply of a product. In 2008, Barrick Gold Corp. was faced with a worldwide shortage of the three-metre-high tires used by the massive ore-moving trucks that are vital to its gold mining activities. It could not afford to have a Cdn$3 million truck sitting idle because it lacked a tire, so Barrick formed an alliance with Yokohama Rubber Co. Ltd. It lent the Japanese tire company US$35 million to help finance the US$50 million expansion of its Onomichi plant in Hiroshima. Barrick agreed to buy 1300 tires a year at direct-from-manufacturing prices beginning in 2009. Over the 10-year life of the deal, Barrick would buy more than Cdn$200 million worth of tires.[25]

The alliance can also involve developing new technology for the user. In 2009, R. R. Donnelley & Sons, a printer that uses digital printing equipment, allied with HP, which produces printing technology. The goal of the alliance was to combine the collective talent, intellectual property, and innovation of the two to develop digital printing solutions for high-speed, inkjet-based digital presses.[26]

Or the alliance can combine the technologies of two companies to create a superior product. In 2007, Walleye Technologies in Massachusetts allied with Terabeam to develop a next generation, handheld, portable imaging technology capable of "seeing" into and through solid objects. Terabeam's expertise in millimetre wave technology allowed Walleye to accelerate development of a new generation of imaging devices.[27]

Customers

An alliance between the company and its customer is also a vertical alliance as a seller and a buyer are involved. For instance, three companies came together (Emerson/Copeland Corporation with 51 percent, Lennox/Heatcraft Technology with 24.5 percent, and American Standard/Trane with 24.5 percent) in a joint venture called Alliance Compressor. Alliance Compressor develops, manufactures, markets, and sells scroll compressors primarily to Lennox and Trane.

An alliance can also help a company improve its market coverage. In 2002, the Stanley Works formed a strategic alliance with Home Depot, the big-box retailer of hardware. Under a five-year agreement, Home Depot used Stanley as its sole national supplier of builders' hardware, raising Stanley's coverage from about half to all of Home Depot's stores. This expanded Stanley's geographic coverage. Home Depot also named Stanley its principal national supplier of pneumatic fastening tools, providing Stanley with increased shelf space and greater market penetration.

Starbucks allied with companies to extend the locations where its coffee was served: Chapters (bookstore cafés), Air Canada (in-flight coffee service), Unilever International (coffee ice cream), PepsiCo (Frappuccino ready-to-drink coffee), and Kraft (ground and whole coffee beans distributed through grocery stores). The various strategic roles that these non-equity alliances play for Starbucks are shown in Exhibit 11.8.[28]

Substitutes

Companies in different industries producing products and services that satisfy the same consumer needs may form an alliance. Dean Foods is a major dairy processor and distributor in the United States. In the late 1990s the demand for soy milk was growing dramatically and consumers were substituting for regular milk. Instead of competing against the soy milk manufacturers, Dean Foods invested in White Wave Inc., the manufacturer of Silk, the leading brand of soymilk. Its initial investment in 2000 gave it 30 percent of the ownership in White Wave. Dean liked the potential for soy milk so much that in 2002 it bought the rest of White Wave. By collaborating with the supplier of a substitute, Dean was able to offer consumers broader choices and in the process discovered for itself an attractive opportunity for growth.

Complementors

Some products and services, when bundled together, provide customers with greater value than when they are acquired separately. Furthermore, bundled products and services can create a powerful combination that puts competitors at a disadvantage and may even lock competitors out of a large part of the market. In the 1980s, Microsoft and Intel informally established the Wintel alliance. It started with the popularity of Microsoft's Windows operating system, which functioned well on personal computers (PCs) using Intel's central processing (CPU) chips. No computer manufacturer dared to be incompatible with the Windows system, so Intel had a ready market for its CPUs. As Microsoft kept increasing processing requirements, Intel kept producing more powerful CPUs. The popularity of the Windows operating system coupled

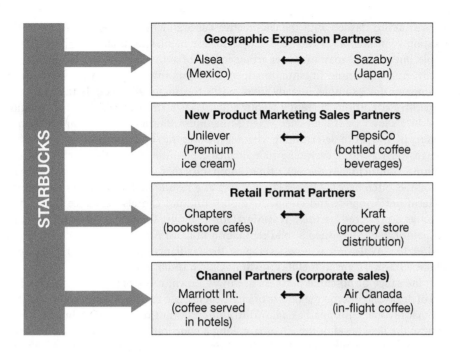

Exhibit 11.8 The Starbucks Universe of Alliances

with Intel's aggressive pricing strategies kept competitors producing operating systems and CPUs down to a handful. Only in the late 1990s did changes allow these competitors to start recovering some market share.

Screening Potential Partners

Knowing where the company might look for partners still leaves open the question of who will make the best partner in an alliance. Determining this involves a two-part screening process. The first is a general screening followed by a tighter screening called due diligence. Management considers five questions of fit when performing the general screening:

- *Strategic fit:* Are the partners' objectives compatible? For how long?
- *Resource and financial fit:* Are the partners willing and able to contribute the resources and competencies?
- *Cultural fit:* Can the partners understand each other? Do they share the same business logic and commitment?
- *Structure, systems, and processes fit:* Can the decision-making and control mechanisms be aligned?
- *Additional fit criteria:* What other key questions should be on the table, such as timing, other alliances, alliance alternatives, environmental context, and competitive pressures?

Because we are interested in alliances as a strategy vehicle, the first question pertains to *strategic fit.* Alliances between complementary equals tend to be the strongest and longest lasting. In some cases, competitive tensions and industry conditions may lead one partner to acquire the other, usually after about seven years. In other cases, the partners remain strong and independent. Some alliances, such as Fuji-Xerox, exemplify true coevolution and are more likely to survive for much longer than seven years. In the case of Fuji-Xerox, this alliance has lasted several decades and has spawned additional complementary alliances. Alliances between weaker and stronger companies can lead the weaker company to a position of strength. Then either the alliance is dissolved or the stronger partner acquires the weaker one. Researchers at McKinsey and Company, a consulting company, have identified lack of strategic fit as a common reason that alliances have failed.[29]

The question of *resource and financial fit* deals with either the availability of a resource or the willingness and ability of a partner to make that resource available. The question of *cultural fit* typically relates to the cultural characteristics of the organizations themselves. In the early years of SEMATECH, for instance, Intel's participation was problematic because Intel's highly competitive culture clashed with the cooperative culture being fostered by the consortium.[30] The question of *structural fit* can be a simple matter of making financial reporting systems compatible, but conflicts may arise over arrangements of authority and decision making.

Finally, in determining fit, situation-specific factors must be taken into consideration. Is the company, for example, already involved in too many alliances? Is the timing right? Do competitive conditions currently favour alliances as a strategy vehicle? How Would You Do That? 11.1 shows what happened when Millennium Pharmaceuticals applied a checklist for assessing partner fit in determining whether to enter into an alliance with a potential partner. The answer was no. Developing rich alliance capabilities that satisfy a checklist such as Millennium's is difficult. At the same time, companies that succeed in developing the requisite capabilities often become better competitors as a result. Such capabilities can contribute to near-term performance and competitive position, and can also enhance the company's reputation as a preferred partner. Wal-Mart, for example, though known as a very aggressive competitor, has established a solid reputation in Latin America as a dependable partner. As noted earlier, Wal-Mart is now leveraging these alliance skills and the reputation built through local partnerships to fuel its growth in China, India, and Japan.

With the range of potential partners narrowed down, more detailed analysis is in order. The level of detail depends on the degree of interdependence that the alliance will create. Simple alliances that involve joint purchasing or distribution do not require much further investigation because the likelihood of the alliance making a contribution to competitive advantage is relatively easy to assess and regimented with a contract. A more complex alliance like a joint venture calls for considerable investigation because the demands of the alliance are much greater, exposing each company to more uncertainty and risk. Detailed analysis helps clarify what the alliance can deliver and what steps need to be taken to mitigate risks due to the alliance. The importance of due diligence is influenced by the reputation of the potential partner as a company with the reputation of being a cheater is not an attractive partner.

Examination of the potential partner's interactions with other companies is a good indicator of its future behaviour and the degree to which it can be trusted. This influences the character of the alliance that the company is willing to form.[31] When the partner can be trusted, one's willingness to make investments in assets customized to the alliance is greater because fear of a hold-up is lessened. A hold-up is possible when one company makes a specific investment tied to the alliance, which has limited alternative use or liquidation value. It occurs when the return on the investment is expropriated by the partner. Trust allows the parties to have difficult discussions that transform the alliance over time, giving it longevity. In addition, trust means that the allies require less information for monitoring and maintaining the alliance. Trust also allows for a simpler governance structure and enables adaptability, even renegotiation of financial terms, to accommodate changes. It also reduces the need for creating new legal agreements for small changes in the arrangement. Finally, trust allows flexibility in arrangements, which promotes learning and the pursuit of opportunities that were not recognized when the alliance was formed. Trust can be eroded when allies work strictly according to the contract.

FOCUS ON ETHICS 11.1
Using a Strategic Alliance to Build Image

Strategic alliances have become a tool to strengthen social responsibility credentials with for-profit and non-profit organizations (NPOs) joining forces to achieve their separate but related missions. These partnerships are charting a mutual course benefiting each of their strategies. In 1999, Starbucks joined forces with humanitarian agency CARE International and eventually contributed more than US$20 million to programs that provide emergency relief and community support in developing countries. Starbucks was recognized by CARE for its humanitarian contributions and gained the promotional line "Coffee That Cares." Other successful cross-sector alliances include City Year and Timberland; the Nature Conservancy and Georgia-Pacific; Bidwell Training Center and Bayer Corporation; and Jumpstart and American Eagle Outfitters.[32]

How much is really being done for the recipients of aid through actions such as Starbucks'? It is it really just "window dressing" rather than providing substantial benefits for others?

STAGE 3: NEGOTIATING AND SETTING UP THE ALLIANCE[33]

Having decided that an alliance is the right vehicle to use and having selected a partner, the partners have to negotiate the character of the alliance. Most negotiations conclude with a contract which reflects the agreement between the partners in the alliance. The contract provides clear commitments, performance expectations, and provides remedies and processes should disputes arise. It works well for simple arrangements such as distribution agreements. As alliances become more complex, contracts become more detailed; yet no matter how detailed they become, they can never anticipate every contingency. Then sticking to terms of the contract can force rigidity that stifles the ability of the alliance to adjust to the evolving situation. And continual referral to a contract creates tension and frustration from which the working relationship never recovers. Contracts are important but an alliance's success is built on a good working relationship that allows informal, day-to-day operating decisions to be made and the exchange of critical information. This needs to be kept in mind when setting up an alliance. Some general thoughts to keep in mind when negotiating the arrangement follow.

Stewardship

Those forming the alliance need to clearly define the strategy of the alliance. This helps the companies stay focused on why they came together in one. It may be created for a specific purpose linked directly to the parent's operations or it may be created to bring together capabilities that equip the alliance to pursue opportunities as they appear. Whatever the motivation, a clearly defined strategy provides a justification for the alliance and means that it is more likely to meet the members' intentions. A strategy that is closely tied to the strategies of the members of the alliance prolongs its life.

Continuing support of the alliance from the members' senior management is also needed. They can keep the reason for the alliance fresh in the minds of those lower in their organizations and use their power to help the alliance overcome resistance to it in their respective companies.

Resource Commitments

The tangible and intangible resources each member is contributing to the alliance need to be clearly specified along with when those resources will be available. That way, the alliance knows what it has to work with—though from the perspective of the alliance's management, they want sufficient resources that they are independent of those forming the alliance. When the alliance faces a more dynamic environment or an opportunistic strategy, a freer exchange of resources, especially skilled people and intellectual property, is required. The alliance also needs to know if there are limits on the resources, including the time and energy of its executives that the parents are willing to provide.

The allies may invest equity in the alliance itself or in each other as "cross-investments." Investing in a separate legal venture such as a joint venture and earning returns based on the success of that venture limits the allies' interest in behaving in ways that hurt the joint venture. Cross-investments are common in Japanese Keiretsus and Korean Chaebols, with many companies clustered around one parent company and holding shares in one another. Cross-investments mean that a company benefits from the successes and suffers from the losses of its partner.

A Governance Structure

A governance structure provides clear roles, information flows, and performance metrics. A good one facilitates an effective working relationship and leads to maximizing the performance of the alliance itself. What is "good" varies because different alliances need different features to succeed. A single governance model simply will not suffice. For example, the governance model for a short-term co-marketing alliance is different from that for a long-term research joint venture. For each situation a governance structure needs to be built around three considerations: role responsibilities, information flows, and performance evaluation.

Role Responsibilities

The roles that various parties play in the alliance need to be defined and their decision-making authority specified. Without this, decision making is slowed down and conflict among the partners is inevitable. The decision-making power is strongly influenced by the value and complexity of resource contributions each member makes to the alliance. When one parent has the relevant operational skills for the joint venture, it should oversee the venture. If both parents have required skills, the parent with the skills that can be transferred on a one-time basis should do so, and the other should oversee the venture. The danger is that tight control by one partner might reduce conflicts and increase manageability but also limit the flexibility and openness of the joint venture to new opportunities. If the skills of both parents are crucial, shared joint management is appropriate. Then the partners can take an active role in capital allocation, risk management, and performance management because these are areas that drive financial performance and protect shareholder interest: The partners should limit their interventions in areas where the joint venture needs independence to ensure competitiveness and market responsiveness such as staffing, pricing, and product development.

Information Flows

All parties need specific information to execute their responsibilities. At the higher levels, the partners in the alliance will want specific information so they can integrate their activities with the alliance and assess its performance. The quality of this information and when the information is expected also needs to be specified.

Performance Evaluation

The partners need to evaluate the performance of the alliance as they do for their own performance. Performance expectations need to be tempered according to the nature of the alliance. Something like a distribution agreement can produce desirable results much sooner than a joint venture. When the ultimate goal takes longer to achieve, milestones that measure progress toward that goal help sustain the commitment of the members because progress is evident. Additional information, both quantitative and qualitative, may be desired by the members so that they can monitor the success of the alliance. These data needs are best clarified at the start so that the members have the information required to feel comfortable. Members who have worked with each other before develop trust in each other, which lessens the amount of information they require from the alliance.

STAGE 4: MANAGING THE ALLIANCE

The capabilities of managing the alliance depend on the demands of the alliance. Requirements are considerably less for an outsourcing agreement than for a joint venture.

Leadership

Leadership is especially important in the early life of an alliance. Leadership skills are used to give focus to the alliance and gain the support of various stakeholders, though the overall structure will have been determined by the alliance partners prior to appointing the manager of the alliance. An effective leader can attract good people and instill their loyalty to the alliance. This loyalty encourages them to work toward the alliance's success.

Staffing

The alliance needs people with the requisite skills. Whether people will join depends in part on the relationship between the alliance and who is controlling it. When the alliance operates as the business unit of one partner, recruiting people with the necessary skills from that partner will be easy. When the alliance draws on both parents, recruiting from both partners is required. However, recruiting managers from the partners is likely to prove difficult if the alliance is entirely separate from the partners' operations.

Culture

When staff come from the partners, cultural clashes are likely. This problem is greater when people who work in the alliance are still part of their respective companies. Then management of the alliance has to get disparate cultures to work together, with people acting in the best interests of the alliance. When the people become part of a separate organization as with a joint venture, the problem is less challenging because management does not have to continually contest with cultures being sustained by the member companies. The difficulty posed by culture conflicts is a reason why picking partners is so important.

Collaboration

The alliance will only work when the resources of the partners are combined and focused on achieving the intended results of the alliance. When these resources are the skills in people who continue to reside in the partners, management needs to build a collaborative relationship among them, possibly requiring that management get the partners to create assignments and incentives that encourage the cooperation of those with critical skills. In working with people from member companies, management also needs to help each person appreciate that the differences among them are often associated with the benefits they bring to the joint venture. Building better understanding of this and respecting these differences helps encourage collaboration.

STAGE 5: ASSESSING STRATEGIC PERFORMANCE OF THE ALLIANCE

The final stage brings us full circle with respect to the alliance. Periodically the alliance needs to be reviewed to see whether it is still the best way of doing things and whether the partner in the alliance is the best partner. If an alliance is the best solution and the partner has worked out well, the company may want to consider buying the partner. If the alliance is still the best solution but the partner has proven less satisfactory than anticipated, it is time to start looking for a new partner. And if the alliance is no longer the best solution, then it is time to terminate it.

This concludes our examination of the process and we now move on to considering specific forms of alliance.

Specific Forms of Alliance

Two types of alliance that are common in Canada and have sufficient uniqueness that they merit special attention are cooperatives and franchises.

COOPERATIVES[34]

Around 9000 cooperatives provide products and services to 17 million members in Canada. Cooperatives are found in virtually every sector of the economy, including agriculture, car rental, day care, caisses populaires and credit unions, funeral services, and housing and renewable energy.

A **cooperative** is a business or enterprise that is owned by an association of people seeking to satisfy common needs such as access to products or services, sale of their products or services, and employment. People are joined together under the legal umbrella of a corporation operating under cooperative principles that include open membership, one vote for each member, capital provided by the members to the extent feasible, limited returns on the capital provided by members, and possible distribution of surplus to members as patronage refunds.

cooperative An association or corporation established to provide products or services on a non-profit basis to those who own and control it—its shareholders or members.

Cooperatives refer to profits as "surplus" because they are generated by overcharging or underpaying members for services and products. Standard practice is to distribute much of this surplus to members annually as patronage refunds in proportion to the member's use of the cooperative or as dividends based on hours worked. The surplus distributed to members is not taxed at the level of the cooperative but becomes taxable income in the hands of members. This gives the cooperative an income tax advantage over corporations, which pay income tax on earnings that are taxed again when owners receive them as dividends.

Challenges Managing Cooperatives

The principles of cooperation can create several challenges for management. These challenges are related to the breadth of membership, the multiple sources of power that each member holds, the personal interests of members, and the management style of the directors.

Broad Membership

The composition of the membership can be an issue when managing a cooperative. One aspect is that the cooperative may seek to attract as many members as possible in order to achieve size. The problem this creates is that the interests of a large group are less homogeneous. The differences are reflected in the creation of cliques among the members who in turn vote for directors who will represent their interests on the board. When their viewpoints are considerably different, directors have a hard time agreeing on anything. Another aspect of the composition of membership is that a powerful group can use its power to get the cooperative's policies and decisions to favour its needs and interests. This benefits the powerful group but is costly for other members and even detrimental to the cooperative.

Multiple Sources of Power

In most businesses the shareholders, investors, and customers are different sets of stakeholders. This allows management to negotiate separately with each group to gain the support of that group. For a cooperative the shareholders, investors, and customers are one and the same. The consequence is that members frustrated in one regard can carry their frustration over to another area. For example, they can refuse to provide capital if they are dissatisfied as customers and they can vote for new directors if they feel that they are not getting enough back as patronage refunds. The implication is that the general manager of the cooperative has to be an astute politician as well as an effective manager.

Personal Interests

The motivations of members can work against the best interests of the cooperative because they are more interested in the success of their own businesses rather than that of the cooperative. Thus they like to seek patronage refunds as high as possible. This takes money out of the cooperative, reducing the equity available to support borrowing, and so limits the ability to finance further investments. The danger is that the plant and equipment of the cooperative becomes antiquated and the cooperative is no longer competitive.

Personal Styles

The directors, when owners of successful though smaller businesses, can believe that all their opinions are correct, though the size of their businesses means that they have not needed nor been exposed to the professional management practices required in a more complex organization and have been uncontested in the management style they use. The consequences are as one would expect. These directors do not appreciate the contribution that professional management can make, are not willing to pay for professional management, and each wants actions taken that reflect his/her personal management style. This produces confrontations in the boardroom.

The overall implication is that, while cooperatives are a common form that serves some purposes well, this form of alliance comes with a number of managerial challenges because of the principles it is based upon.

FRANCHISES

Around 850 franchise systems with more than 80 000 units operate in Canada. Franchising is most commonly associated with the fast-food industry (including Tim Hortons and Krispy Kreme Doughnuts), but it is also used in many other industries including the automotive industry (auto dealerships), the car rental industry, the real estate industry (agencies), the soft-drink industry (bottlers), the hotel industry, and the cleaning industry. Franchising involves a **franchisor** and **franchisees**. The franchisor has something to sell and the franchisee is willing to sell it.

franchisor One who develops a business model and trademarks for a company and then sells to its franchisees the right to use the model and trademarks to do business.

franchisee One who purchases from the franchisor the rights to use a trademarked name and business model to do business and agrees to follow rules, guidelines, and pay fees established by the franchisor.

Contractual agreements specify what the franchisor provides to the franchisee and how much control the franchisor has. The franchisor will use the contract with many franchisees and so has a great incentive to craft the contract carefully. From the perspective of the franchisees, the consequence is a contract that reads as if it is all in favour of the franchisor.

The franchise agreement can provide the franchisee with three different levels of geographic coverage. The greatest coverage comes with a sub-franchise agreement in which the franchisee is given a territory where individual franchises will be sold, usually by the sub-franchisor, who then supervises and administers the franchisees in that area. A multiunit or area development franchise agreement provides the franchisee with charge over an area in which one or more units will be established and operated. An individual franchise agreement provides the least area coverage—a single operation in one location or serving a geographically defined area.

Franchisors like franchising because it supports rapid expansion, avoids certain legal requirements, and provides operational advantages. Rapid expansion is possible because the franchisor does not have to finance the full cost of providing infrastructure to support sales and services. Each franchisee pays for the facilities and equipment at which products and services will be sold. Legal obligations of the franchisor are reduced when the franchise agreement places legal obligations with the franchisee, such as meeting various local laws. Putting some of the legal burden on the franchisee is beneficial because the presence of local ownership can influence the enforcement of regulation and facilitate access to local licences to operate. Operational advantages come from the close management control the franchisee exerts over operations in order to maximize its profits.

Franchisees like franchising because it provides a quick start and the ability to expand rapidly. The quick start comes from the fact that the franchisor has something that customers want to buy and a way of selling it, and provides the franchisee with training on how to sell it. Expansion is possible because the franchisee can buy additional franchises.

While franchising appeals to both the franchisor and the franchisee, there are requirements for success. Here we will consider the basic requirements for a franchisor selling an entire business format such as fast food.

In order to franchise, the franchisor needs a workable concept and proof that it works. The workable concept has three components: the concept, the franchisee operation, and the franchisor operation. The concept has to provide something for which the final customer is willing to pay more for than the cost of providing it. Each operation that will be franchised is a turnkey operation with a fully designed and equipped facility provided along with all the techniques and processes to operate it. As well as providing the turnkey operations, the franchisor has to also have an economic model, management and quality control systems, advertising, and selection processes for franchisees and locations. Franchisors such as Tim Hortons and McDonald's buy or lease properties that they in turn lease to their franchisees.

Proof that the concept works comes from the fact that the franchisor usually has at least one operation that is working according to standard operating procedures. A single operation may be all that is needed if sales volume and profits are high. Franchisors usually have just a few company-owned units because this ties up capital and requires close supervision to ensure that owned units perform well.

When a unit is franchised, the franchisee makes numerous payments to the franchisor. First comes the franchise fee, a one-time fee that covers the cost of becoming a franchisee and an investment to cover the cost of the facility and equipment. Thereafter the franchisee pays continuing fees (typically monthly): a royalty fee for the franchisor's services, advertising fees, cost of products the franchisor supplies to the franchisee, and rental payments on the property.

A key strategic principle for every franchisor with a business that can be successfully adopted is to expand as quickly as possible so that it occupies all the best locations. Otherwise competitors will quickly spot its appeal, copy it, and fill in the optimal locations.

What can go wrong? Problems can come from many sources. The customers can lose interest in the product or service. The competitors can saturate the market with substitute products and services, or worse, they can have copied the business format completely. The franchisor may not have adequately proven the concept or have chosen poor locations or granted so many franchises in close proximity to one another that there are too many for the market volume. The franchisor requires franchisees to accept the franchisor's pricing, products, and processes. Franchisees are not allowed to innovate in any way. Yet periodically the franchisor can require the franchisees to upgrade facilities and equipment, lowering the franchisees' return on their investment. And the franchisor may not achieve uniformity across the franchises, eroding the franchise's brand image. The franchisee rarely has much power in these situations because the contractual agreements were crafted by the franchisor's lawyers. Finally either the franchisor or the franchisee can be incompetent. So while franchising has a lot in its favour, it does have its potential downsides.

The overall implication again is that while franchising is a popular form of alliance, adopting this approach brings with it a number of managerial challenges.

Although alliances are typical vehicles of business strategy, they are also vehicles for corporate and an international strategy. In the first case, the alliance facilitates product or service diversification within an existing market, while in the second case the alliance facilitates entry and competition in another geographic market. Each of these is now explored.

Alliances and Corporate Strategy

In Chapter 9, corporate strategy was largely concerned with two activities: determining the right mix of businesses in the corporate portfolio and ensuring that this mix creates shareholder value. These same decisions will now be considered in terms of alliances. As for portfolio mix, alliances are vehicles for exploring and implementing diversification options. For example, Xerox developed through its office-copier business a set of technologies that could provide access into the intensely competitive desktop-copier and computer-printer businesses. By allying with a strong partner such as Fuji Photo of Japan, it can share the risk and development costs related to an uncertain diversification move. ◆

Staging

Corporations can also use alliances to create value across a portfolio of individual businesses. At first glance, venture capitalists (VCs) and their various investments seem to be independent entities. They represent strategic alliances because the VCs provide capital and managerial expertise while the entrepreneurs provide new products. From a corporate-strategy perspective, the VC company can create more value for its investments by identifying key individuals in one company who could help create value for its other units. The VC company Softbank, for example, leverages its investments in broadband-application and broadband-provider companies by circulating its best and brightest managers and technologists among its wholly owned companies as well as those in which it has investments.[35] Likewise, a diversified company can also broker relationships among its portfolio businesses.

DEDICATED ALLIANCE FUNCTION

Recent research indicates that corporations are more likely to succeed with alliances when they have a dedicated alliance function.[36] Research In Motion (RIM), like many companies that use alliances, has a functional unit dedicated to three tasks: setting up, tracking, and dissolving the company's alliances. The first two tasks are the most critical. Regardless of the levels of trust, learning, and capabilities that an alliance boasts, it will not be productive when the alliance is weak and the fit between partners is poor. Good intentions alone do not make alliances work. Nothing can replace a good strategy that spells out the role of alliances in a company's strategy and partner fit.

The nature of the corporation's alliance mechanism can have significant bearing on its success with alliances. It can be institutionalizing or integrating. Those with an institutionalizing approach typically have more experience doing alliances and so have developed organizational mechanisms that improve efficiency by formalizing decision making and enforcing standardized practices such as how to select partners. Those with an integrating approach have less experience so seek to learn from their successes and mistakes as companies integrate alliances. The difference is that companies that rely heavily on institutionalizing mechanisms have a 50 percent success rate with alliances while companies that rely on integrating mechanisms have a 71 percent success rate. The moral is that allowing learning in the alliance mechanisms is beneficial because it provides flexibility.[37]

Alliances and International Strategy

In 2000, Krispy Kreme entered Canada with franchised outlets. Krispy Kreme Doughnuts Eastern Canada Inc. (KKDEC and later called KremeKo Inc.) was a private, majority-owned Canadian company that was awarded development rights for Eastern Canada, which included Ontario, Quebec, and the four provinces of Atlantic Canada. Meanwhile, KremeWorks, a franchise partnership between the corporation and ICON, LLC, a Seattle-based restaurant management company, was given the development rights for Washington state, Oregon, Hawaii, and British Columbia.

In 2007, Wal-Mart Stores and Bharti Enterprises created a joint venture, Bharti Wal-Mart Private Ltd, in India. The two partners shared ownership 50/50. The joint venture initially established a wholesale distribution and logistics business to provide product to *kirana* stores

India's Bharti Wal-Mart "Best Price" Modern Wholesale cash-and-carry shop near Amritsar.

(tiny mom-and-pop food outlets), produce resellers, restaurants, and other businesses. This was followed with cash-and-carry outlets of 50 000 to 100 000 square feet, offering perishables, grocery items, clothing, consumer durables, and other general merchandise.

Many alliances are international as companies become bigger and their competition becomes global: either they involve partners from different countries or the alliance itself is headquartered in a country different from those of the partners. The reasons that a domestic company allies with a foreign company are the same as those for alliances among domestic companies—it builds competitive advantage by pursuing the company's business or corporate strategy.

Sometimes alliances are made necessary by government policies. Some governments interested in protecting certain industries for cultural or strategic reasons prevent foreign companies from having self-owned businesses. Some governments want to assist their national businesses so they require arrangements that will provide these businesses with resources and technology. In each of these situations alliances allow foreign companies to derive some profits from being engaged in a larger arena.

In international contexts, decisions about internal and external vehicles through which to execute a company's strategy are much more complex than in domestic contexts. Governments, public policies, and national cultures often play significant roles. Also important, of course, are differences in workplace regulations and socioeconomic conditions.

Nor are alliances necessarily the best vehicle for the international arena. Multinational corporations, for instance, may be better than alliances in facilitating the flow of knowledge across borders. Analysis of patent citations by semiconductor companies suggests that multinationals are better than both alliances and market forces in fostering cross-border knowledge transfer, primarily because they can use multiple mechanisms for transferring knowledge and are more flexible in moving, integrating, and developing technical knowledge.[38]

Strategic Alliances in Stable and Dynamic Environments

Competitive advantage is a temporary phenomenon so companies always need to be looking for ways to enhance it. The speed at which they have to do this varies since the rate of change differs across industries. As competition and complexity increase, forming the right alliances can mean the difference between exceptional value creation and value destruction.

Assessing Alliance Fit at Millennium Pharmaceuticals

Evaluating alliance opportunities is not simple, but you do have the advantage of a framework that helps you start the process. The first step is to develop a grid, shown in Exhibit 11.9, that lays out how well the potential partner fits with your company.

Note that you should always include alternative potential partners, since you may be more likely to enter a bad deal when you have nothing to compare it to. This may sound silly, but many CEOs say that some of the most important alliance or acquisition decisions they have made are the decisions not to do them! In this example, Millennium Pharmaceuticals was faced with a huge alliance opportunity with German company Lundberg—it involved lots of cash and a savvy global partner with a great deal of experience. Why, then, would Millennium turn such a deal down? Using the following alliance-fit framework, and setting up Abbott Labs as the comparison alliance, Millennium decided that it was best to pass on the Lundberg alliance (though it turns out that the Abbott alliance was in the works).

- *Strategic fit?* In general, the strategic fit was good. However, Millennium had recently put together a very similar large alliance with Monsanto, and it was not clear how another deal would move Millennium's strategy forward.

- *Resource fit?* Other than money, Lundberg did not bring much to the table in terms of new resources and capabilities. In fact, Millennium would be putting most of its unique capabilities to work, which in turn could stretch its technical and research staff with no benefit other than additional cash in the bank. At the time, Millennium was strong financially.

- *Cultural fit?* The potential partner was a large, private agribusiness company, whereas Millennium was a relatively small, public biotech company. In initial meetings, there was some indication with the potential partner that top management was keen on an alliance but that lower-level managers were out of the loop. Cultural misfit often arises when line managers are not involved in the alliance-building process from the start.

- *Structural fit?* This, too, was a big question mark. Millennium's management had the impression that the partner would not grant it the autonomy or flexibility that it desired in its alliances. Thus, the structure appeared too rigid from Millennium's perspective.

- *Other questions?* Because Millennium was still contemplating other options and partnerships, it was not

as if this was the only opportunity in the market. The top-management team determined that it was not excited about the alliance beyond the fact that the partner had a great reputation and brought lots of cash to the relationship.

So, you are probably asking what happened to Millennium after it passed up such a lucrative deal. Shortly thereafter, Millennium and Abbott formed a five-year alliance primarily for collaborative research and development in the area of metabolic diseases.[39] The companies agreed to share equally the cost of developing, manufacturing, and marketing products on a worldwide basis. The arrangement with Abbott also includes an equity investment by Abbott in Millennium, amounting in total to $250 million over several years and a technology exchange and development agreement.

In another agreement Millennium and Aventis expanded their existing joint development pipeline to include an aggregate of 11 additional discovery projects that were previously pursued outside the joint collaboration by Millennium or Aventis. These new assets included chemokine receptors, kinases, and integrins, which are important as potential drug-development target classes in inflammatory disease research. As a result of this expansion, that alliance yielded approximately 50 jointly funded discovery projects. Soon, Millennium had created more than 20 alliances with leading pharmaceutical and biotechnology companies—close to $2 billion of committed funding. You can learn more about why Millennium sees such a network of alliances as a central vehicle in its strategy—to eventually become a full-fledged pharmaceutical company—through its R&D page at www.millennium.com.

1. In How Would You Do That? 11.1, you learned how Millennium Phar-

maceuticals evaluated a potential alliance partner. Apply the Millennium fit framework to the alliances of another company you are familiar with. Do these appear to be good alliances? Do any of the alliances suggest that your focal company is on a pathway to acquire its partner or be acquired by it?

Exhibit 11.9 Comparing Alliance Opportunities

	Partner A—Lundberg	Partner B—Abbott Labs
Strategic Fit?	Good, but no new learning opportunities	Good and ample learning and growth opportunities
Resource Fit?	Cash resources, but cash is generic	Cash and technology resources, and technology is unique
Cultural Fit?	Likely to be poor	Good
Structural Fit?	Unknown	Good
Other Key Questions? • Capital market demands—who drives strategy here? • Timing—are capital markets hot or cold? • Timing—do we need another deal like this? • Timing—how plentiful and attractive are other alliance options? • Does "no" here mean no more options? • Again, other criteria? • What other key questions should be on the table?	Management was not excited about the deal	Management was excited about the deal—high level of motivation

Stable environments are characterized by mature industries that are populated with well established companies and stable demand for their products and services. This influences the objectives that partners set for their alliances. Typically they seek to consolidate market positions and generate economies of scope and scale using alliances that provide production technologies and market access.[40] Stable environments are much more forgiving of mistakes, such as poor choices in partners or alliance structures. They also provide companies with time to learn from their mistakes and regroup in new alliances. And they allow companies to participate in more alliances because stability makes the maintenance and management of the alliances easier.

In dynamic environments, strategic opportunities and needs are much less certain. In this environment, alliances are used to close resource gaps, create options, and influence environmental developments. The dynamic environment also creates an incentive for quickly forming alliances that amass the resources needed to rapidly pursue opportunities that open up and address competitive threats.

Any diversion of a company's resources or distraction of managerial attention in a dynamic environment can have serious consequences, particularly when dynamism is coupled with technological intensity. If Millennium Pharmaceuticals chooses an unsuitable partner, managing that relationship will take more resources and also increase the risk that a competitor will produce a significant competitive product. Such risks place tremendous pressure on companies not only to use alliances to put together resources but ideally in configurations that competitors find hard to imitate.

The relative stability also helps us to better understand the coevolution model of corporate strategy outlined in Chapter 9. Recall that *coevolution* means complementary evolution when companies are linked together through relationships. In making alliances, a company develops its specific dynamic capabilities in concert with the best resources and capabilities available to it. The alliance changes what the company can do and in the same way changes what the other company in the alliance does, causing both to evolve. As the needs of the company change, it terminates some alliances and adds others, bringing about further evolution. Thus, a company pursuing a growth strategy may drop alliances with those companies moving toward commoditized products and add those with partners who are trying to enhance competitive advantage through differentiation.[41]

FOCUS ON SUSTAINABILITY 11.1

The Co-operative Auto Network: A Transportation Solution for People and the Planet[42]

Communities face increasing traffic and parking congestion as well as a need to improve air quality. One way to address these problems is to find alternatives to private automobile ownership. Car-sharing is an innovative mobility option that allows individuals to pay for and use automobiles—on an as-needed basis—through membership programs. One such program is the Co-operative Auto Network (CAN), which started in Vancouver in 1997 with two vehicles and 16 members. It has since grown to become one of North America's largest car-sharing organizations. Its goal is to get people thinking about automobiles as an *optional* transportation method. Vehicles are there when you need them, but they're only taken after other options such as walking, cycling, or taking transit or cabs are considered first.

In 2010, CAN had a fleet of 235 vehicles located in seven cities in B.C.'s Lower Mainland and on the Island. Members buy a refundable share for $500 when joining the co-op, and then they can use a co-op vehicle when they need it on a fee-for-use basis. All insurance, maintenance, and fuel costs are covered, and members have access to hatchbacks, sedans, minivans, and pickup trucks, depending on their needs at a given time. Co-op members can also exercise their rights of shared ownership and

democratic decision making by voting in the election of the board of directors of this not-for-profit co-op.

CAN has been financially self-sufficient since reaching 500 members in July 2000 and debt-free since reaching 1200 members in May 2003. The growth of CAN makes it more attractive to new members, since it can provide more cars in more locations, better prices, and other benefits to members.

CAN has taken many pro-active measures to promote environmental responsibility and to reduce the number of cars in the Vancouver area. Its fleet of cars includes hybrid vehicles. It has a cross-use agreement with the Nelson Car Share and Victoria Car Share Co-ops. In addition to its efforts to reduce air pollution and green house gas emissions, CAN has helped shape the city by-laws around parking and development. It was instrumental in the creation of a City of Vancouver by-law allowing developers to reduce their parking ratios if car-sharing was incorporated within the building specifications. This enacted legislation is the first of its kind in the world. CAN has also been able to provide vital start-up, promotional, and policy information to car-sharing groups across North America and the world. Since CAN started, many other car-sharing organizations have been created, many of which are cooperative.

Summary of Challenges

1. *Explain why strategic alliances are important and their main features.* Alliances enable partners to enhance their competitive advantage in ways that they could not if they relied on organic growth. Companies participate in alliances because they enhance their competitive advantage. This can come from three different sources: improving operations, enhancing competitive conditions, and enhancing entry and exit. Enhanced competitive advantage is only meaningful, however, if it is sustainable. This fits with the VRINE framework presented in Chapter 3 that resources and capabilities must be valuable, rare, and difficult to imitate. The alliance itself provides the organizational arrangements needed to fulfill the final requirement of the VRINE framework. If an alliance (or network of alliances) satisfies these criteria, it has probably a collaborative advantage that helps one or more of the member companies achieve a competitive advantage over rivals outside the alliance. The major features of strategic alliances are as follows: the alliance is voluntary; it involves the exchange, sharing, or co-development of products, technologies, or services; the companies in it continue to act independently with respect to matters not covered by the alliance; and the arrangement is of limited duration.

2. *Describe the process of building and managing alliances.* The overall process involves five stages. Stage one is building the case for an alliance. Stage two involves identifying possible partners and then screening them to see which one is best. Stage three deals with the negotiation of the alliance. Stage four involves the ongoing management of the alliance. Finally, stage five is the periodic strategic assessment of the alliance. The first four stages of this process are similar to those for a merger or acquisition.

3. *Identify the various forms of strategic alliances.* Alliances can take many forms, starting with simple agreements over functional activities going all the way to joint ventures. A joint venture is the most complex form because it results in the establishment of a third, independent entity. Alliances can be separated into equity and non-equity types. Joint ventures, in which partners contribute cash and other resources to the partnership, fall into the broader category of equity alliances. Non-equity alliances take the form of contracts to supply, produce, market, or distribute a company's goods or services. Sole-sourcing, just-in-time supply agreements, licensing, and co-branding are examples of non-equity alliances. Alliances that involve many participants are *industry associations, cooperatives,* or *consortia*.

4. *Summarize the considerations when negotiating the alliance.* An alliance is a negotiated arrangement and can include whatever those entering the alliance find acceptable and what they consider necessary for the alliance to be successful. There are three general considerations that all negotiations should include. They are stewardship, resource commitments, and governance. Stewardship involves providing the alliance with clear purpose and helping it pursue that purpose. Clear resource commitments are needed so that the alliance has the wherewithal to pursue its strategy. Governance defines the principal aspects of the alliance's organizational structure and systems. Within this are the roles people will play in it, how information will flow, and how performance will be evaluated.

5. *Compare and contrast cooperatives and franchising as strategic vehicles.* Both a cooperative and franchising are alliances that involve many individuals. In other ways they are very different. A cooperative is a singular organization versus franchising, which involves multiple organizations: the franchisor and the franchises run by the franchisees. A cooperative is in control of its strategy, whereas a franchisor dictates strategy to the franchisees. This means that the member who joins a cooperative is less certain about what will happen than the franchisee who has seen data demonstrating potential performance of the franchise. Finally, in a cooperative members have greater freedom of choice while in a franchising operation franchisees, behaviour is bounded by contractual terms.

6. *Understand the characteristics of alliances in stable and dynamic competitive contexts.* Just as business strategies vary according to context, so, too, does the use of alliances as strategy vehicles. In stable environments companies are interested in alliances that give them production technologies or market access as they seek to consolidate market positions and generate economies of scope and scale. In dynamic environments, strategic opportunities and needs are much less certain. In this environment alliances are used to close resource gaps, create options, and influence environmental developments. Although the choice of alliance partners is always important, failure of any one alliance is unlikely to break the company. Stable environments are more forgiving of mistakes, giving companies time to learn from their mistakes and regroup in new alliances. Dynamic environments are much less forgiving. Stakes are much higher because the wrong partnership in a rapidly evolving environment can mean that the company falls behind its competitors.

Review Questions

1. What is a strategic alliance?
2. Do most strategic alliances succeed?
3. What forms can strategic alliances take?
4. What is the difference between equity and a non-equity strategic alliance?
5. Provide an example of a non-equity strategic alliance.
6. Why do companies enter into alliances?
7. What are the three sources an alliance provides for improving competitive advantage?
8. How does the industry structure models help one identify potential alliance partners?
9. How do alliances serve as a vehicle for corporate strategy?
10. What risks do alliances pose to partner companies?
11. How do alliances differ in stable and dynamic contexts?
12. What are the five steps in the process of building and managing an alliance?

Experiential Activities

Group Exercises

1. Increasingly, corporations such as Cisco Systems (www.cisco.com), Corning (www.corning.com), Millennium Pharmaceuticals (www.millennium.com), Orion (www.orion.fi), and Procter & Gamble (P&G) (www.pg.com) claim to have a competitive advantage based on their ability to manage alliances. Develop statements that both defend and critique this proposition. Then identify risks that companies run when their strategy is essentially a network of alliances.

2. Pick one type of alliance from the list found in Exhibit 11.3. Using the internet, find a company that has used this alliance and descriptions of it. Be prepared to describe it, and provide justification for whether you think it is a good alliance.

3. Identify a company and document its alliance activity over the past five to 10 years (visit the website of a public company, particularly the "history" page). Examine the list of officers at the company (these are always detailed in the annual report and often on the company's website). Do they appear to have a dedicated alliance function? What kinds of changes would they have to make if they were to follow the recommendations on implementation levers necessary to achieve an effective dedicated alliance function? What would be the costs and benefits of such a change?

Ethical Debates

1. One of the biggest barriers for companies entering into alliances with partners, and especially foreign ones, is the issue of trust. Would a well-crafted contract overcome this problem by clearly specifying required behaviour?

2. The press has had many articles about clothing companies in North America that have foreign partners and suppliers where working conditions have been seen as abysmal. Is this just a risk of foreign alliances or can companies here do something to manage these situations?

3. Companies are forming alliances with various non-profit organizations. Are they just manipulating their public image or are they really demonstrating a social conscience?

Endnotes

1. The technology is well summarized in "Digital Cinema." Accessed January 17, 2010, at http://en.wikipedia.org/wiki/Digital_cinema. The technology is described in the report compiled by Nenad Puhovski titled "digital film, digital cinema," Standing Committee for New Technologies, Cilect, International Association of Film and Television Schools, Melbourne, 2002. Accessed January 19, 2010, at http://cilect.org/files/archives/Digital%20Film%202002%20Melbourne.pdf.

2. The studios were Buena Vista Pictures Distribution (Disney), Twentieth Century Fox Film Corporation (Fox), Metro-Goldwyn-Mayer (MGM), Paramount Pictures (Paramount), Sony Pictures Entertainment (Sony), Universal Studios (Universal), and Warner Bros. Studios (Warner Brothers).

3. C. Wolf, "Rubbermaid Struggles to Put Lid on Problems: Company's Earnings Tumble after Price Increase Backfires," *Cincinnati Enquirer*, April 8, 1996, p. D1.

4. J. Cook, T. Halevy, and B. Hastie, "Alliances in Consumer Packaged Goods," *McKinsey on Finance* (Autumn 2003): 16–20.

5. KPMG, *Alliances and Networks: The Next Generation* (Amsterdam: KPMG, 1996).

6. Booz Allen & Hamilton, *Institutionalizing Alliance Skills: Secrets of Repeatable Success* (Los Angeles, Booz Allen & Hamilton, 1998).

7. GasKing, "Fuel Facts." Accessed February 4, 2010, at www.gasking.com/facts/index.asp.

8. J. H. Dyer, *Collaborative Advantage: Winning through Extended Enterprise Supplier Networks* (New York: Oxford University Press, 2000).

9. Joe Truini, "Automakers Join to Develop Hybrids," *Waste News*, September 12, 2005.

10. "Neotech Announces Strategic Alliance with O-Two," AMEinfo.com. Accessed January 22, 2010, at www.ameinfo.com/97793.html.

11. Borland press release, November 12, 2007. Accessed September 30, 2008, at www.borland.com/us/company/news/press_releases/2007/11_12_07_borland_and_dmr_form_strategic_alliance.html.

12. David Segal, "Pillow Fights at the Four Seasons," *New York Times*, June 28, 2009. Accessed June 30, 2009, at www.nytimes.com/2009/06/28/business/global/28four.html.

13. Information in this section is drawn from J. H. Dyer, *Collaborative Advantage: Winning through Extended Enterprise Supplier Networks* (New York: Oxford University Press, 2000).

14. Stephen Voss, "BP Says Thunder Horse Platform Delayed Until Mid-2008 (Update3)," Bloomberg.com. Accessed January 22, 2010, at www.bloomberg.com/apps/news?pid=20601085&sid=ac846CQemCaU&refer=Europe.

15. "World Wide Web Consortium." Accessed January 24, 2010, at http://en.wikipedia.org/wiki/World_Wide_Web_Consortium.

16. Adapted from B. Gomes-Casseres, "Competing in Constellations: The Case of Fuji-Xerox," *Strategy and Business* (First Quarter 1997): 4–16; www.fujixerox.co.jp/eng/company/history (accessed July 15, 2005); The Xerox Fact Book (2005–2006). Accessed November 8, 2005, at www.xerox.com; and B. Gomes-Casseres, "Alliance Strategies of Small Firms," *Small Business Economics* 9 (1997): 33–44.

17. Stephen Shaw, *Airline Marketing and Management* 6th Ed. (Burlington, Vermont: Ashgate Pub. Co., 2007).

18. Competition Bureau, "Competitor Collaboration Guidelines: Enforcement Guidelines," Government of Canada, Draft for Public Consultation, May 8, 2009. Accessed January 22, 2010, at http://competitionbureau.gc.ca/eic/site/cb-bc.nsf/vwapj/Competitor-Collaboration-Guidelines-2009-05-08-e.pdf/$file/Competitor-Collaboration-Guidelines-2009-05-08-e.pdf.

19. Theresa Tedesco and Jamie Sturgeon, "Cable Rivals Drop Gloves," *Vancouver Sun*, November 2, 2009. January 22, 2010, at www.vancouversun.com/business/Cable+rivals+drop+gloves/2165527/story.html.

20. Laurel J. Campbell, "Ethnic Papers Redefine 'Mainstream,'" *The Publisher* XC:3(April 2009): 1. Accessed January 22, 2010, at www.communitynews.ca/publisher/200904.pdf.

21. Kazutaka Takechi, "International Strategic Alliances for Local Market Entry: Direct Launches versus Marketing Alliances in Pharmaceuticals," RIETI Discussion Paper Series 08-E -022, Hosei University Tokyo, Japan, July 9, 2008. Accessed January 22, 2010, at www.rieti.go.jp/jp/publications/dp/08e022.pdf.

22. Ashish Nanda and Peter J. Williamson, "Use Joint Ventures to Ease the Pain of Restructuring," *Harvard Business Review* (November/December 1995): 119–128.

23. GE Energy, "GE and BP Form Alliance to Develop and Deploy Hydrogen Power Technologies," News Release, May 24, 2007. Accessed January 22, 2010, at www.geenergyfinancialservices.com/press_room/press_releases/GE_BP_GlobalAlliance_FINAL_May242007.pdf.

24. Mary Ellen Kelly, "Wal-Mart, Cifra Open Third Mexican Club—Club Aurrera—International Retailing Report," *Discount Store News*, November 16, 1992.

25. Barrick Company Release, "Barrick Signs Innovative 10-year Agreement with Yokohama to Secure Tire Supply," January 30, 2008. Accessed February 4, 2010, at www.barrick.com/Theme/Barrick/files/docs_pressrelease/2008.01.30-Yokohama.pdf; and Eric Shackleton, "Barrick Strikes Tire Deal to Secure Supply," *Globe and Mail*, January 31, 2008, p. B8.

26. "RR Donnelley and HP Plan to Create an Alliance to Develop Next-Generation Digital Printing Technology." Accessed January 22, 2010, at http://files.shareholder.com/downloads/RRD/0x0x318518/394c4b7d-3aa4-48b2-9eaa-8f173b227484/RRD_News_2009_9_10_General.pdf.

27. "Walleye Technologies and Terabeam Form Alliance to Develop Handheld, Portable Imaging System Capable of 'Seeing' Into and Through Solid Objects," Press Release, May 30, 2007. Accessed January 22, 2010, at www.walleyetechnologies.com/Walleye%20Terabeam%20Release.pdf.

28. Adapted from J. D. Bamford, B. Gomes-Casseres, and M. S. Robinson, *Mastering Alliance Strategy: A Comprehensive Guide to Design, Management, and Organization* (San Francisco: John Wiley & Sons, 2003), p. 22.

29. J. Bleeke and D. Ernst, "Is Your Strategic Alliance Really a Sale?" *Harvard Business Review* 73:1 (1995): 97–102.

30. L. D. Browning, J. M. Beyer, and J. C. Shetler, "Building Cooperation in a Competitive Industry: SEMATECH," *Academy of Management Journal* 38:1 (1995): 113–151.

31. J. H. Dyer, *Collaborative Advantage: Winning through Extended Enterprise Supplier Networks* (New York: Oxford University Press, 2000).

32. Various articles have described the challenge of managing a joint venture. The points they make are wide ranging and sometimes appear contradictory. They are James Bamford, David Ernst, and David G. Fubini, "Launching a World Class Joint Venture," *Harvard Business Review* 82:2 (February 2004); Robert C. Hill and Don Hellriegel, "Critical Contingencies in Joint Venture Management," *Organizational Science* 5:4 (November 1994): 594–607; Jonathan Hughes and Jeff Weiss, "Simple Rules for Making Alliances Work," *Harvard Business Review* 85:11 (2007):122–131; Rosabeth Moss Kanter, "Collaborative Advantage: The Art of Alliances," *Harvard Business Review* 72:4 (July/August 1994): 96–108; J. Peter Killing, "How to Make a Global Venture Work," *Harvard Business Review* (May/June 1982):

120-127; Dean Elmuti and Yunus Kathawala, "An Overview of Strategic Alliances," *Management Decision* 39:3 (2001): 205.

33. A full description of cooperatives is found in Corporations Canada's policy statement 17.1 issued on September 3, 2008. Accessed February 3, 2010, at www.ic.gc.ca/eic/site/cd-dgc.nsf/eng/cs03954.html; additional description of cooperative principles is Michel Lafleur, "Evaluating Strategy Based on Eight Features of Cooperative Identity," *Cooperative Grocer for Retailers and Cooperators* 116 (January/February 2005). Accessed January 30, 2010, at www.cooperativegrocer.coop/articles/index.php?id=572. Some interesting alternative cooperatives are described in "New Futures: Innovative Uses of the Co-op Model," Canadian Co-operative Association, Ottawa, 2009. Accessed January 30, 2010, at www.coopscanada.coop/public_html/assets/firefly/files/files/Innovative_Co-ops_December_2009_FINAL.pdf. A selection of Canadian cooperatives is identified at http://en.wikipedia.org/wiki/Category:Canadian_cooperatives (accessed January 30, 2010).

34. www.softbank.co.jp (accessed August 12, 2005).

35. Adapted from J. H. Dyer, P. Kale, and H. Singh, "How to Make Strategic Alliances Work," *Sloan Management Review* 42:4 (2001): 37-43.

36. Koen Heimeriks, "Superstition Undermines Alliances," *Harvard Business Review* (April 2009): 20–21.

37. P. Almeida, J. Song, and R. M. Grant, "Are Firms Superior to Alliances and Markets? An Empirical Test of Cross-Border Knowledge Building," *Organization Science* 14 (2002): 157–171.

38. Harbison and Pekar, *Smart Alliances;* E. Bailey and W. Shan, "Sustainable Competitive Advantage Through Alliances," in E. Bowman and B. Kogut, eds., *Redesigning the Firm* (New York: Oxford University Press, 1995).

39. www.mlnm.com/media/strategy/index.asp (accessed November 2, 2010).

40. S. Brown and K. Eisenhardt, *Competing on the Edge* (Boston: Harvard Business School Press, 1997).

41. James E. Austin, *The Collaboration Challenge: How Nonprofits and Businesses Succeed through Strategic Alliances* (Jossey-Bass, 2000).

42. Adam Millard-Ball, Gail Murray, Jessica Ter Schure, Christine Fox, and Jon Burkhardt, "Car-sharing: Where and How It Succeeds," TCRP Report 108, Transit Cooperative Research Program, Federal Transit Administration, United States of America, Washington, D.C., September 2005. Accessed February 4, 2010, at http://onlinepubs.trb.org/onlinepubs/tcrp/tcrp_rpt_108.pdf. Videotaped interview with Tracey Axelsson, cofounder of Vancouver's Co-operative Auto Network, appearing on YouTube as "Peak Moment 34." Accessed February 4, 2010, at www.youtube.com/watch?v=M6U7t5XyxRs. www.cooperativeauto.net/.

12 Mergers and Acquisitions as Vehicles

TD Bank Acquires Canada Trust

Canada's big banks, which were sales-oriented in the late 1990s, became increasingly interested in lowering costs by pursuing economies of scale. In January 1998, the Royal Bank of Canada proposed merging with the Bank of Montreal. In April of the same year, Toronto Dominion Bank (TD Bank) proposed merging with Canadian Imperial Bank of Commerce. The proposals and prospects of branch closures and potential for higher fees associated with less competition triggered consumer outrage. The federal government eventually denied both mergers on the grounds of anti-trust and concerns about customer access to service.

After the denial of the mergers, the six federally chartered banks pursued growth in other ways, ranging from domestic takeover of trust companies to foreign alliances and acquisitions.

TD Canada Trust branch in Toronto.

TD Bank Merges with Canada Trust[1]

In 1999, in the face of increasing competition and new technologies, TD Bank, Canada's fifth-largest bank, sought to reposition its retail banking business by focusing on improving customer satisfaction and reducing costs. Satisfaction could be improved by enhancing service levels and transforming TD Bank's sales-oriented branches into service centres. Costs could be reduced by increasing the size of the business. Pursuit of both of these goals could be facilitated using an appropriate merger.

On February 1, 2000, TD Bank completed its Cdn$8 billion acquisition of CT Financial Services Inc. (Canada Trust, or CT), Canada's largest independent trust. Many Canadians had moved to Canada Trust because they were dissatisfied with the service offered by the big banks, including TD Bank. CT was viewed as the "anti-bank," an image that the company had fostered, and had introduced many "customer friendly" innovations that the major banks later copied. In 1999, CT had 12 000 employees and 429 branches. By 2001, it had 3.7 million customers, Cdn$38 billion in deposits, and Cdn$176 billion in assets.

The deal was approved by the federal government subject to several conditions. First, TD Canada Trust would have to divest itself of 13 branches in Ontario and sell the MasterCard division of Canada Trust since it wanted to hold on to TD's Visa bankcard. Second, customer service and rural service would have to be maintained. Third, those employees who lost their jobs would have to be taken care of financially.

The success of the merger was dependent on building scale and generating higher returns through revenue growth. Given the restrictions on branch closings and layoffs, cost savings would be minimal. This meant that the key to success rested with retaining customers. Retaining customers would be very challenging because trust companies were customer-oriented and had better customer satisfaction ratings. Canada Trust had advertised itself as the better alternative when the Bank of Nova Scotia had bought National Trust in 1998. Now CT had merged with the TD, which had been the most aggressive bank in weaning customers away from face-to-face service.

Integrating the Two Companies

Early actions in the merger focused on combining operations, which involved standardizing customer accounts. Some customers complained about sharply higher service fees while others were concerned about losing personal service, extended hours, and service in rural areas. TD–CT responded with a plan for retaining customers because the merger was not value enhancing if customers left. This required presentation of a united image and quick integration of the two companies.

First in this plan was defining and communicating a compelling vision so customers and employees knew where the business was heading. This was done with full-page newspaper advertisements. Many of these advertisements promised longer hours, better service from tellers, and fair treatment of employees who were laid off. Eighty million dollars was spent on marketing to make public promises and reassure customers that CT's service level would be maintained at the new bank and extended to TD customers.

Within 30 days of the takeover, senior management set about integrating the organization. First, management provided detailed action plans about how employees would be affected. This provided them with certainty about whether they would have a job, whom they would report to, and how their pay and benefits would be affected.

Second, it selected the target system platform that was used to support the processes and products offered by the bank.

Third, it set about converting the branches so that all account information was on one system; all would offer one suite of products, and all branches would display the same signage and promotional material, and there would be a single brand. The conversion was done in four regional waves so the company could learn and adjust with each wave.

Other Actions

The deal was seen as the takeover of a trust company rather than a merger of equals. Yet executives in both companies decided that the Canada Trust service model would be used. Given all the actions taken, the merger appeared to have become a reverse takeover, with Toronto Dominion being the company taken over.

By August 2000, most of the top officials in the new bank were formerly Canada Trust employees. The CEO of the holding company for Canada Trust became the CEO of the integrated company. CT's vice-president of target marketing became the senior vice-president of advertising and marketing services, the vice-president of customer strategy and information became the senior vice-president of strategy and information, and CT's vice-president of marketing and customer strategy became the chief marketing officer.

Canada Trust's advertising agency was chosen for the new bank while in the new logo the name Canada Trust occupied three to four times more space than TD.

Most products, services, and pricing for the merged bank came from Canada Trust. In February 2000, TD accounts were replaced with TD Canada Trust accounts, which had higher monthly transactions fees. All branch employees, however, were given the power temporarily to reverse service charges without obtaining a manager's approval. Furthermore, service charges were frozen for a year.

CT's "red" employees were mixed with TD's "green" employees in each branch. This helped TD's people learn about CT's products, processes, and its approach to customer service.

The key to encouraging people to deliver customer service was using a customer satisfaction model. This was developed using data obtained from customers who were surveyed by phone within 24 hours of their last service experience. Customer experience was then presented in a scorecard for the branch and incentive compensation was linked to performance on the scorecard.

Through the whole conversion process, management continually communicated. For workers there were written communications and face-to-face meetings. For shareholders there were reports on revenue growth and synergies expected over time. For customers there were reports in newspapers and personalized information packages.

What we see in this example is the role of strategy and competition in encouraging acquisitions but then the role of regulation in tempering what was achieved. Then we see the considerable work required to make the two organization behave as one as products, processes, and staffing were combined. ■

Mergers and Acquisitions as Vehicles

The reasons for mergers and acquisitions (M&As) are the same fundamental reasons as those for alliances. In this chapter the distinction between mergers and acquisitions is clarified. Then the process of making a merger or acquisition is described. This description is heavily action-oriented and fits well with many of the organizational concepts that were introduced in Chapter 8, which dealt with strategy implementation. The chapter includes How Would You Do That? 12.1, which describes some of the key ideas that management at Scotiabank keeps in mind when integrating acquisitions in Latin America. The chapter then describes the institutional mechanisms set up by companies with strong records of successful acquisitions. It concludes with a description of the role of M&As in different industry contexts.

DISTINGUISHING BETWEEN MERGERS AND ACQUISITIONS

The terms *merger* and *acquisition* are used interchangeably in the business media as though they are synonymous, but there is an important distinction between them.

A **merger** typically refers to two companies coming together as one and is achieved through the exchange of shares. Both companies' stocks are surrendered and new company stock is issued in its place. For example, when DaimlerChrysler was created it was a new company and its two predecessors, Daimler-Benz and Chrysler, ceased to exist. The merger of two companies of near equal size is referred to as a "merger of equals." When such mergers are announced, the statement usually made is that the new company will combine the best from each of the companies, though those with power in the new business determine whether this really happens.

> **merger** Consolidation or combination of two or more companies.

An **acquisition** typically has one company purchase the assets or shares of the other company with payment made in cash, securities of the buyer, or other assets of value to the seller. In an asset purchase, the assets given by the seller to the buyer become additional assets of the buying company. In a stock purchase, the seller's shares are often kept separate as the company purchased becomes a new subsidiary or operating division. With an acquisition, one company clearly establishes itself as the new owner. From a legal point of view, the target company ceases to exist, the buyer "swallows" the business, and the buyer's stock continues to be traded.

> **acquisition** Strategy by which one company acquires another through stock purchase or exchange.

Being bought out often carries negative connotations for those in the acquired company, so the acquiring company may state that the acquisition is a merger of equals—or allows the CEO of the acquired business to state that it is. This makes the takeover more palatable to those in the acquired business. When the target company does not want to be purchased, the deal is seen as unfriendly and regarded as an acquisition. So in common-day language, the description of the purchase depends on how it is received by the target company's board of directors, employees, and shareholders.

WHY MERGERS AND ACQUISITIONS HAPPEN

Mergers and acquisitions are motivated by the same reasons that motivate alliances such as joint ventures and contractual arrangements. The additional value created by an M&A is said to be derived from synergies due to increased revenue and decreased cost that come from the combination of the two companies. As with other vehicles, M&As allow the company to grow the business faster than is possible with organic growth. M&As are attractive when management is unable to negotiate a contract in which the benefits exceed the costs of the business relationship, management feels a need for greater control over operations, and management seeks to control risk exposure.

Personal factors can also enter into an M&A decision, such as opportunistic behaviour by top executives.[2] Increasing the size of the company can increase personal compensation and enhance personal power of those in top management. And, to the extent that the M&A diversifies the company, the executives' employment risk is reduced.

Mergers and acquisitions can fail for many reasons. The five major reasons, according to Orit Gadiesh and Charles Ormiston, are poor strategic rationale, a mismatch of cultures, difficulties in communicating and leading the organization, poor integration planning and execution, and paying too much for the target company.[3] They believe that a poor strategic rationale for the merger is the most important problem to overcome, as this rationale guides both pre- and post-merger behaviour. This issue alone can lead to the other four causes of merger failure.

The Merger & Acquisition Process

Success in mergers and acquisitions comes from having an organized and logical process that provides disciplined analysis, which allows good judgment. The process goes from strategy to target identification and valuation to integration (see Exhibit 12.1). Working through this process takes a long time, though the actual negotiation of the deal may be done quickly. The six steps in the process will now be examined.

1. IDENTIFYING CANDIDATES

The strategic rationale for using M&As informs what is wanted in the potential candidates. Setting up criteria on this basis means that the targets will fit the strategy and capabilities of the company. For example, a large company might be very successful at acquiring smaller

Exhibit 12.1 The
Merger and Acquisition
Process

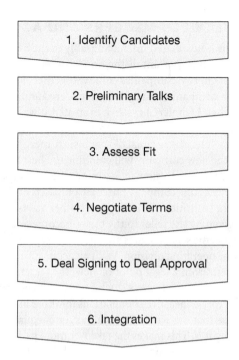

companies and then folding them into its systems, eliminating overhead while streamlining processes. Given this, the criteria become finding small companies with a good customer base that are reasonably priced such that the current owners are willing to sell. Alternatively, the company may need to build capability in a new technology, so this becomes a key criterion when looking for an acquisition.

Identifying potential candidates is one part structured search and one part serendipity. The structured search involves identifying various companies in the industry that satisfy the wants of the company. Many will be identified, but many small companies can easily fall off the radar screen of even effective data gathering. Potential candidates can be subject to a preliminary screening in which problematic companies can be eliminated from further consideration. The companies that pass through the elimination round can then be compared with one another. Popular criteria used in this stage are industry profitability and the company's market position in the industry, unusual resources or capabilities, a target range for size (big enough to make a difference), location, profitability (acquiring distressed companies requires special skills to turn them around), risk exposure, environmental liabilities, union activism, technology, supply chain risk, and culture and values in the target company.

The serendipitous part involves networking by those in charge of identification with others in the industry of interest. Sometimes management of companies for sale will approach the buyer because it has a reputation for buying other companies and treating employees in the acquired companies well. Other times brokers, investment bankers, and lawyers who stand to gain from a deal will "shop" the business for sale. And still other times either the buyer or the seller can hire a third party (a company providing merger, acquisition, and divestment services) to find those it might make a deal with.

2. PRELIMINARY TALKS

The few companies that are identified as attractive candidates are approached and asked about their interest in a merger or an acquisition. The talks can initially involve exploratory talks between chief executive officers about their interest in a possible combination. If the management of each expresses an interest, then the next stage is entered. If there is no immediate interest, occasional casual meetings may occur to see whether management of the candidate company has changed its mind. This relationship can go on for years. When a combination is seen as attractive, the talks are expanded to a broader audience and a formal presentation describing the benefits of combining the two companies may be given.

When one company is interested in buying another that does not want to be bought, the buyer may attempt a hostile takeover. This is an unsolicited offer to purchase the majority or all the shares of the target company. The bidder will offer to buy the shares for a specified period, at a price, with a form of payment and may attach additional conditions to the offer. The hostile tender by the buyer is based on assumptions the buyer makes because it has limited information about the target company. The outcome is determined by how many see the offer by the hostile bidder as an attractive offer relative to the alternatives. Shareholders register their satisfaction with the offer by selling their shares to the company making the hostile offer.

In September 2009, Kraft Foods made a bid to buy Cadbury plc, a British confectionary giant. Kraft's initial offer valued Cadbury shares at 745 British pence each, or a total of £10.2 billion (US$16.7 billion). It offered 40 percent in cash, with the remainder in new Kraft shares. This was rejected by Cadbury's board and called insufficient by some Cadbury shareholders. The British Panel on Takeovers and Mergers told Kraft that it must either make a formal bid or issue a statement that it was walking away from the deal by November 9, 2009. So on November 9, Kraft issued a hostile bid that included the same terms as the earlier offer.

Following the announcement of the bid, Kraft's single biggest shareholder (Warren Buffett, who owned 9.4 percent of Kraft's shares) stated that he opposed Kraft's issuing new shares to finance the acquisition. At the time he thought that the shares were already undervalued and so were an expensive way of paying for the acquisition. Alice Schroeder, a Berkshire investor, said, "He's trying to set the tone for what is a reasonable price for everyone involved. It's a psychological game."[4] Buffett's comments eased fears that Kraft would overpay. Kraft shares soon jumped 4.9 percent to US$28.77, up US$1.34, helping boost the value of the bid by roughly US$600 million to US$16.8 billion, or £10.5 billion, which was 765 pence per share for Cadbury.[5]

Cadbury again rejected Kraft's bid as "insulting" while rumours suggested the U.S.–based Hershey and Italian-based Ferrero might make counter offers. Neither did, and in January 2010 Kraft raised its offer to US$19 billion, of which 60 percent would be in cash. It financed this offer using debt financing and proceeds from the sale of its U.S. pizza business. The new offer raised the amount offered per share of Cadbury by 50 percent over the price it had traded at before Kraft first announced its takeover offer. Still, the price was below the level that a number of Cadbury managers and investors argued that the company was worth. On January 19, Cadbury's board advised its shareholders to accept the offer, which they did in a shareholders' vote on February 2, 2010.[6]

The experience that Kraft had with Cadbury is typical of a hostile takeover. When the two companies are amenable to a deal, a more thorough process is pursued in which additional information is sought and terms of a deal are negotiated.

3. ASSESSING FIT OF THE POTENTIAL CANDIDATE

Having agreed on the possibility of a merger or acquisition, it is time to assess the fit of the targeted company. This includes external and internal analysis. External analysis involves understanding the driving forces in the macro-environment that will affect the industry and the business in terms of its size, growth, and profitability. The competitors in the industry are also identified and assessed from a strategic perspective to determine whether the target company has a good position in the market and a sustainable competitive advantage.

Internal analysis involves learning enough about the other party so that the potential deal can be appropriately valued, the representations and warranties of the other side tested, full disclosure can be made to investors, and post-merger integration can be planned. Both parties agree to respect the confidential information received from the other party during the process. This process is called *due diligence*. When a merger is anticipated, management of each company will want to perform greater due diligence because terms of the deal are much more extensive than when an acquisition is anticipated.

The scope of due diligence has increased as companies have become more complex. Often, due diligence is first done on high-priority items and is then followed by a more detailed process. Generally, the information sought is organized by specific categories, including:

- General Corporate Matters
- Financial, Accounting, and Taxes
- Technology and Intellectual Property
- Product/Service Offerings
- Operations

- Sales and Marketing
- Human Resources and Personnel
- Legal and Regulatory

Within each category, documents are requested and management is questioned. The requested documents include confidential projections, reports, and other documents actually used by the company, as opposed to projections and reports specially created for the M&A process. Traditionally these documents were put in a data room where a detailed record was kept of who saw which version of each document, when, and for how long. With the growth of electronic information, documents are now housed in virtual data rooms that are available online. The questions to management are answered over the phone and in meetings. A major challenge for the company being examined is balancing the demands for information with the need for secrecy so that, if the deal does not go through, its competitiveness is not put at risk.

Many checklists that are publicly available identify data that can be collected in the process, but simply collecting facts is only the start of due diligence. What is wanted is the identification of major forces affecting value and creating risk exposure. These are discovered by researching curious details, anomalies, inconsistencies, and discontinuities in the data. The due diligence process tries the investigator's stamina, care, and capacity for critical thinking because it is typically done under tight time pressures and sellers may make efforts to gloss things over.

Having performed due diligence, management has equipped itself to produce a sound valuation of the proposed combination of the two companies and to produce a plan detailing how the combination of the two companies can be implemented. The detailed understanding of the other business allows management to determine a price-to-pay calculation.

Planning of integration pre-merger is especially critical as companies press to achieve synergies as soon as possible. The due diligence process provides information for a start, but detailed planning is not possible because the deal may not happen. A way to jump-start the integration process is by using third-party expertise in a secure environment (clean rooms). There, the third party can analyze sensitive and competitive data and information from the two companies and prepare plans for integration. One advantage of this approach is that it accelerates the capture of synergies once the deal closes. Even if the deal collapses, using third parties has an advantage. If representatives from the two companies had been working on such sensitive integration plans, they would have to leave their respective companies if the companies are competitors because they would possess confidential information about the other company.

4. NEGOTIATING TERMS

When the two sides are sufficiently in agreement over the general terms of the deal, they may commit their understanding to a term sheet and/or a letter of intent. This confirms the growing level of commitment to the deal and guides lawyers who are drafting the definitive agreement. Most sellers breathe a sigh of relief once a letter of intent has been executed with a buyer. Nothing could be further from the truth, as many points have to be negotiated and disagreement over terms or material adverse changes could derail the negotiation. When negotiations go well, they conclude with a definitive agreement that binds the two parties to completing the transaction. This agreement sets out the details of the deal and commits the directors of both companies to actions that will close the deal.

The design or structure of a deal involves bargaining to find terms that satisfy both sides. This is a complicated process in which one or more objectives are pursued subject to constraints. Changing one term in the deal may be offset by changing other terms in the deal as each term can have multiple effects. The result of this set of interrelationships is that several different combinations of terms may be an attractive deal with no "perfect deal"; that is, one deal that is superior to all others. The terms included in the negotiation are greater with a merger than an acquisition. The reason is that with an acquisition, the owners are giving up any voice in the new organization for a price while in a merger two organizations are being brought together in a manner agreeable to both sides.

The principal terms negotiated in a deal relate to price, form of payment, financing, timing and deadlines, commitments, control and governance, risk management, form of transaction, social issues, and social welfare and community issues. An old axiom states that, while the seller determines the price of his or her company, the buyer sets the terms or "structure." The 10 major terms that could be included in a deal are diagrammed in Exhibit 12.2 and are discussed briefly.[7]

Exhibit 12.2 Ten Potential Terms in a Deal

Price

Price is the amount to be paid/received in the deal. It must be seen as reasonable by each side for the deal to happen. Typically the buyer pays a premium for the target company that exceeds its pre-acquisition price. Over the past 20 years the average premium paid has been between 40 percent and 50 percent.[8] The premium entices the shareholders to sell their shares to the acquiring company. The justification for the premium is the potential synergy that can be created though this is difficult to estimate. The acquisition only produces positive returns when the premium paid is less than the value of synergy actually produced. This is often not the case—in part due to poor integration of the two companies. Another explanation for paying premiums that exceed the potential gains for synergy is hubris, which is related to the personal character of the person driving the deal.[9] *Hubris* is a Greek term denoting excessive pride, overconfidence, or arrogance. Hubristic managers tend to overestimate the value of a potential acquisition and having unrealistic expectations about their ability to create synergies. Hubris may also lead to inadequate due diligence and ignoring negative information that is turned up in the process.[10] Indicators of hubris are praise for the CEO in the media and the CEO's compensation relative to that of peers. The higher the degree of hubris, the greater the price paid for the target company. Glowing press reports puff up CEOs to believe that they can pay more because they are good enough to earn it back. An additional highly favourable press account of the CEO translates to an almost 5 percent premium paid.[11]

Additional explanations for an inappropriate price are related to the process of dealing with acquisitions:

1. Decision bias in that the majority of acquisition announcements use the target company's 52-week trading high when setting the acquisition price.
2. Unfamiliarity with the critical elements of acquisition strategy.
3. Lack of adequate knowledge of the target.
4. Unexpected problems occurring in the integration process.[12]

Price is often negotiated near the end of creating the deal since the amount the buyer is willing to pay is influenced by other terms of the deal.

Form of Payment

The payment of the price can be made in different ways, including fixed payments, contingent payments, and side payments. Fixed payments such as cash and senior debt securities eliminate uncertainty about the value of the transaction to the seller, who receives a known amount. While this shows the buyer is serious in the offer, it also conveys the seller's lack of confidence in owning shares of the buyer's business. Contingent payments are securities with value less certain than cash and senior debt securities. They are made using "junk" bonds, preferred stock, and common stock. They may be used when the buyer is unable to provide fixed payments. Securities will also be used if the seller's shareholders want to delay taxes on the sales. Because their value is uncertain, contingent payments may be made to compensate for changes in the price of stocks between the announcement of the deal and its approval. Side payments are payments to parties other than the owners of the target company. They include payments to executives in the target company, guarantees to employees of work rules, jobs, and training, and guarantees to governments against plant closings and continued investment in the target company.

Financing

This is how the money is raised to make the payment and has implications for taxes (through the tax shield provided by debt), the risk of default, and the future financial flexibility of the buyer. Financial flexibility is measured as excess cash and unused capacity on which the company might call.

Timing and Deadlines

The value of the payment is affected by when the deal is closed and when payments are made, given the present value of money. Immediate payments are certain and of greater value, hence preferred by sellers. But buyers may not have the financial capability to pay immediately so seek to make deferred payments.

Commitments

Deal structure often has specific terms that reduce the uncertainty of what will happen in future. The parties involved make commitments to take responsibility for many issues associated with the deal such as liabilities associated with the environment, products, and pensions. Sometimes commitments include intangible assets (the ownership of patents, brand names, customer lists) and tangible assets (the transfer of certain retail locations). Non-compete clauses for senior executives who might be forced to leave are another form of commitment. Warranties are commitments that each side in the deal makes about certain conditions, and when this is found not to be true, reparations are made.

Control and Governance

This set of terms addresses the form and amount of power stakeholders will have in the new organization. The power of shareholders is influenced through the composition of the board and the limitation of voting power through stand-still agreements. Managerial discretion can also be altered through who has the power to appoint operating executives, the tightening or relation of financial covenants, and the creation of fixed income securities that have a high demand on the target company's cash flow.

Risk Management

Buyers and sellers face risk because of the deal and they seek to mitigate the risk. When the deal involves share-for-share exchange, both sides seek to protect themselves from the risk of changes in share prices. A "collar" is produced by agreeing to a floor on the number of shares the seller receives and a cap on the number of shares the buyer has to pay. When there is a danger of a competing bidder entering the contest, the buyer mitigates this risk with a lockup provision, a toehold equity position, or "topping up" fees. When the risk is that the other side may simply choose to walk away from the deal because it has changed its mind, the other side can include an agreement that "walk away" fees be paid that cover its costs of developing the deal to that point. Finally, buyers will include a material adverse change (MAC) clause in the agreement they sign that allows them to nullify the deal before completion. This clause is triggered by material adverse business or economic changes affecting or involving the target company or its assets prior to the completion of the deal.

Form of the Transaction

The legal reorganization of the business and how it is done has implications for exposure to liabilities and taxes, control, value creation, and continuity. For example, with a cash merger, the seller is immediately subject to taxes while the buyer assumes the liabilities of the target. After the acquisition of the target, its shareholders no longer have any voice in control of the company. With a triangular merger, the buyer forms a subsidiary and capitalizes it with sufficient cash to acquire the stock of the target company. In a reverse triangular merger, the subsidiary merges into the target so that the target company survives as do its tax attributes and liabilities so that the overall transaction is seen as a simple purchase of shares and is not taxable to the seller.

Social Issues

The governance and managerial hierarchy of the new organization must be set. Many merger agreements state the positions that the two CEOs will hold in the new company. Side agreements may state the salaries, perquisites, and responsibilities of these executives. Other agreements include the composition of the board and their compensation.

Social Welfare and Community Issues

Stakeholders associated with the business will be affected by the deal. These effects are plant closings, employee layoffs, changes in charitable contributions, relocation of corporate headquarters, and the like. Sellers of private companies may be highly sensitive about the welfare of their former employees. Concerns of stakeholders about potential changes can be alleviated by agreement or understanding about what the company will do with regard to these stakeholder concerns. Understandings are not enforceable and are rarely stated in the formal merger agreements.

During the negotiations, the two sides grapple with each other as they seek terms that optimize the deal from their perspective. Psychology and self-discipline appear most vividly in this step. The attitudes and appetites of the two sides and the negotiation tactics used have a large influence on price and terms. A deal can acquire emotional momentum, which, once it kicks in, means that nothing can stop the deal from happening. The buyer wants to make the deal at any price. This is most likely to happen when other bidders also want to buy the company. The company that wins by paying beyond what is a rational maximum has the "winner's curse"—it has acquired the company but will never be able to earn back what it paid for the purchase.

Sorting out the structure, like a dance, requires skill and grace as the specific terms of the deal are set. Anticipating pitfalls and knowing how and when to deal with them are part of the art involved in closing the deal.

5. DEAL SIGNING THROUGH APPROVAL

Before the CEOs sign the definitive agreement, a vote by the target's board of directors and possibly by the buyer's board as well is required. If a vote by the shareholders is required, the target's board can recommend whether they approve the deal. Typically the shareholders' vote is done at a special meeting 30 to 60 days after they have received a prospectus laying out the deal. A key component of the prospectus is a "fairness opinion," a letter stating an independent analyst's opinion on the fairness to the target's shareholders of the purchase price, form of payment, and other aspects of the deal. In the time before the meeting, parties can solicit proxies to give them voting power at the meeting. By the time of the shareholders' meeting, the outcome of the vote is predictable because each side has been soliciting proxies allowing it to cast votes for other shareholders.

The formal closing of the deal is scheduled as soon as possible after the shareholders' vote. The buyer wants to get on with integrating the two companies while the seller wants to avoid unforeseen circumstances that might derail the deal. Fast action also means that critical stakeholders such as employees and customers are not left for a long period wondering what is going to happen.

Government approval is often required and the deal cannot be finalized until this is received. The most common form of approval is that of the anti-combines or anti-trust authorities. These agencies promote competition by determining whether the deal will create market power. Other concerns of government regulators include protection of culture, industries, and trade. An example of government intervention occurred when the Canadian government blocked the sale of MacDonald Dettwiler's space division, maker of the Canadarm used in space exploration, to the U.S. company Alliant Techsystems in 2008 after shareholders had overwhelmingly approved the deal. A major concern was that the Canadian Space Agency had invested Cdn$500 million in MacDonald Dettwiler's development and manufacture of Radarsat-2, which would be given to Alliant in the sale.[13]

6. INTEGRATING THE ACQUISITION

Ideally, planning for integrating the two companies begins while due diligence is being conducted. At that stage, plans will be general and then specified in greater detail when more information is available after the deal is completed. Leaving preparation of plans until after the deal is completed slows down integration.

With a plan in hand, the organizational mechanisms need to be created that are in line with pursuing the strategy of the combined companies. The first step is creating an organizational structure. With the structure in place, accountability for achieving both strategic and integration goals is then assigned to positions. Then metrics are determined for measuring the achievement of these goals. With this done, it is time to humanize the mechanism. Humanization starts with selecting leaders who will be in charge—the CEO and the integration manager. With the CEO's leadership, the top two lines in the organization chart can be filled out.

With senior management in place, it is time to learn more about the new company. Major aspects of the new company were learned during the due diligence process conducted before the deal was completed but the workings of the business cannot be penetrated until the deal is completed. The examination explores the new markets and new customer requirements that come with the deal; audits the capabilities of the newly combined company, looking for potential synergies; describes the culture of the new company; and examines differences in governance in terms of leadership, behaviour, and overall identity. Using the knowledge, the senior management team looks for areas where integration can lever the performance of the business. There are six areas that have significant potential (see Exhibit 12.3).

First is setting customer strategy and branding. The focus is on serving the most profitable customers. This requires segmenting the customer base and then determining the value provided to different segments, including brand experience and the level of customer relationship sought.

Second is setting capabilities in line with delivering the company's strategy. Analysis of the value chain shows how these capabilities are used to provide products and services that customers value. Changes in the activities of the value chain and improvements in capabilities improve the value the customer sees and the efficiency with which this is created.

Third is aligning the corporate culture of the two organizations. Cultural alignment requires considerable time so during the integration phase the emphasis is on recognizing and validating the cultures and values of the two companies. A common set of values from the cultures of the two businesses is identified so that communications and interactions are effective in both

Exhibit 12.3 Six Areas of Leverage When Integrating Companies

businesses. In the post-integration phase, further cultural realignment can produce a common corporate culture.

Fourth is creating a common business logic so that people have the same understanding of what will make the new company successful. People in each of the companies being combined will have their own business logic that consists of the assumptions that they think makes their company successful. This logic is the sum of what management has learned about the business and how to use this knowledge to be successful. When everyone shares a common business logic they are able to work together more easily and decisions they make and actions they take are more likely to be compatible.

Fifth is staffing, which involves putting the right people in the right places in the new organization. As each company has capable people, management of the new company wants to select and retain the best. They may pursue this through re-recruitment in which people apply for jobs in the new company and those best suited are put into positions in the new organization.

Sixth is consolidated and rationalized information technology (IT). Each company has its own IT function, which has made its own decisions about information architecture and systems that support the way that the company does business. Consensus is needed on the policies, principles, standards, guidelines, services, common solutions, and specific vendor products that will be used. Some systems will no longer be needed because things are being done in new ways. Criteria need to be set so decisions can be made about which systems will be shut down and which systems will be kept. As systems are highly interdependent, dropping one may affect others. These interrelationships must be recognized when decisions are made about altering systems. The need to alter systems can be avoided by running systems in parallel, but this is likely to be an unacceptable situation for the longer run.

The need to maintain an integrated view of these decisions is evidenced by what happens when one is not taken. In 1994, Manulife Financial acquired the Group Life and Health Business from Confederation Life Insurance Company (Confed). Manulife's group insurance had been very successful with small and medium-sized business customers. Because it had many customers it had developed a limited number of insurance packages that customers could buy and it had automated much of the business using information technology. By buying Confed's business, Manulife was able to expand into serving large businesses. The intent was to cut Confed's high sales and service costs on these large customers by automating the way these customers were handled. Manulife put this into effect after the acquisition and quickly lost customers as customer complaints soared. What management had not recognized was that large customers were often unionized so had very specific insurance needs in order to meet their labour contracts. Acquiring and servicing these accounts was rewarding but people-intensive. These accounts could not be captured nor adequately serviced with a limited number of alternative packages and automated services. Only after losing some major customers did management recognize its mistake and rebuild the human resources and systems need to service large customers well.

As changes are made that bring the two companies together as one, the work of management shifts from managing and integrating two businesses to managing one business.

Acquisition Capability[14]

Companies using M&As as a vehicle for growth have developed core capabilities that give them a competitive advantage at this activity. These capabilities are associated with an experienced team performing the M&As, a standard methodology for doing M&As, and putting an integration manager in charge of pulling the two companies together after the deal is completed.

Having a good team working on the merger and acquisition deal cycle improves the likelihood of good deals. Having people who have worked together on previous deals means they know their roles and those of others. This facilitates communication and coordination. It also provides some emotional resilience because team members have a greater appreciation for the work each does and are more circumspect when the deal does not work out—they do not immediately blame the failure on one individual. Experience gained from multiple deals also improves judgment.

Each team has a process that it uses to work through the cycle. Having an overall process counters the tendency for activities to fragment and go their own ways during implementation.

Two examples of such companies are Cisco Systems and General Electric. After each acquisition the team has reviewed the process and determined what worked and what did not work and uses this to make improvements. They include selecting better targets and better integration processes. The overall process can be documented in a comprehensive guidebook that is used during the integration exercise. The guidebook includes a well-defined, step-by-step methodology based on knowledge and experience from previous integration work. Included in it are templates, principles that flow from the strategy, and values of the business that are used to guide decision making during the integration and the identification of roles and responsibilities and accountability structures. The guidebook provides a road map and time line for integration.

Companies that have performed many integration exercises have learned the value of having an integration manager. Having such a person allows the CEO to focus on running the business while the integration manager makes sure that the integration happens. Having an integration manager committed to making the integration work can help in four ways. First, having one person specifically responsible for integration speeds it up as this manager pushes for plans and decisions and monitors progress against goals so that the integration meets its deadlines. Second, having an integration manager creates a unique position in the organizational structure. This person can cut across the organization, pushing for accomplishment of key tasks, mobilizing joint teams, and facilitating team and executive reviews. Third, the integration manager can forge social contacts between the two organizations by acting as a travelling ambassador. This manager helps others by interpreting the customs, language, and culture of both companies. This manager can also serve as a lightning rod for hot issues. Fourth and finally, the integration manager helps engineer short-term successes that produce performance results. These successes come from identifying critical business synergies and orchestrating the transfer of best practices between companies.

A special set of skills is required to be an effective integration manager. The person has to have a deep knowledge of the acquiring company, have a flexible managerial style, be comfortable with chaos, be self-confident, be independently responsible, and be emotionally and culturally intelligent. Given this rare mix of talents, there are few integration managers so they find themselves in high demand.

Acquisitions in Different Industry Contexts

Not surprisingly, M&A activity varies across industries. It is determined largely by the development phase in which a given industry finds itself and by the extent of industry dynamism. In addition, competitive conditions will determine whether acquisition is a suitable strategy vehicle for a company in a given industry and what the most viable type of acquisition may be. In this section, the role of M&As and industry context in terms of the industry life cycle and the level of industry-wide turbulence is discussed.

M&AS AND INDUSTRY LIFE CYCLE

Recall the model of industry life cycle and industry dynamics that we presented in Chapter 4. In this section, this model is used to illustrate how different types of acquisitions play different roles in each stage.

Introduction

During the introduction stage, acquisitions tend to involve the purchase of start-up companies by well-established companies in related but more mature industry segments. Many partial acquisitions may occur, with established companies making equity investments in start-ups but not acquiring them outright. Thus, at this stage M&As tend to be R&D and product- and market-extension acquisitions. That was the case when Upstream Biosciences Inc. of Vancouver, B.C., acquired all of Pacific Pharma Technologies, also of Vancouver.

Growth

During this phase, we see several types of acquisitions. Established companies from one industry segment may start entering other segments with greater frequency, looking mostly for proven and growing targets. Although some M&A activity may be for R&D, most of it is likely to be for the purpose of acquiring products that are proven and gaining customer acceptance. The geographic roll-up also becomes more common, especially at the end of the growth stage and through the maturity stage. Both Laidlaw and Loewen were examples of corporations taking this approach. In high-velocity industries, industry-convergence acquisitions appear and continue into the maturity stage.

Maturity

At this point, we begin to see overcapacity acquisitions. Why? During the growth stage, the industry witnessed the entry of new companies and aggressive expansion, with numerous competitors jockeying for competitive position. Capacity built during this period often exceeds the long-term needs of the segment, and as demand starts to flatten, companies see consolidation as a way to rationalize the industry. Overcapacity M&A activity continues throughout the decline stage of the cycle. The merger of Domtar and Weyerhaeuser's fine paper business produced the "new" Domtar, North America's largest manufacturer of free-sheet paper. As overall demand for this paper continued dropping, Domtar permanently closed 285 000 tonnes of paper capacity in 2007.

M&AS IN DYNAMIC CONTEXTS

Dynamic contexts are often home to companies that engage in acquisitions at a frantic pace. What is it about dynamic contexts that makes acquisitions such popular strategy vehicles? In Chapter 4, factors were described that can alter an industry landscape, particularly discontinuities and globalization were described. These two factors tend to accelerate acquisitions. Specific factors that we will focus on here are *technological change, demographic change, geopolitical change, trade liberalization,* and *deregulation.*[15]

Technological Change

In high-velocity industries, technological change and innovation happens quickly, and some companies respond with aggressive acquisition campaigns. Canadian technology companies such as Research In Motion and Open Text have used acquisitions to ensure that they stay on the cutting edge of new technology so that innovation and technological change among competitors does not erode their strong competitive positions.

Demographic Change

Demographic changes, such as the aging of the population and mass emigration, may alter customer profiles significantly. Recognizing the increasing number of languages and cultures immigrating to Canada, Rogers Communications purchased the multicultural channel OMNI 1 in 1986. The channel has continued to grow and provide different cultural and language programs, helping to solidify Rogers's market share in this area.

Geopolitical Change

Such events as the fall of the Iron Curtain, the emergence of the European Union, the opening of China, and conflict in the Middle East all have had significant effects on the operations of global companies. In some cases, changes enhance opportunities for acquiring established companies in new locations. In others, they foster divestiture. Numerous companies have entered the Chinese market as the Chinese government opens up its borders. Although there are still regulations and rules that must be followed, such as creating joint ventures with Chinese companies, Canadian companies such as Research In Motion have chosen to enter this high-potential market. And IBM sold its personal computer division to the Chinese company Lenova in 2005, in the process making it a competitor in world markets for personal computers.

Trade Liberalization

Trade liberalization also opens new opportunities for doing business. In the wake of the European Union and the North American Free Trade Agreement (NAFTA), for example, cross-border acquisition activity increased in industries conducting business in those regions. Wal-Mart's acquisition of the successful Mexican retailing giant Cifra is a case in point.

How Scotiabank Effectively Integrates Foreign Acquisitions[16]

Scotiabank, also known as the Bank of Nova Scotia (BNS), is Canada's most international bank, with 50 000 employees serving 10 million customers in 50 countries. Scotiabank decided to build its business in emerging markets because the Canadian market is mature. As of 2006, 50 percent of its employees were outside Canada. Since 2005, for example, Scotiabank acquired Banco in El Salvador, BWS/BSA in Peru, Interfin in Costa Rica, and the Royal Bank of Scotland's business in Colombia. It now has a strong market position in many countries in Latin and South America (its goal is to be in the top three banks in each market) and is making headway in Asia. In these countries it is providing the ever-increasing middle class with many of the financial services that North Americans have taken for granted for a long time. With each acquisition the bank seeks to maintain the customer base and retain employees. Achieving this requires successful integration of acquisitions.

Scotiabank has developed a standard but flexible methodology that speeds up integration because everyone knows what to do. After each integration exercise, the methodology is reviewed so that management learns from the successes and mistakes of the last effort. According to Elmira Hill, vice-president, integration and change projects at Scotiabank International, the number-one factor in the success or failure of any integration is the management of human capital. People drive the success of the integration effort.

Changes that have to be made that affect people are organizational structure, staffing, leadership and management style, and systems.

With each acquisition the new organizational structure has clear accountability for decision making. This helps ensure successful integration by getting important decisions made quickly and decisively. Throughout the rest of the new structure a strong sense of local accountability and ownership of the decisions is encouraged. This gets people involved in the integration and makes success more likely. For the human resources function, physical facilities in the country are all combined in one location to facilitate their integration.

The new organization also has to be staffed. Scotiabank moves quickly in selecting and announcing the senior management appointments, starting with the CEO and several other first-line executives. They then choose the rest of the first-line and second-line executives. The bank likes to use local staff since they know the products, the customers, and the competition. It strives to be the employer of choice wherever it does business so that staff from the acquired company is retained. The bank faces a personnel challenge when staffing the new operation in a country where it already has some operations. Those already working for the bank assume that, because it is taking over the other bank, they will be put in the senior positions. In one case, the acquired company was much larger than present bank operations so the managers of

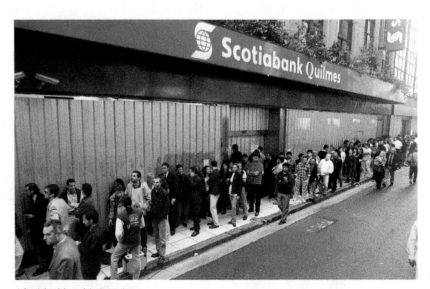

A Scotiabank branch in Argentina.

the acquired bank had better skills for managing the larger organization. Consequently they got the senior positions in the new organization.

Creating the capabilities in the people to lead and manage is also done. Two weeks after senior management is announced, BNS's International Banking division meets with this team to develop the leadership skills needed to manage themselves and the workforce through the uncertainty and ambiguity of integration. The work of leadership does not end with integration but continues with the management of the new business. This also calls for altering the management style in some countries where the style has been very authoritarian. A consequence of this style is that people wait for decisions to be made at the top. Then managers at all levels need to be trained so that they can handle personal accountability.

When the organizations come together, they need to operate on common systems. Eventually the bank will be on one platform, but in the short term it is easier to go with existing systems because this has less impact on the customer. BNS is open-minded about which systems will be used and will talk with personnel from the acquisition to determine which systems

are best. Each department meets for a week and at the end has a high level plan for integration of systems. Having determined what is needed, a great many people need to be trained so that they have the tools and capabilities to manage through the process of change brought on by integration. Only then will they be able to function in the new organization. And this training must continue to provide new employees with the skills and knowledge needed while refreshing and reinforcing these in longer term employees.

Human resources for Scotiabank wants common principles, practices, and policies across the corporation and these are not negotiable—they have to be put in place. To achieve this, corporate headquarters gives considerable support to the local human resources function. In addition, human resources must make sure the new operation complies with all local laws. The bank's purchase of a second operation in Peru created an interesting situation. Peruvian law required that each bank report on loans it made to each employee and his/her family. With the merger, loans by both banks to employees and their families had to be pulled together and reported.

Communication is a critical issue in the turbulence and uncertainty created

when integrating companies. Scotiabank works hard to provide clear, consistent, and frequent communication. This cuts down on rumours and helps reduce concerns so that employees remain positive and focused on looking after customers. A key tool in this activity has been the identification of a communication champion in each branch and each department. These champions meet once a month to raise questions and get answers.

These are the key ideas that Scotiabank has found that help it handle human resources during an integration.

1. Identify a company that has gone through an acquisition in the past five years.

   Was the acquisition friendly or hostile? Were various stakeholders concerned about the takeover? How well has the acquirer appeared to handle the integration? And what has happened to performance of the enlarged company?

A Scotiabank branch in Peru.

Geographic proximity and NAFTA make it cost-effective for Wal-Mart to stock its shelves in the United States with goods assembled in Mexico as well as to provide otherwise more expensive U.S.–made goods to Mexican consumers through Cifra's outlets. Wal-Mart gained improved economies of scope and scale as a result of NAFTA.

Deregulation

Finally, deregulation has had a major impact on the volume of M&A activity in a number of industries. BCE, the parent to Bell Canada, was allowed to operate as a monopoly until 1992 when the CRTC opened the doors to long distance competition for the first time in Canada. The market was further opened to competition in 1997 when the CRTC increased competition for local telephone service by allowing new competitors such as Rogers Cable into the market.

M&As and Coevolution

As with alliances, the use of acquisitions in dynamic contexts fits into the coevolution model of corporate strategy. Recall our definition of coevolution as the orchestration of a web of shifting linkages among evolving businesses. Acquisitions can enable a company to absorb the capabilities of their targets in order to develop specific dynamic capabilities in concert with the best resources and capabilities available on the market. Just as important, acquisitions (at least well-conceived ones) support a specific, focused strategy. Consequently, in keeping with this strategy, certain businesses are periodically pared off through divestitures and others added through acquisitions. If, for instance, the company is pursuing a growth strategy, the coevolution perspective would suggest that it divest slow-growth businesses and products and acquire businesses and products that are operating on the technology frontier or that offer some other basis for future competitive advantage.[17]

FOCUS ON ETHICS 12.1
Kraft Foods Closes Cadbury's Somerdale Plant[18]

In September 2009, Kraft Foods made a hostile bid to buy Cadbury plc, a British confectionary giant, for US$17 billion. During the long and bitter takeover battle that ended in February 2010 with Kraft's acquisition of Cadbury, Kraft said repeatedly that it believed that Cadbury's Somerdale plant in Keynsham, western England, could be kept open. This announcement reversed earlier plans by Cadbury to move production to Poland and close the Somerdale factory, ending 500 associated jobs. Shortly after Kraft completed its takeover in February 2010, it said the Somerdale plant would close by 2011 because it had become clear that it was "unrealistic to reverse the closure program." Executive Vice-President Marc Firestone of Kraft told Britain's Panel on Takeovers and Mergers that he was "truly sorry" for the uncertainty caused by Kraft's backtrack on the factory. He said that Kraft's announcement had been made in good faith and that Kraft had not understood at the time the extent of Cadbury's decision to transfer most production by the middle of the year to new Polish facilities it had invested £100 million in. He added that the company did not plan to shut any more British factories or axe further jobs for the next two years.

"We want to regain the trust of our colleagues, government and public," Firestone told legislators. "We want to develop a stronger growth platform in the U.K. and globally. We understand that in acquiring a British icon we have a responsibility to preserve its heritage."

Lindsay Hoyle, a member of the ruling Labour Party, suggested that Kraft's U-turn on the Somerdale facility was "remote, smug and worst of all duplicitous," while other lawmakers expressed amazement that the U.S. company was not fully aware of Cadbury's plans.

Jacob Rees-Mogg, the Conservative Party candidate for the area where Somerdale is based, had written in a February 15 letter to Britain's Panel on Takeovers and Mergers that Kraft, in backtracking on the closure, broke rules that call for bidders to "prepare statements with the highest degree of care and accuracy" and not to make statements that "while not factually inaccurate may be misleading." On March 5, Rees-Mogg described Kraft's behaviour as "shameful." In an email he said, "It gave people in Keynsham false hope in its prospectus which was either careless or deliberately misleading."

A spokesman for Kraft said in a statement, "Throughout the transaction, it has never been our policy to comment on the U.K. takeover panel. Any questions about the panel therefore should be addressed to the panel itself."

It is unclear what steps if any the panel could take to punish Kraft should it find the company violated the takeover code, and one person familiar with regulatory procedure said that any sanction would amount to little more than a wrist slap—though it would likely add to negative sentiment surrounding the deal.

Do you think that Kraft's management purposefully mislead others about the closing so it was viewed more favourably and the purchase allowed? If not, should it have made promises with full knowledge of the situation?

Summary of Challenges

1. *Know the difference between a merger and an acquisition.* The differences are legally based. A *merger* typically refers to two companies coming together as one and is achieved through the exchange of shares. Both companies' stocks are surrendered and new company stock is issued in its place. An *acquisition* has one company purchase the assets or shares of the target company which then ceases to exist.

   In the business media, however, the terms *merger* and *acquisition* are used interchangeably as though they are synonymous. Those associated with companies that are acquired can be sensitive to the negative connotations that come with this. Hence the buyer may state that the acquisition is a merger of equals or allow the CEO of the acquired business to state that it is. This makes the takeover more palatable to those in the acquired business. When the target company does not want to be purchased, the deal is seen as unfriendly and regarded as an acquisition.

2. *Know why mergers and acquisitions occur.* M&As are motivated by the same reasons that motivate alliances such as joint ventures and contractual arrangements. The additional value created by an M&A is said to be derived from synergies due to increased revenue and decreased cost that come from the combination of the two companies. As with other vehicles, M&As allow the company to grow the business faster than is possible with organic growth. M&As are attractive when management is unable to negotiate a contract in which the benefits exceed the costs of the business relationship, management feels a need for greater control over operations, and management seeks to control risk exposure.

   Personal factors can also enter into the M&A decision, such as opportunistic behaviour by top executives. Increasing the size of the company can increase personal compensation and enhance personal power. And, to the extent that the M&A diversifies the company, the executive's employment risk is reduced.

3. *Explain the role of due diligence when performing a merger or acquisition.* Due diligence is the name given to the analysis of the other company in the deal. The information collected in the process is used to generate the value of the deal, to test the representations and warranties of the other side, to support full disclosure of the implications of the deal to investors, and to plan post-merger integration. Both parties agree to respect the confidential information received from the other party during the process. When a merger is anticipated, management in each company will want to perform greater due diligence because terms of the deal are much more extensive than when an acquisition is anticipated.

4. *Describe the 10 main terms considered when structuring a deal and explain why they matter.* The principal terms negotiated in a deal relate to price, form of payment, financing, timing and deadlines, commitments, control and governance, risk management, form of transaction, social issues, and social welfare and community issues. An old axiom states that, while the seller determines the price of his or her company, the buyer sets the terms or "structure." *Price* is the amount to be paid and received. It must be seen as reasonable by each side for the deal to happen. Price is often negotiated near the end of creating the deal since the amount the buyer is willing to pay is influenced by other terms of the deal. *Form of payment* is what vehicle is used to pay the price. This could be cash, shares, or the transfer of assets. *Financing* is how the money is raised to make the payment and has implications for taxes, the risk of default, and the future financial flexibility of the buyer. *Timing and deadlines* are when the payments are made and when the deal closes. Both will affect the value of the payments given the present value of money. *Commitments* determine who will take responsibility for many of the issues associated with the deal such as liabilities associated with the environment, products, and pensions. *Control and governance* are about the form and amount of power the stakeholders will have in the new organization. *Risk management* deals with various arrangements that control or limit the risk associated with the deal. *Form of the transaction* is the legal reorganization of the business and how it is done which has implications for exposure to liabilities and taxes, control, value creation, and continuity. *Social issues* involve agreement over the governance and management of the new organization. Finally, *social welfare and community issues* are agreements and understandings (not enforceable like agreements) about how decisions will be made that affect stakeholders.

5. *Explain what an integration manager does.* An integration manager is the person who is responsible for integrating two companies. Having an integration manager committed to this helps in four ways. First, having one person specifically responsible for integration speeds it up as this manager pushes for plans and decisions and monitors progress against goals so that the integration meets its deadlines. Second, having an integration manager creates a unique position in the organizational structure. This person can cut across the organization, pushing for accomplishment of key tasks, mobilizing joint teams, and facilitating team and executive reviews. Third, the integration manager can forge social contacts between the two organizations by acting as a travelling ambassador. This manager helps others by interpreting the customs, language, and culture of both companies. This manager can also serve as a lightning rod for hot issues. Fourth and finally, the integration manager helps engineer short-term successes that produce business results. These successes come from identifying critical business synergies and orchestrating the transfer of best practices between companies.

6. *Describe the six major areas to look for leverage when integrating operations of two companies.* First is setting customer strategy and branding. Second is setting capabilities in line with delivering the company's strategy. Third is aligning the corporate culture of the two organizations. Fourth is creating a common business logic so that people have a common understanding of what will make the new company successful. Fifth is staffing, which involves putting the right people in the right places in the new organization. Sixth is consolidated and rationalized

information technology. Decisions about each area should not be made independently as they are different but integrated parts of the company. A change in any one will have implications for other areas.

7. *Discuss the characteristics of acquisitions in different industry contexts.* Different types of acquisitions are seen with greater frequency at different stages of the industry life cycle. During the introduction stage, acquisitions tend to be by companies in related segments acquiring technology (R&D acquisitions) or products of start-ups (product extensions). During the growth phase of the industry life cycle, several types of acquisitions are common. Some R&D acquisitions of a now-proven technology by later-moving established companies from related

industry segments still take place. But given that in the growth phase products have achieved more accepted status, many more product-extension acquisitions are seen. The geographic roll-up tends to appear at the waning stages of the growth phase. In high-velocity industries, industry-convergence acquisitions also start to appear. During the maturity stage, overcapacity acquisitions start to emerge, and roll-ups and product-extension acquisitions continue. Overcapacity acquisitions continue throughout industry decline. Industry turbulence, such as technological change, demographic change, geopolitical change, trade liberalization, and deregulation, are all forms of industry shock that tend to increase acquisition activity because they change the competitive landscape.

Review Questions

1. How is an acquisition different from a merger?
2. Why would a company use a merger or acquisition?
3. What synergies are created through a merger or acquisition?
4. How does a company identify candidates for a merger or acquisition?
5. How important is due diligence when engaged in merger or acquisition discussions?
6. When is price likely to be discussed when negotiating terms of the deal?

7. When should management of the acquirer think about integrating the acquired company with its original company?
8. Explain why serving the role of an integration manager takes a very special individual.
9. Where should management's attention be focused when seeking to improve the performance of the companies during the integration process?
10. How do acquisitions tend to be used in different stages of the industry life cycle?

Experiential Activities

Group Exercises

1. Pick a company of interest to your group. Identify potential acquisition candidates. Explain why these companies would make sense as an acquisition target. Evaluate and describe possible implementation barriers to this acquisition.
2. Pick a large company of interest to your group that has engaged in mergers and acquisitions (M&As). Examine its annual reports over five to 10 years. Assess the information presented on M&As in the annual reports. Do you see any explicit mention of the link between strategy formulation and implementation with respect to the acquisition mentioned in the annual reports? (As a starting place, read the chairman's letter to the shareholders.) How have M&As affected the strategy of the company?

Ethical Debates

1. During the due diligence phase of a pharmaceutical company's acquisition, you discover that an executive of the potential target may have funnelled payments to government regulators overseeing the company's drug approval process. The drug in question is only a minor source of revenue in the target's portfolio of therapies. What should you do?
2. While negotiating a deal, the CEO of the target continues to add contingencies to the deal. In addition, he asks for a "golden parachute" for himself if he convinces the largest shareholder to agree to the deal. The CFO of the target pulls you aside and tells you that he can persuade the largest shareholder to sell and that he can do it for much less than the CEO is asking for in his golden parachute. What should you do?

Endnotes

1. Dennis Campbell and Brent Kazan, "TD Canada Trust (A)," Harvard Business School case number 9-108-005, Revised October 2000; Karen Howlett, "TD Faces New Challenges with Canada Trust Merger," *Globe and Mail*, May 23, 2000, B1; David Roberts, "TD Plans Smoother Merger Steps," *Globe and Mail*, Apr 6, 2001, B4; and Fred Tomczyk, "The TD-Canada Trust Merger: Building a Better Bank," TD Financial Group, Executive Speeches, Speech to the St. Thomas and District Chamber of Commerce in St. Thomas, Ontario, June 12, 2002. Accessed March 29, 2010, at www.td.com/communicate/speeches/12june02.jsp.

2. F. Trautwein, "Merger Motives and Merger Prescriptions," *Strategic Management Journal* 11:4 (1990): 283–296.

3. O. Gadiesh, C. Ormiston, and S. Rovit, "Achieving an M&A's Strategic Goals at Maximum Speed for Maximum Value," *Strategy and Leadership*, 31:3 (2003): 35–41.

4. Dana Cimilluca and Jeffrey Mccracken, "Buffett Hits Kraft on Cadbury," *Wall Street Journal*, January 6, 2010.

5. Berkshire Hathaway Inc., "Statement From Berkshire Hathaway on Authorizing Kraft Share Proposal," January 5, 2010.

6. Dana Cimilluca and Cecilie Rohwedder, "Kraft Wins a Reluctant Cadbury With Help of Clock, Hedge Funds," *Wall Street Journal*, January 20, 2010.

7. Thorough description of the various terms and, indeed, the whole merger and acquisition process is found in Robert A. Bruner, *Applied Mergers and Acquisitions* (Hoboken, New Jersey: John Wiley & Sons, 2004).

8. T. Laamanen, "On the Role of Acquisition Premium in Acquisition Research," *Strategic Management Journal* 28:13 (2007): 1359–1369.

9. R. Roll, "The Hubris Hypothesis of Corporate Takeovers," *Journal of Business* 59:2 (1986): 197–216. .

10. M. A. Hitt, J. S. Harrison, & R. Ireland, *Mergers and Acquisitions: A Guide to Creating Value for Stakeholders* (Oxford, U.K.: Oxford University Press, 2001).

11. Matthew Hayward and Donald Hambrick, "Explaining Premiums Paid for Large Acquisitions: Evidence of CEO Hubris," *Administrative Science Quarterly* (1997): 42, 103–127.

12. M. Baker, X. Pan, & J. Wurgler, *A Reference Point Theory of Mergers and Acquisitions*, 2009. Paper presented at the American Finance Association Meetings, Atlanta, 2010. Accessed March 8, 2010, at http://papers.ssrn.com/ sol3/papers.cfm?abstract_id=1364152##. M. L. Sirower, *The Synergy Trap: How Companies Lose the Acquisition Game* (New York: The Free Press, 1997).

13. Wendy Stueck, "Lost in Space," *Globe and Mail*, May 10, 2008, p. B8.

14. Robert J. Aiello and Michael D. Watkins, "The Fine Art of the Friendly Acquisition," *Harvard Business Review* (November/December 2000), pp. 101–107. Ronald Ashkenas and Suzanne Francis, "Integration Managers: Special Leaders for Special Times," *Harvard Business Review* (November/ December 2000), pp. 108–116.

15. Brunner, *Applied Mergers and Acquisitions*.

16. Elmira Hill, Elizabeth Lorimer, and Blaine Drover, "Structuring for Success: International Banking's Approach to Acquisition Integration," Presentation made for the Conference Board of Canada's conference "Post-Merger Integration Strategies 2006," October 12, 2006.

17. S. L. Brown and K. M. Eisenhardt, *Competing on the Edge: Strategy as Structured Chaos* (Boston, M.A.: Harvard Business School Press, 1998).

18. Associated Press, "UK Unions and Lawmakers Criticize Kraft CEO," *New York Times*, March 16, 2010. Accessed March 28, 2010, at www. nytimes.com/aponline/2010/03/16/business/AP-EU-Kraft-Cadbury.html?_ r=1&scp=3&sq=cadbury&st=cs. Cecilie Rohwedder and Alistair Macdonald, "Kraft Faces Probe on Cadbury," *Wall Street Journal*, March 8, 2010.

13 Considering New Ventures and Corporate Renewal

In this chapter, we challenge you to:

1. Define *new ventures* and *corporate renewal,* then explain how they are related to strategic management.

2. Compare and contrast entrepreneurship and intrapreneurship.

3. Appreciate the professionalization of management.

4. Explain why corporations have a new venture division and what it does.

5. Describe why and when corporate renewal is necessary.

6. Identify the sources of misfit that create the need for corporate renewal.

Mike Lazaridis and Research in Motion[1]

Mike Lazaridis, co-founder of Research In Motion.

Research In Motion (RIM), headquartered in Waterloo, Ontario, was co-founded by Doug Fregin and Mike Lazaridis in 1984.

Education

Lazaridis had been interested in science since childhood in Windsor, Ontario. While in grade six and inspired by the many gadgets of *Star Trek*, he, Fregin, and a third friend experimented with chemicals and electronics. In W. F. Herman Secondary School, he and Fregin spent hours in the school's electronics labs tinkering with the equipment that a wealthy benefactor had donated to the high school. John Micsinzki, the electronics class teacher and an early mentor, told them that whoever puts together wireless and computer technology would be important.

While in high school the boys won the Windsor science fair with a solar-powered water heater that followed the sun. Later, Lazaridis developed a durable, efficient buzzer system that he sold to high schools throughout southwestern Ontario for $600 each, raising enough money to pay for his first year in electrical engineering at the University of Waterloo.

At the University of Waterloo, Lazaridis gained experience as a co-op student, did some computer programming contract work, and collaborated with Fregin, who was then a student in electrical engineering at the University of Windsor. Lazaridis got into contract work when he recognized that he could use his state-of-the-art education to help people. He went out and asked people if they needed work done. He found that their problems could be solved very elegantly and quickly using what he had learned. So he was surprised when, before graduation in 1984, other engineering students were complaining about a lack of jobs because of the recession. He told them there was plenty of work so they dared him to start a business.

The BlackBerry Bold.

RIM Is Started

In 1984, Lazaridis called Fregin, asking him to join him in a new venture that eventually became RIM. Still not finished with his undergraduate program, Lazaridis was setting up a business to count as credits toward his final grade. It was to be a consulting business that designed products using leading-edge electronics and computer science technology. It was financed with $15 000 from a provincial government new venture grant and $15 000 from Lazaridis's parents. At first, Lazaridis attempted to mix business and school, but the tidal wave of activity associated with the business forced him to make a choice. He decided to "take time off" for just two months and a few credits' shy of a degree in electrical engineering. Fregin and Lazaridis got a copy of a request for proposal (RFP) from General Motors that had been circulating for two years and realized that they could do it with some state-of-the-art techniques they had learned in university.

In February 1985, RIM got its first job—a $600 000 contract from General Motors for networked display terminals that could receive updates and scroll messages across LED signs on GM's assembly lines. To complete the contract, RIM hired Mike Barnstijn as a computer programmer after he answered a posting they had put on the local Usenet listings. He fit well—all were enthusiastic about technology, had similar educational backgrounds, and had a big interest in cars. He became RIM's first full-time permanent employee and less than a year later became a partner. RIM soon had a team of three assistants and secretaries, and had to move into a larger office down the street.

The GM deal allowed RIM to explore network technology while making a bit of cash—much of which was reinvested in research. RIM sold the rights to the LED signs to Corman Technologies, the company that was manufacturing them. A further six members were added to RIM's team. All worked long hours, but it was a labour of love as Mike Barnstijn explained, "We worked all day and night back then, but it was what we wanted to do. There is a certain amount of freedom in being part of a very small company, and also a great deal of responsibility. But it was that freedom that all of us really enjoyed."[2]

Getting into Wireless

RIM took on any project that had paying customers while Lazaridis looked for something to get into. He realized the value of wireless data technology in 1987 when he was at a conference and a person mentioned that Coca-Cola in Japan had put in a wireless data system that allowed soft-drink machines to self-report when they needed to be refilled. Then he remembered what Micsinzki had said in high school and he decided that he wanted to connect wireless technology with computer science. Between then and 1992, while the world was fixated on cellular networks, RIM hurled itself into wireless data networks and wireless email software.

The challenge of working with wireless communication was that it was very specific at the time, with cellphones dialling into proprietary servers. Interesting applications were just developing, but no one was lending money for wireless research. Getting into it took a combination of vision and faith 1) that it's going to happen someday, 2) that it has some value, 3) that it can be accomplished in an economic way, and 4) that a business can be built around the development of wireless and grow with it.

With his interest in wireless, Lazaridis was always looking for where the value was. "Push email" looked valuable, but making the technology work was tricky and the company was treating it as a research project. Then one evening Lazaridis sat down at a computer and spent three hours creating a document that became the plan for what eventually became the BlackBerry—at the time he called it an "interactive pager." He saw five improvements needed in wireless networks so they were reliable and power-efficient. This document provided the basic premise for where strategic value was to be found and served as the foundation of RIM's technology for almost a decade.

Professionalization of RIM

In 1992, when the company had 10 employees, Jim Balsillie joined RIM. Balsillie, a chartered accountant, a University of Toronto commerce graduate, and a Harvard M.B.A., invested $125 000 for a one-third stake in the business and took the title of co-CEO. Balsillie was hired because Lazaridis felt he needed a co-pilot. "There were so many complexities in terms of building out the product and growing the company that I realized I needed someone to handle the business side," said Lazaridis. "To me, it was an engineering problem. I defined what I needed, and I started looking—although I had to go through two or three others before I found Jim. But it all began by recognizing my own constraints."[3] Balsillie threw himself into fundraising, which was critical at the time.

Over the next few years RIM frantically developed and launched a series of flops: from the Viking Express wireless email pod to the glitch-heavy RIM 900 Inter@ctive Pager that RIM staff affectionately named the "Bullfrog" or "Hamburger." It was the first pocket-sized two-way pager but steeply priced at $675. Poor market acceptance left Lazaridis and company flirting dangerously with bankruptcy.

Bill Frezza, director of marketing and business development at Ericsson when the company bought into RIM in the mid-1990s, articulated the build-up to the first inception of BlackBerry better than most. "Lazaridis has nine lives" Frezza told *Profit Magazine*, "and each time he built another product that solved one problem but not all, the product failed." He continued, "I like to describe wireless data as a safe with a 10-combo lock. A bunch of us [were] walking around with six of the numbers. Over the years, we would go to the lock and try to open it. Mike went to it again and again. When he came up with all 10 numbers, the BlackBerry popped out."[4]

In 1997, Lazaridis reconceived the product in a white paper that roadmapped the BlackBerry's design. On the opening page, he wrote that RIM's engineers would define the device by outlining what it was not—only then could they say what it was. His title for the paper: "Success Lies in Paradox." In it, he explored the idea that thumbs could be used to type on a tiny keyboard, making it as efficient as a larger one. Lazaridis then created a handheld device, which could produce email simply on a small keyboard and send it securely over a wireless network. The device would always be on, so the user did not have to retrieve email. It also had an address book, memo pad, and calculator.

The original BlackBerry was launched in 1999 and was an instant hit with corporations that could now reach their employees anywhere. Stockbrokers and celebrities were the first market targeted and became early fans of the device. Lazaridis and RIM continued to improve the BlackBerry over the years. By 2001, it could also be used as a cellular telephone and had voice capabilities. A year later, the BlackBerry had hands-free capabilities as well. Such improvements only added to its popularity.

The success of RIM with its BlackBerry is a market capitalization in March 2010 of US$40 billion. Getting there started with an idea and several motivated people. Their perseverance for more than a decade eventually produced a business, which has been astoundingly successful. ■

Considering New Ventures and Corporate Renewal

This chapter deals with two critical phases in the life of a company: the time of creation and the time of resurrection. The time of creation, or birth, of a company with its own strategy is called **new venture creation**. The time of resurrection of an established company with declining performance is called **corporate renewal**. Strategic management is critical in both phases of a company's life, although these stages are far removed from each other. In each situation, strategy provides a common theme that integrates the many decisions management makes for the company to be a success. In the case of the new venture, management has to pull together all the requirements needed to have a successful company. In the case of a corporate renewal, management may need to reconfigure the company around a strategy so that it can be successful.

In the sections that follow, we examine the creation of a new company with its own strategy and the renewal of the strategy of an existing company. By the end of the chapter, you will understand how strategic management is relevant to new enterprises and to challenged enterprises. You will also know how to assess the viability of a young enterprise and to recommend how management of an established company needs to realign its decisions with the strategy.

New Venture Creation

A new venture requires that a new company be created. This is done by an entrepreneur, a person who takes direct responsibility for turning an idea into a profitable finished product through assertive risk-taking and innovation. When this individual does this in an existing organization, the person is called an intrapreneur. Entrepreneurs were at their most brash around 2000 during the height of the high-technology bubble based on the internet. Many entrepreneurs were starting companies that they hoped to sell quickly for astronomical amounts though the businesses were still largely concepts with few or no management resources. The entrepreneurs' interest was to make a lot of money fast. Some were successful, but many more were not. Since the bubble burst, most entrepreneurs take a more disciplined approach to their most critical task—effectively managing the inherent uncertainty of creating value.

All new ventures face similar problem but the emphasis changes depending on the situation. The independent entrepreneur faces the special challenges of obtaining organizational resources and capabilities. In established companies, the corporate intrapreneur faces special challenges that come from working in a larger corporation that is also engaged in other activities.

THE ENTREPRENEUR'S NEW VENTURE

Who an Entrepreneur Is

Entrepreneurs vary tremendously in character, traits, and capabilities. Many people think of the stereotypical individual who starts a high-tech company in a garage. Hewlett-Packard (HP) is the classic example of one that started this way, but it was there for only a short time. Research shows that no matter how important one individual is to an organization, its ultimate success depends as much on the entrepreneurial team as on the lead entrepreneur.[5] This was evidenced in RIM. At Dell, the company would have gone bankrupt in the early 1990s had it not recruited experienced, talented executives from IBM and Apple.

What Entrepreneurs Do

The goal of this section is to understand the entrepreneurial process well enough that we can appreciate its implications for strategic management. A fuller study of entrepreneurship is left to specialized courses on the topic and you are encouraged to take them if you are considering becoming an entrepreneur. The essence of the entrepreneurial process starts with a sound business concept, followed by attracting resources and building an organization around achieving the concept. The process ends when the company has reached the point that it is well organized and ready to be scaled up as sales grow. At this point, the entrepreneurial process is over and the entrepreneur is replaced by professional managers.

The Concept

The starting point for the entrepreneur is the opportunity. The opportunity can spring from many sources but most prominent are changes in technology and insightful thinking. Scientific breakthroughs generated by basic research make the impossible possible. Research at universities has often provided such breakthroughs. For example, Dalsa of Waterloo, Ontario, is a world leader in digital imaging components that grew out of the work of Savas Chamberlain at the University of Waterloo. Widesail Technologies of Montreal, Quebec, has a novel world-leading error-correction technology for digital communications systems that was developed by faculty at McGill University.

The window of opportunity for a company to capture extraordinary value from a technological advance is open for a limited period. Being first to recognize it can give an advantage, but others soon follow through the window unless the barriers to their entry are significant. And sometimes being first to pursue the opportunity does not pay off. Take the example of HD radio, which was developed by iBiquity Digital Corp. Although it has been commercially available since 2004, few consumers are aware of it. When this technology will catch on is unclear at present, and it may never do so.

Insights into new ways to do things are provided by entrepreneurs who challenge orthodoxy, much as did Guy Laliberté, the founder of Cirque du Soleil, when he saw a fresh, new way of presenting the circus. Ray Kroc, founder of McDonald's, also had a fresh insight. He was already a very successful paper cup manufacturer and had begun making milkshake machines. He visited the McDonald brothers intending to sell them these machines. During his visit, the idea of a hamburger chain came to mind. When asked how, he answered, "I can't pretend to know what it is. Certainly it is not some divine vision. Perhaps it is a combination of your background, your instincts and your dreams. Whatever it was at that moment, I suppose I became an entrepreneur and decided to go for broke."[6]

Entrepreneurs are able to escape the accepted standards about the industry and what accounts for the success of those in it. Those orthodox views include:

- Who the customer and consumer are
- The type of interface and interaction with the customer and consumer
- How benefit is defined and value is delivered
- How product/service functionality is defined
- What form the product/service should take
- How processes are structured and managed
- The "ideal" cost and pricing structure

This thinking may serve the current market well, but it creates blind spots. These blind spots are where potential opportunities are found. Consider the examples in Exhibit 13.1 of a few notable opportunities that were ignored by many because of the orthodox thinking of the time.[7] The fortunes of some companies cited may have been different had they capitalized on the opportunities that invention made possible.

Once the concept has been formed, the entrepreneur takes direct responsibility for turning an idea into a profitable finished product through assertive risk-taking and innovation.

Creating a Company[8]

The entrepreneur starts the process by hypothesizing a company model that contains the key aspects of a business strategy (the opportunity, the value created if the company is successful), the resources needed, and how they will be organized. The model contains many implicit and explicit assumptions about uncertain aspects such as how customers will react, how competitors will respond, and whether resources will be available. Further uncertainty comes from the potential interactions among the variables and still more uncertainty comes from factors the entrepreneur has not even considered.

Exhibit 13.1
Orthodoxies That Have
Created Entrepreneurial
Blind Spots

- "This 'telephone' has too many shortcomings to be seriously considered as a means of communication. The device is inherently of no value to us."
  —Western Union internal memo, 1876
- "The wireless music box has no imaginable commercial value. Who would pay for a message sent to nobody in particular?"—David Sarnhoff's associates in response to his urgings for investment in the radio in the 1920s
- "There is no reason anyone would want a computer in their home."—Ken Olson, president, chairman, and founder of Digital Equipment Corp., 1977
- "The concept is interesting and well-formed, but in order to earn better than a 'C,' the idea must be feasible."—A Yale University management professor in response to Fred Smith's paper proposing reliable overnight delivery service. Smith went on to found Federal Express Corp.
- "A cookie store is a bad idea. Besides, the market research reports say America likes crispy cookies, not soft and chewy cookies like you make."
  —Response to Debbi Fields' idea of starting Mrs. Fields' Cookies
- "There will never be a market in selling stock over the Internet."
  —David Komansky, Merrill Lynch chairman & CEO, 1999

The entrepreneur reduces uncertainty through both partial and holistic experimentation. Partial experiments can produce information about a single critical source of uncertainty. These experiments work best when a known unknown is involved and the value and cost of obtaining the information can be quantified. Partial experiments can deal with testing assumptions that are critical to success: potential opportunity killers and big bets. Potential opportunity killers are many but can be characterized as things that the entrepreneur might be unable to change or changes that the entrepreneur will be unable to stop. Big bets (key relationships) are positive things that are anticipated and negative things that will not happen. Each of these can be explored on its own but note that they can be linked. For example, developing a new drug with therapeutic benefits is a big bet because of the potential market for it but its possible toxicity can be an opportunity stopper.

Holistic experiments are used to test all critical sources of uncertainty and their interactions (simultaneously testing multiple variables and interactions among them). All these experiments allow the model to be tested and refined so that uncertainty is reduced. Running holistic experiments can be done on a limited scale. For example, an entrepreneur starting a franchise company put two corporate stores in very different locations. Each experienced operating difficulties. The entrepreneur then went to another market where a successful company operated and from careful analysis of that operation determined 15 changes that needed to be made. After making these changes, the operations became successful. With the model refined and proven, the company formalized its model and then scaled up its franchising outlets across the country.

Experiments need to be carefully managed so that the maximum information is derived from them. The testing of opportunity killers and big bets that can be done at low cost is best done first because there is no need to go further if these are against the business. Objectivity needs to be maintained during the experiments so that the results are a true measure of the experiment. Moreover, experiments need to be conducted long enough to get reasonable information but not drag on too long.

Resources

Performing activities requires resources so the entrepreneur has to pull them into the company. Entrepreneurs often have limited resources so they have to determine imaginative ways to get access to more resources. And yet they may use everything they have simply because they do not have enough resources. Pursuing opportunity with inappropriate and insufficient resources is a significant enterprise risk.

When starting the company, the entrepreneur focuses on affordability of the people being recruited. In the immediate future people most valuable to the start-up are those who are flexible about what they do, possess raw talent and passion, and are energetic. Experience is less important. The entrepreneur starts hiring experienced key people when the business model has stabilized so that the experience and expertise required can be specified clearly. Hiring key people before this point can staff the company with talented but expensive people who do not fit the needs of the start-up.

When seeking other resources, ownership of them is not necessarily required. Numerous start-ups have benefited from using the assets of others at low cost. Nor does the company have to perform all the activities required to produce the product or service it sells. It can get others to perform certain activities through outsourcing and alliances. When outsourcing, the motivations of those the business allies needs to be considered carefully. For example, the entrepreneur can get a distributor to sell the start-up's product. This appears to be the way to relieve the need for a distribution system. But the entrepreneur is implicitly assuming that the distributor will actively sell the company's product. The distributor handling other products that are easier to sell or produce higher commissions will sell those instead at the expense of the start-up achieving its expected sales.

For the new venture, cash is critical because that is what the company uses to buy the services of other resources. Entrepreneurs like to have as much cash as possible to protect against uncertainty. Having a lot of cash, however, can make the entrepreneur careless in how cash is used. This matters because those who provided the cash expect a return on their money. Managing the cash flow is crucial to many small companies, and it can be managed either using a cash budget or a monthly cash-flow statement produced using the balance sheet and income statement. Both approaches can be used to determine when cash flow break-even is expected and when periodic infusions of cash are required.

Companies that must perform considerable research and development before they can generate revenue feel the greatest need for a cash cushion. The rate at which the cash cushion is declining is called the "burn rate." The company that runs out of money (burns up all its cash) before it can generate revenues will be in trouble financially; though if the company still has potential, the entrepreneur can raise more cash from others by giving them some ownership in the company. New companies relying on significant technical breakthroughs are advised to think in terms of stages or series of experiments with each stage defined by a goal that has to be achieved. The company obtains just enough cash to achieve the next stage or run the next experiment. If a goal is not achieved, then losses are limited. Each time a goal is met, the company has a higher valuation when it looks for more money. This allows the entrepreneur to reduce the proportion of equity that has to be given to others to obtain their cash.

Not all companies borrow money to get started. Some finance their growth through the cash flow they generate themselves. These companies are "bootstrapping" themselves. This is more easily done if the company has the following characteristics:

- low upfront capital requirements
- short sales cycles (under a month)
- short payment terms (under a month)
- recurring revenue
- word-of-mouth advertising

Though we do not have Canadian data, a study of *Inc.* magazine's 500 fastest-growing small companies found median start-up capital to be around $22 000 in real terms.[9] The tightening of the world credit markets means that bootstrapping for longer periods will be necessary in future. The cash needs of start-ups can be offset in Canada through several government programs. Investments in innovative technology can receive Scientific Research & Experimental Development (SR&ED) tax credits. Expenses that qualify under the National Research Council-Industrial Research Assistance Program (NRC-IRAP) are partially paid for by the government—typically 50 percent to 70 percent of the developer's/scientist's salary. When seeking resources, the entrepreneur wants to attract attention to the start-up because visibility makes raising money, recruiting employees, establishing partnerships, and closing sales easier.

Organization

Organizational structure of the start-up is flat and fluid. As the complexity of tasks increases, more clearly defined authority and responsibility are needed. Eventually the entrepreneur has to formalize the responsibilities of the individuals. This leads to organizational structure and systems that differentiate who does the work and integrates the work done in the company.

Plans

Many entrepreneurs consider planning of limited use because the plan is based on so many assumptions, visions, and unknowns, although entrepreneurs are aware that they will have to make "the pitch" to various potential stakeholders to interest them in supporting the company. A productive view is to see the plan as nothing more than a detailed version of the pitch.

Producing a solid plan forces the entrepreneur to appreciate the enormity of what has to be accomplished. The process of preparing a plan surfaces issues that might be overlooked or glossed over and holes in thinking. In the plan the major tasks that have to be performed are identified, prioritized, and scheduled. A set of milestones can be erected so that the entrepreneur and others can assess what is being achieved and whether it is on plan. If not on plan, the causes of deviation (possibly because of erroneous assumptions) can be determined and changes made.

Financial projections are a critical part of the plan because they provide a holistic view of the company's revenues and costs, the scale of the company, how much money is needed, and how it will be tied up. Projections typically run five years. The first year can be monthly, the second year quarterly, and the remaining years annually. Financial projections are more realistic when built from the bottom up (by making assumptions about the results produced by various actions) rather than from the top down (by assuming that a certain market share will be achieved). The assumptions need to be clearly stated and tested to make sure that they are realistic. Further experience provided through experimentation can be used to revise initial assumptions and the financial statements accordingly.

The potential stakeholders (investors, recruits, potential board members, and internal staff) whom the entrepreneur approaches expect to see a plan before they will commit to the venture. When it comes to finance, each source of money uses its own criteria to evaluate the plans it receives. Sequoia, a major provider of venture capital, has financed many companies over time. It has determined a set of characteristics associated with start-ups that have the best chance of becoming enduring companies. It looks for these characteristics when it evaluates plans (see Exhibit 13.2).

Professionalization of Management

As the start-up grows, more people are added, increasing the managerial workload. The flexibility of the informal organization, which was beneficial when the company was small, starts to become dysfunctional. The company needs to shift from purely entrepreneurial management to more formal or professional management. Daryl Wyckoff observed this in his study of the U.S. trucking industry and described the region where companies are faced with the need to cross over from entrepreneurial to formal management as the Bermuda Triangle of Management.[10] As with the Bermuda Triangle, the infamous area in the Atlantic Ocean where ships and planes are rumoured to enter but never leave, Wyckoff argued that companies that never complete the shift from informal to formal professional management are apt to fail and disappear. Wyckoff reasoned that the Bermuda Triangle effect is part economic and part managerial. In terms of economics, the operating ratio (expenses as a percentage of revenues) in the trucking industry varied by company size, with large and small companies generally more profitable than mid-sized companies. In terms of management, small companies are informally managed while large companies were professionally managed.

With all growth, leadership is essential. The leader provides the motivation for action and sets the direction and priorities for what is done. One of the first moves when professionalizing management is formalizing the organizational structure and systems, then staffing it with people who have managerial capabilities. Formalization of the organization involves delegation of authority, which is reflected in organizational charts and job descriptions, information systems, performance-based reward systems, standard procedures, and written policies. Accompanying these changes is the need to fill key positions with individuals who have the capacity to perform well as managers—this has been called "bringing in the suits" in recognition that those with professional management skills typically dress more formally than many in start-ups.

As management is formalized, the entrepreneur must rise above direct, hands-on management and start working through others. This calls for personal qualities that are very different from those that were important when starting the new venture. Sometimes the entrepreneur has the ability to survive in the professional organization. But many entrepreneurs enjoy doing the work themselves so resist professionalization and delegation of authority. Those entrepreneurs

Exhibit 13.2   Elements of Sustainable Companies[11]

Start-ups with these characteristics have the best chance of becoming enduring companies. Sequoia seeks to partner with companies that have these characteristics.

Clarity of Purpose
Summarize the company's business on the back of a business card.

Large Markets
Address existing markets poised for rapid growth or change. A market on the path to a $1B potential allows for error and time for real margins to develop.

Rich Customers
Target customers who will move fast and pay a premium for a unique offering.

Focus
Customers will only buy a simple product with a singular value proposition.

Pain Killers
Pick the one thing that is of burning importance to the customer then delight them with a compelling solution.

Think Differently
Constantly challenge conventional wisdom. Take the contrarian route. Create novel solutions. Outwit the competition.

Team DNA
A company's DNA is set in the first 90 days. All team members are the smartest or cleverest in their domain. "A" level founders attract an "A" level team.

Agility
Stealth and speed will usually help beat out large companies.

Frugality
Focus spending on what's critical. Spend only on the priorities and maximize profitability.

Inferno
Start with only a little money. It forces discipline and focus. A huge market with customers yearning for a product developed by great engineers requires very little firepower.

who accept the need for professionalization but do not have the inclination to participate in it leave the organization. This happens when they sell the company and move on or are forced out by the new owner because they are not demonstrating sufficient managerial expertise to satisfy the new owners.

Assessing the New Venture

A strategic assessment of a new venture will depend on where it is in its life. A new company falls into one of four stages:[12]

Stage I: The venture has no product revenues to date and little or no expense history, usually indicating an incomplete team with an idea, plan, and possibly some initial product development.

Stage II: The venture has no product revenues but some expense history suggesting product development is underway.

Stage III: The venture shows product revenues but it is still operating at a loss.

Stage IV: The venture has product revenues and is operating profitably.

The value of the venture increases as it moves from Stage I to Stage IV. A company with no product revenues, little expense history, and an incomplete management team will usually receive a lower valuation than a company with revenue that is operating at a loss. The reason is that the absence of one or more of these elements increases the likelihood that the venture will not succeed. Each successive stage commands higher valuations as the results confirm the ability of the management team, and fundamental uncertainties are reduced.

When a venture reaches Stage IV, much of the uncertainty has been removed and performance of the venture can be assessed using methods described in Chapter 7, albeit with the expectation of high growth. Before this point, the assessment involves considerable judgment in answering the five questions: How attractive is the market opportunity?, Does the company have a sustainable competitive advantage?, What are the prospects for successful implementation?, What are the risks?, and What is the return to the owners? For example, considerable judgment is needed when gauging the size of the market before the product is for sale. Even venture capitalists who have considerable experience making these judgments can make mistakes. They address this by placing greater reliance on their assessment of the entrepreneur. They look especially favourably on a successful serial entrepreneur—an entrepreneur who has demonstrated the ability through previous start-ups to identify a market opportunity, then build a company that serves it. Many serial entrepreneurs enjoy the thrill and wealth-creation possibilities from starting a company and have little interest or even capability in operating a larger company.

Now that we understand what matters when looking at a new venture created by an entrepreneur, we turn to looking at one created by an intrapreneur, an entrepreneur who operates in an existing company. While the overall strategic issues are the same, creating a new venture in an existing company brings its own set of issues.

THE INTRAPRENEUR'S NEW VENTURE

Many corporations have been practising intrapreneurship for at least 25 years since the concept was popularized by Gifford Pinchot.[13] A Canadian example of intrapreneurship is provided by Bell Canada. When the internet became popular and competition flooded the traditional telecommunications industry, Bell Canada sought to respond. It spun off an organization called Bell Advanced Communications (BAC) with Ginny Dybenko as president. Setting up a separate organization made sense because Bell's structure and systems did not support innovation. By operating separately, BAC escaped the top-down command and control of Bell Canada and chose an organizational structure that encouraged its knowledge workers to find innovative solutions. The structure also allowed the organization to feed resources to the workers as needed. The results were an impressive series of value-added products and services that Bell offered its customers: ecommerce, multimedia, interactive TV, high-speed data, and distance learning. Initially peers in Bell treated BAC as a competitor but later saw it as a partner when the new products and services supplemented the declining revenues from Bell's traditional services.[14] Developing new companies internally is likely to grow in the future if corporations have trouble borrowing money for making acquisitions.

From the outside, intrapreneurship looks much easier than entrepreneurship because the intrapreneur can rely on the company to supply the resources needed to create the new venture. Ironically, corporations often lavish *too many resources,* including cash, on new ventures. Having a bountiful supply of resources means that the start-up does not face new markets on the same terms as an independent start-up and so is not really "market tested" for profitability. Aside from resources, the intrapreneurial start-up faces a special set of challenges due to being part of an existing company. For a new venture to be successful in such a situation, 10 recommendations have been put forth. The first seven apply to all cases:[15]

1. **Put the interests of the new venture first.** The leader of the venture has to put its interests ahead of personal interests, unlike the entrepreneur. If the person in charge of the new venture appears to be seeking attention or building an empire, others will see the individual as using corporate resources for personal gain so will not provide support.
2. **Hire motivated people.** The venture needs to be staffed with people who feel the urgency of a start-up and are infected with a love for what is being done. This is a very different mindset than many people who work in large companies have. So the start-up needs to avoid having regular employees of the corporation assigned to it.

3. **Build on what exists.** The corporation can provide resources, but it wants to provide those it already has and stay close to the present arena. This constrains the intrapreneur to opportunities that are related to what the corporation is already doing. In the BAC example, it was closely related to Bell Canada's existing activities.

4. **Do not appear to threaten existing services and products.** Those in the corporation and outside the venture who feel threatened will use their power to fight back because they want to protect the status quo and their positions. Early on those in traditional services resented BAC, seeing it as a competitor. Only later did they see that it helped Bell stay competitive.

5. **Be ready to cooperate.** Corporations have control systems that have to be satisfied. This means that the intrapreneur needs to produce a business plan demonstrating profitability before senior executives will provide the financial commitment needed to see the plan through. Then once the venture has started, the intrapreneur is expected to report progress periodically. When doing this, the intrapreneur uses the opportunity to manage the expectations of senior management.

6. **Have a powerful sponsor.** Those with power in the corporation have the respect of top management so are immune from politics. Having such a sponsor protects the start-up from everyday politics. Apart from providing protection when needed, a good sponsor can provide advice and technical and marketing insights.

7. **Anticipate and jump on tectonic shifts.** The intrapreneur needs to be sensitive to the changing situation both within and outside the company. When major changes occur, determine whether the start-up provides a solution and promote it as such.

An additional three recommendations are directed at isolating the start-up from pressures of being part of a larger company:

8. **Get freedom to operate.** A separate structure and systems for the start-up provides exemption from much of the bureaucracy that works well for improving the efficiency of the corporation's ongoing businesses but gets in the way of creating new sources of value. With new ventures, failures will occur in the process of experimentation. Bell Canada allowed BAC this freedom by setting it up as a separate company.

9. **Get a separate location.** A separate location for the start-up fosters *esprit de corps*, protects resources, and avoids the need to continually explain what is going on to others—out of sight, out of mind.

10. **Attract little attention.** Keeping the venture's profile low lets the project progress without interruption. When people do not know about what the venture is doing, they will not challenge it. When they are aware of it, they will question it.

To provide the isolation that start-ups benefit from, many corporations have set up a separate new venture division.

New Venture Division

The new venture division has its own structure and is exempt from "bureaucratic" policies that distract it from creating new sources of revenue. In many ways, this division acts like a venture capitalist or business incubator, working to provide expertise and resources and impart structure to the process of developing the new opportunity.

The structural approach first became popular in the late 1960s, when 25 percent of the *Fortune* 500 maintained internal venture divisions.[16] The next wave came in the late 1970s and early 1980s, when large players such as Gillette, IBM, Levi Strauss, and Xerox launched internal new venture groups.[17] Then there was the internet boom, when many companies set up divisions to run ecommerce operations that mirrored their traditional brick-and-mortar operations. In 2000, IBM set up a special group to work on "emerging-business opportunities," or EBOs, as it called them. The group's mission was to find areas that are entirely new to IBM and can grow into profitable billion-dollar-plus businesses in five to seven years. IBM launched more than 30 EBOs between 2000 and 2010.[18] By 2007, several had failed but the remaining 22 were producing annual revenue of $15 billion, a figure that was growing at more than 40 percent per year.[19]

Once the business created in the new venture division is well established, it can be added as a division to the corporation, sold to another company, or taken public by selling shares in it to the public. The corporation that holds on to the division is engaging in diversification. When it sells its ownership, it is looking to profit immediately from its creation.

A new venture division can be managed like a venture capital operation—that is, it can be cost-conscious while still encouraging risk taking, experimentation, and novel, market-oriented solutions. However, corporate new venture divisions do not achieve the same return on investment that private equity venture capital companies achieve.[20] Possible explanations are that corporate groups do not possess as high a level of skill and experience in managing venture capital.

This brings us to the end of our coverage of the creation of new ventures. Now we look at the application of strategic management to a very different situation—dealing with mature businesses that are experiencing declining performance.

Corporate Renewal

Corporate renewal addresses a problem that nearly all established companies experience at some point—declining performance. The ultimate measure of distress is the inability of the business to earn sufficient return to cover its cost of capital. At this point the economic rationale for the company's existence is gone. Other financial measures such as unexpected declines in earnings or revenues provide early warning signals that trouble is brewing. Sometimes the source of distress can be uncovered by assessing financial ratios (profitability, operating, liquidity, and debt ratios are a good start) in terms of historical performance of the company or in comparison to industry standards.

All financial indicators are lagging indicators of performance, however. Earlier signals of declining performance include of levels of customer satisfaction and worker dissatisfaction. For example, several quarters of record-breaking numbers of customer complaints about service quality show that customers are frustrated and a decline in sales will inevitably follow. Good managers focus on managing the business such that leading indicators are healthy so they are never surprised by poor financial performance.

Let's now consider causes of distress and what the business can do about them.

CAUSES OF DISTRESS

A company can be thought of as an open system. Management has to make a great many decisions about what the business does, where it does it, and how it does what it does. The key assumption in strategic management is that performance will be best when all decisions made within the business fit together and fit with the environment the business operates in. This is an ideal situation. In reality not all decisions will fit together—there are misfits. Misfits are brought about by changes outside the company (its environment) or inside the company after management has already made decisions about what to do. Management may make some decisions that complement the changes, but this in turn creates misfits with prior decisions it has made.

Externally Induced Misfits

The tools presented in Chapter 4—PESTEL, industry structure, and value-chain analysis tools—can be used to organize your analysis as you search for changes in the relevant environment that have an impact on the performance of the business.

Let's consider the *macro environment* forces identified in Chapter 4 summarized using the acronym PESTEL, which means *p*olitical, *e*conomic, *s*ociocultural, *t*echnological, *e*cological, and *l*egal. Looking at these in turn:

Political

The political arena is where society governs itself. Public concerns coalesce in the political arena, growing out of broader concerns in society, which may then produce legislation that sanctions only certain behaviour. By paying attention to the political arena, management is aware of public concerns and able to react to them before legislation is produced and to influence the legislation when it is produced.

Economic

Economic forces are felt at several levels. In the broader scheme, the level of economic development influences what people have to spend and what the priorities of society are. In the narrower scheme of things, a particular decision is economically sensible, such as whether to use debt to finance a major expansion in capacity.

Sociocultural

As many people make similar choices, they produce social trends such as changes in lifestyles, in the composition of given populations, or in attitudes toward such issues as pollution and personal health. Sometimes these societal changes occur quickly and sometimes they are not trends but rather temporary fads.

Technological

Technology is continually advancing as humans understand more and so can do more. Technology has a direct impact by what it makes possible such as the exploration of space, rapid collection and processing of large amounts of data, and instantaneous communication. The indirect effect is more subtle as it changes the way people behave.

Ecological

The physical environment that business operates in is changing. Forecasts are made of rising ocean levels, increasing global temperatures, more severe storms. All of these will have an impact on what businesses can do and will promote change in what they do.

Legal

Legislation produces rules that alter what is allowed to be done and how it is done. It can produce subsidization of some activities, prohibition of other activities, and strict operating codes for other activities.

Changes in the *value system* can also produce a mismatch for the company. Consider the following changes, which created a mismatch for small wholesalers of sewing equipment. As large retailers grew to dominate the sale of clothing, they demanded that their clothing suppliers be able to manufacture clothing in volumes sufficient to meet their needs. This encouraged the manufacturers to create large-scale capacity on a global basis. In turn the manufacturers required that their suppliers of sewing equipment supply the whole company. Many of the small-scale wholesalers who had supplied sewing equipment to local clothing manufacturers went out of business because their local manufacturers went out of business since they lacked the capability to serve the new global manufacturers.

Changes producing misfits in the more narrowly specified *industry* environment can also be found. The growth of large retailers such as Wal-Mart has reduced the power of consumer goods manufacturers with national brands and increased the opportunities, albeit at lower levels of profitability, for contract manufacturers.

Finally changes in what *competitors* are offering customers can create mismatches. The dynamics of competition are evidenced in the cellphone business, where competitors are continually extending the capability of cellphones by adding features and improving performance.

The overall message is that any change that occurs in the relevant environment of the business has the potential to create a mismatch. The company addresses the mismatches by making changes. If the mismatches are significant, the misfits could be the reason for declining performance.

Internally Induced Misfits

Misfits can be created internally due to managerial preferences, organization, and resources that are out of synchronization with one another or with the environment.

Managers make decisions and take actions for the company. But managers are people who are driven by personal factors: maintaining power, appearing successful, and survival. These drives may lead them to engage in illegal behaviour such as Conrad Black at Hollinger and Garth Drabinsky at Livent. Some apparently successful managers have psychological issues such as a psychopathic personality. Individuals with this behavioural problem tend to produce decisions that ultimately are destructive for the organization.[21]

The organization of the business can produce misfits as the organization lacks the characteristics needed to implement the strategy. For example, the choice of organizational structure may divide power, putting it in the hands of managers who disagree on what should be done to support the strategy. Alternatively, power can be delegated to managers who lack the resources to do what they know needs to be done.

Misfits can occur with the resources of the business when they are less than needed, either because they have deteriorated or because they were never raised to the planned level to address misfits recognized earlier.

DEALING WITH MISFITS

Some misfits are temporary and are introduced when management makes decisions that "stretch" the business. Over time management makes additional decisions that bring all decisions in line with the stretch decisions and a new equilibrium is achieved among the decisions.

Sometimes management has made decisions that produce serious misfits, but these can be tolerated because the value that the business creates for the customer is so great that the costs of the poor choices can be offset and the business still creates superior value for the owner. This situation is found most frequently in high-tech companies where the value creation by the new technology is considerable. Then, as competition increases, management has to rectify the poor decisions it has made as competition reduces the value of the business's offer to the customer. If it does not do this, the costs of the poor choices become so great that the company produces no value for the owners.

When misfits are minor additional decisions have to be made that change the managerial preferences, organization, and resources to bring harmony among decisions that are all in support of the strategy being pursued. Total harmony is not always possible, though, when misfits are due to basic incompatibility among decisions even though each, on balance, seems to be the best choice. When this is true, management's role is to keep the number down and to manage the situation caused by the misfits on a continuing basis. The net result of improving fit will affect revenue, costs, and assets needed, such that the return to capital employed in the business is improved.

The common process for correcting misfits will be described after a description of possible situations in which misfits have occurred.

SITUATIONS OF MISFIT

The greater misfits are and the longer they persist, the worse the performance of the business will become and the more immediate action is needed to address them. This need for change has been classified into four categories: continual corporate renewal, business transformation, turnaround, and business rescue (see Exhibit 13.3).

Let's now look at the actions management takes in each situation.

Continual Corporate Renewal

With continual corporate renewal performance of the company never suffers financially because management is making changes over time as they are needed so that the company

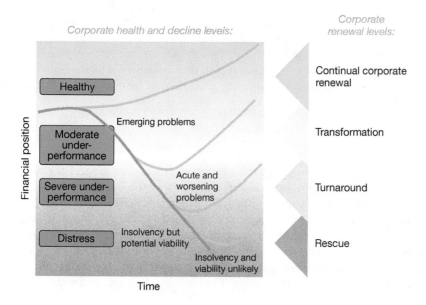

Exhibit 13.3 Corporate Renewal Given Corporate Health and Decline in Performance

evolves with the changing situation. Management performs an ongoing examination of the assumptions on which the strategy is based and assesses whether these assumptions hold true. It anticipates the need to change by looking at the PESTEL factors and determining the implications of changes in them. Management then determines what changes are needed in strategy so the business pursues the opportunities that are opening up and addresses the threats that the changes infer. Management is also continually assessing the internal working of the business, making improvements as possible that address the minor misfits. One of the biggest challenges to making change is getting the internal stakeholders to support change. They often reason that change is unnecessary because company performance is good.

Transformation

With business transformation the need for change is more serious because financial performance has declined. This requires that management take more significant action because it is reacting to a deteriorating situation. Management has to size up the various misfits and seek to eliminate them. This may call for some adjustments to strategy though not necessarily. Getting the support of internal stakeholders is a challenge because many will reason that the decline is only temporary and that performance can be improved by making changes in areas that do not affect them.

Turnaround

In a turnaround situation, performance has declined seriously in terms of acceptable levels of profitability, solvency, liquidity, and cash flow. Misfits are so serious that radical action is needed quickly to return the company to financial health or it may not survive. The many stakeholders involved are emotional: creditors are angry, employees are frightened, customers are wary, and the board of directors is nervous. Management has to generate a plan that reassures stakeholders that the company can be saved. Once it has the support of critical stakeholders, it needs to reverse the causes of distress, resolve the financial crisis, overcome internal constraints and unfavourable industry characteristics, and thereby achieve an improvement in financial performance. The margin for error in decisions is small and the consequences of a mistake are more severe in this situation than the previous situations.

Rescue

The company is in financial distress when it is likely to be insolvent in the near future. At this point strategy is irrelevant and the overriding concern is doing whatever is necessary to keep the company alive. Moving to business rescue proceedings may be initiated either by ordinary company resolution or, failing that, a court order. A business rescue practitioner is appointed to supervise the company and its management on a temporary basis. During this time a moratorium is placed on the rights of claimants against the company. The business rescue practitioner develops and implements a plan to rescue the company by restructuring its affairs, business, property, debt and other liabilities, and equity so that the likelihood of the company continuing to exist on a solvent basis is maximized. The business rescue plan is either adopted or rejected by all parties with voting interests (which include creditors, employees, and shareholders, depending on the circumstances). A plan that is adopted is binding on the company, the creditors, and every holder of the company's securities. If the plan is rejected, the company will be liquidated.

MANAGING CHANGE

Change is rarely a linear process, but thinking about it this way surfaces the magnitude of the effort involved in making it. John Kotter, a professor at the Harvard Business School, has described eight steps when transforming an organization (see Exhibit 13.4).[22]

The first step, establishing a sense of urgency, is used to convey, in the strongest terms, the need for change. The second step is to create a guiding coalition; in essence a group whose members believe in the need for change, are in positions of power to make change happen, work well together, and are good communicators. The next step is to produce a clear and compelling vision that will give direction to the change. The coalition then uses its communication skills

Eight Steps to Transforming Your Organization

Establishing a Sense of Urgency
Examining market and competitive realities
Identifying and discussing crises, potential crises, or major opportunities

1

Forming a Powerful Guiding Coalition
Assembling a group with enough power to lead the change effort
Encouraging the group to work together as a team

2

Creating a Vision
Creating a vision to help direct the change effort
Developing strategies for achieving that vision

3

Communicating the Vision
Using every vehicle possible to communicate the new vision
    and strategies
Teaching new behaviours by the example of the guiding coalition

4

Empowering Others to Act on the Vision
Getting rid of obstacles to change
Changing systems or structures that seriously undermine the vision
Encouraging risk-taking and non-traditional ideas, activities, and actions

5

Planning for and Creating Short-Term Wins
Planning for visible performance improvements
Creating those improvements
Recognizing and rewarding employees involved in the improvements

6

Consolidating Improvements and Producing Still More Change
Using increased credibility to change systems, structures, and
    policies that don't fit the vision
Hiring, promoting, and developing employees who can implement
    the vision
Reinvigorating the process with new projects, themes, and change agents

7

Institutionalizing New Approaches
Articulating the connections between the new behaviours and
    corporate success
Developing the means to ensure leadership development and succession

8

Exhibit 13.4 Essential Transformation Steps

with others and demonstrates what it is communicating through its own actions—it "walks the talk." There is never too much communication when a major transformation is being made. Fifth, others are empowered to act on the vision, which is for all to follow. Sixth, action is directed at short-term wins (think of fixing mismatches) so that people see results. These results are celebrated so that people know that progress is being made as they do the "right" things. Seventh, as the changes add up, more people will recognize change is happening and that it is working. This makes significant changes possible. Taken together, steps six and seven fit well in the staging facet of the strategy diamond. The accumulation of the activities undertaken in steps one through seven will have changed behaviour in a profound way, and the final step is associating the new behaviours with organization success so that this behaviour creates a sustained corporate culture.

Exhibit 13.5   The Levers of Organizational Transformation

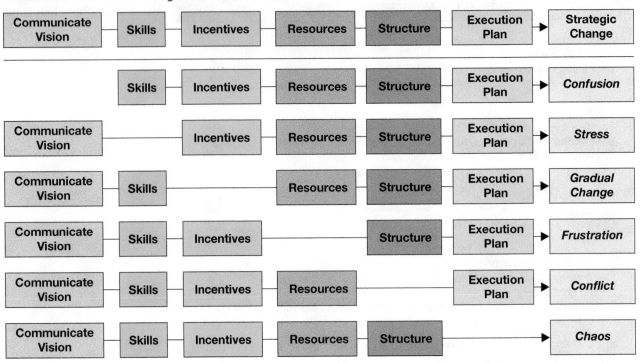

While a general agenda for managing change is provided in Exhibit 13.4, greater specificity for what needs to be changed is provided in Exhibit 13.5, along with the possible repercussions if any particular components are neglected.[23] ◆ The upper path in the model, where all components from vision to an execution plan are included, suggests that strategic change is likely to be achieved, assuming the correct implementation of the components. When any individual component is not addressed in the change, a negative consequence is likely to occur. Let's talk through each of the components in the model, working with the boxes from left to right.

 Arenas

Vision

First, management must have a new vision of the desired end state as was evident in the framework presented in Exhibit 13.4. This new vision must be communicated to all so they know where they are heading and how they can contribute. Supporting the vision is an executive plan that programs the strategic-change process.

Skills

All employees in the organization need to have the skills or be developing the skills required to achieve the strategy expressed in the vision. This has direct implications for both staffing (hiring, firing, and promoting people in the company) and training.

Incentives

Incentives are needed that encourage people to act in ways that support the strategy. This means that incentives have to be tailored to the requirements of the strategy.

Resources

Resources of the quality and in the quantity needed by the strategy have to be provided to the people as they pursue it. Resources can be evaluated using the VRINE framework to gain a richer understanding of the unique opportunities or challenges faced by a particular change effort.

Structure

The organizational structure provides for the allocation of power and resources. Allocating those tasks to individuals with greater power gives these tasks priority.

FOCUS ON SUSTAINABILITY 13.1
Triton Logging[24]

With the development of reservoirs and dams, many acres of forest have been lost. At one estimate the 200 million trees that have been submerged in the world are worth about $50 billion. In British Columbia alone, submerged timber in three vast human-made lakes is worth an estimated $2 billion. The wood from submerged trees is highly valued by craftsmen because the trees have been preserved by cold water and protected from rot and insect infestation. Vancouver Island–based Triton Logging Company has developed a machine called the Sawfish that makes the harvesting of submerged logs possible. This is a boxy, nearly four-tonne remote-controlled submarine with 1.5-metre-long arms and a 1-metre electric chainsaw. It is controlled from the deck of a barge. Under the pilot's watchful eye, the Sawfish attaches an airbag capable of lifting up to 200 kilograms to the tree trunk and then cuts it. Depending upon the size of the tree, when cut it springs from the depths like a rocket thrust into orbit or elevates slowly like a leviathan waking from a long sleep. The Sawfish can cut a tree in three minutes and operate at any depth. Chris Godsall, Triton's CEO, has a B.A. from McGill University and an M.Sc. in Responsibility and Business Practice from the University of Bath (U.K.). In 1995, Godsall co-founded Santropol Roulant, a meals-on-wheels service in downtown Montreal. In 2000, he founded Triton after reflecting on his early days floating logs down to mills. Many sank, but recovery was costly and often unviable using traditional methods. He decided to tap this market, so led the Sawfish design project to automate the harvest. "Mostly it was foolishness that made me think we could do it," he says. He enlisted the help of a dozen contractors to convert a factory built submersible used in the offshore oil industry into the Sawfish.

By using electrical motors and vegetable oil in place of hydraulic fluid, the Sawfish is not affected by restrictions that prohibit the use of petroleum-based oil. Also, by cutting trees rather than pulling them out of the ground, toxic wastes lying on the bottom are undisturbed—disturbing the bottom damages the underwater environment and undoes some of the benefits of retrieving the timber.

Triton has achieved a SmartWood Rediscovered Wood stamp of approval from the Rainforest Alliance. Its "rediscovered timber" fits well with the demands of the environmentally friendly marketplace. Legitimately salvaging wood makes it easier for retailers to sell. Large retailers, including Home Depot and IKEA, which are increasingly buying sustainably harvested wood, find the wood acceptable. Moreover, harvesting these trees means they are not wasted, while healthy forests are spared at least temporarily.

Triton Logging amalgamated with Clark Sustainable Resource Developments Ltd., a private company co-founded by Wayne Dunn, who grew up in rural Saskatchewan, worked in the logging industry, including five years as a logging owner and operator, and is a Sloan Stanford Fellow (1997) with a M.Sc. in Management from the Stanford Graduate School of Business. CSR was launched in 2005 to secure and operate licences to harvest underwater forests in the tropical regions of the world. Dunn has received several international awards for his work in Africa in particular.

By 2012, with this amalgamation, Chris Godsall expects Triton to be supplying 76 million board feet and operating on five continents.

The Sawfish uses an electric chainsaw to cut submerged trees, which then float to the surface because of an airbag attached to the tree.

Execution Plan

All actions being taken need to be organized into a plan that provides for their coordination and sequencing. The plan also facilitates the allocation of responsibility for achieving results and the allocation of resources needed to achieve them.

When all of these components have been adjusted through the change process, the outcome is likely to be successful change. Failure to address every component will undermine the entire change effort and missing just a single component will have a potential consequence for the change effort. For example, without a guiding vision, organization members are likely to be confused about why all these efforts are being undertaken. Failure to have people who possess the skills needed to carry out the efforts will probably produce extreme stress among those who are ill equipped to perform the work. Those who have the wrong incentives will be slow to change what they do or, worse, act in ways that work against the strategy because they

Alan Mulally Turns the Ford Motor Company Around[25]

The recent turnaround of Ford, with its "extreme makeover" elements, is a story that will keep being told. Unlike General Motors and Chrysler, Ford did not go through bankruptcy protection nor take government bailout money. It was just an arduous climb back to profitability. From cutting its massive debt load and getting products out to market, to making the company more competitive on a global scale, Ford has stepped on the gas pedal at the right time and never looked back.

Through the 1990s

Ford was highly successful in the mid-1980s based on the strength and popularity of the Taurus, Lincolns, and pickup trucks, only to lose billions in 1991 and 1992 during an economic recession. Through the mid- to late-1990s, Ford generated record profits building Expeditions, Lincoln Navigators, and pickups on the same platform. But it limped into the 21st century as the profit of US$7.2 billion in 1999 turned into a loss of US$5.4 billion by 2001. In 2001, William Clay Ford, great-grandson of the founder, Henry Ford, became CEO and began a "back-to-basics" campaign to return the carmaker to its roots as a mass producer. In 2002, the company started trying to cut capacity. Cutbacks in Europe were more successful than in North America where executives could not agree on where cuts should be made and unions opposed cutbacks. When Ford celebrated its centennial in June 2003 doubts were growing about its future.

One analyst at UBS, an international bank, went so far as to suggest Ford might not last another decade.

What had gone wrong? Some problems were due to events beyond Ford's control. First and primarily, the fortunes of the western automobile industry follow the economic cycle moving between profitability and loss over time so the booms and busts were to be expected. Second, overcapacity in the global automotive industry held car prices down. Third, the upward trend in the price of gas favoured smaller cards in terms of operating cost. And fourth, foreign producers started competing in the most profitable segment of North America's automotive industry, making more pickup trucks and SUVs and these foreign companies moved production to North America to escape U.S. import duties.

But many problems at Ford were self-induced. First, Ford had not managed its manufacturing well. It was making more cars than customers wanted to buy and while Ford boasted that "Quality is Job One," cars from European and Asian producers were seen as better and more reliable by consumers. Second, Ford found it impossible to get customers to buy small vehicles at prices that produced attractive profits so Ford left the small car market to its foreign competitors. Third, Ford had invested heavily in overseas acquisitions, buying Aston Martin, Jaguar, Volvo, and Land Rover; these acquisitions never produced the expected profits and came to be viewed as a costly diversification that was distracting top management's attention. Fourth, Ford was a dysfunctional organization. It was filled with aggressive politics. Sharp elbows, fierce loyalties, and frequent turf battles were hallmarks of Ford's management culture. And the inability to admit their mistakes was taking its toll.

Mulally becomes CEO

By 2006, Ford's situation was bleak with an anticipated loss of US$17 billion. Bill Ford (then chairman, CEO and COO) and Don LeClair (then Ford's finance director) decided that more money was needed to turn around the North American operations so they started working to acquire loans. To gain credibility for the turnaround, a new chief executive was needed because lenders had little faith in any of the Big Three automotive companies after endless failure to achieve prior plans. Moreover, Bill Ford, after working for five years on Ford's turnaround, was tired, so he went searching for his own replacement as CEO (he remained chairman).

As Bill Ford looked outside the automotive industry, the name of Alan Mulally kept coming up. He had been CEO of Boeing's Commercial Airplanes division for eight years but had been passed over twice in the search for a new CEO for Boeing. Mulally was attractive because of his experience at Boeing dealing with similar suppliers and manufacturing issues as at Ford. Moreover, people at Ford liked him— Don Petersen, the former chairman and CEO of Ford, while serving on Boeing's board of directors, had worked with Mulally. When Bill Ford interviewed Mulally, they were in agreement as to what was needed to produce a turnaround at Ford. So Mulally was made CEO of the Ford Motor Company in September of 2006.

Taking Charge

After accepting the job with Ford, Mulally's first task was to familiarize himself with the organization. He interviewed dozens of employees, analysts, and consultants, and filled five binders with his typed notes. This research allowed him to develop a point of view about the auto business and the company that framed all his future decisions. After this, a plan that identified specific goals for the company needed to be devised, and a process to move the company toward those goals needed to be created and implemented. Meanwhile, Mulally sensed that a recession was coming so he encouraged Ford to borrow as much as it could. The company ended up with US$23.6 billion in loans by pledging all of Ford's North American assets as security.

The Plan

According to Bill Ford, lots of "inspired car guys" worked at Ford and what they needed was direction. Mulally, working with the top management team, crafted a plan to provide this. Key decisions reflected in the plan were as follows:

1. The company's activities would be focused and simplified:

   ■ All cars would carry Ford's familiar blue oval logo. All non-Ford luxury brands would be sold and the Mercury brand would be phased out.

   ■ The number of models would be reduced from 97 down to 36 and could go even lower.

   ■ Eight global Ford platforms (the floor pan and its underpinnings) would be developed. Regional tastes in cars and variations in regulations would be accommodated by building different models like a sedan, hatchback, and small SUV (known internally as "top hats") on the same platform.

2. Ford's vehicles would be "best in class" in quality, fuel efficiency, safety, and value.

3. Cars would be built only if they could be sold profitably. Excess capacity would be eliminated by closing plants, including parts-makers, and reducing staff.

4. The number of dealers in North America would be cut to match production. Outside North America less severe cuts were necessary because they had been made earlier.

5. Ford's product range would be renewed, starting with the popular models. The Fiesta, a small car, and the Fusion, a midsize sedan, would be refreshed. Meanwhile the Taurus, a full-size sedan, would be redesigned and relaunched.

6. International sales in emerging markets would be increased. Ford intended to invest US$4 billion in the Asia Pacific region, with India and China absorbing most of that, and US$2.5 billion in South America, primarily Brazil.

Managing Performance

Mulally drove performance at Ford the same way he had at Boeing. A significant component of this was a meeting called the "Business Plan Review," held early every Thursday in the Thunderbird room. Attending this meeting were

Ford Motor Co. CEO Alan Mulally, left, and Ford Motor Co. Executive Chairman William Ford, Jr., pose beside the next-generation Ford Focus 5-door at the North American International Auto Show in Detroit on January 11, 2010.

Mulally and those who reported directly to him: Ford's four profit centres around the world and the company's 12 functional heads. Outsiders were regularly invited to observe the meeting. Managers reported on how well they were meeting their targets and any problems they were having. In this way, everyone knew the plan, its status, and areas that need special attention. Members might offer solutions to problems in the meetings. When problems could not be fixed, the plan was changed. There were no pre-meetings or briefing books because the meetings were held to let people know where things stood rather than to make decisions.

During the week, Mulally could visit two rooms adjacent to the Thunderbird room whose walls are lined with 280 performance charts, arranged by area of responsibility, with a big picture of the executive in charge in case anyone had doubts as to whom was responsible. The charts were updated weekly. This allowed Mulally to keep his finger on every piece of this large and complex company so that problems could be identified early. He watched all that was happening with intensity and demanded weekly, sometimes daily, updates. Meanwhile the board of directors saw a subset of the data that Mulally saw.

Mulally's Style

Mulally had confidence, discipline, and a fierce desire to win. He was driven:

"I am here to save an American and global icon," he declared.[26] This drive meant that his presence was felt by people throughout the organization.

To let everyone know what he had in mind, Mulally created a plastic card that was given to everyone. On one side was a revised definition of the company's mission, "One Ford," which was one team, one plan, one goal. On the other were four goals or "Expected Behaviors," based on four principles (**FORD**): **F**oster functional and technical excellence; **O**wn working together; **R**ole model Ford values; and **D**eliver results. To Mulally, the mission statement was like a sacred text: "This is me. I wrote it. It's what I believe in. You can't make this shit up."[27]

Mulally's passionate belief in people's ability to meet the challenges he presented made them feel good and created a positive atmosphere. This made his staff want to follow him, fuelled sustainable high performance, and inspired them to create more value.

Ford in 2010

Under Mulally's leadership, the people at Ford have rallied around a simple but compelling plan that focuses resources on the Ford brand, ever improving its competitiveness. Ford's executives now have a shared conviction that they will emerge, along with Toyota and Volkswagen, as one of the three truly global automobile companies.

In 2010, Ford passed Toyota as the No. 2 seller in the United States. Over the year its sales grew 15.2 percent, even though it sold Volvo and closed the Mercury brand. Meanwhile, 219,219 units of the Fusion were sold, making it the first Ford sedan to sell more than 200,000 units in a year since 2004. By comparison, Ford sold 528,349 of its F-Series pickup trucks, so it still has a product mix challenge. Ford was making quarterly profits and was expected to make $7 billion for the year.

HOW WOULD YOU DO THAT? QUESTIONS

1. How Would You Do That? 13.1 presented the turnaround of the Ford Motor Company. Find several articles describing the turnaround of another company and see whether its turnaround followed the same general procedure as Ford's.

2. The introduction to this chapter described how RIM was started. Find an example of another Canadian company that was started by an entrepreneur and describe how the entrepreneur got the concept, the challenges he/she overcame in getting the necessary resources, and how the product or service was sold initially.

are rewarded for doing so. Failure to provide the necessary resources will produce frustration because managers and employees feel that they have little institutional support. An organizational structure that does not allocate power and resources according to the needs of strategy will produce confusion and conflict. Finally, lack of an execution plan will produce a chaotic state as change will not be coordinated and paced.

Summary of Challenges

1. *Define new ventures and corporate renewal, then explain how they are related to strategic management.* A new venture is the creation of a new business while a corporate renewal is the resurrection of an established business with declining financial performance. In each situation, strategy provides a common theme that integrates the many decisions management makes to render the business a success. In the case of the new venture, management has to pull together all the requirements needed to have a successful business. In the case of a corporate renewal, management may need to reconfigure the business around a strategy so that it can be successful.

2. *Compare and contrast entrepreneurship and intrapreneurship.* Both entrepreneurship and intrapreneurship involve creation of a new business. In each case a new concept forms the basis for the business. The big difference is that the entrepreneur faces considerable difficulty assembling the resources needed. In intrapreneurship, the resources are achieved more easily, but much of what can be done and how things are done is limited by the available resources and the organization of the existing company.

3. *Appreciate the professionalization of management.* As the successful business grows, more people are added, increasing the managerial workload. The flexibility of the informal organization, which was beneficial when the business was small, starts to become dysfunctional. What the business needs to do is shift from purely entrepreneurial management to more formal or professional management. This involves both formalization of the organization and staffing it with people who know how to work in this more formal organization. Formalization of the organization involves delegation of authority, which is reflected in organizational charts and job descriptions, information systems, performance-based reward systems, standard procedures, and written policies. Accompanying these changes is the need to fill key positions with individuals who have the capacity to perform well as managers.

4. *Explain why corporations have a new venture division and what it does.* This is a division that has its own structure and is exempt from "bureaucratic" policies that distract it from creating new sources of revenue. In many ways, this division acts like a venture capitalist or business incubator, working to provide expertise and resources and impart structure to the process of developing the new opportunity. A new venture division can be managed like a venture-capital operation—that is, it can be cost conscious while still encouraging risk taking, experimentation, and novel, market-oriented solutions. Once the businesses created in the new venture division are well established, they can be added to the corporation, sold to another company, or taken public through the sale of their stock.

5. *Describe why and when corporate renewal is necessary.* Nearly all established companies experience distress at some point, and corporate renewal prevents companies from vanishing from the face of the competitive landscape. The ultimate signal of distress is declining financial performance. The ultimate measure of distress is the inability of the business to earn sufficient income to cover its cost of capital. Corporate renewal involves fixing mismatches between the decisions that management has made so that all decisions support the pursuit of the company's strategy.

6. *Identify the sources of misfit that create the need for corporate renewal.* Misfits occur when the context within which management has made its decisions changes. Then the decisions that management made no longer fit with the evolving situation. Sources of misfit are both external and internal. External sources are macro changes in politics, economics, society, technology, ecology, and legislation as well as more specific changes by other industries in the value stream, competitive industries, and competitors. Internal sources are due to changes in managerial preferences, resources, and organization as well as the inability to achieve planned changes.

Review Questions

1. What is entrepreneurship?
2. What are the considerations in the entrepreneurial process?
3. How are entrepreneurship and intrapreneurship related to strategy?
4. What is professionalization of management?
5. What is a business plan?
6. How does new venture creation done by the entrepreneur differ from new venture creation done by the intrapreneur?
7. What are some of the external causes of declining company performance?
8. What are some of the internal causes of declining company performance?
9. How does the nature of corporate renewal change as performance continues declining?

Experiential Activities

Group Exercises

1. Entrepreneurship starts with an idea. Brainstorm a set of 10 "wild and crazy" concepts that a new business could be built on. Screen the concepts and rank them in terms of enjoying the greatest market demand, facing the most attractive market structure and size, and providing the greatest profit margins. Which idea is the best when you compare them across the rankings? Is one idea dominant in all rankings?

2. This second exercise relates to corporate renewal. Identify a company that is in dire financial straits. What are the financial symptoms of this distress? What has led to the poor performance of this business? As a group, assemble recommendations for improving the financial performance of this business.

Ethical Debates

1. You are the co-founder and president of a new venture, manufacturing products for the recreational market. Five months after launching the business, one of your key suppliers informs you it can no longer supply you with a critical raw material since you are not a large-quantity user. Without the raw material the business cannot continue. There is a 50/50 chance that your new product may take off, which would let you provide the supplier with a demand estimate that could lead the supplier to think you are a larger prospect and therefore worth investing in as a large-quantity purchaser. What do you do?

2. Your small manufacturing company is in serious financial difficulty. A large order of your products is ready to be delivered to a key customer when you discover that the product is simply not right. It will not meet all performance specifications, will cause problems for your customer, and will require rework in the field; but you know this will not be evident until after the customer has received and paid for the order. If you do not ship the order and receive the payment as expected, your business may be forced into bankruptcy. And if you delay the shipment or inform the customer of these problems, you may lose the order and also go bankrupt. What do you do?

Endnotes

1. Jessica Livingston, "Mike Lazaridis: Cofounder, Research In Motion," in *Founders at Work* (Berkeley, C.A.: Apress, 2007), pp. 141–151; Bill Breen, "Rapid Motion," *Fast Company* 49 (July 2001). Accessed March 2, 2010, at www.fastcompany.com/magazine/49/motion.html?page=0%2C0; John Paczkowski, "D7 Interview: RIM CEO Mike Lazaridis Says It's Not a One-Size-Fits-All Business," All Things Digital, May 27, 2009. Accessed March 2, 1010, at http://d7.allthingsd.com/20090527/d7-interview-mike-lazaridis/; Matt Hartley, "RIM co-CEO Mike Lazaridis on the Next Decade of Black-Berry," *Financial Post*, December 29, 2009. Accessed March 2, 1010, at http://network.nationalpost.com/np/blogs/fpposted/archive/2009/12/29/fp-tech-desk-speaks-to-rim-co-ceo-mike-lazaridis.aspx; Brett Winterford, "RIM founder and CEO, Mike Lazaridis," *ITNews* (Australia), May 5, 2009. Accessed March 2, 1010, at www.itnews.com.au/News/144148,interview-rim-founder-and-ceo-mike-lazaridis.aspx.

2. Daniel Drage "Lazaridis: Wireless Wonder." Accessed December 12, 2010, atwww.businesswings.co.uk/articles/Mike-Lazaridis-wireless-wonder?singlePageView=true.

3. Breen, "Rapid Motion."

4. Drage "Lazaridis: Wireless Wonder."

5. W. Bygrave and J. Timmons, *Venture Capital at the Crossroads* (Boston, M.A.: Harvard Business School Press, 1992).

6. Warren Bennis and Burt Nanus, *Leaders: Strategies for Taking Charge* (New York: HarperBusiness Essentials, 2003) p. 27.

7. Adapted from G. Hamel and C. K. Prahalad, *Competing for the Future* (Boston, M.A.: Harvard Business School Press, 1994).

8. Donald N. Sull "Disciplined Entrepreneurship," *MIT Sloan Management Review* 46:1 (Fall 2004): 71–77; Rita McGrath and Ian C. MacMillan, "Discovery-Driven Planning," *Harvard Business Review* (July, 1995): 44–54.

9. Amar V. Bhide, "Bootstrap Finance: The Art of Start-ups," *Harvard Business Review* 70 (November/December 1992): 109–117.

10. D. Wyckoff, *Organizational Formality and Performance in the Motor Carrier Industry* (Lexington, M.A.: Lexington Books, 1973).

11. "Writing a Business Plan." Accessed March 4, 2010, at www.sequoiacap.com/ideas.

12. PricewaterhouseCoopers United States "The First Key: Understanding the Process." Accessed February 17, 2010, at www.pwc.com/us/en/technology-private-equity/understanding-the-venture-capital-process.jhtml.

13. Gifford Pinchot, *INTRAPRENEURING: Why You Don't Have to Leave the Corporation to Become an Entrepreneur* (New York: HarperCollins, 1986); and Gifford Pinchot and Ron Pellman, *Intrapreneuring in Action: A Handbook for Business Innovation* (San Francisco: Berrett-Koehler, 1999).

14. Cynthia Ross Pedersen, "Fight Paralysis with Intrapreneurship," *Financial Post*, February 03, 2009. Accessed February 16, 2010, at www.financialpost.com/executive/story.html?id=1247229.

15. Guy Kawasaki, *The Art of the Start* (New York: Penguin, 2004); Guy Kawasaki, "The Art of Intrapreneurship," January 04, 2006. Accessed February 17, 2010, at http://blog.guykawasaki.com/2006/01/the_art_of_intr.html#axzz0foj63UdT; David Garvin, "What Every CEO Should Know about Creating New Businesses," *Harvard Business Review* 82:7–8 (July/August 2004): 18–21.

16. N. Fast, *The Rise and Fall of Corporate New Venture Divisions* (Ann Arbor, M.I.: UMI, 1978).

17. R. Gee, "Finding and Commercializing New Business," *Research-Technology Management* 37:1 (1994): 49–56.

18. IBM, "Solutions by Emerging Business Opportunities (EBOs)." Accessed February 25, 2010, at www-05.ibm.com/il/gtu/pdf/catalogue/ebo.pdf.

19. Alan Deutschman, "Building a Better Skunk Works," *Fast Company* (December 19, 2007). Accessed February 25, 2010 at www.fastcompany.com/magazine/92/ibm.html.

20. H. Chesbrough, "Designing Corporate Ventures in the Shadow of Private Venture Capital," *California Management Review* 42:3 (2000): 31–49.

21. Clive Roland Boddy, "The Dark Side of Management Decisions: Organizational Psychopaths," *Management Decision* 44: 10 (2006): 1461–1475.

22. Adapted from J. Kotter, "Why Transformation Efforts Fail," *Harvard Business Review.* (March/April 1995): 59–67.

23. Adapted from A. Marcus, *Management Strategy* (New York: McGraw-Hill, 2004).

24. Larry Greenemeier, "Timber Industry Eyes Logs Under Water: Canada's British Columbia at Forefront, Using 'Sawfish' Submarine," *Grist Magazine*, MSNBC.com, September 13, 2005. Accessed March 2, 1010, at www.msnbc.msn.com/id/9325560/. Phil Whyte, "Timber Treasure of the Deep," *NZ Logger* (August 2007), pp. 35–39. Accessed March 3, 2010, at www.petersonsawmills.com/press_articles_general27.pdf. Sarah Simpson, "Diving for Dead Wood," *Scientific American* (June 2004), pp. 24–25. Gaea Honeycutt, "Timberrrrrrrr . . . Watch That Floating Tree," *Unmanned Systems* 27:3 (March 2009) pp. 35–37.

25. Kathleen Kerwin and Joann Muller, "Bill Ford Takes the Wheel," *Business Week,* November 2001. Accessed January 14, 2011, at www.businessweek.com/bwdaily/dnflash/nov2001/nf2001111_8593.htm; *JD Rucker*, "What Other Automakers Can Learn from Alan Mulally," *Fast Company*, March 6, 2010. Accessed January 14, 2011 at www.fastcompany.com/1573670/what-other-automakers-can-learn-from-alan-mulally; Tony Schwartz, "Alan Mulally—Making Ford a Model for the Future," April 2, 2010 (Accessed January 14, 2011, at blogs.hbr.org/schwartz/2010/04/alan-mulally-making-ford-a-mod.html); and Alex Taylor III, "Fixing up Ford," *Fortune.* Accessed January 14, 2011, at money.cnn.com/2009/05/11/news/companies/mulally_ford.fortune/index.htm.

26. Taylor III, "Fixing up Ford."

27. Taylor III, "Fixing up Ford."

14 Corporate Governance in the Twenty-First Century

In this chapter, we challenge you to:

1. Describe what corporate governance is and why it matters.

2. Explain the three alternative approaches to improving the governance of companies.

3. Compare and contrast corporate governance practices around the world.

4. Identify specific factors that affect the state of governance in Canada.

5. Show how boards of directors are structured and explain the roles they play in corporate governance.

6. Design an executive incentive plan that will serve as a device for corporate governance.

7. Illustrate how the market for corporate control is related to corporate governance.

Corporate Governance in Action at Hewlett-Packard[1]

In 1938, Bill Hewlett and David Packard started Hewlett-Packard (HP) in Palo Alto, California. Packard focused on business operations while Hewlett pursued the big ideas. The first product was an audio oscillator that Hewlett designed and they then manufactured in the garage behind Packard's house. They baked the paint on the panels used to make the product in his wife's oven. (She claimed the roast beef never tasted right after that.) From such modest beginnings, the company went on to become the world's largest manufacturer of electronic instruments.

Along the way, HP became known for its prowess in innovation. The company is credited with making the world's first handheld scientific calculator, one of the first PCs, the first desktop mainframe, and the LaserJet printer. HP's early PCs were durable devices targeted for industrial uses, such as in factory operations, so did not enjoy the strong sales of later makes sold for personal or office use.

In 1999, HP hired Carly Fiorina as its first outsider CEO. She had been a group president in Lucent, a huge conglomerate created in 1996 out of the systems and technology unit of AT&T. Dick Hackborn who was the chair of HP's board at the time saw Fiorina as an ideal candidate for CEO and persuaded the board to hire her. In 2000, Fiorina proposed the acquisition of computer-services business EDS but withdrew the bid after the proposal received a poor reception from HP shareholders. Then in 2002, Fiorina concluded a controversial merger with Compaq Computer Corp. for US$19 billion. This merger met with strong opposition led by Walter Hewlett, a board member and son of company co-founder William Hewlett. Walter claimed that the merger was being pursued by Fiorina because she was desperate to make a strategic decision that would satisfy Wall Street investors.

Debate over the wisdom of the merger continued for years following the closing of the deal. HP management claimed that operating synergies of US$3 billion were realized within two years of the deal closing. However, HP's stock value continued to languish while the price of shares of its major competitor, Dell, grew. This poor financial performance coupled with Fiorina's leadership style prompted questions in the boardroom. By 2004, her relationship with many board members was strained. In January 2005, the directors discussed with Fiorina a list of issues associated with HP's performance. They also proposed that her authority be distributed among HP's division heads. Within a week these confidential board discussions were leaked to the press by one or more board members. Fiorina became very upset and confronted the board, which collectively supported her in maintaining that all conversations with the board were confidential. She then had legal counsel interview each board member to find out who was leaking the information.

Last than a month later the board forced Fiorina to resign as chairman of the board and CEO before the issue of disclosure could be settled. In public statements, the board and succeeding management indicated that Fiorina's dismissal was due to her leadership style and not over differences in strategy. Fiorina had dismissed several top executives in the prior summer. Some suggested that this was a last-ditch effort to find a scapegoat as she attempted to solidify her leadership.

Fiorina was replaced as chair by Patricia Dunn, a member of the board, while she was replaced as CEO by Mark Hurd, one of HP's top executives. Hurd maintained in his early interviews with the press that he would not be changing the strategy, just trying to fix the execution of it.

Dunn pursued two issues as chair: changing the membership of the board and dealing with the leaks. On the first issue, she thought the board needed some new "heavyweight" directors. In looking for new directors, Dunn proposed that

HP's first products were test and measurement devices. Hewlett's audio oscillator—a device used to test sound equipment—was introduced in 1938. HP continued as a leader in this category for years and expanded to making instruments for measurement, medical technology, and chemical analysis.

the board recruit established CEOs from large U.S. companies because they had experience with large, diverse companies such as HP. She ran into resistance with some directors, particularly Tom Perkins, the famous Silicon Valley venture capitalist. He maintained that HP needed directors from high-tech companies who had experience in "fast cycle" industries. He claimed that some of the CEOs Dunn was recruiting had never dealt with products that change every year and that this experience was crucial to proper governance of HP.

On the issue of leaks from the board, Dunn felt that she had a mandate to plug them and so authorized a daring strategy. Private investigators were hired to track down who was leaking information. The investigators felt certain that some directors were lying to them in interviews so they approached phone companies pretending to be certain directors who wanted copies of their billing records. This ruse is now known as "pretexting" and is defined as approaching a company under the pretext of being someone else. This is considered a form of identity theft. Examination of phone records revealed that long-time director George Keyworth had placed phone calls to a reporter at CNet.com who had written stories providing detailed information about the HP board's contemplations. The *Wall Street Journal* estimated that HP's private investigators spent more than US$350,000 to finger Keyworth.

The HP scandal was just getting warmed up at this point. Dunn convened the board and confronted Keyworth without prior notice. Tom Perkins, a member of the board, abruptly quit because he viewed the methods used to entrap Keyworth as unethical. In addition, he maintained that the information that was leaked was inconsequential. HP, in informing the Securities and Exchange Commission, did not disclose Perkins's reasons for leaving the board. This made him so furious that he personally contacted the SEC and the press, giving each the reason for his resignation.

In the months that followed, HP was featured regularly on the front page of the *Wall Street Journal* and the *New York Times* as they competed to uncover what was happening at HP. Dunn and HP maintained that their methods were legal and ethical. When they were pressed on the practice of pretexting, they maintained that they were not in control of the methods used by the investigators. Later examination of internal emails revealed that Dunn and other executives were aware of the methods being used and had acquiesced because they considered the leaks of major importance.

The HP board scandal led to hearings before the U.S. Congress and charges in California courts against the company and specific officers and directors. Eventually, HP agreed to pay a fine of US$14.5 million to settle the "pretexting" scandal. HP also fired Dunn and agreed to pay US$650 000 in civil penalties and US$350 000 to cover the cost of the attorney general's investigation. In addition, a 12-page injunction required that the company adopt a series of corporate governance reforms. HP had to bolster its code of conduct; appoint a new, independent director to serve as the compliance watchdog for the board of directors; and expand the oversight of the company's privacy officer. HP's ethics and compliance officer also had to start reporting to the board's audit committee as well as chairman and CEO. Hurd stated in writing that, "We are pleased to settle this matter with the attorney general and are committed to ensuring that HP regains its standing as a global leader in corporate ethics and responsibility."

This opening vignette illustrates the risk that managers will engage in practices detrimental to the value, health, and vitality of the company. As you learned in Chapters 1 and 2, the CEO and members of the top management team set and guide the vision for the company and are responsible for formulating and implementing the strategy that realizes that vision. Fiorina's mandate, when she was hired by the board as HP's new CEO in 1999, was that she would help formulate and then execute strategy that would restore HP to a dominant position. Six years later, the board decided to dismiss her, as performance problems led them to lose confidence in her leadership. These actions demonstrated the role of the board of directors in governing the corporation. The board's purpose is to translate informed owners' wishes into organizational performance.[2] The vignette also shows that a dynamic process goes on within the board as it seeks to represent the best interests of shareholders. ■

Corporate Governance in the Twenty-First Century

This chapter brings the strategy dialogue full circle as it addresses the responsibility of the chief executive to the board of directors.

Corporate governance involves a set of relationships between a company's management, its board, its shareholders, and other stakeholders. Corporate governance also provides the structure through which the objectives of the company are set, and the means of attaining those objectives and monitoring performance are determined. In this chapter, we look at various aspects of **governance**. First, we establish the need for it and the benefits of good governance. Then the state of governance in various countries is described, with particular attention paid to governance in Canada. This is followed by looking at the role of the board in supervising the management of the company. The chapter then turns to look at various incentives for rewarding executives so that they serve the best interests of shareholders. The chapter then describes agency theory, a way that academics have used to couch governance issues in terms of proper contracting. The chapter concludes with the ultimate remedy of governance—the takeover of the company by a new set of shareholders.

> **governance** The work of the board as it translates informed owners' wishes into organizational performance.

The Need for Governance

The need for governance is most easily demonstrated by situations in which the management of companies was not being controlled and scrutinized by the board. Two telling examples are the cases of Bre-X Minerals and Krispy Kreme Doughnuts, a company that we discussed in Chapter 1.

THE CASE OF BRE-X MINERALS LTD.[3]

A scandal that was Canada's equivalent to the Enron and WorldCom disasters in the United States revolved around Bre-X Minerals Ltd., a junior gold mining company based in Calgary. In 1995, it reported discovering the world's biggest-ever gold deposit alongside the Busang River in Borneo, Indonesia. Bre-X's share price rose to Cdn$286.50 and its market value reached Cdn$6.2 billion—bigger than that of Imperial Oil, Bombardier, Inco, and Molson combined yet it had no sales or profits. The scandal was that the only gold involved was that used to salt exploratory samples of ore from the site.

The fraud began to unravel in March 1997 after Bre-X partnered with U.S. miner Freeport-McMoRan Copper & Gold because the president of Indonesia did not want Bre-X to control the Busang site alone. Freeport began an evaluation of the deposit and found insignificant amounts of gold. Meanwhile the exploration manager of Bre-X Minerals, Michael de Guzman, had fallen from a helicopter to his death in the Indonesian jungle. Bre-X brought in a third-party consulting company, Strathcona Mineral Services, to conduct another review. It shocked Bre-X shareholders with its report on May 4, 1997—the Busang mine was a hoax as the samples had been "salted" with gold from other parts of the world and shavings from gold jewellery. At the open of trading the next day, Bre-X's share price dropped to a mere 6 cents. Trading in Bre-X was soon suspended on the TSX and the NASDAQ and the company filed for bankruptcy protection. Among the major losers were three Canadian public sector organizations: the Ontario Municipal Employees Retirement Board lost Cdn $45 million, the Quebec Public Sector Pension fund lost Cdn $70 million, and the Ontario Teachers' Pension Plan lost Cdn $100 million. There was fallout in the Canadian financial sector also; the fraud proved a major embarrassment for Peter Munk, the head of Barrick Gold, as well as for the head of the Toronto Stock Exchange (resulting in his ouster by 1999), and began a tumultuous realignment of the Canadian stock exchanges, the effects of which were felt for several years.

Looking back at Bre-X, there were red flags that governance was a problem at the mining company. These included the unusual death of de Guzman, the composition of Bre-X's board with only two of the six directors coming from outside the company, having a company executive serve on the board's audit committee, the lack of independent audits, and the willingness of investors and regulators to quickly believe the information the company provided.

THE CASE OF KRISPY KREME

On January 4, 2005, Krispy Kreme Doughnuts Inc. announced that it was filing a financial restatement; its stock had fallen 73 percent over the previous 12 months. How did Krispy Kreme lose so much of its value in such a short period? Governance Metrics International (GMI), which rates the quality of a company's governance practices, had begun evaluating companies in 2002. It first rated Krispy Kreme in June 2003, and compared to all other U.S. companies, Krispy Kreme scored a below-average 4.0 for its corporate governance practices. (On the GMI 10-point scale, an average company earns about 6 points.) Among other things, GMI cited a relatively large number of non-independent directors and related-party transactions and a lack of disclosure about ethical codes of conduct. GMI concluded that the company did not have a strong overall governance record. Seven months later, in January 2004, GMI re-rated the company, and its score had dropped to 2.5. Early warning signals of failures in governance in Krispy Kreme are presented in Exhibit 14.1. At this stage, none of Krispy Kreme's financial woes had been discovered or announced, but the declining GMI scores clearly pointed to risk. Five months later, in May 2004, a shareholder suit was initiated, and in July, an investigation was announced by the U.S. Securities and Exchange Commission (SEC).

However, over this same period, several Wall Street companies were recommending the stock. On August 22, 2003, one had an outperform rating on the stock (even though it was a downgrade from a top pick), and as of January 2005, Krispy Kreme still had an outperform rating. On December 17, 2003, another Wall Street company initiated coverage with a buy recommendation, as did another on March 30, 2004. Another initiated coverage on September 13, 2004, with a hold recommendation, and yet another issued a strong buy on September 28, 2004. GMI is the first to admit that governance should not be the only screen in stock selection, but with this kind of downward move in ratings, one would think that financial analysts would have tempered their enthusiasm.

In October 2004, Krispy Kreme's board of directors established a special committee to conduct an independent investigation of various matters. The committee's work took 10 months and it issued a statement at the conclusion of its work, the critical parts of which are:

> The Krispy Kreme story is one of a newly-public company, experiencing rapid growth that failed to meet its accounting and financial reporting obligations to its shareholders and the public. While some may see the accounting errors discussed in our Summary as relatively small in magnitude, they were critical in a corporate culture driven by a narrowly focused goal of exceeding projected earnings by a penny each quarter.
>
> In our view, Scott A. Livengood, former Chairman of the Board and Chief Executive Officer, and John W. Tate, former Chief Operating Officer, bear primary responsibility for the failure to establish the management tone,

Exhibit 14.1 Early Warning Signals of Problems with Krispy Kreme from GMI

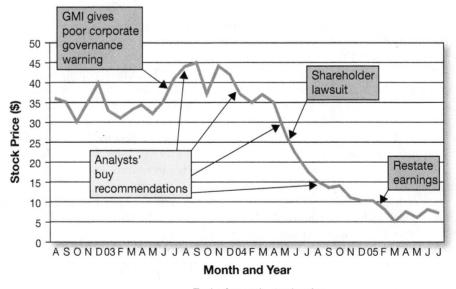

End-of-month stock price

environment and controls essential for meeting the Company's responsibilities as a public company. Krispy Kreme and its shareholders have paid dearly for those failures, as measured by the loss in market value of the Company's shares, a loss in confidence in the credibility and integrity of the Company's management and the considerable costs required to address those failures.[4]

These examples suggest that the management, when left unchecked, does not necessarily operate in ways that serve shareholders' interests. To address this problem, systems of policies and processes have been developed in companies that allow the board to direct and control management's activities. In principle, this should produce higher operating performance. Could careful attention to corporate governance issues have saved investors lots of money? In other words, does corporate governance actually impact the bottom line or is it expensive window dressing?

The Benefits of Good Governance

Good corporate governance leads to efficient allocation as capital is attracted to those companies that earn a higher return on capital invested. Poor governance allows inept or self-interested management to erode the performance of the company. The shareholders are the first to feel the consequences of this because they are residual claimants—the value of the shares they hold is directly related to the profit the company generates. The impact of the company's poor performance is only felt by other stakeholders when poor performance persists.

In principle, the board has a direct influence on strategy formulation and implementation. Researchers have looked at the impact of good governance on performance using achievement in terms of codes of practice related to performance. They have demonstrated that in Europe, emerging countries, and transitional economies corporate governance is associated with higher company earnings and share prices. Studies in Canada and the United States show conflicting results, however. For Canada, a possible explanation for the inconsistent results is that national characteristics affect the analysis. When ownership concentration and excessive or super-voting rights are included in the analysis, a higher quality of governance is associated with higher performance of the company.[5]

Alternative Approaches to Governance

Improved governance of companies has been built on a combination of three approaches: codes of conduct, laws, and contracts. The first approach includes the optional codes of conduct, which include best-practice principles and guidelines provided by industry and investor associations.[6] By 2008, the United States and United Kingdom had 25 distinct codes each. These codes create awareness of the need for and methods for creating stronger corporate governance. The codes tend to be "principles based," providing companies with some discretion when deciding whether to comply with them or to explain deviations from them. The guidelines serve as self-regulatory mechanisms because, while following the guidelines is optional, those who do not comply with them can be expelled from associations or put on some kind of public blacklist. An advantage of the best-practice guidelines is that, as compared to legal measures, they tend to be more flexible and adaptive to changes in the operating environment. However, it leaves vigilance of good practice to the larger community and leaves unclear the specific consequences of not following good practice. Ideally, those companies going beyond what is required by law will maintain the confidence of their shareholders so their share prices will be higher.

The second approach is corporate law, both statutory and judicial. Legal mechanisms are necessary to protect shareholders' rights and interests as the separation between investors and managers has increased with the growth of companies. All countries except those that follow a communist economic system have laws that define private companies and the corporate governance mechanisms that these companies have to implement. As legal mechanisms cannot specify *ex ante* what each party must do in every possible state of the world, they are inevitably incomplete. Courts and other conflict mechanisms fill in some of the gaps in the corporate governance *ex post*. The consequences of non-compliance are clear and supposedly swift although restricted to the jurisdiction of a regulatory body. Rules can quickly produce a response by those who exceed them by setting a minimum of acceptable performance. Unfortunately, those affected by the rules play games with the rules, hoping to find loopholes in them or ways around them.

The third approach is comprised of contractual mechanisms. Parties bargain for contractual terms that address possible dissension *ex ante* instead of relying on the legal system to address problems *ex post*, an exercise that is often costly, time consuming, and uncertain. The search for contractual terms that improve the governance structure tends to involve bargaining over four elements: control, duration, risk of losses, and share of returns. The search for sound contractual terms is guided by agency theory and is described near the end of the chapter.

These three approaches to corporate governance are complementary and mutually reinforcing. Corporate codes can be seen as facilitators and extend belief and trust that companies will subscribe to such principles. They define a playing field, a foundation on which to add needed supporting best practices and contracts. However, when those best practices and contracts fail, lawmakers and regulators have incentives to take legal action.

Corporate Governance Around the World

Although conflicts between managers and owners occur around the globe, the specific nature of the problems and the norms for guarding against them vary markedly. To help promote better governance, the Organisation for Economic Co-operation and Development (OECD) has stated principles for good governance that deal with the rights of shareholders, the equitable treatment of shareholders, the role of stakeholders, disclosure and transparency, and the responsibilities of the board.[7] These principles are universally applicable to all types of corporate governance in countries at all levels of economic development. On this basis, the quality of governance in various countries can be compared. Those with the most open regulatory system and hence highest quality are identified in Exhibit 14.2. This ranking, prepared by Governance-Metrics International, found that companies in Ireland had the best average quality with 7.44, while those in Canada came in at 7.35 and the United States at 7.18. The lowest were in China at 3.01, Mexico at 2.48, and Chile at 1.96.[8]

Governance practices vary across the globe because of differences in history, institutions, laws, and national cultures. Governance in Canada, the United Kingdom, and the United States is based on common law and is shareholder-centric; in other countries, governance is stakeholder-centric as other stakeholders have much greater formal standing. Canadian regulators, lawmakers, and good governance advocates alike look toward the United States and United Kingdom for ideas. Countries with common-law legal systems rely heavily on stock markets to assemble and allocate capital.

In Asia, equity markets are traditionally characterized by smaller capitalization, smaller amounts of capital raised, relatively infrequent turnover, and a concentration of ownership. These characteristics not only have a bearing on how corporate governance standards can be raised but also limit the impact of reforms affecting the balance between governance and overall economic

Exhibit 14.2 The 10 Countries with the Highest Overall Quality of Governance, 2009[9]

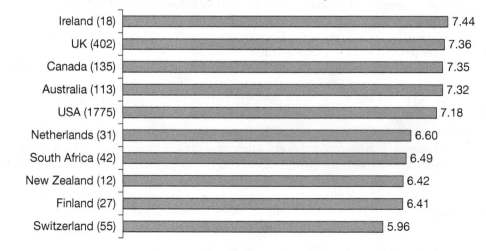

Ireland (18)	7.44
UK (402)	7.36
Canada (135)	7.35
Australia (113)	7.32
USA (1775)	7.18
Netherlands (31)	6.60
South Africa (42)	6.49
New Zealand (12)	6.42
Finland (27)	6.41
Switzerland (55)	5.96

development.[10] Let us now consider governance in the United States, Canada, Germany, and China in detail.

THE UNITED STATES

The first country to issue a code of good governance was the United States in 1978. The U.S. approach to governance tends to rely on compliance with a specific set of rules rather than trust. This was well demonstrated with the radical reforms made in 2002 when the Sarbanes-Oxley Act (colloquially referred to as SOX and Sar-Box for the sake of convenience) dramatically changed the way governance was handled in the United States. These requirements were motivated by corporate scandals at major corporations including Adelphia, Enron, Arthur Andersen, WorldCom, and Tyco—scandals stemming from breaches of trust, failures of responsibility, breakdowns in governance, and lack of candid disclosure.

The act made three specific changes to corporate governance in the United States.[11] First, it brought the role of gatekeepers, including auditors, analysts, and lawyers, into the process of governance. Second, it significantly enhanced the legal status of, and centrality of, the chief executive officer (CEO) and the board's audit committee in governance. Third, internal laws of corporate governance were federalized, creating a new duty of care for the CEO and audit committee and reintroducing serious prohibitions on "conflict of interest" transactions. These changes were reflected in new rules set by the U.S. Securities and Exchange Commission (SEC). This included mandatory listing standards at the New York Stock Exchange and NASDAQ. This led to the harmonization of listing requirements at the two exchanges. All public companies registered in the United States are now required to comply with the act's restrictions and procedures, including filing periodic reports with the U.S. Securities and Exchange Commission (SEC). Other procedures are intended as best practices and not outright requirements. Corporations are required to disclose aspects and then let the market decide what importance to put on that disclosure.

The Sarbanes-Oxley Act led to the creation of the Public Company Accounting Oversight Board, which sets standards and rules for audit reports. All accounting companies that audit public companies must register with the oversight board and the board inspects, investigates, and enforces compliance by these registered companies.

CANADA[12]

Since the mid-1990s, Canada relied on voluntary compliance with codes of conduct, though 35 percent of corporations listed on the TSX were not fully in compliance with even the relatively soft obligation to disclose the extent to which they met the suggested benchmarks.[13] With the U.S. implementation of the Sarbanes-Oxley Act, Canadian authorities switched to a rules-based approach and harmonized rules so that Canadian companies would be "SOX-compliant." This was important because Canadian companies rely heavily on the U.S. market when raising capital as the Canadian market for capital is small. Eligible Canadian companies have privileged access to the U.S. capital using Canadian disclosure documents, which are subject to review only by Canadian securities regulators. They are not subject to the U.S. domestic registration and reporting system. More than half of the Toronto Stock Exchange's market capitalization, in terms of value (approximately 200 issuers), comprises interlisted SEC registrants.

Achieving this harmonization was complicated as Canada has a highly fragmented regulatory and supervisory system for corporate laws and securities laws. The legal framework for corporate governance is governed by the federal Canada Business Corporations Act (CBCA) and provincial or territorial corporate statutes such as the Ontario Business Corporations Act (OBCA) since Canadian companies may be incorporated either federally or provincially.

Meanwhile, securities regulation is administered by the 10 provincial and three territorial governments, each of which has its own legislative and regulatory authority. These bodies coordinate their activities through the Canadian Securities Administrators (CSA), a voluntary umbrella organization of the provincial and territorial securities regulators. In recent years the CSA has developed a system of mutual reliance, which designates one securities regulator as the lead agency when it comes to reviewing applications or disclosure documents from Canadian public companies. As the largest Canadian public companies are listed on the Toronto Stock Exchange (TSX), the Ontario Securities Commission is generally regarded as the lead securities regulatory authority in Canada.

Exhibit 14.3 The 10 Canadian Companies with the Best Governance Overall in 2009[14]

Rank	Company Name	Industry Group	Board Composition	Shareholding and Compensation	Shareholder Rights	Disclosure	Total/100	5-yr % return to investors
1	SNC-Lavalin Group Inc.	Industrials	30	22	30	12	94	202.0
1	Toronto-Dominion Bank	Financials	28	23	32	11	94	70.2
3	Bank of Montreal	Financials	29	22	32	9	92	20.2
4	Bank of Nova Scotia	Financials	26	21	32	12	91	50.5
4	Manulife Financial Corp.	Financials	28	18	33	12	91	-2.7
4	Royal Bank of Canada	Financials	25	23	32	11	91	118.0
7	Canadian Imperial Bank of Commerce	Financials	25	22	32	11	90	18.8
8	Canadian National Railway Co.	Industrials	28	22	28	11	89	88.5
8	Gildan Activewear Inc.	Consumer	27	23	28	11	89	150.0
8	Potash Corp. of Saskatchewan Inc.	Materials	26	22	30	11	89	304.0
9	Sun Life Financial Inc.	Financials	25	22	32	10	89	5.9

In 2002, the Ontario provincial government gave the Ontario Securities Commission the power to make rules for corporate governance through Bill 198 while the TSX imposed disclosure and governance guidelines that brought companies listed with it closer to compliance with SOX. Since then CSA rules have evolved to harmonize Canadian rules with SOX and the consequential rules and guidelines established by the U.S. SEC and stock exchanges.

In the spring of 2010, the Canadian federal government proposed legislation that would create a national securities regulator that would replace the 13 separate provincial and territorial bodies.

Survey Results for Canada

In an effort to improve corporate governance, organizations such as the Canadian Coalition for Good Governance rank companies based on how well they are meeting standards of good governance. Companies answer a set of questions about various aspects of governance (board composition, shareholding and compensation, shareholder rights, and disclosure) and are scored according to their answers. From these scores an overall index is created that is used to rank companies. The 10 companies that scored the best in 2009 are identified in Exhibit 14.3.

Special Factors Influencing Governance in Canada

The ownership of companies in Canada has peculiarities, that set it apart from other countries with common-law histories including the United Kingdom and the United States. These features have implications for efforts that seek to improve governance and hence the equality of shareholders in Canada. Some argue that the differences between the Canadian and United States capital markets justify different approaches to making governance more effective.[15]

Controlling Shareholders

Half the top companies in Canada have controlling shareholders, a greater proportion than in the United Kingdom and the United States. These shareholders usually dominate the board and so are entrusted with the governance of the companies. Families with controlling interest in Canada are the Thomson family (Thomson Corp.), the Weston family (George Weston Ltd.), and the Rogers family (Rogers Communications Inc.). In the case of Rogers, four of the seven company directors are family members.

Controlling shareholders can be good for a company in several circumstances. When those shareholders are brilliant and highly ethical entrepreneurs, being in control lets the company act without concern for short-term share price effects. An example of an owner-controlled company is Nike, run by founder Philip Knight. When controlling shareholders are sophisticated investors, they can monitor and, if necessary, discipline errant managers. Moreover, the very presence of a sophisticated controlling shareholder can reassure smaller investors. In addition, when the controlling shareholders have their own wealth tied up in their companies, they have a clear economic interest in efficient economic management because the better run their companies, the richer they are.

Countries whose large companies are more likely to have controlling shareholders are also countries whose controlling shareholders reap larger private benefits of control. The private benefits of control induce controlling shareholders to run their corporations in ways that need not align with the wishes of public shareholders. In Canada, controlling shareholders appear to benefit from exercising control in spite of measures to eliminate some abuse such as coattail provisions that protect inferior voting shareholders from exclusion during transfers of control blocks and rules opening control block sales to public investors. These gains may be attributed to self-dealing (also called tunnelling and described under business groups) or to their political influence from running great corporate empires. These personal gains negate many other advantages that large shareholders can bring to a company. The consequence is depressed valuations of Canadian companies and flagging total factor productivity.

Conrad Black and his associates at Hollinger drained US$400 million, or 95 percent of Hollinger's adjusted net income, from the company between 1997 and 2003. Much of this was accomplished by having Hollinger pay a "management fee" to a company controlled by Black. In a later trial, he was acquitted of improperly using company money to subsidize his lifestyle, but he was brought down by "non-compete fees" that he paid himself and his co-defendants for agreeing not to compete with themselves. Black and his associates kept the money without passing it on to his company shareholders. Of the total £3.2 million that was stolen from the company, Black personally received £1.7 million, although his lawyer claimed the figure was £1.4 million.[16] Granting Hollinger's shareholders, notably Conrad Black, more rights *vis-à-vis* hired managers would not have checked that scandal because professional managers subject to controlling shareholders seldom defy their masters.

Governance problems also arise where controlling shareholders are either unsophisticated or wield control without owning very many shares. The first problem typically arises in family companies governed by either senile patriarchs or unqualified heirs who fail to appreciate their own competence. The second problem typically occurs where controlling shareholders actually own few shares and wield control using super-voting shares, pyramiding, or other control-magnifying devices.

Dual-Class Shareholders

Over the past 30 years, Canadian companies have made growing use of dual-class share structures. The incidence of superior voting shares in Toronto Stock Exchange (TSX) companies rose from 5 percent in 1975 to more than 15 percent in 1987. In 2005, an estimated 20 percent to 25 percent of companies listed on the TSX used some form of dual-class share structure or special voting rights. Since then the proportion has likely declined. In comparison, in the United States, where rules on dual-class shares are much more restrictive and investor opposition is more vocal, just over 2 percent of companies issue restricted shares.[17]

Examples of this practice include some of Canada's most renowned and largest companies: Bombardier Inc., Magna International Inc., Onex Corp., Power Corporation, Rogers Communications Inc., Shaw Communications Inc., Telus Corporation, and Quebecor, to name only a few. The importance of these dual-class shares is that they disconnect ownership from control of the company. At one point the Bombardier family controlled 59.7 percent of Bombardier's voting rights but held only 17.5 percent of its equity. The Stronach family controlled 75 percent of the votes at Magna but held only 3 percent of its equity. Similarly, the Shaw family controlled 78 percent of the votes at Shaw Communications but held only 4 percent of its equity. It is usually impossible for outside investors to buy the super-voting shares.

Business Groups

Business groups are a common feature of Canadian business.[18] These groups are clusters of listed and unlisted companies that hold control blocks of stock in each other and typically produce pyramid-shaped structure with a controlling shareholder—usually a wealthy family—owning a family company at the top (for example the Desmarais family and the Power Corporation). This company holds voting control blocks in a first tier of listed companies, which hold voting control blocks in a second tier of listed companies, and in turn the second tier companies hold voting control blocks in a third tier, and so on. Pyramidal groups of this sort have tied up hundreds of corporations, both listed and unlisted, in corporate ownership. The Bronfman pyramidal group in the mid-1990s had 16 tiers of ownership. Such pyramiding allows one company to control a huge constellation of companies.

Pyramiding creates a number of problems. First, it gives rise to *self-dealing* or *tunnelling* in which the controlling owner directs one controlled company to take a loss so that another might benefit or so that the controlling owner might benefit personally. These problems are worsened by dual-class shares. Second, it greatly magnifies the political influence and economic control of individuals or families who are at the apex of the pyramid and actually own few shares. Corporate governance problems in business groups have a different flavour from those in freestanding companies with controlling shareholders. This is because conflicts arise between controlling shareholders and public shareholders, and also between the public shareholders of different companies in a group.

Institutional Investors

institutional investors
Institutions that manage large sums of money for third-party investors.

Institutional investors include pensions, mutual funds, insurance companies, endowments, and foundations. In Canada, such investors had financial assets worth more than Cdn$1.5 trillion in 2007. The leading institutional investors include: Alberta Investment Management (Cdn$73.3 billion in 2007), British Columbia Investment Management (Cdn$83.4 billion in 2007), Caisse de dépôt et placement du Québec (Cdn$237.3 billion in 2007), Canada Pension Plan (Cdn$116.6 billion in 2007), and the Ontario Teachers' Pension Plan (Cdn$106 billion in 2006). Most institutional investors are relatively passive: They indicate what they think of a company by buying or selling its stock based on their expectations of its future performance. Pension funds were limited in their ability to leave the Canadian market until 2005 by caps on how much of their holdings could be in foreign investments. This limitation reduced Canadian pension revenues by an estimated Cdn$3 billion a year.[19] They can also be active investors, as are Caisse de dépôt et placement du Québec, the Ontario Municipal Employees Retirement System, and the Ontario Teachers' Pension Plan. Reasons for being active are that their large asset bases gives them power, that their large stock positions make it hard for them to sell underperforming shares, and that they are focused on returns on the investments they make. Pension funds have also been moving into making direct investments in private companies. An example is the Ontario Teachers' Pension Plan's acquisition in 2010, through Teachers' Private Capital (its private investment department), of the Exal Group, the largest specialty manufacturer of aluminum containers in the world.

GERMANY

In Germany, state governments and banks are major owners. It is not unusual for German banks to hold debt and own equity in the same corporation. In addition to the direct voting power that banks have due to their ownership position, banks also control a significant number of proxy voting positions from depositors who use the bank as a trustee for ownership purposes.

Germany governance involves a two-board system (sometimes called a two-tiered board): the management board and the supervisory board. The management board is responsible for managing the enterprise. Its members are jointly accountable for the company's management. The work of the management board is coordinated by its chair. The supervisory board is responsible for appointing, supervising, and advising the members of the management board and is directly involved in decisions of fundamental importance to the enterprise. The work of the supervisory board is coordinated by its chair. The supervisory board is similar to the board of directors, with two major exceptions. First, a portion of the board's seats are allocated to shareholders' representatives and a portion to labour's representatives. The chair of the supervisory board is always a representative of shareholders and has two votes so owners are always more powerful. Second, management executives are not permitted to serve on the supervisory board.

Contrasting the situation in Germany with that of North America, the North American CEO appears to have much more power. In North America, the CEO is often also chairman of the board of the company. In addition, in North America members of the board are elected by shareholders; no seats are allocated to other stakeholders by right. Furthermore, in North America potential board members nominated by people other than the current board are rarely elected to the board. Finally, in North America there are no legal limits on the number of internal members on the board, though in practice this is changing. Conversely, in Germany the CEO has a harder time because it is relatively easy for those other than owners to nominate and elect members to the board.

CHINA

China is perhaps the newest market to face corporate governance issues. With its flagship stock exchanges set up in Shanghai and Shenzhen, the China securities market started in 1990. At that time, only 10 companies were listed on the stock exchanges. After 17 years of exponential growth, the Chinese securities market has reached a considerable size, and Chinese as well as non-Chinese individuals and companies are allowed to own stock. At the end of 2005, well over 1000 companies were listed on Chinese exchanges, with shares owned by Chinese citizens (these types of shares are referred to as A-class shares). The number of companies listed in the local market with shares owned by foreign investors (B-class shares) was 108; among them, 26 companies issued B shares only, while the rest issued both A and B shares. Forty-six companies have overseas listings (H-class shares).[20]

Given China's history of operating as a closed economy, the majority of companies listed on the Chinese exchanges were state-owned enterprises. This heritage is evident in the ownership structure of public companies, where the percentage of state ownership remains relatively high across all industries. The consequence is that Chinese public companies are controlled by state-owned or state-controlled shareholders. The remaining shares are typically owned by a combination of individual and institutional investors.[21] Such government control of public corporations is most often seen in countries where, historically, the government owned the largest companies and gradually privatized them. In Brazil, the government still has veto power over the operations of Embraer and Petrobras, two of the world's largest airplane and oil companies, respectively. French and Russian also have residual government ownership of many large companies.

Role of Board of Directors

The responsibilities of the **board of directors** include setting the company's strategic goals, providing the leadership to put them into effect, supervising the management of the business, and reporting to the shareholders on their stewardship. The board's actions are subject to laws, regulations, and the wishes of the shareholders in the general meeting. The directors are appointed by the shareholders. Who becomes a director may be influenced by who can be considered, how candidates are nominated, and how they are voted upon.

Board practices vary around the world because of differences in national institutions and cultures. Canadian companies, in comparison to U.S. companies have smaller boards with fewer independent directors; have boards that hold more meetings; have directors that sit on a greater number of boards; are less likely to have CEOs also serving as the chairman of the board; are less likely to have compensation, nominating, and corporate governance committees; and have a significantly lower fraction of independent directors sitting on these committees.[22]

Various issues of governance relate to the board of directors. These will now be detailed.

board of directors Group of individuals that formally represents the company's shareholders and oversees the work of top executives.

THE DUAL CHAIRMAN OF THE BOARD/CEO

A common feature of North American boards is that the same individual serves both as the chairman of the board and as the chief executive officer of the company. CEOs tend to like this arrangement. The arguments made for serving dual roles include that specialized information is needed which an outsider does not have, that there is a lack of qualified candidates for one of the positions, and that splitting the roles creates tension because the chairman can overreach his/her boundaries and get involved in the day-to-day management of the company.

In Europe, separate individuals in each role is more common while in Germany the CEO and the chair are always different people.[23] The argument for two separate positions is that the board can then more effectively monitor top executives. When the chief executive officer is chair of the board of directors, the impartiality of the board is compromised. Agency and organizational economic theories predict that when the CEO also holds the dual role of chair, the interests of the owners will be sacrificed to a degree in favour of management.

The pressure for good governance has increased in recent years. This has led several large U.S. companies including Boeing, Walt Disney, and Oracle to split the chair/CEO role into two separate roles. In Canada, the six largest banks all have separate chairmen and CEOs.[24]

INSIDE VERSUS OUTSIDE DIRECTORS

A distinction is made between directors who are employed by the company and those who are not. Those employed by the company are called "inside" directors and typically come from the top management of the company. Those who are not employed by the company are called "outside" directors. From the perspective of good governance, a board consisting mostly of outside directors is preferred because they are seen as more independent in fulfilling their board responsibilities. Being an outsider does not necessarily make a director independent, however, as the director may have business dealings with the company or ties of friendship with the CEO. There have been situations where CEOs have tempered board scrutiny of their activities by providing directors with consulting engagements and use of corporate jets. These relationships can affect how they monitor and advise management. In addition, by virtue of their position, CEOs have considerable control over the information that outside directors receive.

Although watchdog groups clamour for more independent outside directors on boards, outsiders are likely to be limited in their knowledge of the company's business and are probably operating under severe time constraints. The argument has been made that the board is better served with insiders from the executive ranks. For instance, when the company operates in highly technical areas, insiders are best equipped with critical knowledge.[25]

DESIRED BACKGROUND OF THE DIRECTORS

Positive CEO–board interactions are maximized when the selection of outside board members matches the competitive environment facing the company. Companies operating in relatively stable competitive environments get better advice from outside board members drawn from other companies that are strategically related to the company. In stable environments, the knowledge and experience that board members gain in their own companies translates well to the companies they monitor. However, companies operating in a very unstable competitive environment get a more effective board when outside board members come from strategically dissimilar companies. A possible explanation is that in unstable environments, drawing on the broader range of experiences of board members helps the board make better sense of the company's competitive environment.

Research indicates that social ties do not reduce the level of board-monitoring activity and do improve the ability of the CEO to tap board members for advice and counsel on strategic issues. This suggests that social ties between CEOs and board members may increase board involvement rather than decrease it.[26] The same research found that CEOs were more willing to turn to board members for advice when they had social ties to these members—when they considered the relationship to be friendship-based, not solely monitoring-based. This suggests that when CEOs perceive they have a loyal board, they will involve the board more in strategic decision making.

Finally, companies appear to be well served when board members are willing to collaborate with the CEO outside board meetings. In companies where this happens, they perform significantly better than companies that limit CEO/board interactions to purely monitoring roles. There is a trend toward encouraging board members to be more active. For instance, General Electric now requires that its board members spend time at its various facilities around the world in addition to the regular boardroom meetings.

A concern is that CEOs may be tempted to have highly paid CEOs sit on their boards. Landing highly paid CEOs as directors probably leads to a board that is be supportive of paying high wages for CEOs. For instance, research shows that the CEOs of the boards of companies on which Home Depot's former CEO Bob Nardelli sat were overpaid relative to their peers and that Nardelli himself was overpaid.[27]

COMPOSITION OF BOARD COMMITTEES

Boards generally are organized into several committees as each committee focuses on a key board responsibility. The governance committee plays a major role in ensuring that the board meets its responsibilities. It manages the dynamics of the board, setting committees' terms of reference and the criteria for their leadership, and managing dysfunctional behaviour. It also pays attention to whether management respects the board. Moreover, it takes charge of board succession, including moving old directors off and new members meeting the necessary requirements onto the board in a timely manner. The audit committee is responsible for selecting the independent auditor and reviewing the reports provided by that auditor. Good governance suggests that the audit committee be composed only of outsiders because independence is more likely to produce effective monitoring. Another committee is the compensation committee and is charged with setting the level of executive compensation. Having well-paid CEOs serving on this committee is likely to boost the pay of the CEO of the company. Increasingly, those interested in governance are seeking to have a say on the pay of top management.

MONITORING VERSUS ADVISING

In all cases, the general responsibility of the board is to ensure that executives are acting in shareholders' best interests. The board is legally charged with monitoring management, but it can also provide advice and counsel to the CEO and other top executives. Monitoring is the process of the board acting on its legal and fiduciary responsibilities to oversee the executive's behaviour and performance and to take action when necessary to replace management. The chapter opening vignette on HP provides an example of the board in this role. Although increasing emphasis is being placed on the monitoring roles of boards, recent research has shown that just as much, if not more, value is to be had by tapping into the expertise and contacts of the board and using board members as confidants and information sources. On the other hand, many critics of corporate governance argue that CEOs who have social ties and friendships with board members could put shareholders at risk because these relationships may make the board less likely to monitor the CEO effectively.

In the wake of numerous high-profile financial scandals in recent years, boards have been under increasing pressure to exercise their monitoring responsibility with greater vigilance.[28] Part of this pressure comes from laws that require public companies to put particular governance reforms into place.[29] Recent rules such as Sarbanes-Oxley and its Canadian counterparts have caused directors on both sides of the border to emphasize their job as "watchdogs." A concern is that this emphasis detracts from collaboration between the board and management when making significant decisions that shape the company's future.

INTERLOCKING BOARDS

Directors who sit on multiple boards connect with other directors (a characteristic called a *board interlock*). For instance, Bristol-Myers Squibb has both PepsiCo director Robert E. Allen and Coca-Cola director James D. Robinson III sitting on its board. Debate continues as to whether such board interlocks help companies perform better by virtue of their access to better information or simply allow corporations to collude at the expense of the public at large. Although there is no evidence that consumers are generally harmed by such interrelationships at the board level, strategy research has shown that directors themselves may be more effective as monitors if they are linked to certain companies given the competitive standing and environmental turbulence facing the focal companies.[30] Common board ties have been found to influence many important decisions, ranging from the choice of CEO to a company's strategy in the face of failing performance.[31]

Directors can also be conflicted when they sit on several boards. Darren Entwistle was a director on the board of Toronto Dominion Bank (TD) since 2001 and was also CEO of Telus. When BCE Inc. came into play, both the Ontario Teachers' Pension Plan and Telus competed in the bidding. A Teachers bid was being backed by TD Securities, a unit of TD. As a director, Entwistle did not want TD to miss out on lucrative buyout fees, but as CEO of Telus he did not want TD supporting the rival's bid. He resolved his dilemma by resigning from TD's board. Meanwhile, Charlie Baillie, former CEO of TD Bank, still sits on the Telus board.

Having considered how the board is influenced in ways that affect the quality of governance, we now turn to consider CEO compensation. Incentive compensation is an important mechanism used to encourage and motivate managers to do what shareholders want.

Aligning Executives' and Shareholders' Interests

The separation of company ownership from company management produces conflicts of interest because what is best for shareholders is not necessarily what is best for management. The most direct way to align incentives is to require that executives own stock in the company. Less direct is providing incentives that encourage managers to act in the best interests of shareholders. We will now describe the two approaches.

EXECUTIVE STOCK OWNERSHIP

The theory is that as an owner of the company, the manager will behave more like an owner and less like a hired hand. In recent years, many companies have established ownership guidelines and holding requirements for senior executives and their prevalence is expected to continue increasing because they are seen as one of the best forms of governance (see Exhibit 14.4).[32] The ownership program of one company, Dendrite International, is described in Exhibit 14.5.[33]

Stock Ownership Policies

Ownership guidelines require individuals to attain and maintain a certain level of equity ownership in the company. There are two types of programs: traditional stock ownership and retention programs. Traditional stock ownership guidelines establish ownership levels through a multiple-of-salary approach. For example, Sunlife Financial requires that executives hold shares worth six times their salary, while BCE requires that executives hold at least 10 000 shares personally. Retention programs express ownership as a percentage of the gains resulting from the exercise of stock options and other equity-based incentives, such as restricted stock. These two types of programs are sometimes used together. For example, some companies require that executives retain their shares (or some percentage of their shares) acquired through stock options until they own five times their salary in company stock. Holding requirements prohibit individuals from selling a certain percentage of equity acquired in the company for a specified length of time.

Implementing a stock ownership plan takes time. Most CEOs do not have sufficient liquid assets to immediately buy the needed shares when a plan is implemented. Consequently, most companies allow CEOs five years to acquire the required shares. When companies use the retention program, no time requirement is necessary because all that matters is how much is retained from options granted.

Companies are increasingly requiring that their members of the board also own stock, as evidenced in Exhibit 14.5. The level of ownership required is much lower than for CEOs. In 2006, a study of 204 large corporations in the S&P/TSX index found 69 percent had share ownership requirements for their directors while 31 percent left it up to individual directors to decide whether to put their own money on the line.[34] In 2003, 58 percent of 207 companies on the S&P/TSX index had no mandatory ownership requirements for directors. The Canadian Coalition for Good Governance set a guideline that directors hold shares worth three times their salary, although best practice is five times their salary. By 2010, the coalition had relaxed its position and recommended that the board should decide on an appropriate level.[35]

Exhibit 14.4 Comparison of Executive Stock Ownership

	Largest 250 Companies with Stock Ownership Guidelines		
	Number of Companies	Percentage of Companies	Percentage Increase from 2001 to 2004
Executives	142	57	58
Directors	123	49	127

Exhibit 14.5 Establishing Executive-Ownership Requirements at Dendrite International

As an illustration of a recent adopter of an executive stock-ownership plan, consider Dendrite. Dendrite (DRTE), a leading supplier of specialized software to the global pharmaceutical industry that was founded in Australia in 1986 and is now headquartered in Bedmaster, New Jersey, implemented a formal stock-ownership plan for its 20 senior-most executives and all of its non-employee directors. The new program mandates ownership of Dendrite stock, ranging from 15 000 to 100 000 shares, depending on the executive's position.

The ownership requirements set by Dendrite are based on owned common stock, not stock options. Ownership of the predetermined number of shares must be achieved within five years, with an initial number attained in three years. Restrictions have been placed on the receipt of additional equity-based compensation and sale of Dendrite shares until ownership commitments are attained. The executive participants may obtain shares through purchase on the open market, receiving incentive compensation in shares or exercising options and holding shares.

In addition to instituting share-ownership requirements, Dendrite also made changes to its executive compensation program. Executives may now elect to receive incentive compensation in stock instead of cash. If the executive elects to receive stock, these shares are restricted from sale for one year, and the executive will receive a number of options equal to the number of restricted shares. Replacement options will be granted for shares used to exercise vested options.

By the start of 2005, Dendrite's executive stock ownership plan was fully in place. In addition, all of Dendrite's directors—executive and independent—owned at least some Dendrite stock, further aligning the board, top manager, and shareholder interests. While Dendrite is in a highly competitive and dynamic industry, it is notable that since beginning the implementation of the executive stock ownership plan in 2000, the firm has managed to garner shareholders a strong return. For instance, as of the end of 2005 shareholders had earned a three-year average return of 28 percent, versus the S&P 1500 return of 12 percent. Standard and Poor also ranked the firm among the top tier of its peers, in terms of overall performance and outlook.

Is an executive stock ownership plan an easy pathway to competitive advantage? Probably not, but at least it is an important lever in a firm's corporate governance repertoire to provide executives and directors an incentive to see that the right strategy is being executed well.

Company-Related Risk

The ownership requirement can backfire. Executives required to invest heavily in the company cannot diversify their risk exposure as well as shareholders who can spread their risks across many companies. In addition to financial risk, executives risk their human capital—that is, their reputation and future job opportunities—through the employment relationship. In Canada, the CEO and CFO are required to sign off on the company's financial statements according to MI 52-109. In the U.S., the CEO and CFO must certify that the company's financial statements are accurate. They can be jailed if the statements are proven fraudulent or misrepresentative. This increases the pressures of top executives' jobs—an indication of this is that CFO turnover increased by about 23 percent from 2001 to 2003.[36] The impact of this requirement is that executives suffer heavy exposure to company-specific risk, which could lead some to become very risk averse.

EXECUTIVE INCENTIVE COMPENSATION

Executives put a great deal of effort into activities that are rewarded and less on activities that are not rewarded. On this basis, giving incentives that reward actions in line with shareholder interests is a way to bring executives in line with them. For instance, shareholders might be interested in selling the business but management is not interested if its employment is threatened. Management's hesitancy to examine selling opportunities can be eliminated by including a "golden parachute" provision in managers' compensation packages, which offers a significant payment for loss of employment due to an acquisition. Of course, sometimes incentives unwittingly exacerbate conflicts of interest.

A number of mechanisms are frequently used to increase the **incentive alignment** between shareholders and executives. We review some of the common mechanisms in this section, but note that each mechanism has its limitations and that eliminating all possible conflicts of interest is impossible.

incentive alignment Use of incentives to align managerial self-interest with shareholders.

Exhibit 14.6 Comparison of Incentive Pay Usage in the Food Industry

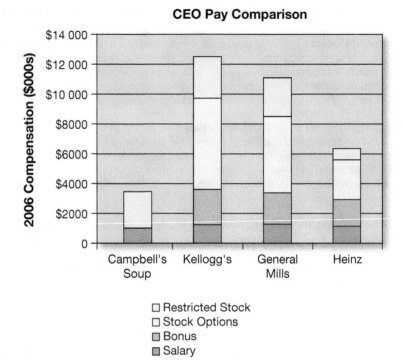

CEO Pay Comparison

☐ Restricted Stock
☐ Stock Options
▨ Bonus
▨ Salary

Incentive Plans

The two most common incentive plans are annual bonus plans and stock options. In recent years, companies have been increasing their reliance on newer approaches, such as restricted stock grants and long-term accounting-based incentive plans. Exhibit 14.6 illustrates how different companies in the food industry emphasize various incentive mechanisms when paying their CEOs.

Bonus Plans

The bonus pool is the total amount of bonus that can be paid to qualified employees in a given year. Shareholders vote on the formula that will be used to determine the size of the pool. The formula is usually related to overall company profitability, the simplest approach being a percentage of net income. The board then evaluates executives' performance on multiple dimensions and allocates a cash award as appropriate at year-end.

Bonus plans are appealing because the board can tie them to multiple desired outcomes, including both financial performance and other important outcomes such as customer satisfaction and quality. In addition, the board can more easily revoke or withhold bonuses than it can other long-term incentives that it loses control of once they are granted. The effectiveness of annual bonus programs is determined by how well the board links them to the achievement of desired objectives.

The bonus-plan incentive has two principal drawbacks. First, when bonuses are tied to accounting indicators of performance, executives may make decisions that maximize their possible bonus payout. For instance, companies are more likely to increase income deferrals when senior executives have reached the maximum payout under terms of their bonus plan.[37] Second, linking pay to annual company performance can produce a short-term bias and inattention to long-term strategic needs. For instance, bonus plans can lead to the underfunding of R&D initiatives.[38] To get around this problem, companies are tying bonus payouts to long-term performance rather than annual performance. These are often called Long-term Incentive Plans, or LTIPS, because incentives are based on company performance over a period longer than one year but exclude other long-term incentives such as restricted stock, stock options, or stock appreciation rights plans.

Stock Option Plans

stock option Incentive device giving an employee the right to buy a share of company stock at a later date for a predetermined price.

The executive stock option plan has been one of the most popular incentive devices over the past 20 years. A **stock option** is a right to buy a number of shares of stock at or after a given date in the future (the exercise date) at a price agreed upon at the time the option is granted (usually the current market price or 95 percent of the current market price). Usually stock option plans impose a vesting period after which the executive can buy the stocks. Some companies have taken a more complicated approach to options. For example, the Bank of Montreal ties the exercise of options closely to performance and extends the right to exercise the option over a longer period. Options are vested at 25 percent a year over a four-year span. There are also price hurdles that must be hit. One-third of the options can be exercised once the share price has risen 50 percent, and another one-third can be exercised once share price has gained over 100 percent.[39]

The attraction of a stock plan is that it simulates stock ownership for an executive who cannot afford to buy a lot of stock. When a company grants a stock option, the executive's cash pay does not increase in the year the option is granted but rather the employee has the right to buy a share of company stock at a later date for a predetermined price. Usually, the price of the stock goes up over time so the employee is able to buy the stock at a price below the market price. Many companies do not require the executive to actually buy the stock; sometimes they allow the executive to receive the difference between the stock price and the option price as compensation at that future date.

The rationale for using stock options is that they motivate executives to act like owners and take reasonable risks that will result in the company's stock price increasing. Advocates of stock options like their supposed win–win attributes: If executives do not create shareholder value in the form of higher stock prices, the options will be worthless and are said to be "under water." Some companies have dealt with this problem by re-pricing the option, lowering the price that the executive buys the stock for so that he/she benefits from the option and stays motivated, even if the stock price has fallen.

Like most incentive plans, options have a downside. They do not make executives bear financial risk like stock ownership does. When executives own stock, their wealth increases if the stock price increases and, conversely, decreases if the stock price decreases. With stock options, only the upside potential is conveyed. The only cost to executives is an opportunity cost. Moreover, executives make decisions quite differently when they have something to lose. The upside potential and downside risks seem to motivate different behaviours. Research shows that stock options may increase excessive risk taking beyond the level of risk desired by shareholders.[40] For instance, executives with large proportions of their pay package derived from stock options tend to pursue aggressive acquisition and divestiture strategies; buying and selling divisions frequently is a key part of their corporate strategy. GE has used stock options heavily historically, so it may be no coincidence that it is one of the most prolific acquirers of companies in the world. Likewise, in the chapter opening vignette, Carly Fiorina was quick to use acquisitions to solve her company's revenue problems rather than exercising patience with internal development programs that would produce organic growth. Conversely, companies run by executives with high levels of stock ownership are much less likely to pursue acquisitions and divestitures and focus more on internal developments.[41]

Restricted Stock

Restricted stock is a recent compensation initiative that is designed to avoid the problems associated with annual bonus plans and stock options. Annual bonuses can encourage short-term behaviour while options are only attractive when the market price is greater than the price at which the share is granted.

Companies can grant shares to executives subject to restrictions that prevent managers from selling the stock or converting it into cash. The restrictions usually entail vesting over a period of three to five years and prohibitions on the sale of the stock for some extended period of time. The popularity of restricted stock has grown significantly in the past several years because of the wave of bad press associated with stock option abuses. With restricted stock grants, the executive has upside incentive associated with the stock but is also exposed to the downside risk. When the stock price drops, the value of the executives restricted stock declines as well. Some boards think they are better at truly aligning the incentives of managers with those of shareholders because restricted stock has real value when granted and not just potential value like stock options.

Doing Some Repairs at Home Depot

Hiring (and firing) and compensating the CEO are some of the chief responsibilities of the board of directors. After all, the CEO is expected to foster the formulation of a leading-edge strategy and champion it. Ultimately, the CEO is held accountable for the strategy's successful execution. When Home Depot and Bob Nardelli parted ways in 2006 because of poor performance, the board decided that the best candidate was Frank Blake, a senior executive of the company. By deciding to hire an insider, the Home Depot board in some ways simplified their job because they would not have to offer a big carrot to recruit an executive from another company to come to Home Depot. When a board goes outside the company to hire a CEO, they usually pay a premium because they need to lure an executive from another position. But, deciding what, and how, to pay the CEO is still a major challenge for the board. The

board's objective is to offer a compensation package that will result in incentives consistent with Home Depot's objectives—incentives that will motivate the CEO to formulate a strategy that achieves the board's vision and mission. When the Home Depot board had identified Blake as the new CEO, they stated that the company's objectives were to improve its strategy and tie CEO pay more closely to company performance.

In setting Blake's pay, three of the key considerations were (1) Blake's prior compensation as an executive vice-president of the company, (2) Nardelli's compensation as the former CEO, and (3) the compensation of the CEO of Home Depot's chief rival, Lowe's. These data are provided in Exhibit 14.7.

With Home Depot's objectives in mind, the board initially offered Blake a contract that included a mixture of incentives, including bonus payments, restricted stock, and stock options.

Surprisingly, Blake rejected the pay package because it was *too* generous and because he was opposed to restricted stock grants. His argument was that restricted stock did not offer enough incentive because, if the stock price declined, he would still have some value in the shares and so make money. He ended up settling on the following package:[42]

Annual salary: $975 000

Annual bonus: A target 100 percent of salary, with the possibility of double salary if performance is high enough

Long-term bonus: A target of $2 500 000, contingent on performance over the next three years

Restricted stock awards: None

Stock options: A present value of $2 500 000 but contingent on increasing stock price

Exhibit 14.7 Pay Comparison Among CEOs

	Salary	Bonus	Restricted Stock	Stock Options
Blake's Pay as EVP	$685 000	$825 000	$2 900 000	$0
Nardelli's Pay as former CEO	$2 200 000	$7 000 000	$14 000 000	$0
CEO Pay at Lowe's	$850 000	$2 600 000	$4 000 000	$0

1. Refer back to Exhibit 14.5, which discussed the establishment of executive stock ownership requirements at Dendrite International. Many business press outlets, such as *BusinessWeek* and *Fortune*, publish articles that are critical of the corporate governance practices, particularly executive compensation, of one company or another. Using these outlets, identify a recent example of a company that has been criticized for its governance practices and determine whether executive or director stock ownership was a factor in this criticism. What action plan for remedying this situation would you propose?

2. Identify a company that is looking for a new CEO (or pick one whose CEO you think should be replaced!). Using How Would You Do That? 14.1 as a model, imagine that a company is turning toward a compensation model that requires the CEO to own stock. What, specifically, do you think the compensation package should look like? How different will your company be from the competition in terms of the compensation package offered to the new CEO? (*Hint:* Pull up competitors' filed documents and annual reports on the internet.) What are the implications of these differences?

THE WELL-DESIGNED COMPENSATION PLAN

A manager's total compensation consists of three components: salary, benefits, and incentive compensation. Managers of larger companies typically receive more compensation than those in smaller companies. In addition, compensation of companies in the same industry tends to be competitive. Companies with low levels of compensation tend to have higher turnover. Also, companies with large pay gaps across top managerial ranks have higher turnover, which appears to undermine their ability to develop managerial talent.[43] In addition, the best-performing companies tend to compensate their second-level managers (i.e., CFO, COO, etc.) at levels more closely related to the pay of the CEO rather than have a star system where the CEO's pay significantly outpaces that of other top managers. A probable explanation is that strategic management is inherently a team function, and huge gaps in pay between the CEO and other officers create an unhealthy social context in which to operate as an effective team.[44] Thus, to maximize performance, companies need to adjust both absolute and relative pay levels to achieve the proper fit with their strategic context. Of the three components, the amount of incentive compensation is the component that the manager is best able to influence through personal efforts.

Most corporate by-laws and securities regulations require that the board and then shareholders approve incentive compensation plans and changes in them. Top management often hires outside consultants to work with the compensation committee of the board to craft the best incentive plan for the company. This plan is then submitted to the board for approval.

The power of incentives aligned with strategy to produce superior performance was demonstrated with the turnaround of General Dynamics in 1991. That year the board of directors hired a new management team. At the time General Dynamics was facing intense competition, cutbacks in military spending, and years of underperformance. The board charged the management team with formulating a strategy to create shareholder wealth. Managerial compensation was linked to shareholder wealth through a combination of bonuses, options, and restricted stock. This pay-for-performance plan is largely credited with motivating the team to devise a strategy that was politically unpopular but economically successful. The team radically altered the company, downsizing, restructuring, and exiting some of its businesses by selling divisions to competitors. By doing this the team created gains for shareholders of approximately $4.5 billion. Scholars suggest that such a dramatic and successful strategy would have been unlikely without these financial incentives.[45] The key to using incentives is finding the appropriate performance metrics (such as those identified in the balanced scorecard) and linking executive pay incentives to these outcomes.

Executives can make a great deal of money from options and restricted stock because any increase in the company's stock price increases compensation. A company's stock price can increase even when a company is losing out to competitors. For this reason evidence suggests that option pay should be used in moderation and balanced with other types of incentives, such as annual bonus plans and stock ownership.

How Would You Do That? 14.1 examines some of the factors that companies should consider when structuring CEO compensation. When establishing CEO pay and aligning it with a company's intended strategy, recognize that boards of directors are often criticized but rarely praised for how they structure CEO incentives.

An Agency Approach to Governance[46]

Agency theory explores how contracts and incentives can be written to motivate individuals so that goal congruence is achieved. When applied to governance of the company, it starts with the assumption that the interests of owners or board members and managers (principals and agents, respectively) are not aligned initially. Directors and managers, for example, want to maximize their own wealth, power, and prestige while safeguarding their reputation, while shareholders want to maximize the value of their assets. Agency theory holds that managers will not act to maximize the returns to shareholders unless appropriate governance structures are implemented in the corporation to safeguard the interests of shareholders.

In agency theory, the person who does the work is called the **agent** while the person who hired the agent is called the **principal.** The potential problems and pitfalls of the relationship can be examined in terms of an agency model that holds three components:

1. **decision rights,** which deal with the control over a particular asset, either to make and implement a decision or to approve, monitor, and reward others for their decisions;
2. **knowledge,** which one uses as an agent, either general knowledge or specific knowledge;
3. **incentives,** which motivate the agent to act in a particular way and are either monetary or non-monetary.

Agents are insulated from the consequences of their decisions by three veils:

1. **a legal veil** shelters agents from decisions that have onerous financial consequences;
2. **an information veil,** in that the principal lacks the information;
3. **a motivational veil,** in that agents are insulated from the consequences of their actions.

Generally, agency failures occur whenever decision rights, the necessary specific and general information, and incentives are not co-located in the same person.

Agency theorists argue that the problems of divergent objectives and information asymmetry can be dealt with through monitoring and incentives. With monitoring, the principal designs the control systems that limit the agent's ability to increase his/her welfare at the expense of the principal's. Audited financial statements are an example of a monitoring system. Monitoring is more effective when the agent's task is well defined and information used is accurate. When the task is not clearly defined or easily monitored, incentive contracting is more attractive. With incentives, the principal defines performance measures that further his/her interest and then provides incentives to the agent for achieving those measures. No incentive arrangement can ensure complete goal congruence because of differences in risk preferences, asymmetry of information, and the costs of monitoring. These differences produce residual loss. The total agency cost is the cost of monitoring, incentive compensation, and residual loss.

In most companies, both monitoring and incentives are used. Executives have incentive contracts while their actions are monitored with audited financial statements.

agent Party, such as a manager, who acts on behalf of another party.

principal Party, such as a shareholder, who hires an agent to act on his/her behalf.

The Market for Corporate Control

The final corporate governance mechanism we review is not a mechanism that the board puts in place to protect shareholders but rather mechanisms used to defend control of companies. The **market for corporate control** reflects the view that every public company is for sale. To explain this, let us take the phrase in its parts. The *market* is the sum of all the possible buyers of corporate stock and the individual shareholders of the company (who might be "sellers" in this market). The term *control* refers to what can be bought and sold in this market—the control of corporations. This is not to be confused with use of the stock market to buy shares. Rather, it is use of the stock market to acquire enough shares of a company that one gains control of the corporation and in so doing takes control away from another. Mergers and acquisitions are all about control, and HP's acquisition of Compaq is one example. Players in the market for control are competitors, corporate raiders, leveraged-buyout companies, company managers, and private equity.

Companies become subject to a battle for control when misbehaviour or underperformance leads to low share prices. The company then becomes the target of a raider or a fight for control, signalling that the company's board and its management have been ineffective or, at the very least, that being acquired by another entity is the only possible way of improving performance. Typically, existing shareholders are paid a premium over the market price of shares by whomever gains corporate control of the company. The new owner has the power and votes needed to determine who the CEO and members of the board of directors are.[47] The result of a change in corporate control is the replacement of management and a change in company strategy. The fear of this happening helps keep the present managers focused on improving the performance of the company.

market for corporate control Control over public corporations is traded, and this theoretically puts some pressure on managers to perform; otherwise their corporation can be taken over.

A change in control is the most costly and emotion-wrenched remedy of governance beyond the replacement of the CEO by a company's board. Although the market for corporate control may serve to discipline management, it is a very costly and time-consuming remedy to implement, and the benefits to the buyer will always be of concern.

The market for corporate control can only be an effective governance mechanism to the extent that the capital markets and governance mechanisms in place in a country allow hostile acquisitions to occur in the first place.

FOCUS ON ETHICS 14.1
Corrupt Practices

Companies doing business or contemplating doing business in countries other than their home country might be subject to domestic laws on foreign activity or other anti-corruption conventions (such as those of the Organization of American States, the United Nations, and the European Union). Many countries have national laws criminalizing bribery of foreign government officials. Bribery is seen as having a detrimental impact on the poor and development, on markets, and on public services. The poor pay for the costs of bribes, either through higher prices or lower quality services, which inhibits development. Bribery also distorts markets. Finally, bribery undermines public confidence in the integrity of public services.

In 1977, the U.S. through its Foreign Corrupt Practices Act (FCPA) made paying bribes to *foreign* government officials a criminal offence for American companies—as well as those foreign companies whose securities are listed in the United States. Other OECD countries did not have equivalent legislation and this raised concerns that the FCPA had created an *un-level* playing field. This need to "level the playing field" provided the motivation for the OECD Convention on Combating Bribery of Foreign Public Officials in International Business Transactions, which came into force in 1999. The convention requires signatories to enact national legislation that criminalizes the act of bribing a foreign public official. As of March 2009, 38 countries had signed the OECD's convention, including the United States, the United Kingdom, Canada, Korea, Japan, and most European

nations. The U.S. amended its Foreign Corrupt Practices Act (FCPA) to bring it into compliance with the OECD convention.

The impact of such laws on companies has been considerable. In 2008, Siemens, the German engineering giant, agreed to pay a record fine of US$1.6 billion to settle bribery allegations made by American and European authorities. The company was charged with paying out more than $1 billion in bribes to win contracts around the world. The company had created its slush fund for paying bribes by paying for non-existent consultant services and then channelling the money into off-the-books accounts. The money was then used to pay bribes to secure orders for major Siemens projects. This was once considered acceptable practice in corporate Germany, especially in big infrastructure projects, a Siemens specialty. Bribery of foreign officials came under threat when Germany criminalized it in 1998. But shutting down the system quickly was difficult since Siemens had been promised payments for long periods. In 2006, German prosecutors revealed their investigation with a series of raids on Siemens' offices. That investigation helped to kick off or accelerate similar inquiries in a dozen different countries, including the United States, Greece, Liechtenstein, Italy, and Austria.

Is it really wrong to pay bribes when bribes are critical to the functioning of governmental agencies in some countries? Those who collect bribes in turn have to pay bribes to others so things "get done."

Summary of Challenges

1. *Describe what corporate governance is and why it matters.* Corporate governance is the means and mechanisms used to ensure that managers act in accordance with shareholders' best interests. It encompasses the system by which organizations are directed and controlled by their shareholders. Evidence suggests that companies with good governance outperform those with poor governance. To the extent that governance helps companies maximize returns and minimize agency costs, companies with good governance may have a competitive advantage.

2. *Explain the three alternative approaches to improving the governance of companies.* Improved governance of companies has been built on a combination of three approaches: codes of conduct, law, and contracts. The first approach includes the optional codes of conduct, which include best-practice principles and guidelines provided by industry and investor associations. The second approach is corporate law, both statutory and judicial. Legal mechanisms are necessary to protect shareholders' rights and interests as the separation between investors

and managers has increased with the growth of companies. The third approach is comprised of contractual mechanisms. Parties bargain for contractual terms that address possible dissension *ex ante* instead of relying on the legal system to address problems *ex post*, an exercise that is often costly, time-consuming, and uncertain. All three approaches are used in each country with the mix determined by the country's history, its institutions, and its approach to business.

3. *Compare and contrast corporate governance practices around the world.* Governance practices differ around the globe in accordance with history, institutions, and cultures. Governance in Canada, the United Kingdom, and the United States is based on common law and is shareholder-centric; in Europe, stakeholders have much greater formal standing, with labour having a much greater voice in what the company does—they are said to be stakeholder-centric. In Asia, corporate governance is also influenced by ownership patterns associated with developing economies. Still, it is possible to assess the overall quality of governance using universal principles such as those of the OECD.

4. *Identify specific factors that affect the state of governance in Canada.* Canada has various features of ownership that make it appear more like a developing economy than one that parallels the United Kingdom and the United States. Half the companies in Canada have controlling shareholders. The private benefits of control induce controlling shareholders to run their corporations in ways that need not align with the wishes of public shareholders. When controlling shareholders actually own few shares, they wield control using super-voting shares, pyramiding, or other control-magnifying devices. Many Canadian companies have a dual-class share structure in which shares with single voting rights are coupled with shares having multiple or super-voting rights. In addition, many large companies in Canada belong to business groups that are pyramid-shaped. Some argue that the differences between the Canadian and American capital markets justify different approaches to pursuing more effective governance.

5. *Show how boards of directors are structured and explain the roles they play in corporate governance.* All publicly held companies are required to have a board of directors that is responsible for ensuring that management acts in shareholders' best interests. The board does much of its work through committees. Among the most important are the governance committee, the audit committee, and the compensation committee. The legal roles of the board include hiring and firing top executives, monitoring management, ensuring that shareholders' interests are protected, establishing executive compensation, and reviewing and approving the company's strategy.

6. *Design an executive incentive plan that will serve as a device for corporate governance.* Incentives can be used to bring management (executive) and shareholder interests into alignment by rewarding executives for doing what is in shareholders' best interests. The two most common incentive plans involve bonuses and stock options. A bonus pay is paid from a bonus pool created as performance goals are achieved. Its potential drawbacks are that it has a short-term bias and that executives may manipulate earnings to achieve it. Stock options are a stronger way to link shareholders' and executives' incentives because they make the executives owners in the company. Stock options have a limitation, however, in that they do not convey a downside financial risk beyond opportunity cost. Recently, long-term incentive plans and restricted stock grants have become popular because they seem to overcome the limitations of bonuses and options.

7. *Illustrate how the market for corporate control is related to corporate governance.* The threat that a company may become the target in a battle for corporate control is an external governance mechanism. The threat becomes likely when bad management produces poor performance, which lowers the price of the company's shares. Then either disgruntled shareholders who want to replace the board and the management or opportunistic investors looking to buy a company on the cheap buy enough shares to take control of the company. On obtaining this control, they will likely replace the existing board and management of the company. This is the harshest control that shareholders can exhibit.

Review Questions

1. Explain what is meant by corporate governance.
2. Why is good governance attractive?
3. When are inside directors beneficial to the functioning of the board of directors?
4. What are the three primary approaches to improving governance?
5. How do boards improve governance of the company?
6. What is the difference between stock options and restricted stock? What are the advantages and disadvantages of each?
7. Who are the principals and agents in the modern corporation? How do their interests differ?
8. What is the market for corporate control? What role does it play in solving or exacerbating the agency problem?
9. What are some primary differences and similarities in governance practices between Canada and other countries?

Experiential Activities

Group Exercises

1. Prior to class, visit the website www.sedar.com, which provides financial documents on Canadian public companies. Pick a company from the list of available companies and then open up a recent Management Information Circular for the company and look at its executive compensation. Note how top executives are being compensated. For the CEO, write down the types and amounts of compensation he/she is receiving. Then look at the corporate governance practices. Note how many board members there are, and how many insiders and outsiders there are on the governance, audit, and compensation committees. Write this down. Then bring your notes to class.

2. Identify a company that is currently subject to an attempted hostile takeover (various online sources can help you do this quickly). What are the dynamics that are involved in this potential takeover? Who are the key stakeholders in this battle? Who do you see benefiting and losing if this takeover is successful? Does it appear that this hostile takeover would create value?

Ethical Debates

1. You serve as lead director on the governance committee of the board. This year three members of the board are resigning so need to be replaced. The CEO/chairman of the board comes up to you before the board meeting at which replacements will be discussed. He tells you that replacements will not be a problem. He has already identified three excellent candidates and offered them the positions. What do you do?

2. You work in the human resources department of a large, international high-tech company. During the annual process of preparing for the closing of year-end books, your manager comes to you and tells you to pull out the documents for executive stock option grants and change the grant date from April 1 to July 13. Why would he do this? What should be done?

Endnotes

1. A fuller accounting of events is found in Anthony Bianco, *The Big Lie* (New York, Public Affairs, 2010) and Michael S. Malone, *Bill and Dave* (New York: Penguin, 2007). The book is worth reading for anyone interested not only in the history of the electronics industry but also in the growth of a corporation.

2. John Carver, *Boards That Make a Difference,* 3rd Ed. (San Francisco: Jossey-Bass, 2006), p. 375.

3. "Bre-X." Accessed April 4, 2010, at http://en.wikipedia.org/wiki/Bre-X; R. J. Finlay, "Bre-X: The Giant Fraud That Started with a Bang Ends with a Regulator's Whimper." Accessed April 4, 2010, at http://finlayongovernance.com/?p=282.

4. "Krispy Kreme Announces Completion of Special Committee Investigation," August 10, 2005, PRNewswire-FirstCall. Accessed April 4, 2010, at http://phx.corporate-ir.net/phoenix.zhtml?c=120929&p=irol-newsArticle&ID=741862&highlight.

5. A review of the literature on governance performance is found in Yves Bozec, Richard Boze, and Mohamed Dia, "Excess Voting Rights, Governance, and Performance," Administrative Sciences Assoc. of Canada, Annual Meeting, Niagara Falls, Ontario, 2009.

6. The explosion in national and transnational codes of conduct is described by Ruth V. Aguilera and Alvaro Cuervo-Cazurra, "Codes of Good Governance," *Corporate Governance: An International Review* 17:3 (2009): 376–387; OECD, *OECD Principles of Corporate Governance* (Paris: OECD Publications Service, 2004). Accessed March 29, 2010, at www.oecd.org/dataoecd/32/18/31557724.pdf. Also www.oecd.org/document/49/0,3343,en_2649_34813_31530865_1_1_1_37439,00.html.

7. OECD, "OECD Principles of Corporate Governance."

8. GovernanceMetrics International, "GMI Announces New Country Rankings for Corporate Governance," September 23, 2009. March 29, 2010, at www.csrwire.com/press/press_release/27699-GMI-Announces-New-Country-Rankings-for-Corporate-Governance.

9. "The Ten Countries with the Highest Overall Quality of Governance." Accessed on March 28, 2010, at www.gmiratings.com/GMI_Country_Rankings_as_of_09_22_2009.pdf.

10. OECD, "White Paper on Corporate Governance in Asia," July 15, 2003. Accessed on April 2, 2010, at www.oecd.org/dataoecd/4/12/2956774.pdf.

11. Lawrence E. Mitchell, "The Sarbanes-Oxley Act and the Reinvention of Corporate Governance?" *Villanova University School of Law's Law Review Symposium Issue* 48:4 (2003): 1189–1216.

12. The history of corporate governance in Canada is described in Harry Swain, Jeff Carruthers, Karen Minden, and Cheryl Urban, "Corporate Governance and Accountability in Canada," Sussex Circle Inc., May 2002. Accessed April 1, 2010, at www.aucc.ca/_pdf/english/programs/.../Final%20report_swain.pdf; The challenges to changing governance in Canada are described in an excellent study by Randall Morck and Bernard Yeung, "Some Obstacles to Good Corporate Governance in Canada and How to Overcome Them," Research Study commissioned by the Task Force to Modernize Securities Legislation in Canada, August 18, 2006. Accessed April 1, 2010, at www.tfmsl.ca/docs/V4%285%29%20Morck.pdf; The current state of governance is described by the Financial Standards Foundation, "Canada: Principles of Corporate Governance," March 2010. Accessed April 2, 2010, at www.estandardsforum.org/canada/standards/principles-of-corporate-governance.

13. J. McFarland, "Companies Don't Respect Governance Rules: Study," *Globe and Mail,* January 20, 2003, p. B1.

14. "Board Games 2009," *Globe and Mail.* Accessed March 29, 2010, at www.theglobeandmail.com/report-on-business/board-games/board-games-2009/article1375949/#custom.

15. Erinn B. Broshko and Kai Li, "Corporate Governance Requirements in Canada and the United States: A Legal and Empirical Comparison of the Principles-based and Rules-based Approaches," June 2006. Accessed April 4, 2010, at http://finance.sauder.ubc.ca/~kaili/BroshkoLi.pdf.

16. David Litterick and Philip Johnston, "Conrad Black Guilty of Multiple Fraud Charges," *Telegraph,* July 15, 2007. Accessed April 4, 2010, at www.telegraph.co.uk/news/worldnews/1557439/Conrad-Black-guilty-of-multiple-fraud-charges.html; Floyd Norris, "Panel Says Conrad Black Ran a 'Corporate Kleptocracy,'" *New York Times,* August 31, 2004. Accessed April 4, 2010, at www.nytimes.com/2004/08/31/business/media/31CND-CONR.html?ex=1251691200&en=9da66a6bf14c0900&ei=5090&partner=rssuserland.

17. Tara Gry, "Dual-Class Share Structures and Best Practices in Corporate Governance," Economics Division, Parliamentary Information and Research Service (PIRS) of the Library of Parliament, August 18, 2005. Accessed May 30, 2010, at www2.parl.gc.ca/Content/LOP/ResearchPublications/prb0526-e.htm.

18. "Canadian controlling shareholders make more extensive use of pyramiding and/or super-voting shares, for their control rights exceed their actual share ownership by a greater margin than in other Common Law countries. In the late 1990s, almost half of the assets of the top 100 listed Canadian companies belonged to companies that were members of pyramidal business groups." Randall Morck and Bernard Yeung, "Some Obstacles to Good Corporate Governance in Canada and How to Overcome Them," Research Study commissioned by the Task Force to Modernize Securities Legislation in Canada, August 18, 2006, p. 299. Accessed April 1, 2010, at www.tfmsl.ca/docs/V4%285%29%20Morck.pdf.

19. Angela Marion Lee, "Canada to End Limit on Foreign Holdings; Proposed Budget Still Must Pass the House of Commons," *Pensions & Investments* (March 7, 2005).

20. www.oecd.org (accessed July 15, 2005).

21. Ibid.

22. Erinn B. Broshko and Kai Li, "Corporate Governance Requirements in Canada and the United States: A Legal and Empirical Comparison of the Principles-Based and Rules-Based Approaches," June 2006. Accessed April 4, 2010, at http://finance.sauder.ubc.ca/~kaili/BroshkoLi.pdf.

23. J. Dahya, A. Lonie, and D. Power, "The Case for Separating the Roles of Chairman and CEO: An Analysis of Stock Market and Accounting Data," *Corporate Governance* 4 (1996): 71, 76. This study examined the impact of separating or combining the roles of CEO and chair in the United Kingdom. The authors found that a "significant positive market reaction . . . followed the separation of the responsibilities of chairman and CEO." Also, companies that announced a separation subsequently performed better than their counterparts based on several accounting measures. Conversely, companies that announced combination of the positions resulted in "the largest negative market response the day after the announcement."

24. Martha Graybow, "More Firms Split CEO and Chairman Roles: Study," Reuters, June 16, 2008. Accessed April 4, 2010, at http://uk.reuters.com/article/ousiv/idUKN1634597920080616.

25. B. Baysinger and R. E. Hoskisson, "The Composition of Boards of Directors and Strategic Control: Effects on Corporate Strategy," *Academy of Management Review* 15 (1990): 72–87.

26. M. A. Carpenter and J. D. Westphal, "The Strategic Context of External Network Ties: Examining the Impact of Director Appointments on Board Involvement in Strategic Decision Making," *Academy of Management Journal* 44 (2001): 639–651.

27. www.thecorporatelibrary.com and www.issproxy.com (accessed July 15, 2005).

28. M. Peers, J. Carreyrou, and B. Orwall, "Vivendi CEO Loses Key Board Support, Endangering His Job," *Wall Street Journal*, July 1, 2002, p. A1; L. Panetta, "It's Not Just What You Do, It's the Way You Do It," *Directors & Boards* 27 (2003): 17–21.

29. www.aicpa.org/info/sarbanes_oxley_summary.htm (accessed November 29, 2005).

30. M. A. Carpenter and J. D. Westphal, "The Strategic Context of External Network Ties: Examining the Impact of Director Appointments on Board Involvement in Strategic Decision Making," *Academy of Management Journal* 44 (2001): 639–651.

31. M. McDonald and J. D. Westphal, "Getting by with the Advice of Their Friends: CEOs' Advice Networks and Firms' Strategic Responses to Poor Performance," *Administrative Science Quarterly* 48 (2003): 1–32; J. D. Westphal and J. W. Fredrickson, "Who Directs Strategic Change? Director Experience, the Selection of New CEOs, and Change in Corporate Strategy," *Strategic Management Journal* 22 (2001): 1113–1138; J. D. Westphal, M. D. Seidel, and K. S. Stewart, "Second-Order Imitation: Uncovering Latent Effects of Board Network Ties," *Administrative Science Quarterly* 46 (2001): 717–747.

32. Adapted from Fredrick W. Cook & Co. Inc., "Stock Ownership Policies: Prevalence and Design of Executive and Director Ownership Policies Among the Top 250 Companies," September 2004. Accessed November 29, 2005, at www.fwcook.com/surveys.html.

33. "Dendrite International Board Mandates New Executive Share Ownership Policy; Program Reflects Positive Expectations," *BusinessWire* (February 8, 2000); Standard & Poor's Quantitative Stock Report; DRTE (Dendrite International), December 17, 2005.

34. SNAGY, "Directors' Share Ownership Plans: How Much Is Just Right?" *Globe and Mail*, April 7, 2009. Accessed April 2, 2010, at www.theglobeandmail.com/archives/article850671.ece.

35. Janet McFarland, "First-Time Directors Excluded: Many Companies Still Have Board Members Who Don't Own Stock," *Globe and Mail*, September 25, 2003, p. B1; Canadian Coalition for Good Governance, "2010 Building High Performance Boards," March 2010. Accessed April 4, 2010, at www.ccgg.ca/site/ccgg/assets/pdf/CCGG_Building_High_Performance_Boards_Final_March_2010.pdf.

36. E. White, "Call It Sarbanes-Oxley Burnout: Finance-Chief Turnover Is Rising," *Wall Street Journal*, April 5, 2005, p. A1.

37. P. M. Healy and J. M. Wahlen, "A Review of the Earnings Management Literature and Its Implications for Standard Setting," *Accounting Horizons* 13 (1999): 365–383.

38. R. E. Hoskisson, M. A. Hitt, and C. W. L. Hill, "Managerial Incentives and Investment in R&D in Large Multiproduct Firms," *Organization Science* 4 (1993): 325–341.

39. Rose M. Patten, "From Implicit to Explicit: Putting Corporate Values and Personal Accountability Front and Centre," *Ivey Business Journal* (September/October 2004).

40. W. G. Sanders, "Behavioral Responses of CEOs to Stock Ownership and Stock Option Pay," *Academy of Management Journal* 44 (2001): 477–492; W. G. Sanders, "Incentive Alignment, CEO Pay Level, and Firm Performance: A Case of 'Heads I Win, Tails You Lose'?" *Human Resource Management* 40 (2001): 159–170.

41. W. G. Sanders, "Behavioral Responses of CEOs to Stock Ownership and Stock Option Pay," *Academy of Management Journal* 44 (2001): 477–492.

42. Home Depot proxy statement filing (form DEF 14A), April 20, 2007.

43. M. Bloom and J. G. Michel, "The Relationships among Organizational Context, Pay Dispersion, and Managerial Turnover," *Academy of Management Journal* 45 (2002): 33–42.

44. M. A. Carpenter and W. G. Sanders, "Top Management Team Compensation: The Missing Link Between CEO Pay and Firm Performance," *Strategic Management Journal* 23 (2002): 367–374.

45. J. Dial and K. J. Murphy, "Incentives, Downsizing, and Value Creation at General Dynamics," *Journal of Financial Economics* 37 (1995): 261–314.

46. An interesting treatise on agency theory applied to governance is Mihnea Moldoveanu and Roger Martin, "Agency Theory and the Design of Efficient Governance Mechanisms," Prepared for the Joint Committee on Corporate Governance, Rotman School of Management, University of Toronto, February 2, 2001. Accessed April 1, 2010, at www.rotman.utoronto.ca/rogermartin/Agencytheory.pdf.

47. A. A. Berle, Jr. and G. C. Means, *The Modern Corporation and Private Property* (New York: McMillan, 1932).

Glossary

acquisition Strategy by which one company acquires another through stock purchase or exchange.

agent Party, such as a manager, who acts on behalf of another party.

alliance A relationship between two or more companies that enhances the effectiveness of the strategy of each.

arbitrage Making profit by taking advantage of the price difference between two or more markets.

arena Area (product, service, distribution channel, geographic markets, technology, etc.) in which a company participates.

backward integration Diversifying into related activities that extend the company's value chain while moving closer to sources of supply.

barriers to entry Conditions under which it is more difficult to join or compete in an industry.

board of directors Group of individuals that formally represents the company's shareholders and oversees the work of top executives.

business strategy Strategy for creating value while competing with rivals in a particular industry.

buyer power Degree to which companies in the buying industry are able to dictate terms on purchase agreements that extract some of the profit that would otherwise go to competitors in the focal industry.

CAGE framework Tool that considers the dimensions of culture, administration, geography and economics when assessing the distance between different markets.

capabilities A company's skill at using its resources to create goods and services; combination of procedures and expertise on which a company relies to produce goods and services.

coevolution Process by which diversification causes two or more interdependent businesses to adapt not only to their environment but also to each other.

commoditization Process during industry evolution by which sales eventually come to depend less on unique product features and more on price.

competitive advantage A company's ability to create *value* in a way that its rivals cannot.

complementor An industry that provides products or services which tend to increase sales in another industry.

conglomeration Diversification of the company into activities that are entirely unrelated to its current value chain.

contractual agreement An exchange of promises or agreement between parties that is often enforceable by the law.

cooperative An association or corporation established to provide products or services on a non-profit basis to those who own and control it—its shareholders or members.

core competence Capability that is central to a corporation's main business operations and allows it to generate new products and services.

corporate renewal The successful outcome from reintegrating the many management decisions of an established company around a strategy.

corporate strategy Strategy for creating value by diversifying into various industries.

cross-subsidizing When a company uses profits from one aspect of a product, service, or region to support its competitive activity.

differentiation Strategic position based on products or offers services with quality, reliability, or prestige that is discernibly higher than that of competitors and for which customers are willing to pay.

differentiator Feature or attribute of a company's product or service (e.g., image, customization, technical superiority, price, quality, and reliability) that helps it beat its competitors in the marketplace.

discovered process People throughout the company have generated strategic ideas from which top management has selected some to further.

diseconomy of scale Condition under which average total costs per unit of production increases as the volume of output increases.

disruptive technology Breakthrough product- or process-related technology that destroys the competencies of incumbent companies in an industry.

distinctive competence Capability that sets a company apart from other companies; something that a company can do that competitors cannot duplicate easily.

dynamic capabilities A company's ability to modify, reconfigure, and upgrade resources and capabilities in order to strategically respond to or generate environmental changes.

economic logic Means by which a company will earn an excess profit by implementing a strategy.

economy of scale Condition under which average total cost for a unit of production is lower at higher levels of output.

economy of scope Condition under which lower total average costs result from sharing resources to produce more than one product or service.

exit barriers Barriers that impose a high cost on the abandonment of a market or product.

exporting Foreign-country entry vehicle in which a company uses an intermediary to perform most foreign marketing functions.

first mover The company that is first to offer a new product or service in a market.

fit Condition in which all decisions made by management may support each other but at a minimum do not contradict each other.

five-forces model Framework for evaluating industry structure according to the effects of rivalry, threat of entry, supplier power, buyer power, and the threat of substitutes.

focused differentiation Strategic position based on targeting products to relatively small segments.

focused low-cost leadership Strategic position based on being a low-cost leader in a narrow market segment.

foreign direct investment (FDI) Foreign-country entry vehicle by which a company commits to the direct ownership of a foreign subsidiary or division.

forward integration Diversifying into related activities that extend the company's value chain while moving closer to final consumers.

franchisee One who purchases from the franchisor the rights to use a trademarked name and business model to do business and agrees to follow rules, guidelines, and pay fees established by the franchisor.

franchisor One who develops a business model and trademarks for a company and then sells to its franchisees the right to use the model and trademarks to do business.

general resources Resources that can be exploited across a wide range of activities.

generic strategies Strategic position designed to reduce the effects of rivalry, including *low-cost, differentiation, focused cost leadership, focused differentiation,* and *integrated positions.*

globalization Evolution of distinct geographic product markets into a state of globally interdependent product markets.

governance The work of the board as it translates informed owners' wishes into organizational performance.

greenfield investment Form of FDI in which a company starts a new foreign business from the ground up.

high-end disruption Disruption that provides a product for a new or emerging segment not being served by existing businesses in the industry.

importing Internationalization strategy by which a company brings a good, service, or capital into the home country from abroad.

incentive alignment Use of incentives to align managerial self-interest with shareholders.

industry life cycle Pattern of evolution followed by an industry inception to current and future states.

innovator's dilemma When incumbents avoid investing in innovative and disruptive technologies because those innovations do not satisfy the needs of their mainstream and most profitable clients.

institutional investors Institutions that manage large sums of money for third-party investors.

integrated position Strategic position in which elements of one position support strong standing in another.

international strategy Process by which a company approaches its cross-border activities and those of competitors and plans to approach them in the future.

key success factor (KSF) Key asset or requisite skill that all companies in an industry must possess in order to be a viable competitor.

learning curve Incremental production costs decline at a constant rate as production experience is gained; the steeper the learning curve, the more rapidly costs decline.

low-cost leadership Strategic position based on producing a good or offering a service while maintaining total costs that are lower than what it takes competitors to offer the same product or service.

low-end disruption Disruption that targets customers who do not need the full product performance provided by existing businesses in the industry.

market for corporate control Control over public corporations is traded, and this theoretically puts some pressure on managers to perform; otherwise their corporation can be taken over.

merger Consolidation or combination of two or more companies.

Minimum Efficient Scale (MES) The minimum scale at which the business fully exploits the economies of scale.

multipoint competition When a company competes against another company in multiple product markets or multiple geographic markets (or both).

new venture creation The creation of a new company that has its own strategy.

offshoring Moving a value chain activity or set of activities to another country, typically where key costs are lower.

outsourcing Activity performed for a company by people other than its full-time employees.

PESTEL analysis Tool for assessing the political, economic, sociocultural, technological, environmental, and legal contexts in which a company operates.

planned process A plan of actions that will put strategy in place is created by top management.

principal Party, such as a shareholder, who hires an agent to act on his or her behalf.

real options Process of maximizing the upside or limiting the downside of an investment opportunity by uncovering and quantifying the options and discussion points embedded within it.

resources Inputs used by companies to create products and services.

rivalry The act of companies in an industry competing for profit.

second mover (often *fast follower*) Second significant company to move into a market, quickly following the first mover.

specialized resources Resources with a narrow range of applicability.

staging Timing and pace of strategic moves.

stakeholder An individual or group whom the business seeks to cooperate with because

they have or control something the business needs as it pursues its strategy.

stock option Incentive device giving an employee the right to buy a share of company stock at a later date for a predetermined price.

straddling Unsuccessful attempt to integrate both low-cost and differentiation positions.

strategic group Subset of companies that, because of similar strategies, resources, and capabilities, compete against one another more intensely than with other companies in an industry.

strategic leadership Managing an overall enterprise and influencing key organizational outcomes.

strategic management Process by which a company manages the formulation and implementation of a strategy.

strategic positioning Means by which managers situate a company relative to its rivals.

strategy formulation Process of developing a strategy.

strategy implementation Process of executing a strategy.

strategy The coordinated means by which an organization pursues its goals and objectives.

supplier power Degree to which companies in the supply industry are able to dictate terms to contracts and thereby extract some of the profit that would otherwise be available to competitors in the focal industry.

takeoff Period during which a new product generates rapid growth and huge sales increases.

threat of new entry Degree to which new competitors can enter an industry and intensify rivalry.

threat of substitutes Degree to which products of one industry can satisfy the same demand as those of another.

value chain Total of primary and support activities through which the company adds value.

value curve A graphical depiction of how a company and major groups of its competitors are competing across its industry's factors of completion.

vehicles Means for entering new arenas (e.g., through acquisitions, alliances, internal development, etc.).

visioned process A vision of where strategy will be taking the company is provided by top management.

willingness to pay Principle of differentiation strategy by which customers are willing to pay more for certain product features.

Index

Credits

CHAPTER 1

2, Tim Hortons is a registered trade mark of the TDL Marks Corporation, Used with permission.
3, AP Photo/Kevork Djansezian, File
9, Rolls-Royce International Limited; Photo courtesy of © Rolls-royce plc
16, CP PHOTO/Richard Lam

CHAPTER 2

24, Courtesy of Xerox Corporation
25, Bob Daemmrich/Corbis
36, Photo supplied by Don A. Pether

CHAPTER 3

44 (top and bottom), Courtesy of Canadel Furniture
53, PhotoEdit/Felicia Martinez

CHAPTER 4

70, David Mager; © 2007 Pearson Education/PH College
71, © Rachel Epstein/PhotoEdit Inc.

CHAPTER 5

106, Amanda Edwards/Getty Images, Inc.
107, GUILLAUME HORCAJUELO/epa/Corbis

111, Corbis/Sygma/Jacques Langevin
115 (top), The Canadian Press Images/Maclean's Magazine/Andrew Tolson
115 (bottom), Getty Images Inc./Matthew Peyton

CHAPTER 6

140, Henry Georgi/All Canada Photos
161, Myrleen Ferguson Cate/PhotoEdit Inc.

CHAPTER 7

170 (top), TODD KOROL/X00147/ Reuters/Corbis
170 (bottom), Alesya/Shutterstock Inc.

CHAPTER 8

198, REUTERS/Chaiwat Subprasom
199, AP Photo/Paul Sakuma

CHAPTER 9

222, The Canadian Press Images/Francis Vachon
223, THE CANADIAN PRESS/Graham Hughes
242, REUTERS/Mark Blinch

CHAPTER 10

252, NewsCom/Justin Sullivan/Getty Images
253, © 2007 Dell Inc. All rights reserved.

258, AP Wide World Photos
282, AFP/Getty Images

CHAPTER 11

286, Christie Digital, © 2008, The Nasdaq Stock Market, Inc. Reprinted with permission.
287 (top), Courtesy of Kenneth F. Harling
287 (bottom), Courtesy of Christie
289, Frank LaBua, Inc.
295, REUTERS/Ho New
309, AFP/Getty Images

CHAPTER 12

316, REUTERS/Mark Blinch
330, REUTERS/Alejandro Kaminetzky
331, Bloomberg via Getty Images

CHAPTER 13

336, REUTERS/David Becker
337, REUTERS/Ina Fassbender
353, Courtesy of Triton Logging Inc.
355, AP Photo/Carlos Osorio

CHAPTER 14

360, AP Wide World Photos/Seth Wenig
361 (top), Courtesy of Hewlett-Packard
361 (bottom), CORBIS-NY/© CORBIS. All rights reserved.

The Fundamentals of Economic Logic

Ratios	How Calculated	Relevance of Concept
Profitability Indicators		
EBIT (Earnings before interest and taxes)	Net sales – operating expenses (also called operating profit)	Represents the amount of cash that such a company will be able to use to pay off creditors.
EBITDA (Earnings before interest, taxes, depreciation, and amortization)	EBIT + depreciation expenses + amortization expenses	A good way of comparing companies within and across industries. EBITDA is essentially the income that a company has free for interest payments.
Net Profit Margin	$$\frac{\text{Profits after taxes}}{\text{Sales}}$$	This number is an indication of how effective a company is at cost control. The higher the net profit margin is, the more effective the company is at converting revenue into actual profit.
Gross Profit Margin	$$\frac{\text{Sales – Cost of goods sold}}{\text{Sales}}$$	A good indication of what the company has left over to cover administrative costs after it has cover the cost of the goods sold
Return on assets	$$\frac{\text{Return after taxes}}{\text{Total assets}}$$ or $$\frac{\text{Profits after taxes + interest}}{\text{Total Assets}}$$	A measure of how effectively a firm uses its total assets.
Return on capital employed (ROCE)	$$\frac{\text{EBIT}}{\text{Total assets – current liabilities}}$$	A measure of the returns that a company is realizing from its capital employed. The ratio can also be seen as representing the efficiency with which capital is being utilized to generate revenue. It is commonly used as a measure for comparing the performance between businesses and for assessing whether a business generates enough returns to pay for its cost of capital.
Return on Equity (ROE)	$$\frac{\text{Profits after taxes}}{\text{Total stockholders' equity}}$$	A measure of how well a company has used reinvested earnings to generate additional earnings.
Return on Investment (ROI)	$$\frac{\text{Operating income}}{\text{Total assets}}$$	How effectively the firm uses its capital to generate profit; the higher the ROI, the better.
Return on Invested Capital (ROIC)	$$\frac{\text{Profits after taxes – Preferred stock dividends}}{\text{Total stockholders' equity + total debt – par value of preferred stock}}$$	How effectively a company uses the money (borrowed or owned) invested in its operations.
EBITDA margin	$$\frac{\text{EBITDA}}{\text{Total revenue}}$$	Measures the extent to which cash operating expenses use up revenue.
Operating Profit Margin	$$\frac{\text{EBIT}}{\text{Total revenue}}$$	A measure of a company's earnings power from ongoing operations. Operating profit margin indicates how effective a company is at controlling the costs and expenses associated with their normal business operations.